CENSUS OF INDIA 1911

CENSUS OF INDIA, 1911

VOLUME - IX

BURMA

PART II - TABLES

C. MORGAN WEBB

GYAN

Published by

Gyan Publishing House
5, Ansari Road
Daryaganj, New Delhi-110002
Phone: 011-47034999, 9811692060
E-mail: books@gyanbooks.com

Distribution Network
gyanbooks.com
India, USA, Canada, UK, Australia

ISBN: 978-81-212-7127-1 (Set) 23 Vols. In 41 Bindings

ISBN: 978-81-212-7471-5 (PB) Vol. IX, Pt. II

First Published, 1912

2nd Impression 2024

Printed at: Gyan Press, Delhi.

CENSUS OF INDIA 1911

Census of India, 1911

VOLUME IX

BURMA

PART II.—TABLES

BY

C. MORGAN WEBB, M.A., I.C.S.
FELLOW OF THE ROYAL STATISTICAL SOCIETY
SUPERINTENDENT, CENSUS OPERATIONS

RANGOON
OFFICE OF THE SUPERINTENDENT, GOVERNMENT PRINTING, BURMA
1912

LIST OF AGENTS

FOR THE

SALE OF GOVERNMENT PUBLICATIONS.

IN INDIA:

THACKER, SPINK & Co., Calcutta and Simla.
W. NEWMAN & Co., Calcutta.
THACKER & Co., Bombay.
HIGGINBOTHAM & Co., MADRAS.
SUPERINTENDENT, AMERICAN BAPTIST MISSION PRESS, Rangoon.
* D. B. TARAPOREVALA & SONS, & Co., 103, Meadow Street, Fort Bombay.

IN ENGLAND:

HENRY S. KING & Co., 65, Cornhill, E.C., London.
CONSTABLE & Co., 10, Orange Street, Leicester Square, W. C.
KEGAN PAUL, TRENCH, TRUBNER & Co., 68-74, Carter Lane, E.C.
BERNARD QUARITCH, 11, Grafton Street, New Bond Street, W.
P. S. KING & SON, 2 & 4, Great Smith Street, Westminster, London, W. S.
GRINDLAY & Co., 54, Parliament Street, S. W.
T. FISHER UNWIN, 1, Adelphi Terrace, London, W. C.
B. H. BLACKWELL, 50 & 51, Broad Street, Oxford.
DEIGHTON BELL & Co., Cambridge.
W. THACKER & Co., 2, Creed Lane, London, E. C.
LUZAC & Co., 46, Great Russell Street, London, W. C.

ON THE CONTINENT:

R. FRIEDLANDER & SOHN, 11, Carlstrasse, Berlin, Germany.
OTTO HARRASSOWITZ, Leipzig, Germany.
KARL W. HIERSEMANN, Leipzig, Germany.
ERNEST LEROUX, 28, Rue Bonaparte, Paris, France.
MARTINUS NIJHOFF, The Hague, Holland.

---

* For the sale of official publications excluding those of the Legislative Department of the Government of Burma.

INTRODUCTORY NOTE.

Considerable changes have been made in the presentation of statistics in this volume of the report. The following tables are being published for the first time :—

Imperial Table XV-B.—Subsidiary occupations of agriculturalists.
Imperial Table XV-D.—Distribution of occupations by religion.
Imperial Table XV-E.—*Parts I to IV.*—Industrial statistics.
Provincial Table I.—Area and population of Townships, States and Special Tracts.
Provincial Table II.—Population of Townships and States by religions.

Table XV A-II has also been expanded by the addition of 470 columns to show—

(i) total workers and dependents ;
(ii) male and female workers having agriculture as a subsidiary occupation.

The addition of these particulars has necessitated the expansion of the statement from 32 to 66 pages. Despite these additions, the size of the statistical volume has been reduced from 431 to 286 pages. This has been accomplished by a combination of the following methods :—

(i) reduction in size of printing for the more lengthy tables ;
(ii) elimination of unnecessary information from Imperial Tables VIII and XIII ;
(iii) Rearrangement of Imperial Tables VII, VIII, X, XI, XIII and XV A-II.

It is anticipated that the rearrangements will facilitate the task of reference. It is believed that the method of tabulating the speakers of the tribal languages of the Province in Table X and the members of the several tribes in Table XIII, besides economising space, has many points of advantage over their separate entry into the columns of the prescribed statement.

TABLE OF CONTENTS.

PART II.—IMPERIAL AND PROVINCIAL TABLES.

PART II.—IMPERIAL TABLE—concluded.

IMPERIAL TABLE I.

Area, Houses and Population.

NOTE 1.—The figures contained in this table are for the whole of Burma except—

(i) the State of East Manglün in the Northern Shan States;

(ii) the unadministered territories to the North of the Myitkyina and Upper Chindwin Districts;

(iii) the unadministered area nominally included in the district of Northern Arakan.

These areas were omitted from Census Operations.

NOTE 2.—The figures for the following areas, which have been embodied in this table, have been estimated only, and are not the result of an actual enumeration of the population.

District.	Portion.	Population Estimated.		
		Persons.	Males.	Females.
Northern Shan States	Kokang ...	25,604	13,389	12,215
	West Manglün ...	18,562	9,061	9,501
Southern Shan States	Brè Tract of Karenni	5,717	2,606	3,111
Pakökku Hill Tracts...	Unadministered Area	9,123	4,478	4,645

NOTE 3.—Details of the population arranged in smaller territorial units, such as the Township and the State, will be found in Provincial Tables I and II at the end of this Volume.

NOTE 4.—In addition to the four specially administered territories whose population is separately shown in this table, the following areas under special administration are attached to districts included in Burma Proper.

District.	Specially Administered Area.
Bhamo ...	Shwegu, Sinlun ... Kachin Hill Tracts.
Myitkyina ...	Myitkyina, Mogaung, Kamaing, Seinbo, Sadón, Sima ... Kachin Hill Tracts.
Katha ...	Katha, Mawlu ... Kachin Hill Tracts.
Ruby Mines ...	Möng Mit State including the Kodaung and Ngadaung Hill Tracts.
Upper Chindwin ...	Kampti State, Thaungdut State.

The populations of these areas have been included with those of the Districts to which they are attached. They are shown separately in Provincial Tables I and II.

NOTE 5.—The areas of certain districts have been changed since 1901. A list of the alterations, with the reasons for them, will be found on page 4.

See page 4.

Serial No.	District or State.	Area in square miles.	Towns.	Villages.	Occupied Houses. Total.	Occupied Houses. In Towns.	Occupied Houses. In Villages.
	1	2	3	4	5	6	7
	Provincial Total	**230,839**	**63**	**37,678**	**2,471,597**	**212,869**	**2,258,728**
	Burma Proper	**164,411**	**63**	**18,640**	**2,171,165**	**212,869**	**1,958,296**
	Arakan Division	***14,807***	***8***	***1,959***	***175,191***	***8,850***	***166,841***
1	Akyab	5,136	1	1,106	108,235	6,844	101,391
2	Northern Arakan	1,500	...	38	5,456	...	5,456
3	Kyaukpyu	4,387	1	594	41,699	885	40,814
4	Sandoway	3,784	1	221	19,801	621	19,180
	Pegu Division	***18,258***	***10***	***2,576***	***407,945***	***70,488***	***337,462***
5	Rangoon	28	1	...	49,676	49,676	...
6	Hanthawaddy	3,048	2	820	106,456	4,617	101,839
7	Tharrawaddy	2,863	3	642	88,057	4,086	83,971
8	Pegu	4,404	1	515	83,221	3,056	80,165
9	Prome	2,915	3	599	80,535	9,048	71,487
	Irrawaddy Division	***18,408***	***17***	***2,757***	***362,406***	***28,371***	***334,035***
10	Bassein	4,127	3	711	82,592	7,933	74,659
11	Henzada...	2,843	5	629	104,600	9,633	94,967
12	Myaungmya	2,642	2	635	65,113	2,150	62,963
13	Ma-ubin	1,648	3	398	59,611	4,396	55,215
14	Pyapôn	2,148	4	384	50,490	4,259	46,231
	Tenasserim Division	***35,886***	***7***	***1,864***	***276,531***	***28,418***	***248,118***
15	Toungoo	6,172	2	632	76,531	6,347	70,184
16	Salween	2,666	...	85	10,755	...	10,755
17	Thatôn	4,892	2	415	76,502	3,588	72,914
18	Amherst	7,059	1	366	64,423	11,147	53,276
19	Tavoy	5,308	1	199	27,811	4,688	23,123
20	Mergui	9,789	1	167	20,509	2,643	17,866
	Magwe Division	***17,575***	***9***	***2,478***	***257,258***	***16,471***	***240,787***
21	Thayetmyo	4,750	2	703	55,959	4,811	51,148
22	Pakôkku...	6,210	1	862	84,696	3,865	80,831
23	Minbu	3,302	3	430	55,589	3,874	51,715
24	Magwe	3,313	3	478	61,014	3,921	57,093
	Mandalay Division	***32,476***	***6***	***2,760***	***177,295***	***40,325***	***136,970***
25	Mandalay	2,117	3	385	77,181	34,883	42,298
26	Bhamo	6,903	1	721	22,118	1,505	20,613
27	Myitkyina	10,977	1	666	17,242	1,570	15,672
28	Katha	7,001	...	580	41,157	...	41,157
29	Ruby Mines	5,478	1	408	19,597	2,367	17,230
	Sagaing Division	***26,182***	***4***	***2,020***	***257,828***	***7,045***	***250,783***
30	Shwebo	5,714	1	669	80,921	2,077	78,844
31	Sagaing	1,825	1	340	70,751	2,439	68,312
32	Lower Chindwin	3,480	1	523	70,623	1,769	68,854
33	Upper Chindwin	15,163	1	488	35,533	760	34,773
	Meiktila Division	***10,819***	***7***	***2,281***	***256,711***	***13,411***	***243,300***
34	Kyauksè	1,274	1	336	27,777	1,503	26,274
35	Meiktila	2,183	1	473	56,930	1,548	55,382
36	Yamèthin	4,255	3	642	77,616	5,362	72,254
37	Myingyan	3,107	2	780	94,388	4,998	89,390
	Specially Administered Territories ...	**66,428**	...	**19,038**	**300,432**	...	**300,432**
38	Northern Shan States	14,294	...	6,109	84,140	...	84,140
39	Southern Shan States	40,434	...	12,118	185,291	...	185,291
40	Pakôkku Hill Tracts	3,700	...	333	5,459	...	5,459
41	Chin Hills	8,000	...	478	25,542	...	25,542

POPULATION.									
PERSONS.			MALES.			FEMALES.			
Total.	Urban.	Rural.	Total.	Urban.	Rural.	Total.	Urban.	Rural.	
8	9	10	11	12	13	14	15	16	Serial No.
12,115,217	1,127,975	10,987,242	6,183,494	680,760	5,502,734	5,931,723	447,215	5,484,508	
10,610,256	1,127,975	9,482,281	5,432,715	680,760	4,751,955	5,177,541	447,215	4,730,826	
839,896	*44,576*	*795,820*	*441,925*	*33,221*	*408,704*	*397,971*	*11,355*	*386,616*	
529,943	37,893	492,050	289,474	29,509	259,965	240,469	8,384	232,085	1
22,234	...	22,234	11,405	...	11,405	10,829	...	10,829	2
184,916	3,323	181,593	89,571	1,896	87,675	95,345	1,427	93,918	3
102,803	3,360	99,443	51,475	1,816	49,659	51,328	1,544	49,784	4
2,073,737	*406,931*	*1,666,806*	*1,136,192*	*274,469*	*861,723*	*937,545*	*132,462*	*805,083*	
293,316	293,316	...	208,111	208,111	...	85,205	85,205	...	5
539,109	24,889	514,220	295,886	18,480	277,406	243,223	6,409	236,814	6
433,320	23,586	409,734	216,442	12,752	203,690	216,878	10,834	206,044	7
429,121	17,104	412,017	229,540	10,232	219,308	199,581	6,872	192,709	8
378,871	48,036	330,835	186,213	24,894	161,319	192,658	23,142	169,516	9
1,869,485	*168,769*	*1,700,716*	*962,918*	*98,466*	*864,447*	*906,572*	*70,303*	*836,269*	
440,988	49,692	391,296	226,773	30,812	195,961	214,215	18,880	195,335	10
532,357	53,296	479,061	264,319	28,405	235,914	268,038	24,891	243,147	11
334,852	13,592	321,260	176,465	8,587	167,878	158,387	5,005	153,382	12
305,073	27,217	277,856	155,715	15,596	140,119	149,358	11,621	137,737	13
256,215	24,972	231,243	139,641	15,066	124,575	116,574	9,906	106,668	14
1,429,294	*144,647*	*1,284,647*	*750,626*	*82,526*	*668,100*	*678,668*	*62,121*	*616,547*	
351,076	26,583	324,493	181,488	15,461	166,027	169,588	11,122	158,466	15
46,608	...	46,608	24,741	...	24,741	21,867	...	21,867	16
416,975	20,519	396,456	217,770	11,262	206,508	199,205	9,257	189,948	17
367,918	57,582	310,336	198,430	35,130	163,300	169,488	22,452	147,036	18
135,293	25,074	110,219	68,667	12,573	56,094	60,626	12,501	54,125	19
111,424	14,889	96,535	59,530	8,100	51,430	51,894	6,789	45,105	20
1,239,032	*82,847*	*1,156,185*	*603,614*	*42,418*	*561,196*	*635,418*	*40,429*	*594,989*	
248,275	24,471	223,804	122,231	12,758	109,473	126,044	11,713	114,331	21
409,909	20,010	389,899	196,159	9,658	186,501	213,750	10,352	203,398	22
263,939	18,101	245,838	128,837	8,904	119,933	135,102	9,197	125,905	23
316,909	20,265	296,644	156,387	11,098	145,289	160,522	9,167	151,355	24
832,969	*184,633*	*648,336*	*426,776*	*98,849*	*327,927*	*406,193*	*85,784*	*320,409*	
340,770	158,139	182,631	170,750	81,345	89,405	170,020	76,794	93,226	25
107,811	9,762	98,049	55,528	6,703	48,825	52,283	3,059	49,224	26
85,577	5,663	79,914	47,863	3,794	44,069	37,714	1,869	35,845	27
198,193	...	198,193	98,148	...	98,148	100,045	...	100,045	28
100,618	11,069	89,549	54,487	7,007	47,480	46,131	4,062	42,069	29
1,155,271	*33,786*	*1,121,485*	*543,289*	*18,150*	*525,139*	*611,982*	*15,636*	*596,346*	
356,363	10,629	345,734	168,070	6,059	162,011	188,293	4,570	183,723	30
312,111	10,937	301,174	147,816	5,427	142,389	164,295	5,510	158,785	31
316,175	8,628	307,547	141,262	4,614	136,648	174,913	4,014	170,899	32
170,622	3,592	167,030	86,141	2,050	84,091	84,481	1,542	82,939	33
1,170,572	*61,786*	*1,108,786*	*567,380*	*32,661*	*534,719*	*603,192*	*29,125*	*574,067*	
141,426	5,877	135,549	68,868	2,900	65,968	72,558	2,977	69,581	34
279,822	7,076	272,746	134,170	3,985	130,185	145,652	3,091	142,561	35
307,419	26,728	280,691	153,223	14,159	139,064	154,196	12,569	141,627	36
441,905	22,105	419,800	211,119	11,617	199,502	230,786	10,488	220,298	37
1,504,961	...	1,504,961	750,779	...	750,779	754,182	...	754,182	
458,952	...	458,952	230,545	...	230,545	228,407	...	228,407	38
900,202	...	900,202	448,705	...	448,705	451,497	...	451,497	39
26,251	...	26,251	12,967	...	12,967	13,284	...	13,284	40
119,556	...	119,556	58,562	...	58,562	60,994	...	60,994	41

Note on changes in District areas as compared with 1901.

Serial No.	District.	Area, 1901.	Area, 1911.	Change.	Remarks.
2	Northern Arakan	5,233	1,500	− 3,753	See Note (*a*).
5	Rangoon ...	19	28	+ 9	See Note (*b*).
6	Hanthawaddy ...	3,023	3,048	+ 25	See Notes (*b*) & (*c*).
7	Tharrawaddy ...	2,851	2,863	+ 12	See Note (*d*).
8	Pegu ...	4,276	4,404	+ 128	See Note (*c*).
11	Henzada ...	2,870	2,843	− 27	See Note (*d*).
12	Myaungmya ...	2,970	2,642	− 328	See Note (*e*).
13	Ma-ubin ...	3,471	1,648	+ 325	See Notes (*d*) & (*e*).
14	Pyapôn ...		2,148		
17	Thatôn ...	5,079	4,892	− 187	See Note (*c*).
18	Amherst ...	7,062	7,059	− 3	See Note (*c*).
23	Minbu ...	3,299	3,302	+ 3	See Note (*f*).
24	Magwe ...	2,913	3,313	+ 400	See Note (*g*).
26	Bhamo ...	4,146	6,903	+ 2,757	See Note (*h*).
27	Myitkyina ...	10,640	10,977	+ 337	See Note (*h*).
28	Katha ...	6,944	7,001	+ 57	See Note (*i*).
29	Ruby Mines ...	5,476	5,478	+ 2	See Note (*i*).
30	Shwebo ...	5,634	5,714	+ 80	See Note (*j*).
31	Sagaing ...	1,862	1,825	− 37	See Note (*f*).
33	Upper Chindwin	19,062	15,163	− 3,899	See Note (*a*).
37	Myingyan ...	3,137	3,107	− 30	See Note (*f*).

(*a*) The unadministered portions of the Northern Arakan and the Upper Chindwin Districts were omitted from the Census in 1901, but their areas were included in the figures for the districts then given.

(*b*) There has been a transfer of congested districts from Hanthawaddy to Rangoon.

(*c*) Pegu and Hanthawaddy Districts have gained by accretion on the right bank of the Sittang. Thatôn and Amherst have suffered (the latter but slightly) from the erosion of the left banks of the Sittang and the Salween respectively.

(*d*) There has been erosion and accretion on the banks of the Irrawaddy affecting the areas of the Tharrawaddy, Henzada and Ma-ubin Districts.

(*e*) A part of the Myaungmya District was added to the old Thôngwa District in the last Census, and the two new districts of Ma-ubin and Pyapôn have since been formed.

(*f*) There have been numerous and intricate transfers between the Minbu, Pakôkku, Sagaing and Myingyan Districts. The total of the present areas does not coincide with that of 1901. Attempts at readjustments of the slight differences found have been made, but without success. The present figures are the result of careful enquiry and calculation.

(*g*) Forest reserves of an area of 400 square miles were omitted in 1901.

(*h*) The areas of the Kachin Hill Tracts of these districts are not known with exactitude. The northern boundary of the Myitkyina District is indeterminate. The areas of the Kachin Hills were excluded from the area given for Bhamo District in 1901.

(*i*) Slight increases are due to the inclusion of inland water areas previously omitted.

(*j*) The Deputy Commissioner reports that there were two errors (of 100 and 20 square miles respectively) in the original Survey of India figures which were quoted in 1901.

IMPERIAL TABLE II.

Variation in Population since 1872.

NOTE 1.—No census was taken in Upper Burma prior to 1891, nor in the Specially Administered Territories prior to 1901.

NOTE 2.—The changes effected in the Thayetmyo district after the annexation were explained in the Note to Imperial Table No. II for 1901.

NOTE 3.—Three districts, Myaungmya, Ma-ubin and Pyapôn, have been formed out of the old districts of Myaungmya and Thôngwa since the census of 1901. The population for the years 1901, 1891, 1881 and 1872 has been adjusted, as far as the available information would permit, to the district areas as constituted on the 10th March 1911.

NOTE 4.—There have been territorial changes in the following districts since the census of 1901 :—

{ Rangoon, Hanthawaddy }

{ Myitkyina, Upper Chindwin }

{ Myingyan., Pakôkku., Minbu., Sagaing. }

Populations for previous years have been adjusted to the district areas as constituted on the 10th March 1911.

NOTE 5.—The increases for the Northern Shan States and the Pakôkku Hill Tracts to the following extent are due to the inclusion of areas previously omitted from Census Operations :—

District.	Previously omitted Areas.	Persons.	Males.	Females.
Northern Shan States.	Kokang ...	25,604	13,389	12,215
	West Manglûn...	18,562	9,061	9,501
Pakôkku Hill Tracts.	Unadministered Territory.	9,123	4,478	4,645

in Population since 1872.

Females.					Variation Increase (+), Decrease (–).				Net Variation in period 1872 to 1911. Increase (+), Decrease (–).	
1911.	1901.	1891.	1881.	1872.	1901 to 1911.	1891 to 1901.	1881 to 1891.	1872 to 1881.		Serial No.
12	13	14	15	16	17	18	19	20	21	
5,931,728	5,148,591	8,784,117	1,745,766	1,811,680	+ 1,624,588	+ 2,768,571	+ 8,985,282	+ 989,628	+ 9,868,069	
5,177,541	4,524,186	8,784,117	1,745,766	1,811,680	+ 1,357,881	+ 1,580,822	+ 8,985,282	+ 989,628	+ 7,868,108	
897,971	*856,516*	*815,684*	*270,278*	*280,600*	+ *77,794*	+ *88,828*	+ *84,684*	+ *108,727*	+ *854,988*	
240,469	213,686	185,891	156,582	128,491	+ 48,277	+ 65,361	+ 56,599	+ 83,035	+ 253,272	1
10,829	10,125	7,028	7,032	4,006	+ 1,552	+ 6,054	+ 129	+ 5,709	+ 13,444	2
95,345	87,752	83,889	74,827	71,121	+ 16,089	+ 4,995	+ 14,529	+ 5,126	+ 40,739	3
51,328	44,952	38,826	31,832	26,982	+ 11,876	+ 12,418	+ 13,327	+ 9,857	+ 47,478	4
987,545	*825,428*	*698,014*	*547,811*	*894,466*	+ *258,099*	+ *297,616*	+ *807,099*	+ *867,846*	+ *1,225,660*	
85,205	70,843	56,079	42,672	36,371	+ 47,886	+ 63,350	+ 47,904	+ 35,431	+ 194,571	5
243,223	216,302	177,503	126,239	82,426	+ 64,847	+ 79,131	+ 99,105	+ 109,059	+ 352,142	6
216,878	194,537	167,945	131,706	85,488	+ 37,750	+ 56,330	+ 67,239	+ 100,799	+ 262,118	7
199,581	156,399	109,123	82,553	51,205	+ 89,549	+ 101,978	+ 52,779	+ 73,940	+ 318,246	8
192,658	187,342	187,364	164,141	138,976	+ 13,067	— 3,173	+ 40,072	+ 48,617	+ 98,583	9
906,572	*797,752*	*626,088*	*478,179*	*887,856*	+ *205,816*	+ *868,550*	+ *810,141*	+ *809,668*	+ *1,189,170*	
214,215	187,450	154,851	127,995	97,727	+ 49,561	+ 70,454	+ 52,804	+ 65,741	+ 238,560	10
268,038	243,001	217,891	181,167	131,979	+ 47,799	+ 46,938	+ 73,721	+ 107,146	+ 275,604	11
158,387	133,791	87,271	45,217	28,631	+ 51,920	+ 101,140	+ 76,423	+ 48,524	+ 278,007	12
149,358	133,187	100,782	89,875	59,124	+ 26,764	+ 64,571	+ 40,423	+ 48,873	+ 180,631	13
116,574	100,323	65,238	33,925	20,395	+ 29,772	+ 80,447	+ 66,770	+ 39,379	+ 216,368	14
678,668	*551,417*	*482,178*	*867,751*	*278,214*	+ *269,786*	+ *247,507*	+ *189,481*	+ *196,648*	+ *852,817*	
169,588	135,630	102,100	86,610	61,741	+ 71,761	+ 67,531	+ 21,399	+ 53,569	+ 214,260	15
21,867	18,373	14,918	14,500	12,608	+ 8,771	+ 6,398	+ 1,430	+ 3,892	+ 20,491	16
199,205	163,302	126,494	120,119	85,628	+ 73,465	+ 76,890	+ 36,679	+ 64,864	+ 251,898	17
169,488	136,243	105,328	76,079	54,234	+ 67,745	+ 66,634	+ 52,801	+ 50,790	+ 237,970	18
66,626	55,405	48,379	43,203	36,211	+ 25,314	+ 15,058	+ 9,933	+ 13,161	+ 63,466	19
51,894	42,464	34,959	27,240	22,792	+ 22,680	+ 14,996	+ 17,189	+ 9,367	+ 64,232	20
685,418	*559,711*	*516,617*	...	...	+ *160,716*	+ *79,252*	...	...	...	
126,044	120,758	124,687	82,252	75,494	+ 8,569	— 10,455	+ 80,601	+ 12,744	+ 91,459	21
213,750	189,288	165,548	...	...	+ 52,277	+ 44,691	...	...	...	22
135,102	122,099	113,499	...	...	+ 29,668	+ 17,498	...	...	...	23
160,522	127,566	111,883	...	...	+ 70,201	+ 27,518	...	...	...	24
406,198	*881,898*	*288,288*	...	...	+ *54,508*	+ *186,081*	...	...	...	
170,020	183,133	190,663	...	...	— 25,737	— 8,548	...	...	...	25
52,283	37,985	18,593	...	...	+ 28,296	+ 37,576	...	...	...	26
37,714	31,571	22,262	...	...	+ 17,050	+ 16,696	...	...	...	27
100,045	89,729	43,836	...	...	+ 21,970	+ 85,675	...	...	...	28
46,131	39,480	12,934	...	...	+ 12,924	+ 53,632	...	...	...	29
611,982	*582,114*	*487,879*	...	...	+ *160,805*	+ *178,008*	...	...	...	
188,293	152,846	122,006	...	...	+ 69,472	+ 56,112	...	...	...	30
164,295	147,961	129,368	...	...	+ 34,342	+ 36,124	...	...	...	31
174,913	154,416	131,525	...	...	+ 39,792	+ 43,067	...	...	...	32
84,481	76,891	54,980	...	...	+ 17,199	+ 42,700	...	...	...	33
608,192	*519,856*	*470,474*	...	...	+ *174,918*	+ *91,085*	...	...	...	
72,558	71,924	63,859	...	...	+ 173	+ 14,631	...	...	...	34
145,652	133,258	115,281	...	...	+ 27,517	+ 35,025	...	...	...	35
154,196	122,813	103,092	...	...	+ 64,222	+ 36,640	...	...	...	36
230,786	191,361	188,242	...	...	+ 83,001	+ 4,739	...	...	...	37
754,182	624,405	...	...	...	+ 267,212	...	...	...	...	
228,407	161,045	...	...	...	+ 137,862	...	...	...	...	38
451,497	412,771	...	...	...	+ 83,848	...	...	...	...	39
13,284	6,567	...	...	...	+ 13,135	...	...	...	...	40
60,994	44,022	...	...	...	+ 32,367	...	...	...	...	41

IMPERIAL TABLE III.

Towns and Village Tracts classified by Population.

NOTE 1.—A return has been made to the definition of "Village" adopted in 1891. It is now equivalent to the Village-tract or the jurisdiction of a Village-Headman. This explains the large decrease in the figures of Column 2 since 1901, when the residential hamlet was adopted as the village unit.

NOTE 2.—In the Specially Administered Territories the residential hamlet has remained the village unit for census purposes.

NOTE 3.—The figures in Column 22 are as comprehensive as the records would permit. There were many instances in which it was impossible from the enumeration books to distinguish between residents and travellers.

Serial No.	District or State.	Total number of inhabited Towns and Village Tracts.	Population.	Under 500.		500-1,000.		1,000-2,000.	
				Number.	Population.	Number.	Population.	Number.	Population.
	1	2	3	4	5	6	7	8	9
	Provincial Total	37,741	12,115,217	30,446	4,278,120	5,229	3,606,645	1,714	2,260,306
	Burma Proper	18,703	10,610,256	11,562	2,920,040	5,107	3,527,419	1,692	2,232,529
	Arakan Division	*1,962*	*839,896*	*1,415*	*361,198*	*448*	*302,736*	*90*	*113,652*
1	Akyab	1,107	529,943	743	193,438	289	195,477	68	86,206
2	Northern Arakan ...	38	22,234	16	5,957	19	12,695	3	3,511
3	Kyaukpyu	595	184,916	503	114,362	81	54,074	10	12,661
4	Sandoway	222	102,803	153	47,441	59	40,490	9	11,274
	Pegu Division	*2,586*	*2,078,787*	*1,215*	*378,722*	*975*	*688,670*	*331*	*440,807*
5	Rangoon	1	293,316	...	...	...	...	...	...
6	Hanthawaddy	822	539,109	402	125,006	297	205,750	104	137,400
7	Tharrawaddy	645	433,320	293	92,258	271	190,040	69	98,619
8	Pegu	516	429,121	189	60,010	202	148,673	101	132,468
9	Prome	602	378,871	331	101,448	205	144,207	57	71,820
	Irrawaddy Division	*2,774*	*1,869,485*	*1,270*	*412,684*	*1,132*	*791,671*	*334*	*488,008*
10	Bassein	714	440,988	358	110,303	289	196,341	61	75,916
11	Henzada	634	532,357	188	71,123	324	232,738	109	153,080
12	Myaungmya	637	334,852	400	122,149	195	140,489	34	41,736
13	Ma-ubin	401	305,073	144	48,144	172	119,715	80	103,840
14	Pyapôn	388	256,215	180	60,965	152	102,388	50	63,436
	Tenasserim Division	*1,871*	*1,429,294*	*845*	*231,861*	*646*	*459,945*	*307*	*400,548*
15	Toungoo	634	351,076	390	92,957	172	120,603	62	82,660
16	Salween	85	46,608	51	16,082	28	19,582	5	5,865
17	Thatôn	417	416,975	101	33,188	167	123,011	119	156,896
18	Amherst	367	367,918	126	41,164	133	95,831	82	108,099
19	Tavoy	200	135,293	100	24,224	74	51,892	22	26,560
20	Mergui	168	111,424	77	24,246	72	49,026	17	20,468
	Magwe Division	*2,482*	*1,239,082*	*1,728*	*488,411*	*546*	*375,076*	*166*	*220,871*
21	Thayetmyo	705	248,275	586	138,292	107	68,161	8	10,782
22	Pakôkku	863	409,909	611	153,371	179	124,454	61	81,348
23	Minbu	433	263,939	249	66,900	128	91,390	46	60,566
24	Magwe	481	316,909	277	79,848	132	91,071	51	67,675
	Mandalay Division	*2,766*	*832,969*	*2,418*	*378,691*	*276*	*154,880*	*60*	*82,978*
25	Mandalay	388	340,770	264	67,010	88	61,200	28	39,157
26	Bhamo	722	107,811	655	79,846	63	12,554	3	4,512
27	Myitkyina	667	85,577	639	53,027	21	14,704	6	8,907
28	Katha	580	198,193	477	114,906	83	52,329	16	20,538
29	Ruby Mines	409	100,618	378	58,902	21	14,043	7	9,864
	Sagaing Division	*2,024*	*1,155,271*	*1,232*	*326,804*	*508*	*357,941*	*237*	*313,980*
30	Shwebo	670	356,363	420	113,653	173	121,843	67	87,881
31	Sagaing	341	312,111	118	39,830	112	80,977	84	112,935
32	Lower Chindwin	524	316,175	298	85,990	147	105,394	68	90,609
33	Upper Chindwin	489	170,622	396	87,331	71	49,727	18	22,555
	Meiktila Division	*2,238*	*1,170,572*	*1,449*	*396,669*	*581*	*396,550*	*167*	*222,685*
34	Kyauksè	337	141,426	239	58,147	81	53,781	14	18,151
35	Meiktila	474	279,822	268	80,238	142	98,290	58	78,362
36	Yamèthin	645	307,419	449	116,665	156	105,432	28	35,697
37	Myingyan	782	441,905	493	141,619	202	139,047	67	90,475
	Specially Administered Territories.	19,038	1,504,961	18,884	1,358,080	122	79,226	22	27,777
38	Northern Shan States ...	6,109	458,952	6,084	425,932	15	9,596	7	8,502
39	Southern Shan States ...	12,118	900,202	12,047	831,435	56	35,074	9	12,105
40	Pakôkku Hill Tracts ...	333	26,251	328	22,868	5	3,383	...	...
41	Chin Hills	478	119,556	425	77,845	46	31,173	6	7,170

Tracts classified by Population.

2,000-5,000.		5,000-10,000.		10,000-20,000.		20,000-50,000.		50,000-100,000.		100,000 and over.		Encampments, Boat and Railway population unclassed.	
Number.	Population.	Number.	Population.	Number.	Population.	Number.	Population.	Number.	Population.	Number.	Population.		Serial No.
10	11	12	13	14	15	16	17	18	19	20	21	22	
284	**748,012**	**43**	**292,573**	**16**	**213,948**	**6**	**172,021**	**1**	**57,582**	**2**	**421,647**	**64,363**	
277	**727,915**	**40**	**276,196**	**16**	**213,948**	**6**	**172,021**	**1**	**57,582**	**2**	**421,647**	**60,959**	
8	***20,110***	...	...	...	...	***1***	***37,893***	...	...	...	...	***4,307***	
6	13,427	...	...	...	...	1	37,893	...	...	...	...	3,502	1
...	...	...	...	...	...	...	...	...	...	...	...	71	2
1	3,323	...	...	...	...	...	...	...	...	...	...	496	3
1	3,360	...	...	...	...	...	...	...	...	...	...	238	4
54	***145,847***	***5***	***37,828***	***4***	***54,098***	***1***	***26,911***	...	...	***1***	***283,348***	***18,006***	
...	...	...	...	...	...	...	...	...	...	1	283,348	9,968	5
17	44,355	...	...	2	24,890	...	...	...	...	...	...	1,708	6
8	22,446	4	28,807	...	...	...	...	...	...	...	...	1,150	7
23	65,842	...	...	1	17,104	...	...	...	...	...	...	5,024	8
6	13,204	1	9,021	1	12,104	1	26,911	...	...	...	—	156	9
22	***58,009***	***13***	***90,857***	***1***	***12,494***	***2***	***62,133***	...	...	...	...	***3,629***	
3	7,681	2	12,611	...	...	1	37,081	...	...	...	...	1,055	10
8	21,235	4	28,244	...	...	1	25,052	...	...	...	...	885	11
6	15,999	2	13,592	...	...	...	...	...	...	...	...	887	12
2	5,604	2	14,717	1	12,494	...	...	...	...	...	...	559	13
3	7,490	3	21,693	...	...	...	...	...	...	...	...	243	14
62	***164,361***	***6***	***37,216***	***3***	***47,827***	***1***	***25,074***	***1***	***57,582***	...	...	***4,880***	
7	19,336	2	15,908	1	18,546	...	...	...	...	...	...	1,066	15
...	...	1	5,019	...	...	...	...	...	...	...	...	60	16
27	76,125	2	11,309	1	14,392	...	...	...	...	...	...	2,054	17
24	59,718	1	4,980	...	...	...	...	1	57,582	...	...	544	18
3	6,446	...	...	...	...	1	25,074	...	...	...	...	1,097	19
1	2,736	...	...	1	14,889	...	...	...	...	...	...	59	20
36	***98,252***	***8***	***51,605***	***2***	***24,467***	***1***	***20,010***	...	...	...	...	***10,840***	
2	5,402	...	...	2	24,467	...	...	...	...	...	...	1,171	21
11	29,292	...	...	...	...	1	20,010	...	...	...	...	1,434	22
6	15,757	4	23,127	...	...	...	...	...	...	...	...	6,199	23
17	47,801	4	28,478	...	...	...	...	...	...	...	...	2,036	24
11	***28,305***	***3***	***23,291***	***2***	***23,043***	...	...	...	...	***1***	***138,299***	***8,532***	
5	13,590	1	7,866	1	11,974	...	...	...	...	1	138,299	1,674	25
...	...	1	9,762	...	...	...	...	...	...	...	...	1,137	26
...	...	1	5,663	...	...	...	...	...	...	...	...	3,276	27
4	9,004	...	...	...	...	...	...	...	...	...	...	1,416	28
2	5,711	...	...	1	11,069	...	...	...	...	...	...	1,029	29
49	***123,269***	***1***	***8,628***	***2***	***21,566***	...	...	...	...	...	...	***3,083***	
9	21,676	...	...	1	10,629	...	...	...	...	...	...	681	30
26	66,485	...	...	1	10,937	...	...	...	...	...	...	947	31
10	24,952	1	8,628	...	...	...	...	...	...	...	...	602	32
4	10,156	...	...	...	...	...	...	...	...	...	...	853	33
35	***89,762***	***4***	***26,771***	***2***	***30,453***	...	...	...	...	...	...	***7,682***	
2	5,261	1	5,886	...	...	...	...	...	...	...	...	200	34
5	11,459	1	7,076	...	...	...	...	...	...	...	...	4,397	35
10	26,242	1	8,083	1	14,074	...	...	...	...	...	...	1,226	36
18	46,800	1	5,726	1	16,379	...	...	...	...	...	...	1,859	37
7	**20,097**	**3**	**16,377**	...	...	...	...	...	...	...	...	**3,404**	
2	6,638	1	5,455	...	...	...	...	...	...	...	...	2,829	38
4	10,091	2	10,922	...	...	...	...	...	...	...	...	575	39
...	...	...	...	...	...	...	...	...	...	...	...	...	40
1	3,368	...	...	...	...	...	...	...	...	...	...	...	41

IMPERIAL TABLE IV.

Towns Classified by Population, with Variation since 1872.

NOTE 1.—Three towns, Pantanaw, Ôkpo and Kawkareik, included in Table IV in 1901, have now been excluded from the list of Census Towns.

NOTE 2.—Pagan Municipality, included in 1901, has been amalgamated with Nyaung-u Notified Area.

NOTE 3.—The following towns have now been included for the first time in this table :—

Insein.	Danubyu.	Myitkyina.	Kindat.
Mogôk.	Pyapôn.	Kyônpyaw.	Bogale.
Syriam.	Wakèma.	Sinbyugyûn.	
Kyaiklat.	Dedayè.	Pyawbwè.	

NOTE 4.—The boundaries of the City of Rangoon have been changed since 1901. Its population for previous years has been adjusted to its area as constituted on 10th March 1911.

NOTE 5.—The populations of the Cantonments of Rangoon and Mandalay included in the figures of this table are :—

Cantonment.	Population.	Males.	Females.
Rangoon	8,381	6,292	2,089
Mandalay	13,385	7,902	5,483

IMPERIAL TABLE IV.—*Towns Classified by*

Serial No.	Town.	District or State.	Municipality, Suburbs, Cantonment, etc.	POPULATION. 1911.	1901.	1891.	1881.	1872.
	1	2	3	4	5	6	7	8
	Provincial Total	...	...	**1,127,975**	**981,542**	**894,758**	...	...
	Class I, 100,000 and over ...	...	...	*481,615*	*429,246*	*370,895*	...	...
1	Rangoon	Rangoon ...	Municipality ...	293,316	245,430	182,080	134,176	98,745
2	Mandalay	Mandalay ...	Municipality ...	138,299	183,816	188,815	...	...
	Class II, 50,000—100,000	...	...	*57,582*	*58,446*	*55,785*	...	...
3	Moulmein	Amherst ...	Municipality ...	57,582	58,446	55,785	53,107	46,472
	Class III, 20,000—50,000	...	...	*172,021*	*161,502*	*152,970*	...	...
4	Akyab	Akyab ...	Municipality ...	37,893	35,680	37,938	33,989	19,230
5	Bassein	Bassein ...	Municipality ...	37,081	31,864	30,177	28,147	20,688
6	Prome	Prome ...	Municipality ...	26,911	27,375	30,022	28,813	31,157
7	Tavoy	Tavoy ...	Municipality ...	25,074	22,371	15,099	13,372	14,469
8	Henzada	Henzada ...	Municipality ...	25,052	24,756	19,762	16,724	15,307
9	Pakôkku	Pakôkku ...	Municipality ...	20,010	19,456	19,972	...	...
	Class IV, 10,000—20,000 ...	...	...	*213,957*	*157,268*	*158,641*	...	...
10	Toungoo	Toungoo ...	Municipality ...	18,546	15,837	19,232	17,199	10,732
11	Pegu	Pegu ...	Municipality ...	17,104	14,132	10,762	5,891	4,416
12	Myingyan	Myingyan ...	Municipality ...	16,379	16,139	19,790	...	...
13	Mergui	Mergui ...	Municipality ...	14,889	11,987	10,137	8,633	9,737
14	Thatôn	Thatôn ...	Municipality ...	14,392	14,342	9,683	6,388	...
15	Pyinmana	Yamèthin ...	Municipality ...	14,074	14,388	12,926	...	...
16	Insein	Hanthawaddy ...	Municipality ...	13,992	...	...	...	...
17	Allan-Ywataung ...	Thayetmyo ...	Municipality ...	12,894	10,207	9,012	5,825	9,697
18	Yandoon	Ma-ubin ...	Municipality ...	12,500	12,779	20,235	12,673	9,680
19	Paungdè	Prome ...	Municipality ...	12,104	11,105	10,233	6,727	5,630
20	Maymyo	Mandalay ...	Notified Area ...	11,974	1,259	228	...	...
21	Thayetmyo	Thayetmyo ...	Municipality ...	11,577	15,824	17,101	16,097	15,142
22	Mogôk	Ruby Mines ...	...	11,069	...	...	...	...
23	Sagaing	Sagaing ...	Municipality ...	10,937	9,643	9,934	...	...
24	Syriam	Hanthawaddy ...	Municipality ...	10,897	...	...	...	...
25	Shwebo	Shwebo ...	Municipality ...	10,629	9,626	9,368	...	...
	Class V, 5,000—10,000 ...	...	...	*229,708*	*162,858*	*143,715*	...	...
26	Bhamo	Bhamo ...	Municipality ...	9,762	10,734	8,048	...	...
27	Letpadan	Tharrawaddy ...	Municipality ...	9,247	8,772	2,151	775	...
28	Shwedaung	Prome ...	Notified Area ...	9,021	10,787	12,424	12,373	12,654
29	Yenangyaung	Magwe ...	Notified Area ...	8,896	3,246	4,258	...	...
30	Mônywa	Lower Chindwin ...	Municipality ...	8,628	7,869	6,316	...	...
31	Kyaiklat	Pyapôn ...	Municipality ...	8,438	...	...	...	...
32	Kyangin	Henzada ...	Municipality ...	8,386	7,183	8,116	7,565	8,477
33	Myanaung	Henzada ...	Municipality ...	8,331	6,351	5,489	5,416	5,636
34	Yamèthin	Yamèthin ...	Municipality ...	8,083	8,680	6,584	...	...
35	Shwegyin	Toungoo ...	Municipality ...	8,037	7,616	8,754	7,519	7,871
36	Amarapura	Mandalay ...	...	7,866	9,103	11,004	...	...
37	Danubyu	Ma-ubin ...	Notified Area ...	7,695	...	...	...	...
38	Salin	Minbu ...	Municipality ...	7,547	7,957	10,345	...	...
39	Gyobingauk ...	Tharrawaddy ...	Municipality ...	7,410	6,030	3,008	837	...
40	Ngathainggyaung ...	Bassein ...	Municipality ...	7,182	7,182	5,608	...	...
41	Meiktila	Meiktila ...	Notified Area ...	7,076	7,203	4,155	...	...
42	Pyapôn	Pyapôn ...	Municipality ...	7,066	...	...	...	...
43	Wakèma	Myaungmya ...	Municipality ...	7,031	...	...	...	...
44	Ma-ubin	Ma-ubin ...	Municipality ...	7,022	6,623	5,327	1,567	...
45	Thônzè	Tharrawaddy ...	Municipality ...	6,929	6,578	2,257	1,505	...
46	Myaungmya	Myaungmya ...	Municipality ...	6,561	4,711	2,929	...	...
47	Taungdwingyi ...	Magwe ...	Municipality ...	6,402	5,941	5,687	...	...
48	Dedayè	Pyapôn ...	...	6,189	...	...	...	...
49	Zalun	Henzada ...	Municipality ...	6,155	6,642	6,006	5,120	...
50	Kyaikto	Thatôn ...	Municipality ...	6,127	6,637	5,164	3,859	...
51	Kyauksè	Kyauksè ...	Municipality ...	5,877	5,420	7,201	...	...
52	Nyaung-u	Myingyan ...	Notified Area ...	5,726	...	...	...	...
53	Myitkyina	Myitkyina ...	...	5,663	...	...	...	...
54	Minbu	Minbu ...	Municipality ...	5,501	5,780	7,270	...	...
55	Kyônpyaw	Bassein ...	Notified Area ...	5,429	...	...	...	...
56	Lemyethna	Henzada ...	Municipality ...	5,372	5,813	5,614	5,355	5,331
57	Sinbyugyûn ...	Minbu ...	...	5,053	...	...	...	...
	Class VI, under 5,000 ...	...	...	*23,092*	*12,222*	*12,752*	...	...
58	Magwe	Magwe ...	Notified Area ...	4,967	6,232	6,673	...	...
59	Pyawbwè	Yamèthin ...	Notified Area ...	4,571	...	...	...	...
60	Kindat	Upper Chindwin ...	...	3,592	...	...	...	...
61	Sandoway	Sandoway ...	Municipality ...	3,360	2,845	2,531	1,617	...
62	Kyaukpyu	Kyaukpyu ...	Municipality ...	3,323	3,145	3,548	3,225	...
63	Bogale	Pyapôn ...	...	3,279	...	...	...	...

Population, with Variation since 1872.

VARIATION. INCREASE (+), DECREASE (−).				Variation in period 1872 to 1911. Increase (+), Decrease (−).	MALES.			FEMALES.			
1901 to 1911.	1891 to 1901.	1881 to 1891.	1872 to 1881.		1911.	1901.	1891.	1911.	1901.	1891.	
9	10	11	12	13	14	15	16	17	18	19	Serial No.
+ 146,438	+ 86,784	...	...	...	680,760	577,670	511,805	447,215	408,872	382,958	
+ *2,869*	+ *58,851*	...	...	...	*277,829*	*268,170*	*219,401*	*158,786*	*161,076*	*151,494*	
+ 47,886	+ 63,350	+ 47,904	+ 35,431	+ 194,571	208,111	174,587	125,898	85,205	70,843	56,182	1
− 45,517	− 4,999	...	...	...	69,718	93,583	93,503	68,581	90,233	95,812	2
− *864*	+ *2,661*	...	...	...	*35,130*	*36,690*	*34,252*	*22,452*	*21,756*	*21,533*	
− 864	+ 2,661	+ 2,678	+ 6,635	+ 11,110	35,130	36,690	34,252	22,452	21,756	21,533	3
+ *10,519*	+ *8,582*	...	...	...	*104,880*	*95,324*	*90,940*	*67,641*	*66,178*	*62,080*	
+ 2,213	− 2,258	+ 3,949	+ 14,759	+ 18,663	29,509	27,581	29,208	8,384	8,099	8,730	4
+ 5,217	+ 1,687	+ 2,030	+ 7,459	+ 16,393	24,246	20,422	19,013	12,835	11,442	11,164	5
− 464	− 2,647	+ 1,209	− 2,344	− 4,246	14,385	14,037	15,533	12,526	13,338	14,489	6
+ 2,703	+ 7,272	+ 1,727	− 1,097	+ 10,605	12,573	10,904	7,166	12,501	11,467	7,933	7
+ 296	+ 4,994	+ 3,038	+ 1,417	+ 9,745	14,009	13,257	10,640	11,043	11,499	9,122	8
+ 554	− 516	...	...	...	9,658	9,123	9,380	10,352	10,333	10,592	9
+ *56,689*	− *1,878*	...	...	...	*124,514*	*84,681*	*86,204*	*89,448*	*72,687*	*72,487*	
+ 2,709	− 3,395	+ 2,033	+ 6,467	+ 7,814	11,106	8,676	10,880	7,440	7,161	8,352	10
+ 2,972	+ 3,370	+ 4,871	+ 1,475	+ 12,688	10,232	8,375	6,060	6,872	5,757	4,702	11
+ 240	− 3,651	...	...	...	8,765	8,273	10,758	7,614	7,866	9,032	12
+ 2,902	+ 1,850	+ 1,504	− 1,104	+ 5,152	8,100	6,169	5,012	6,789	5,818	5,125	13
+ 50	+ 4,659	+ 3,295	...	...	7,982	8,315	5,147	6,410	6,027	4,536	14
− 314	+ 1,462	...	...	...	7,475	7,169	6,597	6,599	7,219	6,329	15
...	...	...	...	...	10,046	...	...	3,946	...	...	16
+ 2,687	+ 1,195	+ 3,187	− 3,872	+ 3,197	6,384	4,816	4,288	6,510	5,391	4,724	17
− 279	− 7,456	+ 7,562	+ 2,993	+ 2,820	6,793	7,028	11,947	5,707	5,751	8,288	18
+ 999	+ 872	+ 3,506	+ 1,097	+ 6,474	6,322	5,623	4,971	5,782	5,482	5,262	19
+ 10,715	+ 1,031	...	...	...	8,008	1,037	226	3,966	222	2	20
− 4,247	− 1,277	+ 1,004	+ 955	− 3,565	6,374	9,101	9,854	5,203	6,723	7,247	21
...	...	...	...	...	7,007	...	...	4,062	...	...	22
+ 1,294	− 291	...	...	...	5,427	4,659	4,906	5,510	4,984	5,028	23
...	...	...	...	...	8,434	...	...	2,463	...	...	24
+ 1,003	+ 258	...	...	...	6,059	5,390	5,558	4,570	4,236	3,810	25
+ *66,850*	+ *19,148*	...	...	...	*125,946*	*86,818*	*78,916*	*108,762*	*76,540*	*69,799*	
− 972	+ 2,686	...	...	...	6,703	7,129	5,547	3,059	3,605	2,501	26
+ 475	+ 6,621	+ 1,376	...	...	5,099	4,705	1,373	4,148	4,067	778	27
− 1,766	− 1,637	+ 51	− 281	− 3,633	4,187	4,892	5,634	4,834	5,895	6,790	28
+ 5,650	− 1,012	...	...	...	5,085	1,736	2,052	3,811	1,510	2,206	29
+ 759	+ 1,553	...	...	...	4,614	4,382	2,935	4,014	3,487	3,381	30
...	...	...	...	...	5,042	...	...	3,396	...	...	31
+ 1,203	− 933	+ 551	− 912	− 91	4,200	3,379	3,788	4,186	3,804	4,328	32
+ 1,980	+ 862	+ 73	− 220	+ 2,695	4,262	3,118	2,554	4,069	3,233	2,935	33
− 597	+ 2,096	...	...	...	4,289	4,522	3,183	3,794	4,158	3,401	34
+ 421	− 1,138	+ 1,235	− 352	+ 166	4,355	4,029	4,658	3,682	3,587	4,096	35
− 1,237	− 1,901	...	...	...	3,619	4,136	5,115	4,247	4,967	5,889	36
...	...	...	...	...	4,426	...	...	3,269	...	...	37
− 410	− 2,388	...	...	...	3,561	3,641	4,850	3,986	4,316	5,495	38
+ 1,380	+ 3,022	+ 2,171	...	...	4,067	3,208	1,623	3,343	2,822	1,385	39
...	+ 1,574	...	...	...	3,677	3,968	2,822	3,505	3,214	2,786	40
− 127	+ 3,048	...	...	...	3,985	4,287	2,437	3,091	2,916	1,718	41
...	...	...	...	...	4,398	...	...	2,668	...	...	42
...	...	...	...	...	4,126	...	...	2,905	...	...	43
+ 399	+ 1,296	+ 3,760	...	...	4,377	4,304	3,607	2,645	2,319	1,720	44
+ 351	+ 4,321	+ 752	...	...	3,586	3,402	1,081	3,343	3,176	1,176	45
+ 1,850	+ 1,782	...	...	...	4,461	2,922	1,664	2,100	1,789	1,265	46
+ 461	+ 254	...	...	...	3,179	2,883	2,919	3,223	3,058	2,768	47
...	...	...	...	...	3,656	...	...	2,533	...	...	48
− 487	+ 636	+ 886	...	...	3,275	3,406	3,227	2,880	3,236	2,779	49
− 510	+ 1,473	+ 1,305	...	...	3,280	3,734	2,757	2,847	2,903	2,407	50
+ 457	− 1,781	...	...	...	2,900	2,712	3,448	2,977	2,708	3,753	51
...	...	...	...	...	2,852	...	...	2,874	...	...	52
...	...	...	...	...	3,794	...	...	1,869	...	...	53
− 279	− 1,490	...	...	...	2,967	2,977	3,886	2,534	2,803	3,384	54
...	...	...	...	...	2,889	...	...	2,540	...	...	55
− 441	+ 199	+ 259	+ 24	+ 41	2,659	2,846	2,756	2,713	2,967	2,858	56
...	...	...	...	...	2,376	...	...	2,677	...	...	57
+ *10,870*	− *580*	...	...	...	*12,961*	*6,587*	*7,092*	*10,181*	*5,685*	*5,660*	
− 1,265	− 441	...	...	...	2,834	3,305	3,589	2,133	2,927	3,084	58
...	...	...	...	...	2,395	...	...	2,176	...	...	59
...	...	...	...	...	2,050	...	...	1,542	...	...	60
+ 515	+ 314	+ 914	...	...	1,816	1,462	1,376	1,544	1,383	1,155	61
+ 178	− 403	+ 323	...	...	1,896	1,770	2,127	1,427	1,375	1,421	62
...	...	...	...	...	1,970	...	...	1,309	...	...	63

IMPERIAL TABLE V.

Towns arranged territorially with Population by Religion.

NOTE 1.—Three towns, Pantanaw, Ôkpo and Kawkareik, included in Table V in 1901, have now been excluded from the list of Census Towns.

NOTE 2.—Pagan Municipality included in 1901 has been amalgamated with Nyaung-u notified area.

NOTE 3.—The following towns have been included for the first time in this table:—

Syriam.	Danubyu.	Dedayè.	Kindat.
Insein.	Pyapôn.	Sinbyugyun.	Pyawbwè.
Kyônpyaw.	Kyaiklat.	Myitkyina.	
Wakèma.	Bogalè.	Mogôk.	

NOTE 4.—Details of population included under other Religions are:—

Belief.	Males.	Females.
Confucian ...	57	14
Agnostic ... Secularist ...	19	16
TOTAL ...	76	30

District or State.	Serial No.	Town, Municipality, Suburbs, Cantonment, etc.		Population. Persons.	Population. Males.	Population. Females.	Buddhist. Persons.	Buddhist. Males.	Buddhist. Females.	Animist. Persons.	Animist. Males.	Animist. Females.
1		2		3	4	5	6	7	8	9	10	11
Provincial Total ...		...	...	**1,127,975**	**680,760**	**447,215**	**693,589**	**346,749**	**346,840**	**24,821**	**21,097**	**3,724**
Arakan Division ...		...	...	**44,576**	**33,221**	**11,355**	**17,035**	**8,957**	**8,078**	**469**	**420**	**49**
Akyab ...	1	Akyab ...	Municipality	37,893	29,509	8,384	12,864	6,790	6,074	392	345	47
Kyaukpyu ...	2	Kyaukpyu ...	Municipality	3,323	1,896	1,427	2,325	1,216	1,109	28	28	...
Sandoway ...	3	Sandoway ...	Municipality	3,360	1,816	1,544	1,846	951	895	49	47	2
Pegu Division ...		...	...	**406,931**	**274,469**	**132,462**	**176,813**	**91,968**	**84,845**	**9,651**	**8,089**	**1,562**
Rangoon ...	4	Rangoon ...	Municipality	293,316	208,111	85,205	97,467	52,137	45,330	7,217	5,936	1,281
Hanthawaddy ...	5	Syriam ...	Municipality	10,897	8,434	2,463	3,311	1,678	1,633	150	138	12
Do. ...	6	Insein ...	Municipality	13,092	10,046	3,046	5,759	4,223	1,536	284	254	30
Tharrawaddy ...	7	Thonzè ..	Municipality	6,929	3,586	3,343	5,515	2,552	2,963	142	126	16
Do. ...	8	Letpadan ...	Municipality	9,247	5,099	4,148	7,102	3,457	3,645	276	249	27
Do. ...	9	Gyobingauk ...	Municipality	7,410	4,067	3,343	6,087	3,022	3,065	142	138	4
Pegu ...	10	Pegu ...	Municipality	17,104	10,232	6,872	10,935	5,443	5,492	563	476	87
Prome ...	11	Prome ...	Municipality	26,911	14,385	12,526	21,691	10,628	11,063	558	484	74
Do. ...	12	Paungdè ...	Municipality	12,104	6,322	5,782	10,587	5,075	5,512	283	258	25
Do. ...	13	Shwedaung ...	Notified Area	9,021	4,187	4,834	8,359	3,753	4,606	36	30	6
Irrawaddy Division		...	...	**168,769**	**98,466**	**70,303**	**126,639**	**64,510**	**62,129**	**3,984**	**3,564**	**420**
Bassein ...	14	Bassein ...	Municipality	37,081	24,246	12,835	21,105	11,517	9,588	540	490	59
Do. ...	15	Ngathainggyaung	Municipality	7,182	3,677	3,505	6,288	3,014	3,274	108	93	15
Do. ...	16	Kyônpyaw ...	Notified Area	5,429	2,889	2,540	4,691	2,306	2,385	112	108	4
Henzada ...	17	Henzada ...	Municipality	25,052	14,009	11,043	19,857	9,978	9,879	348	319	29
Do. ...	18	Zalun ...	Municipality	6,155	3,275	2,880	5,459	2,726	2,733	119	97	22
Do. ...	19	Lemyethna ...	...	5,372	2,659	2,713	5,016	2,388	2,628	42	41	1
Do. ...	20	Myanaung ...	Municipality	8,331	4,262	4,069	7,109	3,379	3,730	157	135	22
Do. ...	21	Kyangin ..	Municipality	8,386	4,200	4,186	7,601	3,642	3,959	56	54	2
Myaungmya ...	22	Myaungmya ...	Municipality	6,561	4,461	2,100	4,486	2,765	1,721	329	310	19
Do. ...	23	Wakèma ...	Municipality	7,031	4,126	2,905	5,460	2,726	2,734	258	244	14
Ma-ubin ...	24	Ma-ubin ...	Municipality	7,022	4,377	2,645	4,573	2,410	2,163	196	172	24
Do. .	25	Yandoon ..	Municipality	12,500	6,793	5,707	10,680	5,359	5,321	175	160	15
Do. ...	26	Danubyu ...	Notified Area	7,695	4,426	3,269	6,327	3,233	3,094	101	93	8
Pyapôn ...	27	Pyapôn ...	Municipality	7,066	4,398	2,668	4,645	2,345	2,300	777	661	116
Do. ...	28	Kyaiklat ...	Municipality	8,438	5,042	3,396	6,277	3,143	3,134	312	289	23
Do. ...	29	Bogalè ...	...	3,279	1,970	1,309	2,503	1,310	1,193	117	108	9
Do. ...	30	Dedayè ...	...	6,189	3,656	2,533	4,542	2,249	2,293	223	190	33
Tenasserim Division		...	...	**144,647**	**82,526**	**62,121**	**93,693**	**46,445**	**47,248**	**4,091**	**3,365**	**726**
Toungoo ...	31	Toungoo ..	Municipality	18,546	11,106	7,440	10,745	5,600	5,145	786	646	140
Do. ...	32	Shwegyin ...	Municipality	8,037	4,355	3,682	6,445	3,254	3,191	72	62	10
Thatôn ...	33	Thatôn ...	Municipality	14,392	7,982	6,410	11,216	5,738	5,478	3	3	...
Do. ...	34	Kyaikto ..	Municipality	6,127	3,280	2,847	4,480	2,125	2,357	239	197	42
Amherst ...	35	Moulmein ...	Municipality	57,582	35,130	22,452	27,014	13,329	13,685	2,172	1,755	417
Tavoy ...	36	Tavoy ...	Municipality	25,074	12,573	12,501	22,816	10,955	11,861	291	275	16
Mergui ...	37	Mergui ...	Municipality	14,889	8,100	6,789	10,977	5,446	5,531	528	427	101
Magwe Division ...		...	...	**82,847**	**42,418**	**40,429**	**73,193**	**35,651**	**37,542**	**1,018**	**851**	**167**
Thayetmyo ...	38	Thayetmyo ...	Municipality	11,577	6,374	5,203	8,697	4,564	4,133	278	176	102
Do. ...	39	Allan-Ywataung	Municipality	12,894	6,384	6,510	11,540	5,434	6,106	6	6	...
Pakôkku ...	40	Pakôkku ...	Municipality	20,010	9,658	10,352	18,780	8,803	9,977	184	155	29
Minbu ..	41	Minbu ...	Municipality	5,501	2,967	2,534	4,417	2,185	2,232	108	97	11
Do. ...	42	Salin ...	Municipality	7,547	3,561	3,986	7,259	3,339	3,920	25	24	1
Do. ...	43	Sinbyugyun ...	...	5,053	2,376	2,677	4,731	2,119	2,612	154	145	9
Magwe ...	44	Magwe ...	Notified Area	4,967	2,834	2,133	3,862	1,997	1,865	81	78	3
Do. ...	45	Yenangyaung ...	Notified Area	8,896	5,085	3,811	7,909	4,324	3,585	145	133	12
Do. ...	46	Taungdwingyi ...	Municipality	6,402	3,179	3,223	5,998	2,886	3,112	37	37	...
Mandalay Division ...		...	...	**184,633**	**98,849**	**85,784**	**132,478**	**63,322**	**69,156**	**4,625**	**3,941**	**684**
Mandalay ...	47	Mandalay ...	Municipality	138,299	69,718	68,581	109,235	51,687	57,548	1,384	1,197	187
Do. ...	48	Amarapura ...	...	7,866	3,619	4,247	7,389	3,376	4,013	15	10	5
Do. ...	49	Maymyo ...	Notified Area	11,974	8,008	3,966	2,869	1,378	1,491	97	70	27
Bhamo ...	50	Bhamo ...	Municipality	9,762	6,703	3,059	4,383	2,229	2,154	1,251	1,045	206
Myitkyina ...	51	Myitkyina ...	...	5,663	3,794	1,869	1,159	583	576	413	377	36
Ruby Mines ...	52	Mogôk ...	...	11,069	7,007	4,062	7,443	4,069	3,374	1,465	1,242	223
Sagaing Division ...		...	...	**33,786**	**18,150**	**15,636**	**25,957**	**12,629**	**13,328**	**282**	**243**	**39**
Shwebo ...	53	Shwebo ...	Municipality	10,629	6,059	4,570	7,253	3,559	3,694	97	87	10
Sagaing ...	54	Sagaing ...	Municipality	10,937	5,427	5,510	9,035	4,286	4,749	62	43	19
Lower Chindwin ...	55	Mônywa ...	Municipality	8,628	4,614	4,014	6,927	3,405	3,522	73	65	8
Upper Chindwin ...	56	Kindat ...	...	3,592	2,050	1,542	2,742	1,379	1,363	50	48	2
Meiktila Division ...		...	...	**61,786**	**32,661**	**29,125**	**47,781**	**23,267**	**24,514**	**701**	**624**	**77**
Kyauksè ...	57	Kyauksè ...	Municipality	5,877	2,900	2,977	5,059	2,342	2,717	25	24	1
Meiktila ...	58	Meiktila ...	Notified Area	7,076	3,985	3,091	4,323	2,120	2,203	39	31	8
Yamèthin ...	59	Yamèthin ...	Municipality	8,083	4,289	3,794	4,706	2,274	2,432	82	71	11
Do. ...	60	Pyinmana ...	Municipality	14,074	7,475	6,599	10,166	4,884	5,282	293	265	28
Do. ...	61	Pyawbwè ...	Notified Area	4,571	2,395	2,176	3,351	1,557	1,794	81	76	5
Myingyan ...	62	Myingyan ...	Municipality	16,379	8,765	7,614	14,794	7,510	7,284	154	136	18
Do. ...	63	Nyaung-u ...	Notified Area	5,726	2,852	2,874	5,382	2,580	2,802	27	21	6

territorially with Population by Religion.

Hindu.			Mahomedan.			Christian.			Sikh.			Jain.			Zoroastrian.			Jew.			Other Religions.			
Persons.	Males.	Females.	Persons.	Males.	Females.	Persons.	Males.	Females.	Persons.	Males.	Females.	Persons.	Males.	Females.	Persons.	Males.	Females.	Persons.	Males.	Females.	Persons.	Males.	Females.	Serial No.
12	13	14	15	16	17	18	19	20	21	22	23	24	25	26	27	28	29	30	31	32	33	34	35	
207,601	**169,412**	**38,189**	**147,907**	**110,039**	**37,868**	**47,099**	**28,148**	**18,951**	**5,191**	**4,191**	**1,000**	**426**	**348**	**78**	**269**	**174**	**95**	**966**	**526**	**440**	**106**	**76**	**30**	
8,840	**8,531**	**309**	**17,553**	**14,845**	**2,708**	**602**	**407**	**195**	**37**	**33**	**4**	**14**	**9**	**5**	...	...	...	**26**	**19**	**7**	...	...	...	
8,521	8,233	288	15,531	13,730	1,801	508	350	158	37	33	4	14	9	5	...	...	...	26	19	7	...	...	...	1
162	151	11	787	487	300	21	14	7	...	...	...	...	...	...	...	...	...	...	...	...	...	...	...	2
157	147	10	1,235	628	607	73	43	30	...	...	...	...	...	...	...	...	...	...	...	...	...	...	...	3
127,264	**104,504**	**22,760**	**63,779**	**51,838**	**11,941**	**26,282**	**15,735**	**10,547**	**1,721**	**1,449**	**272**	**352**	**298**	**54**	**217**	**133**	**84**	**752**	**382**	**370**	**100**	**73**	**27**	
108,350	89,028	19,322	54,634	45,106	9,528	23,044	13,977	9,067	1,263	1,095	168	296	258	38	196	121	75	750	381	369	99	72	27	4
4,702	4,414	288	2,316	1,893	423	354	249	105	56	56	...	6	5	1	2	1	1	...	...	...	...	...	...	5
4,710	3,511	1,199	1,363	1,008	355	1,480	768	712	335	241	94	50	35	15	8	4	4	2	1	1	1	1	...	6
613	509	104	358	233	125	296	163	133	5	3	2	...	...	...	...	...	...	...	...	...	...	...	...	7
1,069	844	225	602	444	158	182	93	89	7	7	...	...	...	...	9	5	4	...	...	...	...	...	...	8
726	587	139	333	256	77	116	59	57	6	5	1	...	...	...	...	...	...	...	...		...	...	...	9
3,638	2,897	741	1,589	1,199	390	350	193	157	29	24	5	...	...	...	...	...	...	...	...	...	...	...	...	10
2,519	1,919	600	1,738	1,149	589	395	196	199	8	7	1	...	...	...	2	2	...	...	...	...	...	...	...	11
688	599	89	500	361	139	34	18	16	12	11	1	...	...	...	...	...	...	...	...	...	...	...	...	12
249	196	53	346	189	157	31	19	12	...	...	...	...	...	...	...	...	...	...	...	...	...	...	...	13
20,797	**18,179**	**2,618**	**13,616**	**9,995**	**3,621**	**3,622**	**2,138**	**1,484**	**31**	**31**	...	**21**	**17**	**4**	**22**	**12**	**10**	**37**	**20**	**17**	...	...	...	
8,666	7,633	1,033	5,212	3,690	1,522	1,497	887	610	...	...	...	3	3	...	22	12	10	27	14	13	...	...	...	14
335	284	51	412	253	159	16	10	6	3	3	...	...	...	...	...	...	...	...	...	...	...	...	...	15
247	222	25	363	244	119	16	9	7	...	...	...	...	...	...	...	...	...	...	...	...	...	...	...	16
2,783	2,369	414	1,351	934	417	700	400	300	3	3	...	...	...	...	...	...	...	10	6	4	...	...	...	17
257	239	18	270	181	89	48	30	18	2	2	...	...	...	...	...	...	...	...	...	...	...	...	...	18
191	161	30	106	59	47	10	5	5	...	...	...	7	5	2	...	...	...	...	...	...	...	...	...	19
346	311	35	675	410	265	41	25	16	...	...	...	3	2	1	...	...	...	...	...	...	...	...	...	20
239	226	13	291	167	124	190	102	88	9	9	...	...	...	...	...	...	...	...	...	...	...	...	...	21
840	731	109	670	526	144	232	126	106	...	...	...	4	3	1	...	...	...	...	...	...	...	...	...	22
622	591	31	633	524	109	54	37	17	...	...	...	4	4	...	...	...	...	...	...	...	...	...	...	23
1,243	1,049	194	693	570	123	317	176	141	...	...	...	...	...	...	...	...	...	...	...	...	...	...	...	24
857	698	159	730	535	195	58	41	17	...	...	...	...	...	...	...	...	...	...	...	...	...	...	...	25
704	660	44	434	300	74	129	80	49	...	...	...	...	...	...	...	...	...	...	...	...	...	...	...	26
907	792	115	542	473	69	188	120	68	7	7	...	...	...	...	...	...	...	...	...	...	...	...	...	27
1,072	963	109	680	579	101	91	62	29	6	6	...	...	...	...	...	...	...	...	...	...	...	...	...	28
491	391	100	159	155	4	9	6	3	...	...	...	...	...	...	...	...	...	...	...	...	...	...	...	29
997	859	138	395	335	60	26	22	4	1	1	...	...	...	...	...	...	...	...	...	...	...	...	...	30
22,699	**17,784**	**4,915**	**18,526**	**11,783**	**6,743**	**5,424**	**2,989**	**2,435**	**92**	**81**	**11**	**36**	**22**	**14**	**4**	**3**	**1**	**82**	**54**	**28**	...	...	...	
2,997	2,328	669	2,636	1,690	946	1,271	750	521	88	77	11	...	...	...	...	...	...	23	15	8	...	...	...	31
549	464	85	713	412	301	258	163	95	...	...	...	...	...	...	...	...	...	...	...	...	...	...	...	32
1,586	1,258	328	1,426	891	535	161	92	69	...	...	...	...	...	...	...	...	...	...	...	...	...	...	...	33
820	571	249	552	373	179	36	16	20	...	...	...	...	...	...	...	...	...	...	...	...	...	...	...	34
15,164	11,761	3,403	10,083	6,663	3,420	3,055	1,563	1,492	4	4	...	36	22	14	4	3	1	50	30	20	...	...	...	35
518	471	47	1,148	679	469	298	190	108	...	...	...	...	...	...	...	...	...	3	3	...	...	...	...	36
1,065	931	134	1,968	1,075	893	345	215	130	...	...	...	...	...	...	...	...	...	6	6	...	...	...	...	37
3,480	**2,651**	**829**	**3,752**	**2,347**	**1,405**	**878**	**546**	**332**	**506**	**364**	**142**	...	...	...	...	...	...	**20**	**8**	**12**	...	...	...	
1,122	759	363	1,091	626	465	381	243	138	8	6	2	...	...	...	...	...	...	...	...	...	...	...	...	38
554	448	106	736	459	277	33	25	8	5	4	1	...	...	...	...	...	...	20	8	12	...	...	...	39
373	295	78	466	294	172	174	91	83	33	20	13	...	...	...	...	...	...	...	...	...	...	...	...	40
369	294	75	347	216	131	101	62	39	159	113	46	...	...	...	...	...	...	...	...	...	...	...	...	41
113	86	27	88	60	28	...	...	...	62	52	10	...	...	...	...	...	...	...	...	...	...	...	...	42
74	47	27	93	64	29	...	...	...	1	1	...	...	...	...	...	...	...	...	...	...	...	...	...	43
368	293	75	370	266	104	67	42	25	219	158	61	...	...	...	...	...	...	...	...	...	...	...	...	44
392	331	61	360	232	128	80	62	18	10	3	7	...	...	...	...	...	...	...	...	...	...	...	...	45
115	98	17	201	130	71	42	21	21	9	7	2	...	...	...	...	...	...	...	...	...	...	...	...	46
17,736	**12,623**	**5,113**	**20,448**	**12,852**	**7,596**	**7,219**	**4,336**	**2,883**	**2,047**	**1,703**	**344**	**2**	**2**	...	**26**	**26**	...	**46**	**41**	**5**	**6**	**3**	**3**	
7,884	5,269	2,615	14,963	8,696	6,267	4,045	2,238	1,807	729	572	157	2	2	...	26	26	...	31	31	...	...	...	...	47
118	74	44	326	149	177	15	7	8	3	3	...	...	...	...	...	...	...	...	...	...	...	...	...	48
4,399	3,323	1,076	2,120	1,625	495	2,403	1,556	847	65	43	22	...	...	...	...	...	...	15	10	5	6	3	3	49
975	811	164	1,743	1,429	314	490	373	117	920	816	104	...	...	...	...	...	...	...	...	...	...	...	...	50
2,949	1,953	996	773	591	182	131	75	56	238	215	23	...	...	...	...	...	...	...	...	...	...	...	...	51
1,411	1,193	218	523	362	161	135	87	48	92	54	38	...	...	...	...	...	...	...	...	...	...	...	...	52
2,538	**1,842**	**696**	**3,050**	**2,047**	**1,003**	**1,599**	**1,116**	**483**	**356**	**271**	**85**	**1**	...	**1**	...	...	...	**3**	**2**	**1**	...	...	...	
1,053	769	284	1,083	783	300	1,120	844	276	22	17	5	1	...	1	...	...	...	...	...	...	...	...	...	53
678	438	240	974	563	411	188	97	91	...	...	...	...	...	...	...	...	...	...	...	...	...	...	...	54
390	298	92	684	473	211	257	146	111	297	227	70	...	...	...	...	...	...	...	...	...	...	...	...	55
417	337	80	309	228	81	34	29	5	37	27	10	...	...	...	...	...	...	3	2	1	...	...	...	56
4,247	**3,298**	**949**	**7,183**	**4,332**	**2,851**	**1,473**	**881**	**592**	**401**	**259**	**142**	...	...	...	...	...	...	...	...	...	...	...	...	
322	250	72	296	190	106	153	81	72	22	13	9	...	...	...	...	...	...	...	...	...	...	...	...	57
905	692	213	1,179	723	456	548	370	178	82	42	33	...	...	...	...	...	...	...	...	...	...	...	...	58
597	444	153	2,274	1,273	1,001	417	222	195	7	5	2	...	...	...	...	...	...	...	...	...	...	...	...	59
1,347	1,032	315	2,126	1,216	910	139	75	64	3	3	...	...	...	...	...	...	...	...	...	...	...	...	...	60
274	201	73	571	370	201	24	15	9	270	176	94	...	...	...	...	...	...	...	...	...	...	...	...	61
714	604	110	538	401	137	162	101	61	17	13	4	...	...	...	...	...	...	...	...	...	...	...	...	62
88	75	13	199	159	40	30	17	13	...	...	...	...	...	...	...	...	...	...	...	...	...	...	...	63

IMPERIAL TABLE VI.

Religion.

NOTE 1.—The populations of the following estimated areas have been entered as Animists in this Table :—

District.	Estimated Area.	Persons.	Males.	Females.
Northern Shan States	Kokang ...	25,604	13,389	12,215
	West Manglün	18,562	9,061	9,501
Southern Shan States	Brè Tracts of Karenni State.	5,717	2,606	3,111
Pakôkku Hill Tracts	Unadministered Area.	9,123	4,478	4,645
	TOTAL ...	59,006	29,534	29,472

NOTE 2.—The following persons of European and Anglo-Indian races, but not professing the Christian religion, are included as Christians in columns 17, 18 and 19 of this Table. They should naturally have been included in columns 35, 36 and 37 of this Table; but it was decided that the members of Christian races should be classed together, even though they might not profess the Christian religion. If a purely religious comparison is required, the necessary transfers can be effected :—

Belief.	Persons.	Males.	Females.
Agnostic ...	50	45	5
Atheist ...	12	12	...
Secularist ...	4	4	...
TOTAL ...	66	61	5

Serial No.	District or State.	Total Population.			Buddhist.			Animist.			Hindu.			Mahomedan.		
		Persons.	Males.	Females.	Persons.	Males.	Females.	Persons.	Males.	Females.	Persons.	Males.	Females.	Persons.	Males.	Females.
	1	2	3	4	5	6	7	8	9	10	11	12	13	14	15	16
	Provincial Total ...	12,115,217	6,183,494	5,931,723	10,384,579	5,113,459	5,271,120	701,473	368,143	333,330	389,679	312,650	77,029	420,777	271,428	149,349
	Burma Proper ...	10,610,256	5,432,715	5,177,541	9,273,865	4,561,249	4,712,616	328,613	183,403	145,210	382,288	306,700	75,588	417,575	269,085	148,490
	Arakan Division ...	839,896	441,925	397,971	561,248	280,251	280,997	75,075	38,626	36,449	15,997	14,755	1,242	186,323	107,506	78,817
1	Akyab ...	529,943	289,474	240,469	302,527	154,935	147,592	33,806	17,501	16,305	14,454	13,418	1,036	178,381	103,124	75,257
2	Northern Arakan ...	22,234	11,405	10,829	1,705	997	708	19,821	9,977	9,844	567	391	176	44	36	8
3	Kyaukpyu ...	184,916	89,571	95,345	165,864	79,099	86,765	14,726	7,718	7,008	590	572	18	3,641	2,130	1,511
4	Sandoway ...	102,803	51,475	51,328	91,062	45,220	45,842	6,632	3,430	3,202	386	374	12	4,257	2,216	2,041
	Pegu Division ...	2,073,737	1,136,192	937,545	1,688,181	844,606	843,575	28,963	21,131	7,832	212,395	169,747	42,648	85,718	67,554	18,164
5	City of Rangoon ...	293,316	208,111	85,205	97,467	52,137	45,330	7,217	5,936	1,281	108,350	89,028	19,322	54,634	45,106	9,528
6	Hanthawaddy ...	539,109	295,886	243,223	447,638	227,611	220,027	4,675	4,024	651	57,137	44,951	12,186	16,307	12,023	4,284
7	Tharrawaddy ...	433,320	216,442	216,878	413,584	202,639	210,945	2,376	1,965	411	7,406	6,125	1,281	3,857	2,667	1,190
8	Pegu ...	429,121	229,540	199,581	369,612	188,279	181,333	5,391	4,110	1,281	34,350	25,357	8,993	7,384	5,399	1,985
9	Prome ...	378,871	186,213	192,658	359,880	173,940	185,940	9,304	5,096	4,208	5,152	4,286	866	3,536	2,359	1,177
	Irrawaddy Division	1,869,485	962,913	906,572	1,712,939	856,877	856,062	11,668	10,449	1,219	42,105	36,512	5,593	28,271	21,115	7,156
10	Bassein ...	440,988	226,773	214,215	391,027	194,614	196,413	2,049	1,864	185	11,822	10,471	1,351	8,107	5,680	2,427
11	Henzada ...	532,357	264,319	268,038	509,310	248,022	261,288	1,466	1,309	157	6,600	5,912	688	4,657	3,074	1,583
12	Myaungmya ...	334,852	176,465	158,387	300,515	153,362	147,153	2,322	2,083	239	6,128	5,486	642	7,103	5,694	1,409
13	Ma-ubin ...	305,073	155,715	149,358	282,669	140,611	142,058	1,651	1,475	176	5,392	4,775	617	4,864	3,615	1,249
14	Pyapôn ...	256,215	139,641	116,574	229,418	119,368	110,050	3,580	3,118	462	12,164	9,869	2,295	3,540	3,052	488
	Tenasserim Division	1,429,294	750,626	678,668	1,204,599	611,494	593,105	63,187	35,970	27,217	59,372	44,807	14,565	51,277	32,293	18,984
15	Toungoo ...	351,076	181,488	169,588	274,870	138,220	136,650	22,355	12,215	10,140	14,220	10,070	4,150	6,369	4,170	2,199
16	Salween ...	46,608	24,741	21,867	20,474	11,213	9,261	25,068	12,725	12,343	274	231	43	408	349	59
17	Thatôn ...	416,975	217,770	199,205	380,244	192,749	187,495	5,958	3,840	2,118	16,805	12,131	4,674	10,221	7,054	3,167
18	Amherst ...	357,918	198,430	159,488	309,904	158,436	151,468	4,338	3,441	897	23,864	18,402	5,462	22,893	14,560	8,333
19	Tavoy ...	135,293	68,667	66,626	129,505	64,908	64,597	1,380	997	383	842	781	61	1,564	908	656
20	Mergui ...	111,424	59,530	51,894	89,602	45,968	43,634	4,088	2,752	1,336	3,367	3,192	175	9,822	5,252	4,570
	Magwe Division ...	1,239,032	603,614	635,418	1,197,596	577,817	619,779	24,823	12,819	12,004	8,639	7,420	1,219	5,736	4,050	1,686
21	Thayetmyo ..	248,275	122,231	126,044	228,058	111,290	116,768	15,232	7,594	7,638	2,186	1,605	581	2,164	1,361	803
22	Pakôkku ...	409,909	196,159	213,750	404,037	192,432	211,605	3,472	1,831	1,641	1,170	1,016	154	894	681	213
23	Minbu ...	263,939	128,837	135,102	253,927	122,133	131,794	5,758	3,056	2,702	2,651	2,449	202	1,061	775	286
24	Magwe ...	316,909	156,387	160,522	311,574	151,962	159,612	361	338	23	2,632	2,350	282	1,617	1,233	384
	Mandalay Division ...	832,969	426,776	406,193	647,543	320,444	327,099	118,132	60,471	57,661	27,849	20,539	7,310	27,354	17,435	9,919
25	Mandalay ...	340,770	170,750	170,020	294,904	141,480	153,424	1,497	1,278	219	16,071	11,192	4,879	20,845	12,236	8,609
26	Bhamo ...	107,811	55,528	52,283	53,490	27,182	26,308	47,722	23,244	24,478	1,652	1,404	248	2,242	1,852	390
27	Myitkyina ...	85,577	47,863	37,714	30,171	16,518	13,653	46,050	24,098	21,952	6,192	4,617	1,575	1,906	1,618	288
28	Katha ...	198,193	98,148	100,045	189,134	92,871	96,263	6,089	2,984	3,105	1,429	1,268	161	1,156	754	402
29	Ruby Mines ...	100,618	54,487	46,131	79,844	42,393	37,451	16,774	8,867	7,907	2,505	2,058	447	1,205	975	230
	Sagaing Division ...	1,155,271	543,289	611,982	1,128,941	526,593	602,348	4,007	2,240	1,767	6,631	5,107	1,524	11,103	6,640	4,463
30	Shwebo ...	356,363	168,070	188,293	344,852	161,070	183,782	111	101	10	2,305	1,841	464	6,326	3,424	2,902
31	Sagaing ..	312,111	147,816	164,295	306,416	144,311	162,105	95	75	20	1,772	1,228	544	2,815	1,710	1,105
32	Lower Chindwin ...	316,175	141,262	174,913	313,839	139,518	174,321	82	74	8	784	629	155	876	635	241
33	Upper Chindwin ...	170,622	86,141	84,481	163,834	81,694	82,140	3,719	1,990	1,729	1,770	1,409	361	1,086	871	215
	Meiktila Division ...	1,170,572	567,380	603,192	1,132,818	543,167	589,651	2,758	1,697	1,061	9,299	7,812	1,487	21,793	12,492	9,301
34	Kyauksè ...	141,426	68,868	72,558	134,928	65,293	69,635	25	24	1	815	682	133	4,954	2,509	2,445
35	Meiktila ...	279,822	134,170	145,652	271,774	128,307	143,467	95	80	15	2,931	2,474	457	4,253	2,800	1,453
36	Yamèthin ...	307,419	153,223	154,196	288,047	141,650	146,397	2,452	1,433	1,019	3,766	3,068	698	11,057	5,956	5,101
37	Myingyan ...	441,905	211,119	230,786	438,069	207,917	230,152	186	160	26	1,787	1,588	199	1,529	1,227	302
	Specially Administered Territories.	1,504,961	750,779	754,182	1,110,714	552,210	558,504	372,860	184,740	188,120	7,391	5,950	1,441	3,202	2,343	859
38	Northern Shan States	458,952	230,545	228,407	335,436	167,904	167,532	110,320	50,217	60,103	2,607	2,250	357	1,241	952	289
39	Southern Shan States	900,202	448,705	451,497	775,156	384,220	390,936	110,131	55,696	54,435	3,282	2,638	644	1,800	1,274	526
40	Pakôkku Hill Tracts	26,251	12,967	13,284	35	22	13	26,051	12,817	13,234	151	115	36	8	7	1
41	Chin Hills ...	119,556	58,562	60,994	87	64	23	117,358	57,010	60,348	1,351	947	404	153	110	43

VI.—*Religion.*

Christian. Persons.	Christian. Males.	Christian. Females.	Sikh. Persons.	Sikh. Males.	Sikh. Females.	Jain. Persons.	Jain. Males.	Jain. Females.	Zoroastrian. Persons.	Zoroastrian. Males.	Zoroastrian. Females.	Jew. Persons.	Jew. Males.	Jew. Females.	Confucian. Persons.	Confucian. Males.	Confucian. Females.	Secularist, Rationalist, and Agnostic. Persons.	Secularist, Rationalist, and Agnostic. Males.	Secularist, Rationalist, and Agnostic. Females.	Serial No.
17	18	19	20	21	22	23	24	25	26	27	28	29	30	31	32	33	34	35	36	37	
220,081	111,033	99,048	6,693	5,527	1,166	495	416	79	300	195	105	1,024	559	465	71	57	14	45	27	18	
199,680	105,815	93,865	6,301	5,210	1,091	495	416	79	300	195	105	1,024	559	465	71	57	14	44	26	18	
1,167	718	449	43	39	4	17	11	6	...	...	...	26	19	7	...	...	...	...	...	...	
605	433	172	37	33	4	17	11	6	...	...	...	26	19	7	...	...	...	...	...	...	1
7	4	3	...	...	...	...	...	...	...	...	...	...	...	...	...	...	...	...	...	...	2
95	52	43	...	...	...	...	...	...	...	...	...	...	...	...	...	...	...	...	...	...	3
460	229	231	6	6	...	...	...	...	...	...	...	...	...	...	...	...	...	...	...	...	4
55,030	30,568	24,462	2,025	1,691	334	335	294	41	228	140	88	762	388	374	71	57	14	29	16	13	
23,044	13,977	9,067	1,263	1,095	168	296	258	38	196	121	75	750	381	369	71	57	14	28	15	13	5
12,647	6,733	5,914	641	495	146	38	35	3	22	11	11	3	2	1	...	...	...	1	1	...	6
6,052	3,011	3,041	27	23	4	1	1	...	8	6	2	9	5	4	...	...	...	...	...	...	7
12,316	6,341	5,975	68	54	14	...	...	...	...	...	...	...	...	...	...	...	...	...	...	...	8
971	506	465	26	24	2	...	...	...	2	2	...	...	...	...	...	...	...	...	...	...	9
74,134	37,662	36,472	191	170	21	88	75	13	33	18	15	55	34	21	...	...	...	...	...	...	
27,927	14,111	13,816	3	3	...	4	4	...	22	12	10	27	14	13	...	...	...	...	...	...	10
10,285	5,070	5,215	14	14	...	14	11	3	1	1	...	10	6	4	...	...	...	...	...	...	11
18,157	9,218	8,939	2	2	...	18	15	3	7	5	2	...	...	...	...	...	...	...	...	...	12
10,474	5,217	5,257	...	...	...	20	19	1	...	...	...	3	3	...	...	...	...	...	...	...	13
7,291	4,046	3,245	172	151	21	32	26	6	3	...	3	15	11	4	...	...	...	...	...	...	14
50,622	25,883	24,739	97	86	11	43	29	14	10	8	2	83	54	29	...	...	...	4	2	2	
33,138	16,712	16,426	88	77	11	5	5	...	3	2	1	24	15	9	...	...	...	4	2	2	15
384	223	161	...	...	...	...	...	...	...	...	...	...	...	...	...	...	...	...	...	...	16
3,738	1,987	1,751	4	4	...	2	2	...	3	3	...	...	...	...	...	...	...	...	...	...	17
6,824	3,531	3,293	5	5	...	36	22	14	4	3	1	50	30	20	...	...	...	...	...	...	18
1,999	1,070	929	...	...	...	...	...	...	...	...	...	3	3	...	...	...	...	...	...	...	19
4,539	2,360	2,179	...	...	...	...	...	...	...	...	...	6	6	...	...	...	...	...	...	...	20
1,508	952	556	686	533	153	9	5	4	3	3	...	32	15	17	...	...	...	...	...	...	
592	357	235	18	12	6	1	1	...	1	1	...	23	10	13	...	...	...	...	...	...	21
284	166	118	50	31	19	...	...	...	2	2	...	...	...	...	...	...	...	...	...	...	22
150	98	52	392	326	66	...	...	...	...	...	...	...	...	...	...	...	...	...	...	...	23
482	331	151	226	164	62	8	4	4	...	...	...	9	5	4	...	...	...	...	...	...	24
9,503	5,658	3,845	2,485	2,146	340	2	2	...	26	26	...	63	47	16	...	...	...	11	8	3	
6,571	3,870	2,701	780	611	169	2	2	...	26	26	...	63	47	16	...	...	...	11	8	3	25
1,785	1,030	755	920	816	104	...	...	...	...	...	...	...	...	...	...	...	...	...	...	...	26
566	349	217	692	663	29	...	...	...	...	...	...	...	...	...	...	...	...	...	...	...	27
383	269	114	2	2	...	...	...	...	...	...	...	...	...	...	...	...	...	...	...	...	28
198	140	58	92	54	38	...	...	...	...	...	...	...	...	...	...	...	...	...	...	...	29
4,229	2,435	1,793	356	271	85	1	...	1	...	...	...	3	2	1	...	...	...	...	...	...	
2,746	1,617	1,129	22	17	5	1	...	1	...	...	...	...	...	...	...	...	...	...	...	...	30
1,013	492	521	...	...	...	...	...	...	...	...	...	...	...	...	...	...	...	...	...	...	31
297	179	118	297	227	70	...	...	...	...	...	...	...	...	...	...	...	...	...	...	...	32
173	148	25	37	27	10	...	...	...	...	...	...	3	2	1	...	...	...	...	...	...	33
3,487	1,938	1,549	417	274	143	...	...	...	...	...	...	...	...	...	...	...	...	...	...	...	
679	345	334	25	15	10	...	...	...	...	...	...	...	...	...	...	...	...	...	...	...	34
678	451	227	91	58	33	...	...	...	...	...	...	...	...	...	...	...	...	...	...	...	35
1,813	928	885	284	188	96	...	...	...	...	...	...	...	...	...	...	...	...	...	...	...	36
317	214	103	17	13	4	...	...	...	...	...	...	...	...	...	...	...	...	...	...	...	37
10,401	5,218	5,183	392	317	75	...	...	...	...	...	...	...	...	...	...	...	...	1	1	...	
348	222	126	...	...	...	...	...	...	...	...	...	...	...	...	...	...	...	...	...	...	38
9,818	4,866	4,952	15	11	4	...	...	...	...	...	...	...	...	...	...	...	...	...	...	...	39
4	4	...	2	2	...	...	...	...	...	...	...	...	...	...	...	...	...	...	...	...	40
231	126	105	375	304	71	...	...	...	...	...	...	...	...	...	...	...	...	1	1	...	41

IMPERIAL TABLE VII.

Age, Sex and Civil Condition.

PART A.—PROVINCIAL SUMMARY (By Religions).

NOTE 1.—This table is divided into two parts. Part A shows the distribution for the Province as a whole, of the total population and of each religion by age, sex and civil condition. Separate statements are also given showing the distribution for Burma Proper and for Specially Administered Territories. Part B shows a similar distribution for each district and each Specially Administered Territory; but in order to economise space, minor religions have been omitted, and longer age periods have been adopted.

NOTE 2.—No records of age were taken in the following areas. Their populations are therefore omitted from this table.

Territory.	Portion.	Population.		
		Persons.	Males.	Females.
Northern Shan States	Kokang ...	25,604	13,389	12,215
	West Manglün	18,562	9,061	9,501
Southern Shan States	Brè Tract of Karenni State.	5,717	2,606	3,111
Pakôkku Hill Tracts	The whole ...	26,251	12,967	13,284
	Total ...	76,134	38,023	38,111

IMPERIAL TABLE VII.—*Age, Sex and Civil Condition.*

PART A.—PROVINCIAL SUMMARY (Whole Province).

	AGE.	POPULATION.			UNMARRIED.			MARRIED.			WIDOWED.		
		Persons.	Males.	Females.	Persons.	Males.	Females.	Persons.	Males.	Females.	Persons.	Males.	Females.
	1	2	3	4	5	6	7	8	9	10	11	12	13
ALL RELIGIONS.	0—1	276,258	134,170	142,088	276,258	134,170	142,088	...	...	...	...	...	...
	1—2	272,896	133,736	139,160	272,896	133,736	139,160	...	...	...	...	...	...
	2—3	333,112	163,221	169,891	333,103	163,216	169,887	9	5	4	...	...	...
	3—4	376,269	185,763	190,506	376,257	185,758	190,499	12	5	7	...	...	...
	4—5	337,042	165,191	171,851	337,017	165,176	171,841	23	14	9	2	1	1
	Total 0—5	*1,595,577*	*782,081*	*813,496*	*1,595,531*	*782,056*	*813,475*	*44*	*24*	*20*	*2*	*1*	*1*
	5—10	1,573,950	784,144	789,806	1,573,692	784,071	789,621	255	72	183	3	1	2
	10—15	1,377,509	714,400	663,109	1,372,107	713,429	658,678	5,236	951	4,285	166	20	146
	15—20	1,118,007	548,748	569,259	917,133	504,069	413,004	190,586	43,008	147,578	10,288	1,671	8,617
	20—25	1,047,189	526,720	520,469	443,475	292,186	151,289	567,858	223,588	344,270	35,856	10,946	24,910
	25—30	1,005,278	528,466	476,812	227,873	160,724	67,149	729,654	350,184	379,470	47,751	17,558	30,193
	30—35	959,031	519,988	439,043	131,988	91,009	40,979	764,534	405,596	358,938	62,509	23,383	39,126
	35—40	756,862	416,295	340,567	74,272	49,953	24,319	617,931	344,213	273,718	64,659	22,129	42,530
	40—45	692,906	365,155	327,751	59,182	36,448	22,734	547,979	302,370	245,609	85,745	26,337	59,408
	45—50	459,548	245,019	214,529	34,173	20,151	14,022	354,968	203,921	151,047	70,407	20,947	49,460
	50—55	453,584	227,471	226,113	35,565	19,262	16,303	313,359	182,359	131,000	104,660	25,850	78,810
	55—60	272,842	136,952	135,890	20,999	10,921	10,078	180,795	107,347	73,448	71,048	18,684	52,364
	60—65	321,844	161,527	160,317	26,232	12,616	13,616	178,035	118,133	59,902	117,577	30,778	86,799
	65—70	147,671	75,936	71,735	13,446	6,956	6,490	75,097	50,949	24,148	59,128	18,031	41,097
	70 and over	257,285	112,569	144,716	25,836	11,507	14,269	85,092	60,387	24,705	146,357	40,615	105,742
	Total ...	**12,039,083**	**6,145,471**	**5,893,612**	**6,551,504**	**3,495,418**	**3,056,086**	**4,611,423**	**2,393,102**	**2,218,321**	**876,156**	**256,951**	**619,205**
BUDDHIST.	0—1	247,995	119,972	128,023	247,995	119,972	128,023	...	...	...	...	...	...
	1—2	243,043	119,054	123,989	243,043	119,054	123,989	...	...	...	...	...	...
	2—3	292,955	143,253	149,702	292,955	143,253	149,702	...	...	...	...	...	...
	3—4	332,616	164,109	168,507	332,616	164,109	168,507	...	...	...	...	...	...
	4—5	299,006	146,150	152,856	299,006	146,150	152,856	...	...	...	...	...	...
	Total 0—5	*1,415,615*	*692,538*	*723,077*	*1,415,615*	*692,538*	*723,077*	...	...	...	...	...	...
	5—10	1,401,609	693,184	708,425	1,401,599	693,184	708,415	10	...	10	...	...	...
	10—15	1,232,952	632,177	600,775	1,229,826	631,848	597,978	2,993	317	2,676	133	12	121
	15—20	969,399	459,826	509,573	802,197	426,365	375,832	157,913	32,135	125,778	9,289	1,326	7,963
	20—25	851,894	396,442	455,452	347,065	212,342	134,723	473,704	175,448	298,256	31,125	8,652	22,473
	25—30	806,072	388,774	417,298	163,830	104,343	59,487	601,579	270,754	330,825	40,663	13,677	26,986
	30—35	775,207	392,117	383,090	91,364	56,390	34,974	632,048	317,719	314,329	51,795	18,008	33,787
	35—40	642,997	335,152	307,845	56,290	33,947	22,343	530,660	283,269	247,391	56,047	17,936	38,111
	40—45	580,508	289,304	291,204	44,792	24,267	20,525	464,290	244,102	220,188	71,426	20,935	50,491
	45—50	406,044	208,786	197,258	28,382	15,290	13,093	315,417	175,634	139,783	62,245	17,862	44,383
	50—55	392,906	190,614	202,292	29,411	14,555	14,856	273,102	154,403	118,699	90,393	21,656	68,737
	55—60	250,457	123,095	127,362	19,013	9,489	9,524	166,162	96,871	69,291	65,282	16,735	48,547
	60—65	288,976	142,413	146,563	23,169	10,501	12,668	160,064	104,475	55,589	105,743	27,437	78,306
	65—70	135,376	67,737	67,639	12,366	6,223	6,143	68,133	45,237	22,896	54,877	16,277	38,600
	70 and over	234,532	101,278	133,254	23,777	10,261	13,516	76,558	53,831	22,727	134,197	37,186	97,011
	Total ...	**10,384,544**	**5,113,437**	**5,271,107**	**5,688,696**	**2,941,543**	**2,747,153**	**3,922,633**	**1,954,195**	**1,968,438**	**773,215**	**217,699**	**555,516**
ANIMIST.	0—1	10,956	5,544	5,412	10,956	5,544	5,412	...	...	...	...	...	...
	1—2	12,674	6,172	6,502	12,674	6,172	6,502	...	...	...	...	...	...
	2—3	17,572	8,656	8,916	17,572	8,656	8,916	...	...	...	...	...	...
	3—4	19,654	9,620	10,034	19,654	9,620	10,034	...	...	...	...	...	...
	4—5	16,727	8,203	8,524	16,727	8,203	8,524	...	...	...	...	...	...
	Total 0—5	*77,583*	*38,195*	*39,388*	*77,583*	*38,195*	*39,388*	...	...	...	...	...	...
	5—10	78,418	42,444	35,974	78,418	42,444	35,974	...	...	...	...	...	...
	10—15	62,219	33,386	28,833	61,923	33,353	28,570	279	31	248	17	2	15
	15—20	55,210	27,748	27,462	46,320	25,557	20,763	8,507	2,064	6,443	383	127	256
	20—25	59,265	29,598	29,667	28,859	19,061	9,798	28,597	9,899	18,698	1,809	638	1,171
	25—30	55,918	29,917	26,001	16,031	12,149	3,882	37,286	16,774	20,512	2,601	994	1,607
	30—35	62,709	33,722	28,987	11,543	7,666	3,877	46,302	24,383	21,919	4,864	1,673	3,191
	35—40	38,296	22,313	15,983	4,295	3,443	852	30,343	17,634	12,709	3,658	1,236	2,422
	40—45	44,815	24,774	20,041	3,419	2,323	1,096	34,132	20,592	13,540	7,264	1,859	5,405
	45—50	20,607	12,073	8,534	1,314	951	363	15,622	10,080	5,542	3,671	1,042	2,629
	50—55	27,309	13,822	13,487	1,685	973	712	18,305	11,239	7,066	7,319	1,610	5,709
	55—60	9,487	5,318	4,169	560	337	223	6,381	4,272	2,109	2,546	709	1,837
	60—65	15,584	7,773	7,811	924	493	431	8,441	5,956	2,485	6,219	1,324	4,895
	65—70	6,375	4,239	2,136	427	228	199	3,777	3,149	628	2,171	862	1,309
	70 and over	11,744	4,948	6,796	869	484	385	3,995	2,890	1,105	6,880	1,574	5,306
	Total ...	**625,539**	**330,270**	**295,269**	**334,170**	**187,657**	**146,513**	**241,967**	**128,963**	**113,004**	**49,402**	**13,690**	**35,752**
HINDU.	0—1	4,465	2,248	2,217	4,465	2,248	2,217	...	...	...	...	...	...
	1—2	3,765	1,964	1,801	3,765	1,964	1,801	...	...	...	...	...	...
	2—3	5,310	2,723	2,587	5,307	2,722	2,585	3	1	2	...	...	...
	3—4	5,870	2,996	2,874	5,862	2,992	2,870	8	4	4	...	...	...
	4—5	4,626	2,443	2,183	4,611	2,434	2,177	15	9	6	...	...	...
	Total 0—5	*24,036*	*12,374*	*11,662*	*24,010*	*12,360*	*11,650*	*26*	*14*	*12*	...	...	...
	5—10	19,932	10,688	9,244	19,722	10,633	9,089	209	55	154	1	..	1
	10—15	18,459	12,895	5,564	17,140	12,422	4,718	1,307	467	840	12	6	6
	15—20	31,690	25,216	6,474	21,987	20,228	1,759	9,519	4,886	4,633	184	102	82
	20—25	61,821	51,932	9,889	31,934	30,935	999	28,819	20,214	8,605	1,068	783	285
	25—30	69,943	59,738	10,205	26,479	25,806	673	41,738	32,565	9,173	1,726	1,367	359
	30—35	60,309	52,109	8,200	17,889	17,353	536	40,051	32,883	7,168	2,369	1,873	496
	35—40	34,499	29,971	4,528	8,236	7,987	249	24,433	20,622	3,811	1,830	1,362	468
	40—45	30,832	26,785	4,047	6,800	6,534	266	21,440	18,534	2,906	2,592	1,717	875
	45—50	12,012	10,199	1,813	2,287	2,186	101	8,271	7,171	1,100	1,454	842	612
	50—55	12,653	10,420	2,233	2,582	2,402	180	7,884	6,838	1,046	2,187	1,180	1,007
	55—60	3,735	2,965	770	704	644	60	2,212	1,895	327	809	426	383
	60—65	5,396	4,182	1,214	1,025	920	105	2,819	2,457	362	1,552	805	747
	65—70	1,525	1,172	353	287	250	37	744	634	110	494	288	206
	70 and over	2,686	1,889	797	493	420	73	1,101	936	165	1,092	533	559
	Total ...	**389,528**	**312,535**	**76,993**	**181,575**	**151,080**	**30,495**	**190,583**	**150,171**	**40,412**	**17,370**	**11,284**	**6,086**

IMPERIAL TABLE VII.—*Age, Sex and Civil Condition.*

PART A.—PROVINCIAL SUMMARY (Whole Province).

	AGE.	POPULATION.			UNMARRIED.			MARRIED.			WIDOWED.		
		Persons.	Males.	Females.	Persons.	Males.	Females.	Persons.	Males.	Females.	Persons.	Males.	Females.
	1	2	3	4	5	6	7	8	9	10	11	12	13
MAHOMEDAN.	0—1	7,902	4,002	3,900	7,902	4,002	3,900	...	...	...	...	...	...
	1—2	8,577	4,189	4,388	8,577	4,189	4,388	...	...	...	...	...	...
	2—3	10,978	5,499	5,479	10,972	5,495	5,477	6	4	2	...	...	...
	3—4	11,595	5,797	5,798	11,394	5,796	5,798	1	1	...	...	...	...
	4—5	10,572	5,343	5,229	10,562	5,337	5,225	8	5	3	2	1	1
	Total 0—5	*49,624*	*24,830*	*24,794*	*49,607*	*24,819*	*24,788*	*15*	*10*	*5*	*2*	*1*	*1*
	5—10	47,711	24,617	23,094	47,678	24,600	23,078	31	16	15	2	1	1
	10—15	39,015	22,877	16,138	38,422	22,750	15,672	590	127	463	3	...	3
	15—20	40,503	25,228	15,275	27,949	21,638	6,311	12,185	3,487	8,698	369	103	266
	20—25	51,268	35,824	15,444	22,589	20,261	2,328	37,204	14,822	22,382	1,475	741	734
	25—30	50,584	37,250	13,294	14,015	12,560	1,455	34,510	23,524	10,986	2,059	1,206	853
	30—35	42,632	31,398	11,234	7,814	7,073	741	32,274	22,877	9,397	2,544	1,448	1,096
	35—40	26,951	20,365	6,586	3,671	3,294	377	21,172	15,900	5,272	2,108	1,171	937
	40—45	24,296	17,246	7,050	2,962	2,563	399	18,455	13,402	5,053	2,879	1,281	1,598
	45—50	13,049	9,435	3,614	1,594	1,367	227	9,624	7,255	2,369	1,831	813	1,018
	50—55	13,719	8,862	4,857	1,342	1,034	308	9,270	6,884	2,386	3,107	944	2,163
	55—60	5,799	3,739	2,060	486	337	149	3,740	2,831	909	1,573	571	1,002
	60—65	7,718	4,913	2,805	774	557	217	4,301	3,547	754	2,643	809	1,834
	65—70	2,748	1,858	890	254	204	50	1,520	1,280	240	974	374	600
	70 and over	5,152	2,939	2,213	430	291	139	2,133	1,798	335	2,589	850	1,739
	Total ...	420,769	271,421	149,348	219,587	143,348	76,239	177,024	117,760	59,264	24,158	10,313	13,845
CHRISTIAN.	0—1	4,750	2,310	2,440	4,750	2,310	2,440	...	...	...	...	...	...
	1—2	4,757	2,327	2,430	4,757	2,327	2,430	...	...	...	...	...	...
	2—3	6,139	3,010	3,129	6,139	3,010	3,129	...	...	...	...	...	...
	3—4	6,372	3,159	3,213	6,369	3,159	3,210	3	..	3	...	...	...
	4—5	6,000	2,999	3,001	6,000	2,999	3,001	...	...	...	...	...	...
	Total 0—5	*28,018*	*13,805*	*14,213*	*28,015*	*13,805*	*14,210*	*3*	...	*3*	...	...	...
	5—10	25,835	12,975	12,860	25,830	12,974	12,856	5	1	4	...	...	...
	10—15	24,516	12,853	11,663	24,467	12,847	11,620	48	6	42	1	...	1
	15—20	20,477	10,168	10,309	18,148	9,801	8,347	2,267	354	1,913	62	13	49
	20—25	20,971	11,239	9,732	11,793	8,379	3,414	8,843	2,765	6,078	335	95	240
	25—30	21,227	11,474	9,753	6,848	5,215	1,633	13,757	6,019	7,738	622	240	382
	30—35	17,103	9,746	7,357	3,030	2,188	842	13,184	7,220	5,964	889	338	551
	35—40	13,406	7,879	5,527	1,624	1,130	494	10,819	6,367	4,452	963	382	581
	40—45	11,891	6,567	5,324	1,111	670	441	9,267	5,410	3,857	1,513	487	1,026
	45—50	7,573	4,283	3,290	568	329	239	5,828	3,593	2,235	1,177	361	816
	50—55	6,829	3,609	3,220	520	273	247	4,678	2,891	1,787	1,631	445	1,186
	55—60	3,319	1,797	1,522	230	110	120	2,254	1,446	808	835	241	594
	60—65	4,133	2,220	1,913	336	141	195	2,385	1,679	706	1,412	400	1,012
	65—70	1,632	918	714	112	51	61	913	640	273	607	227	380
	70 and over	3,147	1,496	1,651	264	108	156	1,290	920	370	1,593	468	1,125
	Total ...	210,077	111,029	99,048	122,896	68,021	54,875	75,541	39,311	36,230	11,640	3,697	7,943
SIKH.	0—1	156	75	81	156	75	81	...	...	...	...	...	...
	1—2	59	25	34	59	25	34	...	...	...	...	...	...
	2—3	116	57	59	116	57	59	...	...	...	...	...	...
	3—4	116	62	54	116	62	54	...	...	...	...	...	...
	4—5	77	40	37	77	40	37	...	...	...	...	...	...
	Total 0—5	*524*	*259*	*265*	*524*	*259*	*265*	...	...	...	...	...	...
	5—10	265	152	113	265	152	113	...	...	...	...	...	...
	10—15	178	123	55	165	121	44	13	2	11	...	...	...
	15—20	543	451	92	391	380	11	151	71	80	1	...	1
	20—25	1,687	1,488	199	1,081	1,069	12	567	383	184	39	36	3
	25—30	1,265	1,078	187	580	573	7	614	435	179	71	70	1
	30—35	882	750	132	299	294	5	540	414	126	43	42	1
	35—40	545	493	52	134	133	1	374	324	50	37	36	1
	40—45	443	397	46	83	79	4	303	263	40	57	55	2
	45—50	204	190	14	24	24	...	153	140	13	27	26	1
	50—55	111	105	6	16	16	...	81	76	5	14	13	1
	55—60	20	18	2	3	2	1	15	15	...	2	1	1
	60—65	12	10	2	3	3	...	6	5	1	3	2	1
	65—70	2	1	...	...	...	...	1	1	...	...	...	...
	70 and over	11	10	1	2	2	...	7	6	1	2	2	...
	Total ...	6,691	5,525	1,166	2,570	2,207	463	2,825	2,135	690	296	283	13
JAIN.	0—1	2	1	1	2	1	1	...	...	...	...	...	...
	1—2	4	1	3	4	1	3	...	...	...	...	...	...
	2—3	3	2	1	3	2	1	...	...	...	...	...	...
	3—4	6	3	3	6	3	3	...	...	...	...	...	...
	4—5	4	1	3	4	1	3	...	...	...	...	...	...
	Total 0—5	*19*	*8*	*11*	*19*	*8*	*11*	...	...	...	...	...	...
	5—10	14	6	8	14	6	8	...	...	...	...	...	...
	10—15	9	8	1	8	7	1	1	1	...	...	...	...
	15—20	43	30	13	29	24	5	14	6	8	...	...	...
	20—25	113	96	17	67	66	1	45	30	15	1	...	1
	25—30	104	89	15	30	28	2	73	60	13	1	1	...
	30—35	79	75	4	20	19	1	59	56	3	...	...	...
	35—40	52	48	4	6	6	...	43	40	3	3	2	1
	40—45	32	29	3	6	6	...	23	22	1	3	1	2
	45—50	9	8	1	...	...	...	8	7	1	1	1	...
	50—55	13	13	...	7	7	...	6	6	...	...	...	...
	55—60	3	2	1	1	...	1	2	2	...	...	...	...
	60—65	3	2	1	...	...	...	3	2	1	...	...	...
	65—70	...	...	...	...	...	...	...	...	...	...	...	...
	70 and over	2	2	...	...	...	...	2	2	...	...	...	...
	Total ...	495	416	79	207	177	30	279	234	45	9	5	4

IMPERIAL TABLE VII.—*Age, Sex and Civil Condition.*

PART A.—PROVINCIAL SUMMARY (Whole Province).

	AGE.	POPULATION.			UNMARRIED.			MARRIED.			WIDOWED.		
		Persons.	Males.	Females.	Persons.	Males.	Females.	Persons.	Males.	Females.	Persons.	Males.	Females.
	1	2	3	4	5	6	7	8	9	10	11	12	13
ZOROASTRIAN.	0—1	5	3	2	5	3	2	...	...	...	...	...	...
	1—2	2	...	2	2	...	2	...	...	...	...	...	...
	2—3	9	4	5	9	4	5	...	...	...	...	...	...
	3—4	10	4	6	10	4	6	...	...	...	...	...	...
	4—5	2	2	...	2	2	...	...	...	...	...	...	...
	Total 0—5	*28*	*13*	*15*	*28*	*13*	*15*	...	...	...	...	...	...
	5—10	23	16	7	23	16	7	...	...	...	...	...	...
	10—15	33	18	15	30	18	12	3	...	3	...	...	...
	15—20	18	9	9	14	8	6	4	1	3	...	...	...
	20—25	32	19	13	18	14	4	14	5	9	...	...	...
	25—30	44	32	12	17	14	3	25	17	8	2	1	1
	30—35	37	26	11	13	11	2	24	15	9	...	...	...
	35—40	28	23	5	6	5	1	21	18	3	1	...	1
	40—45	20	12	8	3	1	2	15	10	5	2	1	1
	45—50	13	12	1	1	1	...	12	11	1	...	...	...
	50—55	10	6	4	2	2	...	6	3	3	2	1	1
	55—60	3	2	1	...	...	...	3	2	1	...	...	...
	60—65	6	4	2	...	...	...	4	3	1	2	1	1
	65—70	3	2	1	...	...	...	3	2	1	...	...	...
	70 and over	2	1	1	...	...	...	2	1	1	...	...	...
	Total ...	300	195	105	155	103	52	136	88	48	9	4	5
JEW.	0—1	26	15	11	26	15	11	...	...	...	...	...	...
	1—2	15	4	11	15	4	11	...	...	...	...	...	...
	2—3	29	17	12	29	17	12	...	...	...	...	...	...
	3—4	28	12	16	28	12	16	...	...	...	...	...	...
	4—5	26	9	17	26	9	17	...	...	...	...	...	...
	Total 0—5	*124*	57	*67*	*124*	57	*67*	...	...	...	...	...	...
	5—10	136	59	77	136	59	77	...	...	...	...	...	...
	10—15	121	59	62	119	59	60	2	...	2	...	...	...
	15—20	115	64	51	91	62	29	24	2	22	...	...	...
	20—25	121	69	52	56	48	8	61	20	41	4	1	3
	25—30	99	58	41	29	26	3	64	30	34	6	2	4
	30—35	58	34	24	11	10	1	43	23	20	4	1	3
	35—40	79	43	36	7	5	2	62	36	26	10	2	8
	40—45	62	36	26	3	3	...	50	32	18	9	1	8
	45—50	32	29	3	2	2	...	29	27	2	1	...	1
	50—55	30	17	13	...	...	...	23	16	7	7	1	6
	55—60	14	11	3	1	1	...	13	10	3	...	...	...
	60—65	14	8	6	1	1	...	10	7	3	3	...	3
	65—70	10	9	1	...	...	...	6	6	...	4	3	1
	70 and over	9	6	3	1	1	...	4	3	1	4	2	2
	Total ...	1,024	559	465	581	334	247	291	212	179	52	13	39
CONFUCIAN.	0—1	...	...	...	...	...	...	...	...	...	...	...	...
	1—2	...	...	...	...	...	...	...	...	...	...	...	...
	2—3	1	...	1	1	...	1	...	...	...	...	...	...
	3—4	1	...	1	1	...	1	...	...	...	...	...	...
	4—5	1	...	1	1	...	1	...	...	...	...	...	...
	Total 0—5	*3*	...	*3*	*3*	...	*3*	...	...	...	...	...	...
	5—10	7	3	4	7	3	4	...	...	...	...	...	...
	10—15	3	1	2	3	1	2	...	...	...	...	...	...
	15—20	4	4	...	2	2	...	2	2	...	...	...	...
	20—25	10	9	1	8	8	...	2	1	1	...	...	...
	25—30	13	13	...	9	9	...	4	4	...	...	...	...
	30—35	12	10	2	4	4	...	7	6	1	1	...	1
	35—40	7	6	1	2	2	...	4	3	1	1	1	...
	40—45	2	2	...	1	1	...	1	1	...	...	...	...
	45—50	3	2	1	1	1	...	2	1	1	...	...	...
	50—55	2	2	...	...	...	...	2	2	...	...	...	...
	55—60	4	4	...	...	...	...	3	3	...	1	1	...
	60—65	1	1	...	...	...	...	1	1	...	...	...	...
	65—70	...	...	...	...	...	...	...	...	...	...	...	...
	70 and over	...	...	...	...	...	...	...	...	...	...	...	...
	Total ...	71	57	14	40	31	9	28	24	4	3	2	1
SECULARIST, RATIONALIST, AND AGNOSTIC.	0—1	1	...	1	1	...	1	...	...	...	...	...	...
	1—2	...	...	...	...	...	...	...	...	...	...	...	...
	2—3	...	...	...	...	...	...	...	...	...	...	...	...
	3—4	1	1	...	1	1	...	...	...	...	...	...	...
	4—5	1	1	...	1	1	...	...	...	...	...	...	...
	Total 0—5	*3*	*2*	*1*	*3*	*2*	*1*	...	...	...	...	...	...
	5—10	...	...	...	...	...	...	...	...	...	...	...	...
	10—15	4	3	1	4	3	1	...	...	...	...	...	...
	15—20	5	4	1	5	4	1	...	...	...	...	...	...
	20—25	7	4	3	5	3	2	2	1	1	...	...	...
	25—30	9	3	6	5	1	4	4	2	2	...	...	...
	30—35	3	1	2	1	1	...	2	...	2	...	...	...
	35—40	2	2	...	1	1	...	...	...	...	1	1	...
	40—45	5	3	2	2	1	1	3	2	1	...	...	...
	45—50	2	2	...	...	...	...	2	2	...	...	...	...
	50—55	2	1	1	...	...	...	2	1	1	...	...	...
	55—60	1	1	...	1	1	...	...	...	...	...	...	...
	60—65	1	1	...	...	...	...	1	1	...	...	...	...
	65—70	1	...	1	...	...	...	...	...	...	1	...	1
	70 and over	...	...	...	...	...	...	...	...	...	...	...	...
	Total ...	45	27	18	27	17	10	16	9	7	2	1	1

IMPERIAL TABLE VII.—*Age, Sex and Civil Condition.*

PART A.—PROVINCIAL SUMMARY (Burma Proper).

	AGE.	POPULATION.			UNMARRIED.			MARRIED.			WIDOWED.		
		Persons.	Males.	Females.	Persons.	Males.	Females.	Persons.	Males.	Females.	Persons.	Males.	Females.
	1	2	3	4	5	6	7	8	9	10	11	12	13
ALL RELIGIONS.	0—1	245,555	119,090	126,465	245,555	119,090	126,465	...	...	...	...	...	...
	1—2	242,279	118,649	123,630	242,279	118,649	123,630	...	...	...	...	...	...
	2—3	293,826	144,151	149,675	293,817	144,146	149,671	9	5	4	...	...	...
	3—4	331,217	163,620	167,597	331,205	163,615	167,590	12	5	7	...	...	...
	4—5	295,870	145,272	150,598	295,846	145,258	150,588	22	13	9	2	1	1
	Total 0—5	*1,408,747*	*690,782*	*717,965*	*1,408,702*	*690,758*	*717,944*	*43*	*23*	*20*	*2*	*1*	*1*
	5—10	1,376,130	682,803	693,327	1,375,876	682,734	693,142	251	68	183	3	1	2
	10—15	1,228,264	636,557	591,707	1,223,345	635,626	587,719	4,772	913	3,859	147	18	129
	15—20	989,849	486,948	502,901	813,077	447,151	365,926	169,136	38,490	130,646	7,636	1,307	6,329
	20—25	934,259	474,642	459,617	393,937	259,575	134,362	511,197	206,103	305,094	29,125	8,964	20,161
	25—30	896,320	477,460	418,860	204,122	143,833	60,289	652,849	319,131	333,718	32,349	14,496	24,853
	30—35	834,640	457,316	377,324	118,246	82,648	35,598	666,741	356,239	310,502	49,653	18,429	31,224
	35—40	673,815	373,217	300,598	69,273	46,546	22,727	552,181	307,872	244,309	52,361	18,799	33,562
	40—45	596,384	315,012	281,372	54,864	33,822	21,042	470,622	258,908	211,714	70,898	22,282	48,616
	45—50	410,844	218,129	192,715	32,058	18,738	13,320	317,023	181,203	135,820	61,763	18,188	43,575
	50—55	386,944	194,328	192,616	32,803	17,687	15,116	267,306	154,633	112,673	86,835	22,008	64,827
	55—60	244,736	121,861	122,875	19,896	10,316	9,580	161,571	94,958	66,613	63,269	16,587	46,682
	60—65	278,350	140,550	137,800	24,440	11,862	12,578	154,796	101,757	53,039	99,114	26,931	72,183
	65—70	131,296	66,375	64,921	12,164	6,030	6,134	66,377	44,291	22,086	52,755	16,054	36,701
	70 and over	219,678	96,735	122,943	24,145	10,784	13,361	72,670	50,906	21,764	122,863	35,045	87,818
	Total ...	**10,610,256**	**5,432,715**	**5,177,541**	**5,806,948**	**3,098,110**	**2,708,838**	**4,067,535**	**2,115,495**	**1,952,040**	**735,773**	**219,110**	**516,663**
BUDDHISTS.	0—1	222,930	107,621	115,309	222,930	107,621	115,309	...	...	...	...	...	...
	1—2	219,909	107,433	112,476	219,909	107,433	112,476	...	...	...	...	...	...
	2—3	263,535	128,651	134,884	263,535	128,651	134,884	...	...	...	...	...	...
	3—4	298,699	147,201	151,498	298,699	147,201	151,498	...	...	...	...	...	...
	4—5	266,617	130,324	136,293	266,617	130,324	136,293	...	...	...	...	...	...
	Total 0—5	*1,271,690*	*621,230*	*650,460*	*1,271,690*	*621,230*	*650,460*	...	...	...	...	...	...
	5—10	1,246,762	615,913	630,849	1,246,752	615,913	630,839	10	...	10	...	...	...
	10—15	1,114,256	570,467	543,789	1,111,382	570,151	541,231	2,745	304	2,441	129	12	117
	15—20	868,671	411,143	457,528	721,494	381,553	339,941	140,345	28,564	111,781	6,832	1,026	5,806
	20—25	768,797	358,502	410,295	311,206	188,371	122,835	432,266	163,150	269,116	25,325	6,981	18,344
	25—30	723,319	350,935	372,384	146,348	91,947	54,401	543,359	247,888	295,471	33,612	11,100	22,512
	30—35	681,446	344,577	336,869	82,475	50,300	32,175	557,402	280,446	276,956	41,569	13,831	27,738
	35—40	577,257	301,357	275,900	52,351	31,250	21,101	479,287	254,993	224,294	45,619	15,114	30,505
	40—45	506,252	250,808	255,444	41,502	22,203	19,299	404,591	210,940	193,651	60,159	17,665	42,494
	45—50	367,034	187,165	179,869	26,587	14,057	12,530	285,037	157,584	127,453	55,410	15,524	39,886
	50—55	340,918	164,276	176,642	27,156	13,198	13,958	237,361	132,542	104,819	76,401	18,536	57,865
	55—60	227,423	110,665	116,758	18,059	8,960	9,099	150,425	86,748	63,677	58,939	14,957	43,982
	60—65	253,642	125,243	128,399	21,680	9,883	11,797	141,404	91,184	50,220	90,558	24,176	66,382
	65—70	123,018	60,903	62,115	11,301	5,377	5,924	61,959	40,748	21,211	49,758	14,778	34,980
	70 and over	203,380	88,065	115,315	22,352	9,604	12,748	66,367	45,948	20,419	114,661	32,513	82,148
	Total ...	**9,273,865**	**4,561,249**	**4,712,616**	**5,112,335**	**2,633,997**	**2,478,338**	**3,502,558**	**1,741,039**	**1,761,519**	**658,972**	**186,213**	**472,759**
ANIMIST.	0—1	5,862	3,077	2,785	5,862	3,077	2,785	...	...	...	...	...	...
	1—2	5,673	2,956	2,717	5,673	2,956	2,717	...	...	...	...	...	...
	2—3	8,349	4,525	3,824	8,349	4,525	3,824	...	...	...	...	...	...
	3—4	9,155	4,708	4,447	9,155	4,708	4,447	...	...	...	...	...	...
	4—5	8,497	4,414	4,083	8,497	4,414	4,083	...	...	...	...	...	...
	Total 0—5	*37,536*	*19,680*	*17,856*	*37,536*	*19,680*	*17,856*	...	...	...	...	...	...
	5—10	37,432	19,330	18,102	37,432	19,330	18,102	...	...	...	...	...	...
	10—15	33,097	18,014	15,083	32,986	18,005	14,981	108	9	99	3	...	3
	15—20	29,282	15,486	13,796	24,069	14,203	9,866	5,011	1,215	3,796	202	68	134
	20—25	31,976	17,230	14,746	16,347	11,481	4,866	14,688	5,386	9,302	941	363	578
	25—30	32,547	18,738	13,809	10,613	8,451	2,162	20,580	9,697	10,883	1,354	590	764
	30—35	34,622	20,540	14,082	7,221	5,875	1,346	25,027	13,667	11,360	2,374	998	1,376
	35—40	22,694	14,380	8,374	3,479	2,965	514	17,294	10,534	6,760	1,921	821	1,100
	40—45	24,084	14,281	9,803	2,537	1,896	641	17,691	11,224	6,467	3,856	1,161	2,695
	45—50	11,576	7,309	4,267	1,063	831	232	8,545	5,804	2,741	1,968	674	1,294
	50—55	13,350	7,484	5,866	1,226	795	431	8,488	5,743	2,745	3,636	946	2,690
	55—60	4,666	2,812	1,854	427	273	154	3,057	2,120	937	1,182	419	763
	60—65	7,743	4,150	3,593	641	369	272	4,049	3,003	1,046	3,053	778	2,275
	65—70	2,453	1,563	890	220	152	68	1,276	1,016	260	957	395	562
	70 and over	5,555	2,466	3,089	618	369	249	1,884	1,375	509	3,053	722	2,331
	Total ...	**328,613**	**183,403**	**145,210**	**176,415**	**104,675**	**71,740**	**127,698**	**70,793**	**56,905**	**24,500**	**7,935**	**16,565**
HINDU	0—1	4,339	2,201	2,138	4,339	2,201	2,138	...	...	...	...	...	...
	1—2	3,635	1,882	1,753	3,635	1,882	1,753	...	...	...	...	...	...
	2—3	5,161	2,643	2,518	5,158	2,642	2,516	3	1	2	...	...	...
	3—4	5,729	2,925	2,804	5,721	2,921	2,800	8	4	4	...	...	...
	4—5	4,513	2,382	2,131	4,499	2,374	2,125	14	8	6	...	...	...
	Total 0—5	*23,377*	*12,033*	*11,344*	*23,352*	*12,020*	*11,332*	*25*	*13*	*12*	...	...	...
	5—10	19,501	10,443	9,058	19,295	10,392	8,903	205	51	154	1	...	1
	10—15	18,214	12,748	5,466	16,919	12,276	4,643	1,283	466	817	12	6	6
	15—20	31,347	24,969	6,378	21,795	20,041	1,754	9,372	4,828	4,544	180	100	80
	20—25	60,666	50,962	9,704	31,324	30,333	991	28,297	19,862	8,435	1,045	767	278
	25—30	68,602	58,556	10,046	25,950	25,281	669	40,967	31,946	9,021	1,685	1,329	356
	30—35	59,052	51,031	8,021	17,534	17,033	501	39,200	32,168	7,032	2,318	1,830	488
	35—40	33,795	29,351	4,444	8,101	7,854	247	23,914	20,182	3,732	1,780	1,315	465
	40—45	30,263	26,256	4,007	6,725	6,459	266	20,991	18,119	2,872	2,547	1,678	869
	45—50	11,803	10,006	1,797	2,258	2,157	101	8,115	7,028	1,087	1,430	821	609
	50—55	12,485	10,265	2,220	2,555	2,375	180	7,777	6,738	1,039	2,153	1,152	1,001
	55—60	2,677	2,018	759	696	637	59	2,194	1,871	323	787	410	377
	60—65	5,343	4,136	1,207	1,019	914	105	2,788	2,428	360	1,536	794	742
	65—70	1,513	1,162	351	284	248	36	736	627	109	493	287	206
	70 and over	2,650	1,864	786	490	417	73	1,086	924	162	1,074	523	551
	Total ...	**382,288**	**306,700**	**75,588**	**178,297**	**148,437**	**29,860**	**186,950**	**147,251**	**39,699**	**17,041**	**11,022**	**6,019**

Imperial Table VII.—*Age, Sex and Civil Condition.*
PART A.—PROVINCIAL SUMMARY (Burma Proper).

Religion	Age.	Population.			Unmarried.			Married.			Widowed.		
		Persons.	Males.	Females.	Persons.	Males.	Females.	Persons.	Males.	Females.	Persons.	Males.	Females.
	1	2	3	4	5	6	7	8	9	10	11	12	13
MAHOMEDAN.	0—1	7,810	3,958	3,852	7,810	3,958	3,852	...	...	...	...	...	...
	1—2	8,530	4,164	4,366	8,530	4,164	4,366	...	...	...	...	...	...
	2—3	10,895	5,452	5,443	10,889	5,448	5,441	6	4	2	...	...	...
	3—4	11,520	5,757	5,763	11,519	5,756	5,763	1	1	...	...	...	...
	4—5	10,511	5,301	5,210	10,501	5,295	5,206	8	5	3	2	1	1
	Total 0—5	*49,265*	*24,632*	*24,634*	*49,219*	*24,621*	*24,628*	*15*	*10*	*5*	*2*	*1*	*1*
	5—10	47,465	24,487	22,978	47,432	24,470	22,962	31	16	15	2	1	1
	10—15	38,881	22,796	16,085	38,290	22,671	15,619	588	125	463	3	...	3
	15—20	40,293	25,097	15,196	27,815	21,522	6,293	12,111	3,473	8,638	367	102	265
	20—25	50,833	35,491	15,342	22,363	20,043	2,320	27,005	14,714	12,291	1,465	734	731
	25—30	50,119	36,930	13,189	13,862	12,413	1,449	34,217	23,327	10,890	2,040	1,190	850
	30—35	42,295	31,068	11,127	7,716	6,080	736	31,969	22,671	9,298	2,510	1,417	1,093
	35—40	26,633	20,098	6,535	3,603	3,228	375	20,951	15,724	5,227	2,079	1,146	933
	40—45	24,039	17,019	7,020	2,923	2,525	398	18,262	13,234	5,028	2,854	1,260	1,594
	45—50	12,917	9,311	3,606	1,577	1,351	226	9,531	7,168	2,363	1,809	792	1,017
	50—55	13,623	8,784	4,839	1,331	1,024	307	9,197	6,821	2,376	3,095	939	2,156
	55—60	5,757	3,703	2,054	483	334	149	3,711	2,802	909	1,563	567	996
	60—65	7,692	4,894	2,798	769	553	216	4,290	3,536	754	2,633	805	1,828
	65—70	2,735	1,852	883	252	203	49	1,516	1,277	239	967	372	595
	70 and over	5,127	2,923	2,204	428	289	139	2,123	1,791	332	2,576	843	1,733
	Total ...	417,575	269,085	148,490	218,093	142,227	75,866	175,517	116,689	58,828	23,965	10,169	13,796
CHRISTIAN.	0—1	4,435	2,144	2,291	4,435	2,144	2,291	...	...	...	...	...	...
	1—2	4,457	2,186	2,271	4,457	2,186	2,271	...	...	...	...	...	...
	2—3	5,737	2,804	2,933	5,737	2,804	2,933	...	...	...	...	...	...
	3—4	5,968	2,955	3,013	5,965	2,955	3,010	3	...	3	...	...	...
	4—5	5,629	2,804	2,825	5,629	2,804	2,825	...	...	...	...	...	...
	Total 0—5	*26,226*	*12,893*	*13,333*	*26,223*	*12,893*	*13,330*	*3*	...	*3*	...	...	...
	5—10	24,547	12,405	12,142	24,542	12,404	12,138	5	1	4	...	...	...
	10—15	23,476	12,327	11,149	23,447	12,321	11,126	29	6	23	...	...	...
	15—20	19,536	9,698	9,838	17,378	9,350	8,020	2,104	329	1,775	54	11	43
	20—25	20,074	10,819	9,255	11,503	8,180	3,323	8,265	2,556	5,709	306	83	223
	25—30	20,264	11,079	9,185	6,701	5,112	1,589	12,979	5,748	7,231	584	219	365
	30—35	16,312	9,251	7,061	2,963	2,132	831	12,509	6,803	5,706	840	316	524
	35—40	12,768	7,519	5,249	1,591	1,105	486	10,262	6,047	4,215	915	367	548
	40—45	11,227	6,213	5,014	1,091	660	431	8,716	5,085	3,631	1,420	468	952
	45—50	7,272	4,117	3,156	549	318	231	5,604	3,446	2,158	1,120	353	767
	50—55	6,411	3,386	3,025	511	271	240	4,370	2,692	1,678	1,530	423	1,107
	55—60	3,168	1,725	1,443	225	108	117	2,148	1,385	763	795	232	563
	60—65	3,893	2,101	1,792	327	139	188	2,240	1,587	653	1,326	375	951
	65—70	1,562	883	679	107	50	57	880	614	266	575	219	356
	70 and over	2,943	1,399	1,544	254	102	152	1,195	856	339	1,494	441	1,053
	Total ...	199,680	105,815	93,865	117,412	65,153	52,259	71,309	37,155	34,154	10,959	3,507	7,452
SIKH.	0—1	145	70	75	145	70	75	...	...	...	...	...	...
	1—2	54	23	31	54	23	31	...	...	...	...	...	...
	2—3	107	53	54	107	53	54	...	...	...	...	...	...
	3—4	100	54	46	100	54	46	...	...	...	...	...	...
	4—5	69	34	35	69	34	35	...	...	...	...	...	...
	Total 0—5	*475*	*234*	*241*	*475*	*234*	*241*	...	...	...	...	...	...
	5—10	243	141	102	243	141	102	...	...	...	...	...	...
	10—15	170	116	54	157	114	43	13	2	11	...	...	...
	15—20	535	444	91	385	374	11	149	70	79	1	...	1
	20—25	1,630	1,441	189	1,040	1,028	12	552	378	174	38	35	3
	25—30	1,200	1,027	173	558	551	7	577	412	165	65	64	1
	30—35	824	703	121	288	283	5	499	384	115	37	36	1
	35—40	501	451	50	127	126	1	343	295	48	31	30	1
	40—45	398	353	45	71	67	4	279	239	40	48	47	1
	45—50	182	168	14	20	20	...	138	125	13	24	23	1
	50—55	100	94	6	15	15	...	74	69	5	11	10	1
	55—60	20	18	2	3	2	1	15	15	...	2	1	1
	60—65	12	10	2	3	3	...	6	5	1	3	2	1
	65—70	1	1	...	...	...	...	1	1	...	...	...	...
	70 and over	10	9	1	2	2	...	7	6	1	1	1	...
	Total ...	6,301	5,210	1,091	3,387	2,960	427	2,653	2,001	652	261	249	12
JAIN.	0—1	2	1	1	2	1	1	...	...	...	...	...	...
	1—2	4	1	3	4	1	3	...	...	...	...	...	...
	2—3	3	2	1	3	2	1	...	...	...	...	...	...
	3—4	6	3	3	6	3	3	...	...	...	...	...	...
	4—5	4	1	3	4	1	3	...	...	...	...	...	...
	Total 0—5	*19*	*8*	*11*	*19*	*8*	*11*	...	...	...	...	...	...
	5—10	14	6	8	14	6	8	...	...	...	...	...	...
	10—15	9	8	1	8	7	1	1	1	...	...	...	...
	15—20	43	30	13	29	24	5	14	6	8	...	...	...
	20—25	113	96	17	67	66	1	45	30	15	1	...	1
	25—30	104	89	15	30	28	2	73	60	13	1	1	...
	30—35	79	75	4	20	19	1	59	56	3	...	...	...
	35—40	52	48	4	6	6	...	43	40	3	3	2	1
	40—45	32	29	3	6	6	...	23	22	1	3	1	2
	45—50	9	8	1	...	...	...	8	7	1	1	1	...
	50—55	13	13	...	7	7	...	6	6	...	...	...	...
	55—60	3	2	1	1	...	1	2	2	...	...	...	...
	60—65	3	2	1	...	...	...	3	2	1	...	...	...
	65—70	...	...	...	...	...	...	...	...	...	...	...	...
	70 and over	2	2	...	...	...	...	2	2	...	...	...	...
	Total ...	495	416	79	207	177	30	279	234	45	9	5	4

IMPERIAL TABLE VII.—*Age, Sex and Civil Condition.*

PART A.—PROVINCIAL SUMMARY (Burma Proper).

AGE.	POPULATION.			UNMARRIED.			MARRIED.			WIDOWED.		
	Persons.	Males.	Females.	Persons.	Males.	Females.	Persons.	Males.	Females.	Persons.	Males.	Females.
1	2	3	4	5	6	7	8	9	10	11	12	13
ZOROASTRIAN.												
0—1	5	3	2	5	3	2	...	...	...	...	...	...
1—2	2	...	2	2	...	2	...	...	...	...	...	...
2—3	9	4	5	9	4	5	...	...	...	...	...	...
3—4	10	4	6	10	4	6	...	...	...	...	...	...
4—5	2	2	...	2	2	...	...	...	...	...	...	...
Total 0—5	*28*	*13*	*15*	*28*	*13*	*15*	...	...	...	...	...	...
5—10	23	16	7	23	16	7	...	...	...	...	...	...
10—15	33	18	15	30	18	12	3	...	3	...	...	...
15—20	18	9	9	14	8	6	4	1	3	...	...	...
20—25	32	19	13	18	14	4	14	5	9	...	...	...
25—30	44	32	12	17	14	3	25	17	8	2	1	1
30—35	27	26	11	13	11	2	24	15	9	...	...	...
35—40	28	23	5	6	5	1	21	18	3	1	...	1
40—45	20	12	8	3	1	2	15	10	5	2	1	1
45—50	13	12	1	1	1	...	12	11	1	...	...	...
50—55	10	6	4	2	2	...	6	3	3	2	1	1
55—60	3	2	1	...	...	...	3	2	1	...	...	...
60—65	6	4	2	...	...	...	4	3	1	2	1	1
65—70	3	2	1	...	...	...	3	2	1	...	...	...
70 and over	2	1	1	...	...	...	2	1	1	...	...	...
Total ...	300	195	105	155	103	52	136	88	48	9	4	5
JEW.												
0—1	26	15	11	26	15	11	...	...	...	...	...	...
1—2	15	4	11	15	4	11	...	...	...	...	...	...
2—3	29	17	12	29	17	12	...	...	...	...	...	...
3—4	28	12	16	28	12	16	...	...	...	...	...	...
4—5	26	9	17	26	9	17	...	...	...	...	...	...
Total 0—5	*124*	*57*	*67*	*124*	*57*	*67*	...	...	...	...	...	...
5—10	136	59	77	136	59	77	...	...	...	...	...	...
10—15	121	59	62	119	59	60	2	...	2	...	...	...
15—20	115	64	51	91	62	29	24	2	22	...	...	...
20—25	121	69	52	56	48	8	61	20	41	4	1	3
25—30	99	58	41	29	26	3	64	30	34	6	2	4
30—35	58	34	24	11	10	1	43	23	20	4	1	3
35—40	79	43	36	7	5	2	62	36	26	10	2	8
40—45	62	36	26	3	3	...	50	32	18	9	1	8
45—50	32	29	3	2	2	...	29	27	2	1	...	1
50—55	30	17	13	...	...	...	23	16	7	7	1	6
55—60	14	11	3	1	1	...	13	10	3	...	...	...
60—65	14	8	6	1	1	...	10	7	3	3	...	3
65—70	10	9	1	...	...	...	6	6	...	4	3	1
70 and over	9	6	3	1	1	...	4	3	1	4	2	2
Total ..	1,024	559	465	581	334	247	391	212	179	52	13	39
CONFUCIAN.												
0—1	...	...	...	...	...	...	...	...	...	...	...	...
1—2	...	...	...	...	...	...	...	...	...	...	...	...
2—3	1	...	1	1	...	1	...	...	...	...	...	...
3—4	1	...	1	1	...	1	...	...	...	...	...	...
4—5	1	...	1	1	...	1	...	...	...	...	...	...
Total 0—5 ...	*3*	...	*3*	*3*	...	*3*	...	...	...	...	...	...
5—10	7	3	4	7	3	4	...	...	...	...	...	...
10—15	3	1	2	3	1	2	...	...	...	...	...	...
15—20	4	4	...	2	2	...	2	2	...	...	...	...
20—25	10	9	1	8	8	...	2	1	1	...	...	...
25—30	13	13	...	9	9	...	4	4	...	...	...	...
30—35	12	10	2	4	4	...	7	6	1	1	...	1
35—40	7	6	1	2	2	...	4	3	1	1	1	...
40—45	2	2	...	1	1	...	1	1	...	...	...	...
45—50	3	2	1	1	1	...	2	1	1	...	...	...
50—55	2	2	...	...	...	...	2	2	...	...	...	...
55—60	4	4	...	...	...	...	3	3	...	1	1	...
60—65	1	1	...	...	...	...	1	1	...	...	...	...
65—70	...	...	...	...	...	...	...	...	...	...	...	...
70 and over	...	...	...	...	...	...	...	...	...	...	...	...
Total ...	71	57	14	40	31	9	28	24	4	2	1	1
SECULARIST, RATIONALIST AND AGNOSTIC.												
0—1	1	...	1	1	...	1	...	...	...	...	...	...
1—2	...	...	...	...	...	...	...	...	...	...	...	...
2—3	...	...	...	...	...	...	...	...	...	...	...	...
3—4	1	1	...	1	1	...	...	...	...	...	...	...
4—5	1	1	...	1	1	...	...	...	...	...	...	...
Total 0—5	*3*	*2*	*1*	*3*	*2*	*1*	...	...	...	...	...	...
5—10	...	...	...	...	...	...	...	...	...	...	...	...
10—15	4	3	1	4	3	1	...	...	...	...	...	...
15—20	5	4	1	5	4	1	...	...	...	...	...	...
20—25	7	4	3	5	3	2	2	1	1	...	...	...
25—30	9	3	6	5	1	4	4	2	2	...	...	...
30—35	3	1	2	1	1	...	2	...	2	...	...	...
35—40	1	1	...	...	...	...	...	...	...	1	1	...
40—45	5	3	2	2	1	1	3	2	1	...	...	...
45—50	2	2	...	...	...	...	2	2	...	...	...	...
50—55	2	1	1	...	...	...	2	1	1	...	...	...
55—60	1	1	...	1	1	...	...	...	...	...	...	...
60—65	1	1	...	...	...	...	1	1	...	...	...	...
65—70	1	...	1	...	...	...	...	...	...	1	...	1
70 and over	...	...	...	...	...	...	...	...	...	...	...	...
Total ...	44	26	18	26	16	10	16	9	7	2	1	1

IMPERIAL TABLE VII.—*Age, Sex and Civil Condition.*

PART A.—PROVINCIAL SUMMARY (Specially Administered Territories).

AGE.	POPULATION.			UNMARRIED.			MARRIED.			WIDOWED.		
	Persons.	Males.	Females.	Persons.	Males.	Females.	Persons.	Males.	Females.	Persons.	Males.	Females.
1	2	3	4	5	6	7	8	9	10	11	12	13
ALL RELIGIONS.												
0—1	30,703	15,080	15,623	30,703	15,080	15,623	...	...	...	...	...	...
1—2	30,617	15,087	15,530	30,617	15,087	15,530	...	...	...	...	...	...
2—3	39,286	19,070	20,216	39,286	19,070	20,216	...	...	...	...	...	...
3—4	45,052	22,143	22,909	45,052	22,143	22,909	...	...	...	...	...	...
4—5	41,172	19,919	21,253	41,171	19,918	21,253	1	1	...	...	...	...
Total 0—5	*186,830*	*91,299*	*95,531*	*186,829*	*91,298*	*95,531*	*1*	*1*	...	..	...	...
5—10	197,820	101,341	96,479	197,816	101,337	96,479	4	4	...	...	...	...
10—15	149,245	77,843	71,402	148,762	77,803	70,959	464	38	426	19	2	17
15—20	128,158	61,800	66,358	104,056	56,918	47,138	21,450	4,518	16,932	2,652	364	2,288
20—25	112,930	52,078	60,852	49,538	32,611	16,927	56,661	17,485	39,176	6,731	1,982	4,749
25—30	108,958	51,006	57,952	23,751	16,891	6,860	76,805	31,053	45,752	8,402	3,062	5,340
30—35	124,391	62,672	61,719	13,742	8,361	5,381	97,793	49,357	48,436	12,856	4,954	7,902
35—40	83,047	43,078	39,969	4,999	3,407	1,592	65,750	36,341	29,409	12,298	3,330	8,968
40—45	96,522	50,143	46,379	4,318	2,626	1,692	77,357	43,462	33,895	14,847	4,055	10,792
45—50	48,704	26,890	21,814	2,115	1,413	702	37,945	22,718	15,227	8,644	2,759	5,885
50—55	66,640	33,143	33,497	2,762	1,575	1,187	46,053	27,726	18,327	17,825	3,842	13,983
55—60	28,106	15,091	13,015	1,103	605	498	19,224	12,389	6,835	7,779	2,097	5,682
60—65	43,494	20,977	22,517	1,792	754	1,038	23,239	16,376	6,863	18,463	3,847	14,616
65—70	16,375	9,561	6,814	1,282	926	356	8,720	6,658	2,062	6,373	1,977	4,396
70 and over	37,607	15,834	21,773	1,691	783	908	12,422	9,481	2,941	23,494	5,570	17,924
Total ...	**1,428,827**	**712,756**	**716,071**	**744,556**	**397,308**	**347,248**	**543,888**	**277,607**	**266,281**	**140,383**	**37,841**	**102,542**
BUDDHIST.												
0—1	25,065	12,351	12,714	25,065	12,351	12,714	...	...	...	...	...	...
1—2	23,134	11,621	11,513	23,134	11,621	11,513	...	...	...	...	...	...
2—3	29,420	14,602	14,818	29,420	14,602	14,818	...	...	...	...	...	...
3—4	33,917	16,908	17,009	33,917	16,908	17,009	...	...	...	...	...	...
4—5	32,389	15,826	16,563	32,389	15,826	16,563	...	..	...	...	...	...
Total 0—5	*143,925*	*71,308*	*72,617*	*143,925*	*71,308*	*72,617*	...	...	...	...	...	...
5—10	154,847	77,271	77,576	154,847	77,271	77,576	...	...	...	...	...	...
10—15	118,696	61,710	56,986	118,444	61,697	56,747	248	13	235	4	...	4
15—20	100,728	48,683	52,045	80,703	44,812	35,891	17,568	3,571	13,997	2,457	300	2,157
20—25	83,097	37,940	45,157	35,859	23,971	11,888	41,438	12,298	29,140	5,800	1,671	4,129
25—30	82,753	37,839	44,914	17,482	12,396	5,086	58,220	22,866	35,354	7,051	2,577	4,474
30—35	93,761	47,540	46,221	8,889	6,090	2,799	74,646	37,273	37,373	10,226	4,177	6,049
35—40	65,740	33,795	31,945	3,939	2,697	1,242	51,373	28,276	23,097	10,428	2,822	7,606
40—45	74,256	38,496	35,760	3,290	2,064	1,226	59,699	33,162	26,537	11,267	3,270	7,997
45—50	39,010	21,621	17,389	1,795	1,233	562	30,380	18,050	12,330	6,835	2,338	4,497
50—55	51,988	26,338	25,650	2,255	1,357	898	35,741	21,861	13,880	13,992	3,120	10,872
55—60	23,034	12,430	10,604	954	529	425	15,737	10,123	5,614	6,343	1,778	4,565
60—65	35,334	17,170	18,164	1,489	618	871	18,660	13,291	5,369	15,185	3,261	11,924
65—70	12,358	6,834	5,524	1,065	846	219	6,174	4,489	1,685	5,119	1,499	3,620
70 and over	31,152	13,213	17,939	1,425	657	768	10,191	7,883	2,308	19,536	4,673	14,863
Total ...	**1,110,679**	**552,188**	**558,491**	**576,361**	**307,546**	**268,815**	**420,075**	**213,156**	**206,919**	**114,243**	**31,486**	**82,757**
ANIMIST.												
0—1	5,094	2,467	2,627	5,094	2,467	2,627	...	...	...	...	...	...
1—2	7,001	3,216	3,785	7,001	3,216	3,785	...		...	...	...	...
2—3	9,223	4,131	5,092	9,223	4,131	5,092	...	...	...	...	...	...
3—4	10,499	4,912	5,587	10,499	4,912	5,587	...	...	...	...	...	...
4—5	8,230	3,789	4,441	8,230	3,789	4,441	...	...	...	...	...	...
Total 0—5	*40,047*	*18,515*	*21,532*	*40,047*	*18,515*	*21,532*	...	...	...	...	...	...
5—10	40,986	23,114	17,872	40,986	23,114	17,872	...	...	...	...	...	...
10—15	29,122	15,372	13,750	28,937	15,348	13,589	171	22	149	14	2	12
15—20	25,928	12,262	13,666	22,251	11,354	10,897	3,496	849	2,647	181	59	122
20—25	27,289	12,368	14,921	12,512	7,580	4,932	13,909	4,513	9,396	868	275	593
25—30	23,371	11,179	12,192	5,418	3,698	1,720	16,706	7,077	9,629	1,247	404	843
30—35	28,087	13,182	14,905	4,322	1,791	2,531	21,275	10,716	10,559	2,490	675	1,815
35—40	15,602	7,993	7,609	816	478	338	13,049	7,100	5,949	1,737	415	1,322
40—45	20,731	10,493	10,238	882	427	455	16,441	9,368	7,073	3,408	698	2,710
45—50	9,031	4,764	4,267	251	120	131	7,077	4,276	2,801	1,703	368	1,335
50—55	13,959	6,338	7,621	459	178	281	9,817	5,496	4,321	3,683	664	3,019
55—60	4,821	2,506	2,315	133	64	69	3,324	2,152	1,172	1,364	291	1,074
60—65	7,841	3,623	4,218	283	124	159	4,392	2,953	1,439	3,166	546	2,620
65—70	3,922	2,676	1,246	207	76	131	2,501	2,133	368	1,214	467	747
70 and over	6,189	2,482	3,707	251	115	136	2,111	1,515	596	3,827	852	2,975
Total ...	**296,926**	**146,867**	**150,059**	**157,755**	**82,982**	**74,773**	**114,269**	**58,170**	**56,099**	**24,902**	**5,715**	**19,187**
HINDU.												
0—1	126	47	79	126	47	79	...	...	...	...	...	...
1—2	130	82	48	130	82	48	...	...	...	...	...	...
2—3	149	80	69	149	80	69	...	...	...	...	...	...
3—4	141	71	70	141	71	70	...	...	...	...	...	...
4—5	113	61	52	112	60	52	1	1	...	...	...	...
Total 0—5	*659*	*341*	*318*	*658*	*340*	*318*	*1*	*1*	...	...	...	...
5—10	431	245	186	427	241	186	4	4	...	...	...	...
10—15	245	147	98	221	146	75	24	1	23	...	...	...
15—20	343	247	96	192	187	5	147	58	89	4	2	2
20—25	1,155	970	185	610	602	8	522	352	170	23	16	7
25—30	1,341	1,182	159	529	525	4	771	619	152	41	38	3
30—35	1,257	1,078	179	355	320	35	851	715	136	51	43	8
35—40	704	620	84	135	133	2	519	440	79	50	47	3
40—45	569	529	40	75	75	...	449	415	34	45	39	6
45—50	209	193	16	29	29	...	156	143	13	24	21	3
50—55	168	155	13	27	27	...	107	100	7	34	28	6
55—60	58	47	11	8	7	1	28	24	4	22	16	6
60—65	53	46	7	6	6	...	31	29	2	16	11	5
65—70	12	10	2	3	2	1	8	7	1	1	1	...
70 and over	36	25	11	3	3	...	15	12	3	18	10	8
Total ...	**7,240**	**5,835**	**1,405**	**3,278**	**2,643**	**635**	**3,633**	**2,980**	**732**	**329**	**272**	**57**

Imperial Table VII.—*Age, Sex and Civil Condition.*

PART A.—PROVINCIAL SUMMARY (Specially Administered Territories).

Religion	AGE	Population Persons	Population Males	Population Females	Unmarried Persons	Unmarried Males	Unmarried Females	Married Persons	Married Males	Married Females	Widowed Persons	Widowed Males	Widowed Females
	1	2	3	4	5	6	7	8	9	10	11	12	13
MAHOMEDAN.	0—1	92	44	48	92	44	48	...	...	...	...	...	...
	1—2	47	25	22	47	25	22	...	...	...	...	...	...
	2—3	83	47	36	83	47	36	...	...	...	...	...	...
	3—4	75	40	35	75	40	35	...	...	...	...	...	...
	4—5	61	42	19	61	42	19	...	...	...	...	...	...
	Total 0—5	*358*	*198*	*160*	*358*	*198*	*160*	...	...	...	...	...	...
	5—10	246	130	116	246	130	116	...	...	...	...	...	...
	10—15	134	81	53	132	79	53	2	2	...	...	...	...
	15—20	220	131	79	134	116	18	74	14	60	2	1	1
	20—25	435	333	102	226	218	8	199	108	91	10	7	3
	25—30	465	360	105	153	147	6	293	197	96	19	16	3
	30—35	437	330	107	98	93	5	305	206	99	34	31	3
	35—40	318	267	51	68	66	2	221	176	45	29	24	4
	40—45	257	227	30	39	38	1	193	168	25	25	21	4
	45—50	132	124	8	17	16	1	93	87	6	22	21	1
	50—55	96	78	18	11	10	1	73	63	10	12	5	7
	55—60	42	36	6	3	3	...	29	29	...	10	4	6
	60—65	26	19	7	5	4	1	11	11	...	10	4	6
	65—70	13	6	7	2	1	1	4	3	1	7	2	5
	70 and over	25	16	9	2	2	...	10	7	3	13	7	6
	Total ...	**3,194**	**2,336**	**858**	**1,494**	**1,121**	**373**	**1,507**	**1,071**	**436**	**193**	**144**	**49**
CHRISTIAN.	0—1	315	166	149	315	166	149	...	...	...	...	...	...
	1—2	300	141	159	300	141	159	...	...	...	...	...	...
	2—3	402	206	196	402	206	196	...	...	...	...	...	...
	3—4	404	204	200	404	204	200	...	...	...	...	...	...
	4—5	371	195	176	371	195	176	...	...	...	...	...	...
	Total 0—5	*1,792*	*912*	*880*	*1,792*	*912*	*880*	...	...	...	...	...	...
	5—10	1,288	570	718	1,288	570	718	...	...	...	...	...	...
	10—15	1,040	526	514	1,020	526	494	19	...	19	1	...	1
	15—20	941	470	471	770	443	327	163	25	138	8	2	6
	20—25	897	420	477	290	199	91	578	209	369	29	12	17
	25—30	963	395	568	147	103	44	778	271	507	38	21	17
	30—35	791	495	296	67	56	11	675	417	258	49	22	27
	35—40	638	360	278	33	25	8	557	320	237	48	15	33
	40—45	664	354	310	20	10	10	551	325	226	93	19	74
	45—50	300	166	134	19	11	8	224	147	77	57	8	49
	50—55	418	223	195	9	2	7	308	199	109	101	22	79
	55—60	151	72	79	5	2	3	106	61	45	40	9	31
	60—65	240	119	121	9	2	7	145	92	53	86	25	61
	65—70	70	35	35	5	1	4	33	26	7	32	8	24
	70 and over	204	97	107	10	6	4	95	64	31	99	27	72
	Total ...	**10,397**	**5,214**	**5,183**	**5,484**	**2,868**	**2,616**	**4,232**	**2,156**	**2,076**	**681**	**190**	**491**
SIKH.	0—1	11	5	6	11	5	6	...	...	...	...	...	...
	1—2	5	2	3	5	2	3	...	...	...	...	...	...
	2—3	9	4	5	9	4	5	...	...	...	...	...	...
	3—4	16	8	8	16	8	8	...	...	...	...	...	...
	4—5	8	6	2	8	6	2	...	...	...	...	...	...
	Total 0—5	*49*	*25*	*24*	*49*	*25*	*24*	...	...	...	...	...	...
	5—10	22	11	11	22	11	11	...	...	...	...	...	...
	10—15	8	7	1	8	7	1	...	...	...	...	...	...
	15—20	8	7	1	6	6	...	2	1	1	...	...	...
	20—25	57	47	10	41	41	...	15	5	10	1	1	...
	25—30	65	51	14	22	22	...	37	23	14	6	6	...
	30—35	58	47	11	11	11	...	41	30	11	6	6	...
	35—40	44	42	2	7	7	...	31	29	2	6	6	...
	40—45	45	44	1	12	12	...	24	24	...	9	8	1
	45—50	22	22	...	4	4	...	15	15	...	3	3	...
	50—55	11	11	...	1	1	...	7	7	...	3	3	...
	55—60	...	...	...	...	...	...	...	...	...	...	...	...
	60—65	...	...	...	...	...	...	...	...	...	...	...	...
	65—70	...	...	...	...	...	...	...	...	...	...	...	...
	70 and over	1	1	...	...	...	...	...	...	...	1	1	...
	Total ...	**390**	**315**	**75**	**183**	**147**	**36**	**172**	**134**	**38**	**25**	**24**	**1**
AGNOSTIC.	0—1	...	...	...	...	...	...	...	...	...	...	...	...
	1—2	...	...	...	...	...	...	...	...	...	...	...	...
	2—3	...	...	...	...	...	...	...	...	...	...	...	...
	3—4	...	...	...	...	...	...	...	...	...	...	...	...
	4—5	...	...	...	...	...	...	...	...	...	...	...	...
	Total 0—5	...	...	...	...	...	...	...	...	...	...	...	...
	5—10	...	...	...	...	...	...	...	...	...	...	...	...
	10—15	...	...	...	...	...	...	...	...	...	...	...	...
	15—20	...	...	...	...	...	...	...	...	...	...	...	...
	20—25	...	...	...	...	...	...	...	...	...	...	...	...
	25—30	...	...	...	...	...	...	...	...	...	...	...	...
	30—35	1	1	...	1	1	...	...	...	...	...	...	...
	35—40	...	...	...	...	...	...	...	...	...	...	...	...
	40—45	...	...	...	...	...	...	...	...	...	...	...	...
	45—50	...	...	...	...	...	...	...	...	...	...	...	...
	50—55	...	...	...	...	...	...	...	...	...	...	...	...
	55—60	...	...	...	...	...	...	...	...	...	...	...	...
	60—65	...	...	...	...	...	...	...	...	...	...	...	...
	65—70	...	...	...	...	...	...	...	...	...	...	...	...
	70 and over	...	...	...	...	...	...	...	...	...	...	...	...
	Total ...	**1**	**1**	...	**1**	**1**	...	...	...	...	...	...	...

IMPERIAL TABLE VII.

Age, Sex and Civil Condition.

PART B.—DETAILS BY DISTRICTS.

NOTE.—The boundaries of the City of Rangoon coincide with those of the District of Rangoon. Separate figures are therefore not needed for the City. Separate figures are given for the City of Mandalay.

IMPERIAL TABLE VII.—*Age, Sex and Civil Condition.*

PART B—DETAILS BY DISTRICTS.

AGE.	POPULATION. Persons.	Males.	Females.	UNMARRIED. Persons.	Males.	Females.	MARRIED. Persons.	Males.	Females.	WIDOWED. Persons.	Males.	Females.
1	2	3	4	5	6	7	8	9	10	11	12	13
AKYAB.												
All Religions ...	*529,943*	*289,474*	*240,469*	*261,714*	*149,742*	*111,972*	*222,741*	*122,758*	*99,983*	*45,488*	*16,974*	*28,514*
0—5	67,867	34,340	33,527	67,867	34,340	33,527	...	...	...	...	...	...
5—10	68,084	33,978	34,106	68,084	33,978	34,106	...	...	..	...	...	...
10—15	59,053	31,954	27,099	58,376	31,940	26,436	634	14	620	43	...	43
15—20	49,729	26,270	23,459	34,357	23,697	10,660	14,430	2,419	12,011	942	154	788
20—40	177,966	102,970	74,996	26,916	22,083	4,833	135,488	73,148	62,340	15,562	7,739	7,823
40—60	82,875	47,239	35,636	4,299	2,735	1,564	61,107	38,601	22,506	17,469	5,903	11,566
60 and over	24,369	12,723	11,646	1,815	969	846	11,082	8,576	2,506	11,472	3,178	8,294
Buddhist ...	*302,527*	*154,935*	*147,592*	*145,174*	*79,631*	*65,543*	*126,423*	*64,331*	*62,092*	*30,930*	*10,973*	*19,957*
0—5	35,632	17,934	17,698	35,632	17,934	17,698	...	...	...	...	...	...
5—10	37,998	19,010	18,988	37,998	19,010	18,988	...	..	...	...	...	...
10—15	35,235	18,281	16,954	34,905	18,281	16,624	288	...	288	42	...	42
15—20	28,116	13,964	14,152	20,561	13,044	7,517	6,839	838	6,001	716	82	634
20—40	97,821	50,763	47,058	12,579	9,516	3,063	74,802	36,381	38,421	10,440	4,866	5,574
40—60	52,010	27,415	24,595	2,362	1,322	1,040	37,835	22,198	15,637	11,813	3,895	7,918
60 and over	15,715	7,568	8,147	1,137	524	613	6,659	4,914	1,745	7,919	2,130	5,789
Animist ...	*33,896*	*17,501*	*16,395*	*16,424*	*8,833*	*7,591*	*15,382*	*7,829*	*7,553*	*2,090*	*839*	*1,251*
0—5	4,699	2,605	2,094	4,699	2,605	2,094	...	...	...	...	...	...
5—10	3,482	1,326	2,156	3,482	1,326	2,156	...	...	...	...	...	...
10—15	3,742	2,032	1,710	3,742	2,032	1,710	...	...	...	...	...	...
15—20	3,269	1,589	1,680	2,437	1,402	1,035	787	169	618	45	18	27
20—40	11,542	6,013	5,529	1,605	1,140	465	9,323	4,527	4,796	614	346	268
40—60	5,495	3,010	2,485	214	132	82	4,503	2,608	1,895	778	270	508
60 and over	1,667	926	741	245	196	49	769	525	244	653	205	448
Hindu ...	*14,454*	*13,418*	*1,036*	*5,674*	*5,248*	*426*	*7,894*	*7,403*	*491*	*886*	*767*	*119*
0—5	359	209	150	359	209	150	...	...	...	...	...	...
5—10	348	201	147	348	201	147	...	...	...	...	...	...
10—15	418	320	98	407	320	87	10	...	10	1	...	1
15—20	1,465	1,365	100	1,163	1,144	19	293	213	80	9	8	1
20—40	8,868	8,496	372	3,039	3,025	14	5,379	5,048	331	450	423	27
40—60	2,618	2,502	116	319	313	6	1,997	1,934	63	302	255	47
60 and over	378	325	53	39	36	3	215	208	7	124	81	43
Mahomedan ...	*178,881*	*103,124*	*75,257*	*94,010*	*55,724*	*38,286*	*72,815*	*43,026*	*29,789*	*11,556*	*4,374*	*7,182*
0—5	27,125	13,562	13,563	27,125	13,562	13,563	...	...	...	...	...	...
5—10	26,207	13,417	12,790	26,207	13,417	12,790	...	...	...	...	...	...
10—15	19,610	11,295	8,315	19,274	11,281	7,993	336	14	322	...	...	...
15—20	16,821	9,316	7,505	10,141	8,071	2,070	6,508	1,199	5,309	172	46	126
20—40	59,380	37,415	21,965	9,488	8,227	1,261	45,846	27,096	18,750	4,046	2,092	1,954
40—60	22,648	14,228	8,420	1,385	955	430	16,697	11,798	4,899	4,566	1,475	3,091
60 and over	6,590	3,891	2,699	390	211	179	3,428	2,919	509	2,772	761	2,011
NORTHERN ARAKAN.												
All Religions ...	*22,234*	*11,405*	*10,829*	*9,883*	*5,479*	*4,404*	*10,639*	*5,335*	*5,304*	*1,712*	*591*	*1,121*
0—5	2,380	1,175	1,205	2,380	1,175	1,205	...	...	...	...	...	...
5—10	2,590	1,340	1,250	2,590	1,340	1,250	...	...	...	...	...	...
10—15	2,428	1,352	1,076	2,405	1,351	1,054	22	1	21	1	...	1
15—20	2,169	1,045	1,124	1,495	886	609	622	137	485	52	22	30
20—40	7,516	3,784	3,732	925	677	248	6,130	2,870	3,260	461	237	224
40—60	3,773	1,979	1,794	64	37	27	3,097	1,761	1,336	612	181	431
60 and over	1,378	730	648	24	13	11	768	566	202	586	151	435
Buddhist ...	*1,795*	*997*	*798*	*882*	*512*	*370*	*780*	*434*	*346*	*133*	*51*	*82*
0—5	220	92	128	220	92	128	...	...	...	...	...	...
5—10	213	114	99	213	114	99	...	...	...	...	...	...
10—15	171	96	75	168	96	72	3	...	3	...	...	...
15—20	184	108	76	144	99	45	37	8	29	3	1	2
20—40	629	375	254	127	106	21	466	249	217	36	20	16
40—60	289	160	129	6	2	4	232	142	90	51	16	35
60 and over	89	52	37	4	3	1	42	35	7	43	14	29
Animist ...	*19,821*	*9,977*	*9,844*	*8,688*	*4,724*	*3,964*	*9,581*	*4,731*	*4,850*	*1,552*	*522*	*1,030*
0—5	2,109	1,061	1,048	2,109	1,061	1,048	...	...	...	...	...	...
5—10	2,320	1,191	1,129	2,320	1,191	1,129	...	...	...	...	...	...
10—15	2,203	1,223	980	2,188	1,223	965	15	...	15	...	...	...
15—20	1,942	915	1,027	1,328	766	562	566	128	438	48	21	27
20—40	6,561	3,166	3,395	673	446	227	5,473	2,510	2,963	415	210	205
40—60	3,401	1,745	1,656	50	27	23	2,802	1,563	1,239	549	155	394
60 and over	1,285	676	609	20	10	10	725	530	195	540	136	404

IMPERIAL TABLE VII.—*Age, Sex and Civil Condition.*

PART B—DETAILS BY DISTRICTS.

AGE.	POPULATION.			UNMARRIED.			MARRIED.			WIDOWED.		
	Persons.	Males.	Females.	Persons.	Males.	Females.	Persons.	Males.	Females.	Persons	Males.	Females.
1	2	3	4	5	6	7	8	9	10	11	12	13
KYAUKPYU.												
All Religions ...	***184,916***	***89,571***	***95,845***	***88,855***	***45,935***	***42,920***	***80,274***	***39,687***	***40,637***	***15,787***	***3,999***	***11.788***
0—5	22,275	10,993	11,282	22,275	10,993	11,282	...	...	...	...	...	...
5—10	23,871	12,015	11,856	23,871	12,015	11,856	...	...	...	...	...	...
10—15	19,888	10,208	9,680	19,825	10,200	9,625	63	8	55	...	...	...
15—20	16,889	8,021	8,868	12,546	7,165	5,381	4,092	807	3,285	251	49	202
20—40	57,897	27,615	30,282	7,497	4,432	3,065	45,926	21,753	24,173	4,474	1,430	3,044
40—60	32,559	15,675	16,884	1,918	801	1,117	24,721	13,475	11,246	5,920	1,399	4,521
60 and over	11,537	5,044	6,493	923	329	594	5,472	3,594	1,878	5,142	1,121	4,021
Buddhist ...	***165,864***	***79,099***	***86,765***	***79,682***	***40,676***	***39,006***	***71,629***	***34,953***	***36,676***	***14,558***	***3,470***	***11,088***
0—5	19,614	9,683	9,931	19,614	9,683	9,931	...	...	...	...	...	...
5—10	21,377	10,687	10,690	21,377	10,687	10,690	...	...	...	...	...	...
10—15	18,135	9,231	8,904	18,072	9,223	8,849	63	8	55	...	...	...
15—20	15,251	7,188	8,063	11,500	6,474	5,026	3,500	665	2,835	251	49	202
20—40	51,058	23,699	27,359	6,477	3,608	2,869	40,513	18,898	21,615	4,068	1,193	2,875
40—60	29,648	13,995	15,653	1,765	697	1,068	22,460	12,077	10,383	5,423	1,221	4,202
60 and over	10,781	4,616	6,165	877	304	573	5,093	3,305	1,788	4,811	1,007	3,804
Animist ...	***14,726***	***7,718***	***7,008***	***7.221***	***3,955***	***3,266***	***6,710***	***3,410***	***3,300***	***795***	***353***	***442***
0—5	2,294	1,131	1,163	2,294	1,131	1,163	...	...	...	...	...	...
5—10	2,155	1,113	1,042	2,155	1,113	1,042	...	...	...	...	...	...
10—15	1,409	803	606	1,409	803	606	...	...	...	...	...	...
15—20	1,257	609	648	789	509	280	468	100	368	...	...	...
20—40	4,918	2,558	2,360	482	354	128	4,191	2,050	2,141	245	154	91
40—60	2,110	1,178	932	60	33	27	1,740	1,028	712	310	117	193
60 and over	583	326	257	32	12	20	311	232	79	240	82	158
Mahomedan ...	***3,641***	***2,130***	***1,511***	***1,607***	***990***	***617***	***1,637***	***1,004***	***633***	***397***	***136***	***261***
0—5	344	169	175	344	169	175	...	...	...	...	...	...
5—10	312	200	112	312	200	112	...	...	...	...	...	...
10—15	317	152	165	317	152	165	...	...	...	...	...	...
15—20	328	175	153	214	140	74	114	35	79	...	...	...
20—40	1,510	964	546	344	276	68	1,028	628	400	138	60	78
40—60	681	391	290	68	46	22	438	295	143	175	50	125
60 and over	149	79	70	8	7	1	57	46	11	84	26	58
SANDOWAY.												
All Religions ...	***102,808***	***51,475***	***51,328***	***52,940***	***27,865***	***25,075***	***42,859***	***21,602***	***21,257***	***7,004***	***2,008***	***4,996***
0—5	14,352	7,010	7,342	14,352	7,010	7,342	...	...	...	...	...	...
5—10	13,813	7,028	6,785	13,813	7,028	6,785	...	...	...	...	...	...
10—15	12,131	6,449	5,682	12,131	6,449	5,682	...	...	...	...	...	...
15—20	10,278	4,965	5,313	7,942	4,493	3,449	2,213	456	1,757	123	16	107
20—40	31,210	15,624	15,586	3,775	2,419	1,356	25,550	12,519	13,031	1,885	686	1,199
40—60	15,554	7,753	7,801	566	295	271	12,350	6,760	5,590	2,638	698	1,940
60 and over	5,465	2,646	2,819	361	171	190	2,746	1,867	879	2,358	608	1,750
Buddhist ...	***91,062***	***45,220***	***45,842***	***46,944***	***24,579***	***22,365***	***37,961***	***18,957***	***19,004***	***6,157***	***1,684***	***4,473***
0—5	12,749	6,200	6,549	12,749	6,200	6,549	...	...	...	...	...	...
5—10	12,313	6,280	6,033	12,313	6,280	6,033	...	...	...	...	...	...
10—15	10,833	5,747	5,086	10,833	5,747	5,086	...	...	...	...	...	...
15—20	9,179	4,435	4,744	7,102	4,011	3,091	1,975	412	1,563	102	12	90
20—40	27,248	13,402	13,846	3,109	1,934	1,175	22,508	10,920	11,588	1,631	548	1,083
40—60	13,874	6,822	7,052	502	250	252	11,030	5,980	5,050	2,342	592	1,750
60 and over	4,866	2,334	2,532	336	157	179	2,448	1,645	803	2,082	532	1,550
Animist ...	***6,632***	***3,430***	***3,202***	***3,347***	***1,802***	***1,545***	***2,845***	***1,459***	***1,386***	***440***	***169***	***271***
0—5	962	494	468	962	494	468	...	...	...	...	...	...
5—10	855	435	420	855	435	420	...	...	...	...	...	...
10—15	740	387	353	740	387	353	...	...	...	...	...	...
15—20	616	281	335	472	260	212	138	17	121	6	4	2
20—40	2,151	1,116	1,035	270	190	76	1,747	852	895	134	70	64
40—60	993	555	438	34	26	8	802	470	332	157	59	98
60 and over	315	162	153	14	6	8	158	120	38	143	36	107
Mahomedan ...	***4,257***	***2,216***	***2,041***	***2,260***	***1,220***	***1,040***	***1,661***	***891***	***770***	***336***	***105***	***231***
0—5	550	265	285	550	265	285	...	...	...	...	...	...
5—10	575	282	293	575	282	293	...	...	...	...	...	...
10—15	503	285	218	503	285	218	...	...	...	...	...	...
15—20	425	207	218	320	186	134	90	21	69	15	...	15
20—40	1,405	769	636	284	186	98	1,030	539	491	91	44	47
40—60	565	290	275	23	13	10	429	249	180	113	28	85
60 and over	234	118	116	5	3	2	112	82	30	117	33	84

IMPERIAL TABLE VII.—*Age, Sex and Civil Condition.*

PART B.—DETAILS BY DISTRICTS.

District	AGE.	POPULATION. Persons.	POPULATION. Males.	POPULATION. Females.	UNMARRIED. Persons.	UNMARRIED. Males.	UNMARRIED. Females.	MARRIED. Persons.	MARRIED. Males.	MARRIED. Females.	WIDOWED. Persons.	WIDOWED. Males.	WIDOWED. Females.
	1	2	3	4	5	6	7	8	9	10	11	12	13
RANGOON.	*All Religions* ...	*293,816*	*208,111*	*85,205*	*125,907*	*86,830*	*39,077*	*152,474*	*115,848*	*86,681*	*14,985*	*5,488*	*9,497*
	0—5	18,681	9,450	9,231	18,636	9,426	9,210	43	23	20	2	1	1
	5—10	19,259	10,034	9,225	19,143	9,984	9,159	113	49	64	3	1	2
	10—15	20,426	12,370	8,056	19,680	11,997	7,683	735	371	364	11	2	9
	15—20	28,967	19,940	9,027	21,790	16,323	5,467	7,056	3,587	3,469	121	30	91
	20—40	151,793	118,607	33,186	42,124	35,770	6,354	105,508	80,847	24,661	4,161	1,990	2,171
	40—60	45,089	32,528	12,561	3,915	2,890	1,025	34,581	27,460	7,121	6,593	2,178	4,415
	60 and over	9,101	5,182	3,919	619	440	179	4,438	3,506	932	4,044	1,236	2,808
	Buddhist ...	*97,467*	*52,137*	*45,330*	*53,368*	*30,131*	*23,237*	*36,212*	*19,719*	*16,493*	*7,887*	*2,287*	*5,600*
	0—5	9,233	4,616	4,617	9,233	4,616	4,617	...	...	...	...	...	...
	5—10	9,702	4,938	4,764	9,701	4,938	4,763	1	...	1	...	...	...
	10—15	10,047	5,362	4,685	9,983	5,348	4,635	61	14	47	3	...	3
	15—20	10,162	5,327	4,835	8,749	5,052	3,697	1,361	268	1,093	52	7	45
	20—40	36,871	20,855	16,016	13,455	8,863	4,592	21,762	11,435	10,327	1,654	557	1,097
	40—60	16,060	8,450	7,610	1,807	1,022	785	10,863	6,528	4,335	3,390	900	2,490
	60 and over	5,392	2,589	2,803	440	292	148	2,164	1,474	690	2,788	823	1,965
	Animist ...	*7,217*	*5,936*	*1,281*	*3,692*	*3,069*	*623*	*3,319*	*2,763*	*556*	*206*	*104*	*102*
	0—5	343	207	136	343	207	136	...	...	...	...	...	...
	5—10	332	197	135	332	197	135	...	...	...	...	...	...
	10—15	332	206	126	323	201	122	9	5	4	...	...	...
	15—20	549	428	121	482	381	101	66	47	19	1	...	1
	20—40	4,221	3,656	565	1,934	1,830	104	2,233	1,794	439	54	32	22
	40—60	1,293	1,119	174	254	232	22	930	839	91	109	48	61
	60 and over	147	123	24	24	21	3	81	78	3	42	24	18
	Hindu ...	*108,350*	*89,028*	*19,322*	*33,110*	*26,932*	*6,178*	*71,554*	*60,340*	*11,214*	*3,686*	*1,756*	*1,930*
	0—5	4,427	2,239	2,188	4,402	2,226	2,176	25	13	12	...	...	...
	5—10	4,359	2,306	2,053	4,277	2,270	2,007	81	36	45	1	...	1
	10—15	4,655	3,312	1,343	4,146	3,042	1,104	504	268	236	5	2	3
	15—20	9,476	7,637	1,839	5,883	5,499	384	3,560	2,125	1,435	33	13	20
	20—40	67,421	58,317	9,104	13,475	13,025	450	52,568	44,467	8,101	1,378	825	553
	40—60	16,281	13,957	2,324	863	808	55	13,722	12,436	1,286	1,696	713	983
	60 and over	1,731	1,260	471	64	62	2	1,094	995	99	573	203	370
	Mahomedan ...	*54,634*	*45,106*	*9,528*	*20,846*	*16,871*	*3,975*	*31,991*	*27,362*	*4,629*	*1,797*	*873*	*924*
	0—5	2,397	1,236	1,161	2,380	1,225	1,155	15	10	5	2	1	1
	5—10	2,625	1,487	1,138	2,597	1,474	1,123	26	12	14	2	1	1
	10—15	3,096	2,260	836	2,955	2,182	773	138	78	60	3	...	3
	15—20	6,136	5,070	1,066	4,452	3,976	476	1,660	1,084	576	24	10	14
	20—40	31,249	27,476	3,773	7,854	7,456	398	22,734	19,587	3,147	661	433	228
	40—60	7,875	6,660	1,215	561	521	40	6,560	5,825	735	754	314	440
	60 and over	1,256	917	339	47	37	10	858	766	92	351	114	237
	Christian ...	*23,044*	*13,977*	*9,067*	*13,573*	*8,827*	*4,746*	*8,212*	*4,787*	*3,425*	*1,259*	*363*	*896*
	0—5	2,087	1,069	1,018	2,084	1,069	1,015	3	...	3	...	...	...
	5—10	2,067	1,025	1,042	2,062	1,024	1,038	5	1	4	...	...	...
	10—15	2,143	1,143	1,000	2,128	1,140	988	15	3	12	...	...	...
	15—20	2,375	1,277	1,098	2,032	1,253	779	332	24	308	11	...	11
	20—40	10,549	7,090	3,459	4,822	4,032	790	5,365	2,945	2,420	362	113	249
	40—60	3,292	2,110	1,182	402	282	120	2,281	1,644	637	609	184	425
	60 and over	531	263	268	43	27	16	211	170	41	277	66	211
HANTHAWADDY.	*All Religions* ...	*539,109*	*295,886*	*243,223*	*311,012*	*178,226*	*132,786*	*197,292*	*105,770*	*91,522*	*30,805*	*11,890*	*18,915*
	0—5	69,283	33,742	35,541	69,283	33,742	35,541	...	...	...	...	...	...
	5—10	65,771	32,687	33,084	65,770	32,687	33,083	1	...	1	...	...	...
	10—15	60,208	31,697	28,511	59,930	31,697	28,233	278	...	278	...	...	...
	15—20	51,597	27,202	24,395	43,205	25,329	17,876	8,161	1,843	6,318	231	30	201
	20—40	185,513	109,625	75,888	59,369	45,215	14,154	118,708	61,120	57,588	7,436	3,290	4,146
	40—60	80,259	45,794	34,465	10,306	7,547	2,759	57,395	33,639	23,756	12,558	4,608	7,950
	60 and over	26,478	15,139	11,339	3,149	2,009	1,140	12,749	9,168	3,581	10,580	3,962	6,618
	Buddhist ...	*447,638*	*227,611*	*220,027*	*257,830*	*136,085*	*121,745*	*162,792*	*81,968*	*80,824*	*27,016*	*9,558*	*17,458*
	0—5	61,749	29,870	31,879	61,749	29,870	31,879	...	...	...	...	...	...
	5—10	59,452	29,333	30,119	59,452	29,333	30,119	...	...	...	...	...	...
	10—15	54,181	27,773	26,408	54,008	27,773	26,235	173	...	173	...	...	...
	15—20	43,584	21,103	22,481	36,771	19,832	16,939	6,605	1,241	5,364	208	30	178
	20—40	137,850	70,792	67,058	36,649	23,619	13,030	95,152	44,937	50,215	6,049	2,236	3,813
	40—60	67,127	35,640	31,487	6,659	4,158	2,501	49,477	27,731	21,746	10,991	3,751	7,240
	60 and over	23,695	13,100	10,595	2,542	1,500	1,042	11,385	8,059	3,326	9,768	3,541	6,227

IMPERIAL TABLE VII.—*Age, Sex and Civil Condition.*

PART B.—DETAILS BY DISTRICTS.

District	AGE.	POPULATION. Persons.	Males.	Females.	UNMARRIED. Persons.	Males.	Females.	MARRIED. Persons.	Males.	Females.	WIDOWED. Persons.	Males.	Females.
	1	2	3	4	5	6	7	8	9	10	11	12	13
HANTHAWADDY—*concluded.*	***Animist* ..**	***4,675***	***4,024***	***651***	***2,991***	***2,667***	***324***	***1,465***	***1,176***	***289***	***219***	***181***	***38***
	0—5	357	237	120	357	237	120	...	...	...	...	...	...
	5—10	283	200	83	283	200	83	...	...	..	...	...	...
	10—15	253	200	53	253	200	53	...	...	..	...	...	...
	15—20	277	232	45	242	218	24	35	14	21	...	...	...
	20—40	2,401	2,143	258	1,489	1,455	34	843	627	216	69	61	8
	40—60	937	858	79	324	316	8	512	463	49	101	79	22
	60 and over	167	154	13	43	41	2	75	72	3	49	41	8
	***Hindu* ...**	***57,137***	***44,951***	***12,186***	***33,361***	***28,079***	***5,282***	***21,661***	***15,416***	***6,245***	***2,115***	***1,456***	***659***
	0—5	4,113	2,153	1,960	4,113	2,153	1,960	...	...	...	...	...	...
	5—10	3,213	1,693	1,520	3,213	1,693	1,520	...	...	...	...	...	...
	10—15	3,066	2,171	895	2,964	2,171	793	102	...	102	...	...	...
	15—20	4,855	3,890	965	3,767	3,426	341	1,066	464	602	22	...	22
	20—40	32,591	27,385	5,206	16,280	15,788	492	15,425	10,874	4,551	886	723	163
	40—60	7,932	6,597	1,335	2,638	2,513	125	4,451	3,563	888	843	521	322
	60 and over	1,367	1,062	305	386	335	51	617	515	102	364	212	152
	***Mahomedan* ...**	***16,307***	***12,023***	***4,284***	***9,078***	***6,984***	***2,094***	***6,536***	***4,619***	***1,917***	***698***	***420***	***278***
	0—5	1,439	717	722	1,439	717	722	...	...	...	...	...	...
	5—10	1,288	710	578	1,287	710	577	1	...	1	...	...	...
	10—15	1,260	790	470	1,257	790	467	3	...	3	...	...	...
	15—20	1,745	1,332	413	1,314	1,218	96	431	114	317	...	...	...
	20—40	7,793	6,381	1,412	3,160	2,992	168	4,371	3,195	1,176	262	194	68
	40—60	2,174	1,622	552	495	445	50	1,421	1,045	376	258	132	126
	60 and over	608	471	137	126	112	14	309	265	44	173	94	79
	***Christian* ...**	***12,647***	***6,733***	***5,914***	***7,451***	***4,158***	***3,293***	***4,459***	***2,322***	***2,137***	***737***	***253***	***484***
	0—5	1,576	735	841	1,576	735	841	...	...	...	...	...	...
	5—10	1,503	736	767	1,503	736	767	...	...	...	...	...	...
	10—15	1,417	742	675	1,417	742	675	...	...	...	...	...	...
	15—20	1,087	611	476	1,087	611	476	...	...	...	...	..	...
	20—40	4,444	2,571	1,873	1,645	1,216	429	2,642	1,291	1,351	157	64	93
	40—60	1,985	991	994	171	97	74	1,459	778	681	355	116	239
	60 and over	635	347	288	52	21	31	358	253	105	225	73	152
THARRAWADDY.	***All Religions* ...**	***433,320***	***216,442***	***216,878***	***238,880***	***123,985***	***114,895***	***167,659***	***84,859***	***82,800***	***26,781***	***7,598***	***19,183***
	0—5	60,629	29,588	31,041	60,629	29,588	31,041	...	...	...	...	...	...
	5—10	59,187	29,269	29,918	59,187	29,269	29,918	...	...	...	...	...	...
	10—15	53,783	27,659	26,124	53,497	27,638	25,859	280	21	259	6	...	6
	15—20	40,664	19,572	21,092	33,394	18,033	15,361	7,073	1,513	5,560	197	26	171
	20—40	135,676	68,254	67,422	25,853	16,204	9,649	102,956	49,941	53,015	6,867	2,109	4,758
	40—60	61,093	30,523	30,570	4,365	2,325	2,040	46,075	25,625	20,450	10,653	2,573	8,080
	60 and over	22,288	11,577	10,711	1,955	928	1,027	11,275	7,759	3,516	9,058	2,890	6,168
	***Buddhist* ...**	***413,584***	***202,639***	***210,945***	***227,916***	***115,990***	***111,926***	***159,956***	***79,666***	***80,290***	***25,712***	***6,983***	***18,729***
	0—5	58,830	28,642	30,188	58,830	28,642	30,188	...	...	...	...	...	...
	5—10	57,551	28,394	29,157	57,551	28,394	29,157	...	...	...	...	...	...
	10—15	52,144	26,655	25,489	51,875	26,642	25,233	263	13	250	6	...	6
	15—20	39,011	18,493	20,518	32,061	17,084	14,977	6,759	1,387	5,372	191	22	169
	20—40	126,626	61,272	65,354	22,027	12,659	9,368	98,105	46,766	51,339	6,494	1,847	4,647
	40—60	57,996	28,215	29,781	3,754	1,759	1,995	43,981	24,089	19,892	10,261	2,367	7,894
	60 and over	21,426	10,968	10,458	1,818	810	1,008	10,848	7,411	3,437	8,760	2,747	6,013
	***Animist* ...**	***2,376***	***1,965***	***411***	***1,306***	***1,100***	***206***	***935***	***757***	***178***	***135***	***108***	***27***
	0—5	232	164	68	232	164	68	...	...	...	...	...	...
	5—10	191	123	68	191	123	68	...	...	...	...	...	...
	10—15	169	135	34	169	135	34	...	...	...	...	...	...
	15—20	121	92	29	89	70	19	32	22	10	...	...	...
	20—40	1,094	945	149	510	495	15	533	406	127	51	44	7
	40—60	472	422	50	93	91	2	324	286	38	55	45	10
	60 and over	97	84	13	22	22	...	46	43	3	29	19	10
	***Hindu* ...**	***7,406***	***6,125***	***1,281***	***4,105***	***3,595***	***510***	***2,922***	***2,236***	***686***	***379***	***294***	***85***
	0—5	441	237	204	441	237	204	...	...	...	...	...	...
	5—10	346	200	146	346	200	146	...	...	...	...	...	...
	10—15	328	254	74	315	246	69	13	8	5	...	...	...
	15—20	543	451	92	406	382	24	135	67	68	2	2	...
	20—40	4,307	3,752	555	2,173	2,128	45	1,965	1,482	483	169	142	27
	40—60	1,195	1,019	176	367	352	15	691	573	118	137	94	43
	60 and over	246	212	34	57	50	7	118	106	12	71	56	15

IMPERIAL TABLE VII.—*Age, Sex and Civil Condition.*

PART B.—DETAILS BY DISTRICTS.

District	AGE.	POPULATION. Persons.	POPULATION. Males.	POPULATION. Females.	UNMARRIED. Persons.	UNMARRIED. Males.	UNMARRIED. Females.	MARRIED. Persons.	MARRIED. Males.	MARRIED. Females.	WIDOWED. Persons.	WIDOWED. Males.	WIDOWED. Females.
	1	2	3	4	5	6	7	8	9	10	11	12	13
THARRAWADDY—*concluded.*	***Mahomedan*** ...	*3,857*	*2,667*	*1,190*	*2,089*	*1,486*	*603*	*1,621*	*1,086*	*535*	*147*	*95*	*52*
	0—5	390	179	211	390	179	211	...	...	...	...	...	...
	5—10	362	200	162	362	200	162	...	...	...	...	...	...
	10—15	328	196	132	324	196	128	4	...	4	...	...	...
	15—20	324	200	124	228	168	60	92	30	62	4	2	2
	20—40	1,729	1,317	412	648	610	38	1,028	670	358	53	37	16
	40—60	555	432	123	103	101	2	402	303	99	50	28	22
	60 and over	169	143	26	34	32	2	95	83	12	40	28	12
	Christian ...	*6,052*	*3,011*	*3,041*	*3,437*	*1,791*	*1,646*	*2,208*	*1,102*	*1,106*	*407*	*118*	*289*
	0—5	733	363	370	733	363	370	...	...	...	...	...	...
	5—10	736	351	385	736	351	385	...	...	...	...	...	...
	10—15	814	419	395	814	419	395	...	...	...	...	...	...
	15—20	663	335	328	608	328	280	55	7	48	...	...	...
	20—40	1,890	943	947	475	294	181	1,315	610	705	100	39	61
	40—60	867	430	437	47	22	25	670	369	301	150	39	111
	60 and over	349	170	179	24	14	10	168	116	52	157	40	117
PEGU.	***All Religions*** ...	*429,121*	*229,540*	*199,581*	*245,799*	*137,702*	*108,097*	*158,552*	*82,667*	*75,885*	*24,770*	*9,171*	*15,599*
	0—5	57,138	28,209	28,929	57,138	28,209	28,929	...	...	...	...	...	...
	5—10	55,456	27,707	27,749	55,446	27,697	27,749	10	10	...	...	...	...
	10—15	50,904	27,203	23,701	50,610	27,073	23,537	294	130	164	...	...	...
	15—20	40,994	20,384	20,610	34,127	19,033	15,094	6,754	1,312	5,442	113	39	74
	20—40	142,212	79,595	62,617	39,925	29,775	10,150	95,974	47,288	48,686	6,313	2,532	3,781
	40—60	62,399	35,120	27,279	6,496	4,686	1,810	45,659	26,783	18,876	10,244	3,651	6,593
	60 and over	20,018	11,322	8,696	2,057	1,229	828	9,861	7,144	2,717	8,100	2,949	5,151
	Buddhist ...	*369,612*	*188,279*	*181,333*	*212,398*	*112,831*	*99,567*	*135,620*	*68,060*	*67,560*	*21,594*	*7,388*	*14,206*
	0—5	51,247	25,177	26,070	51,247	25,177	26,070	...	...	...	...	...	...
	5—10	50,397	24,991	25,406	50,397	24,991	25,406	...	...	...	...	...	...
	10—15	46,274	24,211	22,063	46,246	24,211	22,035	28	...	28	...	...	...
	15—20	36,097	17,052	19,045	30,351	16,090	14,261	5,656	939	4,717	90	23	67
	20—40	114,178	58,445	55,733	27,996	18,618	9,378	80,894	38,012	42,882	5,288	1,815	3,473
	40—60	53,534	28,536	24,998	4,487	2,831	1,656	40,187	22,764	17,423	8,860	2,941	5,919
	60 and over	17,885	9,867	8,018	1,674	913	761	8,855	6,345	2,510	7,356	2,609	4,747
	Animist ...	*5,891*	*4,110*	*1,281*	*8,258*	*2,657*	*601*	*1,788*	*1,218*	*566*	*850*	*285*	*115*
	0—5	526	326	200	526	326	200	...	...	...	...	...	...
	5—10	463	282	181	463	282	181	...	...	...	...	...	...
	10—15	399	297	102	399	297	102	...	...	...	...	...	...
	15—20	398	270	128	328	256	72	66	11	55	4	3	1
	20—40	2,510	2,064	446	1,280	1,249	31	1,117	724	393	113	91	22
	40—60	911	718	193	224	212	12	523	411	112	164	95	69
	60 and over	184	153	31	38	35	3	77	72	5	69	46	23
	Hindu ...	*34,850*	*25,857*	*8,993*	*18,630*	*14,976*	*3,654*	*13,965*	*9,324*	*4,641*	*1,755*	*1,057*	*698*
	0—5	3,048	1,568	1,480	3,048	1,568	1,480	...	...	...	...	...	...
	5—10	2,365	1,306	1,059	2,355	1,296	1,059	10	10	...	...	...	...
	10—15	2,130	1,493	637	1,873	1,363	510	257	130	127	...	...	...
	15—20	2,693	2,039	654	1,927	1,724	203	755	304	451	11	11	...
	20—40	17,750	14,020	3,730	7,769	7,496	273	9,370	6,070	3,300	611	454	157
	40—60	5,250	4,133	1,117	1,423	1,327	96	3,052	2,383	669	775	423	352
	60 and over	1,114	798	316	235	202	33	521	427	94	358	169	189
	Mahomedan ...	*7,884*	*5,899*	*1,985*	*4,472*	*3,452*	*1,020*	*2,564*	*1,709*	*855*	*848*	*238*	*110*
	0—5	721	360	361	721	360	361	...	...	...	...	...	...
	5—10	617	338	279	617	338	279	...	...	...	...	...	...
	10—15	594	383	211	586	383	203	8	...	8	...	...	...
	15—20	623	438	185	482	401	81	136	37	99	5	...	5
	20—40	3,615	2,916	699	1,738	1,661	77	1,731	1,144	587	146	111	35
	40—60	943	754	189	262	250	12	564	422	142	117	82	35
	60 and over	271	210	61	66	59	7	125	106	19	80	45	35
	Christian ...	*12,316*	*6,341*	*5,975*	*7,005*	*3,757*	*3,248*	*4,592*	*2,335*	*2,257*	*719*	*249*	*470*
	0—5	1,594	778	816	1,594	778	816	...	...	...	...	...	...
	5—10	1,610	789	821	1,610	789	821	...	...	...	...	...	...
	10—15	1,502	815	687	1,502	815	687	...	...	...	...	...	...
	15—20	1,181	585	596	1,038	562	476	140	21	119	3	2	1
	20—40	4,112	2,109	2,003	1,120	730	390	2,838	1,319	1,519	154	60	94
	40—50	1,754	972	782	97	63	34	1,331	801	530	326	108	218
	60 and over	563	293	270	44	20	24	283	194	89	236	79	157

IMPERIAL TABLE VII.—*Age, Sex and Civil Condition.*

PART B.—DETAILS BY DISTRICTS.

District	AGE.	POPULATION.			UNMARRIED.			MARRIED.			WIDOWED.		
		Persons.	Males.	Females.	Persons.	Males.	Females.	Persons.	Males.	Females.	Persons.	Males.	Females.
	1	2	3	4	5	6	7	8	9	10	11	12	13
PROME.	*All Religions* ...	378,871	186,213	192,658	201,823	103,639	98,184	144,376	73,002	71,874	32,672	9,572	23,100
	0— 5	49,672	23,929	25,743	49,672	23,929	25,743	...	...	...	...	...	...
	5—10	48,874	24,514	24,360	48,874	24,514	24,360	...	...	...	...	...	...
	10—15	46,776	23,765	23,011	46,679	23,750	22,929	90	13	77	7	2	5
	15—20	36,719	17,641	19,078	30,405	16,274	14,131	6,000	1,298	4,702	314	69	245
	20—40	118,130	58,221	59,909	21,717	12,814	8,903	88,011	42,877	45,134	8,402	2,530	5,872
	40—60	55,745	26,775	28,970	3,106	1,649	1,457	40,146	21,995	18,151	12,493	3,131	9,362
	60 and over	22,955	11,368	11,587	1,370	709	661	10,129	6,819	3,310	11,456	3,840	7,616
	Buddhist ...	359,880	173,940	185,940	191,893	97,030	94,863	136,755	68,003	68,752	31,232	8,907	22,325
	0— 5	47,672	22,948	24,724	47,672	22,948	24,724	...	...	...	...	...	...
	5—10	47,105	23,591	23,514	47,105	23,591	23,514	...	...	...	...	...	...
	10—15	45,183	22,885	22,298	45,116	22,885	22,231	62	...	62	5	...	5
	15—20	35,103	16,665	18,438	29,172	15,438	13,734	5,637	1,170	4,467	294	57	237
	20—40	110,010	52,221	57,789	18,855	10,260	8,595	83,189	39,684	43,505	7,966	2,277	5,689
	40—60	52,802	24,817	27,985	2,689	1,273	1,416	38,144	20,637	17,507	11,969	2,907	9,062
	60 and over	22,005	10,813	11,192	1,284	635	649	9,723	6,512	3,211	10,998	3,666	7,332
	Animist ...	9,304	5,096	4,208	4,908	2,769	2,139	3,585	2,087	1,548	811	290	521
	0— 5	1,319	653	666	1,319	653	666	...	...	...	...	...	...
	5—10	1,118	583	535	1,118	583	535	...	...	...	...	...	...
	10—15	976	502	474	976	502	474	...	...	...	...	...	...
	15—20	768	377	391	602	337	265	158	38	120	8	2	6
	20—40	2,977	1,818	1,159	765	590	175	2,021	1,143	878	191	85	106
	40—60	1,545	852	693	105	85	20	1,154	671	483	286	96	190
	60 and over	601	311	290	23	19	4	252	185	67	326	107	219
	Hindu ...	5,152	4,286	866	2,594	2,274	320	2,221	1,765	456	337	247	90
	0— 5	226	103	123	226	103	123	...	...	...	...	...	...
	5—10	208	116	92	208	116	92	...	...	...	...	...	...
	10—15	232	172	60	207	157	50	23	13	10	2	2	...
	15—20	439	350	89	304	279	25	126	63	63	9	8	1
	20—40	3,126	2,749	377	1,384	1,364	20	1,590	1,262	328	152	123	29
	40—60	775	681	94	220	216	4	420	374	46	135	91	44
	60 and over	146	115	31	45	39	6	62	53	9	39	23	16
	Mahomedan ...	3,536	2,359	1,177	1,877	1,270	607	1.427	987	440	232	102	130
	0— 5	338	167	171	338	167	171	...	...	...	...	...	...
	5—10	307	162	145	307	162	145	...	...	...	...	...	...
	10—15	286	160	126	281	160	121	5	...	5	...	...	...
	15—20	343	210	133	265	185	80	75	23	52	3	2	1
	20—40	1,649	1,232	417	591	515	76	976	677	299	82	40	42
	40—60	472	335	137	79	66	13	315	241	74	78	28	50
	60 and over	141	93	48	16	15	1	56	46	10	69	32	37
BASSEIN.	*All Religions* ...	440,988	226,773	214,215	254,497	136,049	118,448	163,936	83,326	80,610	22,555	7,398	15,157
	0— 5	56,081	27,154	28,927	56,081	27,154	28,927	...	...	...	...	...	...
	5—10	59,543	29,457	30,086	59,543	29,457	30,086	...	...	...	...	...	...
	10—15	55,772	29,119	26,653	55,746	29,113	26,633	26	6	20	...	...	...
	15—20	44,086	21,129	22,957	37,292	19,613	17,679	6,621	1,484	5,137	173	32	141
	20—40	140,827	74,907	65,920	37,410	25,332	12,078	98,228	47,632	50,596	5,189	1,943	3,246
	40—60	63,738	33,864	29,874	6,377	4,194	2,183	48,276	26,826	21,450	9,085	2,844	6,241
	60 and over	20,941	11,143	9,798	2,048	1,186	862	10,785	7,378	3,407	8,108	2,579	5,529
	Buddhist ...	391,027	194,614	196,413	226,324	117,817	108,507	144,522	70,618	73,904	20,181	6,179	14,002
	0— 5	51,321	24,788	26,533	51,321	24,788	26,533	...	...	...	...	...	...
	5—10	54,692	26,998	27,694	54,692	26,998	27,694	...	...	...	...	...	...
	10—15	51,022	26,523	24,499	51,008	26,519	24,489	14	4	10	...	...	...
	15—20	39,346	18,373	20,973	33,228	17,120	16,108	5,971	1,236	4,735	147	17	130
	20—40	119,401	59,326	60,075	29,209	18,286	10,923	85,788	39,618	46,170	4,404	1,422	2,982
	40—60	56,251	28,678	27,573	5,073	3,107	1,966	42,987	23,153	19,834	8,191	2,418	5,773
	60 and over	18,994	9,928	9,066	1,793	999	794	9,762	6,607	3,155	7,439	2,322	5,117
	Animist ...	2,049	1,864	185	1,150	1,065	85	826	735	91	73	64	9
	0— 5	143	111	32	143	111	32	...	...	...	...	...	...
	5—10	117	105	12	117	105	12	...	...	...	...	...	...
	10—15	80	67	13	78	65	13	2	2	...	...	...	...
	15—20	121	101	20	109	94	15	12	7	5	...	...	...
	20—40	1,118	1,036	82	576	564	12	510	442	68	32	30	2
	40—60	401	376	25	112	111	1	259	242	17	30	23	7
	60 and over	69	68	1	15	15	...	43	42	1	11	11	...

IMPERIAL TABLE VII.—*Age, Sex and Civil Condition.*

PART B.—DETAILS BY DISTRICTS.

AGE.	POPULATION.			UNMARRIED.			MARRIED.			WIDOWED.		
	Persons.	Males.	Females.	Persons.	Males.	Females.	Persons.	Males.	Females.	Persons.	Males.	Females.
1	2	3	4	5	6	7	8	9	10	11	12	13
BASSEIN—*concluded.*												
Hindu ...	*11,822*	*10,471*	*1,351*	*5,907*	*5,375*	*532*	*5,425*	*4,692*	*733*	*490*	*404*	*86*
0— 5	340	182	158	340	182	158	...	...	...	...	...	...
5—10	311	170	141	311	170	141	...	...	...	...	...	...
10—15	354	270	84	351	270	81	3	...	3	...	...	...
15—20	907	782	125	684	640	44	210	132	78	13	10	3
20—40	7,689	7,043	646	3,499	3,421	78	3,935	3,393	542	255	229	26
40—60	1,940	1,769	171	640	615	25	1,138	1,034	104	162	120	42
60 and over	281	255	26	82	77	5	139	133	6	60	45	15
Mahomedan ...	*8,107*	*5,680*	*2,427*	*4,690*	*3,337*	*1,353*	*2,939*	*2,054*	*885*	*478*	*289*	*189*
0— 5	732	389	343	732	389	343	...	...	...	...	...	...
5—10	648	299	349	648	299	349	...	...	...	...	...	...
10—15	631	350	281	624	350	274	7	...	7	...	...	...
15—20	814	530	284	653	475	178	148	50	98	13	5	8
20—40	3,899	3,081	818	1,695	1,537	158	1,991	1,395	596	213	149	64
40—60	1,071	802	269	275	234	41	636	476	160	160	92	68
60 and over	312	229	83	63	53	10	157	133	24	92	43	49
Christian ...	*27,927*	*14,111*	*13,816*	*16,392*	*8,432*	*7,960*	*10,205*	*5,218*	*4,987*	*1,330*	*461*	*869*
0— 5	3,540	1,682	1,858	3,540	1,682	1,858	...	...	...	...	...	...
5—10	3,770	1,882	1,888	3,770	1,882	1,888	...	...	...	...	...	...
10—15	3,676	1,906	1,770	3,676	1,906	1,770	...	...	...	...	...	...
15—20	2,894	1,340	1,554	2,615	1,281	1,334	279	59	220	...	...	...
20—40	8,697	4,404	4,293	2,420	1,513	907	5,992	2,778	3,214	285	113	172
40—60	4,065	2,234	1,831	276	126	150	3,250	1,918	1,332	539	190	349
60 and over	1,285	663	622	95	42	53	684	463	221	506	158	348
HENZADA.												
All Religions ...	*532,357*	*264,319*	*268,038*	*305,401*	*158,061*	*147,340*	*194,181*	*96,384*	*97,797*	*32,775*	*9,874*	*22,901*
0— 5	69,962	34,286	35,676	69,962	34,286	35,676	...	...	...	...	...	...
5—10	72,202	35,560	36,642	72,202	35,560	36,642	...	...	...	...	...	...
10—15	71,404	38,535	32,869	71,090	38,535	32,555	294	...	294	20	...	20
15—20	52,594	24,791	27,803	45,317	23,290	22,027	6,977	1,457	5,520	300	44	256
20—40	163,128	81,092	82,036	37,932	22,038	15,894	117,918	56,709	61,209	7,278	2,345	4,933
40—60	73,669	34,925	38,744	6,387	3,103	3,284	54,373	28,337	26,036	12,909	3,485	9,424
60 and over	29,398	15,130	14,268	2,511	1,249	1,262	14,619	9,881	4,738	12,268	4,000	8,268
Buddhist ...	*509,310*	*248,922*	*260,388*	*292,132*	*149,097*	*143,035*	*185,423*	*90,428*	*94,995*	*31,755*	*9,397*	*22,358*
0— 5	67,779	33,192	34,587	67,779	33,192	34,587	...	...	...	...	...	...
5—10	70,148	34,576	35,572	70,148	34,576	35,572	...	...	...	...	..	...
10—15	69,329	37,325	32,004	69,031	37,325	31,706	278	...	278	20	...	20
15—20	50,366	23,363	27,003	43,446	22,006	21,440	6,626	1,315	5,311	294	42	252
20—40	152,932	73,371	79,561	33,614	18,302	15,312	112,310	52,905	59,405	7,008	2,164	4,844
40—60	70,269	32,529	37,740	5,733	2,539	3,194	52,048	26,682	25,366	12,488	3,308	9,180
60 and over	28,487	14,566	13,921	2,381	1,157	1,224	14,161	9,526	4,635	11,945	3,883	8,062
Animist ...	*1,466*	*1,309*	*157*	*822*	*757*	*65*	*588*	*506*	*82*	*56*	*46*	*10*
0— 5	103	80	23	103	80	23	...	...	...	...	...	...
5—10	52	38	14	52	38	14	...	...	...	...	...	...
10—15	72	61	11	72	61	11	...	...	...	...	...	...
15—20	82	72	10	76	72	4	6	...	6	...	...	...
20—40	842	764	78	437	426	11	384	318	66	21	20	1
40—60	265	251	14	77	75	2	170	162	8	18	14	4
60 and over	50	43	7	5	5	...	28	26	2	17	12	5
Hindu ...	*6,600*	*5,912*	*688*	*3,639*	*3,282*	*357*	*2,726*	*2,433*	*293*	*235*	*197*	*38*
0— 5	232	122	110	232	122	110	...	...	...	...	...	...
5—10	190	112	78	190	112	78	...	...	...	...	...	...
10—15	242	191	51	239	191	48	3	...	3	...	...	...
15—20	581	520	61	434	422	12	144	96	48	3	2	1
20—40	4,158	3,867	291	2,172	2,071	101	1,887	1,702	185	99	94	5
40—60	1,036	958	78	326	321	5	616	564	52	94	73	21
60 and over	161	142	19	46	43	3	76	71	5	39	28	11
Mahomedan ...	*4,657*	*3,074*	*1,583*	*2,724*	*1,850*	*874*	*1,742*	*1,137*	*605*	*191*	*87*	*104*
0— 5	545	260	285	545	260	285	...	...	...	...	...	...
5—10	461	221	240	461	221	240	...	...	...	...	...	...
10—15	418	231	187	412	231	181	6	...	6	...	...	...
15—20	454	290	164	341	264	77	111	26	85	2	...	2
20—40	1,987	1,495	492	812	740	72	1,127	731	396	48	24	24
40—60	633	454	179	129	111	18	408	298	110	96	45	51
60 and over	159	123	36	24	23	1	90	82	8	45	18	27

IMPERIAL TABLE VII.—*Age, Sex and Civil Condition.*

PART B.—DETAILS BY DISTRICTS.

District	AGE.	POPULATION.			UNMARRIED.			MARRIED.			WIDOWED.		
		Persons.	Males.	Females.	Persons.	Males.	Females.	Persons.	Males.	Females.	Persons.	Males.	Females.
	1	2	3	4	5	6	7	8	9	10	11	12	13
HENZADA—*concluded.*	***Christian*** ...	*10,285*	*5,070*	*5,215*	*6,059*	*3,055*	*3,004*	*3,688*	*1,868*	*1,820*	*538*	*147*	*391*
	0—5	1,301	631	670	1,301	631	670	...	...	...	...	...	...
	5—10	1,349	613	736	1,349	613	736	...	...	...	...	...	...
	10—15	1,342	727	615	1,335	727	608	7	...	7	...	...	...
	15—20	1,109	544	565	1,019	525	494	89	19	70	1	...	1
	20—40	3,185	1,573	1,612	883	485	398	2,200	1,045	1,155	102	43	59
	40—60	1,458	726	732	117	53	64	1,128	628	500	213	45	168
	60 and over	541	256	285	55	21	34	264	176	88	222	59	163
MYAUNGMYA.	***All Religions*** ...	*334,852*	*176,465*	*158,387*	*190,104*	*104,464*	*85,640*	*127,985*	*65,932*	*62,053*	*16,763*	*6,069*	*10,694*
	0—5	46,524	22,779	23,745	46,524	22,779	23,745	...	...	...	...	...	...
	5—10	44,940	22,257	22,683	44,940	22,257	22,683	...	...	...	...	...	...
	10—15	40,128	20,879	19,249	40,053	20,879	19,174	68	...	68	7	...	7
	15—20	31,788	15,930	15,858	26,098	14,845	11,253	5,560	1,078	4,482	130	7	123
	20—40	108,487	59,963	48,524	27,127	20,262	6,865	77,481	38,105	39,376	3,879	1,596	2,283
	40—60	47,172	25,876	21,296	3,970	2,657	1,313	36,486	20,863	15,623	6,716	2,356	4,360
	60 and over	15,813	8,781	7,032	1,392	785	607	8,390	5,886	2,504	6,031	2,110	3,921
	Buddhist ...	*300,515*	*153,362*	*147,153*	*169,058*	*89,652*	*79,406*	*116,072*	*58,354*	*57,718*	*15,385*	*5,356*	*10,029*
	0—5	42,737	20,828	21,909	42,737	20,828	21,909	...	...	...	...	...	...
	5—10	41,561	20,513	21,048	41,561	20,513	21,048	...	...	...	...	...	...
	10—15	37,015	19,078	17,937	36,940	19,078	17,862	68	...	68	7	...	7
	15—20	28,608	13,817	14,791	23,342	12,874	10,468	5,142	940	4,202	124	3	121
	20—40	93,291	48,384	44,907	20,140	13,826	6,314	69,701	33,230	36,471	3,450	1,328	2,122
	40—60	42,651	22,716	19,935	3,090	1,858	1,232	33,409	18,787	14,622	6,152	2,071	4,081
	60 and over	14,652	8,026	6,626	1,248	675	573	7,752	5,397	2,355	5,652	1,954	3,698
	Animist ...	*2,922*	*2,683*	*239*	*1,830*	*1,726*	*104*	*990*	*869*	*121*	*102*	*88*	*14*
	0—5	221	185	36	221	185	36	...	...	...	...	...	...
	5—10	132	109	23	132	109	23	...	...	...	...	...	...
	10—15	123	104	19	123	104	19	...	...	...	...	...	...
	15—20	149	139	10	138	133	5	11	6	5	...	...	...
	20—40	1,681	1,570	111	1,027	1,010	17	619	530	89	35	30	5
	40—60	542	505	37	172	168	4	318	292	26	52	45	7
	60 and over	74	71	3	17	17	...	42	41	1	15	13	2
	Hindu ...	*6,128*	*5,486*	*642*	*3,820*	*3,558*	*262*	*2,140*	*1,796*	*344*	*168*	*132*	*36*
	0—5	231	129	102	231	129	102	...	...	...	...	...	...
	5—10	167	100	67	167	100	67	...	...	...	...	...	...
	10—15	265	235	30	265	235	30	...	...	...	...	...	...
	15—20	652	589	63	541	526	15	110	62	48	1	1	...
	20—40	3,959	3,650	309	2,280	2,242	38	1,599	1,337	262	80	71	9
	40—60	768	705	63	302	294	8	397	363	34	69	48	21
	60 and over	86	78	8	34	32	2	34	34	...	18	12	6
	Mahomedan ...	*7,103*	*5,694*	*1,409*	*4,684*	*3,919*	*765*	*2,250*	*1,642*	*608*	*169*	*133*	*36*
	0—5	557	283	274	557	283	274	...	...	...	...	...	...
	5—10	476	258	218	476	258	218	...	...	...	...	...	...
	10—15	440	283	157	440	283	157	...	...	...	...	...	...
	15—20	688	552	136	574	511	63	113	40	73	1	1	...
	20—40	3,988	3,499	489	2,339	2,293	46	1,567	1,140	427	82	66	16
	40—60	787	676	111	261	257	4	466	372	94	60	47	13
	60 and over	167	143	24	37	34	3	104	90	14	26	19	7
	Christian ...	*18,157*	*9,218*	*8,939*	*10,696*	*5,595*	*5,101*	*6,522*	*3,263*	*3,259*	*939*	*360*	*579*
	0—5	2,778	1,354	1,424	2,778	1,354	1,424	...	...	...	...	...	...
	5—10	2,601	1,276	1,325	2,601	1,276	1,325	...	...	...	...	...	...
	10—15	2,285	1,179	1,106	2,285	1,179	1,106	...	...	...	...	...	...
	15—20	1,689	832	857	1,502	800	702	183	30	153	4	2	2
	20—40	5,548	2,842	2,706	1,330	880	450	3,986	1,861	2,125	232	101	131
	40—60	2,423	1,273	1,150	144	79	65	1,896	1,049	847	383	145	238
	60 and over	833	462	371	56	27	29	457	323	134	320	112	208
MA-UBIN.	***All Religions*** ...	*305,073*	*155,715*	*149,358*	*176,767*	*93,644*	*83,123*	*111,269*	*56,314*	*54,955*	*17,037*	*5,757*	*11,280*
	0—5	41,840	20,364	21,476	41,840	20,364	21,476	...	...	...	...	...	...
	5—10	40,439	20,104	20,335	40,439	20,104	20,335	...	...	...	...	...	...
	10—15	37,463	19,467	17,996	37,396	19,465	17,931	64	2	62	3	...	3
	15—20	29,525	14,376	15,149	25,328	13,429	11,899	4,077	915	3,162	120	32	88
	20—40	95,107	49,256	45,851	26,025	16,881	9,144	65,268	31,077	34,191	3,814	1,298	2,516
	40—60	44,006	23,245	20,761	4,199	2,555	1,644	33,212	18,545	14,667	6,595	2,145	4,450
	60 and over	16,693	8,903	7,790	1,540	846	694	8,648	5,775	2,873	6,505	2,282	4,223

Imperial Table VII.—*Age, Sex and Civil Condition.*

PART B.—DETAILS BY DISTRICTS.

District	AGE.	POPULATION. Persons.	POPULATION. Males.	POPULATION. Females.	UNMARRIED. Persons.	UNMARRIED. Males.	UNMARRIED. Females.	MARRIED. Persons.	MARRIED. Males.	MARRIED. Females.	WIDOWED. Persons.	WIDOWED. Males.	WIDOWED. Females.
	1	2	3	4	5	6	7	8	9	10	11	12	13
MA-UBIN—*concluded.*	***Buddhist*** ...	*282,669*	*140,611*	*142,058*	*163,805*	*84,194*	*79,111*	*103,335*	*51,119*	*52,216*	*16,029*	*5,298*	*10,781*
	0—5	39,606	19,210	20,396	39,606	19,210	20,396	...	...	...	...	...	...
	5—10	38,415	19,084	19,331	38,415	19,084	19,331	...	...	...	...	...	...
	10—15	35,429	18,244	17,185	35,370	18,244	17,126	56	...	56	3	...	3
	15—20	27,453	13,037	14,416	23,548	12,208	11,340	3,792	803	2,989	113	26	87
	20—40	85,239	41,762	43,477	21,395	12,739	8,656	60,293	27,876	32,417	3,551	1,147	2,404
	40—60	40,792	20,947	19,845	3,555	1,959	1,596	31,018	17,014	14,004	6,219	1,974	4,245
	60 and over	15,735	8,327	7,408	1,416	750	666	8,176	5,426	2,750	6,143	2,151	3,992
	Animist ...	*1,651*	*1,475*	*176*	*1,016*	*937*	*79*	*575*	*494*	*81*	*60*	*44*	*16*
	0—5	112	86	26	112	86	26	...	...	...	...	...	...
	5—10	74	50	24	74	50	24	...	...	...	...	...	...
	10—15	81	67	14	79	65	14	2	2	...	...	...	...
	15—20	109	99	10	98	92	6	10	6	4	1	1	...
	20—40	915	842	73	545	538	7	352	289	63	18	15	3
	40—60	294	273	21	89	87	2	180	168	12	25	18	7
	60 and over	66	58	8	19	19	...	31	29	2	16	10	6
	Hindu ...	*5,892*	*4,775*	*617*	*8,388*	*3,104*	*284*	*1,840*	*1,538*	*302*	*164*	*133*	*31*
	0—5	238	129	109	238	129	109	...	...	...	...	...	...
	5—10	193	110	83	193	110	83	...	...	...	...	...	...
	10—15	229	185	44	229	185	44	...	...	...	...	...	...
	15—20	458	408	50	377	362	15	80	46	34	1	...	1
	20—40	3,330	3,081	249	1,984	1,958	26	1,287	1,072	215	59	51	8
	40—60	799	728	71	316	311	5	416	367	49	67	50	17
	60 and over	145	134	11	51	49	2	57	53	4	37	32	5
	Mahomedan ...	*4,864*	*3,615*	*1,249*	*2,893*	*2 228*	*665*	*1,808*	*1,297*	*511*	*163*	*90*	*73*
	0—5	484	226	258	484	226	258	...	...	...	...	...	...
	5—10	387	211	176	387	211	176	...	...	...	...	...	...
	10—15	400	278	122	394	278	116	6	...	6	...	...	...
	15—20	452	333	119	356	296	60	93	34	59	3	3	...
	20—40	2,397	1,971	426	1,117	1,069	48	1,220	867	353	60	35	25
	40—60	627	507	120	142	137	5	422	336	86	63	34	29
	60 and over	117	89	28	13	11	2	67	60	7	37	18	19
	Christian ...	*10,474*	*5,217*	*5,257*	*6,151*	*3,167*	*2,984*	*3,702*	*1,858*	*1,844*	*621*	*192*	*429*
	0—5	1,400	713	687	1,400	713	687	...	...	...	...	...	...
	5—10	1,370	649	721	1,370	649	721	...	...	...	...	...	...
	10—15	1,324	693	631	1,324	693	631	...	...	...	...	...	...
	15—20	1,048	495	553	947	469	478	99	24	75	2	2	...
	20—40	3,209	1,583	1,626	972	565	407	2,111	968	1,143	126	50	76
	40—60	1,493	789	704	97	61	36	1,175	659	516	221	69	152
	60 and over	630	295	335	41	17	24	317	207	110	272	71	201
PYAPÔN.	***All Religions*** ...	*256,215*	*139,641*	*116,574*	*147,758*	*84,655*	*63,103*	*95,111*	*49,843*	*45,268*	*13,346*	*5,143*	*8,208*
	0—5	34,757	17,013	17,744	34,757	17,013	17,744	...	...	...	...	...	...
	5—10	32,615	16,123	16,492	32,604	16,118	16,486	11	5	6	...	...	...
	10—15	28,681	14,833	13,848	28,648	14,811	13,837	33	22	11	...	...	...
	15—20	24,264	12,750	11,514	19,131	11,689	7,442	4,943	1,026	3,917	190	35	155
	20—40	86,331	50,601	35,730	26,847	20,867	5,980	56,315	28,395	27,920	3,169	1,339	1,830
	40—60	37,729	21,643	16,086	4,351	3,328	1,023	27,983	16,280	11,703	5,395	2,035	3,360
	60 and over	11,838	6,678	5,160	1,420	829	591	5,826	4,115	1,711	4,592	1,734	2,858
	Buddhist ...	*229,418*	*119,368*	*110,050*	*130,674*	*70,876*	*59,798*	*86,193*	*43,839*	*42,354*	*12,551*	*4,653*	*7,898*
	0—5	32,423	15,801	16,622	32,423	15,801	16,622	...	...	...	...	...	...
	5—10	30,695	15,062	15,633	30,695	15,062	15,633	...	...	...	...	...	...
	10—15	26,803	13,527	13,276	26,803	13,527	13,276	...	...	...	...	...	...
	15—20	21,827	10,871	10,956	17,052	9,934	7,118	4,595	905	3,690	180	32	148
	20—40	72,465	39,241	33,224	19,311	13,680	5,631	50,268	24,421	25,847	2,886	1,140	1,746
	40—60	34,178	18,770	15,408	3,151	2,200	951	25,929	14,718	11,211	5,098	1,852	3,246
	60 and over	11,027	6,096	4,931	1,239	672	567	5,401	3,795	1,606	4,387	1,629	2,758
	Animist ...	*3,580*	*3,118*	*462*	*2,325*	*2,083*	*242*	*1,159*	*976*	*183*	*96*	*59*	*37*
	0—5	211	146	65	211	146	65	...	...	...	...	...	...
	5—10	226	168	58	226	168	58	...	...	...	...	...	...
	10—15	192	156	36	192	156	36	...	...	...	...	...	...
	15—20	272	262	10	258	248	10	14	14	...	...	...	...
	20—40	1,996	1,793	203	1,240	1,176	64	729	600	129	27	17	10
	40—60	571	504	67	170	163	7	346	307	39	55	34	21
	60 and over	112	89	23	28	26	2	70	55	15	14	8	6

IMPERIAL TABLE VII.—*Age, Sex and Civil Condition.*

PART B.—DETAILS BY DISTRICTS.

District	AGE.	POPULATION. Persons.	POPULATION. Males.	POPULATION. Females.	UNMARRIED. Persons.	UNMARRIED. Males.	UNMARRIED. Females.	MARRIED. Persons.	MARRIED. Males.	MARRIED. Females.	WIDOWED. Persons.	WIDOWED. Males.	WIDOWED. Females.
	1	2	3	4	5	6	7	8	9	10	11	12	13
PYAPÔN—*concluded.*	*Hindu* ...	*12,164*	*9,869*	*2,295*	*8,047*	*7,086*	*1,011*	*3,797*	*2,582*	*1,215*	*320*	*251*	*69*
	0—5	841	436	405	841	436	405	...	...	...	...	...	...
	5—10	612	345	267	604	343	261	8	2	6	...	...	...
	10—15	665	536	129	642	519	123	23	17	6	...	...	...
	15—20	1,129	943	186	938	869	69	186	74	112	5	...	5
	20—40	7,066	6,017	1,049	4,218	4,108	110	2,697	1,785	912	151	124	27
	40—60	1,593	1,392	201	714	685	29	767	620	147	112	87	25
	60 and over	258	200	58	90	76	14	116	84	32	52	40	12
	Mahomedan ...	*8,540*	*8,052*	*488*	*2,200*	*1,949*	*251*	*1,247*	*1,038*	*209*	*93*	*65*	*28*
	0—5	173	82	91	173	82	91	...	...	...	...	...	...
	5—10	151	95	56	148	92	56	3	3	...	...	...	...
	10—15	168	123	45	159	118	41	9	5	4	...	...	...
	15—20	343	292	51	279	256	23	59	33	26	5	3	2
	20—40	2,126	1,953	173	1,215	1,188	27	876	737	139	35	28	7
	40—60	463	408	55	189	176	13	250	214	36	24	18	6
	60 and over	116	99	17	37	37	...	50	46	4	29	16	13
	Christian ...	*7,291*	*4,046*	*3,245*	*4,363*	*2,570*	*1,793*	*2,643*	*1,361*	*1,282*	*285*	*115*	*170*
	0—5	1,102	544	558	1,102	544	558	...	...	...	...	...	...
	5—10	921	447	474	921	447	474	...	...	...	...	...	...
	10—15	839	478	361	839	478	361	...	...	...	...	...	...
	15—20	671	362	309	584	362	222	87	...	87	...	...	...
	20—40	2,547	1,484	1,063	780	632	148	1,698	822	876	69	30	39
	40—60	892	543	349	112	90	22	674	409	265	106	44	62
	60 and over	319	188	131	25	17	8	184	130	54	110	41	69
TOUNGOO.	*All Religions* ...	*351,076*	*181,488*	*169,588*	*192,007*	*104,113*	*87,894*	*135,947*	*69,638*	*66,309*	*28,122*	*7,737*	*15,385*
	0—5	47,121	23,218	23,903	47,121	23,218	23,903	...	...	...	...	...	...
	5—10	47,240	23,964	23,276	47,138	23,964	23,174	102	...	102	...	...	...
	10—15	42,045	22,209	19,836	41,719	22,169	19,550	326	40	286	...	...	...
	15—20	31,876	15,074	16,802	25,216	13,937	11,279	6,311	1,094	5,217	349	43	306
	20—40	112,094	59,052	53,042	24,954	17,448	7,506	81,248	39,213	42,035	5,892	2,391	3,501
	40—60	52,810	28,341	24,469	4,193	2,565	1,628	38,969	22,686	16,283	9,648	3,090	6,558
	60 and over	17,890	9,630	8,260	1,666	812	854	8,991	6,605	2,386	7,233	2,213	5,020
	Buddhist ...	*274,870*	*138,220*	*136,650*	*149,841*	*78,551*	*70,790*	*107,746*	*54,118*	*53,628*	*17,783*	*5,551*	*12,232*
	0—5	36,645	17,945	18,700	36,645	17,945	18,700	...	...	...	...	...	...
	5—10	38,387	19,005	19,382	38,387	19,005	19,382	...	...	...	...	...	...
	10—15	34,426	18,162	16,264	34,320	18,122	16,198	106	40	66	...	..	...
	15—20	24,986	11,363	13,623	19,648	10,702	8,946	5,043	634	4,409	295	27	268
	20—40	83,745	42,246	41,499	16,168	10,556	5,612	63,324	30,127	33,197	4,253	1,563	2,690
	40—60	41,766	21,600	20,166	2,861	1,599	1,262	31,673	17,819	13,854	7,232	2,182	5,050
	60 and over	14,915	7,899	7,016	1,312	622	690	7,600	5,498	2,102	6,003	1,779	4,224
	Animist ...	*22,355*	*12,215*	*10,140*	*13,175*	*7,499*	*5,676*	*7,847*	*3,966*	*3,881*	*1,333*	*750*	*1,083*
	0—5	3,025	1,592	1,433	3,025	1,592	1,433	...	...	...	...	...	...
	5—10	3,023	1,603	1,420	3,023	1,603	1,420	...	...	...	...	...	...
	10—15	2,296	1,223	1,073	2,275	1,223	1,052	21	...	21	...	...	...
	15—20	1,993	963	1,030	1,737	917	820	244	46	198	12	...	12
	20—40	7,714	4,298	3,416	2,645	1,892	753	4,537	2,170	2,367	532	236	296
	40—60	3,312	1,979	1,333	371	236	135	2,119	1,408	711	822	335	487
	60 and over	992	557	435	99	36	63	426	342	84	467	179	288
	Hindu ...	*14,220*	*10,070*	*4,150*	*6,788*	*5,260*	*1,528*	*6,465*	*4,172*	*2,293*	*967*	*638*	*329*
	0—5	1,618	801	817	1,618	801	817	...	...	...	...	...	...
	5—10	1,115	582	533	1,013	582	431	102	...	102	...	...	...
	10—15	838	487	351	651	487	164	187	...	187	...	...	...
	15—20	1,082	812	270	560	528	32	507	274	233	15	10	5
	20—40	7,016	5,433	1,583	2,435	2,371	64	4,198	2,749	1,449	383	313	70
	40—60	2,098	1,661	437	432	415	17	1,287	1,008	279	379	238	141
	60 and over	453	294	159	79	76	3	184	141	43	190	77	113
	Mahomedan ...	*6,369*	*4,170*	*2,199*	*3,774*	*2,607*	*1,167*	*2,197*	*1,359*	*838*	*398*	*204*	*194*
	0—5	631	313	318	631	313	318	...	...	...	...	...	...
	5—10	616	311	305	616	311	305	...	...	...	...	...	...
	10—15	568	325	243	556	325	231	12	...	12	...	...	...
	15—20	641	390	251	493	338	155	139	49	90	9	3	6
	20—40	2,789	2,030	759	1,207	1,086	121	1,428	851	577	154	93	61
	40—60	889	642	247	219	191	28	522	376	146	148	75	73
	60 and over	235	159	76	52	43	9	96	83	13	87	33	54

IMPERIAL TABLE VII.—*Age, Sex and Civil Condition.*

PART B.—DETAILS BY DISTRICTS.

	AGE.	POPULATION.			UNMARRIED.			MARRIED.			WIDOWED.		
		Persons.	Males.	Females.	Persons.	Males.	Females.	Persons.	Males.	Females.	Persons.	Males.	Females.
	1	2	3	4	5	6	7	8	9	10	11	12	13
TOUNGOO—*concluded.*	***Christian*** ...	***33,138***	***16,712***	***16,426***	***18,861***	***10,137***	***8,724***	***12,144***	***5,989***	***6,155***	***2,133***	***586***	***1,547***
	0—5	5,189	2,559	2,630	5,189	2,559	2,630	...	...	...	...	...	...
	5—10	4,095	2,461	1,634	4,095	2,461	1,634	...	...	...	...	...	...
	10—15	3,914	2 010	1,904	3,914	2,010	1,904	...	...	...	...	...	...
	15—20	3,255	1,529	1,726	2,762	1,437	1,325	475	89	386	18	3	15
	20—40	10,663	4,990	5,673	2,469	1,513	956	7,631	3,298	4,333	563	179	384
	40—60	4,727	2,442	2,285	308	122	186	3,353	2,061	1,292	1,066	259	807
	60 and over	1,295	721	574	124	35	89	685	541	144	486	145	341
SALWEEN.	***All Religions*** ...	***46,608***	***24,741***	***21,867***	***26,430***	***14,745***	***11,685***	***16,037***	***8,211***	***7,826***	***4,141***	***1,785***	***2,356***
	0—5	7,162	3,679	3,483	7,162	3,679	3,483	...	...	...	...	...	...
	5—10	6,245	3,320	2,925	6,245	3,320	2,925	...	...	...	...	...	...
	10—15	4,370	2,370	2,000	4,334	2,367	1,967	31	3	28	5	...	5
	15—20	3,859	1,854	2,005	3,248	1,789	1,459	589	64	525	22	1	21
	20—40	16,610	8,588	8,022	4,587	3,104	1,483	10,799	4,950	5,849	1,224	534	690
	40—60	6,810	4,043	2,767	686	397	289	4,078	2,766	1,312	2,046	880	1,166
	60 and over	1,552	887	665	168	89	79	540	428	112	844	370	474
	Buddhist ...	***20,474***	***11,213***	***9,261***	***11,840***	***6,624***	***4,716***	***7,829***	***8,722***	***8,607***	***1,805***	***867***	***938***
	0—5	3,232	1,671	1,561	3,232	1,671	1,561	...	...	...	...	...	...
	5—10	2,802	1,500	1,302	2,802	1,500	1,302	...	...	...	...	...	...
	10—15	2,042	1,146	896	2,031	1,146	885	9	...	9	2	...	2
	15—20	1,622	808	814	1,306	781	525	302	26	276	14	1	13
	20—40	7,152	3,851	3,301	1,657	1,299	358	4,925	2,260	2,665	570	292	278
	40—60	2,968	1,836	1,132	267	195	72	1,835	1,232	603	866	409	457
	60 and over	656	401	255	45	32	13	258	204	54	353	165	188
	Animist ...	***25,068***	***12,725***	***12,848***	***14,521***	***7,669***	***6,852***	***8,272***	***4,176***	***4,096***	***2,275***	***880***	***1,395***
	0—5	3,839	1,954	1,885	3,839	1,954	1,885	...	...	...	...	...	...
	5—10	3,375	1,780	1,595	3,375	1,780	1,595	...	...	...	...	...	...
	10—15	2,250	1,174	1,076	2,229	1,174	1,055	18	...	18	3	...	3
	15—20	2,154	998	1,156	1,883	967	916	263	31	232	8	...	8
	20—40	8,896	4,278	4,618	2,694	1,574	1,120	5,574	2,478	3,096	628	226	402
	40—60	3,676	2,071	1,605	381	165	216	2,146	1,453	693	1,149	453	696
	60 and over	878	470	408	120	55	65	271	214	57	487	201	286
THATÔN.	***All Religions*** ...	***416,975***	***217,770***	***199,205***	***251,878***	***186,510***	***115,868***	***148,408***	***72,923***	***70,485***	***21,689***	***8,837***	***18,352***
	0—5	63,650	31,707	31,943	63,650	31,707	31,943	...	...	...	...	...	...
	5—10	59,685	30,019	29,666	59,685	30,019	29,666	...	...	...	...	...	...
	10—15	49,730	25,891	23,839	49,324	25,875	23,449	398	16	382	8	...	8
	15—20	39,816	19,424	20,392	34,562	18,379	16,183	5,047	1,011	4,036	207	34	173
	20—40	130,237	69,469	60,768	36,545	25,298	11,247	88,322	41,902	46,420	5,370	2,269	3,101
	40—60	53,831	29,818	24,013	5,673	3,814	1,859	39,676	22,950	16,726	8,482	3,054	5,428
	60 and over	20,026	11,442	8,584	2,439	1,418	1,021	9,965	7,044	2,921	7,622	2,980	4,642
	Buddhist ...	***380,244***	***192,749***	***187,495***	***229,369***	***120,283***	***109,136***	***131,244***	***65,525***	***65,719***	***19,631***	***6,991***	***12,640***
	0—5	59,613	29,642	29,971	59,613	29,642	29,971	...	...	...	...	...	...
	5—10	56,063	28,155	27,908	56,063	28,155	27,908	...	...	...	...	...	...
	10—15	46,852	24,141	22,711	46,486	24,125	22,361	358	16	342	8	...	8
	15—20	36,897	17,525	19,372	32,224	16,618	15,606	4,513	901	3,612	160	6	154
	20—40	113,998	57,328	56,670	28,840	18,214	10,626	80,505	37,375	43,130	4,653	1,739	2,914
	40—60	48,414	25,752	22,662	4,110	2,397	1,713	36,587	20,758	15,829	7,717	2,597	5,120
	60 and over	18,407	10,206	8,201	2,033	1,082	951	9,281	6,475	2,806	7,093	2,649	4,444
	Animist ...	***5,958***	***3,840***	***2,118***	***3,595***	***2,408***	***1,187***	***2,018***	***1,235***	***783***	***345***	***197***	***148***
	0—5	718	402	316	718	402	316	...	...	...	...	...	...
	5—10	723	397	326	723	397	326	...	...	...	...	...	...
	10—15	599	374	225	599	374	225	...	...	...	...	...	...
	15—20	438	275	163	389	254	135	48	20	28	1	1	..
	20—40	2,191	1,474	717	924	777	147	1,179	643	536	88	54	34
	40—60	1,010	700	310	180	154	26	670	463	207	160	83	77
	60 and over	279	218	61	62	50	12	121	109	12	96	59	37
	Hindu ...	***16,805***	***12,131***	***4,674***	***9,991***	***7,784***	***2,207***	***5,799***	***3,592***	***2,207***	***1,015***	***755***	***260***
	0—5	1,615	812	803	1,615	812	803	...	...	...	...	...	...
	5—10	1,315	651	664	1,315	651	664	...	...	...	...	...	...
	10—15	1,004	648	356	979	648	331	25	...	25	...	...	...
	15—20	1,258	899	359	949	818	131	285	63	222	24	18	6
	20—40	8,309	6,524	1,785	4,046	3,874	172	3,852	2,301	1,551	411	349	62
	40—60	2,585	2,049	536	898	824	74	1,351	998	353	336	227	109
	60 and over	719	548	171	189	157	32	286	230	56	244	161	83

Imperial Table VII.—*Age, Sex and Civil Condition.*

PART B.—DETAILS BY DISTRICTS.

District	AGE.	POPULATION. Persons.	Males.	Females.	UNMARRIED. Persons.	Males.	Females.	MARRIED. Persons.	Males.	Females.	WIDOWED. Persons.	Males.	Females.
	1	2	3	4	5	6	7	8	9	10	11	12	13
THATÔN—*concluded.*	***Mahomedan*** ...	*10,221*	*7,054*	*8,167*	*6,606*	*4,809*	*1,797*	*8,121*	*1,931*	*1,190*	*494*	*814*	*180*
	0—5	1,158	577	581	1,158	577	581	...	...	...	...	...	...
	5—10	1,068	566	502	1,068	560	502	...	...	...	...	...	...
	10—15	819	472	347	805	472	333	14	...	14	...	...	...
	15—20	896	565	331	704	536	174	171	26	145	21	9	12
	20—40	4,478	3,451	1,027	2,306	2,142	164	2,000	1,194	806	172	115	57
	40—60	1,336	1,038	298	428	401	27	727	527	200	181	110	71
	60 and over ...	466	385	81	137	121	16	209	184	25	120	80	40
	Christian ...	*8,738*	*1,987*	*1,751*	*2,810*	*1,269*	*1,041*	*1,224*	*638*	*586*	*204*	*80*	*124*
	0—5	545	273	272	545	273	272	...	...	...	...	...	...
	5—10	515	249	266	515	249	266	...	...	...	...	...	...
	10—15	456	256	200	455	256	199	1	...	1	...	...	...
	15—20	327	160	167	296	159	137	30	1	29	1	...	1
	20—40	1,254	685	569	424	286	138	784	387	397	46	12	34
	40—60	486	279	207	57	38	19	341	204	137	88	37	51
	60 and over ...	155	85	70	18	8	10	68	46	22	69	31	38
AMHERST.	***All Religions*** ...	*867,918*	*198,480*	*169,488*	*216,851*	*120,847*	*96,504*	*131,636*	*70,143*	*61,493*	*19,431*	*7,940*	*11,491*
	0—5	53,534	26,673	26,861	53,534	26,673	26,681	...	...	...	...	...	...
	5—10	51,016	25,672	25,344	51,016	25,672	25,344	...	...	...	...	...	...
	10—15	42,898	22,737	20,161	42,875	22,737	20,138	23	...	23	...	...	...
	15—20	36,133	18,373	17,760	31,125	17,386	13,739	4,849	966	3,883	159	21	138
	20—40	116,845	66,145	50,700	31,904	23,426	8,478	80,011	40,449	39,562	4,930	2,270	2,660
	40—60	49,896	28,605	21,291	4,692	3,388	1,304	37,867	22,338	15,529	7,337	2,879	4,458
	60 and over	17,596	10,225	7,371	1,705	1,065	640	8,886	6,390	2,496	7,005	2,770	4,235
	Buddhist ...	*809,904*	*158,436*	*151,468*	*185,750*	*98,583*	*87,167*	*107,936*	*53,677*	*54,259*	*16,218*	*6,176*	*10,042*
	0—5	47,954	23,696	24,258	47,954	23,696	24,258	...	...	...	...	...	...
	5—10	45,274	22,657	22,617	45,274	22,657	22,617	...	...	...	...	...	...
	10—15	38,169	19,863	18,306	38,149	19,863	18,286	20	...	20	...	...	...
	15—20	31,026	15,184	15,842	27,274	14,587	12,687	3,602	576	3,026	150	21	129
	20—40	91,474	46,833	44,641	22,721	15,100	7,621	64,813	30,090	34,723	3,940	1,643	2,297
	40—60	41,003	21,855	19,148	3,040	1,915	1,125	31,909	17,728	14,181	6,054	2,212	3,842
	60 and over	15,004	8,348	6,656	1,338	765	573	7,592	5,283	2,309	6,074	2,300	3,774
	Animist ...	*4,888*	*8,441*	*897*	*2,648*	*2,063*	*485*	*1,648*	*1,210*	*838*	*247*	*168*	*79*
	0—5	452	320	132	452	320	132	...	...	...	...	...	...
	5—10	447	318	129	447	318	129	...	...	...	...	...	...
	10—15	363	264	99	360	264	96	3	...	3	...	...	...
	15—20	279	216	63	254	209	45	25	7	18	...	...	...
	20—40	1,713	1,396	317	834	764	70	809	582	227	70	50	20
	40—60	842	710	132	163	153	10	576	495	81	103	62	41
	60 and over	242	217	25	38	35	3	130	126	4	74	56	18
	Hindu ...	*28,864*	*18,402*	*5,462*	*11,158*	*8,945*	*2,208*	*11,285*	*8,551*	*2,734*	*1,426*	*906*	*520*
	0—5	1,441	769	672	1,441	769	672	...	...	...	...	...	...
	5—10	1,532	813	719	1,532	813	719	...	...	...	...	...	...
	10—15	1,275	863	412	1,275	863	412	...	...	...	...	...	...
	15—20	1,790	1,283	507	1,165	1,013	152	625	270	355	...	...	...
	20—40	12,547	10,389	2,158	4,563	4,390	173	7,510	5,651	1,859	474	348	126
	40—60	4,250	3,501	749	983	924	59	2,664	2,213	451	603	364	239
	60 and over	1,029	784	245	194	173	21	486	417	69	349	194	155
	Mahomedan ...	*22,893*	*14,560*	*8,333*	*13,011*	*8,440*	*4,571*	*8,689*	*5,567*	*3,132*	*1,198*	*568*	*630*
	0—5	2,771	1,405	1,366	2,771	1,405	1,366	...	...	...	...	...	...
	5—10	2,849	1,441	1,408	2,849	1,441	1,408	...	...	...	...	...	...
	10—15	2,163	1,262	901	2,163	1,262	901	...	...	...	...	...	...
	15—20	2,221	1,291	930	1,664	1,179	485	548	112	436	9	...	9
	20—40	8,971	6,399	2,572	3,058	2,720	338	5,552	3,485	2,067	361	194	167
	40—60	2,902	2,053	849	409	352	57	2,063	1,509	554	430	192	238
	60 and over	1,016	709	307	97	81	16	526	451	75	393	177	216
	Christian ...	*6,824*	*3,531*	*3,293*	*4,339*	*2,285*	*2,054*	*2,141*	*1,122*	*1,019*	*344*	*124*	*220*
	0—5	906	478	428	906	478	428	...	...	...	...	...	...
	5—10	902	439	463	902	439	463	...	...	...	...	...	...
	10—15	925	484	441	925	484	441	...	...	...	...	...	...
	15—20	803	388	415	756	387	369	47	1	46	...	...	...
	20—40	2,095	1,099	996	715	442	273	1,297	624	673	83	33	50
	40—60	892	479	413	97	44	53	648	386	262	147	49	98
	60 and over	301	164	137	38	11	27	149	111	38	114	42	72

Imperial Table VII.—*Age, Sex and Civil Condition.*

PART B.—DETAILS BY DISTRICTS.

District	AGE.	POPULATION. Persons.	POPULATION. Males.	POPULATION. Females.	UNMARRIED. Persons.	UNMARRIED. Males.	UNMARRIED. Females.	MARRIED. Persons.	MARRIED. Males.	MARRIED. Females.	WIDOWED. Persons.	WIDOWED. Males.	WIDOWED. Females.
	1	2	3	4	5	6	7	8	9	10	11	12	13
TAVOY.	***All Religions*** ...	*135,293*	*68,667*	*66,626*	*77,539*	*39,995*	*37,544*	*50,318*	*26,369*	*23,949*	*7,436*	*2,303*	*5,133*
	0—5	19,097	9,748	9,349	19,097	9,748	9,349	...	...	...	...	...	...
	5—10	18,472	9,254	9,218	18,471	9,254	9,217	1	...	1	...	...	...
	10—15	16,102	8,536	7,566	16,035	8,474	7,561	57	52	5	10	10	...
	15—20	11,846	5,378	6,468	10,525	4,944	5,581	1,283	424	859	38	10	28
	20—40	40,809	21,355	19,454	11,044	6,430	4,614	28,163	14,467	13,696	1,602	458	1,144
	40—60	20,688	10,507	10,181	1,573	818	755	16,313	8,845	7,468	2,802	844	1,958
	60 and over	8,279	3,889	4,390	794	327	467	4,501	2,581	1,920	2,984	981	2,003
	Buddhist ...	*129,505*	*64,908*	*64,597*	*74,144*	*37,675*	*36,469*	*48,183*	*25,041*	*23,142*	*7,178*	*2,192*	*4,986*
	0—5	18,531	9,457	9,074	18,531	9,457	9,074	...	...	...	...	...	...
	5—10	17,912	8,961	8,951	17,912	8,961	8,951	...	...	...	...	...	...
	10—15	15,606	8,265	7,341	15,545	8,204	7,341	51	51	...	10	10	...
	15—20	11,290	5,055	6,235	10,064	4,655	5,409	1,189	390	799	37	10	27
	20—40	38,266	19,508	18,758	9,904	5,415	4,489	26,828	13,668	13,160	1,534	425	1,109
	40—60	19,869	9,951	9,918	1,427	682	745	15,756	8,467	7,289	2,686	802	1,884
	60 and over	8,031	3,711	4,320	761	301	460	4,359	2,465	1,894	2,911	945	1,966
	Animist ...	*1,880*	*997*	*883*	*944*	*724*	*220*	*401*	*255*	*146*	*35*	*18*	*17*
	0—5	130	70	60	130	70	60	...	...	...	...	...	...
	5—10	134	81	53	134	81	53	...	...	...	...	...	...
	10—15	143	86	57	143	86	57	...	...	...	...	...	...
	15—20	99	62	37	84	59	25	14	3	11	1	...	1
	20—40	632	514	118	405	381	24	220	129	91	7	4	3
	40—60	171	127	44	42	41	1	114	79	35	15	7	8
	60 and over	71	57	14	6	6	...	53	44	9	12	7	5
	Mahomedan ...	*1,564*	*908*	*656*	*824*	*478*	*346*	*652*	*401*	*251*	*88*	*29*	*59*
	0—5	139	75	64	139	75	64	...	...	...	...	...	...
	5—10	174	82	92	174	82	92	...	...	...	...	...	...
	10—15	127	55	72	127	55	72	...	...	...	...	...	...
	15—20	173	92	81	133	75	58	40	17	23	...	...	...
	20—40	646	407	239	213	159	54	412	240	172	21	8	13
	40—60	231	147	84	27	25	2	163	110	53	41	12	29
	60 and over	74	50	24	11	7	4	37	34	3	26	9	17
	Christian ...	*1,999*	*1,070*	*929*	*1,105*	*617*	*488*	*793*	*417*	*376*	*101*	*36*	*65*
	0—5	265	126	139	265	126	139	...	...	...	...	...	...
	5—10	235	117	118	235	117	118	...	...	...	...	...	...
	10—15	207	118	89	207	118	89	...	...	...	...	...	...
	15—20	232	126	106	206	117	89	26	9	17	...	...	...
	20—40	717	399	318	170	125	45	521	264	257	26	10	16
	40—60	270	142	128	16	10	6	207	119	88	47	13	34
	60 and over	73	42	31	6	4	2	39	25	14	28	13	15
MERGUI.	***All Religions*** ...	*111,424*	*59,530*	*51,894*	*64,471*	*35,917*	*28,554*	*41,429*	*21,711*	*19,718*	*5,524*	*1,902*	*3,622*
	0—5	14,335	7,095	7,240	14,335	7,095	7,240	...	...	...	...	...	...
	5—10	15,923	8,231	7,692	15,923	8,231	7,692	...	...	...	...	...	...
	10—15	13,272	7,068	6,204	13,266	7,068	6,198	6	...	6	...	...	...
	15—20	10,663	5,257	5,406	9,455	5,052	4,403	1,162	202	960	46	3	43
	20—40	36,040	20,123	15,917	9,965	7,449	2,516	24,840	12,213	12,627	1,235	461	774
	40—60	15,875	8,771	7,104	1,166	811	355	12,526	7,226	5,300	2,183	734	1,449
	60 and over	5,316	2,985	2,331	361	211	150	2,895	2,070	825	2,060	704	1,356
	Buddhist ..	*89,602*	*45,968*	*43,634*	*52,023*	*28,018*	*24,005*	*33,028*	*16,433*	*16,595*	*4,551*	*1,517*	*3,034*
	0—5	11,928	5,863	6,065	11,928	5,863	6,065	...	...	...	...	...	...
	5—10	13,355	6,889	6,466	13,355	6,889	6,466	...	...	...	...	...	...
	10—15	11,006	5,758	5,248	11,005	5,758	5,247	1	...	1	...	...	...
	15—20	8,642	4,061	4,581	7,626	3,927	3,699	974	131	843	42	3	39
	20—40	27,638	14,324	13,314	7,040	4,936	2,104	19,592	9,026	10,566	1,006	362	644
	40—60	12,755	6,731	6,024	790	495	295	10,174	5,650	4,524	1,791	586	1,205
	60 and over	4,278	2,342	1,936	279	150	129	2,287	1,626	661	1,712	566	1,146
	Animist ...	*4,088*	*2,752*	*1,336*	*2,214*	*1,544*	*670*	*1,694*	*1,121*	*573*	*180*	*87*	*93*
	0—5	391	204	187	391	204	187	...	...	...	...	...	...
	5—10	389	214	175	389	214	175	...	...	...	...	...	...
	10—15	335	204	131	335	204	131	...	...	...	...	...	...
	15—20	315	188	127	298	188	110	17	...	17	...	...	...
	20—40	1,660	1,164	496	628	569	59	987	573	414	45	22	23
	40—60	775	608	167	143	135	8	559	434	125	73	39	34
	60 and over	223	170	53	30	30	...	131	114	17	62	26	36

IMPERIAL TABLE VII.—*Age, Sex and Civil Condition.*

PART B.—DETAILS BY DISTRICTS.

AGE.	POPULATION. Persons.	POPULATION. Males.	POPULATION. Females.	UNMARRIED. Persons.	UNMARRIED. Males.	UNMARRIED. Females.	MARRIED. Persons.	MARRIED. Males.	MARRIED. Females.	WIDOWED. Persons.	WIDOWED. Males.	WIDOWED. Females.
1	2	3	4	5	6	7	8	9	10	11	12	13
MERGUI—*concluded.*												
Hindu ...	*3,367*	*3,192*	*175*	*1,822*	*1,751*	*71*	*1,504*	*1,412*	*92*	*41*	*29*	*12*
0— 5	59	23	36	59	23	36	...	...	...	...	...	...
5—10	52	33	19	52	33	19	...	...	...	...	...	...
10—15	172	163	9	172	163	9	...	...	...	...	...	...
15—20	392	385	7	336	335	1	56	50	6	...	...	...
20—40	2,287	2,210	77	1,102	1,100	2	1,168	1,095	73	17	15	2
40—60	345	325	20	86	82	4	243	233	10	16	10	6
60 and over	60	53	7	15	15	...	37	34	3	8	4	4
Mahomedan ...	*9,822*	*5,252*	*4,570*	*5,696*	*3,157*	*2,539*	*3,564*	*1,886*	*1,678*	*562*	*209*	*353*
0— 5	1,256	647	609	1,256	647	609	...	...	...	...	...	...
5—10	1,498	777	721	1,498	777	721	...	...	...	...	...	...
10—15	1,168	635	533	1,163	635	528	5	...	5	...	...	...
15—20	947	453	494	828	432	396	115	21	94	4	...	4
20—40	3,040	1,657	1,383	830	584	246	2,086	1,025	1,061	124	48	76
40—60	1,393	780	613	99	71	28	1,074	633	441	220	76	144
60 and over	520	303	217	22	11	11	284	207	77	214	85	129
Christian ...	*4,539*	*2,360*	*2,179*	*2,710*	*1,441*	*1,269*	*1,639*	*859*	*780*	*190*	*60*	*130*
0— 5	701	358	343	701	358	343	...	...	...	...	...	...
5—10	629	318	311	629	318	311	...	...	...	...	...	...
10—15	591	308	283	591	308	283	...	...	...	...	...	...
15—20	366	169	197	366	169	197	...	...	...	...	...	...
20—40	1,412	765	647	362	257	105	1,007	494	513	43	14	29
40—60	606	326	280	47	27	20	476	276	200	83	23	60
60 and over	234	116	118	14	4	10	156	89	67	64	23	41
THAYETMYO.												
All Religions ...	*248,275*	*122,231*	*126,044*	*130,287*	*66,760*	*63,527*	*98,340*	*49,537*	*48,803*	*19,648*	*5,934*	*13,714*
0— 5	33,181	16,161	17,020	33,181	16,161	17,020	...	...	...	...	...	...
5—10	32,998	16,333	16,665	32,998	16,333	16,665	...	...	...	...	...	...
10—15	30,205	15,269	14,936	30,054	15,269	14,785	145	...	145	6	...	6
15—20	21,636	10,544	11,092	17,774	9,692	8,082	3,661	798	2,863	201	54	147
20—40	75,790	37,078	38,712	12,689	7,554	5,135	58,521	27,958	30,563	4,580	1,566	3,014
40—60	38,013	18,795	19,218	2,303	1,137	1,166	28,425	15,699	12,726	7,285	1,959	5,326
60 and over	16,452	8,051	8,401	1,288	614	674	7,588	5,082	2,506	7,576	2,355	5,221
Buddhist ...	*228,058*	*111,290*	*116,768*	*120,145*	*61,147*	*58,998*	*89,730*	*44,821*	*44,909*	*18,183*	*5,322*	*12,861*
0— 5	30,689	14,942	15,747	30,689	14,942	15,747	...	...	...	...	...	...
5—10	30,608	15,160	15,448	30,608	15,160	15,448	...	...	...	...	...	...
10—15	28,078	14,160	13,918	27,948	14,160	13,788	124	...	124	6	...	6
15—20	19,878	9,629	10,249	16,433	8,897	7,536	3,268	689	2,579	177	43	134
20—40	68,688	33,032	35,656	11,183	6,406	4,777	53,329	25,282	28,047	4,176	1,344	2,832
40—60	34,816	16,950	17,866	2,103	1,014	1,089	25,993	14,180	11,813	6,720	1,756	4,964
60 and over	15,301	7,417	7,884	1,181	568	613	7,016	4,670	2,346	7,104	2,179	4,925
Animist ...	*15,232*	*7,594*	*7,638*	*7,636*	*3,922*	*3,714*	*6,590*	*3,350*	*3,240*	*1,006*	*322*	*684*
0— 5	1,978	952	1,026	1,978	952	1,026	...	...	...	...	...	...
5—10	1,893	916	977	1,893	916	977	...	...	...	...	...	...
10—15	1,743	881	862	1,728	881	847	15	...	15	...	...	...
15—20	1,341	666	675	1,066	596	470	261	65	196	14	5	9
20—40	4,876	2,375	2,501	755	484	271	3,887	1,798	2,089	234	93	141
40—60	2,466	1,317	1,149	123	57	66	1,946	1,150	796	397	110	287
60 and over	935	487	448	93	36	57	481	337	144	361	114	247
Hindu ...	*2,186*	*1,605*	*581*	*1,016*	*752*	*264*	*926*	*661*	*265*	*244*	*192*	*52*
0— 5	205	104	101	205	104	101	...	...	...	...	...	...
5—10	188	98	90	188	98	90	...	...	...	...	...	...
10—15	138	88	50	133	88	45	5	...	5	...	...	...
15—20	169	113	56	96	83	13	68	27	41	5	3	2
20—40	1,043	849	194	343	332	11	601	425	176	99	92	7
40—60	343	276	67	43	41	2	216	176	40	84	59	25
60 and over	100	77	23	8	6	2	36	33	3	56	38	18
Mahomedan ...	*2,164*	*1,361*	*803*	*1,108*	*691*	*417*	*879*	*587*	*292*	*177*	*83*	*94*
0— 5	240	126	114	240	126	114	...	...	...	...	...	...
5—10	241	128	113	241	128	113	...	...	...	...	...	...
10—15	202	123	79	201	123	78	1	...	1	...	...	...
15—20	210	124	86	149	104	45	56	17	39	5	3	2
20—40	867	595	272	246	187	59	556	375	181	65	33	32
40—60	312	207	105	26	19	7	223	161	62	63	27	36
60 and over	92	58	34	5	4	1	43	34	9	44	20	24

IMPERIAL TABLE VII.—*Age, Sex and Civil Condition.*

PART B.—DETAILS BY DISTRICTS.

District	AGE.	POPULATION. Persons.	Males.	Females.	UNMARRIED. Persons.	Males.	Females.	MARRIED. Persons.	Males.	Females.	WIDOWED. Persons.	Males.	Females.
	1	2	3	4	5	6	7	8	9	10	11	12	13
PAKÔKKU.	***All Religions*** ...	***409,909***	***196,159***	***213,750***	***220,467***	***111,145***	***109,822***	***156,876***	***77,847***	***79,029***	***32,566***	***7,167***	***25,399***
	0—5	**57,417**	28,414	29,003	57,417	28,414	29,003	...	...	...	...	...	...
	5—10	**55,904**	27,320	28,584	55,904	27,320	28,584	...	...	...	...	...	...
	10—15	**47,166**	24,134	23,032	47,152	24,134	23,018	14	...	14	...	...	...
	15—20	**37,413**	17,438	19,975	30,865	15,924	14,941	6,269	1,473	4,796	279	41	238
	20—40	**115,770**	55,216	60,554	21,651	12,260	9,391	87,521	41,414	46,107	6,598	1,542	5,056
	40—60	**65,605**	31,148	34,457	4,758	2,084	2,674	49,351	26,666	22,685	11,496	2,398	9,098
	60 and over	**30,634**	12,489	18,145	2,720	1,009	1,711	13,721	8,294	5,427	14,193	3,186	11,007
	Buddhist ...	***404,037***	***192,432***	***211,605***	***217,580***	***109,282***	***108,248***	***154,248***	***76,083***	***78,165***	***32,259***	***7,067***	***25,192***
	0—5	**56,763**	28,083	28,680	56,763	28,083	28,680	...	...	...	...	...	...
	5—10	**55,312**	27,015	28,297	55,312	27,015	28,297	...	...	...	...	...	...
	10—15	**46,653**	23,853	22,800	46,642	23,853	22,789	11	...	11	...	...	...
	15—20	**36,979**	17,152	19,827	30,518	15,676	14,842	6,184	1,435	4,749	277	41	236
	20—40	**113,279**	53,457	59,822	20,924	11,642	9,282	85,855	40,316	45,539	6,500	1,499	5,001
	40—60	**64,628**	30,490	34,138	4,662	2,010	2,652	48,583	26,117	22,466	11,383	2,363	9,020
	60 and over	**30,423**	12,382	18,041	2,709	1,003	1,706	13,615	8,215	5,400	14,099	3,164	10,935
	Animist ...	***3,472***	***1,831***	***1,641***	***1,798***	***1,006***	***792***	***1,443***	***772***	***671***	***231***	***53***	***178***
	0—5	**460**	233	227	460	233	227	...	...	...	...	...	...
	5—10	**460**	231	229	460	231	229	...	...	...	...	...	...
	10—15	**420**	222	198	420	222	198	...	...	...	...	...	...
	15—20	**247**	144	103	212	139	73	35	5	30	...	...	...
	20—40	**1,174**	646	528	208	163	45	906	466	440	60	17	43
	40—60	**542**	279	263	31	16	15	424	245	179	87	18	69
	60 and over	**169**	76	93	7	2	5	78	56	22	84	18	66
	Hindu ...	***1,170***	***1,016***	***154***	***535***	***429***	***106***	***607***	***563***	***44***	***28***	***24***	***4***
	0—5	**69**	38	31	69	38	31	...	...	...	...	...	...
	5—10	**48**	25	23	48	25	23	...	...	...	...	...	...
	10—15	**21**	18	3	21	18	3	...	...	...	...	...	...
	15—20	**88**	76	12	59	55	4	29	21	8	...	...	...
	20—40	**722**	651	71	299	256	43	407	381	26	16	14	2
	40—60	**214**	201	13	38	36	2	166	156	10	10	9	1
	60 and over	**8**	7	1	1	1	...	5	5	...	2	1	1
MINBU.	***All Religions*** ...	***263,939***	***128,837***	***135,102***	***138,318***	***71,253***	***67,065***	***102,923***	***51,597***	***51,326***	***22,698***	***5,987***	***16,711***
	0—5	**36,567**	17,968	18,599	36,567	17,968	18,599	...	...	...	...	...	...
	5—10	**33,786**	16,696	17,090	33,786	16,696	17,090	...	...	...	...	...	...
	10—15	**29,379**	14,678	14,701	29,330	14,662	14,668	48	16	32	1	...	1
	15—20	**23,420**	11,311	12,109	18,890	10,362	8,528	4,344	930	3,414	186	19	167
	20—40	**77,675**	38,761	38,914	15,124	9,463	5,661	57,929	27,774	30,155	4,622	1,524	3,098
	40—60	**42,928**	20,642	22,286	3,080	1,454	1,626	31,812	17,165	14,647	8,036	2,023	6,013
	60 and over	**20,184**	8,781	11,403	1,541	648	893	8,790	5,712	3,078	9,853	2,421	7,432
	Buddhist ...	***253,927***	***122,133***	***131,794***	***133,128***	***67,747***	***65,381***	***98,630***	***48,684***	***49,946***	***22,169***	***5,702***	***16,467***
	0—5	**35,380**	17,363	18,017	35,380	17,363	18,017	...	...	...	...	...	...
	5—10	**32,766**	16,151	16,615	32,766	16,151	16,615	...	...	...	...	...	...
	10—15	**28,625**	14,256	14,369	28,581	14,243	14,330	43	13	30	1	...	1
	15—20	**22,612**	10,790	11,822	18,259	9,905	8,354	4,170	867	3,303	183	18	165
	20—40	**73,215**	35,368	37,847	13,686	8,118	5,568	55,070	25,850	29,220	4,459	1,400	3,059
	40—60	**41,529**	19,649	21,880	2,943	1,334	1,609	30,746	16,388	14,358	7,840	1,927	5,913
	60 and over	**19,800**	8,556	11,244	1,513	633	880	8,601	5,566	3,035	9,686	2,357	7,329
	Animist ...	***5,758***	***3,056***	***2,702***	***3,105***	***1,713***	***1,392***	***2,317***	***1,215***	***1,102***	***336***	***128***	***208***
	0—5	**935**	472	463	935	472	463	...	...	...	...	...	...
	5—10	**829**	428	401	829	428	401	...	...	...	...	...	...
	10—15	**579**	301	278	579	301	278	...	...	...	...	...	...
	15—20	**473**	244	229	378	228	150	93	15	78	2	1	1
	20—40	**1,821**	985	836	317	241	76	1,455	716	739	49	28	21
	40—60	**822**	475	347	52	38	14	634	390	244	136	47	89
	60 and over	**299**	151	148	15	5	10	135	94	41	149	52	97
	Hindu ...	***2,651***	***2,449***	***202***	***1,213***	***1,132***	***81***	***1,341***	***1,232***	***109***	***97***	***85***	***12***
	0—5	**80**	46	34	80	46	34	...	...	...	...	...	...
	5—10	**59**	37	22	59	37	22	...	...	...	...	...	...
	10—15	**58**	44	14	54	41	13	4	3	1	...	...	...
	15—20	**230**	208	22	174	169	5	55	39	16	1	...	1
	20—40	**1,826**	1,741	85	783	779	4	980	902	78	63	60	3
	40—60	**354**	331	23	55	53	2	272	258	14	27	20	7
	60 and over	**44**	42	2	8	7	1	30	30	...	6	5	1

IMPERIAL TABLE VII.—*Age, Sex and Civil Condition.*

PART B.—DETAILS BY DISTRICTS.

	AGE.	POPULATION.			UNMARRIED.			MARRIED.			WIDOWED.		
		Persons.	Males.	Females.	Persons.	Males.	Females.	Persons.	Males.	Females.	Persons.	Males.	Females.
	1	2	3	4	5	6	7	8	9	10	11	12	13
MINBU—*concluded.*	***Mahomedan*** ...	*1,061*	*775*	*286*	*647*	*896*	*151*	*438*	*325*	*113*	*76*	*54*	*22*
	0—5	114	61	53	114	61	53	...	...	...	...	...	...
	5—10	104	65	39	104	65	39	...	...	...	...	...	...
	10—15	89	55	34	89	55	34	...	...	...	...	...	...
	15—20	87	56	31	63	47	16	24	9	15	...	...	...
	20—40	484	387	97	158	150	8	282	208	74	44	29	15
	40—60	150	124	26	17	17	...	111	89	22	22	18	4
	60 and over	33	27	6	2	1	1	21	19	2	10	7	3
MAGWE.	***All Religions*** ...	*316,909*	*156,387*	*160,522*	*181,815*	*92,852*	*88,963*	*115,512*	*58,816*	*56,696*	*20,082*	*5,219*	*14,863*
	0—5	42,893	20,754	22,139	42,893	20,754	22,139	...	...	...	...	...	...
	5—10	44,021	21,979	22,042	44,018	21,976	22,042	3	3	...	...	...	...
	10—15	38,792	19,191	19,601	38,777	19,179	19,598	15	12	3	...	...	...
	15—20	28,918	14,202	14,716	25,457	13,570	11,887	3,312	609	2,703	149	23	126
	20—40	91,325	46,184	45,141	23,755	14,039	9,716	63,845	31,047	32,798	3,725	1,098	2,627
	40—60	48,816	24,239	24,577	4,404	2,094	2,310	37,176	20,346	16,830	7,236	1,799	5,437
	60 and over	22,144	9,838	12,306	2,011	740	1,271	11,161	6,799	4,362	8,972	2,299	6,673
	Buddhist ...	*311,574*	*151,962*	*159,612*	*178,206*	*89,670*	*88,536*	*113,421*	*57,173*	*56,248*	*19,947*	*5,119*	*14,828*
	0—5	42,544	20,560	21,984	42,544	20,560	21,984	...	...	...	...	...	...
	5—10	43,764	21,839	21,925	43,764	21,839	21,925	...	...	...	...	...	...
	10—15	38,537	19,010	19,527	38,537	19,010	19,527	...	...	...	...	...	...
	15—20	28,433	13,793	14,640	25,076	13,217	11,859	3,208	553	2,655	149	23	126
	20—40	88,181	43,432	44,749	22,111	12,442	9,669	62,391	29,928	32,463	3,679	1,062	2,617
	40—60	48,061	23,560	24,501	4,183	1,881	2,302	36,704	19,930	16,774	7,174	1,749	5,425
	60 and over	22,054	9,768	12,286	1,991	721	1,270	11,118	6,762	4,356	8,945	2,285	6,660
	Hindu ...	*2,632*	*2,350*	*282*	*1,603*	*1,504*	*99*	*970*	*803*	*167*	*59*	*43*	*16*
	0—5	113	69	44	113	69	44	...	...	...	...	...	...
	5—10	59	36	23	56	33	23	3	3	...	...	...	...
	10—15	90	80	10	77	70	7	13	10	3	...	...	...
	15—20	269	246	23	217	214	3	52	32	20	...	...	...
	20—40	1,707	1,560	147	978	961	17	713	587	126	16	12	4
	40—60	354	330	24	147	143	4	175	159	16	32	28	4
	60 and over	40	29	11	15	14	1	14	12	2	11	3	8
	Mahomedan ...	*1,617*	*1,233*	*384*	*886*	*684*	*202*	*686*	*516*	*170*	*45*	*33*	*12*
	0—5	135	70	65	135	70	65	...	...	...	...	...	...
	5—10	105	50	55	105	50	55	...	...	...	...	..	...
	10—15	110	65	45	108	63	45	2	2	...	...	...	...
	15—20	152	115	37	106	93	13	46	22	24	...	...	...
	20—40	853	711	142	392	370	22	444	327	117	17	14	3
	40—60	234	201	33	37	35	2	178	151	27	19	15	4
	60 and over	28	21	7	3	3	...	16	14	2	9	4	5
MANDALAY (CITY INCLUDED).	***All Religions*** ...	*340,770*	*170,750*	*170,020*	*174,654*	*93,796*	*80,858*	*130,055*	*66,802*	*63,253*	*36,061*	*10,152*	*25,909*
	0—5	40,185	19,720	20,465	40,185	19,720	20,465	...	...	...	...	...	...
	5—10	38,239	18,957	19,282	38,239	18,957	19,282	...	...	...	...	...	...
	10—15	36,387	18,397	17,990	36,272	18,366	17,906	108	27	81	7	4	3
	15—20	30,866	14,891	15,975	25,134	13,498	11,636	5,367	1,339	4,028	365	54	311
	20—40	109,761	58,400	51,361	27,937	19,302	8,635	74,056	36,279	37,777	7,768	2,819	4,949
	40—60	60,910	29,859	31,051	5,019	2,934	2,085	41,510	23,176	18,334	14,381	3,749	10,632
	60 and over	24,422	10,526	13,896	1,868	1,019	849	9,014	5,981	3,033	13,540	3,526	10,014
	Buddhist ...	*294,904*	*141,480*	*153,424*	*150,460*	*78,011*	*72,449*	*112,011*	*54,853*	*57,158*	*32,433*	*8,616*	*23,817*
	0—5	35,893	17,647	18,246	35,893	17,647	18,246	...	...	...	...	...	...
	5—10	34,246	16,977	17,269	34,246	16,977	17,269	...	...	...	...	...	...
	10—15	32,824	16,467	16,357	32,766	16,447	16,319	53	18	35	5	2	3
	15—20	26,921	12,612	14,309	22,189	11,571	10,618	4,405	1,001	3,404	327	40	287
	20—40	88,483	42,926	45,557	19,593	12,251	7,342	62,253	28,490	33,763	6,637	2,185	4,452
	40—60	53,937	25,241	28,696	4,064	2,203	1,861	36,985	19,884	17,101	12,888	3,154	9,734
	60 and over	22,600	9,610	12,990	1,709	915	794	8,315	5,460	2,855	12,576	3,235	9,341
	Animist ...	*1,497*	*1,278*	*219*	*861*	*741*	*120*	*551*	*463*	*88*	*85*	*74*	*11*
	0—5	92	55	37	92	55	37	...	...	...	...	...	...
	5—10	48	28	20	48	28	20	...	...	...	...	...	...
	10—15	72	44	28	72	44	28	...	...	...	...	...	...
	15—20	114	96	18	101	85	16	13	11	2	...	...	...
	20—40	841	758	83	467	452	15	331	264	67	43	42	1
	40—60	270	239	31	70	66	4	169	150	19	31	23	8
	60 and over	60	58	2	11	11	...	38	38	...	11	9	2

Imperial Table VII.—*Age, Sex and Civil Condition.*

PART B.—DETAILS BY DISTRICTS.

District	Age.	Population.			Unmarried.			Married.			Widowed.		
		Persons.	Males.	Females.	Persons.	Males.	Females.	Persons.	Males.	Females.	Persons.	Males.	Females.
	1	2	3	4	5	6	7	8	9	10	11	12	13
MANDALAY (CITY INCLUDED)—*concluded.*	***Hindu*** ...	*16,071*	*11,192*	*4,879*	*7,344*	*5,367*	*1,977*	*7,367*	*5,188*	*2184*	*1,360*	*642*	*718*
	0—5	1,350	653	697	1,350	653	697	...	...	...	...	...	...
	5—10	1,105	560	545	1,105	560	545	...	...	...	...	...	...
	10—15	940	532	408	885	521	364	53	9	44	2	2	...
	15—20	1,166	728	438	730	555	175	421	164	257	15	9	6
	20—40	8,384	6,543	1,841	2,854	2,699	155	5,033	3,541	1,492	497	303	194
	40—60	2,555	1,882	673	382	349	33	1,651	1,313	338	522	220	302
	60 and over	571	294	277	38	30	8	209	156	53	324	108	216
	Mahomedan ...	*20,845*	*12,236*	*8,609*	*11,129*	*6,510*	*4,619*	*7,944*	*5,060*	*2,884*	*1,772*	*666*	*1,106*
	0—5	2,155	1,016	1,139	2,155	1,016	1,139	...	...	...	...	...	...
	5—10	2,093	1,033	1,060	2,093	1,033	1,060	...	...	...	...	...	...
	10—15	1,827	988	839	1,827	988	839	...	...	...	...	...	...
	15—20	1,940	1,055	885	1,484	901	583	434	150	284	22	4	18
	20—40	8,552	5,699	2,853	3,110	2,278	832	4,981	3,193	1,788	461	228	233
	40—60	3,255	1,965	1,290	367	242	125	2,141	1,437	704	747	286	461
	60 and over	1,023	480	543	93	52	41	388	280	108	542	148	394
	Christian ...	*6,571*	*3,870*	*2,701*	*4,368*	*2,759*	*1,609*	*1,819*	*979*	*840*	*884*	*132*	*252*
	0—5	636	318	318	636	318	318	...	...	...	...	...	...
	5—10	701	332	369	701	332	369	...	...	...	...	...	...
	10—15	696	351	345	694	351	343	2	...	2	...	...	...
	15—20	638	331	307	559	324	235	78	6	72	1	1	...
	20—40	2,919	1,990	929	1,634	1,357	277	1,170	585	585	115	48	67
	40—60	819	469	350	129	68	61	509	344	165	181	57	124
	60 and over	162	79	83	15	9	6	60	44	16	87	26	61
MANDALAY CITY.	***All Religions*** ...	*138,299*	*69,718*	*68,581*	*68,520*	*37,110*	*31,410*	*53,395*	*28,207*	*25,188*	*16,384*	*4,401*	*11,983*
	0—5	14,211	6,891	7,320	14,211	6,891	7,320	...	...	...	...	...	...
	5—10	13,804	6,805	6,999	13,804	6,805	6,999	...	...	...	...	...	...
	10—15	13,514	6,737	6,777	13,510	6,737	6,773	4	...	4	...	...	...
	15—20	12,648	6,242	6,406	10,245	5,638	4,607	2,253	569	1,684	150	35	115
	20—40	48,338	26,437	21,901	13,436	9,126	4,310	31,290	16,039	15,251	3,612	1,272	2,340
	40—60	25,352	12,410	12,942	2,569	1,498	1,071	16,231	9,227	7,004	6,552	1,685	4,867
	60 and over	10,432	4,196	6,236	745	415	330	3,617	2,372	1,245	6,070	1,409	4,661
	Buddhist ...	*109,235*	*51,687*	*57,548*	*53,357*	*27,621*	*25,736*	*42,006*	*20,699*	*21,307*	*13,872*	*3,367*	*10,505*
	0—5	11,598	5,653	5,945	11,598	5,653	5,945	...	...	...	...	...	...
	5—10	11,308	5,563	5,745	11,308	5,563	5,745	...	...	...	...	...	...
	10—15	11,150	5,452	5,698	11,150	5,452	5,698	...	...	..	...	...	...
	15—20	10,020	4,744	5,276	8,233	4,356	3,877	1,660	364	1,296	127	24	103
	20—40	35,399	17,331	18,068	8,526	5,251	3,275	23,982	11,220	12,762	2,891	860	2,031
	40—60	20,671	9,401	11,270	1,903	998	905	13,254	7,113	6,141	5,514	1,290	4,224
	60 and over	9,089	3,543	5,546	639	348	291	3,110	2,002	1,108	5,340	1,193	4,147
	Animist ...	*1,384*	*1,197*	*187*	*796*	*696*	*100*	*506*	*429*	*77*	*82*	*72*	*10*
	0—5	78	48	30	78	48	30	...	...	...	...	...	...
	5—10	38	25	13	38	25	13	...	...	...	...	...	...
	10—15	67	41	26	67	41	26	...	...	...	...	...	...
	15—20	106	91	15	94	81	13	12	10	2	...	...	...
	20—40	790	717	73	445	431	14	303	245	58	42	41	1
	40—60	249	221	28	64	60	4	156	139	17	29	22	7
	60 and over	56	54	2	10	10	...	35	35	...	11	9	2
	Hindu ...	*7,884*	*5,269*	*2,615*	*3,449*	*2,423*	*1,026*	*3,622*	*2,460*	*1,162*	*813*	*386*	*427*
	0—5	635	298	337	635	298	337	...	...	...	...	...	...
	5—10	539	271	268	539	271	268	...	...	...	...	...	...
	10—15	447	263	184	443	263	180		...	4	...	...	...
	15—20	565	329	236	366	248	118	192	74	118	7	7	...
	20—40	3,903	2,923	980	1,229	1,131	98	2,416	1,633	783	258	159	99
	40—60	1,405	997	408	212	193	19	875	661	214	318	143	175
	60 and over	390	188	202	25	19	6	135	92	43	230	77	153
	Mahomedan ...	*14,963*	*8,696*	*6,267*	*7,865*	*4,477*	*3,388*	*5,806*	*3,779*	*2,026*	*1,293*	*440*	*853*
	0—5	1,458	672	786	1,458	672	786	...	...	...	...	...	...
	5—10	1,421	695	726	1,421	695	726	...	...	...	...	...	...
	10—15	1,329	719	610	1,329	719	610	...	...	...	...	...	...
	15—20	1,433	789	644	1,092	675	417	326	111	215	15	3	12
	20—40	6,166	4,059	2,107	2,216	1,493	723	3,636	2,410	1,226	314	156	158
	40—60	2,381	1,413	968	289	193	96	1,552	1,049	503	540	171	369
	60 and over	775	349	426	60	30	30	291	209	82	424	110	314

IMPERIAL TABLE VII.—*Age, Sex and Civil Condition.*

PART B.—DETAILS BY DISTRICTS.

District	Age.	Population. Persons.	Population. Males.	Population. Females.	Unmarried. Persons.	Unmarried. Males.	Unmarried. Females.	Married. Persons.	Married. Males.	Married. Females.	Widowed. Persons.	Widowed. Males.	Widowed. Females.
	1	2	3	4	5	6	7	8	9	10	11	12	13
MANDALAY CITY —concluded.	***Christian*** ...	*4,045*	*2,238*	*1,807*	*2,608*	*1,516*	*1,092*	*1,138*	*606*	*532*	*299*	*116*	*183*
	0—5	389	193	196	389	193	196	...	...	...	...	...	...
	5—10	458	224	234	458	224	234	...	...	...	...	...	...
	10—15	498	249	249	498	249	249	...	...	...	...	...	...
	15—20	463	239	224	412	235	177	50	3	47	1	1	...
	20—40	1,541	954	587	748	561	187	700	349	351	93	44	49
	40—60	579	321	258	94	48	46	345	222	123	140	51	89
	60 and over	117	58	59	9	6	3	43	32	11	65	20	45
BHAMO.	***All Religions*** ...	*107,811*	*55,528*	*52,283*	*56,831*	*31,039*	*25,792*	*42,314*	*22,529*	*19,785*	*8,666*	*1,960*	*6,706*
	0—5	12,518	6,129	6,389	12,518	6,129	6,389	...	...	...	...	...	...
	5—10	12,394	6,242	6,152	12,394	6,242	6,152	..	...	...	...	...	...
	10—15	12,044	6,190	5,854	12,040	6,190	5,850	4	...	4	...	...	...
	15—20	10,129	5,129	5,000	8,399	4,736	3,663	1,634	386	1,248	96	7	89
	20—40	36,463	19,479	16,984	9,749	6,794	2,955	24,688	12,007	12,681	2,026	678	1,348
	40—60	18,609	9,957	8,652	1,264	774	490	13,566	8,452	5,114	3,779	731	3,048
	60 and over	5,654	2,402	3,252	467	174	293	2,422	1,684	738	2,765	544	2,221
	Buddhist ...	*53,490*	*27,182*	*26,308*	*28,492*	*15,270*	*13,222*	*21,021*	*10,786*	*10,235*	*3,977*	*1,126*	*2,851*
	0—5	7,626	3,715	3,911	7,626	3,715	3,911	...	...	...	...	..	...
	5—10	6,653	3,335	3,318	6,653	3,335	3,318	...	...	...	...	...	...
	10—15	5,684	2,872	2,812	5,684	2,872	2,812	...	...	...	...	...	...
	15—20	4,952	2,439	2,513	4,010	2,267	1,743	867	165	702	75	7	68
	20—40	15,828	8,403	7,425	3,465	2,527	938	11,498	5,540	5,958	865	336	529
	40—60	9,243	4,798	4,445	694	417	277	7,072	3,995	3,077	1,477	386	1,091
	60 and over	3,504	1,620	1,884	360	137	223	1,584	1,086	498	1,560	397	1,163
	Animist ...	*47,722*	*23,244*	*24,478*	*25,121*	*13,232*	*11,889*	*18,259*	*9,405*	*8,854*	*4,342*	*607*	*3,735*
	0—5	4,443	2,183	2,260	4,443	2,183	2,260	...	...	...	...	...	...
	5—10	5,410	2,741	2,669	5,410	2,741	2,669	...	...	...	...	...	...
	10—15	6,044	3,119	2,925	6,040	3,119	2,921	4	...	4	...	...	...
	15—20	4,601	2,274	2,327	3,974	2,123	1,851	610	151	459	17	...	17
	20—40	16,767	7,803	8,964	4,736	2,809	1,927	11,033	4,801	6,232	998	193	805
	40—60	8,411	4,400	4,011	417	226	191	5,819	3,900	1,919	2,175	274	1,901
	60 and over	2,046	724	1,322	101	31	70	793	553	240	1,152	140	1,012
	Hindu ...	*1,652*	*1,404*	*248*	*674*	*567*	*107*	*913*	*776*	*137*	*65*	*61*	*4*
	0—5	115	69	46	115	69	46	...	...	...	...	...	...
	5—10	68	34	34	68	34	34	...	...	...	...	...	...
	10—15	36	28	8	36	28	8	...	...	...	...	...	...
	15—20	84	65	19	44	44	...	40	21	19	...	...	...
	20—40	1,042	930	112	354	339	15	653	556	97	35	35	...
	40—60	293	268	25	57	53	4	211	190	21	25	25	...
	60 and over	14	10	4	...	...	...	9	9	...	5	1	4
	Mahomedan ...	*2,242*	*1,852*	*390*	*1,035*	*854*	*181*	*1,088*	*900*	*188*	*119*	*98*	*21*
	0—5	131	67	64	131	67	64	...	...	...	...	...	...
	5—10	114	53	61	114	53	61	...	...	...	...	...	...
	10—15	75	49	26	75	49	26	...	...	...	...	...	...
	15—20	204	167	37	148	136	12	56	31	25	...	...	...
	20—40	1,386	1,236	150	517	499	18	800	668	132	69	69	...
	40—60	297	255	42	44	44	...	219	188	31	34	23	11
	60 and over	35	25	10	6	6	...	13	13	...	16	6	10
	Christian ...	*1,785*	*1,030*	*755*	*1,000*	*643*	*357*	*669*	*366*	*303*	*116*	*21*	*95*
	0—5	153	74	79	153	74	79	...	...	...	...	...	...
	5—10	128	63	65	128	63	65	...	...	...	...	...	...
	10—15	191	110	81	191	110	81	...	...	...	...	...	...
	15—20	169	80	89	129	72	57	36	8	28	4	...	4
	20—40	796	514	282	347	290	57	424	213	211	25	11	14
	40—60	293	166	127	52	34	18	186	122	64	55	10	45
	60 and over	55	23	32	...	...	...	23	23	...	32	...	32
MYITKYINA.	***All Religions*** ...	*85,577*	*47,863*	*37,714*	*46,217*	*27,483*	*18,734*	*33,037*	*18,380*	*14,657*	*6,328*	*2,000*	*4,328*
	0—5	8,730	4,352	4,378	8,730	4,352	4,378	...	...	...	...	...	...
	5—10	9,703	4,977	4,726	9,703	4,977	4,726	...	...	...	...	...	...
	10—15	8,195	4,238	3,957	8,144	4,235	3,909	51	3	48	...	...	...
	15—20	7,357	3,920	3,437	5,941	3,566	2,375	1,360	345	1,015	56	9	47
	20—40	33,586	20,319	13,267	11,749	9,172	2,577	20,065	10,380	9,685	1,772	767	1,005
	40—60	14,197	8,315	5,882	1,556	1,008	548	9,844	6,426	3,418	2,797	881	1,916
	60 and over	3,809	1,742	2,067	394	173	221	1,717	1,226	491	1,698	343	1,355

Imperial Table VII.—*Age, Sex and Civil Condition.*

PART B.—DETAILS BY DISTRICTS.

District	AGE.	POPULATION. Persons.	POPULATION. Males.	POPULATION. Females.	UNMARRIED. Persons.	UNMARRIED. Males.	UNMARRIED. Females.	MARRIED. Persons.	MARRIED. Males.	MARRIED. Females.	WIDOWED. Persons.	WIDOWED. Males.	WIDOWED. Females.
	1	2	3	4	5	6	7	8	9	10	11	12	13
MYITKYINA—*concluded.*	***Buddhist*** ...	*30,171*	*16,518*	*13,653*	*15,796*	*9,185*	*6,611*	*12,220*	*6,409*	*5,811*	*2,166*	*924*	*1,231*
	0—5	3,794	1,896	1,898	3,794	1,896	1,898	...	...	...	...	...	...
	5—10	3,604	1,800	1,804	3,604	1,800	1,804	...	...	...	...	...	...
	10—15	3,078	1,551	1,527	3,078	1,551	1,527	...	...	...	...	...	...
	15—20	2,342	1,183	1,159	1,764	1,086	678	550	95	455	28	2	26
	20—40	10,440	6,207	4,233	2,832	2,372	460	7,039	3,500	3,539	569	335	234
	40—60	5,514	3,212	2,302	559	398	161	4,036	2,398	1,638	919	416	503
	60 and over	1,399	669	730	165	82	83	595	416	179	639	171	468
	Animist ...	*46,050*	*24,098*	*21,952*	*25,609*	*14,471*	*11,138*	*16,584*	*8,771*	*7,813*	*3,857*	*856*	*3,001*
	0—5	4,075	2,000	2,075	4,075	2,000	2,075	...	...	...	...	...	...
	5—10	5,401	2,814	2,587	5,401	2,814	2,587	...	...	...	...	...	...
	10—15	4,718	2,474	2,244	4,699	2,474	2,225	19	...	19	...	...	...
	15—20	4,559	2,424	2,135	3,880	2,226	1,654	654	192	462	25	6	19
	20—40	17,635	9,437	8,198	6,545	4,460	2,085	10,044	4,659	5,385	1,046	318	728
	40—60	7,353	3,942	3,411	794	416	378	4,792	3,146	1,646	1,767	380	1,387
	60 and over	2,309	1,007	1,302	215	81	134	1,075	774	301	1,019	152	867
	Hindu ...	*6,192*	*4.617*	*1,575*	*3,219*	*2,466*	*753*	*2,804*	*2,024*	*780*	*169*	*127*	*42*
	0—5	666	338	328	666	338	328	...	...	...	...	...	...
	5—10	555	286	269	555	286	269	...	...	...	...	...	...
	10—15	277	138	139	250	136	114	27	2	25	...	...	...
	15—20	281	179	102	158	137	21	122	42	80	1	...	1
	20—40	3.413	2,815	598	1,447	1,435	12	1,894	1,329	565	72	51	21
	40—60	931	818	113	131	126	5	728	629	99	72	63	9
	60 and over	69	43	26	12	8	4	33	22	11	24	13	11
	Mahomedan ...	*1,906*	*1,618*	*288*	*887*	*759*	*128*	*945*	*806*	*139*	*74*	*53*	*21*
	0—5	113	70	43	113	70	43	...	...	...	...	...	...
	5—10	87	47	40	87	47	40	...	...	...	...	...	...
	10—15	75	44	31	70	43	27	5	1	4	...	...	...
	15—20	112	90	22	86	78	8	25	12	13	1	...	1
	20—40	1, 253	1,134	119	494	485	9	719	618	101	40	31	9
	40—60	237	210	27	35	34	1	182	161	21	20	15	5
	60 and over	29	23	6	2	2	...	14	14	...	13	7	6
KATHA.	***All Religions*** ...	*198,193*	*98,148*	*100,045*	*104,605*	*54,882*	*50,223*	*81,000*	*40,608*	*40,892*	*12,588*	*3,158*	*9,430*
	0—5	28,972	13,999	14,973	28,972	13,999	14,973	...	...	...	...	...	...
	5—10	25,277	12,246	13,031	25,277	12,246	13,031	...	...	...	...	...	...
	10—15	21,654	10,769	10,885	21,639	10,769	10,870	15	...	15	...	...	...
	15—20	17,101	7,958	9,143	13,580	7,346	6,234	3,351	578	2,773	170	34	136
	20—40	60,308	30,780	29,528	11,584	8,364	3,220	46,118	21,496	24,622	2,606	920	1,686
	40—60	34,694	17,808	16,886	2,299	1,215	1,084	27,082	15,350	11,732	5,313	1,243	4,070
	60 and over	10,187	4,588	5,599	1,254	443	811	4.434	3,184	1,250	4,499	961	3,538
	Buddhist ...	*189,134*	*92,871*	*96,263*	*99,777*	*51,386*	*48,891*	*77,675*	*38,596*	*39,079*	*11,682*	*2,889*	*8,793*
	0—5	28,043	13,528	14,515	28,043	13,528	14,515	...	...	...	...	...	...
	5—10	24,295	11,748	12,547	24,295	11,748	12,547	...	...	...	...	...	...
	10—15	20,881	10,396	10,485	20,869	10,396	10,473	12	...	12	...	...	...
	15—20	16,410	7,610	8,800	12,983	7,018	5,965	3,260	559	2,701	167	33	134
	20—40	56,508	28,301	28,207	10,214	7,188	3,026	44,028	20,315	23,713	2,266	798	1,468
	40—60	33,239	16,876	16,363	2,145	1,080	1,065	26,106	14,664	11,442	4,988	1,132	3,856
	60 and over	9.758	4,412	5,346	1,228	428	800	4,269	3,058	1,211	4,261	926	3,335
	Animist ...	*6,089*	*2,984*	*3,105*	*3,373*	*1,870*	*1,503*	*1,982*	*984*	*998*	*734*	*130*	*604*
	0—5	693	344	349	693	344	349	...	...	...	...	...	...
	5—10	808	408	400	808	408	400	...	...	...	...	...	...
	10—15	630	300	330	630	300	330	...	...	...	...	...	...
	15—20	545	269	276	499	259	240	46	10	36	...	...	...
	20—40	2,130	1,070	1,060	683	519	164	1,183	493	690	264	58	206
	40—60	912	460	452	46	32	14	614	378	236	252	50	202
	60 and over	371	133	238	14	8	6	139	103	36	218	22	196
	Hindu ...	*1,429*	*1 268*	*161*	*698*	*629*	*69*	*686*	*551*	*85*	*95*	*88*	*7*
	0—5	70	41	29	70	41	29	...	...	...	...	...	...
	5—10	48	31	17	48	31	17	...	...	...	...	...	...
	10—15	36	23	13	33	23	10	3	...	3	...	...	...
	15—20	51	37	14	35	32	3	15	4	11	1	1	...
	20—40	913	838	75	431	422	9	435	373	62	47	43	4
	40—60	284	274	10	74	73	1	171	163	8	39	38	1
	60 and over	27	24	3	7	7	...	12	11	1	8	6	2

IMPERIAL TABLE VII.—*Age, Sex and Civil Condition.*

PART B.—DETAILS BY DISTRICTS.

AGE.	POPULATION. Persons.	Males.	Females.	UNMARRIED. Persons.	Males.	Females.	MARRIED. Persons.	Males.	Females.	WIDOWED. Persons.	Males.	Females.
1	2	3	4	5	6	7	8	9	10	11	12	13
KATHA—concluded.												
Mahomedan ...	*1,156*	*754*	*402*	*532*	*340*	*192*	*556*	*368*	*188*	*68*	*46*	*22*
0— 5	122	59	63	122	59	63	...	...	...	...	...	...
5—10	94	46	48	94	46	48	...	...	...	...	...	...
10—15	82	37	45	82	37	45	...	...	...	...	...	...
15—20	73	31	42	45	26	19	26	5	21	2	...	2
20—40	557	410	147	166	153	13	366	238	128	25	19	6
40—60	204	155	49	22	19	3	153	116	37	29	20	9
60 and over	24	16	8	1	...	1	11	9	2	12	7	5
RUBY MINES.												
All Religions ...	*100,618*	*54,487*	*46,131*	*52,222*	*29,768*	*22,454*	*40,142*	*21,584*	*18,558*	*8,254*	*3,135*	*5,119*
0— 5	12,347	6,050	6,297	12,347	6,050	6,297	...	...	...	...	...	...
5—10	11,597	5,804	5,793	11,597	5,804	5,793	...	...	...	...	...	...
10—15	9,678	4,936	4,742	9,655	4,932	4,723	23	4	19	...	...	...
15—20	8,403	4,285	4,118	6,782	3,889	2,893	1,509	358	1,151	112	38	74
20—40	34,861	20,254	14,607	9,647	7,630	2,017	23,237	11,592	11,645	1,977	1,032	945
40—60	17,642	10,282	7,360	1,626	1,173	453	12,806	7,835	4,971	3,210	1,274	1,936
60 and over	6,090	2,876	3,214	568	290	278	2,567	1,795	772	2,955	791	2,164
Buddhist ...	*79,844*	*42,393*	*37,451*	*41,244*	*23,128*	*18,116*	*32,032*	*16,633*	*15,399*	*6,568*	*2,632*	*3,936*
0— 5	10,099	4,880	5,219	10,099	4,880	5,219	...	...	...	...	...	...
5—10	9,352	4,606	4,746	9,352	4,606	4,746	...	...	...	...	...	...
10—15	7,965	4,067	3,898	7,945	4,065	3,880	20	2	18	...	...	...
15—20	6,627	3,292	3,335	5,323	3,004	2,319	1,198	256	942	106	32	74
20—40	26,522	14,866	11,656	6,795	5,424	1,371	18,185	8,629	9,556	1,542	813	729
40—60	14,440	8,328	6,112	1,246	908	338	10,613	6,335	4,278	2,581	1,085	1,496
60 and over	4,839	2,354	2,485	484	241	243	2,016	1,411	605	2,339	702	1,637
Animist ...	*16,774*	*8,867*	*7,907*	*9,287*	*5,298*	*3,989*	*5,977*	*3,212*	*2,765*	*1,510*	*357*	*1,153*
0— 5	1,904	1,000	904	1,904	1,000	904	...	...	...	...	...	...
5—10	2,015	1,053	962	2,015	1,053	962	...	...	...	...	...	...
10—15	1,578	786	792	1,578	786	792	...	...	...	...	...	...
15—20	1,520	804	716	1,314	751	563	201	48	153	5	5	...
20—40	5,984	3,364	2,620	2,114	1,493	621	3,524	1,731	1,793	346	140	206
40—60	2,583	1,391	1,192	286	174	112	1,738	1,082	656	559	135	424
60 and over	1,190	469	721	76	41	35	514	351	163	600	77	523
Hindu ...	*2,505*	*2,058*	*447*	*1,078*	*893*	*185*	*1,317*	*1,073*	*244*	*110*	*92*	*18*
0— 5	211	111	100	211	111	100	...	...	...	...	...	...
5—10	132	87	45	132	87	45	...	...	...	...	...	...
10—15	77	50	27	77	50	27	...	...	...	...	...	...
15—20	154	117	37	95	93	2	59	24	35	...	...	...
20—40	1,548	1,343	205	506	496	10	974	788	186	68	59	9
40—60	354	328	26	54	53	1	267	248	19	33	27	6
60 and over	29	22	7	3	3	...	17	13	4	9	6	3
Mahomedan ...	*1,205*	*975*	*230*	*462*	*349*	*113*	*685*	*578*	*107*	*58*	*48*	*10*
0— 5	90	39	51	90	39	51	...	...	...	...	...	...
5—10	73	44	29	73	44	29	...	...	...	...	...	...
10—15	51	32	19	49	30	19	2	2	...	...	...	...
15—20	89	67	22	43	37	6	45	29	16	1	1	...
20—40	648	562	86	171	164	7	459	381	78	18	17	1
40—60	222	200	22	31	30	1	159	146	13	32	24	8
60 and over	32	31	1	5	5	...	20	20	...	7	6	1
SHWEBO.												
All Religions ...	*356,363*	*168,070*	*188,293*	*188,870*	*93,715*	*95,155*	*139,037*	*67,887*	*71,150*	*28,456*	*6,468*	*21,988*
0— 5	49,129	23,563	25,566	49,129	23,563	25,566	...	...	...	...	...	...
5—10	46,589	23,534	23,055	46,580	23,534	23,046	9	...	9	...	...	...
10—15	40,086	19,730	20,356	39,813	19,698	20,115	270	32	238	3	...	3
15—20	31,557	14,450	17,107	25,295	12,689	12,606	6,015	1,708	4,307	247	53	194
20—40	96,527	45,363	51,164	18,617	10,525	8,092	73,288	33,718	39,570	4,622	1,120	3,502
40—60	64,063	29,582	34,481	5,487	2,362	3,125	47,593	24,945	22,648	10,983	2,275	8,708
60 and over	28,412	11,848	16,564	3,949	1,344	2,605	11,862	7,484	4,378	12,601	3,020	9,581
Buddhist ...	*344,852*	*161,070*	*183,782*	*182,293*	*89,542*	*92,751*	*134,757*	*65,292*	*69,465*	*27,802*	*6,236*	*21,566*
0— 5	47,581	22,785	24,796	47,581	22,785	24,796	...	...	...	...	...	...
5—10	45,307	22,913	22,394	45,298	22,913	22,385	9	...	9	...	...	...
10—15	38,995	19,150	19,845	38,722	19,118	19,604	270	32	238	3	...	3
15—20	30,656	13,983	16,673	24,608	12,271	12,337	5,814	1,664	4,150	234	48	186
20—40	92,115	42,159	49,956	16,972	8,979	7,993	70,678	32,142	38,536	4,465	1,038	3,427
40—60	62,307	28,471	33,836	5,237	2,172	3,065	46,345	24,115	22,230	10,725	2,184	8,541
60 and over	27,891	11,609	16,282	3,875	1,304	2,571	11,641	7,339	4,302	12,375	2,966	9,409

Imperial Table VII.—*Age, Sex and Civil Condition.*

PART B.—DETAILS BY DISTRICTS.

District	AGE.	POPULATION. Persons.	POPULATION. Males.	POPULATION. Females.	UNMARRIED. Persons.	UNMARRIED. Males.	UNMARRIED. Females.	MARRIED. Persons.	MARRIED. Males.	MARRIED. Females.	WIDOWED. Persons.	WIDOWED. Males.	WIDOWED. Females.
	1	2	3	4	5	6	7	8	9	10	11	12	13
SHWEBO—*concluded.*	***Hindu*** ...	*2,305*	*1,841*	*464*	*1,213*	*1,003*	*210*	*990*	*760*	*230*	*102*	*78*	*24*
	0—5	200	105	95	200	105	95	...	...	...	...	...	...
	5—10	138	78	60	138	78	60	...	...	...	...	...	...
	10—15	105	74	31	105	74	31	...	...	...	...	...	...
	15—20	144	101	43	91	84	7	52	17	35	1	...	1
	20—40	1,255	1,076	179	555	545	10	662	497	165	38	34	4
	40—60	401	356	45	105	102	3	246	219	27	50	35	15
	60 and over	62	51	11	19	15	4	30	27	3	13	9	4
	Mahomedan ...	*6,326*	*3,424*	*2,902*	*3,450*	*1,925*	*1,525*	*2,469*	*1,387*	*1,082*	*407*	*112*	*295*
	0—5	950	481	469	950	481	469	...	...	...	...	...	...
	5—10	842	413	429	842	413	429	...	...	...	...	...	...
	10—15	710	375	335	710	375	335	...	...	...	...	...	...
	15—20	520	242	278	388	216	172	120	21	99	12	5	7
	20—40	1,943	1,199	744	428	366	62	1,433	806	627	82	27	55
	40—60	997	560	437	90	55	35	764	467	297	143	38	105
	60 and over	364	154	210	42	19	23	152	93	59	170	42	128
	Christian ...	*2,746*	*1,617*	*1,129*	*1,838*	*1,176*	*662*	*778*	*414*	*364*	*130*	*27*	*103*
	0—5	384	180	204	384	180	204	...	...	...	...	...	...
	5—10	292	123	169	292	123	169	...	...	...	...	...	...
	10—15	272	128	144	272	128	144	...	...	...	...	...	...
	15—20	227	115	112	198	109	89	29	6	23	...	...	...
	20—40	1,143	866	277	631	604	27	490	256	234	22	6	16
	40—60	335	173	162	49	27	22	221	128	93	65	18	47
	60 and over	93	32	61	12	5	7	38	24	14	43	3	40
SAGAING.	***All Religions*** ...	*312,111*	*147,816*	*164,295*	*173,494*	*86,272*	*87,222*	*112,852*	*55,307*	*57,545*	*25,765*	*6,237*	*19,528*
	0—5	42,516	20,678	21,838	42,516	20,678	21,838	...	...	...	...	...	...
	5—10	40,603	20,013	20,590	40,603	20,013	20,590	...	...	...	...	...	...
	10—15	37,442	19,011	18,431	37,433	19,011	18,422	9	...	9	...	...	...
	15—20	30,035	14,013	16,022	25,595	12,783	12,812	4,141	1,172	2,969	299	58	241
	20—40	83,162	39,383	43,779	19,242	10,347	8,895	58,890	27,773	31,117	5,030	1,263	3,767
	40—60	51,843	23,578	28,265	5,032	2,155	2,877	37,838	19,386	18,452	8,973	2,037	6,936
	60 and over	26,510	11,140	15,370	3,073	1,285	1,788	11,974	6,976	4,998	11,463	2,879	8,584
	Buddhist ...	*306,416*	*144,311*	*162,105*	*170,551*	*84,468*	*86,083*	*110,511*	*53,770*	*56,741*	*25,354*	*6,073*	*19,281*
	0—5	41,837	20,346	21,491	41,837	20,346	21,491	...	...	...	...	...	...
	5—10	39,987	19,700	20,287	39,987	19,700	20,287	...	...	...	...	...	...
	10—15	36,954	18,769	18,185	36,946	18,769	18,177	8	...	8	...	...	...
	15—20	29,565	13,739	15,826	25,245	12,542	12,703	4,034	1,142	2,892	286	55	231
	20—40	80,887	37,778	43,109	18,582	9,781	8,801	57,393	26,795	30,598	4,912	1,202	3,710
	40—60	50,922	22,966	27,956	4,911	2,062	2,849	37,205	18,934	18,271	8,806	1,970	6,836
	60 and over	26,264	11,013	15,251	3,043	1,268	1,775	11,871	6,899	4,972	11,350	2,846	8,504
	Hindu ...	*1,772*	*1,228*	*544*	*845*	*595*	*250*	*825*	*577*	*248*	*102*	*56*	*46*
	0—5	224	117	107	224	117	107	...	...	...	...	...	...
	5—10	145	74	71	145	74	71	...	...	...	...	...	...
	10—15	103	59	44	102	59	43	1	...	1	...	...	...
	15—20	96	60	36	56	49	7	37	10	27	3	1	2
	20—40	829	635	194	246	237	9	559	382	177	24	16	8
	40—60	315	251	64	60	54	6	208	169	39	47	28	19
	60 and over	60	32	28	12	5	7	20	16	4	28	11	17
	Mahomedan ...	*2,815*	*1,710*	*1,105*	*1,464*	*871*	*593*	*1,134*	*751*	*383*	*217*	*88*	*129*
	0—5	312	145	167	312	145	167	...	...	...	...	...	...
	5—10	324	167	157	324	167	157	...	...	...	...	...	...
	10—15	272	132	140	272	132	140	...	...	...	...	...	...
	15—20	245	141	104	188	125	63	51	14	37	6	2	4
	20—40	1,117	795	322	316	265	51	731	493	238	70	37	33
	40—60	422	263	159	40	28	12	300	205	95	82	30	52
	60 and over	123	67	56	12	9	3	52	39	13	59	19	40
	Christian ...	*1,013*	*492*	*521*	*580*	*290*	*290*	*345*	*182*	*163*	*88*	*20*	*68*
	0—5	138	65	73	138	65	73	...	...	...	...	...	...
	5—10	137	64	73	137	64	73	...	...	...	...	...	...
	10—15	108	47	61	108	47	61	...	...	...	...	...	...
	15—20	119	64	55	96	58	38	19	6	13	4	...	4
	20—40	290	145	145	81	49	32	188	88	100	21	8	13
	40—60	163	83	80	15	5	10	111	69	42	37	9	28
	60 and over	58	24	34	5	2	3	27	19	8	26	3	23

IMPERIAL TABLE VII.—*Age, Sex and Civil Condition.*

PART B.—DETAILS BY DISTRICTS.

District	AGE.	POPULATION. Persons.	POPULATION. Males.	POPULATION. Females.	UNMARRIED. Persons.	UNMARRIED. Males.	UNMARRIED. Females.	MARRIED. Persons.	MARRIED. Males.	MARRIED. Females.	WIDOWED. Persons.	WIDOWED. Males.	WIDOWED. Females.
	1	2	3	4	5	6	7	8	9	10	11	12	13
LOWER CHINDWIN.	***All Religions*** ...	*316,175*	*141,262*	*174,913*	*167,066*	*79,472*	*87,594*	*115,606*	*55,790*	*59,816*	*33,503*	*6,000*	*27,503*
	0—5	43,830	21,372	22,458	43,830	21,372	22,458	...	...	...	...	...	...
	5—10	42,480	20,195	22,285	42,480	20,195	22,285	...	...	...	...	...	...
	10—15	34,711	17,306	17,405	34,596	17,279	17,317	107	27	80	8	...	8
	15—20	28,709	12,429	16,280	23,232	11,035	12,197	5,109	1,319	3,790	368	75	293
	20—40	82,515	35,557	46,958	15,659	6,938	8,721	60,315	27,502	32,813	6,541	1,117	5,424
	40—60	52,703	22,502	30,201	4,429	1,632	2,797	37,224	19,200	18,024	11,050	1,670	9,380
	60 and over	31,227	11,901	19,326	2,840	1,021	1,819	12,851	7,742	5,109	15,536	3,138	12,398
	Buddhist ...	*313,839*	*139,518*	*174,321*	*166,015*	*78,711*	*87,304*	*114,439*	*54,899*	*59,540*	*33,385*	*5,908*	*27,477*
	0—5	43,602	21,271	22,331	43,602	21,271	22,331	..	...	...	...	...	...
	5—10	42,298	20,093	22,205	42,298	20,093	22,205	...	...	...	...	...	...
	10—15	34,583	17,220	17,363	34,472	17,195	17,277	103	25	78	8	...	8
	15—20	28,517	12,291	16,226	23,095	10,925	12,170	5,055	1,291	3,764	367	75	292
	20—40	81,313	34,586	46,727	15,314	6,607	8,707	59,525	26,922	32,603	6,474	1,057	5,417
	40—60	52,353	22,200	30,153	4,395	1,600	2,795	36,942	18,953	17,989	11,016	1,647	9,369
	60 and over	31,173	11,857	19,316	2,839	1,020	1,819	12,814	7,708	5,106	15,520	3,129	12,391
UPPER CHINDWIN.	***All Religions*** ...	*170,622*	*86,141*	*84,481*	*88,790*	*47,054*	*41,736*	*69,745*	*35,964*	*33,781*	*12,087*	*3,123*	*8,964*
	0—5	23,670	11,589	12,081	23,670	11,589	12,081	...	...	...	...	...	...
	5—10	21,006	10,369	10,637	21,006	10,369	10,637	...	...	...	...	...	...
	10—15	18,236	9,042	9,194	18,143	9,040	9,103	93	2	91	...	...	...
	15—20	15,609	7,720	7,889	12,385	7,047	5,338	3,061	657	2,404	163	16	147
	20—40	53,013	27,537	25,476	10,814	7,496	3,318	39,445	19,022	20,423	2,754	1,019	1,735
	40—60	29,975	15,547	14,428	1,880	1,095	785	23,099	13,265	9,834	4,996	1,187	3,809
	60 and over	9,113	4,337	4,776	892	418	474	4,047	3,018	1,029	4,174	901	3,273
	Buddhist ...	*163,834*	*81,694*	*82,140*	*85,610*	*44,880*	*40,730*	*66,523*	*33,902*	*32,621*	*11,701*	*2,912*	*8,789*
	0—5	23,022	11,252	11,770	23,022	11,252	11,770	...	...	...	...	...	...
	5—10	20,474	10,082	10,392	20,474	10,082	10,392	...	...	...	...	...	...
	10—15	17,826	8,808	9,018	17,739	8,808	8,931	87	...	87	...	...	...
	15—20	15,103	7,427	7,676	12,010	6,790	5,220	2,935	623	2,312	158	14	144
	20—40	49,758	25,258	24,500	9,817	6,597	3,220	37,329	17,739	19,590	2,612	922	1,690
	40—60	28,713	14,631	14,082	1,691	946	745	22,207	12,590	9,617	4,815	1,095	3,720
	60 and over	8,938	4,236	4,702	857	405	452	3,965	2,950	1,015	4,116	881	3,235
	Animist ...	*3,719*	*1,990*	*1,729*	*1,830*	*1,063*	*767*	*1,644*	*831*	*813*	*246*	*96*	*149*
	0—5	429	218	211	429	218	211	...	...	...	...	...	...
	5—10	366	197	169	366	197	169	...	...	...	...	...	...
	10—15	292	163	129	292	163	129	...	...	...	...	...	...
	15—20	363	202	161	289	183	106	70	18	52	4	1	3
	20—40	1,458	763	695	351	260	91	1,027	461	566	80	42	38
	40—60	696	397	299	75	36	39	497	315	182	124	46	78
	60 and over	115	50	65	28	6	22	50	37	13	37	7	30
	Hindu ...	*1,770*	*1,409*	*361*	*761*	*633*	*128*	*905*	*687*	*218*	*104*	*84*	*20*
	0—5	114	66	48	114	66	48	...	...	...	...	...	...
	5—10	97	56	41	97	56	41	...	...	...	...	...	...
	10—15	65	38	27	61	38	23	4	...	4	...	...	...
	15—20	80	48	32	45	39	6	34	8	26	1	1	...
	20—40	1,032	861	171	370	366	4	618	457	161	44	38	6
	40—60	346	313	33	70	69	1	231	205	26	45	39	6
	60 and over	36	27	9	4	4	...	18	17	1	14	6	8
KYAUKSE.	***All Religions*** ...	*141,426*	*68,868*	*72,558*	*67,316*	*34,345*	*32,971*	*60,105*	*30,276*	*29,829*	*14,005*	*4,247*	*9,758*
	0—5	17,278	7,921	9,357	17,278	7,921	9,357	..	...	...	...	...	...
	5—10	16,846	7,479	9,367	16,845	7,478	9,367	1	1	...	...	...	...
	10—15	14,609	7,936	6,673	14,585	7,912	6,673	24	24	...	...	...	...
	15—20	12,236	5,848	6,388	9,411	5,148	4,263	2,625	656	1,969	200	44	156
	20—40	41,071	20,720	20,351	6,789	4,466	2,323	31,504	15,085	16,419	2,778	1,169	1,609
	40—60	28,351	14,109	14,242	1,644	1,010	634	21,114	11,444	9,670	5,593	1,655	3,938
	60 and over	11,035	4,855	6,180	764	410	354	4,837	3,066	1,771	5,434	1,379	4,055
	Buddhist ...	*134,928*	*65,293*	*69,635*	*64,100*	*32,503*	*31,597*	*57,401*	*28,737*	*28,664*	*13,427*	*4,053*	*9,374*
	0—5	16,424	7,492	8,932	16,424	7,492	8,932	...	...	...	...	...	...
	5—10	16,135	7,135	9,000	16,135	7,135	9,000	...	...	...	...	...	...
	10—15	13,923	7,574	6,349	13,920	7,571	6,349	3	3	...	...	...	...
	15—20	11,667	5,563	6,104	9,008	4,908	4,100	2,469	611	1,858	190	44	146
	20—40	38,868	19,382	19,486	6,306	4,056	2,250	29,914	14,215	15,699	2,648	1,111	1,537
	40—60	27,268	13,461	13,807	1,557	938	619	20,340	10,958	9,382	5,371	1,565	3,806
	60 and over	10,643	4,686	5,957	750	403	347	4,675	2,950	1,725	5,218	1,333	3,885

IMPERIAL TABLE VII.—*Age, Sex and Civil Condition.*

PART B.—DETAILS BY DISTRICTS.

District	AGE.	POPULATION.			UNMARRIED.			MARRIED.			WIDOWED.		
		Persons.	Males.	Females.	Persons.	Males.	Females.	Persons.	Males.	Females.	Persons.	Males.	Females.
	1	2	3	4	5	6	7	8	9	10	11	12	13
KYAUKSÈ—*concluded.*	***Mahomedan*** ...	*4,954*	*2,509*	*2,445*	*2,460*	*1,814*	*1,146*	*1,988*	*1,036*	*952*	*506*	*159*	*347*
	0—5	704	356	348	704	356	348	...	...	...	..	...	...
	5—10	573	277	296	572	276	296	1	1	...	...	...	...
	10—15	592	310	282	571	289	282	21	21	...	...	...	...
	15—20	468	219	249	332	184	148	126	35	91	10	...	10
	20—40	1,461	779	682	230	178	52	1,124	555	569	107	46	61
	40—60	810	434	376	43	30	13	575	327	248	192	77	115
	60 and over	346	134	212	8	1	7	141	97	44	197	36	161
MEIKTILA.	***All Religions*** ...	*279,822*	*134,170*	*145,652*	*158,798*	*78,714*	*80,084*	*100,673*	*50,848*	*49,830*	*20,351*	*4,613*	*15,738*
	0—5	37,212	17,896	19,316	37,212	17,896	19,316	...	...	...	...	...	...
	5—10	38,453	18,658	19,795	38,453	18,658	19,795	..	...	...	...	...	...
	10—15	33,232	16,389	16,843	33,232	16,389	16,843	...	...	...	...	...	...
	15—20	24,648	11,257	13,391	21,600	10,579	11,021	2,889	657	2,232	159	21	138
	20—40	79,270	38,723	40,547	20,650	11,851	8,799	54,656	25,930	28,726	3,964	942	3,022
	40—60	45,769	22,042	23,727	4,975	2,290	2,685	33,593	18,161	15,432	7,201	1,591	5,610
	60 and over	21,238	9,205	12,033	2,676	1,051	1,625	9,535	6,095	3,440	9,027	2,059	6,968
	Buddhist ...	*271,774*	*128,307*	*143,467*	*154,465*	*75,529*	*78,936*	*97,259*	*48,335*	*48,924*	*20,050*	*4,443*	*15,607*
	0—5	36,391	17,495	18,896	36,391	17,495	18,896	...	...	...	...	...	...
	5—10	37,758	18,294	19,464	37,758	18,294	19,464	...	...	...	...	...	...
	10—15	32,734	16,105	16,629	32,734	16,105	16,629	...	...	...	...	...	...
	15—20	24,108	10,908	13,200	21,209	10,286	10,923	2,747	602	2,145	152	20	132
	20—40	75,133	35,371	39,762	18,991	10,262	8,729	52,286	24,237	28,049	3,856	872	2,984
	40—60	44,585	21,044	23,541	4,730	2,057	2,673	32,776	17,469	15,307	7,079	1,518	5,561
	60 and over	21,065	9,090	11,975	2,652	1,030	1,622	9,450	6,027	3,423	8,963	2,033	6,930
	Hindu ...	*2,931*	*2,474*	*457*	*1,428*	*1,229*	*199*	*1,395*	*1,158*	*237*	*108*	*87*	*21*
	0—5	172	72	100	172	72	100	...	...	...	...	...	...
	5—10	121	70	51	121	70	51	...	...	...	...	...	...
	10—15	72	47	25	72	47	25	...	...	...	...	...	...
	15—20	164	137	27	126	119	7	36	17	19	2	1	1
	20—40	1,862	1,652	210	802	789	13	1,015	823	192	45	40	5
	40—60	483	446	37	124	121	3	315	291	24	44	34	10
	60 and over	57	50	7	11	11	0	29	27	2	17	12	5
	Mahomedan ...	*4,253*	*2,800*	*1,453*	*2,358*	*1,548*	*810*	*1,731*	*1,183*	*548*	*164*	*69*	*95*
	0—5	530	264	266	530	264	266	...	...	...	...	...	...
	5—10	496	255	241	496	255	241	...	...	...	...	...	...
	10—15	376	207	169	376	207	169	...	...	...	...	...	...
	15—20	336	190	146	239	153	86	93	37	56	4	...	4
	20—40	1,797	1,341	456	597	557	40	1,144	758	386	56	26	30
	40—60	616	487	129	108	102	6	446	353	93	62	32	30
	60 and over	102	56	46	12	10	2	48	35	13	42	11	31
YAMÈTHIN.	***All Religions*** ...	*307,419*	*153,223*	*154,196*	*168,538*	*89,043*	*79,495*	*119,497*	*59,892*	*60,105*	*19,384*	*4,788*	*14,596*
	0—5	41,822	20,352	21,470	41,822	20,352	21,470	...	...	...	...	...	...
	5—10	41,967	20,706	21,261	41,967	20,706	21,261	...	...	...	...	...	...
	10—15	37,064	19,166	17,898	36,946	19,101	17,845	117	65	52	1	...	1
	15—20	27,071	12,912	14,159	21,740	11,871	9,869	5,076	1,014	4,062	255	27	228
	20—40	91,077	46,355	44,722	19,399	13,510	5,889	67,747	31,616	36,131	3,931	1,229	2,702
	40—60	47,999	24,375	23,624	4,377	2,568	1,809	36,870	20,350	16,520	6,752	1,457	5,295
	60 and over	20,419	9,357	11,062	2,287	935	1,352	9,687	6,347	3,340	8,445	2,075	6,370
	Buddhist ...	*288,047*	*141,650*	*146,397*	*158,089*	*82,581*	*75,508*	*111,807*	*54,714*	*57,093*	*18,151*	*4,355*	*13,796*
	0—5	39,390	19,125	20,265	39,390	19,125	20,265	...	...	...	...	...	...
	5—10	39,929	19,661	20,268	39,929	19,661	20,268	...	...	...	...	...	...
	10—15	35,269	18,182	17,087	35,162	18,119	17,043	107	63	44	...	...	...
	15—20	25,313	11,944	13,369	20,390	11,033	9,357	4,681	888	3,793	242	23	219
	20—40	83,490	41,272	42,218	17,071	11,522	5,549	62,837	28,682	34,155	3,582	1,068	2,514
	40—60	45,107	22,540	22,567	3,957	2,238	1,719	34,881	19,006	15,875	6,269	1,296	4,973
	60 and over	19,549	8,926	10,623	2,190	883	1,307	9,301	6,075	3,226	8,058	1,968	6,090
	Animist ...	*2,452*	*1,433*	*1,019*	*1,300*	*834*	*466*	*951*	*531*	*420*	*201*	*68*	*133*
	0—5	283	145	138	283	145	138	...	...	...	...	...	...
	5—10	255	160	95	255	160	95	...	...	...	...	...	...
	10—15	210	119	91	210	119	91	...	...	...	...	...	...
	15—20	243	132	111	197	119	78	46	13	33	...	...	...
	20—40	918	565	353	273	223	50	595	321	274	50	21	29
	40—60	421	252	169	67	58	9	265	165	100	89	29	60
	60 and over	122	60	62	15	10	5	45	32	13	62	18	44

IMPERIAL TABLE VII.—*Age, Sex and Civil Condition.*

PART B.—DETAILS BY DISTRICTS.

District	Age.	Population.			Unmarried.			Married.			Widowed.		
		Persons.	Males.	Females.	Persons.	Males.	Females.	Persons.	Males.	Females.	Persons.	Males.	Females.
	1	2	3	4	5	6	7	8	9	10	11	12	13
YAMÈTHIN—*concluded.*	***Hindu*** ...	*3,766*	*3,068*	*698*	*1,845*	*1,547*	*298*	*1,782*	*1,419*	*363*	*139*	*102*	*37*
	0—5	265	142	123	265	142	123	...	...	...	...	...	...
	5—10	169	91	78	169	91	78	...	...	...	...	...	...
	10—15	134	86	48	123	84	39	10	2	8	1	...	1
	15—20	226	169	57	148	132	16	77	36	41	1	1	...
	20—40	2,308	1,993	315	962	932	30	1,284	1,013	271	62	48	14
	40—60	595	526	69	161	151	10	378	337	41	56	38	18
	60 and over	69	61	8	17	15	2	33	31	2	19	15	4
	Mahomedan ...	*11,057*	*5,956*	*5,101*	*8,162*	*3,459*	*2,703*	*4,116*	*2,275*	*1,841*	*779*	*222*	*557*
	0—5	1,541	775	766	1,541	775	766	...	...	...	...	...	...
	5—10	1,381	682	699	1,381	682	699	...	...	...	...	...	...
	10—15	1,276	687	589	1,276	687	589	...	...	...	...	...	...
	15—20	1,073	569	504	835	499	336	228	67	161	10	3	7
	20—40	3,562	2,063	1,499	888	676	212	2,467	1,310	1,157	207	77	130
	40—60	1,608	900	708	178	113	65	1,141	708	433	289	79	210
	60 and over	616	280	336	63	27	36	280	190	90	273	63	210
	Christian ...	*1,813*	*928*	*885*	*987*	*511*	*476*	*723*	*386*	*337*	*103*	*31*	*72*
	0—5	288	137	151	288	137	151	...	...	...	...	...	...
	5—10	208	98	110	208	98	110	...	...	...	...	...	...
	10—15	162	84	78	162	84	78	...	...	...	...	...	...
	15—20	194	82	112	157	76	81	35	6	29	2	...	2
	20—40	662	368	294	158	110	48	479	248	231	25	10	15
	40—60	236	129	107	12	6	6	181	113	68	43	10	33
	60 and over	63	30	33	2	...	2	28	19	9	33	11	22
MYINGYAN.	***All Religions*** ...	*441,905*	*211,119*	*230,786*	*248,644*	*123,614*	*125,030*	*161,698*	*80,069*	*81,629*	*31,563*	*7,436*	*24,127*
	0—5	64,128	31,712	32,416	64,128	31,712	32,416	...	...	...	...	...	...
	5—10	59,053	28,762	30,291	59,053	28,762	30,291	...	...	...	...	...	...
	10—15	51,918	25,874	26,044	51,916	25,872	26,044	2	2	...	...	...	...
	15—20	40,180	19,265	20,915	34,440	17,830	16,610	5,487	1,398	4,089	253	37	216
	20—40	122,537	57,680	64,857	28,081	14,967	13,114	88,409	41,277	47,132	6,047	1,436	4,611
	40—60	71,226	33,527	37,699	7,186	2,983	4,203	52,729	28,075	24,654	11,311	2,469	8,842
	60 and over	32,863	14,299	18,564	3,840	1,488	2,352	15,071	9,317	5,754	13,952	3,494	10,458
	Buddhist ...	*438,069*	*207,917*	*230,152*	*246,887*	*122,172*	*124,715*	*159,734*	*78,387*	*81,347*	*31,448*	*7,358*	*24,090*
	0—5	63,897	31,595	32,302	63,897	31,595	32,302	...	...	...	...	...	...
	5—10	58,862	28,666	30,196	58,862	28,666	30,196	...	...	...	...	...	...
	10—15	51,745	25,754	25,991	51,743	25,752	25,991	2	2	...	...	...	...
	15—20	39,838	18,996	20,842	34,205	17,621	16,584	5,382	1,338	4,044	251	37	214
	20—40	120,219	55,575	64,644	27,251	14,158	13,093	86,966	40,017	46,949	6,002	1,400	4,602
	40—60	70,709	33,082	37,627	7,099	2,900	4,199	52,346	27,744	34,602	11,264	2,438	8,826
	60 and over	32,799	14,249	18,550	3,830	1,480	2,350	15,038	9,286	5,752	13,931	3,483	10,448
	Hindu ...	*1,787*	*1,588*	*199*	*721*	*640*	*81*	*1,017*	*910*	*107*	*49*	*38*	*11*
	0—5	74	36	38	74	36	38	...	...	...	...	...	...
	5—10	59	32	27	59	32	27	...	...	...	...	...	...
	10—15	47	39	8	47	39	8	...	...	...	...	...	...
	15—20	146	125	21	100	96	4	46	29	17	...	...	...
	20—40	1,201	1,123	78	395	391	4	789	715	74	17	17	...
	40—60	232	211	21	42	42	...	170	154	16	20	15	5
	60 and over	28	22	6	4	4	...	12	12	...	12	6	6
	Mahomedan ...	*1,529*	*1,227*	*302*	*770*	*605*	*165*	*721*	*601*	*120*	*38*	*21*	*17*
	0—5	113	57	56	113	57	56	...	...	...	...	...	...
	5—10	101	51	50	101	51	50	...	...	...	...	...	...
	10—15	82	54	28	82	54	28	...	...	...	...	...	...
	15—20	151	112	39	97	83	14	53	29	24	1	...	1
	20—40	869	779	90	337	325	12	512	441	71	20	13	7
	40—60	187	154	33	36	32	4	139	115	24	12	7	5
	60 and over	26	20	6	4	3	1	17	16	1	5	1	4
NORTHERN SHAN STATES.	***All Religions*** ...	*414,786*	*208,095*	*206,691*	*219,165*	*117,987*	*101,178*	*155,756*	*79,443*	*76,313*	*39,865*	*10,665*	*29,200*
	0—5	55,174	27,127	28,047	55,174	27,127	28,047	...	...	...	...	...	...
	5—10	56,542	28,516	28,026	56,542	28,516	28,026	...	...	...	...	...	...
	10—15	43,427	22,213	21,214	43,326	22,213	21,113	101	...	101	...	...	...
	15—20	37,060	18,159	18,901	30,776	17,099	13,677	5,375	972	4,403	909	88	821
	20—40	122,769	61,876	60,893	28,468	19,934	8,534	84,955	38,317	46,638	9,346	3,625	5,721
	40—60	69,231	36,687	32,544	3,194	2,077	1,117	52,575	30,990	21,585	13,462	3,620	9,842
	60 and over	30,583	13,517	17,066	1,685	1,021	664	12,750	9,164	3,586	16,148	3,332	12,816

IMPERIAL TABLE VII.—*Age, Sex and Civil Condition.*

PART B.—DETAILS BY DISTRICTS.

AGE.	POPULATION. Persons.	POPULATION. Males.	POPULATION. Females.	UNMARRIED. Persons.	UNMARRIED. Males.	UNMARRIED. Females.	MARRIED. Persons.	MARRIED. Males.	MARRIED. Females.	WIDOWED. Persons.	WIDOWED. Males.	WIDOWED. Females.
1	2	3	4	5	6	7	8	9	10	11	12	13
NORTHERN SHAN STATES—*concluded.*												
Buddhist ...	*335,436*	*167,904*	*167,532*	*177,538*	*95,133*	*82,405*	*125,115*	*63,459*	*61,656*	*32,783*	*9,312*	*23,471*
0—5	46,036	22,822	23,214	46,036	22,822	23,214	...	...	...	...	...	...
5—10	47,210	23,382	23,828	47,210	23,382	23,828	...	...	...	...	...	...
10—15	35,200	17,999	17,201	35,142	17,999	17,143	58	...	58	...	...	...
15—20	29,694	14,346	15,348	24,354	13,599	10,755	4,475	670	3,805	865	77	788
20—40	95,487	47,549	47,938	20,588	14,581	6,007	66,989	29,814	37,175	7,910	3,154	4,756
40—60	56,581	30,209	26,372	2,635	1,791	844	43,071	25,292	17,779	10,875	3,126	7,749
60 and over	25,228	11,597	13,631	1,573	959	614	10,522	7,683	2,839	13,133	2,955	10,178
Animist ...	*75,154*	*36,767*	*38,387*	*39,769*	*21,312*	*18,457*	*28,562*	*14,298*	*14,264*	*6,823*	*1,157*	*5,666*
0—5	8,834	4,139	4,695	8,834	4,139	4,695	...	...	...	...	...	...
5—10	9,133	5,030	4,103	9,133	5,030	4,103	...	...	...	...	...	...
10—15	8,063	4,098	3,965	8,024	4,098	3,926	39	...	39	...	...	...
15—20	7,113	3,628	3,485	6,252	3,349	2,903	821	269	552	40	10	30
20—40	24,699	12,087	12,612	6,960	4,450	2,510	16,423	7,264	9,159	1,316	373	943
40—60	12,017	5,905	6,112	460	189	271	9,073	5,304	3,769	2,484	412	2,072
60 and over	5,295	1,880	3,415	106	57	49	2,206	1,461	745	2,983	362	2,621
Hindu ...	*2,607*	*2,250*	*357*	*1,040*	*904*	*136*	*1,408*	*1,214*	*194*	*159*	*132*	*27*
0—5	158	79	79	158	79	79	...	...	...	...	...	...
5—10	84	49	35	84	49	35	...	...	...	...	...	...
10—15	69	49	20	65	49	16	4	...	4	...	...	...
15—20	130	103	27	78	77	1	50	25	25	2	1	1
20—40	1,779	1,611	168	590	585	5	1,106	955	151	83	71	12
40—60	363	343	20	63	63	...	239	226	13	61	54	7
60 and over	24	16	8	2	2	...	9	8	1	13	6	7
Mahomedan ...	*1,241*	*952*	*289*	*604*	*491*	*113*	*562*	*402*	*160*	*75*	*59*	*16*
0—5	100	60	40	100	60	40	...	...	...	...	...	...
5—10	83	38	45	83	38	45	...	...	...	...	...	...
10—15	50	35	15	50	35	15	...	...	...	...	...	...
15—20	80	55	25	55	48	7	25	7	18	...	...	...
20—40	687	550	137	284	278	6	372	247	125	31	25	6
40—60	219	196	23	29	29	...	156	139	17	34	28	6
60 and over	22	18	4	3	3	...	9	9	...	10	6	4
SOUTHERN SHAN STATES.												
All Religions ...	*894,485*	*446,099*	*448,386*	*459,143*	*245,209*	*213,934*	*342,875*	*175,376*	*167,499*	*92,467*	*25,514*	*66,953*
0—5	113,188	55,297	57,891	113,187	55,296	57,891	1	1	...	...	...	...
5—10	125,299	64,792	60,507	125,295	64,788	60,507	4	4	...	...	...	...
10—15	94,135	49,639	44,496	93,838	49,599	44,239	288	38	250	9	2	7
15—20	80,253	38,408	41,845	64,019	34,902	29,117	14,538	3,239	11,299	1,696	267	1,429
20—40	267,195	128,109	139,086	53,591	35,430	18,161	184,629	83,540	101,089	28,975	9,139	19,836
40—60	152,715	79,471	73,244	6,355	3,824	2,531	114,420	67,146	47,274	31,940	8,501	23,439
60 and over	61,700	30,383	31,317	2,858	1,370	1,488	28,995	21,408	7,587	29,847	7,605	22,242
Buddhist ...	*775,156*	*384,220*	*390,936*	*398,790*	*212,392*	*186,398*	*294,911*	*149,659*	*145,252*	*81,455*	*22,169*	*59,286*
0—5	97,875	48,482	49,393	97,875	48,482	49,393	...	...	...	...	...	...
5—10	107,629	53,883	53,746	107,629	53,883	53,746	...	...	...	...	...	...
10—15	83,495	43,710	39,785	83,301	43,697	39,604	190	13	177	4	...	4
15—20	71,031	34,335	36,696	56,348	31,212	25,136	13,091	2,900	10,191	1,592	223	1,369
20—40	229,813	109,524	120,289	45,572	30,564	15,008	158,650	70,871	87,779	25,591	8,089	17,502
40—60	131,697	68,666	63,031	5,659	3,392	2,267	98,477	57,895	40,582	27,561	7,379	20,182
60 and over	53,616	25,620	27,996	2,406	1,162	1,244	24,503	17,980	6,523	26,707	6,478	20,229
Animist ...	*104,414*	*53,090*	*51,324*	*52,751*	*28,261*	*24,490*	*41,551*	*21,871*	*19,680*	*10,112*	*2,958*	*7,154*
0—5	13,078	5,659	7,419	13,078	5,659	7,419	...	...	...	...	...	...
5—10	16,078	10,158	5,920	16,078	10,158	5,920	...	...	...	...	...	...
10—15	9,465	5,340	4,125	9,398	5,316	4,082	63	22	41	4	2	2
15—20	8,048	3,443	4,605	6,780	3,123	3,657	1,174	280	894	94	40	54
20—40	31,421	14,663	16,758	6,449	3,498	2,951	21,871	10,296	11,575	3,101	869	2,232
40—60	18,837	9,386	9,451	554	320	234	14,271	8,069	6,202	4,012	997	3,015
60 and over	7,487	4,441	3,046	414	187	227	4,172	3,204	968	2,901	1,050	1,851
Hindu ...	*3,282*	*2,638*	*644*	*1,640*	*1,332*	*308*	*1,511*	*1,190*	*321*	*131*	*116*	*15*
0—5	297	162	135	296	161	135	1	1	...	...	...	...
5—10	212	130	82	208	126	82	4	4	...	...	...	...
10—15	127	69	58	113	68	45	14	1	13	...	...	...
15—20	167	124	43	98	95	3	67	28	39	2	1	1
20—40	1,965	1,682	283	858	817	41	1,044	807	237	63	58	5
40—60	450	414	36	58	57	1	341	313	28	51	44	7
60 and over	64	57	7	9	8	1	40	36	4	15	13	2

IMPERIAL TABLE VII.—*Age, Sex and Civil Condition.*

PART B.—DETAILS BY DISTRICTS.

District	AGE.	POPULATION.			UNMARRIED.			MARRIED.			WIDOWED.		
		Persons.	Males.	Females.	Persons.	Males.	Females.	Persons.	Males.	Females.	Persons.	Males.	Females.
	1	2	3	4	5	6	7	8	9	10	11	12	13
SOUTHERN SHAN STATES—*concluded.*	*Mahomedan* ...	*1,800*	*1,274*	*526*	*821*	*580*	*241*	*861*	*609*	*252*	*118*	*85*	*33*
	0—5	232	127	105	232	127	105	...	...	...	...	...	...
	5—10	153	84	69	153	84	69	...	...	...	...	...	...
	10—15	80	43	37	78	41	37	2	2	...	...	...	...
	15—20	124	71	53	74	63	11	48	7	41	2	1	1
	20—40	892	685	207	238	224	14	593	407	186	61	54	7
	40—60	277	241	36	40	37	3	202	181	21	35	23	12
	60 and over	42	23	19	6	4	2	16	12	4	20	7	13
	Christian ...	*9,818*	*4,866*	*4,952*	*5,136*	*2,641*	*2,495*	*4,033*	*2,040*	*1,993*	*649*	*185*	*464*
	0—5	1,705	867	838	1,705	867	838	...	...	...	...	...	...
	5—10	1,226	537	689	1,226	537	689	...	...	...	...	...	...
	10—15	968	477	491	948	477	471	19	...	19	1	...	1
	15—20	883	435	448	719	409	310	158	24	134	6	2	4
	20—40	3,094	1,546	1,548	471	324	147	2,465	1,154	1,311	158	68	90
	40—60	1,451	762	689	44	18	26	1,127	686	441	280	58	222
	60 and over	491	242	249	23	9	14	264	176	88	204	57	147
CHIN HILLS.	*All Religions* ...	*119,556*	*58,562*	*60,994*	*66,248*	*84,112*	*82,136*	*45,257*	*22,788*	*22,469*	*8,051*	*1,662*	*6,389*
	0—5	18,468	8,875	9,593	18,468	8,875	9,593	...	...	...	...	...	...
	5—10	15,979	8,033	7,946	15,979	8,033	7,946	...	...	...	...	...	...
	10—15	11,683	5,991	5,692	11,958	5,991	5,607	75	...	75	10	...	10
	15—20	10,845	5,233	5,612	9,261	4,917	4,344	1,537	307	1,230	47	9	38
	20—40	39,362	18,849	20,513	9,971	5,906	4,065	27,425	12,379	15,046	1,966	564	1,402
	40—60	18,026	9,109	8,917	749	318	431	13,584	8,159	5,425	3,693	632	3,061
	60 and over	5,193	2,472	2,721	222	72	150	2,636	1,943	693	2,335	457	1,878
	Animist ...	*117,858*	*57,010*	*60,848*	*65,235*	*83,409*	*81,826*	*44,156*	*22,001*	*22,155*	*7,967*	*1,600*	*6,367*
	0—5	18,135	8,717	9,418	18,135	8,717	9,418	...	...	...	...	...	...
	5—10	15,775	7,926	7,849	15,775	7,926	7,849	...	...	...	...	...	...
	10—15	11,594	5,934	5,660	11,515	5,934	5,581	69	...	69	10	...	10
	15—20	10,767	5,191	5,576	9,219	4,882	4,337	1,501	300	1,201	47	9	38
	20—40	38,229	17,972	20,257	9,659	5,599	4,060	26,645	11,846	14,799	1,925	527	1,398
	40—60	17,688	8,810	8,878	711	280	431	13,315	7,919	5,396	3,662	611	3,051
	60 and over	5,170	2,460	2,710	221	71	150	2,626	1,936	690	2,323	453	1,870
	Hindu ...	*1,351*	*947*	*404*	*598*	*407*	*191*	*714*	*516*	*198*	*39*	*24*	*15*
	0—5	204	100	104	204	100	104	...	...	...	...	...	...
	5—10	135	66	69	135	66	69	...	...	...	...	...	...
	10—15	49	29	20	43	29	14	6	...	6	...	...	...
	15—20	46	20	26	16	15	1	30	5	25	...	...	...
	20—40	713	557	156	181	178	3	513	364	149	19	15	4
	40—60	191	167	24	18	18	...	160	143	17	13	6	7
	60 and over	13	8	5	1	1	...	5	4	1	7	3	4

IMPERIAL TABLE VIII.

Education by Religion and Age.

PART A.—PROVINCIAL SUMMARY.

NOTE 1.—This Table is divided into two parts. Part A gives provincial details for each religion returned. Part B gives details for individual districts, the figures for minor religions being omitted.

2.—The populations of the Pakôkku Hill Tracts, and of the estimated areas of Kokang and West Manglün in the Northern Shan States and the Brè Tract in Karenni (Southern Shan States), are omitted from this Table. The figures for these omitted areas are given on page 25.

3.—An analysis of the Christian population literate in English gives the following figures.

	Age.	Persons.	Males.	Females.
Europeans and Allied Races and Anglo-Indians.	Total ...	22,884	15,634	7,250
	0—10	1,126	636	490
	10—15	1,373	740	633
	15—20	2,471	1,394	1,077
	20 and over	17,914	12,864	5,050
Other Christians ...	Total ...	7,130	5,073	2,057
	0—10	741	333	408
	10—15	1,777	1,031	746
	15—20	1,103	750	353
	20 and over	3,509	2,959	550

Imperial Table VIII.—*Education by Religion and Age.*

PART A.—PROVINCIAL SUMMARY (Whole Province).

Religion.	AGE.	Population.									Literate in English.		
		Total.			Literate.			Illiterate.					
		Persons.	Males.	Females.	Persons.	Males.	Females.	Persons.	Males.	Females.	Persons.	Males.	Females.
1	2	3	4	5	6	7	8	9	10	11	12	13	14
ALL RELIGIONS.	Total ...	*12,039,083*	*6,145,471*	*5,893,612*	*2,670,878*	*2,312,883*	*357,995*	*9,368,205*	*3,832,588*	*5,535,617*	*67,837*	*55,803*	*12,034*
	0—10	3,169,527	1,566,225	1,603,302	61,760	43,542	18,218	3,107,767	1,522,683	1,585,084	2,562	1,498	1,064
	10—15	1,377,509	714,400	663,109	253,133	204,084	49,049	1,124,376	510,316	614,060	6,497	4,665	1,832
	15—20	1,118,007	548,748	569,259	324,498	262,684	61,814	793,509	286,064	507,445	9,823	7,878	1,945
	20 and over	6,374,040	3,316,098	3,057,942	2,031,487	1,802,573	228,914	4,342,553	1,513,525	2,829,028	48,955	41,762	7,193
BUDDHIST.	Total ...	*10,384,544*	*5,113,437*	*5,271,107*	*2,423,629*	*2,107,738*	*315,891*	*7,960,915*	*3,005,699*	*4,955,216*	*21,189*	*19,916*	*1,273*
	0—10	2,817,224	1,385,722	1,431,502	54,398	39,110	15,288	2,762,826	1,346,612	1,416,214	313	245	68
	10—15	1,232,952	632,177	600,775	235,116	191,823	43,293	997,836	440,354	557,482	2,247	1,992	255
	15—20	969,399	459,826	509,573	299,085	244,142	54,943	670,314	215,684	454,630	4,399	4,108	291
	20 and over	5,364,969	2,635,712	2,729,257	1,835,030	1,632,663	202,367	3,529,939	1,003,049	2,526,890	14,230	13,571	659
ANIMIST.	Total ...	*625,539*	*330,270*	*295,269*	*20,459*	*19,588*	*871*	*605,080*	*310,682*	*294,398*	*470*	*443*	*27*
	0—10	156,001	80,639	75,362	261	222	39	155,740	80,417	75,323	19	19	...
	10—15	62,219	33,386	28,833	936	828	108	61,283	32,558	28,725	28	24	4
	15—20	55,210	27,748	27,462	1,418	1,274	144	53,792	26,474	27,318	77	75	2
	20 and over	352,109	188,497	163,612	17,844	17,264	580	334,265	171,233	163,032	346	325	21
HINDU.	Total ...	*389,528*	*312,535*	*76,993*	*75,905*	*71,835*	*4,070*	*313,623*	*240,700*	*72,923*	*9,260*	*8,858*	*402*
	0—10	43,968	23,062	20,906	1,255	936	319	42,713	22,126	20,587	177	139	38
	10—15	18,459	12,895	5,564	2,930	2,503	427	15,529	10,392	5,137	507	444	63
	15—20	31,690	25,216	6,474	5,910	5,226	684	25,780	19,990	5,790	856	782	74
	20 and over	295,411	251,362	44,049	65,810	63,170	2,640	229,601	188,192	41,409	7,720	7,493	227
MAHOMEDAN.	Total ..	*420,769*	*271,421*	*149,348*	*75,028*	*63,455*	*11,573*	*345,741*	*207,966*	*137,775*	*5,924*	*5,204*	*720*
	0—10	97,335	49,447	47,888	1,713	1,172	541	95,622	48,275	47,347	120	96	24
	10—15	39,015	22,877	16,138	5,031	3,680	1,351	33,984	19,197	14,787	441	365	76
	15—20	40,503	25,228	15,275	8,375	6,560	1,815	32,128	18,668	13,460	795	693	102
	20 and over	243,916	173,869	70,047	59,909	52,043	7,866	184,007	121,826	62,181	4,568	4,050	518
CHRISTIAN.	Total ...	*210,077*	*111,029*	*99,048*	*71,696*	*46,689*	*25,007*	*138,381*	*64,340*	*74,041*	*30,014*	*20,707*	*9,307*
	0—10	53,853	26,780	27,073	3,994	2,034	1,960	49,859	24,746	25,113	1,867	969	898
	10—15	24,516	12,853	11,663	8,902	5,111	3,791	15,614	7,742	7,872	3,150	1,771	1,379
	15—20	20,477	10,168	10,309	9,345	5,206	4,139	11,132	4,962	6,170	3,574	2,144	1,430
	20 and over	111,231	61,228	50,003	49,455	34,338	15,117	61,776	26,890	34,886	21,423	15,823	5,600
SIKH.	Total ...	*6,691*	*5,525*	*1,166*	*3,002*	*2,774*	*228*	*3,689*	*2,751*	*938*	*209*	*176*	*33*
	0—10	789	411	378	43	19	24	746	392	354	1	...	1
	10—15	178	123	55	87	66	21	91	57	34	18	13	5
	15—20	543	451	92	229	187	42	314	264	50	23	13	10
	20 and over	5,181	4,540	641	2,643	2,502	141	2,538	2,038	500	167	150	17
JAIN.	Total ...	*495*	*416*	*79*	*207*	*187*	*20*	*288*	*229*	*59*	*51*	*48*	*3*
	0—10	33	14	19	5	3	2	28	11	17	...	...	...
	10—15	9	8	1	7	7	...	2	1	1	1	1	...
	15—20	43	30	13	25	22	3	18	8	10	11	10	1
	20 and over	410	364	46	170	155	15	240	209	31	39	37	2
ZOROASTRIAN.	Total ...	*300*	*195*	*105*	*221*	*148*	*73*	*79*	*47*	*32*	*181*	*124*	*57*
	0—10	51	29	22	11	7	4	40	22	18	9	6	3
	10—15	33	18	15	28	17	11	5	1	4	24	16	8
	15—20	18	9	9	15	6	9	3	3	...	13	5	8
	20 and over	198	139	59	167	118	49	31	21	10	135	97	38
JEW.	Total ...	*1,024*	*559*	*465*	*650*	*406*	*244*	*374*	*153*	*221*	*491*	*297*	*194*
	0—10	260	116	144	74	34	40	186	82	104	53	22	31
	10—15	121	59	62	91	45	46	30	14	16	77	36	41
	15—20	115	64	51	88	54	34	27	10	17	70	44	26
	20 and over	528	320	208	397	273	124	131	47	84	291	195	96
CONFUCIAN.	Total ...	*71*	*57*	*14*	*36*	*36*	...	*35*	*21*	*14*	*3*	*3*	...
	0—10	10	3	7	3	3	...	7	...	7	...	...	...
	10—15	3	1	2	1	1	...	2	...	2	...	...	...
	15—20	4	4	...	3	3	...	1	1	...	1	1	...
	20 and over	54	49	5	29	29	...	25	20	5	2	2	...
SECULARIST, RATIONALIST, AND AGNOSTIC.	Total ...	*45*	*27*	*18*	*45*	*27*	*18*	...	...	...	*45*	*27*	*18*
	0—10	3	2	1	3	2	1	...	...	...	3	2	1
	10—15	4	3	1	4	3	1	...	...	...	4	3	1
	15—20	5	4	1	5	4	1	...	...	...	4	3	1
	20 and over	33	18	15	33	18	15	...	...	...	34	19	15

IMPERIAL TABLE VIII.—*Education by Religion and Age.*

PART A.—PROVINCIAL SUMMARY (Burma Proper).

Religion.	AGE.	Population. Total. Persons.	Total. Males.	Total. Females.	Literate. Persons.	Literate. Males.	Literate. Females.	Illiterate. Persons.	Illiterate. Males.	Illiterate. Females.	Literate in English. Persons.	Literate in English. Males.	Literate in English. Females.
1	2	3	4	5	6	7	8	9	10	11	12	13	14
ALL RELIGIONS.	TOTAL ...	*10,610,256*	*5,432,715*	*5,177,541*	*2,599,778*	*2,245,898*	*353,880*	*8,010,478*	*3,186,817*	*4,823,661*	*67,098*	*55,143*	*11,955*
	0—10	2,784,877	1,373,585	1,411,292	60,690	42,860	17,830	2,724,187	1,330,725	1,393,462	2,535	1,480	1,055
	10—15	1,228,264	636,557	591,707	246,101	197,460	48,641	982,163	439,097	543,066	6,464	4,638	1,826
	15—20	989,849	486,948	502,901	315,320	254,110	61,210	674,529	232,838	441,691	9,774	7,841	1,933
	20 and over	5,607,266	2,935,625	2,671,641	1,977,667	1,751,468	226,199	3,629,599	1,184,157	2,445,442	48,325	41,184	7,141
BUDDHIST.	TOTAL ...	*9,273,865*	*4,561,249*	*4,712,616*	*2,357,431*	*2,045,338*	*312,093*	*6,916,434*	*2,515,911*	*4,400,523*	*21,033*	*19,763*	*1,270*
	0—10	2,518,452	1,237,143	1,281,309	53,426	38,493	14,933	2,465,026	1,198,650	1,266,376	307	239	68
	10—15	1,114,256	570,467	543,789	228,355	185,439	42,916	885,901	385,028	500,873	2,239	1,984	255
	15—20	868,671	411,143	457,528	290,260	235,873	54,387	578,411	175,270	403,141	4,389	4,098	291
	20 and over	4,772,486	2,342,496	2,429,990	1,785,390	1,585,533	199,857	2,987,096	756,963	2,230,133	14,098	13,442	656
ANIMIST.	TOTAL ...	*328,613*	*183,403*	*145,210*	*20,019*	*19,167*	*852*	*308,594*	*164,236*	*144,358*	*467*	*440*	*27*
	0—10	74,968	39,010	35,958	260	222	38	74,708	38,788	35,920	19	19	...
	10—15	33,097	18,014	15,083	918	810	108	32,179	17,204	14,975	28	24	4
	15—20	29,282	15,486	13,796	1,362	1,226	136	27,920	14,260	13,660	77	75	2
	20 and over	191,266	110,893	80,373	17,479	16,909	570	173,787	93,984	79,803	343	322	21
HINDU.	TOTAL ...	*382,288*	*306,700*	*75,588*	*73,187*	*69,192*	*3,995*	*309,101*	*237,508*	*71,593*	*9,092*	*8,690*	*402*
	0—10	42,878	22,476	20,402	1,221	907	314	41,657	21,569	20,088	172	134	38
	10—15	18,214	12,748	5,466	2,866	2,443	423	15,348	10,305	5,043	502	439	63
	15—20	31,347	24,969	6,378	5,791	5,114	677	25,556	19,855	5,701	848	774	74
	20 and over	289,849	246,507	43,342	63,309	60,728	2,581	226,540	185,779	40,761	7,570	7,343	227
MAHOMEDAN.	TOTAL ...	*417,575*	*269,085*	*148,490*	*74,210*	*62,685*	*11,525*	*343,365*	*206,400*	*136,965*	*5,853*	*5,136*	*717*
	0—10	96,731	49,119	47,612	1,702	1,163	539	95,029	47,956	47,073	120	96	24
	10—15	38,881	22,796	16,085	5,014	3,664	1,350	33,867	19,132	14,735	441	365	76
	15—20	40,293	25,097	15,196	8,320	6,511	1,809	31,973	18,586	13,387	793	691	102
	20 and over	241,670	172,073	69,597	59,174	51,347	7,827	182,496	120,726	61,770	4,499	3,984	515
CHRISTIAN.	TOTAL ...	*199,680*	*105,815*	*93,865*	*70,900*	*46,061*	*24,839*	*128,780*	*59,754*	*69,026*	*29,680*	*20,445*	*9,235*
	0—10	50,773	25,298	25,475	3,946	2,008	1,938	46,827	23,290	23,537	1,851	962	889
	10—15	23,476	12,327	11,149	8,731	4,966	3,765	14,745	7,361	7,384	3,130	1,757	1,373
	15—20	19,536	9,698	9,838	9,223	5,111	4,112	10,313	4,587	5,726	3,545	2,127	1,418
	20 and over	105,895	58,492	47,403	49,000	33,976	15,024	56,895	24,516	32,379	21,154	15,599	5,555
SIKH.	TOTAL ...	*6,301*	*5,210*	*1,091*	*2,873*	*2,652*	*221*	*3,428*	*2,558*	*870*	*203*	*171*	*32*
	0—10	718	375	343	39	18	21	679	357	322	1	...	1
	10—15	170	116	54	86	65	21	84	51	33	18	13	5
	15—20	535	444	91	228	186	42	307	258	49	23	13	10
	20 and over	4,878	4,275	603	2,520	2,383	137	2,358	1,892	466	161	145	16
JAIN.	TOTAL ...	*495*	*416*	*79*	*207*	*187*	*20*	*288*	*229*	*59*	*51*	*48*	*3*
	0—10	33	14	19	5	3	2	28	11	17	...	...	...
	10—15	9	8	1	7	7	...	2	1	1	1	1	...
	15—20	43	30	13	25	22	3	18	8	10	11	10	1
	20 and over	410	364	46	170	155	15	240	209	31	39	37	2
ZOROASTRIAN.	TOTAL ...	*300*	*195*	*105*	*221*	*148*	*73*	*79*	*47*	*32*	*181*	*124*	*57*
	0—10	51	29	22	11	7	4	40	22	18	9	6	3
	10—15	33	18	15	28	17	11	5	1	4	24	16	8
	15—20	18	9	9	15	6	9	3	3	...	13	5	8
	20 and over	198	139	59	167	118	49	31	21	10	135	97	38
JEW.	TOTAL ...	*1,024*	*559*	*465*	*650*	*406*	*244*	*374*	*153*	*221*	*491*	*297*	*194*
	0—10	260	116	144	74	34	40	186	82	104	53	22	31
	10—15	121	59	62	91	45	46	30	14	16	77	36	41
	15—20	115	64	51	88	54	34	27	10	17	70	44	26
	20 and over	528	320	208	397	273	124	131	47	84	291	195	96
CONFUCIAN.	TOTAL ...	*71*	*57*	*14*	*36*	*36*	...	*35*	*21*	*14*	*3*	*3*	...
	0—10	10	3	7	3	3	...	7	...	7	...	...	...
	10—15	3	1	2	1	1	...	2	...	2	...	...	...
	15—20	4	4	...	3	3	...	1	1	...	1	1	...
	20 and over	54	49	5	29	29	...	25	20	5	2	2	...
SECULARIST, RATIONALIST, AND AGNOSTIC.	TOTAL ...	*44*	*26*	*18*	*44*	*26*	*18*	...	...	...	*44*	*26*	*18*
	0—10	3	2	1	3	2	1	...	...	...	3	2	1
	10—15	4	3	1	4	3	1	...	...	...	4	3	1
	15—20	5	4	1	5	4	1	...	...	...	4	3	1
	20 and over	32	17	15	32	17	15	...	...	...	33	18	15

IMPERIAL TABLE VIII.—*Education by Religion and Age.*

PART A.—PROVINCIAL SUMMARY (Specially Administered Territories).

Religion.	AGE.	POPULATION. Total. Persons.	Total. Males.	Total. Females.	Literate. Persons.	Literate. Males.	Literate. Females.	Illiterate. Persons.	Illiterate. Males.	Illiterate. Females.	LITERATE IN ENGLISH. Persons.	Males.	Females.
1	2	3	4	5	6	7	8	9	10	11	12	13	14
ALL RELIGIONS.	TOTAL ...	*1,428,827*	*712,756*	*716,071*	*71,100*	*66,985*	*4,115*	*1,357,727*	*645,771*	*711,956*	739	660	79
	0—10	384,650	192,640	192,010	1,070	682	388	383,580	191,958	191,622	27	18	9
	10—15	149,245	77,843	71,402	7,032	6,624	408	142,213	71,219	70,994	33	27	6
	15—20	128,158	61,800	66,358	9,178	8,574	604	118,980	53,226	65,754	49	37	12
	20 and over	766,774	380,473	386,301	53,820	51,105	2,715	712,954	329,368	383,586	630	578	52
BUDDHIST.	TOTAL ...	*1,110,679*	*552,188*	*558,491*	*66,198*	*62,400*	*3,798*	*1,044,481*	*489,788*	*554,693*	*156*	*153*	*3*
	0—10	298,772	148,579	150,193	972	617	355	297,800	147,962	149,838	6	6	...
	10—15	118,696	61,710	56,986	6,761	6,384	377	111,935	55,326	56,609	8	8	...
	15—20	100,728	48,683	52,045	8,825	8,269	556	91,903	40,414	51,489	10	10	...
	20 and over	592,483	293,216	299,267	49,640	47,130	2,510	542,843	246,086	296,757	132	129	3
ANIMIST.	TOTAL ...	*296,926*	*146,867*	*150,059*	*440*	*421*	*19*	*296,486*	*146,446*	*150,040*	*3*	*3*	...
	0—10	81,033	41,629	39,404	1	...	1	81,032	41,629	39,403	...	...	...
	10—15	29,122	15,372	13,750	18	18	...	29,104	15,354	13,750	...	...	...
	15—20	25,928	12,262	13,666	56	48	8	25,872	12,214	13,658	...	...	...
	20 and over	160,843	77,604	83,239	365	355	10	160,478	77,249	83,229	3	3	...
HINDU.	TOTAL ...	*7,240*	*5,835*	*1,405*	*2,718*	*2,643*	75	*4,522*	*3,192*	*1,330*	*168*	*168*	...
	0—10	1,090	586	504	34	29	5	1,056	557	499	5	5	...
	10—15	245	147	98	64	60	4	181	87	94	5	5	...
	15—20	343	247	96	119	112	7	224	135	89	8	8	...
	20 and over	5,562	4,855	707	2,501	2,442	59	3,061	2,413	648	150	150	...
MAHOMEDAN.	TOTAL ...	*3,194*	*2,336*	*858*	*818*	*770*	*48*	*2,376*	*1,566*	*810*	*71*	*68*	*3*
	0—10	604	328	276	11	9	2	593	319	274	...	...	...
	10—15	134	81	53	17	16	1	117	65	52	...	...	...
	15—20	210	131	79	55	49	6	155	82	73	2	2	...
	20 and over	2,246	1,796	450	735	696	39	1,511	1,100	411	69	66	3
CHRISTIAN.	TOTAL ...	*10,397*	*5,214*	*5,183*	*796*	*628*	*168*	*9,601*	*4,586*	*5,015*	*334*	*262*	*72*
	0—10	3,080	1,482	1,598	48	26	22	3,032	1,456	1,576	16	7	9
	10—15	1,040	526	514	171	145	26	869	381	488	20	14	6
	15—20	941	470	471	122	95	27	819	375	444	29	17	12
	20 and over	5,336	2,736	2,600	455	362	93	4,881	2,374	2,507	269	224	45
SIKH.	TOTAL ...	*390*	*315*	*75*	*129*	*122*	*7*	*261*	*193*	*68*	*6*	*5*	*1*
	0—10	71	36	35	4	1	3	67	35	32	...	...	...
	10—15	8	7	1	1	1	...	7	6	1	...	...	...
	15—20	8	7	1	1	1	...	7	6	1	...	...	...
	20 and over	303	265	38	123	119	4	180	146	34	6	5	1
SECULARIST, RATIONALIST, AND AGNOSTIC.	TOTAL ...	*1*	*1*	...	*1*	*1*	...	...	...	...	*1*	*1*	...
	0—10	...	...	...	...	...	...	...	...	...	...	...	...
	10—15	...	...	...	...	...	...	...	...	...	...	...	...
	15—20	...	...	...	...	...	...	...	...	...	...	...	...
	20 and over	1	1	...	1	1	...	...	...	...	1	1	...

IMPERIAL TABLE VIII.

Education by Religion and Age.

PART B.—DETAILS BY DISTRICTS.

NOTE.—Figures for Mandalay City are separately given.

IMPERIAL TABLE VIII.—*Education by Religion and Age.*

PART B.—DETAILS BY DISTRICTS.

District.	AGE.	POPULATION. Total. Persons.	Total. Males.	Total. Females.	Literate. Persons.	Literate. Males.	Literate. Females.	Illiterate. Persons.	Illiterate. Males.	Illiterate. Females.	LITERATE IN ENGLISH. Persons.	Males.	Females.
1	2	3	4	5	6	7	8	9	10	11	12	13	14
AKYAB.	*All Religions* ...	*529,943*	*289,474*	*240,469*	*79,229*	*72,879*	*6,350*	*450,714*	*216,595*	*234,119*	*1,519*	*1,866*	*158*
	0—10	135,951	68,318	67,633	1,040	760	280	134,911	67,558	67,353	40	26	14
	10—15	59,053	31,954	27,099	5,206	4,501	705	53,847	27,453	26,394	120	100	20
	15—20	49,729	26,270	23,459	7,694	6,940	754	42,035	19,330	22,705	219	194	25
	20 and over	285,210	162,932	122,278	65,289	60,678	4,611	219,921	102,254	117,667	1,140	1,046	94
	Buddhist ...	*302,527*	*154,935*	*147,592*	*67,831*	*61,917*	*5,914*	*234,696*	*93,018*	*141,678*	*778*	*741*	*82*
	0—10	73,630	36,944	36,686	851	628	223	72,779	36,316	36,463	8	6	2
	10—15	35,235	18,281	16,954	4,785	4,149	636	30,450	14,132	16,318	79	72	7
	15—20	28,116	13,964	14,152	6,784	6,084	700	21,332	7,880	13,452	140	133	7
	20 and over	165,546	85,746	79,800	55,411	51,056	4,355	110,135	34,690	75,445	546	530	16
	Animist ...	*33,896*	*17,501*	*16,395*	*429*	*421*	*8*	*33,467*	*17,080*	*16,387*	*6*	*6*	...
	0—10	8,181	3,931	4,250	16	15	1	8,165	3,916	4,249	...	...	...
	10—15	3,742	2,032	1,710	14	12	2	3,728	2,020	1,708	...	...	...
	15—20	3,269	1,589	1,680	19	19	...	3,250	1,570	1,680	1	1	...
	20 and over	18,704	9,949	8,755	380	375	5	18,324	9,574	8,750	5	5	...
	Hindu ...	*14,454*	*13,418*	*1,036*	*3,896*	*3,853*	*43*	*10,558*	*9,565*	*993*	*85*	*82*	*3*
	0—10	707	410	297	15	14	1	692	396	296	2	2	...
	10—15	418	320	98	60	57	3	358	263	95	2	1	1
	15—20	1,465	1,365	100	347	342	5	1,118	1,023	95	8	8	...
	20 and over	11,864	11,323	541	3,474	3,440	34	8,390	7,883	507	23	21	2
	Mahomedan ...	*178,381*	*103,124*	*75,257*	*6,578*	*6,322*	*256*	*171,803*	*96,802*	*75,001*	*228*	*220*	*8*
	0—10	53,332	26,979	26,353	126	84	42	53,206	26,895	26,311	2	...	2
	10—15	19,610	11,295	8,315	313	262	51	19,297	11,033	8,264	13	13	...
	15—20	16,821	9,316	7,505	504	473	31	16,317	8,843	7,474	36	34	2
	20 and over	88,618	55,534	33,084	5,635	5,503	132	82,983	50,031	32,952	177	173	4
NORTHERN ARAKAN.	*All Religions* ...	*22,234*	*11,405*	*10,829*	*726*	*691*	*35*	*21,508*	*10,714*	*10,794*	*21*	*18*	*3*
	0—10	4,970	2,515	2,455	1	1	...	4,969	2,514	2,455	...	...	...
	10—15	2,428	1,352	1,076	28	27	1	2,400	1,325	1,075	...	...	...
	15—20	2,169	1,045	1,124	56	53	3	2,113	992	1,121	1	1	...
	20 and over	12,667	6,493	6,174	641	610	31	12,026	5,883	6,143	20	17	3
	Buddhist ...	*1,795*	*997*	*798*	*406*	*385*	*21*	*1,389*	*612*	*777*	*13*	*12*	*1*
	0—10	433	206	227	1	1	...	432	205	227	...	...	...
	10—15	171	96	75	17	17	...	154	79	75	..	...	...
	15—20	184	108	76	45	42	3	139	66	73	1	1	...
	20 and over	1,007	587	420	343	325	18	664	262	402	12	11	1
	Animist ...	*19,821*	*9,977*	*9,844*	*50*	*50*		*19,771*	*9,927*	*9,844*	...	...	...
	0—10	4,429	2,252	2,177	...	...	...	4,429	2,252	2,177	...	...	...
	10—15	2,203	1,223	980	..	...	...	2,203	1,223	980	...	...	...
	15—20	1,942	915	1,027	1	1	...	1,941	914	1,027	...	...	...
	20 and over	11,247	5,587	5,660	49	49	...	11,198	5,538	5,660	...	...	...
KYAUKPYU.	*All Religions* ...	*184,916*	*89,571*	*95,345*	*28,468*	*26,137*	*2,331*	*156,448*	*63,434*	*93,014*	*209*	*194*	*15*
	0—10	46,146	23,008	23,138	428	341	87	45,718	22,667	23,051	2	1	1
	10—15	19,888	10,208	9,680	1,738	1,519	219	18,150	8,689	9,461	5	4	1
	15—20	16,889	8,021	8,868	2,726	2,438	288	14,163	5,583	8,580	17	14	3
	20 and over	101,993	48,334	53,659	23,576	21,839	1,737	78,417	26,495	51,922	185	175	10
	Buddhist ...	*165,864*	*79,099*	*86,765*	*27,736*	*25,512*	*2,224*	*138,128*	*53,587*	*84,541*	*165*	*156*	*9*
	0—10	40,991	20,370	20,621	413	334	79	40,578	20,036	20,542	...	...	...
	10—15	18,135	9,231	8,904	1,694	1,497	197	16,441	7,734	8,707	4	4	...
	15—20	15,251	7,188	8,063	2,652	2,386	266	12,599	4,802	7,797	15	12	3
	20 and over	91,487	42,310	49,177	22,977	21,295	1,682	68,510	21,015	47,495	146	140	6
	Animist ...	*14,726*	*7,718*	*7,008*	*88*	*76*	*12*	*14,638*	*7,642*	*6,996*	...	...	...
	0—10	4,449	2,244	2,205	2	1	1	4,447	2,243	2,204	...	...	...
	10—15	1,409	803	606	4	1	3	1,405	802	603	...	...	...
	15—20	1,257	609	648	7	4	3	1,250	605	645	...	...	...
	20 and over	7,611	4,062	3,549	75	70	5	7,536	3,992	3,544	...	...	...
	Mahomedan ...	*3,641*	*2,130*	*1,511*	*490*	*405*	*85*	*3,151*	*1,725*	*1,426*	*20*	*18*	*2*
	0—10	656	369	287	8	4	4	648	365	283	...	...	...
	10—15	317	152	165	33	15	18	284	137	147	...	...	...
	15—20	328	175	153	51	33	18	277	142	135	1	1	...
	20 and over	2,340	1,434	906	398	353	45	1,942	1,081	861	19	17	2

IMPERIAL TABLE VIII.—*Education by Religion and Age.*

PART B.—DETAILS BY DISTRICTS.

District.	AGE.	POPULATION.									LITERATE IN ENGLISH.		
		Total.			Literate.			Illiterate.					
		Persons.	Males.	Females.	Persons.	Males.	Females.	Persons.	Males.	Females.	Persons.	Males.	Females.
1	2	3	4	5	6	7	8	9	10	11	12	13	14
SANDOWAY.	***All Religions*** ...	***102,803***	***51,475***	***51,328***	***19,931***	***17,873***	***2,058***	***82,872***	***33,602***	***49,270***	***249***	***237***	***12***
	0—10	28,165	14,038	14,127	301	211	90	27,864	13,827	14,037	4	3	1
	10—15	12,131	6,449	5,682	1,624	1,351	273	10,507	5,098	5,409	23	23	...
	15—20	10,278	4,965	5,313	2,417	2,049	368	7,861	2,916	4,945	44	43	1
	20 and over	52,229	26,023	26,206	15,589	14,262	1,327	36,640	11,761	24,879	178	168	10
	Buddhist ...	***91,062***	***45,220***	***45,842***	***18,461***	***16,646***	***1,815***	***72,601***	***28,574***	***44,027***	***90***	***89***	***1***
	0—10	25,062	12,480	12,582	255	181	74	24,807	12,299	12,508	1	1	...
	10—15	10,833	5,747	5,086	1,448	1,215	233	9,385	4,532	4,853	11	11	...
	15—20	9,179	4,435	4,744	2,259	1,931	328	6,920	2,504	4,416	19	19	...
	20 and over	45,988	22,558	23,430	14,499	13,319	1,180	31,489	9,239	22,250	59	58	1
	Animist ...	***6,632***	***3,430***	***3,202***	***231***	***218***	***13***	***6,401***	***3,212***	***3,189***	***2***	***2***	...
	0—10	1,817	929	888	...	...	...	1,817	929	888	...	...	...
	10—15	740	387	353	13	13	...	727	374	353	...	...	...
	15—20	616	281	335	12	12	...	604	269	335	...	...	...
	20 and over	3,459	1,833	1,626	206	193	13	3,253	1,640	1,613	2	2	...
	Mahomedan ...	***4,257***	***2,216***	***2,041***	***924***	***767***	***157***	***3,333***	***1,449***	***1,884***	***98***	***97***	***1***
	0—10	1,125	547	578	38	25	13	1,087	522	565	...	...	...
	10—15	503	285	218	128	101	27	375	184	191	9	9	...
	15—20	425	207	218	112	82	30	313	125	188	18	18	...
	20 and over	2,204	1,177	1,027	646	559	87	1,558	618	940	71	70	1
RANGOON.	***All Religions*** ...	***293,316***	***208,111***	***85,205***	***121,978***	***91,348***	***30,630***	***171,838***	***116,763***	***54,575***	***31,472***	***25,204***	***6,268***
	0—10	37.940	19,484	18,456	4,424	2,698	1,726	33,516	16,786	16,730	1,188	685	503
	10—15	20,426	12,370	8,056	10,303	6,876	3,427	10,123	5,494	4,629	3,050	2,180	870
	15—20	28,967	19,940	9,027	14,354	9,821	4,533	14,613	10,119	4,494	4,412	3,447	965
	20 and over	205,983	156,317	49,666	92,897	71,953	20,944	113,086	84,364	28,722	22,822	18,892	3,930
	Buddhist ...	***97,467***	***52,137***	***45,330***	***54,229***	***36,923***	***17,306***	***43,238***	***15,214***	***28,024***	***7,888***	***7,252***	***636***
	0—10	18,935	9,554	9,381	2,178	1,364	814	16,757	8,190	8,567	153	114	39
	10—15	10,047	5,362	4.685	5,806	3,859	1,947	4,241	1,503	2,738	935	805	130
	15—20	10,162	5,327	4,835	7,104	4,505	2,599	3,058	822	2,236	1,715	1,572	143
	20 and over	58,323	31,894	26,429	39,141	27,195	11,946	19,182	4,699	14,483	5,085	4,761	324
	Animist ...	***7,217***	***5,936***	***1,281***	***3,099***	***2,956***	***143***	***4,118***	***2,980***	***1,138***	***208***	***200***	***8***
	0—10	675	404	271	23	19	4	652	385	267	4	4	...
	10—15	332	206	126	77	58	19	255	148	107	11	9	2
	15—20	549	428	121	221	194	27	328	234	94	23	22	1
	20 and over	5,661	4,898	763	2,778	2,685	93	2,883	2,213	670	170	165	5
	Hindu ...	***108,350***	***89,028***	***19,322***	***22,951***	***21,278***	***1,673***	***85,399***	***67,750***	***17,649***	***5,096***	***4,857***	***239***
	0—10	8,786	4,545	4,241	491	340	151	8,295	4,205	4,090	102	79	23
	10—15	4,655	3,312	1,343	1,050	859	191	3,605	2,453	1,152	304	273	31
	15—20	9,476	7,637	1,839	2,071	1,759	312	7.405	5,878	1,527	514	466	48
	20 and over	85,433	73,534	11,899	19,339	18,320	1,019	66,094	55,214	10,880	4,176	4,039	137
	Mahomedan ...	***54,634***	***45,106***	***9,528***	***23,164***	***17,721***	***5,443***	***31,470***	***27,385***	***4,085***	***3,395***	***2,740***	***655***
	0—10	5,022	2,723	2,299	598	394	204	4,424	2,329	2,095	58	39	19
	10—15	3,096	2,260	836	1,513	1,058	455	1.583	1,202	381	293	225	68
	15—20	6,136	5,070	1,066	2,797	2,099	698	3,339	2,971	368	456	365	91
	20 and over	40,380	35,053	5,327	18,256	14,170	4,086	22,124	20,883	1,241	2,588	2,111	477
	Christian ...	***23,044***	***13,977***	***9,067***	***16,920***	***11,186***	***5,734***	***6,124***	***2,791***	***3,333***	***14,259***	***9,747***	***4,512***
	0—10	4,154	2,094	2,060	1,054	542	512	3,100	1,552	1,548	820	424	396
	10—15	2,143	1,143	1,000	1,735	968	767	408	175	233	1,418	818	600
	15—20	2,375	1,277	1,098	1,987	1,137	850	388	140	248	1,628	977	651
	20 and over	14,372	9,463	4,909	12,144	8,539	3,605	2,228	924	1,304	10,393	7.528	2,865
HANTHAWADDY.	***All Religions*** ...	***539,109***	***295,886***	***243,223***	***181,142***	***145,897***	***35,245***	***357,967***	***149,989***	***207,978***	***3,172***	***2,609***	***563***
	0—10	135,054	66,429	68,625	5,437	3,715	1,722	129,617	62,714	66,903	107	55	52
	10—15	60,208	31,697	28,511	19,537	14,255	5,282	40,671	17,442	23,229	248	173	75
	15—20	51,597	27,202	24,395	23,376	16,814	6,562	28,221	10,388	17,833	399	320	79
	20 and over	292,250	170,558	121,692	132,792	111,113	21,679	159,458	59,445	100,013	2,418	2,061	357
	Buddhist ...	***447,638***	***227,611***	***220,027***	***160,694***	***127,916***	***32,778***	***286,944***	***99,695***	***187,249***	***810***	***753***	***57***
	0—10	121,201	59,203	61,998	4,922	3,400	1,522	116,279	55,803	60,476	6	3	3
	10—15	54,181	27,773	26,408	18,201	13,259	4,942	35,980	14,514	21,466	63	58	5
	15—20	43,584	21,103	22,481	21,374	15,196	6,178	22,210	5,907	16,303	134	124	10
	20 and over	228,672	119,532	109,140	116,197	96,061	20,136	112,475	23,471	89,004	607	568	39

IMPERIAL TABLE VIII.—*Education by Religion and Age.*

PART B.—DETAILS BY DISTRICTS.

District.	AGE.	Population. Total. Persons.	Males.	Females.	Literate. Persons.	Males.	Females.	Illiterate. Persons.	Males.	Females.	Literate in English. Persons.	Males.	Females.
1	2	3	4	5	6	7	8	9	10	11	12	13	14
HANTHAWADDY—*concluded.*	***Animist*** ...	*4,675*	*4,024*	*651*	*1,597*	*1,554*	*43*	*3,078*	*2,470*	*608*	*12*	*12*	...
	0—10	640	437	203	25	23	2	615	414	201	...	...	...
	10—15	253	200	53	71	67	4	182	133	49	...	...	...
	15—20	277	232	45	95	88	7	182	144	38	1	1	...
	20 and over	3,505	3,155	350	1,406	1,376	30	2,099	1,779	320	11	11	...
	Hindu ..	*57,137*	*44,951*	*12,186*	*9,579*	*9,083*	*496*	*47,558*	*35,868*	*11,690*	*572*	*557*	*15*
	0—10	7,326	3,846	3,480	150	109	41	7,176	3,737	3,439	10	9	1
	10—15	3,066	2,171	895	402	357	45	2,664	1,814	850	37	35	2
	15—20	4,855	3,890	965	814	729	85	4,041	3,161	880	68	67	1
	20 and over	41,890	35,044	6,846	8,213	7,888	325	33,677	27,156	6,521	457	446	11
	Mahomedan ...	*16,307*	*12,023*	*4,284*	*4,458*	*4,082*	*376*	*11,849*	*7,941*	*3,908*	*165*	*160*	*5*
	0—10	2,727	1,427	1,300	79	56	23	2,648	1,371	1,277	...	...	...
	10—15	1,260	790	470	325	265	60	935	525	410	4	4	...
	15—20	1,745	1,332	413	543	469	74	1,202	863	339	13	12	1
	20 and over	10,575	8,474	2,101	3,511	3,292	219	7,064	5,182	1,882	148	144	4
	Christian ...	*12,647*	*6,733*	*5,914*	*4,524*	*2,994*	*1,530*	*8,123*	*3,739*	*4,384*	*1,572*	*1,093*	*479*
	0—10	3,079	1,471	1,608	255	125	130	2,824	1,346	1,478	91	43	48
	10—15	1,417	742	675	518	291	227	899	451	448	141	75	66
	15—20	1,087	611	476	524	309	215	563	302	261	176	110	66
	20 and over	7,064	3,909	3,155	3,227	2,269	958	3,837	1,640	2,197	1,164	865	299
THARRAWADDY.	***All Religions*** ...	*433,320*	*216,442*	*216,878*	*128,459*	*110,007*	*18,452*	*304,861*	*106,435*	*198,426*	*1,251*	*1,083*	*168*
	0—10	119,816	58,857	60,959	2,988	2,117	871	116,828	56,740	60,088	49	29	20
	10—15	53,783	27,659	26,124	14,076	11,148	2,928	39,707	16,511	23,196	203	159	44
	15—20	40,664	19,572	21,092	16,766	13,291	3,475	23,898	6,281	17,617	284	265	19
	20 and over	219,057	110,354	108,703	94,629	83,451	11,178	124,428	26,903	97,525	715	630	85
	Buddhist ...	*413,584*	*202,639*	*210,945*	*122,940*	*105,492*	*17,448*	*290,644*	*97,147*	*193,497*	*626*	*599*	*27*
	0—10	116,381	57,036	59,345	2,797	2,007	790	113,584	55,029	58,555	9	8	1
	10—15	52,144	26,655	25,489	13,485	10,745	2,740	38,659	15,910	22,749	83	79	4
	15—20	39,011	18,493	20,518	16,129	12,845	3,284	22,882	5,648	17,234	169	168	1
	20 and over	206,048	100,455	105,593	90,529	79,895	10,634	115,519	20,560	94,959	365	344	21
	Animist ...	*2,376*	*1,965*	*411*	*702*	*683*	*19*	*1,674*	*1,282*	*392*	*5*	*5*	...
	0—10	423	287	136	17	16	1	406	271	135	...	...	...
	10—15	169	135	34	47	46	1	122	89	33	1	1	...
	15—20	121	92	29	30	27	3	91	65	26	1	1	...
	20 and over	1,663	1,451	212	608	594	14	1,055	857	198	3	3	...
	Hindu ...	*7,406*	*6,125*	*1,281*	*1,390*	*1,347*	*43*	*6,016*	*4,778*	*1,238*	*92*	*89*	*3*
	0—10	787	437	350	17	14	3	770	423	347	2	2	...
	10—15	328	254	74	50	45	5	278	209	69	2	2	...
	15—20	543	451	92	83	75	8	460	376	84	5	5	...
	20 and over	5,748	4,983	765	1,240	1,213	27	4,508	3,770	738	83	80	3
	Mahomedan ...	*3,857*	*2,667*	*1,190*	*1,073*	*952*	*121*	*2,784*	*1,715*	*1,069*	*59*	*59*	...
	0—10	752	379	373	26	16	10	726	363	363	3	3	...
	10—15	328	196	132	87	69	18	241	127	114	5	5	...
	15—20	324	200	124	115	97	18	209	103	106	8	8	...
	20 and over	2,453	1,892	561	845	770	75	1,608	1,122	486	43	43	...
	Christian ...	*6,052*	*3,011*	*3,041*	*2,330*	*1,516*	*814*	*3,722*	*1,495*	*2,227*	*460*	*324*	*136*
	0—10	1,469	714	755	131	64	67	1,338	650	688	34	15	19
	10—15	814	419	395	407	243	164	407	176	231	112	72	40
	15—20	663	335	328	407	246	161	256	89	167	100	83	17
	20 and over	3,106	1,543	1,563	1,385	963	422	1,721	580	1,141	214	154	60
PEGU.	***All Religions*** ...	*429,121*	*229,540*	*199,581*	*135,121*	*110,863*	*24,258*	*294,000*	*118,677*	*175,323*	*1,548*	*1,377*	*171*
	0—10	112,594	55,916	56,678	3,964	2,745	1,219	108,630	53,171	55,459	28	21	7
	10—15	50,904	27,203	23,701	15,217	11,697	3,520	35,687	15,506	20,181	152	137	15
	15—20	40,994	20,384	20,610	17,476	12,976	4,500	23,518	7,408	16,110	240	206	34
	20 and over	224,629	126,037	98,592	98,464	83,445	15,019	126,165	42,592	83,573	1,128	1,013	115
	Buddhist ...	*369,612*	*188,279*	*181,333*	*123,676*	*101,124*	*22,552*	*245,936*	*87,155*	*158,781*	*707*	*684*	*23*
	0—10	101,644	50,168	51,476	3,694	2,565	1,129	97,950	47,603	50,347	9	9	...
	10—15	46,274	24,211	22,063	14,311	11,031	3,280	31,963	13,180	18,783	88	87	1
	15—20	36,097	17,052	19,045	16,331	12,125	4,206	19,766	4,927	14,839	142	137	5
	20 and over	185,597	96,848	88,749	89,340	75,403	13,937	96,257	21,445	74,812	468	451	17

IMPERIAL TABLE VIII—*Education by Religion and Age.*

PART B.—DETAILS BY DISTRICTS.

District.	AGE.	Population. Total. Persons.	Total. Males.	Total. Females.	Literate. Persons.	Literate. Males.	Literate. Females.	Illiterate. Persons.	Illiterate. Males.	Illiterate. Females.	Literate in English. Persons.	Literate in English. Males.	Literate in English. Females.
1	2	3	4	5	6	7	8	9	10	11	12	13	14
PEGU—*concluded.*	***Animist*** ...	*5,391*	*4,110*	*1,281*	*1,381*	*1,352*	*29*	*4,010*	*2,758*	*1,252*	*12*	*12*	...
	0—10	989	608	381	23	20	3	966	588	378	...	...	...
	10—15	399	297	102	58	53	5	341	244	97	1	1	...
	15—20	398	270	128	78	75	3	320	195	125	5	5	...
	20 and over	3,605	2,935	670	1,222	1,204	18	2,383	1,731	652	6	6	...
	Hindu ...	*34,850*	*25,857*	*8,993*	*4,261*	*4,118*	*143*	*30,089*	*21,239*	*8,850*	*239*	*237*	*2*
	0—10	5,413	2,874	2,539	60	54	6	5,353	2,820	2,533	1	1	...
	10—15	2,130	1,493	637	204	188	16	1,926	1,305	621	15	15	...
	15—20	2,693	2,039	654	351	325	26	2,342	1,714	628	16	15	1
	20 and over	24,114	18,951	5,163	3,646	3,551	95	20,468	15,400	5,068	207	206	1
	Mahomedan ...	*7,384*	*5,399*	*1,985*	*2,302*	*2,115*	*187*	*5,082*	*3,284*	*1,798*	*119*	*117*	*2*
	0—10	1,338	698	640	47	38	9	1,291	660	631	1	1	...
	10—15	594	383	211	170	147	23	424	236	188	4	4	...
	15—20	623	438	185	228	192	36	395	246	149	6	6	...
	20 and over	4,829	3,880	949	1,857	1,738	119	2,972	2,142	830	108	106	2
	Christian ...	*12,316*	*6,341*	*5,975*	*3,492*	*2,146*	*1,346*	*8,824*	*4,195*	*4,629*	*468*	*324*	*144*
	0—10	3,204	1,567	1,637	140	68	72	3,064	1,499	1,565	16	9	7
	10—15	1,502	815	687	474	278	196	1,028	537	491	44	30	14
	15—20	1,181	585	596	488	259	229	693	326	367	71	43	28
	20 and over	6,429	3,374	3,055	2,390	1,541	849	4,039	1,833	2,206	337	242	95
PROME.	***All Religions*** ...	*378,871*	*186,213*	*192,658*	*103,691*	*91,832*	*11,859*	*275,180*	*94,381*	*180,799*	*786*	*713*	*73*
	0—10	98,546	48,443	50,103	1,815	1,116	699	96,731	47,327	49,404	9	6	3
	10—15	46,776	23,765	23,011	10,237	8,264	1,973	36,539	15,501	21,038	48	36	12
	15—20	36,719	17,641	19,078	13,410	11,263	2,147	23,309	6,378	16,931	116	109	7
	20 and over	196,830	96,364	100,466	78,229	71,189	7,040	118,601	25,175	93,426	613	562	51
	Buddhist ...	*359,880*	*173,940*	*185,940*	*100,205*	*88,801*	*11,404*	*259,675*	*85,139*	*174,536*	*479*	*460*	*19*
	0—10	94,777	46,539	48,238	1,742	1,077	665	93,035	45,462	47,573	1	1	...
	10—15	45,183	22,885	22,298	10,025	8,123	1,902	35,158	14,762	20,396	31	24	7
	15—20	35,103	16,665	18,438	13,085	11,002	2,083	22,018	5,663	16,355	93	89	4
	20 and over	184,817	87,851	96,966	75,353	68,599	6,754	109,464	19,252	90,212	354	346	8
	Animist ...	*9,304*	*5,096*	*4,208*	*855*	*831*	*24*	*8,449*	*4,265*	*4,184*	*6*	*6*	...
	0—10	2,437	1,236	1,201	...	...	...	2,437	1,236	1,201	...	...	...
	10—15	976	502	474	42	37	5	934	465	469	1	1	...
	15—20	768	377	391	62	59	3	706	318	388	2	2	..
	20 and over	5,123	2,981	2,142	751	735	16	4,372	2,246	2,126	3	3	...
	Hindu ..	*5,152*	*4,286*	*866*	*914*	*879*	*35*	*4,238*	*3,407*	*831*	*55*	*52*	*3*
	0—10	434	219	215	6	6	...	428	213	215	1	1	...
	10—15	232	172	60	24	20	4	208	152	56	2	1	1
	15—20	439	350	89	74	65	9	365	285	80	3	2	1
	20 and over	4,047	3,545	502	810	788	22	3,237	2,757	480	49	48	1
	Mahomedan ...	*3,536*	*2,359*	*1,177*	*1,221*	*999*	*222*	*2,315*	*1,360*	*955*	*57*	*55*	*2*
	0—10	645	329	316	36	18	18	609	311	298	1	1	...
	10—15	286	160	126	86	53	33	200	107	93	3	3	...
	15—20	343	210	133	150	109	41	193	101	92	6	6	...
	20 and over	2,262	1,660	602	949	819	130	1,313	841	472	47	45	2
BASSEIN.	***All Religions*** ...	*440,993*	*226,778*	*214,215*	*122,055*	*100,692*	*21,363*	*318,933*	*126,081*	*192,852*	*1,769*	*1,429*	*340*
	0—10	115,624	56,611	59,013	3,012	1,986	1,026	112,612	54,625	57,987	31	15	16
	10—15	55,772	29,119	26,653	12,103	9,115	2,988	43,669	20,004	23,665	153	105	48
	15—20	44,086	21,129	22,957	16,361	12,397	3,964	27,725	8,732	18,993	344	258	86
	20 and over	225,506	119,914	105,592	90,579	77,194	13,385	134,927	42,720	92,207	1,241	1,051	190
	Buddhist ...	*391,027*	*194,614*	*196,413*	*109,367*	*91,448*	*17,919*	*281,660*	*103,166*	*178,494*	*573*	*548*	*25*
	0—10	106,013	51,786	54,227	2,642	1,794	848	103,371	49,992	53,379	6	4	2
	10—15	51,022	26,523	24,499	10,948	8,454	2,494	40,074	18,069	22,005	61	59	2
	15—20	39,346	18,373	20,973	14,750	11,433	3,317	24,596	6,940	17,656	138	135	3
	20 and over	194,646	97,932	96,714	81,027	69,767	11,260	113,619	28,165	85,454	368	350	18
	Animist ...	*2,049*	*1,864*	*185*	*625*	*606*	*19*	*1,424*	*1,258*	*166*	*12*	*12*	...
	0—10	260	216	44	...	...	...	260	216	44	...	...	...
	10—15	80	67	13	20	19	1	60	48	12	...	...	...
	15—20	121	101	20	6	1	5	115	100	15	1	1	...
	20 and over	1,588	1,480	108	599	586	13	989	894	95	11	11	...

IMPERIAL TABLE VIII.—*Education by Religion and Age.*

PART B.—DETAILS BY DISTRICTS.

District.	AGE.	POPULATION. Total. Persons.	Total. Males.	Total. Females.	Literate. Persons.	Literate. Males.	Literate. Females.	Illiterate. Persons.	Illiterate. Males.	Illiterate. Females.	LITERATE IN ENGLISH. Persons.	LITERATE IN ENGLISH. Males.	LITERATE IN ENGLISH. Females.
1	2	3	4	5	6	7	8	9	10	11	12	13	14
BASSEIN—*concluded.*	***Hindu*** ...	*11,822*	*10,471*	*1,351*	*1,703*	*1,646*	*57*	*10,119*	*8,825*	*1,294*	*100*	*95*	*5*
	0—10	651	352	299	4	2	2	647	350	297	...	...	...
	10—15	354	270	84	41	36	5	313	234	79	1	1	...
	15—20	907	782	125	105	99	6	802	683	119	10	9	1
	20 and over	9,910	9,067	843	1,553	1,509	44	8,357	7,558	799	89	85	4
	Mahomedan ...	*8,107*	*5,680*	*2,427*	*1,917*	*1,660*	*257*	*6,190*	*4,020*	*2,170*	*116*	*110*	*6*
	0—10	1,380	688	692	35	20	15	1,345	668	677	4	4	...
	10—15	631	350	281	107	85	22	524	265	259	5	4	1
	15—20	814	530	284	285	240	45	529	290	239	17	15	2
	20 and over	5,282	4,112	1,170	1,490	1,315	175	3,792	2,797	995	90	87	3
	Christian ...	*27,927*	*14,111*	*13,816*	*8,416*	*5,316*	*3,100*	*19,511*	*8,795*	*10,716*	*1,047*	*752*	*295*
	0—10	7,310	3,564	3,746	331	170	161	6,979	3,394	3,585	21	7	14
	10—15	3,676	1,906	1,770	982	520	462	2,694	1,386	1,308	82	40	42
	15—20	2,894	1,340	1,554	1,213	623	590	1,681	717	964	176	97	79
	20 and over	14,047	7,301	6,746	5,890	4,003	1,887	8,157	3,298	4,859	768	608	160
HENZADA.	***All Religions*** ...	*532,357*	*264,319*	*268,038*	*162,587*	*136,574*	*26,013*	*369,770*	*127,745*	*242,025*	*1,414*	*1,205*	*209*
	0—10	142,164	69,846	72,318	4,197	2,829	1,368	137,967	67,017	70,950	34	26	8
	10—15	71,404	38,535	32,869	18,176	14,359	3,817	53,228	24,176	29,052	208	167	41
	15—20	52,594	24,791	27,803	21,390	16,738	4,652	31,204	8,053	23,151	289	235	54
	20 and over	266,195	131,147	135,048	118,824	102,648	16,176	147,371	28,499	118,872	883	777	106
	Buddhist ...	*509,310*	*248,922*	*260,388*	*155,812*	*130,898*	*24,414*	*353,998*	*118,024*	*235,974*	*672*	*641*	*31*
	0—10	137,927	67,768	70,159	3,960	2,711	1,249	133,967	65,057	68,910	12	9	3
	10—15	69,329	37,325	32,004	17,418	13,865	3,553	51,911	23,460	28,451	102	95	7
	15—20	50,366	23,363	27,003	20,467	16,128	4,339	29,899	7,235	22,664	142	135	7
	20 and over	251,688	120,466	131,222	113,467	98,194	15,273	138,221	22,272	115,949	416	402	14
	Animist ...	*1,466*	*1,309*	*157*	*692*	*665*	*27*	*774*	*644*	*130*	*2*	*2*	...
	0—10	155	118	37	7	5	2	148	113	35	...	...	...
	10—15	72	61	11	20	20	...	52	41	11	...	...	...
	15—20	82	72	10	46	43	3	36	29	7	1	1	...
	20 and over	1,157	1,058	99	619	597	22	538	461	77	1	1	...
	Hindu ...	*6,600*	*5,912*	*688*	*1,524*	*1,470*	*54*	*5,076*	*4,442*	*634*	*110*	*105*	*5*
	0—10	422	234	188	13	8	5	409	226	183	...	...	...
	10—15	242	191	51	48	43	5	194	148	46	3	3	...
	15—20	581	520	61	113	105	8	468	415	53	5	4	1
	20 and over	5,355	4,967	388	1,350	1,314	36	4,005	3,653	352	102	98	4
	Mahomedan ...	*4,657*	*3,074*	*1,583*	*1,464*	*1,265*	*199*	*3,193*	*1,809*	*1,384*	*64*	*63*	*1*
	0—10	1,006	481	525	40	26	14	966	455	511	1	1	...
	10—15	418	231	187	108	80	28	310	151	159	3	3	...
	15—20	454	290	164	180	136	44	274	154	120	6	6	...
	20 and over	2,779	2,072	707	1,136	1,023	113	1,643	1,049	594	54	53	1
	Christian ...	*10,285*	*5,070*	*5,215*	*3,572*	*2,257*	*1,315*	*6,713*	*2,813*	*3,900*	*564*	*393*	*171*
	0—10	2,650	1,244	1,406	175	79	96	2,475	1,165	1,310	21	16	5
	10—15	1,342	727	615	581	351	230	761	376	385	99	66	33
	15—20	1,109	544	565	584	326	258	525	218	307	135	89	46
	20 and over	5,184	2,555	2,629	2,232	1,501	731	2,952	1,054	1,898	309	222	87
MYAUNGMYA.	***All Religions*** ...	*334,852*	*176,465*	*158,387*	*91,953*	*76,482*	*15,471*	*242,899*	*99,983*	*142,916*	*629*	*535*	*94*
	0—10	91,464	45,036	46,428	2,148	1,473	675	89,316	43,563	45,753	15	13	2
	10—15	40,128	20,879	19,249	8,619	6,603	2,016	31,509	14,276	17,233	69	54	15
	15—20	31,788	15,930	15,858	11,103	8,368	2,735	20,685	7,562	13,123	98	81	17
	20 and over	171,472	94,620	76,852	70,083	60,038	10,045	101,389	34,582	66,807	447	387	60
	Buddhist ...	*300,515*	*153,362*	*147,153*	*83,748*	*70,123*	*13,625*	*216,767*	*83,239*	*133,528*	*335*	*302*	*33*
	0—10	84,298	41,341	42,957	1,952	1,363	589	82,346	39,978	42,368	7	7	...
	10—15	37,015	19,078	17,937	7,897	6,139	1,758	29,118	12,939	16,179	51	44	7
	15—20	28,608	13,817	14,791	10,237	7,798	2,439	18,371	6,019	12,352	76	63	13
	20 and over	150,594	79,126	71,468	63,662	54,823	8,839	86,932	24,303	62,629	201	188	13
	Animist ...	*2,922*	*2,683*	*239*	*1,074*	*1,055*	*19*	*1,848*	*1,628*	*220*	*6*	*6*	...
	0—10	353	294	59	11	9	2	342	285	57	...	...	...
	10—15	123	104	19	37	34	3	86	70	16	...	...	...
	15—20	149	139	10	50	49	1	99	90	9	1	1	...
	20 and over	2,297	2,146	151	976	963	13	1,321	1,183	138	5	5	...

IMPERIAL TABLE VIII.—*Education by Religion and Age.*

PART B.—DETAILS BY DISTRICTS.

District.	AGE.	POPULATION. Total. Persons.	Total. Males.	Total. Females.	Literate. Persons.	Literate. Males.	Literate. Females.	Illiterate. Persons.	Illiterate. Males.	Illiterate. Females.	LITERATE IN ENGLISH. Persons.	Males.	Females.
1	2	3	4	5	6	7	8	9	10	11	12	13	14
MYAUNGMYA—*concluded.*	***Hindu*** ...	***6,128***	***5,486***	***642***	***997***	***959***	***38***	***5,131***	***4,527***	***604***	***30***	***28***	***2***
	0—10	398	229	169	4	3	1	394	226	168	...	...	...
	10—15	265	235	30	37	36	1	228	199	29	...	...	...
	15—20	652	589	63	88	83	5	564	506	58	1	1	...
	20 and over	4,813	4,433	380	868	837	31	3,945	3,596	349	29	27	2
	Mahomedan ...	***7,103***	***5,694***	***1,409***	***1,459***	***1,378***	***86***	***5,644***	***4,321***	***1,323***	***24***	***24***	...
	0—10	1,033	541	492	15	10	5	1,018	531	487	...	...	...
	10—15	440	283	157	67	55	12	373	228	145	1	1	...
	15—20	688	552	136	115	102	13	573	450	123	1	1	...
	20 and over	4,942	4,318	624	1,262	1,206	56	3,680	3,112	568	22	22	...
	Christian ...	***18,157***	***9,218***	***8,939***	***4,664***	***2,962***	***1,702***	***13,493***	***6,256***	***7,237***	***234***	***175***	***59***
	0—10	5,379	2,630	2,749	166	88	78	5,213	2,542	2,671	8	6	2
	10—15	2,285	1,179	1,106	581	339	242	1,704	840	864	17	9	8
	15—20	1,689	832	857	612	335	277	1,077	497	580	19	15	4
	20 and over	8,804	4,577	4,227	3,305	2,200	1,105	5,499	2,377	3,122	190	145	45
MA-UBIN.	***All Religions*** ...	***305,073***	***155,715***	***149,358***	***91,806***	***75,519***	***16,287***	***213,267***	***80,196***	***133,071***	***733***	***640***	***93***
	0—10	82,279	40,468	41,811	2,866	1,962	904	79,413	38,506	40,907	8	5	3
	10—15	37,463	19,467	17,996	10,576	8,114	2,462	26,887	11,353	15,534	92	78	14
	15—20	29,525	14,376	15,149	11,908	8,945	2,963	17,617	5,431	12,186	171	145	26
	20 and over	155,806	81,404	74,402	66,456	56,498	9,958	89,350	24,906	64,444	462	412	50
	Buddhist ...	***282,669***	***140,611***	***142,058***	***86,028***	***70,826***	***15,202***	***196,641***	***69,785***	***126,856***	***411***	***390***	***21***
	0—10	78,021	38,294	39,727	2,702	1,873	829	75,319	36,421	38,898	5	3	2
	10—15	35,429	18,244	17,185	9,990	7,706	2,284	25,439	10,538	14,901	61	59	2
	15—20	27,453	13,037	14,416	11,231	8,489	2,742	16,222	4,548	11,674	112	104	8
	20 and over	141,766	71,036	70,730	62,105	52,758	9,347	79,661	18,278	61,383	233	224	9
	Animist ...	***1,651***	***1,475***	***176***	***524***	***504***	***20***	***1,127***	***971***	***156***	***2***	***2***	...
	0—10	186	136	50	2	2	...	184	134	50	...	...	...
	10—15	81	67	14	26	26	...	55	41	14	...	...	...
	15—20	109	99	10	42	38	4	67	61	6	...	...	...
	20 and over	1,275	1,173	102	454	438	16	821	735	86	2	2	...
	Hindu ...	***5,392***	***4,775***	***617***	***938***	***919***	***19***	***4,454***	***3,856***	***598***	***51***	***48***	***3***
	0—10	431	239	192	14	14	...	417	225	192	2	2	...
	10—15	229	185	44	26	24	2	203	161	42	...	...	...
	15—20	458	408	50	64	63	1	394	345	49	4	4	...
	20 and over	4,274	3,943	331	834	818	16	3,440	3,125	315	45	42	3
	Mahomedan ...	***4,864***	***3,615***	***1,249***	***1,325***	***1,232***	***93***	***3,539***	***2,383***	***1,156***	***43***	***41***	***2***
	0—10	871	437	434	26	13	13	845	424	421	...	...	...
	10—15	400	278	122	89	82	7	311	196	115	3	3	...
	15—20	452	333	119	151	133	18	301	200	101	11	11	...
	20 and over	3,141	2,567	574	1,059	1,004	55	2,082	1,563	519	29	27	2
	Christian ...	***10,474***	***5,217***	***5,257***	***2,990***	***2,037***	***953***	***7,484***	***3,180***	***4,304***	***226***	***159***	***67***
	0—10	2,770	1,362	1,408	122	60	62	2,648	1,302	1,346	1	...	1
	10—15	1,324	693	631	445	276	169	879	417	462	28	16	12
	15—20	1,048	495	553	420	222	198	628	273	355	44	26	18
	20 and over	5,332	2,667	2,665	2,003	1,479	524	3,329	1,188	2,141	153	117	36
PYAPÔN.	***All Religions*** ...	***256,215***	***139,641***	***116,574***	***92,510***	***77,430***	***15,080***	***163,705***	***62,211***	***101,494***	***467***	***418***	***49***
	0—10	67,372	33,136	34,236	2,393	1,733	660	64,979	31,403	33,576	3	3	...
	10—15	28,681	14,833	13,848	9,017	7,104	1,913	19,664	7,729	11,935	15	13	2
	15—20	24,264	12,750	11,514	11,782	8,901	2,881	12,482	3,849	8,633	72	63	9
	20 and over	135,898	78,922	56,976	69,318	59,692	9,626	66,580	19,230	47,350	377	339	38
	Buddhist ...	***229,418***	***119,368***	***110,050***	***86,168***	***71,959***	***14,209***	***143,250***	***47,409***	***95,841***	***232***	***232***	...
	0—10	63,118	30,863	32,255	2,258	1,639	619	60,860	29,224	31,636	...	...	...
	10—15	26,803	13,527	13,276	8,579	6,782	1,797	18,224	6,745	11,479	6	6	..
	15—20	21,827	10,871	10,956	11,188	8,455	2,733	10,639	2,416	8,223	43	43	...
	20 and over	117,670	64,107	53,563	64,143	55,083	9,060	53,527	9,024	44,503	183	183	...
	Animist ...	***3,580***	***3,118***	***462***	***1,156***	***1,121***	***35***	***2,424***	***1,997***	***427***	***5***	***5***	...
	0—10	437	314	123	15	13	2	422	301	121	...	...	...
	10—15	192	156	36	42	38	4	150	118	32	...	...	...
	15—20	272	262	10	77	75	2	195	187	8	1	1	...
	20 and over	2,679	2,386	293	1,022	995	27	1,657	1,391	266	4	4	...

Imperial Table VIII.—*Education by Religion and Age.*

PART B.—DETAILS BY DISTRICTS.

District.	Age.	Population. Total. Persons.	Total. Males.	Total. Females.	Literate. Persons.	Literate. Males.	Literate. Females.	Illiterate. Persons.	Illiterate. Males.	Illiterate. Females.	Literate in English. Persons.	Literate in English. Males.	Literate in English. Females.
1	2	3	4	5	6	7	8	9	10	11	12	13	14
PYAPÔN—*concluded.*	***Hindu*** ...	*12,164*	*9,869*	*2,295*	*1,976*	*1,910*	*66*	*10,188*	*7,959*	*2,229*	*53*	*53*	...
	0—10	1,453	781	672	30	27	3	1,423	754	669	...	...	...
	10—15	665	536	129	91	85	6	574	451	123	...	...	...
	15—20	1,129	943	186	156	144	12	973	799	174	6	6	...
	20 and over	8,917	7,609	1,308	1,699	1,654	45	7,218	5,955	1,263	47	47	...
	Mahomedan ...	*3,540*	*3,052*	*488*	*915*	*860*	*55*	*2,625*	*2,192*	*433*	*16*	*16*	...
	0—10	324	177	147	19	12	7	305	165	140	...	...	...
	10—15	168	123	45	36	31	5	132	92	40	...	...	...
	15—20	343	292	51	72	65	7	271	227	44	4	4	...
	20 and over	2,705	2,460	245	788	752	36	1,917	1,708	209	12	12	...
	Christian ...	*7,291*	*4,046*	*3,245*	*2,255*	*1,542*	*713*	*5,036*	*2,504*	*2,532*	*160*	*111*	*49*
	0—10	2,023	991	1,032	70	41	29	1,953	950	1,003	2	2	...
	10—15	839	478	361	267	166	101	572	312	260	9	7	2
	15—20	671	362	309	286	160	126	385	202	183	18	9	9
	20 and over	3,758	2,215	1,543	1,632	1,175	457	2,126	1,040	1,086	131	93	38
TOUNGOO.	***All Religions*** ...	*351,076*	*181,488*	*169,588*	*77,611*	*67,020*	*10,591*	*273,465*	*114,468*	*158,997*	*2,030*	*1,606*	*424*
	0—10	94,361	47,182	47,179	1,979	1,387	592	92,382	45,795	46,587	90	53	37
	10—15	42,045	22,209	19,836	7,892	6,394	1,498	34,153	15,815	18,338	281	204	77
	15—20	31,876	15,074	16,802	8,915	7,046	1,869	22,961	8,028	14,933	422	328	94
	20 and over	182,794	97,023	85,771	58,825	52,193	6,632	123,969	44,830	79,139	1,237	1,021	216
	Buddhist ...	*274,870*	*138,220*	*136,650*	*67,700*	*59,819*	*7,881*	*207,170*	*78,401*	*128,769*	*610*	*585*	*25*
	0—10	75,032	36,950	38,082	1,582	1,178	404	73,450	35,772	37,678	7	7	...
	10—15	34,426	18,162	16,264	6,754	5,655	1,099	27,672	12,507	15,165	62	58	4
	15—20	24,986	11,363	13,623	7,589	6,194	1,395	17,397	5,169	12,228	134	123	11
	20 and over	140,426	71,745	68,681	51,775	46,792	4,983	88,651	24,953	63,698	407	397	10
	Animist ...	*22,355*	*12,215*	*10,140*	*1,038*	*990*	*48*	*21,317*	*11,225*	*10,092*	*10*	*9*	*1*
	0—10	6,048	3,195	2,853	14	12	2	6,034	3,183	2,851	...	...	...
	10—15	2,296	1,223	1,073	57	49	8	2,239	1,174	1,065	2	2	...
	15—20	1,993	963	1,030	77	64	13	1,916	899	1,017	...	...	...
	20 and over	12,018	6,834	5,184	890	865	25	11,128	5,969	5,159	8	7	1
	Hindu ...	*14,220*	*10,070*	*4,150*	*1,511*	*1,424*	*87*	*12,709*	*8,646*	*4,063*	*117*	*109*	*8*
	0—10	2,733	1,383	1,350	15	10	5	2,718	1,373	1,345	1	...	1
	10—15	838	487	351	46	37	9	792	450	342	4	4	...
	15—20	1,082	812	270	118	106	12	964	706	258	25	23	2
	20 and over	9,567	7,388	2,179	1,332	1,271	61	8,235	6,117	2,118	87	82	5
	Mahomedan ...	*6,369*	*4,170*	*2,199*	*1,552*	*1,365*	*187*	*4,817*	*2,805*	*2,012*	*113*	*109*	*4*
	0—10	1,247	624	623	30	19	11	1,217	605	612	...	...	...
	10—15	568	325	243	121	97	24	447	228	219	4	4	...
	15—20	641	390	251	214	175	39	427	215	212	24	23	1
	20 and over	3,913	2,831	1,082	1,187	1,074	113	2,726	1,757	969	85	82	3
	Christian ...	*33,138*	*16,712*	*16,426*	*5,763*	*3,383*	*2,380*	*27,375*	*13,329*	*14,046*	*1,075*	*693*	*382*
	0—10	9,284	5,020	4,264	334	165	169	8,950	4,855	4,095	78	42	36
	10—15	3,914	2,010	1,904	911	554	357	3,003	1,456	1,547	209	136	73
	15—20	3,255	1,529	1,726	910	501	409	2,345	1,028	1,317	245	166	79
	20 and over	16,685	8,153	8,532	3,608	2,163	1,445	13,077	5,990	7,087	543	349	194
SALWEEN.	***All Religions*** ...	*46,608*	*24,741*	*21,867*	*1,246*	*1,138*	*108*	*45,362*	*23,603*	*21,759*	*49*	*44*	*5*
	0—10	13,407	6,999	6,408	16	10	6	13,391	6,989	6,402	...	...	...
	10—15	4,370	2,370	2,000	132	115	17	4,238	2,255	1,983	...	...	...
	15—20	3,859	1,854	2,005	90	82	8	3,769	1,772	1,997	1	1	...
	20 and over	24,972	13,518	11,454	1,008	931	77	23,964	12,587	11,377	48	43	5
	Buddhist ...	*20,474*	*11,213*	*9,261*	*988*	*917*	*71*	*19,486*	*10,296*	*9,190*	*14*	*13*	*1*
	0—10	6,034	3,171	2,863	7	2	5	6,027	3,169	2,858	...	...	...
	10—15	2,042	1,146	896	104	96	8	1,938	1,050	888	...	...	...
	15—20	1,622	808	814	74	70	4	1,548	738	810	...	...	...
	20 and over	10,776	6,088	4,688	803	749	54	9,973	5,339	4,634	14	13	1
	Animist ...	*25,068*	*12,725*	*12,343*	*47*	*46*	*1*	*25,021*	*12,679*	*12,342*	*2*	*2*	...
	0—10	7,214	3,734	3,480	4	4	...	7,210	3,730	3,480	...	...	...
	10—15	2,250	1,174	1,076	5	5	...	2,245	1,169	1,076	...	...	...
	15—20	2,154	998	1,156	4	4	...	2,150	994	1,156	1	1	...
	20 and over	13,450	6,819	6,631	34	33	1	13,416	6,786	6,630	1	1	...

IMPERIAL TABLE VIII.—*Education by Religion and Age.*

PART B.—DETAILS BY DISTRICTS.

District.	AGE.	POPULATION.									LITERATE IN ENGLISH.		
		Total.			Literate.			Illiterate.					
		Persons.	Males.	Females.	Persons.	Males.	Females.	Persons.	Males.	Females.	Persons.	Males.	Females.
1	2	3	4	5	6	7	8	9	10	11	12	13	14
THATÔN.	***All Religions*** ...	***416,975***	***217,770***	***199,205***	***70,165***	***58,849***	***11,316***	***346,810***	***158,921***	***187,889***	***859***	***762***	***97***
	0—10	123,335	61,726	61,609	2,079	1,433	646	121,256	60,293	60,963	11	6	5
	10—15	49,730	25,891	23,839	7,795	6,097	1,698	41,935	19,794	22,141	51	39	12
	15—20	39,816	19,424	20,392	9,370	7,285	2,085	30,446	12,139	18,307	127	108	19
	20 and over	204,094	110,729	93,365	50,921	44,034	6,887	153,173	66,695	86,478	670	609	61
	Buddhist ...	***380,244***	***192,749***	***187,495***	***64,728***	***54,018***	***10,710***	***315,516***	***138,736***	***176,780***	***419***	***395***	***24***
	0—10	115,676	57,797	57,879	1,916	1,312	604	113,760	56,485	57,275	4	4	...
	10—15	46,852	24,141	22,711	7,406	5,791	1,615	39,446	18,350	21,096	32	27	5
	15—20	36,897	17,525	19,372	8,835	6,869	1,966	28,062	10,656	17,406	82	75	7
	20 and over	180,819	93,286	87,533	46,571	40,041	6,530	134,248	53,245	81,003	301	289	12
	Animist ...	***5,958***	***3,840***	***2,118***	***679***	***644***	***35***	***5,279***	***3,196***	***2,083***	***8***	***8***	...
	0—10	1,441	799	642	8	8	...	1,433	791	642	...	...	...
	10—15	599	374	225	67	61	6	532	313	219	...	...	...
	15—20	438	275	163	66	56	10	372	219	153	...	...	...
	20 and over	3,480	2,392	1,088	538	519	19	2,942	1,873	1,069	8	8	...
	Hindu ...	***16,805***	***12,131***	***4,674***	***2,180***	***2,082***	***98***	***14,625***	***10,049***	***4,576***	***137***	***136***	***1***
	0—10	2,930	1,463	1,467	61	53	8	2,869	1,410	1,459	...	...	...
	10—15	1,004	648	356	113	106	7	891	542	349	2	2	...
	15—20	1,258	899	359	159	140	19	1,099	759	340	13	13	...
	20 and over	11,613	9,121	2,492	1,847	1,783	64	9,766	7,338	2,428	122	121	1
	Mahomedan ...	***10,221***	***7,054***	***3,167***	***1,802***	***1,617***	***185***	***8,419***	***5,437***	***2,982***	***138***	***136***	***2***
	0—10	2,226	1,143	1,083	50	37	13	2,176	1,106	1,070	...	...	...
	10—15	819	472	347	118	90	28	701	382	319	3	2	1
	15—20	896	565	331	219	180	39	677	385	292	13	13	...
	20 and over	6,280	4,874	1,406	1,415	1,310	105	4,865	3,564	1,301	122	121	1
	Christian ...	***3,738***	***1,987***	***1,751***	***772***	***489***	***283***	***2,966***	***1,498***	***1,468***	***222***	***152***	***70***
	0—10	1,060	522	538	43	22	21	1,017	500	517	7	2	5
	10—15	456	256	200	91	49	42	365	207	158	14	8	6
	15—20	327	160	167	91	40	51	236	120	116	22	10	12
	20 and over	1,895	1,049	846	547	378	169	1,348	671	677	179	132	47
AMHERST.	***All Religions*** ...	***367,918***	***198,430***	***169,488***	***66,826***	***56,235***	***10,591***	***301,092***	***142,195***	***158,897***	***4,176***	***3,147***	***1,029***
	0—10	104,550	52,345	52,205	1,815	1,239	576	102,735	51,106	51,629	218	123	95
	10—15	42,898	22,737	20,161	5,980	4,437	1,543	36,918	18,300	18,618	599	333	266
	15—20	36,133	18,373	17,760	8,155	6,282	1,873	27,978	12,091	15,887	766	571	195
	20 and over	184,337	104,975	79,362	50,876	44,277	6,599	133,461	60,698	72,763	2,593	2,120	473
	Buddhist ...	***309,904***	***158,436***	***151,468***	***54,562***	***46,280***	***8,282***	***255,342***	***112,156***	***143,186***	***1,568***	***1,489***	***79***
	0—10	93,228	46,353	46,875	1,337	962	375	91,891	45,391	46,500	19	19	...
	10—15	38,169	19,863	18,306	4,900	3,781	1,119	33,269	16,082	17,187	178	144	34
	15—20	31,026	15,184	15,842	6,845	5,372	1,473	24,181	9,812	14,369	347	329	18
	20 and over	147,481	77,036	70,445	41,480	36,165	5,315	106,001	40,871	65,130	1,024	997	27
	Animist ...	***4,338***	***3,441***	***897***	***1,199***	***1,125***	***74***	***3,139***	***2,316***	***823***	***51***	***50***	***1***
	0—10	899	638	261	23	19	4	876	619	257	...	...	...
	10—15	363	264	99	97	79	18	266	185	81	3	3	...
	15—20	279	216	63	113	104	9	166	112	54	15	15	...
	20 and over	2,797	2,323	474	966	923	43	1,831	1,400	431	33	32	1
	Hindu ...	***23,864***	***18,402***	***5,462***	***3,315***	***3,066***	***249***	***20,549***	***15,336***	***5,213***	***374***	***355***	***19***
	0—10	2,973	1,582	1,391	79	59	20	2,894	1,523	1,371	9	9	...
	10—15	1,275	863	412	145	117	28	1,130	746	384	17	14	3
	15—20	1,790	1,283	507	221	173	48	1,569	1,110	459	51	45	6
	20 and over	17,826	14,674	3,152	2,870	2,717	153	14,956	11,957	2,999	297	287	10
	Mahomedan ...	***22,893***	***14,560***	***8,333***	***4,687***	***4,158***	***529***	***18,206***	***10,402***	***7,804***	***287***	***283***	***4***
	0—10	5,620	2,846	2,774	107	75	32	5,513	2,771	2,742	...	...	...
	10—15	2,163	1,262	901	289	214	75	1,874	1,048	826	13	13	...
	15—20	2,221	1,291	930	464	380	84	1,757	911	846	38	37	1
	20 and over	12,889	9,161	3,728	3,827	3,489	338	9,062	5,672	3,390	236	233	3
	Christian ...	***6,824***	***3,531***	***3,293***	***2,997***	***1,559***	***1,438***	***3,827***	***1,972***	***1,855***	***1,859***	***947***	***912***
	0—10	1,808	917	891	263	121	142	1,545	796	749	181	89	92
	10—15	925	484	441	546	245	301	379	239	140	385	158	227
	15—20	803	388	415	502	243	259	301	145	156	310	140	170
	20 and over	3,288	1,742	1,546	1,686	950	736	1,602	792	810	983	560	423

Imperial Table VIII.—*Education by Religion and Age.*

PART B.—DETAILS BY DISTRICTS.

District.	AGE.	Population. Total. Persons.	Total. Males.	Total. Females.	Literate. Persons.	Literate. Males.	Literate. Females.	Illiterate. Persons.	Illiterate. Males.	Illiterate. Females.	Literate in English. Persons.	Literate in English. Males.	Literate in English. Females.
1	2	3	4	5	6	7	8	9	10	11	12	13	14
TAVOY.	*All Religions* ...	*135,293*	*68,667*	*66,626*	*24,478*	*21,579*	*2,899*	*110,815*	*47,088*	*63,727*	*404*	*380*	*24*
	0—10	37,569	19,002	18,567	576	426	150	36,993	18,576	18,417	33	29	4
	10—15	16,102	8,536	7,566	2,062	1,642	420	14,040	6,894	7,146	31	31	...
	15—20	11,846	5,378	6,468	2,833	2,331	502	9,013	3,047	5,966	89	87	2
	20 and over	69,776	35,751	34,025	19,007	17,180	1,827	50,769	18,571	32,198	251	233	18
	Buddhist ...	*129,505*	*64,908*	*64,597*	*23,428*	*20,764*	*2,664*	*106,077*	*44,144*	*61,933*	*230*	*230*	...
	0—10	36,443	18,418	18,025	509	374	135	35,934	18,044	17,890	1	1	...
	10—15	15,606	8,265	7,341	1,960	1,574	386	13,646	6,691	6,955	16	16	...
	15—20	11,290	5,055	6,235	2,704	2,239	465	8,586	2,816	5,770	63	63	...
	20 and over	66,166	33,170	32,996	18,255	16,577	1,678	47,911	16,593	31,318	150	150	...
	Animist ...	*1,380*	*997*	*383*	*88*	*87*	*1*	*1,292*	*910*	*382*	*1*	*1*	...
	0—10	264	151	113	1	1	...	263	150	113	...	...	...
	10—15	143	86	57	3	2	1	140	84	56	...	...	...
	15—20	99	62	37	1	1	...	98	61	37	...	...	...
	20 and over	874	698	176	83	83	...	791	615	176	1	1	...
	Mahomedan ...	*1,564*	*908*	*656*	*341*	*251*	*90*	*1,223*	*657*	*566*	*27*	*26*	*1*
	0—10	313	157	156	37	31	6	276	126	150	22	22	...
	10—15	127	55	72	36	24	12	91	31	60	...	...	...
	15—20	173	92	81	49	32	17	124	60	64	4	4	...
	20 and over	951	604	347	219	164	55	732	440	292	1	...	1
	Christian ...	*1,999*	*1,070*	*929*	*486*	*348*	*138*	*1,513*	*722*	*791*	*126*	*103*	*23*
	0—10	500	243	257	26	17	9	474	226	248	8	4	4
	10—15	207	118	89	58	38	20	149	80	69	13	13	...
	15—20	232	126	106	57	38	19	175	88	87	6	4	2
	20 and over	1,060	583	477	345	255	90	715	328	387	99	82	17
MERGUI.	*All Religions* ...	*111,424*	*59,530*	*51,894*	*20,733*	*17,759*	*2,974*	*90,691*	*41,771*	*48,920*	*328*	*282*	*46*
	0—10	30,258	15,326	14,932	409	265	144	29,849	15,061	14,788	8	5	3
	10—15	13,272	7,068	6,204	1,585	1,198	387	11,687	5,870	5,817	13	10	3
	15—20	10,663	5,257	5,406	2,261	1,748	513	8,402	3,509	4,893	46	41	5
	20 and over	57,231	31,879	25,352	16,478	14,548	1,930	40,753	17,331	23,422	261	226	35
	Buddhist ...	*89,602*	*45,968*	*43,634*	*18,400*	*15,855*	*2,545*	*71,202*	*30,113*	*41,089*	*133*	*126*	*7*
	0—10	25,283	12,752	12,531	368	242	126	24,915	12,510	12,405	1	1	...
	10—15	11,006	5,758	5,248	1,430	1,094	336	9,576	4,664	4,912	4	3	1
	15—20	8,642	4,061	4,581	2,051	1,606	445	6,591	2,455	4,136	30	28	2
	20 and over	44,671	23,397	21,274	14,551	12,913	1,638	30,120	10,484	19,636	98	94	4
	Animist ...	*4,088*	*2,752*	*1,336*	*318*	*315*	*3*	*3,770*	*2,437*	*1,333*	*2*	*2*	...
	0—10	780	418	362	2	2	...	778	416	362	...	...	...
	10—15	335	204	131	10	10	...	325	194	131	...	...	...
	15—20	315	188	127	12	11	1	303	177	126	...	...	...
	20 and over	2,658	1,942	716	294	292	2	2,364	1,650	714	2	2	...
	Hindu ...	*3,367*	*3,192*	*175*	*240*	*232*	*8*	*3,127*	*2,960*	*167*	*20*	*20*	...
	0—10	111	56	55	1	...	1	110	56	54	...	...	...
	10—15	172	163	9	6	5	1	166	158	8	..	...	...
	15—20	392	385	7	17	15	2	375	370	5	...	...	...
	20 and over	2,692	2,588	104	216	212	4	2,476	2,376	100	20	20	...
	Mahomedan .	*9,822*	*5,252*	*4,570*	*1,194*	*981*	*213*	*8,628*	*4,271*	*4,357*	*46*	*44*	*2*
	0—10	2,754	1,424	1,330	19	12	7	2,735	1,412	1,323	...	...	...
	10—15	1,168	635	533	83	56	27	1,085	579	506	6	6	...
	15—20	947	453	494	118	83	35	829	370	459	6	6	...
	20 and over	4,953	2,740	2,213	974	830	144	3,979	1,910	2,069	34	32	2
	Christian ...	*4,539*	*2,360*	*2,179*	*575*	*370*	*205*	*3,964*	*1,990*	*1,974*	*127*	*90*	*37*
	0—10	1,330	676	654	19	9	10	1,311	667	644	7	4	3
	10—15	591	308	283	56	33	23	535	275	260	3	1	2
	15—20	366	169	197	62	32	30	304	137	167	10	7	3
	20 and over	2,252	1,207	1,045	438	296	142	1,814	911	903	107	78	29
THAYET-MYO.	*All Religions* ...	*248,275*	*122,231*	*126,044*	*63,606*	*58,272*	*5,334*	*184,669*	*63,959*	*120,710*	*696*	*647*	*49*
	0—10	66,179	32,494	33,685	1,024	776	248	65,155	31,718	33,437	7	6	1
	10—15	30,205	15,269	14,936	5,734	5,042	692	24,471	10,227	14,244	63	50	13
	15—20	21,636	10,544	11,092	6,929	6,102	827	14,707	4,442	10,265	85	76	9
	20 and over	130,255	63,924	66,331	49,919	46,352	3,567	80,336	17,572	62,764	541	515	26

Imperial Table VIII.—*Education by Religion and Age.*

PART B.—DETAILS BY DISTRICTS.

District.	AGE.	Population. Total. Persons.	Total. Males.	Total. Females.	Literate. Persons.	Literate. Males.	Literate. Females.	Illiterate. Persons.	Illiterate. Males.	Illiterate. Females.	Literate in English. Persons.	Literate in English. Males.	Literate in English. Females.
1	2	3	4	5	6	7	8	9	10	11	12	13	14
THAYETMYO—*concluded.*	***Buddhist*** ...	*228,058*	*111,290*	*116,768*	*61,320*	*56,214*	*5,106*	*166,738*	*55,076*	*111,662*	*308*	*295*	*13*
	0—10	61,297	30,102	31,195	975	740	235	60,322	29,362	30,960	...	...	...
	10—15	28,078	14,160	13,918	5,609	4,944	665	22,469	9,216	13,253	36	29	7
	15—20	19,878	9,629	10,249	6,729	5,929	800	13,149	3,700	9,449	54	50	4
	20 and over	118,805	57,399	61,406	48,007	44,601	3,406	70,798	12,798	58,000	218	216	2
	Animist ...	*15,282*	*7,594*	*7,688*	*685*	*655*	*30*	*14,547*	*6,939*	*7,608*	*4*	*4*	...
	0—10	3,871	1,868	2,003	11	9	2	3,860	1,859	2,001	...	...	...
	10—15	1,743	881	862	27	26	1	1,716	855	861	...	...	...
	15—20	1,341	666	675	54	51	3	1,287	615	672	3	3	...
	20 and over	8,277	4,179	4,098	593	569	24	7,684	3,610	4,074	1	1	...
	Hindu ...	*2,186*	*1,605*	*581*	*538*	*511*	*27*	*1,648*	*1,094*	*554*	*63*	*59*	*4*
	0—10	393	202	191	4	4	...	389	198	191	3	3	...
	10—15	138	88	50	28	21	7	110	67	43	10	8	2
	15—20	169	113	56	42	40	2	127	73	54	6	6	...
	20 and over	1,486	1,202	284	464	446	18	1,022	756	266	44	42	2
	Mahomedan ...	*2,164*	*1,361*	*808*	*731*	*625*	*106*	*1,433*	*736*	*697*	*88*	*87*	*1*
	0—10	481	254	227	21	14	7	460	240	220	1	1	...
	10—15	202	123	79	55	44	11	147	79	68	10	9	1
	15—20	210	124	86	87	71	16	123	53	70	12	12	...
	20 and over	1,271	860	411	568	496	72	703	364	339	65	65	...
PAKÔKKU.	***All Religions*** ...	*409,909*	*196,159*	*213,750*	*83,313*	*74,079*	*9,234*	*326,596*	*122,080*	*204,516*	*443*	*391*	*52*
	0—10	113,321	55,734	57,587	1,254	882	372	112,067	54,852	57,215	13	8	5
	10—15	47,166	24,134	23,032	6,767	5,506	1,261	40,399	18,628	21.771	51	48	3
	15—20	37,413	17,438	19,975	9,777	7,981	1,796	27,636	9,457	18,179	75	70	5
	20 and over	212,009	98,853	113,156	65,515	59,710	5,805	146,494	39,143	107,351	304	265	39
	Buddhist ...	*404,087*	*192,482*	*211,605*	*82,072*	*72,974*	*9,098*	*321,965*	*119,458*	*202,507*	*275*	*252*	*23*
	0—10	112,075	55,098	56,977	1,231	869	362	110,844	54,229	56,615	4	3	1
	10—15	46,653	23,853	22,800	6,721	5,470	1,251	39,932	18,383	21,549	43	42	1
	15—20	36,979	17,152	19,827	9,668	7,889	1,779	27,311	9,263	18,048	66	63	3
	20 and over	208,330	96,329	112,001	64,452	58,746	5,706	143,878	37,583	106,295	162	144	18
	Animist ...	*3,472*	*1,831*	*1,641*	*251*	*231*	*20*	*3,221*	*1,600*	*1,621*	*2*	*2*	...
	0—10	920	464	456	3	2	1	917	462	455	...	...	...
	10—15	420	222	198	13	12	1	407	210	197	1	1	...
	15—20	247	144	103	28	27	1	219	117	102	...	...	...
	20 and over	1,885	1,001	884	207	190	17	1,678	811	867	1	1	...
	Hindu ...	*1,170*	*1,016*	*154*	*455*	*429*	*26*	*715*	*587*	*128*	*38*	*86*	*2*
	0—10	117	63	54	5	3	2	112	60	52	...	...	...
	10—15	21	18	3	3	3	...	18	15	3	...	...	...
	15—20	88	76	12	38	35	3	50	41	9	3	3	...
	20 and over	944	859	85	409	388	21	535	471	64	35	33	2
MINBU.	***All Religions*** ...	*263,939*	*128,837*	*135,102*	*62,497*	*58,112*	*4,385*	*201,442*	*70,725*	*130,717*	*394*	*374*	*20*
	0—10	70,353	34,664	35,689	706	549	157	69,647	34,115	35,532	3	2	1
	10—15	29,379	14,678	14,701	4,305	3,798	507	25,074	10,880	14,194	41	39	2
	15—20	23,420	11,311	12,109	7,169	6,537	632	16,251	4,774	11,477	74	69	5
	20 and over	140,787	68,184	72,603	50,317	47,228	3,089	90,470	20,956	69,514	276	264	12
	Buddhist ...	*253,927*	*122,133*	*131,794*	*61,227*	*56,927*	*4,300*	*192,700*	*65,206*	*127,494*	*259*	*256*	*3*
	0—10	68,146	33,514	34,632	690	538	152	67,456	32,976	34,480	2	2	...
	10—15	28,625	14,256	14,369	4,233	3,738	495	24,392	10,518	13,874	31	31	...
	15—20	22,612	10,790	11,822	7,057	6,438	619	15,555	4,352	11,203	66	63	3
	20 and over	134,544	63,573	70,971	49,247	46,213	3,034	85,297	17,360	67,937	160	160	...
	Animist ...	*5,758*	*3,056*	*2,702*	*344*	*339*	*5*	*5,414*	*2,717*	*2,697*	*1*	*1*	...
	0—10	1,764	900	864	...	...	...	1,764	900	864	...	...	...
	10—15	579	301	278	19	18	1	560	283	277	...	...	...
	15—20	473	244	229	27	27	...	446	217	229	1	1	...
	20 and over	2,942	1,611	1,331	298	294	4	2,644	1,317	1,327	...	...	...
	Hindu ...	*2,651*	*2,449*	*202*	*520*	*504*	*16*	*2,131*	*1,945*	*186*	*43*	*41*	*2*
	0—10	139	83	56	3	3	...	136	80	56	...	...	...
	10—15	58	44	14	10	10	...	48	34	14	1	1	...
	15—20	230	208	22	41	38	3	189	170	19	1	...	1
	20 and over	2,224	2,114	110	466	453	13	1,758	1,661	97	41	40	1

IMPERIAL TABLE VIII.—*Education by Religion and Age.*

PART B.—DETAILS BY DISTRICTS.

District.	AGE.	Population. Total. Persons.	Total. Males.	Total. Females.	Literate. Persons.	Literate. Males.	Literate. Females.	Illiterate. Persons.	Illiterate. Males.	Illiterate. Females.	Literate in English. Persons.	Literate in English. Males.	Literate in English. Females.
1	2	3	4	5	6	7	8	9	10	11	12	13	14
MINBU—*concluded.*	***Mahomedan*** ...	***1,061***	***775***	***286***	***296***	***261***	***35***	***765***	***514***	***251***	***17***	***17***	...
	0—10	218	126	92	8	4	4	210	122	88	...	...	...
	10—15	89	55	34	26	18	8	63	37	26	1	1	...
	15—20	87	56	31	36	27	9	51	29	22	3	3	...
	20 and over	667	538	129	226	212	14	441	326	115	13	13	...
MAGWE.	***All Religions*** ...	***316,909***	***156,387***	***160,522***	***77,722***	***78,547***	***4,175***	***239,187***	***82,840***	***156,347***	***523***	***484***	***39***
	0—10	86,914	42,733	44,181	1,246	1,009	237	85,668	41,724	43,944	6	3	3
	10—15	38,792	19,191	19,601	6,074	5,591	483	32,718	13,600	19,118	16	16	...
	15—20	28,918	14,202	14,716	9,336	8,775	561	19,582	5,427	14 155	33	29	4
	20 and over	162,285	80,261	82,024	61,066	58,172	2,894	101,219	22,089	79,130	468	436	32
	Buddhist ...	***311,574***	***151,962***	***159,612***	***75,828***	***71,806***	***4,022***	***235,746***	***80,156***	***155,590***	***208***	***200***	***8***
	0—10	86,308	42,399	43,909	1,213	990	223	85,095	41,409	43,686	1	1	...
	10—15	38,537	19,010	19,527	5,995	5,534	461	32,542	13,476	19,066	13	13	...
	15—20	28,433	13,793	14,640	9,195	8,655	540	19,238	5,138	14,100	23	21	2
	20 and over	158,296	76,760	81,536	59,425	56,627	2,798	98,871	20,133	78,738	171	165	6
	Hindu ...	***2,632***	***2,350***	***282***	***652***	***632***	***20***	***1,980***	***1,718***	***262***	***45***	***45***	...
	0—10	172	105	67	2	2	...	170	103	67	...	...	...
	10—15	90	80	10	19	18	1	71	62	9	...	...	...
	15—20	269	246	23	40	39	1	229	207	22	1	1	...
	20 and over	2,101	1,919	182	591	573	18	1,510	1,346	164	44	44	...
	Mahomedan ...	***1,617***	***1,233***	***384***	***665***	***607***	***58***	***952***	***626***	***326***	***39***	***39***	...
	0—10	240	120	120	9	5	4	231	115	116	...	...	...
	10—15	110	65	45	34	21	13	76	44	32	1	1	...
	15—20	152	115	37	70	58	12	82	57	25	4	4	...
	20 and over	1,115	933	182	552	523	29	563	410	153	34	34	...
MANDALAY (CITY INCLUDED).	***All Religions*** ...	***340,770***	***170,750***	***170,020***	***94,541***	***77,646***	***16,895***	***246,229***	***93,104***	***153,125***	***5,410***	***4,255***	***1,155***
	0—10	78,424	38,677	39,747	2,054	1,380	674	76,370	37,297	39,073	336	184	152
	10—15	36,387	18,397	17,990	8,396	6,533	1,863	27,991	11,864	16,127	564	364	200
	15—20	30,866	14,891	15,975	11,242	8,730	2,512	19,624	6,161	13,463	700	527	173
	20 and over	195,093	98,785	96,308	72,849	61,003	11,846	122,244	37,782	84,462	3,810	3,180	630
	Buddhist ...	***294,904***	***141,480***	***153,424***	***78,652***	***65,101***	***13,551***	***216,252***	***76,379***	***139,873***	***998***	***934***	***64***
	0—10	70,139	34,624	35,515	1,514	1,089	425	68,625	33,535	35,090	23	16	7
	10—15	32,824	16,467	16,357	7,246	5,817	1,429	25,578	10,650	14,928	106	91	15
	15—20	26,921	12,612	14,309	9,600	7,592	2,008	17,321	5,020	12,301	233	216	17
	20 and over	165,020	77,777	87,243	60,292	50,603	9,689	104,728	27,174	77,554	636	611	25
	Animist ...	***1,497***	***1,278***	***219***	***727***	***657***	***70***	***770***	***621***	***149***	***38***	***36***	***2***
	0—10	140	83	57	7	6	1	133	77	56	...	...	...
	10—15	72	44	28	21	17	4	51	27	24	2	2	...
	15—20	114	96	18	51	45	6	63	51	12	8	7	1
	20 and over	1,171	1,055	116	648	589	59	523	466	57	28	27	1
	Hindu ...	***16,071***	***11,192***	***4,879***	***4,282***	***3,952***	***330***	***11,789***	***7,240***	***4,549***	***596***	***571***	***25***
	0—10	2,455	1,213	1,242	87	55	32	2,368	1,158	1,210	14	10	4
	10—15	940	532	408	209	164	45	731	368	363	51	41	10
	15—20	1,166	728	438	348	298	50	818	430	388	44	44	...
	20 and over	11,510	8,719	2,791	3,638	3,435	203	7,872	5,284	2,588	487	476	11
	Mahomedan ...	***20,845***	***12,236***	***8,609***	***6,025***	***4,584***	***1,441***	***14,820***	***7,652***	***7,168***	***273***	***261***	***12***
	0—10	4,248	2,049	2,199	72	37	35	4,176	2,012	2,164	7	5	2
	10—15	1,827	988	839	372	240	132	1,455	748	707	18	16	2
	15—20	1,940	1,055	885	701	479	222	1,239	576	663	45	41	4
	20 and over	12,830	8,144	4,686	4,880	3,828	1,052	7,950	4,316	3,634	203	199	4
	Christian ...	***6,571***	***3,870***	***2,701***	***4,459***	***3,010***	***1,449***	***2,112***	***860***	***1,252***	***1,757***	***748***	***1,009***
	0—10	1,337	650	687	363	188	175	974	462	512	283	150	133
	10—15	696	351	345	531	287	244	165	64	101	374	208	166
	15—20	638	331	307	510	292	218	128	39	89	346	206	140
	20 and over	3,900	2,538	1,362	3,055	2,243	812	845	295	550	754	184	570
MANDALAY CITY.	***All Religions*** ...	***138,299***	***69,718***	***68,581***	***54,166***	***41,760***	***12,406***	***84,133***	***27,958***	***56,175***	***3,151***	***2,477***	***674***
	0—10	28,015	13,696	14,319	1,247	822	425	26,768	12,874	13,894	199	122	77
	10—15	13,514	6,737	6,777	4,783	3,447	1,336	8,731	3,290	5,441	387	259	128
	15—20	12,648	6,242	6,406	6,482	4,637	1,845	6,166	1,605	4,561	533	411	122
	20 and over	84,122	43,043	41,079	41,654	32,854	8,800	42,468	10,189	32,279	2,032	1,685	347

IMPERIAL TABLE VIII.—*Education by Religion and Age.*

PART B.—DETAILS BY DISTRICTS.

District.	AGE.	Population. Total. Persons.	Total. Males.	Total. Females.	Literate. Persons.	Literate. Males.	Literate. Females.	Illiterate. Persons.	Illiterate. Males.	Illiterate. Females.	Literate in English. Persons.	Literate in English. Males.	Literate in English. Females.
1	2	3	4	5	6	7	8	9	10	11	12	13	14
MANDALAY CITY—*concluded.*	***Buddhist*** ...	*109,285*	*51,687*	*57,548*	*48,308*	*33,407*	*9,901*	*65,927*	*18,280*	*47,647*	*858*	*794*	*59*
	0—10	22,906	11,216	11,690	899	620	279	22,007	10,596	11,411	20	13	7
	10—15	11,150	5,452	5,698	3,947	2,934	1,013	7,203	2,518	4,685	100	87	13
	15—20	10,020	4,744	5,276	5,273	3,824	1,449	4,747	920	3,827	221	205	16
	20 and over	65,159	30,275	34,884	33,189	26,029	7,160	31,970	4,246	27,724	512	489	23
	Animist ...	*1,384*	*1,197*	*187*	*623*	*603*	*20*	*761*	*594*	*167*	*29*	*29*	...
	0—10	116	73	43	6	6	...	110	67	43	...	...	...
	10—15	67	41	26	19	15	4	48	26	22	2	2	...
	15—20	106	91	15	42	40	2	64	51	13	4	4	...
	20 and over	1,095	992	103	556	542	14	539	450	89	23	23	...
	Hindu ...	*7,884*	*5,269*	*2,615*	*2,355*	*2,170*	*185*	*5,529*	*3,099*	*2,430*	*247*	*234*	*13*
	0—10	1,174	569	605	41	32	9	1,133	537	596	4	4	...
	10—15	447	263	184	113	94	19	334	169	165	12	10	2
	15—20	565	329	236	171	142	29	394	187	207	17	15	2
	20 and over	5,698	4,108	1,590	2,030	1,902	128	3,668	2,206	1,462	214	205	9
	Mahomedan ...	*14,963*	*8,696*	*6,267*	*4,934*	*3,599*	*1,335*	*10,029*	*5,097*	*4,932*	*207*	*196*	*11*
	0—10	2,879	1,367	1,512	66	33	33	2,813	1,334	1,479	7	5	2
	10—15	1,329	719	610	318	197	121	1,011	522	489	18	16	2
	15—20	1,433	789	644	601	403	198	832	386	446	42	38	4
	20 and over	9,322	5,821	3,501	3,949	2,966	983	5,373	2,855	2,518	140	137	3
	Christian ...	*4,045*	*2,238*	*1,807*	*2,585*	*1,661*	*924*	*1,460*	*577*	*883*	*1,745*	*1,181*	*564*
	0—10	847	417	430	230	126	104	617	291	326	165	97	68
	10—15	498	249	249	372	199	173	126	50	76	245	138	107
	15—20	463	239	224	370	211	159	93	28	65	238	146	92
	20 and over	2,237	1,333	904	1,613	1,125	488	624	208	416	1,097	800	297
BHAMO.	***All Religions*** ...	*107,811*	*55,528*	*52,288*	*11,780*	*10,600*	*1,180*	*96,081*	*44,928*	*51,158*	*551*	*495*	*56*
	0—10	24,912	12,371	12,541	198	114	84	24,714	12,257	124,57	5	2	3
	10—15	12,044	6,190	5,854	827	682	145	11,217	5,508	5,709	24	21	3
	15—20	10,129	5,129	5,000	1,179	971	208	8,950	4,158	4,792	38	30	8
	20 and over	60,726	31,838	28,888	9,526	8,833	693	51,200	23,005	28,195	484	442	42
	Buddhist ...	*53,490*	*27,182*	*26,308*	*9,106*	*8,171*	*935*	*44,384*	*19,011*	*25,373*	*95*	*81*	*14*
	0—10	14,279	7,050	7,229	163	88	75	14,116	6,962	7,154	...	...	...
	10—15	5,684	2,872	2,812	688	562	126	4,996	2,310	2,686	10	8	2
	15—20	4,952	2,439	2,513	978	801	177	3,974	1,638	2,336	23	20	3
	20 and over	28,575	14,821	13,754	7,277	6,720	557	21,298	8,101	13,197	62	53	9
	Animist ...	*47,722*	*23,244*	*24,478*	*436*	*425*	*11*	*47,286*	*22,819*	*24,467*	...	...	...
	0—10	9,853	4,924	4,929	12	12	...	9,841	4,912	4,929	...	...	...
	10—15	6,044	3,119	2,925	47	44	3	5,997	3,075	2,922	...	...	...
	15—20	4,601	2,274	2,327	44	44	...	4,557	2,230	2,327	...	...	...
	20 and over	27,224	12,927	14,297	333	325	8	26,891	12,602	14,289	...	...	...
	Hindu ...	*1,652*	*1,404*	*248*	*559*	*526*	*33*	*1,093*	*878*	*215*	*58*	*50*	*8*
	0—10	183	103	80	7	4	3	176	99	77	...	...	...
	10—15	36	28	8	18	17	1	18	11	7	4	4	..
	15—20	84	65	19	19	17	2	65	48	17	4	3	1
	20 and over	1,349	1,208	141	515	488	27	834	720	114	45	43	2
	Mahomedan ...	*2,242*	*1,852*	*390*	*673*	*627*	*46*	*1,569*	*1,225*	*344*	*41*	*41*	...
	0—10	245	120	125	2	1	1	243	119	124	...	...	...
	10—15	75	49	26	21	16	5	54	33	21	5	5	...
	15—20	204	167	37	60	52	8	144	115	29	2	2	...
	20 and over	1,718	1,516	202	590	558	32	1,128	958	170	34	34	...
	Christian ...	*1,785*	*1,030*	*755*	*529*	*435*	*94*	*1,256*	*595*	*661*	*338*	*299*	*39*
	0—10	281	137	144	13	8	5	268	129	139	5	2	3
	10—15	191	110	81	46	36	10	145	74	71	5	4	1
	15—20	169	80	89	48	29	19	121	51	70	8	4	4
	20 and over	1,144	703	441	422	362	60	722	341	381	320	289	31
MYITKYINA.	***All Religions*** ...	*85,577*	*47,863*	*37,714*	*11,191*	*10,490*	*701*	*74,386*	*37,373*	*37,013*	*387*	*358*	*29*
	0—10	18,433	9,329	9,104	235	183	52	18,198	9,146	9,052	11	8	3
	10—15	8,195	4,238	3,957	716	619	97	7,479	3,619	3,860	8	8	...
	15—20	7,357	3,920	3,437	1,268	1,162	106	6,089	2,758	3,331	10	7	3
	20 and over	51,592	30,376	21,216	8,972	8,526	446	42,620	21,850	20,770	358	335	23

IMPERIAL TABLE VIII.—*Education by Religion and Age.*

PART B.—DETAILS BY DISTRICTS.

District.	AGE.	POPULATION.									LITERATE IN ENGLISH.		
		Total.			Literate.			Illiterate.					
		Persons.	Males.	Females.	Persons.	Males.	Females.	Persons.	Males.	Females.	Persons.	Males.	Females.
1	2	3	4	5	6	7	8	9	10	11	12	13	14
MYITKYINA—*concluded.*	***Buddhist*** ...	*30,171*	*16,518*	*13,653*	*7,236*	*6,719*	*517*	*22,935*	*9,799*	*13,136*	*53*	*52*	*1*
	0—10	7,398	3,696	3,702	169	128	41	7,229	3,568	3,661	1	1	...
	10—15	3,078	1,551	1,527	603	525	78	2,475	1,026	1,449	1	1	...
	15—20	2,342	1,183	1,159	1,065	983	82	1,277	200	1,077	2	1	1
	20 and over	17,353	10,088	7,265	5,399	5,083	316	11,954	5,005	6,949	49	49	...
	Animist ...	*46,050*	*24,098*	*21,952*	*413*	*398*	*15*	*45,637*	*23,700*	*21,937*	*6*	*6*	...
	0—10	9,476	4,814	4,662	...	...	...	9,476	4,814	4,662	...	...	...
	10—15	4,718	2,474	2,244	23	19	4	4,695	2,455	2,240	...	...	..
	15—20	4,559	2,424	2,135	30	19	11	4,529	2,405	2,124	...	...	...
	20 and over	27,297	14,386	12,911	360	360	...	26,937	14,026	12,911	6	6	...
	Hindu ...	*6,192*	*4,617*	*1,575*	*2,279*	*2,197*	*82*	*3,913*	*2,420*	*1,493*	*119*	*117*	*2*
	0—10	1,221	624	597	49	43	6	1,172	581	591	4	2	2
	10—15	277	138	139	57	49	8	220	89	131	3	3	...
	15—20	281	179	102	94	91	3	187	88	99	1	1	...
	20 and over	4,413	3,676	737	2,079	2,014	65	2,334	1,662	672	111	111	...
	Mahomedan ...	*1,906*	*1,618*	*288*	*603*	*556*	*47*	*1,303*	*1,062*	*241*	*33*	*32*	*1*
	0—10	200	117	83	9	7	2	191	110	81	...	...	...
	10—15	75	44	31	26	21	5	49	23	26	2	2	...
	15—20	112	90	22	44	38	6	68	52	16	1	1	...
	20 and over	1,519	1,367	152	524	490	34	995	877	118	30	29	1
KATHA.	***All Religions*** ...	*198,193*	*98,148*	*100,045*	*45,602*	*43,295*	*2,307*	*152,591*	*54,853*	*97,738*	*269*	*235*	*34*
	0—10	54,249	26,245	28,004	833	681	152	53,416	25,564	27,852	4	3	1
	10—15	21,654	10,769	10,885	4,063	3,744	319	17,591	7,025	10,566	6	4	2
	15—20	17,101	7,958	9,143	4,795	4,459	336	12,306	3,499	8,807	13	8	5
	20 and over	105,189	53,176	52,013	35,911	34,411	1,500	69,278	18,765	50,513	246	220	26
	Buddhist ...	*189,134*	*92,871*	*96,263*	*44,532*	*42,364*	*2,168*	*144,602*	*50,507*	*94,095*	*56*	*53*	*3*
	0—10	52,338	25,276	27,062	805	662	143	51,533	24,614	26,919	...	...	...
	10—15	20,881	10,396	10,485	4,025	3,719	306	16,856	6,677	10,179	1	1	...
	15—20	16,410	7,610	8,800	4,736	4,417	319	11,674	3,193	8,481	1	1	...
	20 and over	99,505	49,589	49,916	34,966	33,566	1,400	64,539	16,023	48,516	54	51	3
	Animist ...	*6,089*	*2,984*	*3,105*	*30*	*29*	*1*	*6,059*	*2,955*	*3,104*	...	...	...
	0—10	1,501	752	749	...	...	...	1,501	752	749	...	...	..
	10—15	630	300	330	1	...	1	629	300	329	...	...	...
	15—20	545	269	276	3	3	...	542	266	276	...	...	...
	20 and over	3,413	1,663	1,750	26	26	...	3,387	1,637	1,750	...	...	...
	Hindu ...	*1,429*	*1,268*	*161*	*443*	*419*	*24*	*986*	*849*	*137*	*61*	*60*	*1*
	0—10	118	72	46	11	8	3	107	64	43	1	1	...
	10—15	36	23	13	6	4	2	30	19	11	2	1	1
	15—20	51	37	14	14	12	2	37	25	12	3	3	...
	20 and over	1,224	1,136	88	412	395	17	812	741	71	55	55	...
	Mahomedan ...	*1,156*	*754*	*402*	*891*	*815*	*76*	*765*	*439*	*326*	*23*	*22*	*1*
	0—10	216	105	111	10	6	4	206	99	107	..	...	...
	10—15	82	37	45	23	15	8	59	22	37	...	...	...
	15—20	73	31	42	27	17	10	46	14	32	...	...	...
	20 and over	785	581	204	331	277	54	454	304	150	23	22	1
RUBY MINES.	***All Religions*** ...	*100,618*	*54,487*	*46,131*	*16,726*	*14,860*	*1,866*	*83,892*	*39,627*	*44,265*	*279*	*235*	*44*
	0—10	23,944	11,854	12,090	482	326	156	23,462	11,528	11,934	9	8	1
	10—15	9,678	4,936	4,742	1,348	1,012	336	8,330	3,924	4,406	20	15	5
	15—20	8,403	4,285	4,118	1,708	1,365	343	6,695	2,920	3,775	14	12	2
	20 and over	58,593	33,412	25,181	13,188	12,157	1,031	45,405	21,255	24,150	236	200	36
	Buddhist ...	*79,844*	*42,393*	*37,451*	*14,968*	*13,319*	*1,649*	*64,876*	*29,074*	*35,802*	*78*	*74*	*4*
	0—10	19,451	9,486	9,965	425	285	140	19,026	9,201	9,825	1	1	...
	10—15	7,965	4,067	3,898	1,293	979	314	6,672	3,088	3,584	9	7	2
	15—20	6,627	3,292	3,335	1,577	1,269	308	5,050	2,023	3,027	6	5	1
	20 and over	45,801	25,548	20,253	11,673	10,786	887	34,128	14,762	19,366	62	61	1
	Animist ...	*16,774*	*8,867*	*7,907*	*451*	*352*	*99*	*16,323*	*8,515*	*7,808*	*58*	*43*	*15*
	0—10	3,919	2,053	1,866	24	16	8	3,895	2,037	1,858	2	2	...
	10—15	1,578	786	792	19	10	9	1,559	776	783	5	3	2
	15—20	1,520	804	716	39	24	15	1,481	780	701	3	3	...
	20 and over	9,757	5,224	4,533	369	302	67	9,388	4,922	4,466	48	35	13

IMPERIAL TABLE VIII.—*Education by Religion and Age.*

PART B.—DETAILS BY DISTRICTS.

District.	AGE.	POPULATION. Total. Persons.	Total. Males.	Total. Females.	Literate. Persons.	Literate. Males.	Literate. Females.	Illiterate. Persons.	Illiterate. Males.	Illiterate. Females.	LITERATE IN ENGLISH. Persons.	Males.	Females.
1	2	3	4	5	6	7	8	9	10	11	12	13	14
RUBY MINES—*concluded.*	***Hindu*** ...	***2,505***	***2,058***	***447***	***909***	***852***	***57***	***1,596***	***1,206***	***390***	***56***	***56***	...
	0—10	343	198	145	17	13	4	326	185	141	...	...	...
	10—15	77	50	27	24	20	4	53	30	23	5	5	...
	15—20	154	117	37	65	54	11	89	63	26	3	3	...
	20 and over	1,931	1,693	238	803	765	38	1,128	928	200	48	48	...
	Mahomedan ...	***1,205***	***975***	***280***	***227***	***208***	***24***	***978***	***772***	***206***	...	...	...
	0—10	163	83	80	7	6	1	156	77	79	...	...	...
	10—15	51	32	19	9	2	7	42	30	12	...	...	...
	15—20	89	67	22	21	16	5	68	51	17	...	...	...
	20 and over	902	793	109	190	179	11	712	614	98	...	...	...
SHWEBO.	***All Religions*** ...	***356,868***	***168,070***	***188,298***	***85,736***	***72,058***	***13,678***	***270,627***	***96,012***	***174,615***	***1,066***	***917***	***149***
	0—10	95,718	47,097	48,621	2,139	1,537	602	93,579	45,560	48,019	81	48	33
	10—15	40,086	19,730	20,356	7,883	6,293	1,590	32,203	13,437	18,766	52	28	24
	15—20	31,557	14,450	17,107	9,733	7,878	1,855	21,824	6,572	15,252	112	97	15
	20 and over	189,002	86,793	102,209	65,981	56,350	9,631	123,021	30,443	92,578	821	744	77
	Buddhist ...	***344,852***	***161,070***	***183,782***	***82,286***	***69,253***	***13,033***	***262,566***	***91,817***	***170,749***	***170***	***161***	***9***
	0—10	92,888	45,698	47,190	1,966	1,431	535	90,922	44,267	46,655	...	...	...
	10—15	38,995	19,150	19,845	7,510	6,090	1,420	31,485	13,060	18,425	8	8	...
	15—20	30,656	13,983	16,673	9,342	7,653	1,689	21,314	6,330	14,984	52	52	...
	20 and over	182,313	82,239	100,074	63,468	54,079	9,389	118,845	28,160	90,685	110	101	9
	Hindu ...	***2,805***	***1,841***	***464***	***677***	***636***	***41***	***1,628***	***1,205***	***423***	***121***	***114***	***7***
	0—10	338	183	155	20	17	3	318	166	152	4	4	...
	10—15	105	74	31	23	17	6	82	57	25	5	3	2
	15—20	144	101	43	43	36	7	101	65	36	10	9	1
	20 and over	1,718	1,483	235	591	566	25	1,127	917	210	102	98	4
	Mahomedan ...	***6,826***	***3,424***	***2,902***	***1,309***	***1,031***	***278***	***5,017***	***2,393***	***2,624***	***47***	***47***	...
	0—10	1,792	894	898	32	24	8	1,760	870	890	1	1	...
	10—15	710	375	335	232	122	110	478	253	225	5	5	...
	15—20	520	242	278	197	102	95	323	140	183	3	3	...
	20 and over	3,304	1,913	1,391	848	783	65	2,456	1,130	1,326	38	38	...
	Christian ...	***2,746***	***1,617***	***1,129***	***1,400***	***1,080***	***320***	***1,346***	***537***	***809***	***714***	***582***	***132***
	0—10	676	303	373	119	64	55	557	239	318	73	41	32
	10—15	272	128	144	116	63	53	156	65	91	32	10	22
	15—20	227	115	112	148	85	63	79	30	49	44	30	14
	20 and over	1,571	1,071	500	1,017	868	149	554	203	351	565	501	64
SAGAING.	***All Religions*** ...	***312,111***	***147,816***	***164,295***	***70,769***	***64,189***	***6,580***	***241,342***	***83,627***	***157,715***	***498***	***396***	***102***
	0—10	83,119	40,691	42,428	1,522	1,233	289	81 597	39,458	42,139	29	15	14
	10—15	37,442	19,011	18,431	8,326	7,262	1,064	29,116	11,749	17,367	54	36	18
	15—20	30,035	14,013	16,022	9,251	7,949	1,302	20,784	6,064	14,720	66	49	17
	20 and over	161,515	74,101	87,414	51,670	47,745	3,925	109,845	26,356	83,489	349	296	53
	Buddhist ...	***306,416***	***144,311***	***162,105***	***69,032***	***62,775***	***6,257***	***237,384***	***81,536***	***155,848***	***169***	***162***	***7***
	0—10	81,824	40,046	41,778	1,457	1,192	265	80,367	38,854	41,513	3	2	1
	10—15	36,954	18,769	18,185	8,194	7,184	1,010	28,760	11,585	17,175	19	19	...
	15—20	29,565	13,739	15,826	9,065	7,812	1,253	20,500	5,927	14,573	31	29	2
	20 and over	158,073	71,757	86,316	50,316	46,587	3,729	107,757	25,170	82,587	116	112	4
	Hindu ...	***1,772***	***1,228***	***544***	***481***	***439***	***42***	***1,291***	***789***	***502***	***183***	***95***	***88***
	0—10	369	191	178	12	5	7	357	186	171	8	1	7
	10—15	103	59	44	27	17	10	76	42	34	19	10	9
	15—20	96	60	36	36	29	7	60	31	29	11	4	7
	20 and over	1,204	918	286	406	388	18	798	530	268	95	80	15
	Mahomedan ...	***2,815***	***1,710***	***1,105***	***847***	***705***	***142***	***1,968***	***1,005***	***963***	***84***	***84***	...
	0—10	636	312	324	22	17	5	614	295	319	3	3	...
	10—15	272	132	140	63	38	25	209	94	115	2	2	...
	15—20	245	141	104	98	71	27	147	70	77	7	7	...
	20 and over	1,662	1,125	537	664	579	85	998	546	452	22	22	...
	Christian ..	***1,018***	***492***	***521***	***871***	***238***	***138***	***642***	***259***	***383***	***159***	***102***	***57***
	0—10	275	129	146	30	18	12	245	111	134	15	9	6
	10—15	108	47	61	40	21	19	68	26	42	13	4	9
	15—20	119	64	55	47	32	15	72	32	40	15	7	8
	20 and over	511	252	259	254	162	92	257	90	167	116	82	34

IMPERIAL TABLE VIII.—*Education by Religion and Age.*

PART B.—DETAILS BY DISTRICTS.

District.	AGE.	Population. Total. Persons.	Total. Males.	Total. Females.	Literate. Persons.	Literate. Males.	Literate. Females.	Illiterate. Persons.	Illiterate. Males.	Illiterate. Females.	Literate in English. Persons.	Literate in English. Males.	Literate in English. Females.
1	2	3	4	5	6	7	8	9	10	11	12	13	14
LOWER CHINDWIN.	*All Religions* ...	*816,175*	*141,262*	*174,918*	*54,448*	*51,069*	*8,379*	*261,727*	*90,193*	*171,534*	*315*	*288*	*82*
	0—10	86,310	41,567	44,743	807	639	168	85,503	40,928	44,575	6	4	2
	10—15	34,711	17,306	17,405	4,238	3,826	412	30,473	13,480	16,993	26	22	4
	15—20	28,709	12,429	16,280	6,163	5,595	568	22,546	6,834	15,712	64	60	4
	20 and over	166,445	69,960	96,485	43,240	41,009	2,231	123,205	28,951	94,254	219	197	22
	Buddhist ...	*818,839*	*139,518*	*174,821*	*58,600*	*50,845*	*3,255*	*260,239*	*89,173*	*171,066*	*184*	*172*	*12*
	0—10	85,900	41,364	44,536	783	623	160	85,117	40,741	44,376	2	1	1
	10—15	34,583	17,220	17,363	4,190	3,797	393	30,393	13,423	16,970	13	12	1
	15—20	28,517	12,291	16,226	6,086	5,535	551	22,431	6,756	15,675	50	47	3
	20 and over	164,839	68,643	96,196	42,541	40,390	2,151	122,298	28,253	94,045	119	112	7
UPPER CHINDWIN.	*All Religions* ...	*170,622*	*86,141*	*84,481*	*45,210*	*42,738*	*2,472*	*125,412*	*43,403*	*82,009*	*227*	*214*	*18*
	0—10	44,676	21,958	22,718	921	765	156	43,755	21,193	22,562	7	5	2
	10—15	18,236	9,042	9,194	3,588	3,248	340	14,648	5,794	8,854	5	5	...
	15—20	15,609	7,720	7,889	5,660	5,205	455	9,949	2,515	7,434	15	15	...
	20 and over	92,101	47,421	44,680	35,041	33,520	1,521	57,060	13,901	43,159	200	189	11
	Buddhist ...	*163,884*	*81,694*	*82,140*	*44,086*	*41,626*	*2,410*	*119,798*	*40,068*	*79,730*	*98*	*97*	*1*
	0—10	43,496	21,334	22,162	900	749	151	42,596	20,585	22,011	...	...	...
	10—15	17,826	8,808	9,018	3,554	3,219	335	14,272	5,589	8,683	3	3	...
	15—20	15,103	7,427	7,676	5,608	5,163	445	9,495	2,264	7,231	11	11	...
	20 and over	87,409	44,125	43,284	33,974	32,495	1,479	53,435	11,630	41,805	84	83	1
	Animist ...	*3,719*	*1,990*	*1,729*	*39*	*87*	*2*	*3,680*	*1,953*	*1,727*	...	...	...
	0—10	795	415	380	...	...	...	795	415	380	...	...	...
	10—15	292	163	129	1	1	...	291	162	129	...	...	...
	15—20	363	202	161	5	5	...	358	197	161	...	...	...
	20 and over	2,269	1,210	1,059	33	31	2	2,236	1,179	1,057	...	...	...
	Hindu ...	*1,770*	*1,409*	*361*	*583*	*561*	*22*	*1,187*	*848*	*339*	*36*	*36*	...
	0—10	211	122	89	5	4	1	206	118	88	...	...	...
	10—15	65	38	27	12	11	1	53	27	26	1	1	...
	15—20	80	48	32	21	16	5	59	32	27	1	1	...
	20 and over	1,414	1,201	213	545	530	15	869	671	198	34	34	...
KYAUKSE.	*All Religions* ...	*141,426*	*68,868*	*72,558*	*30,846*	*28,125*	*2,721*	*110,580*	*40,743*	*69,837*	*306*	*265*	*41*
	0—10	34,124	15,400	18,724	891	674	217	33,233	14,726	18,507	15	11	4
	10—15	14,609	7,936	6,673	2,759	2,269	490	11,850	5,667	6,183	31	24	7
	15—20	12,236	5,848	6,388	3,371	2,876	495	8,865	2,972	5,893	61	54	7
	20 and over	80,457	39,684	40,773	23,825	22,306	1,519	56,632	17,378	39,254	199	176	23
	Buddhist ...	*134,928*	*65,293*	*69,635*	*29,450*	*26,909*	*2,541*	*105,478*	*38,384*	*67,094*	*138*	*126*	*12*
	0—10	32,559	14,627	17,932	778	574	204	31,781	14,053	17,728	4	2	2
	10—15	13,923	7,574	6,349	2,626	2,176	450	11,297	5,398	5,899	15	11	4
	15—20	11,667	5,563	6,104	3,221	2,758	463	8,446	2,805	5,641	33	30	3
	20 and over	76,779	37,529	39,250	22,825	21,401	1,424	53,954	16,128	37,826	86	83	3
	Mahomedan ...	*4,954*	*2,509*	*2,445*	*886*	*775*	*111*	*4,068*	*1,784*	*2,384*	*46*	*45*	*1*
	0—10	1,277	633	644	99	90	9	1,178	543	635	6	6	...
	10—15	592	310	282	94	62	32	498	248	250	11	10	1
	15—20	468	219	249	108	81	27	360	138	222	12	12	...
	20 and over	2,617	1,347	1,270	585	542	43	2,032	805	1,227	17	17	...
MEIKTILA.	*All Religions* ...	*279,822*	*134,170*	*145,652*	*57,809*	*54,697*	*3,112*	*222,013*	*79,473*	*142,540*	*1,445*	*1,330*	*115*
	0—10	75,665	36,554	39,111	1,297	1,141	156	74,368	35,413	38,955	51	31	20
	10—15	33,232	16,389	16,843	4,532	4,139	393	28,700	12,250	16,450	51	43	8
	15—20	24,648	11,257	13,391	6,411	5,829	582	18,237	5,428	12,809	77	72	5
	20 and over	146,277	69,970	76,307	45,569	43,588	1,981	100,708	26,382	74,326	1,266	1,184	82
	Buddhist ...	*271,774*	*128,307*	*143,467*	*55,560*	*52,705*	*2,855*	*216,214*	*75,602*	*140,612*	*758*	*740*	*18*
	0—10	74,149	35,789	38,360	1,204	1,084	120	72,945	34,705	38,240	4	4	...
	10—15	32,734	16,105	16,629	4,446	4,071	375	28,288	12,034	16,254	22	22	...
	15—20	24,108	10,908	13,200	6,262	5,726	536	17,846	5,182	12,664	54	54	...
	20 and over	140,783	65,505	75,278	43,648	41,824	1,824	97,135	23,681	73,454	673	660	13
	Hindu ...	*2,931*	*2,474*	*457*	*947*	*889*	*58*	*1,984*	*1,585*	*399*	*185*	*184*	*1*
	0—10	293	142	151	22	16	6	271	126	145	4	4	...
	10—15	72	47	25	19	17	2	53	30	23	3	3	...
	15—20	164	137	27	44	36	8	120	101	19	4	4	...
	20 and over	2,402	2,148	254	862	820	42	1,540	1,328	212	174	173	1

IMPERIAL TABLE VIII.—*Education by Religion and Age.*

PART B.—DETAILS BY DISTRICTS.

District.	AGE.	Population. Total. Persons.	Total. Males.	Total. Females.	Literate. Persons.	Literate. Males.	Literate. Females.	Illiterate. Persons.	Illiterate. Males.	Illiterate. Females.	Literate in English. Persons.	Literate in English. Males.	Literate in English. Females.
1	2	3	4	5	6	7	8	9	10	11	12	13	14
MEIKTILA —*concluded.*	***Mahomedan*** ...	***4,258***	***2,800***	***1,458***	***720***	***670***	***50***	***3,538***	***2,130***	***1,408***	***82***	***81***	***1***
	0—10	1,026	519	507	18	12	6	1,008	507	501	2	1	1
	10—15	376	207	169	38	32	6	338	175	163	4	4	...
	15—20	336	190	146	65	52	13	271	138	133	6	6	...
	20 and over	2,515	1,884	631	599	574	25	1,916	1,310	606	70	70	...
YAMÈTHIN.	***All Religions*** ...	***307,419***	***153,223***	***154,196***	***69,116***	***64,196***	***4,920***	***238,303***	***89,027***	***149,276***	***777***	***629***	***148***
	0—10	83,789	41,058	42,731	1,256	984	272	82,533	40,074	42,459	65	33	32
	10—15	37,064	19,166	17,898	5,954	5,314	640	31,110	13,852	17,258	73	59	14
	15—20	27,071	12,912	14,159	7,472	6,667	805	19,599	6,245	13,354	104	83	21
	20 and over	159,495	80,087	79,408	54,434	51,231	3,203	105,061	28,856	76,205	535	454	81
	Buddhist ...	***288,047***	***141,650***	***146,397***	***65,325***	***60,895***	***4,430***	***222,722***	***80,755***	***141,967***	***224***	***206***	***18***
	0—10	79,319	38,786	40,533	1,145	913	232	78,174	37,873	40,301	6	4	2
	10—15	35,269	18,182	17,087	5,630	5,061	569	29,639	13,121	16,518	30	29	1
	15—20	25,313	11,944	13,369	7,074	6,355	719	18,239	5,589	12,650	36	33	3
	20 and over	148,146	72,738	75,408	51,476	48,566	2,910	96,670	24,172	72,498	152	140	12
	Animist ...	***2,452***	***1,433***	***1,019***	***292***	***279***	***18***	***2,160***	***1,154***	***1,006***	***10***	***10***	...
	0—10	538	305	233	...	...	...	538	305	233	...	...	...
	10—15	210	119	91	16	16	...	194	103	91	...	...	...
	15—20	243	132	111	28	24	4	215	108	107	6	6	...
	20 and over	1,461	877	584	248	239	9	1,213	638	575	4	4	...
	Hindu ...	***3,766***	***3,068***	***698***	***728***	***681***	***42***	***3,048***	***2,387***	***656***	***99***	***96***	***3***
	0—10	434	233	201	7	7	...	427	226	201	...	...	...
	10—15	134	86	48	24	18	6	110	68	42	4	4	...
	15—20	226	169	57	34	28	6	192	141	51	5	5	...
	20 and over	2,972	2,580	392	658	628	30	2,314	1,952	362	90	87	3
	Mahomedan ...	***11,057***	***5,956***	***5,101***	***2,181***	***1,944***	***237***	***8,876***	***4,012***	***4,864***	***95***	***93***	***2***
	0—10	2,922	1,457	1,465	37	37	...	2,885	1,420	1,465	6	6	...
	10—15	1,276	687	589	236	190	46	1,040	497	543	9	7	2
	15—20	1,073	569	504	283	233	50	790	336	454	22	22	...
	20 and over	5,786	3,243	2,543	1,625	1,484	141	4,161	1,759	2,402	58	58	...
	Christian ...	***1,813***	***928***	***885***	***454***	***289***	***165***	***1,359***	***639***	***720***	***333***	***209***	***124***
	0—10	496	235	261	61	27	34	435	208	227	53	23	30
	10—15	162	84	78	38	22	16	124	62	62	26	15	11
	15—20	194	82	112	40	18	22	154	64	90	32	15	17
	20 and over	961	527	434	315	222	93	646	305	341	222	156	66
MYINGYAN.	***All Religions*** ...	***441,905***	***211,119***	***230,786***	***98,201***	***91,121***	***7,080***	***343,704***	***119,998***	***223,706***	***427***	***386***	***41***
	0—10	123,181	60,474	62,707	1,937	1,540	397	121,244	58,934	62,310	9	5	4
	10—15	51,918	25,874	26,044	8,688	7,766	922	43,230	18,108	25,122	18	10	8
	15—20	40,180	19,265	20,915	11,413	10,261	1,152	28,767	9,004	19,763	76	66	10
	20 and over	226,626	105,506	121,120	76,163	71,554	4,609	150,463	33,952	116,511	324	305	19
	Buddhist ...	***438,069***	***207,917***	***230,152***	***96,594***	***89,617***	***6,977***	***341,475***	***118,300***	***223,175***	***208***	***194***	***14***
	0—10	122,759	60,261	62,498	1,922	1,531	391	120,837	58,730	62,107	5	3	2
	10—15	51,745	25,754	25,991	8,634	7,721	913	43,111	18,033	25,078	10	4	6
	15—20	39,838	18,996	20,842	11,263	10,129	1,134	28,575	8,867	19,708	50	46	4
	20 and over	223,727	102,906	120,821	74,775	70,236	4,539	148,952	32,670	116,282	143	141	2
	Hindu ...	***1,787***	***1,588***	***199***	***597***	***583***	***14***	***1,190***	***1,005***	***185***	***44***	***44***	...
	0—10	133	68	65	...	...	...	133	68	65	...	...	...
	10—15	47	39	8	8	8	...	39	31	8	...	...	...
	15—20	146	125	21	45	45	...	101	80	21	4	4	...
	20 and over	1,461	1,356	105	544	530	14	917	826	91	40	40	...
	Mahomedan ...	***1,529***	***1,227***	***302***	***660***	***624***	***36***	***869***	***603***	***266***	***30***	***30***	...
	0—10	214	108	106	4	2	2	210	106	104	...	...	...
	10—15	82	54	28	21	18	3	61	36	25	...	...	...
	15—20	151	112	39	69	60	9	82	52	30	4	4	...
	20 and over	1,082	953	129	566	544	22	516	409	107	26	26	...
N. SHAN STATES.	***All Religions*** ...	***414,786***	***208,095***	***206,691***	***19,804***	***18,708***	***1,096***	***394,982***	***189,387***	***205,595***	***241***	***218***	***23***
	0—10	111,716	55,643	56,073	491	346	145	111,225	55,297	55,928	7	3	4
	10—15	43,427	22,213	21,214	2,385	2,255	130	41,042	19,958	21,084	7	7	...
	15—20	37,060	18,159	18,901	2,396	2,250	146	34,664	15,909	18,755	15	12	3
	20 and over	222,583	112,080	110,503	14,532	13,857	675	208,051	98,223	109,828	212	196	16

IMPERIAL TABLE VIII.—*Education by Religion and Age.*

PART B.—DETAILS BY DISTRICTS.

District.	AGE.	POPULATION. Total. Persons.	Total. Males.	Total. Females.	Literate. Persons.	Literate. Males.	Literate. Females.	Illiterate. Persons.	Illiterate. Males.	Illiterate. Females.	LITERATE IN ENGLISH. Persons.	Males.	Females.
1	2	3	4	5	6	7	8	9	10	11	12	13	14
NORTHERN SHAN STATES—*concluded.*	***Buddhist*** ...	***335,436***	***167,904***	***167,532***	***17,970***	***16,967***	***1,008***	***317,466***	***150,937***	***166,529***	***56***	***54***	***2***
	0—10	93,246	46,204	47,042	461	327	134	92,785	45,877	46,908	...	...	...
	10—15	35,200	17,999	17,201	2,320	2,193	127	32,880	15,806	17,074	1	1	...
	15—20	29,694	14,346	15,348	2,294	2,167	127	27,400	12,179	15,221	1	1	...
	20 and over	177,296	89,355	87,941	12,895	12,280	615	164,401	77,075	87,326	54	52	2
	Animist ...	***75,154***	***36,767***	***38,387***	***203***	***203***	...	***74,951***	***36,564***	***38,387***	***3***	...	***3***
	0—10	17,967	9,169	8,798	...	...	...	17,967	9,169	8,798	...	...	...
	10—15	8,063	4,098	3,965	...	...	...	8,063	4,098	3,965	...	...	...
	15—20	7,113	3,628	3,485	...	...	...	7,113	3,628	3,485	...	...	...
	20 and over	42,011	19,872	22,139	203	203	...	41,808	19,669	22,139	3	...	3
	Hindu ...	***2,607***	***2,250***	***357***	***1,057***	***1,025***	***32***	***1,550***	***1,225***	***325***	***57***	***57***	...
	0—10	242	128	114	11	8	3	231	120	111	1	1	...
	10—15	69	49	20	25	24	1	44	25	19	...	...	...
	15—20	130	103	27	48	42	6	82	61	21	3	3	...
	20 and over	2,166	1,970	196	973	951	22	1,193	1,019	174	53	53	...
	Mahomedan ...	***1,241***	***952***	***289***	***393***	***371***	***22***	***848***	***581***	***267***	***18***	***18***	...
	0—10	183	98	85	6	5	1	177	93	84	...	...	...
	10—15	50	35	15	11	11	...	39	24	15	...	...	...
	15—20	80	55	25	25	21	4	55	34	21	...	...	...
	20 and over	928	764	164	351	334	17	577	430	147	18	18	...
SOUTHERN SHAN STATES.	***All Religions*** ...	***894,485***	***446,099***	***448,386***	***50,590***	***47,614***	***2,976***	***843,895***	***398,485***	***445,410***	***458***	***408***	***50***
	0—10	238,487	120,089	118,398	563	328	235	237,924	119,761	118,163	20	15	5
	10—15	94,135	49,639	44,496	4,610	4,337	273	89,525	45,302	44,223	24	18	6
	15—20	80,253	38,408	41,845	6,738	6,284	454	73,515	32,124	41,391	28	24	4
	20 and over	481,610	237,963	243,647	38,679	36,665	2,014	442,931	201,298	241,633	386	351	35
	Buddhist ...	***775,156***	***384,220***	***390,936***	***48,182***	***45,392***	***2,790***	***726,974***	***338,828***	***388,146***	***98***	***97***	***1***
	0—10	205,504	102,365	103,139	510	289	221	204,994	102,076	102,918	6	6	...
	10—15	83,495	43,710	39,785	4,441	4,191	250	79,054	39,519	39,535	7	7	...
	15—20	71,031	34,335	36,696	6,528	6,100	428	64,503	28,235	36,268	8	8	...
	20 and over	415,126	203,810	211,316	36,703	34,812	1,891	378,423	168,998	209,425	77	76	1
	Animist ...	***104,414***	***53,090***	***51,324***	***170***	***158***	***12***	***104,244***	***52,932***	***51,312***	...	...	...
	0—10	29,156	15,817	13,339	...	...	...	29,156	15,817	13,339	...	...	...
	10—15	9,465	5,340	4,125	4	4	...	9,461	5,336	4,125	...	...	...
	15—20	8,048	3,443	4,605	33	28	5	8,015	3,415	4,600	...	...	...
	20 and over	57,745	28,490	29,255	133	126	7	57,612	28,364	29,248	...	...	...
	Hindu ...	***3,282***	***2,638***	***644***	***1,268***	***1,234***	***34***	***2,014***	***1,404***	***610***	***100***	***100***	...
	0—10	509	292	217	20	18	2	489	274	215	4	4	...
	10—15	127	69	58	25	24	1	102	45	57	4	4	...
	15—20	167	124	43	59	58	1	108	66	42	5	5	...
	20 and over	2,479	2,153	326	1,164	1,134	30	1,315	1,019	296	87	87	...
	Mahomedan ...	***1,800***	***1,274***	***526***	***390***	***366***	***24***	***1,410***	***908***	***502***	***47***	***45***	***2***
	0—10	385	211	174	4	3	1	381	208	173	...	...	...
	10—15	80	43	37	6	5	1	74	38	36	...	...	...
	15—20	124	71	53	28	26	2	96	45	51	2	2	...
	20 and over	1,211	949	262	352	332	20	859	617	242	45	43	2
	Christian ...	***9,818***	***4,866***	***4,952***	***564***	***450***	***114***	***9,254***	***4,416***	***4,838***	***204***	***158***	***46***
	0—10	2,931	1,404	1,527	29	18	11	2,902	1,386	1,516	10	5	5
	10—15	968	477	491	134	113	21	834	364	470	13	7	6
	15—20	883	435	448	90	72	18	793	363	430	13	9	4
	20 and over	5,036	2,550	2,486	311	247	64	4,725	2,303	2,422	168	137	31

IMPERIAL TABLE VIII.—*Education by Religion and Age.*

PART B.—DETAILS BY DISTRICTS.

District.	AGE.	Population. Total. Persons.	Males.	Females.	Literate. Persons.	Males.	Females.	Illiterate. Persons.	Males.	Females.	Literate in English. Persons.	Males.	Females.
1	2	3	4	5	6	7	8	9	10	11	12	13	14
CHIN HILLS.	*All Religions* ...	*119,656*	*68,662*	*60,994*	*706*	*668*	*48*	*118,850*	*67,899*	*60,951*	*40*	*84*	*6*
	0—10	34,447	16,908	17,539	16	8	8	34,431	16,900	17,531	...	...	...
	10—15	11,683	5,991	5,692	37	32	5	11,646	5,959	5,687	2	2	...
	15—20	10,845	5,233	5,612	44	40	4	10,801	5,193	5,608	6	1	5
	20 and over	62,581	30,430	32,151	609	583	26	61,972	29,847	32,125	32	31	1
	Animist ...	*117,868*	*67,010*	*60,348*	*67*	*60*	*7*	*117,291*	*66,950*	*60,341*	...	...	...
	0—10	33,910	16,643	17,267	1	...	1	33,909	16,643	17,266	...	...	...
	10—15	11,594	5,934	5,660	14	14	...	11,580	5,920	5,660	...	...	...
	15—20	10,767	5,191	5,576	23	20	3	10,744	5,171	5,573	...	...	...
	20 and over	61,087	29,242	31,845	29	26	3	61,058	29,216	31,842	...	...	...
	Hindu ...	*1,351*	*947*	*404*	*393*	*384*	*9*	*958*	*563*	*395*	*11*	*11*	...
	0—10	339	166	173	3	3	...	336	163	173	...	...	...
	10—15	49	29	20	14	12	2	35	17	18	1	1	...
	15—20	46	20	26	12	12	...	34	8	26	...	...	...
	20 and over	917	732	185	364	357	7	553	375	178	10	10	...

IMPERIAL TABLE IX.

Education by Ten Selected Tribes and Races.

NOTE.—The entries in this table are not exhaustive for the populations of the ten selected tribes and races. During the process of sorting, every individual who obviously belonged to one of the ten categories was included. But there were many members who were enumerated as belonging to sub-tribes or subdivisions of the main categories, and whose exact tribal classification was not determined until the process of tabulation was commenced. It was then impossible without a disproportionate amount of labour to commence sorting afresh for those who had been thereby excluded. This table therefore comprises all the members of the ten selected tribes and races who were enumerated either under their general tribal or racial names, or under their more easily identified subdivisions. The figures for the Talaing, Arakanese, Kachin, Danu, and Taungthu agree with those given for these races in Table XIII, showing that the analysis in this table is comprehensive for these races. It is not comprehensive for the Karen, Shan, Chin, Wa-Palaung and Chinese races.

IMPERIAL TABLE IX.—*Education by*

TRIBE OR RACE.	LOCALITY.	POPU TOTAL. Persons.	Males.	Females.
1	2	3	4	5
Talaing	Amherst and Thatôn Districts principally, but extending westwards into Pegu, Hanthawaddy and Pyapôn Districts.	320,629	159,235	161,394
Karen	Tenasserim Division, the Southern Shan States and the rural portions of the Deltaic plain Districts.	903,626	450,971	452,655
Arakanese	Arakan Division and Bassein District ...	344,123	177,089	167,034
Shan	Northern and Southern Shan States, the Northern Hill Districts and the Eastern Districts of the Deltaic plain.	941,724	465,609	476,115
Chin	The Arakan Division, the Chin Hills, the Pakôkku Hill Tracts and the western portions of the Pakôkku, Minbu, Thayetmyo, Prome and Henzada Districts.	243,066	119,373	123,693
Kachin	The Northern Hill Districts and the Northern Shan States.	162,368	80,764	81,604
Wa-Palaung	The Northern and Southern Shan States and the specially administered areas attached to the Ruby Mines District.	150,375	74,600	75,775
Danu	The Northern and Southern Shan States and Mandalay District.	70,947	35,264	35,683
Taungthu	Southern Shan States and Thatôn District	183,054	91,597	91,457
Chinese	Distributed all over Burma, but principally in the Deltaic plains, the Tenasserim Coast, the Northern and Southern Shan States, and the Districts of Myitkyina, Bhamo and Ruby Mines.	104,641	79,830	24,811

Selected Tribes and Races.

LATION.

Literate.			Illiterate.			Literate in English.		
Persons.	Males.	Females.	Persons.	Males.	Females.	Persons.	Males.	Females.
6	7	8	9	10	11	12	13	14
70,833	58,256	12,577	249,796	100,979	148,817	619	334	285
114,152	86,098	28,054	789,474	364,873	424,601	4,277	3,045	1,232
58,022	54,790	3,232	286,101	122,299	163,802	1,165	1,081	84
94,962	84,340	10,622	846,762	381,269	465,493	140	118	22
6,923	6,473	450	236,143	112,900	123,243	39	33	6
1,449	937	512	160,919	79,827	81,092	14	13	1
4,202	3,172	1,030	146,173	71,428	74,745	...	...	...
9,400	8,112	1,288	61,547	27,152	34,395	2	...	2
10,553	8,227	2,326	172,501	83,370	89,131	18	13	5
28,321	25,578	2,743	76,320	54,252	22,068	1,912	1,842	70

IMPERIAL TABLE X.

Language.

General Scheme of Language Classification.

Part.	Head of Classification.	Pages.
A I	Vernaculars of Burma	92 to 95
A II	Vernaculars of India beyond Burma	96 & 97
B	Non-Indian Asiatic Languages	97
C	European Languages	97

Detailed Scheme of Classification adopted for the Vernaculars of Burma.

FAMILY.	SUB-FAMILY.	*Branch.*	Group.	Sub-Group.	Columns.
Malayo-Polynesian	......	......	Malay ...	......	50, 51 & 52
Austro-Asiatic ...	Mōn-Khmēr	......	Mōn-Khmēr Palaung-Wa Miao-Yao ...	....	44, 45 & 46 47, 48 & 49
Tibeto-Chinese	Tibeto-Burmese ...	Assam-Burmese	Kuki-Chin	Old Kuki Southern Chin	26, 27 & 28
				Unclassed ...	23, 24 & 25
			Kachin	Unclassed ...	14, 15 & 16
				Kachin-Burma Hybrids	17, 18 & 19
			Lolo ...	......	20, 21 & 22
			Burma ...	......	5 to 13
	Siamese-Chinese ...		Sinitic ...	......	35 to 43
			Tai ...	......	29 to 34

NOTE 1.—The above scheme of classification involves two departures from the authorised scheme based on the results of the Linguistic Survey of India. A new group (the Miao-Yao) has been introduced into the Mōn-Khmēr Sub-Family, and the Lisaw Sub-Group has been treated as a separate group and re-named the Lolo-Group. The reasons for these changes are given in Chapter IX of the Report Volume.

NOTE 2.—The arrangement of groups in the detailed scheme of classification is based on general linguistic considerations; the arrangement of columns in the table itself is adopted rather to provincial conditions.

NOTE 3.—The entry of the number of persons speaking each separate language recorded would have expanded this table to about 250 columns, the majority of which would have contained one entry only. As the utility of a statistical table varies with its degree of concentration, a method of avoiding such an undue expansion by the use of what may be termed "Remainder columns", has been adopted. Extremely localised vernaculars have been grouped together in the main table and analysed separately in a series of supplementary tables on page 98. The number of columns has thereby been reduced to 82. The reduction involves no diminution in the amount of statistical matter presented, and tends to simplify rather than to confuse the scheme of classification.

NOTE 4.—No attempt at uniformity has been made in the analytic tables on page 98. The form giving the greatest amount of information in the least space has been adopted for each grouping.

NOTE 5.—An analysis of the persons speaking Sgau-Karen and Pwo-Karen (columns 35, 36 and 37) has not been made, as the number of persons entered simply as Karen is so great as to render any such analysis valueless.

NOTE 6.—A linguistic analysis of the population of the estimated areas has been effected, and the figures are included in this Table.

Imperial Table X.—

Serial No.	District or State.	Population. Persons.	Population. Males.	Population. Females.	TIBETO-CHINESE — TIBETO-BURMESE SUB-FAMILY— Burma Group. Burmese. Persons.	Burmese. Males.	Burmese. Females.	Arakanese. Persons.	Arakanese. Males.	Arakanese. Females.	Other Languages of the Burma Group. Persons.	Other Languages of the Burma Group. Males.	Other Languages of the Burma Group. Females.
	1	2	3	4	5	6	7	8	9	10	11	12	13
	Provincial Total ...	12,115,217	6,183,494	5,931,723	7,883,299	3,855,510	4,027,789	323,962	161,994	161,968	110,581	55,639	54,942
	Burma Proper ...	10,610,256	5,432,715	5,177,541	7,813,491	3,821,568	3,991,983	323,958	161,991	161,967	17,977	8,610	9,367
	Arakan Division ...	839,896	441,925	397,971	239,946	119,745	120,201	322,782	161,335	161,447	5,233	2,549	2,684
1	Akyab ...	529,943	289,474	240,469	93,480	47,069	46,411	208,527	107,828	100,699	626	260	366
2	Northern Arakan ...	22,234	11,405	10,829	80	59	21	80	50	30	4,607	2,289	2,318
3	Kyaukpyu ...	184,916	89,571	95,345	82,769	40,067	42,702	84,050	39,509	44,541	...	...	...
4	Sandoway ...	102,803	51,475	51,328	63,617	32,550	31,067	30,125	13,948	16,177	...	...	...
	Pegu Division ...	2,073,737	1,136,192	937,545	1,593,355	794,104	799,251	176	137	39	9	1	8
5	City of Rangoon ...	293,316	208,111	85,205	97,364	49,444	47,920	173	137	36	1	1	...
6	Hanthawaddy ...	539,109	295,886	243,223	411,307	209,926	201,381	...	...	...	5	...	5
7	Tharrawaddy ...	433,320	216,442	216,878	392,856	192,291	200,565	...	...	...	...	...	...
8	Pegu ...	429,121	229,540	199,581	337,913	171,511	166,402	3	...	3	3	...	3
9	Prome ...	378,871	186,213	192,658	353,915	170,932	182,983	...	...	...	...	...	...
	Irrawaddy Division.	1,869,485	962,913	906,572	1,449,457	726,140	723,317	955	487	468	...	...	...
10	Bassein ...	440,988	226,773	214,215	323,064	161,208	161,856	832	393	439	...	...	...
11	Henzada ...	532,357	264,319	268,038	473,699	231,966	241,733	8	...	8	...	...	...
12	Myaungmya ...	334,852	176,465	158,387	222,875	113,051	109,824	99	80	19	...	...	...
13	Ma-ubin ...	305,073	155,715	149,358	207,996	104,273	103,723	2	...	2	...	...	...
14	Pyapôn ...	256,215	139,641	116,574	221,825	115,642	106,181	14	14	...	...	...	...
	Tenasserim Division	1,429,294	750,626	678,668	682,806	343,950	338,856	2	2	...	68	43	25
15	Toungoo ...	351,076	181,488	169,588	238,166	119,121	119,045	...	...	...	34	11	23
16	Salween ...	46,608	24,741	21,867	1,647	1,017	630	...	...	...	...	...	...
17	Thatôn ...	416,975	217,770	199,205	150,097	76,223	73,874	...	...	...	15	15	...
18	Amherst ...	367,918	198,430	169,488	99,073	50,269	48,804	...	...	...	19	17	2
19	Tavoy ...	135,293	68,667	66,626	121,699	60,632	61,067	...	...	...	...	...	...
20	Mergui ...	111,424	59,530	51,894	72,124	36,688	35,436	2	2	...	...	...	...
	Magwe Division.	1,239,032	603,614	635,418	1,169,586	564,345	605,241	1	...	1	...	...	...
21	Thayetmyo ...	248,275	122,231	126,044	223,912	109,505	114,407	...	...	...	...	...	...
22	Pakôkku ...	409,909	196,159	213,750	393,653	187,182	206,471	...	...	...	...	...	...
23	Minbu ...	263,939	128,837	135,102	242,123	116,483	125,640	...	...	...	...	...	...
24	Magwe ...	316,909	156,387	160,522	309,898	151,175	158,723	1	...	1	...	...	...
	Mandalay Division ...	832,969	426,776	405,193	473,287	233,269	240,018	4	4	...	11,204	5,546	5,658
25	Mandalay (including City).	340,770	170,750	170,020	309,081	148,512	160,509	...	...	...	14	14	...
	Mandalay City ...	*138,299*	*69,718*	*68,581*	*121,258*	*57,195*	*64,063*	...	...	...	...	...	...
26	Bhamo ...	107,811	55,528	52,283	25,172	13,039	12,133	...	...	...	297	234	63
27	Myitkyina ...	85,577	47,863	37,714	8,237	4,679	3,558	...	...	...	624	391	233
28	Katha ...	198,193	98,148	100,045	90,119	45,024	45,095	4	4	...	10,154	4,900	5,254
29	Ruby Mines ...	100,618	54,487	46,131	40,738	22,015	18,723	...	...	...	115	7	108
	Sagaing Division ...	1,155,271	543,289	611,982	1,060,962	491,940	569,022	9	9	...	394	234	160
30	Shwebo ...	356,363	168,070	188,293	350,392	163,542	186,850	...	...	...	88	65	23
31	Sagaing ...	312,111	147,816	164,295	309,150	145,583	163,567	...	...	...	...	...	...
32	Lower Chindwin ...	316,175	141,262	174,913	314,121	139,599	174,522	...	...	...	...	...	...
33	Upper Chindwin ...	170,622	85,141	84,481	87,299	43,216	44,083	9	9	...	306	169	137
	Meiktila Division ...	1,170,572	567,380	603,192	1,144,052	548,015	596,077	29	17	12	1,069	237	832
34	Kyauksè ...	141,426	68,868	72,558	139,440	67,230	72,210	...	...	...	...	...	...
35	Meiktila ...	279,822	134,170	145,652	272,844	128,818	144,026	13	13	...	675	44	631
36	Yamèthin ...	307,419	153,223	154,196	293,331	143,872	149,459	3	3	...	393	192	201
37	Myingyan ...	441,905	211,119	230,786	438,477	208,095	230,382	13	1	12	1	1	...
	Specially Administered Territories.	1,504,961	750,779	754,182	69,808	34,002	35,806	4	3	1	92,604	47,029	45,575
38	Northern Shan States	458,952	230,545	228,407	6,928	3,613	3,315	4	3	1	10,672	5,588	5,084
39	Southern Shan States	900,202	448,705	451,497	62,789	30,328	32,461	...	...	...	81,932	41,441	40,491
40	Pakôkku Hill Tracts	26,251	12,967	13,284	34	20	14	...	...	...	...	...	...
41	Chin Hills ...	119,556	58,562	60,994	57	41	16	...	...	...	...	...	...

Language.

FAMILY.

ASSAM-BURMESE BRANCH.

KACHIN GROUP.						LOLO GROUP.			KUKI-CHIN GROUP.						
Kachin.			Kachin-Burma Hybrids.			Lolo Group.			Chin (Unspecified).			Other Chin Dialects.			
Persons.	Males.	Females.	Persons.	Males.	Females.	Persons.	Males.	Females.	Persons.	Males.	Females.	Persons.	Males.	Females.	Serial No.
14	15	16	17	18	19	20	21	22	23	24	25	26	27	28	
169,424	83,450	85,964	730	509	221	65,548	33,030	32,518	233,661	114,552	119,109	61,622	30,794	30,828	
99,237	50,320	48,917	477	363	114	4,408	1,992	2,416	115,884	57,352	58,532	35,420	17,901	17,519	
...	...	...	...	...	...	...	...	...	44,081	22,466	21,615	28,633	14,425	14,208	
...	...	...	...	...	...	...	...	...	19,027	9,523	9,504	14,265	7,165	7,100	1
...	...	...	...	...	...	...	...	...	2,360	1,204	1,156	14,368	7,260	7,108	2
...	...	...	..	...	...	...	...	...	14,736	7,704	7,032	...	...	...	3
...	...	...	...	...	...	...	...	...	7,958	4,035	3,923	...	...	...	4
44	23	21	...	...	...	...	...	...	13,899	7,081	6,818	...	...	...	
44	23	21	...	...	...	...	...	...	4	4	...	...	...	...	5
...	...	...	...	...	...	...	...	...	94	36	58	...	...	...	6
...	...	...	...	...	...	...	...	...	1,386	692	694	...	...	...	7
...	...	...	...	...	...	...	...	...	1,245	801	444	...	...	...	8
...	...	...	...	...	...	...	...	..	11,170	5,548	5,622	...	...	...	9
2	2	...	...	...	...	...	...	...	5,337	2,595	2,742	...	...	...	
...	...	...	...	...	...	...	...	...	509	281	228	...	...	...	10
2	2	...	...	...	...	...	...	...	4,743	2,239	2,504	...	...	...	11
...	...	...	...	...	...	...	...	...	74	73	1	...	...	...	12
...	...	...	...	...	...	...	...	...	9	...	9	...	...	...	13
...	...	...	...	...	...	...	...	...	2	2	..	...	...	...	14
...	...	...	...	...	...	...	...	...	238	116	122	...	...	...	
...	..	...	...	...	...	...	...	...	113	54	59	...	...	...	15
...	...	...	...	...	...	...	...	...	26	26	...	...	...	...	16
...	...	...	...	...	...	...	...	...	1	1	...	...	...	...	17
...	...	...	...	...	...	...	...	...	1	1	...	...	...	...	18
...	...	...	...	...	...	...	...	...	...	...	...	...	...	...	19
...	...	...	...	...	...	...	..	...	97	34	63	...	...	...	20
...	...	...	...	...	...	...	...	...	47,275	22,854	24,321	6,787	3,476	3,311	
...	...	...	...	.	...	...	...	...	20,370	9,709	10,661	...	...	...	21
...	...	...	...	...	...	...	...	...	6,941	3,456	3,485	6,787	3,476	3,311	22
...	...	...	...	...	...	...	...	...	17,665	8,628	9,037	...	...	...	23
...	...	...	...	...	...	...	...	...	2,199	1,061	1,138	...	...	...	24
97,249	49,390	47,959	397	283	114	4,408	1,992	2,416	1,783	480	1,303	...	...	...	
39	36	3	...	...	...	...	...	...	4	4	...	...	...	...	25
37	36	1	...	...	...	...	...	...	4	4	...	...	...	...	
42,955	21,126	21,829	45	45	...	909	450	459	...	...	...	...	...	...	26
39,274	19,768	19,506	65	47	18	1,518	773	745	...	...	...	...	...	...	27
6,046	2,948	3,098	17	17	...	...	...	...	...	...	...	...	...	...	28
9,035	5,512	3,523	270	174	96	1,981	769	1,212	1,779	476	1,303	...	...	...	29
1,807	887	920	...	...	...	...	...	...	2,083	1,108	975	...	...	...	
17	16	1	...	...	...	...	...	...	...	...	...	...	...	...	30
...	...	...	...	...	...	...	..	...	...	...	...	...	...	...	31
...	...	...	...	...	...	...	...	...	...	...	...	...	...	...	32
1,790	871	919	...	...	..	...	...	...	2,083	1,108	975	...	...	...	33
35	18	17	80	80	...	...	...	...	1,288	652	636	...	...	...	
...	...	...	...	...	...	...	...	...	...	...	...	...	...	...	34
...	...	...	80	80	...	...	...	...	...	...	...	...	...	...	35
35	18	17	...	...	...	...	...	...	1,275	640	635	...	...	...	36
...	...	...	...	...	...	...	...	...	13	12	1	...	...	...	37
70,177	33,130	37,047	253	146	107	61,140	31,038	30,102	117,777	57,200	60,577	26,202	12,893	13,309	
69,620	32,987	36,633	213	109	104	3,591	1,829	1,762	98	97	1	...	...	...	38
557	143	414	40	37	3	57,549	29,209	28,340	10	10	...	...	...	...	39
...	...	...	...	...	...	...	...	...	2	2	...	26,051	12,817	13,234	40
...	...	...	...	...	...	...	...	...	117,667	57,091	60,576	151	76	75	41

Serial No.	District or State.	TIBETO-CHINESE FAMILY. SIAMESE-CHINESE. TAI GROUP. Shan (Unspecified). Persons.	Males.	Females.	Other Shan Dialects. Persons.	Males.	Females.	SINITIC. Sgau Karen, Pwo-Karen and Karen (Unspecified). Persons.	Males.	Females.
	1	29	30	31	32	33	34	35	36	37
	Provincial Total	897,878	445,823	452,785	70,797	35,986	34,811	850,756	425,748	425,008
	Burma Proper	290,648	146,094	144,554	8,878	5,037	3,841	816,231	408,616	407,615
	Arakan Division	59	32	27	...	...	...	46	6	40
1	Akyab	45	18	27	...	...	...	30	1	29
2	Northern Arakan	...	...	...	...	...	...	...	...	...
3	Kyaukpyu	2	2	...	...	...	...	3	3	...
4	Sandoway	12	12	...	...	...	...	13	2	11
	Pegu Division	18,601	9,126	9,475	3	1	2	104,566	52,483	52,083
5	City of Rangoon	278	132	146	...	...	...	1,046	659	387
6	Hanthawaddy	6,542	3,030	3,512	...	...	...	41,522	20,290	21,232
7	Tharrawaddy	3,859	1,887	1,972	...	...	...	22,836	11,351	11,485
8	Pegu	7,154	3,680	3,474	1	1	...	35,223	18,225	16,998
9	Prome	768	397	371	2	...	2	3,939	1,958	1,981
	Irrawaddy Division	1,394	680	714	1	1	...	332,125	164,618	167,507
10	Bassein	295	172	123	...	...	...	95,419	46,986	48,433
11	Henzada	600	256	344	1	1	...	41,650	20,020	21,630
12	Myaungmya	245	140	105	...	...	...	95,935	49,307	46,628
13	Ma-ubin	220	79	141	...	...	...	85,546	41,407	44,139
14	Pyapôn	34	33	1	...	...	...	13,575	6,898	6,677
	Tenasserim Division ...	31,302	16,885	14,417	8,874	5,035	3,839	375,266	189,256	186,010
15	Toungoo	12,691	6,466	6,225	...	...	...	73,225	37,491	35,734
16	Salween	3,725	2,255	1,470	...	...	...	40,512	20,853	19,659
17	Thatôn	5,021	2,654	2,367	...	...	...	167,829	84,616	83,213
18	Amherst	9,837	5,486	4,351	...	...	...	66,838	32,557	34,281
19	Tavoy	28	24	4	...	...	...	10,776	5,581	5,195
20	Mergui	...	...	...	8,874	5,035	3,839	16,086	8,158	7,928
	Magwe Division	58	22	36	...	...	...	31	10	21
21	Thayetmyo	5	3	2	...	...	...	24	7	17
22	Pakôkku	2	...	2	...	...	...	2	1	1
23	Minbu	22	8	14	...	...	...	4	1	3
24	Magwe	29	11	18	...	...	...	1	1	...
	Mandalay Division	160,500	79,616	80,884	...	...	...	326	227	99
25	Mandalay (including City) ...	3,514	1,821	1,693	...	...	...	30	17	13
	Mandalay City	*107*	*87*	*10*	...	...	...	*17*	*8*	*9*
26	Bhamo	26,811	13,142	13,669	...	...	...	97	42	55
27	Myitkyina	22,545	11,800	10,745	...	...	...	14	8	6
28	Katha	89,257	42,971	46,286	...	...	...	121	108	13
29	Ruby Mines	18,373	9,882	8,491	...	...	...	64	52	12
	Sagaing Division	77,297	38,920	38,377	...	...	...	288	241	47
30	Shwebo	1,221	639	582	...	...	...	115	93	22
31	Sagaing	13	1	12	...	...	...	5	2	3
32	Lower Chindwin	11	7	4	...	...	...	94	84	10
33	Upper Chindwin	76,052	38,273	37,779	...	...	...	74	62	12
	Meiktila Division	1,437	813	624	...	...	...	3,583	1,775	1,808
34	Kyauksè	84	44	40	...	...	...	1	...	1
35	Meiktila	144	76	68	...	...	...	...	...	...
36	Yamèthin	1,109	600	509	...	...	...	3,563	1,760	1,803
37	Myingyan	100	93	7	...	...	...	19	15	4
	Specially Administered Territories.	606,930	299,729	307,201	61,919	30,949	30,970	34,526	17,132	17,398
38	Northern Shan States ...	234,217	115,668	118,549	...	...	...	432	415	17
39	Southern Shan States ...	372,710	184,058	188,652	61,919	30,949	30,970	34,084	16,713	17,371
40	Pakôkku Hill Tracts ...	...	...	...	...	...	...	...	...	...
41	Chin Hills	3	3	...	...	...	...	9	4	5

Language.

						AUSTRO-ASIATIC FAMILY.						MALAYO-POLYNESIAN FAMILY.			
SUB-FAMILY.						MÖN KHMĔR SUB-FAMILY.									
GROUP.						MÖN KHMER PROPER.			PALAUNG, WA AND MIAO-YAO GROUPS.			MALAY GROUP.			
Taungthu.			Other Karen dialects.			Talaing.			Other Mön Khmĕr Languages.			Malayan Languages.			
Persons.	Males.	Females.	Persons.	Males.	Females.	Persons.	Males.	Females.	Persons.	Males.	Females.	Persons.	Males.	Females.	Serial No.
38	39	40	41	42	43	44	45	46	47	48	49	50	51	52	
168,306	84,522	83,824	48,281	24,509	23,772	179,443	91,301	88,142	166,677	83,912	82,765	6,061	3,192	2,869	
43,136	21,994	21,142	3,874	3,572	302	179,252	91,113	88,139	21,726	10,779	10,947	6,029	3,164	2,865	
...	...	...	...	...	...	...	...	...	...	...	...	...	...	...	
...	...	...	...	...	...	...	...	...	...	...	...	...	...	...	1
...	...	...	...	...	...	...	...	...	...	...	...	...	...	...	2
...	...	...	...	...	...	...	...	...	...	...	...	...	...	...	3
...	...	...	...	...	...	...	...	...	...	...	...	...	...	...	4
1,292	688	604	2	3	...	1,960	980	980	...	...	...	25	13	12	
1	1	...	...	...	...	22	10	12	...	...	...	25	13	12	5
100	55	45	3	3	...	782	376	406	...	...	...	...	...	...	6
...	...	...	...	...	...	1	1	...	...	...	...	...	...	...	7
1,191	632	559	...	...	...	1,155	593	562	...	...	...	...	...	...	8
...	...	...	...	...	...	...	...	...	...	...	...	...	...	...	9
...	...	...	15	9	6	2,186	1,047	1,139	...	...	...	...	...	...	
...	...	...	...	...	...	922	453	469	...	...	...	...	...	...	10
...	...	...	...	...	...	399	138	261	...	...	...	...	...	...	11
...	...	...	12	9	3	456	189	267	...	...	...	...	...	...	12
...	...	...	3	...	3	326	214	112	...	...	...	...	...	...	13
...	...	...	...	...	...	83	53	30	...	...	...	...	...	...	14
41,678	21,232	20,446	3,852	3,555	296	175,127	89,108	86,019	3	...	3	5,975	3,128	2,847	
6,009	3,069	2,940	330	143	187	103	51	52	3	...	3	...	...	...	15
8	8	...	9	...	9	4	4	...	...	...	...	...	...	...	16
32,639	16,582	16,057	13	...	13	34,805	17,601	17,204	...	...	...	...	...	...	17
3,017	1,568	1,449	3,499	3,412	87	139,970	71,319	68,651	...	...	...	...	...	...	18
2	2	...	...	...	...	110	58	52	...	...	...	...	...	...	19
3	3	...	...	...	...	135	75	60	...	...	...	5,975	3,128	2,847	20
...	...	...	...	...	...	1	...	1	29	14	15	4	3	1	
...	...	...	...	...	...	...	...	...	...	...	...	...	...	...	21
...	...	...	...	...	...	...	...	...	...	...	...	4	3	1	22
...	...	...	...	...	...	1	...	1	29	14	15	...	...	...	23
...	...	...	...	...	...	...	...	...	...	...	...	...	...	...	24
9	5	4	...	...	...	78	78	...	21,649	10,704	10,925	8	8	...	
...	...	...	...	...	...	...	...	...	3	...	3	...	...	...	25
...	...	...	...	...	...	78	78	...	3	...	3	...	...	...	26
...	...	...	...	...	...	...	...	...	221	121	100	8	8	...	27
...	...	...	...	...	...	...	...	...	606	377	329	...	...	...	28
9	5	4	...	...	...	...	...	...	20,819	10,326	10,493	...	...	...	29
...	...	...	5	5	...	...	...	...	...	...	...	17	12	5	
...	...	...	5	5	...	...	...	...	...	...	...	1	1	...	30
...	...	...	...	...	...	...	...	...	...	...	...	13	10	3	31
...	...	...	...	...	...	...	...	...	...	...	...	3	1	2	32
...	...	...	...	...	...	...	...	...	...	...	...	...	...	...	33
157	69	88	...	...	...	...	...	...	45	41	4	...	...	...	
39	10	29	...	...	...	...	...	...	...	...	...	...	...	...	34
115	56	59	...	...	...	...	...	...	2	2	...	...	...	...	35
3	3	...	...	...	...	...	...	...	43	39	4	...	...	...	36
...	...	...	...	...	...	...	...	...	...	...	...	...	...	...	37
125,190	62,528	62,672	44,407	20,937	23,470	91	88	3	144,951	73,133	71,818	32	28	4	
212	16	196	97	1	96	9	6	3	94,237	47,529	46,708	32	28	4	38
124,978	62,508	62,476	44,310	20,936	23,374	82	82	...	50,714	25,604	25,110	...	...	...	39
...	...	...	...	...	...	...	...	...	...	...	...	...	...	...	40
...	...	...	...	...	...	...	...	...	...	...	...	...	...	...	41

VERNACULARS OF INDIA

Serial No.	District or State.	Tamil. Persons.	Tamil. Males.	Tamil. Females.	Telugu. Persons.	Telugu. Males.	Telugu. Females.	Oriya. Persons.	Oriya. Males.	Oriya. Females.	Bengali. Persons.	Bengali. Males.	Bengali. Females.
	1	53	54	55	56	57	58	59	60	61	62	63	64
	Provincial Total ...	125,670	87,917	37,753	123,162	102,875	20,287	19,112	18,276	836	248,310	164,405	83,905
	Burma Proper ...	125,496	87,779	37,717	122,833	102,626	20,207	17,969	17,148	821	247,851	164,035	83,816
	Arakan Division ...	1,523	1,372	151	649	629	20	1,630	1,610	20	184,743	109,628	75,115
1	Akyab ...	1,192	1,178	14	573	554	19	1,489	1,474	15	181,509	107,394	74,115
2	Northern Arakan ...	49	34	15	5	5	...	10	7	3	189	173	16
3	Kyaukpyu ...	256	137	119	40	39	1	72	71	1	2,525	1,634	891
4	Sandoway ...	26	23	3	31	31	...	59	58	1	520	427	93
	Pegu Division ...	79,059	54,297	24,762	83,904	70,686	13,218 (a)	9,199	8,676	523	29,290	26,961	2,329
5	City of Rangoon ...	42,408	29,446	12,968	53,358	46,117	7,241	2,174	1,899	275	21,089	19,678	1,411
6	Hanthawaddy ...	20,549	13,647	6,902	16,415	13,448	2,967	3,401	3,255	146	5,133	4,702	431
7	Tharrawaddy ...	1,840	1,466	374	2,450	1,974	476	609	587	22	937	727	210
8	Pegu ...	12,509	8,475	4,034	10,021	7,743	2,278	2,798	2,722	76	1,621	1,388	233
9	Prome ...	1,753	1,263	490	1,660	1,404	256	217	213	4	510	466	44
	Irrawaddy Division ...	12,540	9,777	2,763	15,490	13,461	2,029	1,958	1,883	75	10,778	9,457	1,321
10	Bassein ...	2,122	1,606	516	6,236	5,578	658	134	117	17	2,994	2,494	500
11	Henzada ...	1,349	1,037	312	1,546	1,372	174	1,251	1,228	23	659	617	42
12	Myaungmya ...	2,360	1,995	365	2,383	2,121	262	144	144	...	2,706	2,509	197
13	Ma-ubin ...	634	489	145	1,237	1,043	194	283	259	24	1,821	1,610	211
14	Pyapôn ...	6,075	4,650	1,425	4,088	3,347	741	146	135	11	2,598	2,227	371
	Tenasserim Division ...	24,457	17,237	7,220	18,158	14,128	4,030	1,907	1,829	78	16,129	12,223	3,906
15	Toungoo ...	1,871	1,420	451	2,952	2,427	525	768	763	5	884	718	166
16	Salween ...	4	3	1	15	15	...	...	...	...	333	294	39
17	Thatôn ...	10,878	7,537	3,341	4,052	3,091	961	270	263	7	3,636	3,036	600
18	Amherst ...	11,223	7,875	3,348	8,168	5,806	2,362	783	718	65	10,713	7,693	3,020
19	Tavoy ...	302	263	39	268	194	74	11	10	1	221	190	31
20	Mergui ...	179	139	40	2,703	2,595	108	75	75	...	342	292	50
	Magwe Division ...	1,537	1,006	531	1,679	1,548	131	1,218	1,205	13	1,133	1,040	93
21	Thayetmyo ...	774	435	339	271	227	44	56	55	1	321	300	21
22	Pakôkku ...	138	94	44	133	127	6	30	30	...	258	223	35
23	Minbu ...	299	245	54	427	402	25	1,054	1,042	12	150	138	12
24	Magwe ...	326	232	94	848	792	56	78	78	...	404	379	25
	Mandalay Division ...	4,090	2,550	1,540	1,015	689	326	604	600	4	3,856	2,999	857
25	Mandalay (including City).	3,426	2,004	1,422	707	419	288	129	129	...	2,460	1,731	729
	Mandalay City ...	*1,859*	*1,147*	*712*	*334*	*239*	*95*	...	...	...	*1,237*	*1,006*	*231*
26	Bhamo ...	119	87	32	84	66	18	12	12	...	318	298	20
27	Myitkyina ...	109	75	34	49	36	13	229	228	1	444	383	61
28	Katha ...	181	137	44	35	30	5	230	227	3	189	176	13
29	Ruby Mines ...	255	247	8	140	138	2	4	4	...	445	411	34
	Sagaing Division ...	964	630	334	356	234	122	463	374	89	991	889	102
30	Shwebo ...	556	356	200	137	97	40	134	134	...	255	208	47
31	Sagaing ...	235	154	81	160	102	58	197	129	68	357	336	21
32	Lower Chindwin ...	127	88	39	25	15	10	42	35	7	166	144	22
33	Upper Chindwin ...	46	32	14	34	20	14	90	76	14	213	201	12
	Meiktila Division ...	1,326	910	416	1,582	1,251	331	990	971	19	931	838	93
34	Kyauksè ...	48	35	13	46	24	22	44	43	1	52	50	2
35	Meiktila ...	564	364	200	219	164	55	425	417	8	240	207	33
36	Yamèthin ...	536	350	186	1,015	782	233	329	319	10	230	190	40
37	Myingyan ...	178	161	17	308	281	21	192	192	...	409	391	18
	Specially Administered Territories.	174	138	36	329	249	80	1,143	1,128	15	459	370	89
38	Northern Shan States	80	64	16	44	43	1	807	794	13	148	95	53
39	Southern Shan States	76	62	14	68	42	26	336	334	2	303	271	32
40	Pakôkku Hill Tracts	2	2	...	1	1	...	...	...	...	1	1	...
41	Chin Hills ...	16	10	6	216	163	53	...	...	...	7	3	4

Language.

BEYOND BURMA.						NON-INDIAN ASIATIC LANGUAGES.						EUROPEAN LANGUAGES.						
Hindi Languages.			Other Indian Languages.			Chinese.			Other Asiatic Languages.			English.			Other European Languages.			
Persons.	Males.	Females.	Persons.	Males.	Females.	Persons.	Males.	Females.	Persons.	Males.	Females.	Persons.	Males.	Females.	Persons.	Males.	Females.	Serial No.
65	66	67	68	69	70	71	72	73	74	75	76	77	78	79	80	81	82	
184,882	150,833	34,049	42,159	33,400	8,752	108,877	78,364	30,513	1,141	560	581	24,355	15,756	8,599	820	647	173	
182,046	148,452	33,594	37,351	29,592	7,759	69,919	55,801	14,118	1,138	557	581	24,111	15,876	8,235	836	663	173	
8,982	6,890	2,092	463	346	117	645	578	67	15	...	15	466	314	152	...	...	...	
8,144	6,199	1,945	102	87	15	501	441	60	15	...	15	418	283	135	...	...	...	1
188	122	66	292	198	94	...	...	...	...	...	...	6	4	2	...	...	...	2
387	337	50	8	8	...	58	53	5	...	...	...	10	7	3	...	...	...	3
263	232	31	61	53	8	86	84	2	...	...	...	32	20	12	...	...	...	4
84,863	69,970	14,893	11,166	9,461	1,705	26,473	22,226	4,247	548	239	309	12,744	8,706	4,038	568	460	108	
39,000	33,600	5,400	9,947	7,728	2,219	13,594	11,169	2,425	524	217	307	11,729	7,391	4,338	535	442	93	5
25,640	20,920	4,720	1,367	998	369	4,793	4,243	550	...	...	...	1,436	952	484	20	5	15	6
4,315	3,524	791	201	170	31	1,881	1,682	199	3	...	3	144	88	56	8	8	...	7
12,580	9,143	3,437	584	528	56	4,797	3,903	894	14	2	12	309	193	116	...	...	...	8
3,328	2,783	545	67	37	30	1,408	1,129	279	7	...	7	126	82	44	1	1	...	9
23,285	20,575	2,710	1,125	907	218	11,899	10,679	1,220	108	33	75	770	502	268	60	60	...	
5,522	5,009	513	90	78	12	2,276	2,043	233	76	20	56	449	287	162	48	48	...	10
4,357	3,697	660	312	211	101	1,617	1,431	186	8	4	4	148	92	56	8	8	...	11
4,357	3,943	414	182	151	31	1,944	1,706	238	6	...	6	70	43	27	4	4	...	12
4,948	4,468	480	...	...	...	1,991	1,832	159	9	4	5	48	37	11	...	...	...	13
4,101	3,458	643	541	467	74	3,071	2,667	404	9	5	4	55	43	12	...	...	...	14
26,715	19,835	6,880	2,446	2,139	307	11,180	9,178	2,002	304	202	102	2,678	1,461	1,217	130	94	36	
10,679	7,147	3,532	398	341	57	2,185	1,884	301	30	14	16	614	353	261	21	15	6	15
253	206	47	38	35	3	12	10	2	...	...	...	22	15	7	...	...	...	16
4,749	3,684	1,065	370	317	53	2,441	2,049	392	...	...	...	156	98	58	3	3	...	17
8,614	6,995	1,619	1,548	1,359	189	2,990	2,547	443	43	21	22	1,498	721	777	84	66	18	18
818	701	117	6	5	1	897	878	19	3	3	...	149	123	26	3	3	...	19
1,602	1,102	500	86	82	4	2,655	1,810	845	228	164	64	239	141	98	19	7	12	20
6,659	5,540	1,119	1,164	949	215	1,317	1,102	215	49	29	20	604	471	123	...	...	...	
1,945	1,471	474	127	110	17	233	216	17	25	10	15	212	183	29	...	...	...	21
1,112	979	133	276	205	71	448	290	158	19	19	...	106	74	32	...	...	...	22
1,121	981	140	662	557	105	318	299	19	...	...	...	64	39	25	...	...	...	23
2,481	2,109	372	99	77	22	318	297	21	5	...	5	282	235	47	...	...	...	24
17,928	14,380	3,538	14,236	11,128	3,108	16,074	10,010	6,064	57	36	21	2,969	1,738	1,231	48	24	24	
10,740	8,364	2,376	5,948	4,293	1,655	1,427	1,224	203	43	22	21	3,222	2,141	1,081	43	19	24	25
6,748	*5,154*	*1,594*	*3,899*	*2,789*	*1,110*	*1,258*	*1,102*	*156*	...	...	...	*1,502*	*939*	*563*	*36*	*12*	*24*	
1,693	1,505	188	2,220	1,967	253	6,447	3,030	3,417	11	11	...	318	271	47	4	4	...	26
3,123	2,462	661	4,495	3,583	912	4,086	3,224	862	...	...	...	151	121	30	...	...	...	27
1,154	1,019	135	163	146	17	389	337	52	3	3	...	131	101	30	...	...	...	28
1,208	1,030	178	1,510	1,139	371	3,725	2,195	1,530	...	...	...	147	104	43	1	1	...	29
5,269	4,311	958	2,864	2,294	570	586	485	101	11	8	3	998	802	196	7	6	1	
2,090	1,735	355	434	381	53	303	283	20	1	1	...	710	610	100	4	4	...	30
1,176	924	252	497	352	145	134	119	15	3	...	3	168	102	66	3	2	1	31
715	597	118	660	522	138	141	125	16	7	7	...	63	38	25	...	...	...	32
1,188	955	233	1,273	1,039	234	108	58	50	...	...	...	57	52	5	...	...	...	33
8,455	7,051	1,404	2,787	2,368	429	1,745	1,643	102	46	30	16	880	590	290	13	9	4	
1,453	1,228	225	55	44	11	122	121	1	...	...	...	77	45	32	4	4	...	34
1,829	1,552	277	1,858	1,647	211	500	483	17	19	19	...	364	271	93	7	3	4	35
3,741	3,030	711	535	389	146	831	786	45	5	...	5	330	197	133	...	...	...	36
1,432	1,241	191	339	288	51	292	253	39	22	11	11	111	79	32	2	2	...	37
2,836	2,381	455	4,801	2,808	993	38,958	22,563	16,395	3	3	...	244	180	64	4	4	...	
1,169	984	185	1,264	1,049	215	35,003	19,569	15,434	...	...	...	73	56	17	2	2	...	38
1,332	1,127	205	2,323	1,768	555	3,938	2,977	961	3	3	...	147	107	40	2	2	...	39
4	4	...	154	118	36	...	...	...	...	...	...	2	2	...	...	...	...	40
331	266	65	1,060	873	187	17	17	...	...	...	...	22	15	7	...	...	...	41

Analysis of columns {12, 13 / 27, 28 / 42, 43}

OTHER BURMESE LANGUAGES.

Language.	District.	Persons. M. Column 12.	Persons. F. Column 13.
Taungyo	......	9,569	9,748
	Southern Shan States	9,534	9,659
	Other districts ...	35	89
Intha ...	......	27,707	28,173
	Southern Shan States	27,705	28,167
	Other districts ...	2	6
Danu ...	......	10,076	8,618
	Northern Shan States	5,588	5,056
	Southern Shan States	4,202	2,665
	Meiktila ...	35	591
	Yamèthin ...	167	179
	Other districts ...	84	127
Hpôn ...	Myitkyina ..	157	185
Tavoyan	......	44	2
	Thatôn ...	13	...
	Amherst ...	17	2
	Mandalay ...	14	...
Kadu ...	......	5,537	5,532
	Katha ...	4,900	5,254
	Myitkyina ...	234	48
	Bhamo ...	161	63
	Upper Chindwin ...	169	137
	Other districts ...	73	30
Chaungtha	......	1,205	1,309
	Northern Arakan ...	1,056	1,038
	Akyab ..	150	271
Mrö ...	......	1,343	1,375
	Northern Arakan ...	1,233	1,280
	Akyab ...	110	95
	Total ...	55,639	54,942

OTHER CHIN LANGUAGES.

Language.	District.	Column 27.	Column 28.
Taungtha	......	8,817	8,427
	Akyab ...	5,341	5,116
	Pakôkku ...	3,476	3,311
Khami ...	......	8,230	8,201
	Akyab ...	1,333	1,453
	Northern Arakan ...	6,897	6,748
Ann ...	Northern Arakan ...	235	239
Chaw ...	Northern Arakan ...	128	121
Daingnet	Akyab	445	474
M'hang	Akyab	8	15
Thet	Akyab	38	42
Yindu	Pakôkku Hill Tracts	2,138	2,210
Chinbôk	Pakôkku Hill Tracts	8,916	9,263
Chinbôn	Pakôkku Hill Tracts	818	782
Baungshe	Pakôkku Hill Tracts	945	979
Siyin ...	Chin Hills ..	76	75
	Total ...	30,794	30,828

OTHER KAREN LANGUAGES.

Language.	District.	Column 42.	Column 43.
Karenni	......	11,257	9,946
	Southern Shan States	7,685	9,644
	Amherst ..	3,412	87
	Toungoo ...	143	187
	Other districts ..	17	28
Karennet	......	494	234
	Southern Shan States	493	138
	Other districts ...	1	96
Karenbyu	Southern Shan States	420	357
Zayein	Southern Shan States	2,574	2,318
Sinsin	Southern Shan States	522	377
Brè	Southern Shan States	3,149	3,769
Manô	Southern Shan States	955	1,227
Yinbaw	Southern Shan States	1,032	1,134
Padaung	Southern Shan States	4,106	4,410
	Total ...	24,509	23,772

Analysis of columns {18, 19 / 21, 22 / 48, 49}

Columns in Imperial Table X.	Language and Group.	Southern Shan States. Males.	Southern Shan States. Females.	Northern Shan States. Males.	Northern Shan States. Females.	Ruby Mines. Males.	Ruby Mines. Females.	Myitkyina. Males.	Myitkyina. Females.	Bhamo. Males.	Bhamo. Females.	Other Districts. Males.	Other Districts. Females.	Total. Males.	Total. Females.
18, 19	Kachin-Burma Hybrids.	37	3	109	104	174	96	47	18	45	...	97	...	509	221
	Tsi (Szi-Lepai)	...	...	...	...	122	83	...	...	...	...	...	...	122	83
	Maingtha ...	37	3	...	...	52	13	47	18	45	...	97	...	279	37
	Maru ...	...	...	109	104	...	...	...	...	...	...	...	...	108	101
21, 22	Lolo Group ...	29,209	28,340	1,829	1,762	769	1,212	773	745	450	459	...	...	33,030	32,518
	Lolo (Myen)...	...	...	166	173	...	...	...	...	...	...	...	...	166	173
	Lisu ...	772	680	1,643	1,563	769	1,212	773	745	450	459	...	...	4,407	4,659
	Lahu (Muhso)	9,355	9,099	20	26	...	...	...	...	...	...	...	...	9,375	9,125
	Kwi (Lahu Hsi)	2,007	1,917	...	...	...	...	...	...	...	...	...	...	2,007	1,917
	Akha (Kaw)	16,666	16,259	...	...	...	...	...	...	...	...	...	...	16,666	16,259
	Akö ...	409	385	...	...	...	...	...	...	...	...	...	...	409	385
48, 49	Other Mön Khmër languages.	25,604	25,110	47,529	46,708	10,326	10,493	277	329	121	100	55	25	83,912	82,765
	Palaung ...	18,313	17,878	43,999	43,164	10,100	10,493	...	...	121	100	55	25	72,588	71,660
	Yin (Riang)...	2,359	2,515	53	77	...	...	...	...	...	...	...	...	2,412	2,592
	Wa ...	2,677	2,630	3,197	3,192	226	...	277	329	...	...	...	...	6,397	6,151
	En ...	1,895	1,789	...	...	...	...	...	...	...	...	...	...	1,895	1,789
	Pyin ...	153	120	...	...	...	...	...	...	...	...	...	...	153	120
	Yao ...	136	138	...	...	...	...	...	...	...	...	...	...	136	138
	Miao (Hmeng)	51	40	280	275	...	...	...	...	...	...	...	...	331	315

Analysis of columns 33, 34 and 51, 52.

OTHER SHAN LANGUAGES.

Language.	District.	Males, column 33.	Females, column 34.
Khün	Southern Shan States ...	23,925	24,483
Lü	Southern Shan States ...	6,892	6,370
Daye	Southern Shan States ...	111	114
Siamese	......	5,058	3,844
	Mergui	5,035	3,839
	Other Districts ...	23	5
	Total ...	35,985	34,811

MALAYAN LANGUAGES.

Language.	District.	Column 51.	Column 52.
Malay	......	2,237	1,953
	Mergui	2,173	1,931
	Other Districts ...	64	22
Salon (Mawken) ...	Mergui	955	916
	Total ...	3,192	2,869

Analysis of columns 69 and 70.

Family.	Sub-Family.	Branch.	Group.	Language.	Males, column 69.	Females, column 70.
Indo-European	Aryan	Iranian ...	Western ...	Persian ...	163	77
		Indian ..	Eastern ...	Pushto ...	1,490	97
			North-Western.	Sindhi ...	70	15
				Marathi ...	1,362	349
				Goanese ...	342	9
			Western ...	Gujerati ...	6,049	1,847
				Punjabi ...	19,493	3,445
				Marwari ...	382	122
			Northern ...	Garhwali ...	...	3
				Naipali ...	2,325	1,647
			South-Western.	Singalese ...	102	48
			Eastern ...	Assamese ...	81	70
				Total ..	31,857	7,729
Dravidian ..	...		... ...	Malayalam ...	719	17
Semitic ...	...	...	......	Arabic ...	130	71
Tibeto-Chinese	Tibeto-Burman.	Assam-Burmese.	......	Manipuri ...	694	935
				Grand Total ...	33,400	8,752

Analysis of columns {66, 67 / 75, 76 / 81, 82}

HINDI LANGUAGES.

Language.	Males, column 66.	Females, column 67.
Urdu ...	7,445	1,929
Hindi ...	32,624	7,481
Hindustani	110,583	24,632
Nagri ...	181	7
Total ...	150,833	34,049

OTHER ASIATIC LANGUAGES.

Language.	Males, column 75.	Females, column 76.
Armenian ..	26	3
Hebrew ...	259	217
Caucassian	18	2
Turkish ...	5	...
Japanese ...	199	359
Phillipino ... (Tagala)	53	...
Total ..	560	581

OTHER EUROPEAN LANGUAGES.

Language.	Males, column 81.	Females, column 82.
Greek ...	46	4
Italian ...	115	7
French ...	72	63
Spanish ...	7	9
Portuguese ...	159	53
Finnish ...	2	...
Russian ...	8	14
Hungarian ...	...	1
Bulgarian ...	1	...
Norwegian	27	...
Dutch ...	36	5
Swedish ...	4	...
Danish ...	1	...
German ...	169	17
Total ...	647	173

IMPERIAL TABLE XI.

Birth-Place.

NOTE 1.—This table, comprising nine parts, is printed in three sections arranged according to the following scheme of classification.

Serial No.	Part.	Birth-Place.	Section.	Page.
1	A I.	Born in India—within the Province of Burma ... In—(i) Burma Proper. (ii) Specially Administered Territories.	I	100—111
2	A II.	Born in India—beyond Burma ... ... In—(*a*) Contiguous Province of Eastern Bengal and Assam— (i) British Territory. (ii) Feudatory States. (*b*) Other Provinces and States in India— (i) British Territory. (ii) Feudatory States. (*c*) French and Portuguese Settlements. (*d*) India, unspecified.	II	112—123
3	B	Born in other Asiatic Countries		
4	C	Born in Europe	III	124—135
5	D	Born in Africa		
6	E	Born in America		
7	F	Born in Australasia		
8	H	Birth-place unspecified		
9	...	Not enumerated by birth-place		

NOTE 2.—In Part A II, the details given for the following districts or States—Chittagong, Ganjam, Vizagapatam, Godavery, Tanjore, Fyzabad, Cochin, and Travancore, are also included in the totals of the main Province or State to which they belong.

NOTE 3.—In Part C, details are given for the separate portions of the United Kingdom as well as for the combined total.

NOTE 4.—Part G.—Born at Sea—being blank has been omitted.

NOTE 5.—The last Part (not enumerated by birth-place) comprises the populations of the estimated portions of the Northern and Southern Shan States and the Pakôkku Hill Tracts.

PROVINCE, DISTRICT, OR

Serial No.	District, State, Province, or Country where born.	Whole Province. Persons.	Whole Province. Males.	Whole Province. Females.	Akyab. Persons.	Akyab. Males.	Akyab. Females.	Northern Arakan. Persons.	Northern Arakan. Males.	Northern Arakan. Females.
	1	2	3	4	5	6	7	8	9	10
	A. BORN IN INDIA.	11,958,945	6,076,040	5,882,905	529,304	288,919	240,385	22,039	11,260	10,779
	I.* Within the Province of Burma.	11,465,246	5,652,871	5,812,375	485,505	249,915	235,590	21,557	10,881	10,676
	(i) Within Burma Proper	10,016,791	4,934,670	5,082,121	485,494	249,908	235,586	21,557	10,881	10,676
	Arakan Division	*797,546*	*402,266*	*395,280*	*484,953*	*249,490*	*235,463*	*21,551*	*10,878*	*10,673*
1	Akyab	483,946	248,862	235,084	482,467	247,886	234,581	130	66	64
2	Northern Arakan ...	21,273	10,706	10,567	28	...	28	21,214	10,686	10,528
3	Kyaukpyu	188,287	90,931	97,356	2,393	1,590	803	1	...	1
4	Sandoway	104,040	51,767	52,273	65	14	51	206	126	80
	Pegu Division	*1,691,507*	*837,517*	*853,990*	*294*	*234*	*60*	*3*	*2*	*1*
5	City of Rangoon ...	132,479	67,459	65,020	245	190	55	2	1	1
6	Hanthawaddy ...	441,101	219,907	221,194	8	8	...	...	...	...
7	Tharrawaddy ...	406,514	199,732	206,782	6	3	3	...	...	...
8	Pegu	312,028	155,311	156,717	12	12	...	...	...	...
9	Prome	399,385	195,108	204,277	23	21	2	1	1	...
	Irrawaddy Division ...	*1,650,882*	*818,806*	*832,676*	*38*	*24*	*14*	*1*	...	*1*
10	Bassein	424,856	212,103	212,753	26	16	10	...	...	...
11	Henzada	532,012	261,783	270,229	12	8	4	...	...	...
12	Myaungmya	259,057	129,395	129,662	...	...	...	...	...	...
13	Ma-ubin	285,670	141,401	144,269	...	...	...	1	...	1
14	Pyapôn	149,287	73,624	75,663	...	...	...	...	...	...
	Tenasserim Division ...	*1,308,524*	*662,214*	*646,810*	*24*	*9*	*15*	...	...	...
15	Toungoo	281,779	141,811	139,968	9	4	5	...	...	...
16	Salween	45,083	23,532	21,551	...	...	...	...	...	...
17	Thatôn	393,453	197,775	195,678	...	...	...	...	...	...
18	Amherst	346,277	176,377	169,900	11	5	6	...	...	...
19	Tavoy	137,161	69,118	68,043	2	...	2	...	...	...
20	Mergui	104,771	53,601	51,170	2	...	2	...	...	...
	Lower Burma Unspecified	*125*	*76*	*49*	...	...	...	...	...	...
	Magwe Division	*1,325,101*	*646,601*	*678,500*	*38*	*24*	*14*	*1*	...	*1*
21	Thayetmyo	274,574	135,269	139,305	16	12	4	1	...	1
22	Pakôkku	439,196	213,030	226,166	2	2	...	...	...	...
23	Minbu	280,301	136,589	143,712	19	9	10	...	...	...
24	Magwe	331,030	161,713	169,317	1	1	...	...	...	...
	Mandalay Division ...	*791,526*	*390,960*	*400,566*	*67*	*50*	*17*	*1*	*1*	...
25	Mandalay (including City).	358,195	176,588	181,607	67	50	17	1	1	...
26	Bhamo	89,540	43,677	45,863	...	...	...	...	...	...
27	Myitkyina	64,836	32,761	32,075	...	...	...	...	...	...
28	Katha	196,401	96,495	99,906	...	...	...	...	...	...
29	Ruby Mines	82,554	41,439	41,115	...	...	...	...	...	...
	Sagaing Division... ...	*1,222,241*	*581,108*	*641,188*	*13*	*11*	*2*	...	...	...
30	Shwebo	382,006	182,219	199,787	4	2	2	...	...	...
31	Sagaing	334,834	160,480	174,354	9	9	...	...	...	...
32	Lower Chindwin ...	325,016	147,475	177,541	...	...	...	...	...	...
33	Upper Chindwin ...	180,385	90,929	89,456	...	...	...	...	...	...
	Meiktila Division... ...	*1,229,134*	*595,474*	*633,660*	*67*	*66*	*1*	...	...	...
34	Kyauksè	132,898	64,684	68,214	61	61	...	...	...	...
35	Meiktila	314,436	151,163	163,273	1	1	...	...	...	...
36	Yamèthin	300,449	147,572	152,877	1	1	...	...	...	...
37	Myingyan	481,351	232,055	249,296	4	3	1	...	...	...
	Upper Burma Unspecified	*205*	*153*	*52*	...	...	...	...	...	...
	(ii) Within Specially Administered Territories.	1,448,455	718,201	730,254	11	7	4	...	...	...
38	Northern Shan States	408,584	202,655	205,929	1	1	...	...	...	...
39	Southern Shan States	904,305	449,554	454,751	10	6	4	...	...	...
40	Pakôkku Hill Tracts	16,968	8,349	8,619	...	...	...	...	...	...
41	Chin Hills	118,598	57,643	60,955	...	...	...	..	...	...

Birth-Place.

STATE WHERE ENUMERATED.

Kyaukpyu.			Sandoway.			City of Rangoon.			Hanthawaddy.			
Persons.	Males.	Females.	Persons.	Males.	Females.	Persons.	Males.	Females.	Persons.	Males.	Females.	Serial No.
11	12	13	14	15	16	17	18	19	20	21	22	
184,862	89,523	95,339	102,711	51,385	51,326	275,885	193,630	82,255	534,372	291,626	242,746	
183,540	88,245	95,295	101,930	50,641	51,289	122,407	62,914	59,493	474,433	241,481	232,952	
183,540	88,245	95,295	101,926	50,637	51,289	122,200	62,822	59,378	472,417	240,382	232,035	
182,651	*87,716*	*94,935*	*101,843*	*50,246*	*51,097*	*598*	*457*	*141*	*72*	*60*	*12*	
280	163	117	20	17	3	414	310	104	28	23	5	1
2	2	...	...	...	...	11	10	1	...	...	...	2
182,099	87,388	94,711	1,270	729	541	84	73	11	2	...	2	3
270	163	107	100,053	49,500	50,553	89	64	25	42	37	5	4
45	*33*	*12*	*159*	*115*	*44*	*100,164*	*49,660*	*50,494*	*431,663*	*214,655*	*217,008*	
14	9	5	16	10	6	91,446	44,332	47,114	7,270	4,037	3,233	5
...	...	...	3	1	2	4,266	2,559	1,707	410,285	203,173	207,112	6
6	5	1	3	3	...	891	557	334	7,037	3,855	3,182	7
4	1	3	3	3	...	1,669	1,119	550	2,786	1,441	1,345	8
21	18	3	134	98	36	1,882	1,093	789	4,285	2,149	2,136	9
49	*34*	*15*	*163*	*126*	*37*	*4,877*	*3,172*	*1,705*	*7,402*	*4,551*	*2,851*	
36	24	12	84	65	19	1,140	650	490	853	605	248	10
1	1	...	70	52	18	1,380	932	448	2,207	1,313	894	11
...	...	...	8	8	...	340	265	75	235	196	39	12
10	7	3	1	1	...	1,118	730	388	3,058	1,822	1,236	13
2	2	...	...	...	...	899	595	304	1,049	615	434	14
135	*65*	*70*	*12*	*7*	*5*	*6,050*	*3,129*	*2,921*	*1,940*	*1,444*	*496*	
129	61	68	1	1	...	723	418	305	620	511	109	15
...	...	...	...	...	...	4	2	2	29	4	25	16
1	1	...	...	...	...	217	149	68	221	181	40	17
2	1	1	4	3	1	4,146	2,107	2,039	913	658	255	18
1	...	1	7	3	4	729	332	397	128	70	58	19
2	2	...	...	...	...	231	121	110	29	20	9	20
1	...	*1*	...	...	...	*28*	*12*	*16*	*18*	*18*	...	
614	*369*	*245*	*186*	*105*	*81*	*1,165*	*737*	*428*	*9,580*	*5,546*	*4,034*	
212	118	94	171	94	77	410	212	198	1,357	966	391	21
6	2	4	2	2	...	414	291	123	3,416	2,268	1,148	22
387	243	144	12	8	4	211	135	76	2,804	1,470	1,334	23
9	6	3	1	1	...	130	99	31	2,003	842	1,161	24
34	*19*	*15*	*43*	*29*	*14*	*6,336*	*3,652*	*2,684*	*4,448*	*2,679*	*1,769*	
34	19	15	42	29	13	6,189	3,561	2,628	4,397	2,633	1,764	25
...	...	...	...	...	...	32	20	12	8	7	1	26
...	...	...	...	...	...	43	24	19	...	...	...	27
...	...	...	1	...	1	39	24	15	33	32	1	28
...	...	...	...	...	...	33	23	10	10	7	3	29
7	*6*	*1*	*15*	*8*	*7*	*1,717*	*1,169*	*548*	*11,699*	*7,880*	*3,769*	
1	1	...	7	5	2	435	310	125	5,399	3,386	2,013	30
...	...	...	...	...	...	514	336	178	2,766	1,861	905	31
6	5	1	8	3	5	689	471	218	3,377	2,534	843	32
...	...	...	...	...	...	79	52	27	57	49	8	33
4	*3*	*1*	*5*	*1*	*4*	*1,247*	*820*	*427*	*5,692*	*3,596*	*2,096*	
...	...	...	...	...	...	31	25	6	101	87	14	34
1	1	...	...	...	...	331	243	88	1,906	1,257	649	35
3	2	1	4	1	3	205	117	88	135	90	45	36
...	...	...	1	...	1	680	435	245	3,550	2,162	1,388	37
...	...	...	...	...	...	*28*	*14*	*14*	*3*	*3*	...	
...	...	...	4	4	...	207	92	115	2,016	1,099	917	
...	...	...	...	...	...	64	34	30	717	376	341	38
...	...	...	4	4	...	140	55	85	1,299	723	576	39
...	...	...	...	...	...	...	...	...	...	...	...	40
...	...	...	...	...	...	3	3	...	...	...	...	41

IMPERIAL TABLE XI.—

Serial No.	District, State, Province, or Country where born.	PROVINCE, DISTRICT, OR STATE — THARRAWADDY. Persons.	Males.	Females.	PEGU. Persons.	Males.	Females.	PROME. Persons.	Males.	Females.
	1	23	24	25	26	27	28	29	30	31
	A. BORN IN INDIA.	431,691	214,963	216,728	424,972	225,892	199,080	377,806	185,267	192,539
	I. Within the Province of Burma.	422,809	207,368	215,441	391,075	199,298	191,777	372,247	180.463	191,784
	(i) Within Burma Proper	421,552	206,766	214,786	387,659	197,460	190,199	371,960	180,327	191,633
	Arakan Division ...	*16*	*8*	*8*	*91*	*70*	*21*	*148*	*93*	*55*
1	Akyab	7	3	4	64	54	10	56	20	36
2	Northern Arakan ...	2	2	...	10	1	9	...	...	...
3	Kyaukpyu	3	2	1	6	6	...	13	9	4
4	Sandoway	4	1	3	11	9	2	79	64	15
	Pegu Division	*399,525*	*195,088*	*204,437*	*325,683*	*162,441*	*163,242*	*358,880*	*173,162*	*185,718*
5	City of Rangoon ...	580	300	280	6,292	3,393	2,899	401	254	147
6	Hanthawaddy ...	600	345	255	8,503	4,630	3,873	209	125	84
7	Tharrawaddy ...	378,693	184,481	194,212	10,324	5,485	4,839	2,106	1,048	1,058
8	Pegu	271	156	115	296,691	146,781	149,910	55	27	28
9	Prome	19,381	9,806	9,575	3,873	2,152	1,721	356,109	171,708	184,401
	Irrawaddy Division ...	*3,268*	*1,746*	*1,522*	*2,879*	*1,296*	*1,083*	*1,641*	*859*	*782*
10	Bassein	227	122	105	346	192	154	111	73	38
11	Henzada	2,786	1,512	1,274	1,019	558	461	1,452	747	705
12	Myaungmya	7	2	5	87	30	57	10	6	4
13	Ma-ubin	218	95	123	726	411	315	58	27	31
14	Pyapôn	30	15	15	201	105	96	10	6	4
	Tenasserim Division ...	*339*	*172*	*167*	*17,419*	*9,192*	*8,227*	*250*	*127*	*123*
15	Toungoo	215	92	123	9,086	4,876	4,210	133	67	66
16	Salween	...	...	...	2	1	1	...	...	...
17	Thatôn	15	12	3	7,070	3,591	3,479	12	7	5
18	Amherst	89	60	29	960	532	428	54	27	27
19	Tavoy	13	4	9	181	103	78	18	14	4
20	Mergui	7	4	3	120	89	31	33	12	21
	Lower Burma Unspecified	...	...	...	...	...	...	*8*	*5*	*3*
	Magwe Division ...	*11,894*	*6,184*	*5,710*	*5,780*	*3,447*	*2,333*	*8,368*	*4,532*	*3,831*
21	Thayetmyo	3,809	1,924	1,885	632	340	292	6,266	3,340	2,926
22	Pakôkku	874	505	369	2,628	1,690	938	248	174	74
23	Minbu	851	473	378	595	357	238	374	254	120
24	Magwe	6,360	3,282	3,078	1,925	1,060	865	1,475	764	711
	Mandalay Division ...	*1,672*	*897*	*775*	*3,784*	*2,313*	*1,471*	*1,476*	*816*	*660*
25	Mandalay (including City).	1,667	895	772	3,650	2,225	1,425	1,470	812	658
26	Bhamo	1	...	1	45	33	12	2	...	2
27	Myitkyina	1	1	...	17	10	7	1	1	...
28	Katha	1	1	...	62	40	22	3	3	...
29	Ruby Mines	2	...	2	10	5	5	...	...	...
	Sagaing Division ...	*3,130*	*1,741*	*1,389*	*10,074*	*6,025*	*4,049*	*634*	*385*	*249*
30	Shwebo	1,313	722	591	3,385	1,986	1,399	96	52	44
31	Sagaing	476	250	226	2,320	1,393	927	185	122	63
32	Lower Chindwin ...	1,318	761	557	4.137	2,530	1,607	329	194	135
33	Upper Chindwin ...	23	8	15	232	116	116	24	17	7
	Meiktila Division ...	*1,708*	*930*	*778*	*22,449*	*12,676*	*9,773*	*560*	*348*	*212*
34	Kyauksè	14	3	11	339	213	126	...	...	...
35	Meiktila	241	149	92	14,038	7,825	6,213	98	55	43
36	Yamèthin	21	12	9	2,781	1,593	1,188	11	8	3
37	Myingyan	1,432	766	666	5,291	3,045	2,246	451	285	166
	Upper Burma Unspecified	...	...	...	...	...	...	...	...	...
	(ii) Within Specially Administered Territories.	1,257	602	655	3,416	1,838	1,578	287	136	151
38	Northern Shan States	345	165	180	648	447	201	97	61	36
39	Southern Shan States	912	437	475	2,768	1,391	1,377	190	75	115
40	Pakôkku Hill Tracts	...	...	...	...	...	...	...	...	...
41	Chin Hills	...	...	...	...	...	...	...	...	...

Birth-Place.

WHERE ENUMERATED.

Bassein.			Henzada.			Myaungmya.			Ma-ubin.			
Persons.	Males.	Females.	Persons.	Males.	Females.	Persons.	Males.	Females.	Persons.	Males.	Females.	Serial No.
32	33	34	35	36	37	38	39	40	41	42	43	
438,448	224,512	213,936	530,826	262,912	267,914	332,165	173,958	158,207	303,482	154,219	149,263	
423,279	210,704	212,575	522,844	255,621	267,223	321,540	164,017	157,523	295,831	147,162	148,669	
423,218	210,661	212,557	522,758	255,586	267,172	321,443	163,941	157,502	295,816	147,156	148,660	
4,970	2,442	2,528	214	138	76	337	270	67	11	6	5	
119	49	70	25	14	11	56	41	15	9	4	5	1
...	...	...	...	...	...	2	2	...	...	...	...	2
2,216	1,003	1,213	15	15	...	41	41	...	...	...	...	3
2,635	1,390	1,245	174	109	65	238	186	52	2	2	...	4
1,655	1,004	651	6,550	3,508	3,042	6,028	3,414	2,614	6,744	3,821	2,923	
712	437	275	623	382	241	2,478	1,384	1,094	2,814	1,553	1,261	5
59	28	31	368	183	185	731	454	277	1,526	557	969	6
158	100	58	2,696	1,383	1,313	606	323	283	760	616	144	7
55	24	31	96	31	65	750	415	335	144	101	43	8
671	415	256	2,767	1,529	1,238	1,463	838	625	1,500	994	506	9
410,386	203,450	206,936	493,299	239,891	253,408	288,034	144,881	143,153	269,040	132,530	136,510	
399,666	197,937	201,729	1,634	806	828	11,087	5,954	5,133	3,174	2,006	1,168	10
9,268	4,713	4,555	490,086	238,244	251,842	6,934	3,868	3,066	9,069	5,047	4,022	11
440	243	197	55	30	25	256,730	127,899	128,831	720	414	306	12
976	542	434	1,511	802	709	11,106	6,032	5,074	255,043	124,480	130,563	13
36	15	21	13	9	4	2,177	1,128	1,049	1,034	583	451	14
230	174	56	174	88	86	428	134	294	127	79	48	
57	46	11	57	28	29	163	51	112	32	17	15	15
...	...	...	1	...	1	10	...	10	...	...	...	16
3	3	...	24	20	4	32	22	10	1	1	...	17
152	110	42	73	33	40	147	47	100	66	55	11	18
16	14	2	3	...	3	26	14	12	24	6	18	19
2	1	1	16	7	9	50	...	50	4	...	4	20
...	...	...	...	...	...	...	...	...	...	...	...	
2,151	1,264	887	9,869	5,115	4,754	14,898	8,135	6,763	7,767	4,081	3,786	
211	131	80	4,017	2,065	1,952	3,152	1,654	1,498	711	364	347	21
1,323	752	571	4,000	2,074	1,926	3,843	2,253	1,590	2,900	1,559	1,341	22
477	281	196	1,244	629	615	5,439	2,763	2,676	2,993	1,475	1,518	23
140	100	40	608	347	261	2,464	1,465	999	1,163	633	530	24
1,147	756	391	3,211	1,851	1,360	2,191	1,404	787	2,338	1,302	1,036	
1,127	742	385	3,185	1,839	1,346	2,171	1,384	787	2,333	1,300	1,033	25
10	4	6	11	7	4	3	3	...	2	2	...	26
1	1	...	...	...	...	1	1	...	...	...	...	27
...	...	...	5	1	4	12	12	...	...	...	...	28
9	9	...	10	4	6	4	4	...	3	...	3	29
1,838	1,074	764	6,361	3,340	3,021	4,728	2,963	1,765	5,687	3,103	2,584	
556	336	220	1,422	744	678	1,589	955	634	1,989	990	999	30
517	284	233	2,288	1,227	1,061	877	519	358	2,523	1,425	1,098	31
762	451	311	2,637	1,359	1,278	2,200	1,449	751	1,162	675	487	32
3	3	...	14	10	4	62	40	22	13	13	...	33
841	497	344	3,074	1,650	1,424	4,799	2,740	2,059	4,102	2,284	1,818	
36	18	18	51	19	32	46	35	11	29	20	9	34
27	18	9	157	69	88	184	119	65	186	165	21	35
18	15	3	9	...	9	32	19	13	22	22	...	36
760	446	314	2,857	1,562	1,295	4,537	2,567	1,970	3,865	2,077	1,788	37
...	...	...	6	5	1	...	...	...	...	...	...	
61	43	18	86	35	51	97	76	21	15	6	9	
6	5	1	49	32	17	10	9	1	...	...	..	38
55	38	17	37	3	34	87	67	20	15	6	9	39
...	...	...	...	...	...	...	...	...	...	...	...	40
...	...	...	...	...	...	...	...	...	...	...	...	41

IMPERIAL TABLE XI.—

Serial No.	District, State, Province, or Country where born.	PROVINCE, DISTRICT, OR STATE								
		PYAPÔN.			TOUNGOO.			SALWEEN.		
		Persons.	Males.	Females.	Persons.	Males.	Females.	Persons.	Males.	Females.
	1	44	45	46	47	48	49	50	51	52
	A. BORN IN INDIA.	**253,566**	**137,245**	**116,821**	**348.914**	**179,539**	**169,375**	**46,523**	**24,680**	**21,843**
	I. Within the Province of Buma.	**238,185**	**124,166**	**114,019**	**334,548**	**168,525**	**166,028**	**45,980**	**24,178**	**21,802**
	(i) Within Burma Proper	**238,080**	**124,082**	**114,018**	**327,477**	**164.787**	**162,690**	**45,050**	**23,567**	**21.483**
	Arakan Division	***36***	***36***	...	...	...	...	***2***	***1***	***1***
1	Akyab	36	36	...	...	...	...	1	...	1
2	Northern Arakan ...	...	...	...	...	...	...	...	...	...
3	Kyaukpyu	...	...	...	...	...	...	1	1	...
4	Sandoway	...	...	...	...	...	...	...	...	...
	Pegu Division	***26,665***	***14,186***	***12,479***	***10,729***	***5,742***	***4,987***	***53***	***40***	***13***
5	City of Rangoon ...	9,511	4,864	4,647	1,753	1,196	557	29	19	10
6	Hanthawaddy ...	12,171	6,457	5,714	913	280	633	2	1	1
7	Tharrawaddy ...	1,108	589	519	1,119	642	477	2	2	...
8	Pegu	1,880	1,076	804	4,840	2,505	2,335	10	8	2
9	Prome	1,995	1,200	795	2,104	1,119	985	10	10	...
	Irrawaddy Division ...	***164,408***	***82,046***	***82,362***	***945***	***668***	***277***	***9***	***7***	***2***
10	Bassein	5,015	2,741	2,274	167	92	75	4	2	2
11	Henzada	5,085	3,029	2,056	400	300	100	1	1	...
12	Myaungmya	...	...	...	170	164	6	...	...	...
13	Ma-ubin	10,887	5,913	4.974	145	70	75	3	3	...
14	Pyapôn	143,421	70,363	73,058	63	42	21	1	1	...
	Tenasserim Division ...	***546***	***476***	***70***	***269,405***	***134,282***	***135,128***	***44,899***	***23,458***	***21,446***
15	Toungoo	173	162	11	265,172	132,403	132,769	111	66	45
16	Salween	...	...	...	204	103	101	44,617	23,277	21,340
17	Thatôn	23	23	...	3,580	1,500	2,080	139	80	59
18	Amherst	258	200	58	386	241	145	32	30	2
19	Tavoy	92	91	1	55	35	20	...	...	...
20	Mergui	...	...	...	8	...	8	...	...	...
	Lower Burma Unspecified	...	...	...	...	...	..	...	...	...
	Magwe Division	***25,489***	***13,902***	***11,587***	***4,539***	***2,513***	***2,026***	***5***	***5***	...
21	Thayetmyo	4,236	2,173	2,063	2,495	1,248	1,247	...	...	...
22	Pakôkku	5,552	3,273	2,279	357	301	56	1	1	...
23	Minbu	12,759	6,811	5,948	389	248	141	3	3	...
24	Magwe	2,942	1,645	1,297	1,298	716	582	1	1	...
	Mandalay Division ...	***3,259***	***2,052***	***1,207***	***2,772***	***1,565***	***1,207***	***59***	***43***	***16***
25	Mandalay (including City).	3,252	2,047	1,205	2,561	1,407	1,154	59	43	16
26	Bhamo	6	4	2	139	92	47	...	...	...
27	Myitkyina	1	1	...	...	...	...	...	...	...
28	Katha	...	...	...	66	64	2	...	...	...
29	Ruby Mines	...	...	...	6	2	4	...	...	...
	Sagaing Division	***10,077***	***6,600***	***3,477***	***6,434***	***3,361***	***3,073***	***15***	***10***	***5***
30	Shwebo	2,788	1,897	891	5,301	2,655	2,646	12	7	5
31	Sagaing	4,571	2,713	1,858	555	328	227	...	...	...
32	Lower Chindwin ...	2,683	1,955	728	557	370	187	3	3	...
33	Upper Chindwin ...	35	35	...	21	8	13	...	...	...
	Meiktila Division ...	***7,600***	***4,764***	***2,836***	***32,653***	***16,656***	***15,997***	***8***	***8***	...
34	Kyauksè	167	114	53	238	171	67	...	...	...
35	Meiktila	974	737	237	11,495	5,920	5,575	4	4	...
36	Yamèthin	28	26	2	18,099	9,123	8,976	3	3	...
37	Myingyan ...	6,431	3,887	2,544	2,821	1,442	1,379	1	1	...
	Upper Burma Unspecified	...	...	...	...	...	...	...	...	...
	(ii) Within Specially Administered Territories.	**105**	**104**	**1**	**7,071**	**3,738**	**3,333**	**930**	**611**	**319**
38	Northern Shan States	...	...	...	1,571	758	813	101	53	48
39	Southern Shan States	105	104	1	5,500	2,980	2,520	829	558	271
40	Pakôkku Hill Tracts	...	...	...	...	...	...	...	...	...
41	Chin Hills	...	...	...	...	...	...	...	...	...

Birth-Place.

WHERE ENUMERATED.

Thatôn.			Amherst.			Tavoy.			Mergui.			
Persons.	Males.	Females.	Persons.	Males.	Females.	Persons.	Males.	Females.	Persons.	Males.	Females.	Serial No.
53	54	55	56	57	58	59	60	61	62	63	64	
414,522	215,724	198,798	363,536	194,946	168,590	134,322	67,723	66,599	109,472	57,784	51,688	
396,953	201,097	195,856	341,379	174,913	166,466	133,388	66,839	66,549	105,702	54,182	51,520	
395,013	199,798	195,215	339,223	173,386	165,837	133,388	66,839	66,549	105,279	53,953	51,326	
81	*24*	*7*	*24*	*14*	*10*	*1*	...	*1*	*4*	*4*	...	
28	23	5	17	10	7	1	...	1	2	2	...	1
1	...	1	...	...	...	...	...	...	1	1	...	2
1	...	1	2	1	1	...	...	...	...	...	...	3
1	1	...	5	3	2	...	...	...	1	1	...	4
3,973	*2,354*	*1,619*	*1,734*	*1,065*	*669*	*274*	*224*	*50*	*189*	*144*	*45*	
1,639	964	675	1,138	648	490	222	183	39	157	126	31	5
315	186	129	151	99	52	6	6	...	3	1	2	6
98	66	32	81	56	25	4	3	1	5	3	2	7
1,713	986	727	171	132	39	18	11	7	10	4	6	8
208	152	56	193	130	63	24	21	3	14	10	4	9
573	*361*	*212*	*375*	*266*	*109*	*26*	*20*	*6*	*26*	*22*	*4*	
131	82	49	170	122	48	17	15	2	8	8	...	10
218	147	71	132	84	48	7	4	3	13	10	3	11
13	10	3	50	42	8	1	...	1	2	1	1	12
170	108	62	16	11	5	1	1	...	2	2	...	13
41	14	27	7	7	...	...	...	...	1	1	...	14
387,648	*194,982*	*192,666*	*335,348*	*170,758*	*164,585*	*132,964*	*66,522*	*66,442*	*104,810*	*53,643*	*51,167*	
967	542	425	205	148	57	23	19	4	39	29	10	15
128	81	47	53	37	16	...	...	...	...	...	...	16
376,954	189,057	187,897	4,874	2,903	1,971	11	8	3	7	6	1	17
9,186	5,047	4,139	328,027	166,180	161,847	194	126	68	429	232	197	18
376	236	140	2,008	1,361	647	132,686	66,330	66,356	575	347	228	19
37	19	18	176	129	47	50	39	11	103,760	53,029	50,731	20
1	*1*	...	*1*	...	*1*	...	...	...	...	...	...	
395	*310*	*85*	*229*	*177*	*52*	*17*	*6*	*11*	*187*	*93*	*94*	
46	35	11	17	10	7	4	1	3	1	1	...	21
280	213	67	124	100	24	1	1	...	2	1	1	22
33	28	5	60	47	13	4	3	1	179	87	92	23
36	34	2	28	20	8	8	1	7	5	4	1	24
926	*684*	*242*	*1,101*	*772*	*329*	*89*	*56*	*33*	*43*	*35*	*8*	
888	656	232	1,062	745	317	87	55	32	43	35	8	25
15	12	3	9	4	5	...	...	...	...	...	...	26
1	1	...	...	...	...	1	...	1	...	...	...	27
18	12	6	24	17	7	1	1	...	...	...	...	28
4	3	1	6	6	...	...	...	...	...	...	...	29
792	*588*	*204*	*237*	*185*	*52*	*6*	*6*	...	*17*	*11*	*6*	
357	259	98	63	55	8	4	4	...	8	4	4	30
86	59	27	35	29	6	...	...	...	5	4	1	31
344	265	79	123	88	35	2	2	...	4	3	1	32
5	5	...	16	13	3	...	...	...	...	...	...	33
674	*494*	*180*	*179*	*149*	*30*	*11*	*6*	*6*	*1*	*1*	...	
19	19	...	10	4	6	4	1	3	...	...	...	34
340	245	95	53	50	3	1	...	1	1	1	...	35
172	117	55	6	4	2	1	...	1	...	...	...	36
143	113	30	110	91	19	5	4	1	...	...	...	37
...	...	...	...	...	...	...	...	...	2	...	2	
1,940	1,299	641	2,158	1,527	628	...	...	...	423	229	194	
398	213	185	128	55	73	...	...	...	...	...	...	38
1,542	1,086	456	2,025	1,469	556	...	...	...	423	229	194	39
...	...	...	...	...	...	...	...	...	...	...	...	40
...	...	...	3	3	...	...	...	...	...	...	...	41

Serial No.	District, State, Province, or Country where born.	PROVINCE, DISTRICT, OR — THAYETMYO. Persons.	Males.	Females.	PAKÔKKU. Persons.	Males.	Females.	MINBU. Persons.	Males.	Females.
	1	65	66	67	68	69	70	71	72	73
	A. BORN IN INDIA.	247,879	121,871	126,008	409,632	195,919	213,713	263,591	128,512	135,079
	I. Within the Province of Burma.	245,685	120,039	125,646	407,955	194,420	213,535	260,368	125,502	134,866
	(i) Within Burma Proper	245,667	120,035	125,632	407,899	194,397	213,502	260,349	125,496	134,853
	Arakan Division	*81*	*41*	*40*	*18*	*13*	*5*	*56*	*40*	*16*
1	Akyab	6	5	1	12	12	...	17	13	4
2	Northern Arakan ...	...	...	...	...	...	...	...	...	...
3	Kyaukpu	45	21	24	1	...	1	27	16	11
4	Sandoway	30	15	15	5	1	4	12	11	1
	Pegu Division	*1,180*	*763*	*417*	*351*	*186*	*165*	*548*	*302*	*241*
5	City of Rangoon ...	162	99	63	135	63	72	206	125	81
6	Hanthawaddy ...	51	27	24	14	5	9	60	33	27
7	Tharrawaddy ...	102	57	45	38	27	11	36	19	17
8	Pegu	31	16	15	38	24	14	38	13	25
9	Prome	834	564	270	126	67	59	203	112	91
	Irrawaddy Division ...	*385*	*221*	*164*	*152*	*92*	*60*	*689*	*298*	*391*
10	Bassein	59	40	19	26	21	5	132	77	55
11	Henzada	183	135	48	74	45	29	252	98	154
12	Myaungmya	21	5	16	6	1	5	42	16	26
13	Ma-ubin	85	35	50	42	25	17	142	54	88
14	Pyapôn	37	6	31	4	...	4	121	53	68
	Tenasserim Division ...	*166*	*81*	*85*	*56*	*37*	*19*	*134*	*67*	*67*
15	Toungoo	56	33	23	19	11	8	28	18	10
16	Salween	3	...	3	...	...	...	...	...	...
17	Thatôn	1	...	1	6	6	...	4	3	1
18	Amherst	47	23	24	22	16	6	55	28	27
19	Tavoy	12	2	10	8	3	5	3	1	2
20	Mergui	47	23	24	1	1	...	44	17	27
	Lower Burma Unspecified	*2*	...	*2*	...	...	...	...	...	...
	Magwe Division ...	*242,848*	*118,358*	*124,490*	*404,179*	*192,311*	*211,868*	*255,128*	*122,847*	*132,281*
21	Thayetmyo	240,045	116,962	123,083	135	77	58	1,443	729	714
22	Pakôkku	154	84	70	403,516	191,897	211,619	2,932	1,440	1,492
23	Minbu	875	461	414	471	288	183	248,012	119,256	128,756
24	Magwe	1,774	851	923	57	49	8	2,741	1,422	1,319
	Mandalay Division ...	*374*	*235*	*139*	*298*	*179*	*119*	*551*	*274*	*277*
25	Mandalay (including City).	349	212	137	290	173	117	518	256	262
26	Bhamo	2	2	...	3	3	...	2	2	...
27	Myitkyina	1	...	1	1	1	...	...	...	...
28	Katha	1	1	...	1	...	1	2	1	1
29	Ruby Mines	21	20	1	3	2	1	29	15	14
	Sagaing Division ...	*313*	*165*	*148*	*558*	*398*	*160*	*203*	*125*	*78*
30	Shwebo	45	24	21	45	31	14	38	18	20
31	Sagaing	96	43	53	44	32	12	116	65	51
32	Lower Chindwin ..	169	95	74	441	313	128	48	41	7
33	Upper Chindwin ...	3	3	...	23	17	6	1	1	...
	Meiktila Division ...	*318*	*171*	*147*	*2,290*	*1,185*	*1,105*	*3,044*	*1,543*	*1,501*
34	Kyauksè	3	3	...	7	1	6	7	1	6
35	Meiktila	37	18	19	84	71	13	75	30	45
36	Yamèthin	23	12	11	11	7	4	39	21	18
37	Myingyan	255	138	117	2,188	1,106	1,082	2,923	1,491	1,432
	Upper Burma Unspecified	...	...	...	*2*	*1*	*1*	*1*	...	*1*
	(ii) Within Specially Administered Territories.	18	4	14	56	23	33	19	6	13
38	Northern Shan States	9	4	5	3	1	2	18	5	13
39	Southern Shan States	9	...	9	3	...	3	1	1	...
40	Pakôkku Hill Tracts	...	...	...	...	...	...	...	...	...
41	Chin Hills	...	...	...	50	22	28	...	...	...

Birth-Place.

STATE WHERE ENUMERATED.

Magwe.			Mandalay (including City).			Mandalay City.			Bhamo.			
Persons.	Males.	Females.	Persons.	Males.	Females.	Persons.	Males.	Females.	Persons.	Males.	Females.	Serial No.
74	75	76	77	78	79	80	81	82	83	84	85	
316,524	156,020	160,504	337,039	167,595	169,444	136,584	68,227	68,357	99,547	50,894	48,653	
312,716	152,613	160,103	318,653	152,362	166,291	125,436	58,973	66,463	95,637	47,361	48,276	
312,694	152,610	160,084	317,706	151,779	165,927	125,178	58,822	66,356	92,469	46,192	46,277	
28	*18*	*10*	*116*	*64*	*51*	*102*	*57*	*45*	*88*	*24*	*9*	
14	12	2	54	32	22	53	32	21	1	1	...	1
...	...	...	...	...	...	...	...	...	...	...	...	2
...	...	...	25	2	23	21	...	21	25	22	3	3
9	1	8	36	30	6	28	25	3	7	1	6	4
951	*547*	*404*	*1,960*	*1,166*	*794*	*1,451*	*879*	*572*	*114*	*77*	*87*	
299	182	117	1,365	785	580	1,028	590	438	81	53	28	5
62	29	33	52	41	11	39	29	10	...	...	...	6
167	112	55	117	69	48	97	61	36	10	7	3	7
33	14	19	121	79	42	68	56	12	4	4	...	8
390	210	180	305	192	113	219	143	76	19	13	6	9
322	*182*	*140*	*441*	*293*	*148*	*370*	*268*	*102*	*108*	*56*	*52*	
76	46	30	140	96	44	109	79	30	71	31	40	10
159	98	61	203	118	85	176	114	62	18	9	9	11
7	2	5	17	15	2	16	14	2	...	...	...	12
53	21	32	70	59	11	63	59	4	18	15	3	13
27	15	12	11	5	6	6	2	4	1	1	...	14
81	*59*	*22*	*828*	*487*	*341*	*642*	*406*	*236*	*67*	*38*	*29*	
34	19	15	297	182	115	224	148	76	38	16	22	15
...	...	...	...	...	...	...	...	...	7	6	1	16
8	7	1	39	26	13	21	16	5	...	...	...	17
32	26	6	414	216	198	341	193	148	20	14	6	18
1	1	...	73	60	13	53	46	7	2	2	...	19
6	6	...	5	3	2	3	3	...	...	...	...	20
...	...	...	7	...	7	...	...	...	...	...	...	
305,055	*148,219*	*156,836*	*876*	*579*	*297*	*552*	*398*	*154*	*131*	*27*	*104*	
2,510	1,380	1,130	205	114	91	146	86	60	27	15	12	21
1,489	942	547	311	261	50	163	121	42	101	11	90	22
1,259	759	500	163	128	35	151	119	32	2	...	2	23
299,797	145,138	154,659	197	76	121	92	72	20	1	1	...	24
855	*468*	*387*	*299,356*	*141,612*	*157,744*	*110,687*	*50,635*	*60,052*	*91,501*	*45,655*	*45,846*	
799	445	354	298,900	141,290	157,610	110,364	50,402	59,962	3,186	2,723	463	25
28	15	13	167	105	62	127	76	51	86,477	41,887	44,590	26
...	...	...	30	18	12	14	14	...	67	50	17	27
27	7	20	144	106	38	91	70	21	1,128	776	352	28
1	1	...	115	93	22	91	73	18	643	219	424	29
271	*188*	*83*	*11,654*	*6,015*	*5,639*	*9,758*	*5,040*	*4,718*	*397*	*232*	*165*	
46	23	23	2,609	1,405	1,204	1,964	1,088	876	254	172	82	30
98	73	25	5,002	2,612	2,390	3,936	2,059	1,877	58	40	18	31
124	89	35	3,952	1,941	2,011	3,768	1,839	1,929	78	13	65	32
3	3	...	91	57	34	85	54	31	7	7	...	33
5,136	*2,934*	*2,202*	*2,372*	*1,491*	*881*	*1,524*	*1,067*	*457*	*92*	*57*	*35*	
5	5	...	743	417	326	346	221	125	8	4	4	34
384	202	182	895	587	308	594	421	173	36	21	15	35
345	178	167	314	188	126	230	160	70	34	20	14	36
4,402	2,549	1,853	420	299	121	354	265	89	14	12	2	37
...	...	...	*97*	*72*	*25*	*97*	*72*	*25*	*26*	*26*	...	
22	3	19	947	583	364	258	151	107	3,168	1,169	1,999	
20	3	17	790	534	256	192	141	51	1,673	727	946	38
...	...	...	157	49	108	66	10	56	1,495	442	1,053	39
...	...	...	...	...	...	...	...	...	...	...	...	40
2	...	2	...	...	...	...	...	...	...	...	...	41

Serial No.	District, State, Province, or Country where born.	PROVINCE, DISTRICT, OR								
		MYITKYINA.			KATHA.			RUBY MINES.		
		Persons.	Males.	Females.	Persons.	Males.	Females.	Persons.	Males.	Females.
	1	86	87	88	89	90	91	92	93	94
	A. BORN IN INDIA.	79,749	43,649	36,100	197,428	97,578	99,850	95,926	50,588	45,338
	I. Within the Province of Burma.	75,003	39,277	35,726	195,635	95,925	99,710	93,806	48,708	45,098
	(i) Within Burma Proper	73,630	38,416	35,214	195,175	95,761	99,414	89,400	45,958	43,442
	Arakan Division	*22*	*21*	*1*	*20*	*10*	*10*	*7*	*5*	*2*
1	Akyab	19	19	...	3	1	2	6	5	1
2	Northern Arakan ...	2	2	...	...	...	...	...	...	...
3	Kyaukpyu	...	...	...	3	1	2	1	...	1
4	Sandoway	1	...	1	14	8	6	...	...	...
	Pegu Division	*122*	*75*	*47*	*267*	*175*	*92*	*175*	*119*	*56*
5	City of Rangoon ...	84	51	33	184	116	68	120	82	38
6	Hanthawaddy ...	10	7	3	18	13	5	2	2	...
7	Tharrawaddy ...	2	1	1	16	12	4	29	19	10
8	Pegu	7	4	3	23	17	6	9	5	4
9	Prome	19	12	7	26	17	9	15	11	4
	Irrawaddy Division ...	*53*	*31*	*22*	*67*	*44*	*23*	*87*	*25*	*12*
10	Bassein	39	23	16	18	12	6	18	14	4
11	Henzada	13	7	6	41	25	16	18	10	8
12	Myaungmya	...	...	...	1	1	...	1	1	...
13	Ma-ubin	1	1	...	5	5	...	...	...	...
14	Pyapôn	...	...	...	2	1	1	...	...	...
	Tenasserim Division ...	*100*	*62*	*38*	*169*	*135*	*84*	*119*	*92*	*27*
15	Toungoo	58	33	25	98	79	19	87	69	18
16	Salween	...	...	...	...	...	...	...	...	...
17	Thatôn	6	2	4	...	...	...	...	...	...
18	Amherst	34	26	8	57	42	15	32	23	9
19	Tavoy	2	1	1	14	14	...	...	...	...
20	Mergui	...	...	...	...	...	...	...	...	...
	Lower Burma Unspecified	*3*	...	*3*	...	...	...	...	...	...
	Magwe Division	*385*	*287*	*98*	*120*	*95*	*25*	*143*	*106*	*87*
21	Thayetmyo	16	7	9	12	7	5	4	4	...
22	Pakôkku	340	253	87	55	45	10	107	92	15
23	Minbu	3	2	1	34	30	4	13	4	9
24	Magwe	26	25	1	19	13	6	19	6	13
	Mandalay Division ...	*70,325*	*35,971*	*34,354*	*189,539*	*92,280*	*97,259*	*85,685*	*43,435*	*42,250*
25	Mandalay (including City).	1,010	652	358	1,140	680	460	2,429	1,481	948
26	Bhamo	1,034	637	397	460	266	194	883	436	447
27	Myitkyina	63,924	32,108	31,816	267	163	104	42	39	3
28	Katha	4,239	2,510	1,729	187,152	90,898	96,254	1,619	992	627
29	Ruby Mines	118	64	54	520	273	247	80,712	40,487	40,225
	Sagaing Division	*2,444*	*1,855*	*589*	*4,913*	*2,973*	*1,940*	*2,979*	*2,002*	*977*
30	Shwebo	496	330	166	4,431	2,649	1,782	2,645	1,751	894
31	Sagaing	52	28	24	261	145	116	190	121	69
32	Lower Chindwin ...	253	177	76	151	134	17	133	120	13
33	Upper Chindwin ...	1,643	1,320	323	70	45	25	11	10	1
	Meiktila Division	*149*	*87*	*62*	*80*	*49*	*31*	*255*	*174*	*81*
34	Kyauksè	70	53	17	29	16	13	45	30	15
35	Meiktila	24	3	21	5	4	1	53	33	20
36	Yamèthin	40	18	22	24	13	11	124	94	30
37	Myingyan	15	13	2	22	16	6	33	17	16
	Upper Burma Unspecified	*27*	*27*	...	...	...	...	...	...	...
	(ii) Within Specially Administered Territories.	1,373	861	512	460	164	296	4,406	2,750	1,656
38	Northern Shan States	953	518	435	270	146	124	3,080	1,886	1,194
39	Southern Shan States	312	266	46	190	18	172	1,326	864	462
40	Pakôkku Hill Tracts	21	...	21	...	...	...	...	...	...
41	Chin Hills	87	77	10	...	...	...	...	...	...

Birth-Place.

STATE WHERE ENUMERATED.

Shwebo.			Sagaing.			Lower Chindwin.			Upper Chindwin.			
Persons.	Males.	Females.	Persons.	Males.	Females.	Persons.	Males.	Females.	Persons.	Males.	Females.	Serial No.
95	96	97	98	99	100	101	102	103	104	105	106	
355,621	167,382	188,239	312,014	147,729	164,285	316,058	141,173	174,885	170,296	85,906	84,390	
353,168	165,328	187,840	310,252	146,227	164,025	314,535	139,868	174,667	167,575	83,646	83,929	
353,107	165,277	187,830	310,221	146,212	164,009	314,504	139,837	174,667	166,997	83,317	83,680	
2	*1*	*1*	*10*	*5*	*5*	*6*	*1*	*5*	*8*	*6*	*2*	
2	1	1	5	2	3	1	1	...	5	4	1	1
...	...	...	...	...	...	...	...	...	...	...	...	2
...	...	...	2	2	...	...	...	...	...	...	...	3
...	...	...	3	1	2	5	...	5	3	2	1	4
1,164	*923*	*241*	*347*	*216*	*131*	*193*	*113*	*80*	*107*	*77*	*30*	
513	334	179	223	150	73	90	54	36	49	29	20	5
521	508	13	15	9	6	23	11	12	18	18	...	6
38	35	3	26	11	15	11	7	4	6	4	2	7
54	26	28	29	12	17	15	14	1	11	9	2	8
38	20	18	54	34	20	54	27	27	23	17	6	9
154	*98*	*56*	*276*	*135*	*141*	*107*	*56*	*51*	*42*	*27*	*15*	
20	6	14	49	21	28	42	22	20	15	9	6	10
89	65	24	136	65	71	48	21	27	15	11	4	11
19	11	8	...	...	...	1	1	...	4	3	1	12
23	14	9	54	38	16	14	10	4	6	2	4	13
3	2	1	37	11	26	2	2	...	2	2	...	14
182	*139*	*43*	*116*	*81*	*35*	*116*	*80*	*36*	*110*	*87*	*23*	
138	109	29	75	52	23	75	56	19	84	68	16	15
...	...	...	...	...	...	7	3	4	...	...	...	16
31	27	4	4	4	...	1	1	...	4	3	1	17
12	2	10	33	22	11	29	18	11	17	13	4	18
1	1	...	4	3	1	2	1	1	4	2	2	19
...	...	...	...	...	...	2	1	1	1	1	...	20
8	*7*	*1*	*1*	...	*1*	...	...	...	*1*	*1*	...	
166	*89*	*77*	*697*	*392*	*305*	*941*	*574*	*367*	*950*	*581*	*369*	
80	37	43	31	17	14	58	28	30	42	26	16	21
52	32	20	561	296	265	846	519	327	792	483	309	22
23	15	8	40	27	13	9	6	3	113	69	44	23
11	5	6	65	52	13	28	21	7	3	3	...	24
2,762	*1,491*	*1,271*	*2,320*	*1,107*	*1,213*	*386*	*202*	*184*	*1,940*	*1,140*	*800*	
2,220	1,226	994	2,236	1,069	1,167	368	191	177	584	345	239	25
10	5	5	5	...	5	5	4	1	26	22	4	26
3	3	...	16	8	8	6	6	...	156	90	66	27
483	223	260	55	26	29	6	...	6	1,172	683	489	28
46	34	12	8	4	4	1	1	...	2	...	2	29
348,391	*162,341*	*186,050*	*304,963*	*143,515*	*161,448*	*312,471*	*138,611*	*173,860*	*163,739*	*81,335*	*82,404*	
344,138	159,965	184,173	862	423	439	165	109	56	564	361	203	30
2,899	1,607	1,292	303,687	142,840	160,847	481	298	183	55	34	21	31
1,265	708	557	366	206	160	293,207	127,606	165,601	3,945	2,560	1,385	32
89	61	28	48	46	2	18,618	10,598	8,020	159,175	78,380	80,795	33
278	*188*	*90*	*1,490*	*760*	*730*	*284*	*200*	*84*	*98*	*61*	*37*	
40	23	17	144	68	76	20	13	7	7	1	6	34
28	22	6	144	74	70	13	8	5	11	8	3	35
52	42	10	37	20	17	9	4	5	27	13	14	36
158	101	57	1,165	598	567	242	175	67	53	39	14	37
...	...	...	*1*	*1*	...	...	...	...	*2*	*2*	...	
56	**46**	**10**	**31**	**15**	**16**	**31**	**31**	...	**578**	**329**	**249**	
42	33	9	7	3	4	26	26	...	7	6	1	38
14	13	1	20	12	8	5	5	...	136	136	...	39
...	...	...	...	...	...	...	...	...	...	...	...	40
...	...	...	4	...	4	...	...	...	435	187	248	41

IMPERIAL TABLE XI.—

PROVINCE, DISTRICT, OR

Serial No.	District, State, Province, or Country where born.	Kyauksè. Persons.	Males.	Females.	Meiktila. Persons.	Males.	Females.	Yamèthin. Persons.	Males.	Females.
	1	107	108	109	110	111	112	113	114	115
	A. BORN IN INDIA.	141,285	68,735	72,550	279,327	133,699	145,628	306,287	152,146	154,141
	I. Within the Province of Burma.	140,219	67,832	72,387	274,783	129,698	145,085	301,471	148,222	153,249
	(i) Within Burma Proper	140,001	67,717	72,284	274,377	129,450	144,927	300,807	147,814	152,993
	Arakan Division	*5*	*5*	...	*22*	*21*	*1*	*8*	*4*	*4*
1	Akyab	1	1	...	21	21	...	3	...	3
2	Northern Arakan ...	...	...	...	...	...	..	...	...	...
3	Kyaukpyu	3	3	...	1	...	1	2	1	1
4	Sandoway	1	1	...	...	...	...	3	3	...
	Pegu Division	*199*	*125*	*74*	*331*	*195*	*136*	*1,355*	*777*	*578*
5	City of Rangoon ...	144	84	60	122	59	63	710	436	274
6	Hanthawaddy ...	8	8	...	50	50	...	51	32	19
7	Tharrawaddy ...	13	5	8	28	24	4	58	22	36
8	Pegu	21	16	5	91	39	52	230	129	101
9	Prome	13	12	1	40	23	17	306	158	148
	Irrawaddy Division ...	*127*	*51*	*76*	*107*	*68*	*89*	*144*	*87*	*57*
10	Bassein	39	15	24	23	10	13	48	32	16
11	Henzada	46	29	17	52	35	17	63	38	25
12	Myaungmya	22	...	22	6	5	1	10	9	1
13	Ma-ubin	15	4	11	13	11	2	13	6	7
14	Pyapôn	5	3	2	13	7	6	10	2	8
	Tenasserim Division ...	*128*	*72*	*51*	*280*	*151*	*129*	*2,421*	*1,275*	*1,146*
15	Toungoo	72	27	45	183	93	90	2,091	1,084	1,007
16	Salween	...	...	...	...	...	...	4	4	...
17	Thatôn	10	10	...	14	12	2	46	39	7
18	Amherst	21	15	6	58	26	32	120	68	52
19	Tavoy	20	20	...	25	20	5	36	16	20
20	Mergui	...	...	...	...	...	...	124	64	60
	Lower Burma Unspecified	...	...	...	*3*	*3*	...	*7*	*5*	*2*
	Magwe Division	*133*	*83*	*50*	*191*	*122*	*69*	*7,540*	*3,940*	*3,600*
21	Thayetmyo	41	36	5	64	41	23	1,910	977	933
22	Pakôkku	37	13	24	53	46	7	32	23	9
23	Minbu	38	24	14	31	8	23	182	60	122
24	Magwe	17	10	7	43	27	16	5,416	2,880	2,536
	Mandalay Division ...	*2,509*	*1,347*	*1,162*	*1,139*	*676*	*463*	*1,613*	*841*	*772*
25	Mandalay (including City).	2,484	1,326	1,158	910	468	442	1,581	824	757
26	Bhamo	9	7	2	31	26	5	13	6	7
27	Myitkyina	8	7	1	175	175	...	2	1	1
28	Katha	7	7	...	14	5	9	9	7	2
29	Ruby Mines	1	...	1	9	2	7	8	3	5
	Sagaing Division... ...	*3,299*	*1,605*	*1,694*	*295*	*155*	*140*	*534*	*340*	*194*
30	Shwebo	285	159	126	50	24	26	217	173	44
31	Sagaing	2,943	1,402	1,541	227	117	110	142	68	74
32	Lower Chindwin ...	71	44	27	16	12	4	169	98	71
33	Upper Chindwin ...	...	...	...	2	2	...	6	1	5
	Meiktila Division	*133,606*	*64,429*	*69,177*	*272,009*	*128,059*	*143,950*	*287,185*	*140,545*	*146,640*
34	Kyauksè	128,508	62,037	66,471	405	231	174	713	396	317
35	Meiktila	3,061	1,344	1,717	270,233	127,095	143,138	8,105	4,051	4,054
36	Yamèthin	189	82	107	603	293	310	276,683	135,208	141,475
37	Myingyan	1,848	966	882	768	440	328	1,684	890	794
	Upper Burma Unspecified	...	...	...	...	...	...	...	...	...
	(ii) Within Specially Administered Territories.	218	115	103	406	248	158	664	408	256
38	Northern Shan States	7	3	4	103	30	73	109	5	104
39	Southern Shan States	211	112	99	303	218	85	555	403	152
40	Pakôkku Hill Tracts	...	...	...	...	...	...	...	...	...
41	Chin Hills	...	...	...	...	...	...	...	...	...

Birth-Place.

STATE WHERE ENUMERATED.

Myingyan.			Northern Shan States.			Southern Shan States.			Pakôkku Hill Tracts.			Chin Hills.			
Persons.	Males.	Females.	Persons.	Males.	Females.	Persons.	Males.	Females.	Persons.	Males.	Females	Persons.	Males.	Females.	Serial No.
116	117	118	119	120	121	122	123	124	125	126	127	128	129	130	
441,626	210,868	230,758	404,356	201,390	202,966	889,191	442,039	447,152	17,029	8,408	8,621	119,122	58,232	60,890	
439,575	208,951	230,624	401,731	198,992	202,739	886,247	439,484	446,763	16,988	8,376	8,612	118,117	57,435	60,682	
439,430	208,813	230,617	4,312	2,401	1,911	2,850	1,913	937	39	26	13	107	85	22	
44	*26*	*18*	*8*	*8*	...	*10*	*10*	...	...	...	...	...	...	...	
9	4	5	2	2	...	5	5	...	...	...	...	...	...	...	1
...	...	...	...	...	...	...	...	...	...	...	...	...	...	...	2
3	3	...	1	1	...	1	1	...	...	...	...	...	...	...	3
32	19	13	...	...	...	4	4	...	...	...	...	...	...	...	4
828	*577*	*251*	*193*	*116*	*77*	*119*	*89*	*30*	*2*	*1*	*1*	*6*	*6*	...	
455	353	102	128	75	53	64	44	20	1	1	...	2	2	...	5
16	13	3	5	2	3	6	6	...	...	...	...	...	...	...	6
74	51	23	15	8	7	22	19	3	...	...	...	3	3	...	7
59	32	27	14	8	6	22	17	5	...	...	...	...	...	...	8
224	128	96	31	23	8	5	3	2	1	...	1	1	1	...	9
666	*549*	*117*	*32*	*26*	*6*	*25*	*12*	*13*	*2*	*1*	*1*	7	4	*3*	
107	93	14	16	12	4	15	7	8	2	1	1	5	3	2	10
446	392	54	12	10	2	2	1	1	...	...	...	2	1	1	11
24	11	13	1	1	...	7	3	4	...	...	...	...	...	...	12
62	40	22	3	3	...	1	1	...	...	...	...	...	...	...	13
27	13	14	...	...	...	...	...	...	...	...	...	...	...	...	14
261	*202*	*59*	*107*	*82*	*25*	*341*	*249*	*92*	...	...	...	4	2	2	
185	147	38	73	57	16	172	117	55	...	...	...	1	...	1	15
...	...	...	1	1	...	13	13	...	...	...	...	...	...	...	16
8	2	6	2	...	2	85	69	16	...	...	...	...	...	...	17
44	31	13	28	23	5	70	49	21	...	...	...	3	2	1	18
11	9	2	2	1	1	1	1	...	...	...	...	...	...	...	19
13	13	...	1	...	1	...	...	...	...	...	...	...	...	...	20
...	...	...	...	...	...	*36*	*24*	*12*	...	...	...	...	...	...	
2,343	*1,416*	*927*	*33*	*21*	*12*	*25*	*18*	*7*	*20*	*17*	*3*	*30*	*24*	*6*	
161	105	56	15	12	3	4	2	2	...	...	...	7	5	2	21
1,793	1,088	705	8	3	5	4	4	...	20	17	3	20	19	1	22
179	117	62	5	2	3	13	9	4	...	...	...	3	...	3	23
210	106	104	5	4	1	4	3	1	...	...	...	...	...	...	24
1,167	*643*	*524*	*3,193*	*1,729*	*1,464*	*994*	*684*	*310*	*9*	*5*	*4*	*13*	*10*	*3*	
1,118	625	493	2,900	1,538	1,362	884	585	299	3	1	2	1	...	1	25
26	11	15	31	16	15	44	38	6	1	1	...	...	...	...	26
9	...	9	36	28	8	17	17	...	5	3	2	4	4	...	27
14	7	7	61	37	24	2	2	...	...	...	...	...	...	...	28
...	...	...	165	110	55	47	42	5	...	...	...	8	6	2	29
929	*502*	*427*	*343*	*203*	*140*	*129*	*103*	*26*	*6*	*2*	*4*	*34*	*27*	*7*	
72	37	35	240	143	97	65	46	19	4	1	3	6	5	1	30
686	347	339	40	24	16	27	23	4	...	...	...	3	2	1	31
165	112	53	58	33	25	37	34	3	2	1	1	25	20	5	32
6	6	...	5	3	2	...	...	...	...	...	...	...	...	...	33
433,192	*204,898*	*228,294*	*401*	*219*	*182*	*1,168*	*724*	*444*	...	...	...	*13*	*12*	*1*	
149	111	38	344	186	158	505	298	207	...	...	...	...	...	...	34
758	438	320	18	9	9	424	276	148	...	...	...	10	10	...	35
95	52	43	24	18	6	224	136	88	...	...	...	1	...	1	36
432,190	204,297	227,893	15	6	9	15	14	1	...	...	...	2	2	...	37
...	...	...	*7*	*2*	*5*	*3*	...	*3*	...	...	...	...	...	...	
145	138	7	397,419	196,591	200,828	883,397	437,571	445,826	16,949	8,350	8,599	118,010	57,350	60,660	
5	3	2	397,297	196,493	200,804	28	18	10	...	...	...	2	2	...	38
140	135	5	118	97	21	883,367	437,551	445,816	2	1	1	...	...	...	39
...	...	...	...	...	...	...	...	...	16,947	8,349	8,598	...	...	...	40
...	...	...	4	1	3	2	2	...	...	...	...	118,008	57,348	60,660	41

Serial No.	District, State, Province, or Country where born.	PROVINCE, DISTRICT, OR — Whole Province. Persons.	Whole Province. Males.	Whole Province. Females.	Akyab. Persons.	Akyab. Males.	Akyab. Females.	Northern Arakan. Persons.	Northern Arakan. Males.	Northern Arakan. Females.
	1	2	3	4	5	6	7	8	9	10
	A. BORN IN INDIA.									
	II. Beyond Burma	493,699	423,169	70,530	43,799	39,004	4,795	482	379	103
	(a) Contiguous Province ...	76,414	72,272	4,142	30,811	27,966	2,845	82	76	6
	Eastern Bengal and Assam—									
42	(i) British Territory ...	75,736	71,739	3,997	30,808	27,963	2,845	82	76	6
	Chittagong	*63,968*	*60,261*	*3,707*	*30,521*	*27,715*	*2,806*	*82*	*76*	*6*
43	(ii) States of Eastern Bengal and Assam.	678	533	145	3	3	...	...	...	...
	(b) Non-Contiguous Provinces	414,326	348,321	66,005	12,970	11,020	1,950	400	303	97
	(i) British Territory ...	406,286	341,613	64,673	12,840	10,914	1,926	400	303	97
44	Ajmer-Merwara	199	196	3	...	...	...	...	...	...
45	Andamans and Nicobars ...	451	427	24	...	...	...	...	...	...
46	Baluchistan	30	27	3	...	...	...	...	...	...
47	Bengal	67,981	55,617	12,364	9,066	7,329	1,737	293	225	68
48	Bombay (including Aden)...	12,782	10,646	2,136	274	226	48	...	...	...
49	Central Provinces and Berar	548	417	131	2	2	...	...	...	...
50	Coorg	5	4	1	...	...	...	...	...	...
51	Madras	247,360	205,907	41,453	2,636	2,565	71	92	67	25
	Ganjam	*21,266*	*20,279*	*987*	*41*	*34*	*7*	...	...	...
	Vizagapatam ...	*19,341*	*16,455*	*2,886*	...	...	...	...	...	...
	Godavery	*19,406*	*17,312*	*2,094*	*14*	*14*	...	...	...	...
	Tanjore	*5,952*	*4,734*	*1,218*	...	...	...	...	...	...
52	North-West Frontier Province.	740	704	36	75	66	9	...	...	...
53	Punjab	25,595	22,572	3,023	120	108	12	7	4	3
54	United Provinces of Agra and Oudh.	50,595	45,096	5,499	667	618	49	8	7	1
	Fyzabad	*15,024*	*13,537*	*1,487*	*162*	*146*	*16*	...	...	...
	(ii) States and Agencies ...	8,040	6,708	1,332	130	106	24	...	...	...
55	Baroda	136	121	15	...	...	...	...	...	...
56	Bengal States	771	759	12	...	...	...	...	...	...
57	Bombay States	39	29	10	...	...	..	...	...	...
58	Central India Agency ...	221	166	55	...	...	...	...	...	...
59	Central Provinces States ...	75	73	2	...	...	...	...	...	...
60	Hyderabad	1,575	1,302	273	13	13	...	...	...	...
61	Kashmir	433	275	158	...	...	...	...	...	...
62	Madras States	881	649	232	...	...	...	...	...	...
	Cochin	*53*	*46*	*7*	...	...	...	...	...	...
	Travancore	*124*	*76*	*48*	...	...	...	...	...	...
63	Mysore	933	823	110	...	...	...	...	...	...
64	North-West Frontier (Agencies and Tribal Areas).	3	1	2	...	...	...	...	...	...
65	Punjab States	505	411	94	5	4	1	...	...	...
66	Rajputana Agency ...	1,780	1,497	283	112	89	23	...	...	...
67	United Provinces States ...	688	602	86	...	...	...	...	...	...
	(c) French and Portuguese Settlements.	845	740	105	18	18	...	...	...	...
	(d) India (unspecified) ...	2,114	1,836	278	...	...	...	...	...	...
	B. Born in other Asiatic Countries	88,268	70,368	17,900	489	423	66	190	141	49
68	Afghanistan	109	109	...	...	...	...	...	...	...
69	Arabia	133	101	32	...	...	...	...	...	...
70	Armenia	3	3	...	...	...	...	...	...	...
71	Bhûtan	4	4	...	...	...	...	...	...	...
72	Ceylon	846	752	94	...	...	...	..	...	...
73	China	75,365	60,699	14,666	456	409	47	...	...	...
74	French Indo-China ...	1	...	1	...	...	...	...	...	...
75	Hongkong	6	1	5	...	...	...	...	...	...
76	Japan	666	310	356	15	...	15	...	...	...
77	Maldives	3	3	...	...	...	...	...	...	...
78	Mongolia	1	1	...	...	...	...	...	...	...
79	Nepal	5,997	4,783	1,214	16	13	3	190	141	49
80	Persia	147	123	24	2	1	1	...	...	...
81	Russian Turkistan	2	2	...	...	...	...	...	...	...
82	Siam	3,995	2,706	1,289	...	...	...	...	...	...
83	Straits Settlements and Malaya.	789	655	134	...	...	...	...	...	...
84	Turkey in Asia	200	115	85	...	...	...	...	...	...
85	Asia (unspecified)	1	1	...	...	...	...	...	...	...

Birth-Place.

STATE WHERE ENUMERATED.

Kyaukpyu.			Sandoway.			City of Rangoon.			Hanthawaddy.			
Persons.	Males.	Females.	Persons.	Males.	Females.	Persons.	Males.	Females.	Persons.	Males.	Females.	Serial No.
11	12	13	14	15	16	17	18	19	20	21	22	
1,322	1,278	44	781	744	37	153,478	130,716	22,762	59,939	50,145	9,794	
943	906	37	246	242	4	17,397	17,045	352	11,235	11,143	92	
943	906	37	246	242	4	17,350	17,001	349	11,232	11,143	89	42
937	*900*	*37*	*246*	*242*	*4*	*14,721*	*14,512*	*209*	*3,760*	*3,673*	*87*	
...	...	...	...	...	...	47	44	3	3	...	3	43
379	372	7	535	502	33	135,148	112,850	22,298	48,382	38,694	9,688	
377	370	7	535	502	33	132,847	111,168	21,679	47,955	38,304	9,651	
...	...	...	...	...	...	190	187	3	...	...	...	44
...	...	...	...	...	...	441	420	21	4	4	...	45
...	...	...	...	...	...	7	5	2	...	...	...	46
159	155	4	247	238	9	9,265	7,655	1,610	1,771	306	1,465	47
7	6	1	6	3	3	5,463	4,161	1,302	263	216	47	48
...	...	...	...	...	...	250	184	66	15	15	...	49
...	...	...	...	...	...	4	3	1	...	...	...	50
148	146	2	167	160	7	90,828	74,377	16,451	40,449	33,096	7,353	51
...	...	...	...	...	...	*9,307*	*8,636*	*671*	*4,713*	*4,713*	...	
24	*24*	...	...	...	...	*13,629*	*11,754*	*1,875*	*658*	*658*	...	
1	*1*	...	...	...	...	*16,642*	*15,038*	*1,604*	*438*	*438*	...	
...	...	...	...	...	...	*4,656*	*3,827*	*829*	...	...	...	
...	...	...	...	...	...	97	86	11	...	...	...	52
18	18	...	89	79	10	3,957	3,493	464	1,405	1,119	286	53
45	45	...	26	22	4	22,345	20,597	1,748	4,048	3,548	500	54
5	*5*	...	...	...	...	*6,892*	*6,365*	*527*	*2,617*	*2,312*	*305*	
2	2	...	...	...	...	2,301	1,682	619	427	390	37	
...	...	...	...	...	...	39	24	15	...	...	...	55
...	...	...	...	...	...	1	...	1	...	...	...	56
...	...	...	...	...	...	..	...	...	...	...	...	57
...	...	...	...	...	...	48	1	47	...	...	...	58
...	...	...	...	...	...	...	...	...	...	...	...	59
...	...	...	...	...	...	706	549	157	294	259	35	60
...	...	...	...	...	...	377	220	157	...	...	...	61
...	...	...	...	...	...	161	109	52	...	...	...	62
...	...	...	...	...	...	*47*	*40*	*7*	...	...	...	
...	...	...	...	...	...	*114*	*69*	*45*	...	...	...	
...	...	...	...	...	...	235	177	58	87	86	1	63
...	...	...	...	...	...	2	...	2	...	...	...	64
...	...	...	...	...	...	21	14	7	...	...	...	65
2	2	...	...	...	...	708	585	123	46	45	1	66
...	...	...	...	...	...	3	3	...	...	...	...	67
...	...	...	...	...	...	733	639	94	...	...	...	
...	...	...	...	...	...	200	182	18	322	308	14	
52	47	5	89	87	2	13,240	10,982	2,258	4,270	3,851	419	
...	...	...	...	...	...	58	58	...	...	..	...	68
...	...	...	...	...	...	59	47	12	...	...	...	69
...	...	...	...	...	...	3	3	...	...	...	...	70
...	...	...	...	...	...	...	...	...	...	...	...	71
...	...	...	1	1	...	219	162	57	47	42	5	72
52	47	5	87	85	2	11,759	9,991	1,768	4,182	3,775	407	73
...	...	...	...	...	...	...	...	...	...	...	...	74
...	...	...	...	...	...	...	...	...	...	...	...	75
...	...	...	...	...	...	341	129	212	3	...	3	76
...	...	...	...	...	...	3	3	...	...	...	...	77
...	...	...	...	...	...	1	1	...	...	...	...	78
...	...	...	1	1	...	122	114	8	5	5	...	79
...	...	...	...	...	...	122	105	17	2	2	...	80
...	...	...	...	...	...	...	...	...	2	2	...	81
...	...	...	...	...	...	36	27	9	...	...	...	82
...	...	...	...	...	...	334	242	92	28	24	4	83
...	...	...	...	...	...	...	...	...	...	...	...	84
...	...	...	...	...	...	183	100	83	1	1	...	85

IMPERIAL TABLE XI.—

Serial No.	District, State, Province, or Country where born.	PROVINCE, DISTRICT, OR								
		THARRAWADDY.			PEGU.			PROME.		
		Persons.	Males.	Females.	Persons.	Males.	Females.	Persons.	Males.	Females.
	1	23	24	25	26	27	28	29	30	31
	A. BORN IN INDIA.									
	II. Beyond Burma	**8,882**	**7,595**	**1,287**	**33,897**	**26,594**	**7,303**	**5,559**	**4,804**	**755**
	(a) Contiguous Province ...	**3**	...	**3**	**987**	**936**	**51**	**273**	**269**	**4**
	Eastern Bengal and Assam—									
42	(i) British Territory ...	3	...	3	987	936	51	273	269	4
	Chittagong	*3*	...	*3*	*891*	*860*	*31*	*272*	*268*	*4*
43	(ii) States of Eastern Bengal and Assam	...	...	...	...	...	...	...	...	...
	(b) Non-Contiguous Provinces	**8,868**	**7,585**	**1,283**	**32,890**	**25,641**	**7,249**	**5,277**	**4,526**	**751**
	(i) British Territory ...	**8,835**	**7,577**	**1,258**	**32,619**	**25,397**	**7,222**	**4,489**	**3,742**	**747**
44	Ajmer-Merwara	...	...	...	...	...	...	...	...	...
45	Andamans and Nicobars ...	1	1	...	1	1	...	...	...	...
46	Baluchistan	...	...	...	...	...	...	...	...	...
47	Bengal	1,691	1,483	208	6,207	4,663	1,544	256	161	95
48	Bombay (including Aden) ..	106	98	8	577	553	24	143	109	34
49	Central Provinces and Berar	...	...	...	15	15	...	...	...	...
50	Coorg	...	...	...	...	...	...	...	...	...
51	Madras	5,640	4,825	815	21,259	16,690	4,569	3,652	3,077	575
	Ganjam	...	...	...	*2,975*	*2,869*	*106*	...	...	...
	Visagapatam ...	...	...	...	*1,372*	*1,103*	*269*	*41*	*39*	*2*
	Godavery	...	...	...	*279*	*260*	*19*	...	...	...
	Tanjore	...	...	...	*763*	*582*	*181*	*1*	...	*1*
52	North-West Frontier Province.	...	...	...	9	8	1	...	...	...
53	Punjab	262	232	30	472	421	51	151	124	27
54	United Provinces of Agra and Oudh.	1,135	938	197	4,079	3,046	1,033	287	271	16
	Fyzabad	*1,106*	*926*	*180*	*801*	*801*	...	*144*	*136*	*8*
	(ii) States and Agencies ...	**33**	**8**	**25**	**271**	**244**	**27**	**788**	**784**	**4**
55	Baroda	...	...	...	...	...	...	...	...	...
56	Bengal States	...	...	...	17	17	...	742	742	...
57	Bombay States	6	...	6	7	7	...	...	...	...
58	Central India Agency ...	...	...	...	...	...	...	...	...	...
59	Central Provinces States ...	...	...	...	...	...	...	...	...	...
60	Hyderabad	1	1	...	97	86	11	34	30	4
61	Kashmir	...	...	...	...	...	...	...	...	...
62	Madras States	...	...	...	4	1	3	...	...	...
	Cochin	...	...	...	...	...	...	...	...	...
	Travancore	...	...	...	*4*	*1*	*3*	...	...	...
63	Mysore	9	7	2	15	13	2	...	...	...
64	North-West Frontier (Agencies and Tribal Areas).	...	...	...	...	...	...	...	...	...
65	Punjab States	...	...	...	...	...	...	...	...	...
66	Rajputana Agency ...	17	...	17	111	100	11	12	12	...
67	United Provinces States ...	...	...	...	20	20	...	...	...	...
	(c) French and Portuguese Settlements.	**11**	**10**	**1**	**20**	**17**	**3**	...	...	...
	(d) India (unspecified) ...	...	...	...	...	...	...	**9**	**9**	...
	B. Born in other Asiatic Countries	**1,608**	**1,466**	**142**	**4,105**	**3,615**	**490**	**1,015**	**909**	**106**
68	Afghanistan	...	...	...	...	...	...	...	...	...
69	Arabia	...	...	...	6	4	2	...	...	...
70	Armenia	...	...	...	...	...	...	...	...	...
71	Bhûtan	...	...	...	...	...	...	...	...	...
72	Ceylon	10	6	4	48	39	9	7	4	3
73	China	1,595	1,457	138	3,896	3,475	421	984	891	93
74	French Indo-China	...	...	...	...	...	...	...	...	...
75	Hongkong	...	...	...	5	...	5	1	1	...
76	Japan	...	...	...	14	2	12	7	...	7
77	Maldives	...	...	...	...	...	...	...	...	...
78	Mongolia	...	...	...	...	...	...	...	...	...
79	Nepal	3	3	...	...	...	...	10	10	...
80	Persia	...	...	...	...	...	...	...	...	...
81	Russian Turkistan ...	...	...	...	...	...	...	...	...	...
82	Siam	...	...	...	76	46	30	3	...	3
83	Straits Settlements and Malaya.	...	...	...	60	49	11	3	3	...
84	Turkey in Asia	...	...	...	...	...	...	...	...	...
85	Asia (unspecified)	...	...	...	...	...	...	...	...	...

Birth-Place.

STATE WHERE ENUMERATED.

Bassein.			Henzada.			Myaungmya.			Ma-ubin.			
Persons.	Males.	Females.	Persons.	Males.	Females.	Persons.	Males.	Females.	Persons.	Males.	Females.	Serial No.
32	33	34	35	36	37	38	39	40	41	42	43	
15,169	13,808	1,361	7,982	7,291	691	10,625	9,941	684	7,651	7,057	594	
2,024	1,966	58	377	370	7	1,225	1,176	49	1,144	1,129	15	
2,024	1,966	58	377	370	7	1,217	1,170	47	1,144	1,129	15	42
1,927	*1,877*	*50*	*370*	*363*	*7*	*1,173*	*1,132*	*41*	*1,130*	*1,115*	*15*	
...	...	...	...	...	...	8	6	2	...	...	...	43
13,145	11,842	1,303	7,605	6,921	684	9,379	8,746	633	6,507	5,928	579	
13,047	11,747	1,300	7,492	6,813	679	9,327	8,695	632	6,417	5,838	579	
...	...	...	...	...	...	...	...	...	...	...	...	44
...	...	...	...	...	...	...	...	...	...	...	...	45
...	...	...	...	...	...	...	...	...	...	...	...	46
3,456	3,191	265	2,340	2,161	179	2,845	2,729	116	1,442	1,349	93	47
74	56	18	107	106	1	164	150	14	44	44	...	48
14	14	...	1	1	...	...	...	...	2	2	...	49
...	...	...	...	...	...	...	...	...	...	...	...	50
8,820	7,853	967	4,384	3,935	449	5,503	5,046	457	4,461	4,002	459	51
853	*764*	*89*	...	...	...	*86*	*86*	..	...	...	...	
191	*181*	*10*	*58*	*58*	...	*1*	*1*	...	...	...	...	
648	*583*	*65*	...	...	...	...	...	...	...	...	...	
33	*27*	*6*	...	...	...	*8*	*8*	...	...	...	...	
...	...	...	4	4	...	...	...	...	...	...	...	52
118	106	12	264	243	21	277	259	18	153	144	9	53
565	527	38	392	363	29	538	511	27	315	297	18	54
163	*154*	*9*	*133*	*122*	*11*	*51*	*45*	*6*	...	...	...	
98	95	3	113	108	5	52	51	1	90	90	...	
...	...	...	...	...	...	...	...	...	87	87	...	55
...	...	...	...	...	...	...	...	...	...	...	...	56
...	...	...	2	2	...	...	...	...	...	...	...	57
...	...	...	...	...	...	...	...	...	...	...	...	58
...	...	...	...	...	...	...	...	...	...	...	...	59
40	37	3	84	81	3	21	21	...	...	...	...	60
...	...	...	...	...	...	...	...	...	3	3	...	61
...	...	...	...	...	...	...	...	...	...	...	...	62
...	...	...	...	...	...	...	...	...	...	...	...	
...	...	...	...	...	...	...	...	...	...	...	...	
...	...	...	2	2	...	13	13	...	...	...	...	63
...	...	...	...	...	...	...	...	...	...	...	...	64
...	...	...	...	...	...	...	...	...	...	...	...	65
58	58	...	25	23	2	18	17	1	...	...	...	66
...	...	...	...	...	...	...	...	...	...	...	...	67
...	...	...	...	...	...	...	...	...	...	...	...	
...	...	...	...	...	...	21	19	2	...	...	...	
2,242	2,084	208	1,487	1,375	112	2,671	2,497	174	1,563	1,474	89	
...	...	...	...	...	...	...	...	...	...	...	...	68
14	8	6	...	...	...	...	...	...	...	...	...	69
...	...	...	...	...	...	...	...	...	...	...	...	70
...	...	...	...	...	...	...	...	...	...	...	...	71
20	20	...	63	63	...	2	2	...	...	...	...	72
2,165	1,990	175	1,407	1,302	105	2,649	2,482	167	1,556	1,472	84	73
...	...	...	...	...	...	...	...	...	...	...	...	74
...	...	...	...	...	...	...	...	...	...	...	...	75
42	15	27	4	...	4	7	1	6	6	1	5	76
...	...	...	...	...	...	...	...	...	...	...	...	77
...	...	...	...	...	...	...	...	...	...	...	...	78
...	...	...	...	...	...	2	2	...	...	...	...	79
...	...	...	...	...	...	...	...	...	...	...	...	80
...	...	...	...	...	...	...	...	...	...	...	...	81
...	...	...	2	...	2	...	...	...	...	...	...	82
1	1	...	11	10	1	11	10	1	1	1	...	83
...	...	...	...	...	...	...	...	...	...	...	...	84
...	...	...	...	...	...	...	...	...	...	...	...	85

Serial No.	District, State, Province, or Country where born.	PROVINCE, DISTRICT, OR								
		PYAPÔN.			TOUNGOO.			SALWEEN.		
		Persons.	Males.	Females.	Persons.	Males.	Females.	Persons.	Males.	Females.
	1	44	45	46	47	48	49	50	51	52
	A. BORN IN INDIA.									
	II. Beyond Burma	15,381	13,079	2,302	14,366	11,014	3,352	543	502	41
	(a) Contiguous Province ...	1,644	1,496	148	693	645	48	260	250	10
	Eastern Bengal and Assam—									
42	(i) British Territory ...	1,644	1,496	148	693	645	48	258	248	10
	Chittagong	*1,510*	*1,362*	*148*	*624*	*578*	*46*	*258*	*248*	*10*
43	(ii) States of Eastern Bengal and Assam.	...	...	...	...	...	...	2	2	...
	(b) Non-Contiguous Provinces	13,722	11,568	2,154	13,612	10,308	3,304	283	252	31
	(i) British Territory ...	13,572	11,441	2,131	13,543	10,272	3,271	281	250	31
44	Ajmer-Merwara ...	...	...	...	...	...	...	...	...	...
45	Andamans and Nicobars ...	...	...	...	...	...	...	...	...	...
46	Baluchistan	...	...	...	...	...	...	...	...	...
47	Bengal	2,195	1,897	298	6,221	4,230	1,991	174	150	24
48	Bombay (including Aden)...	193	168	25	83	68	15	17	17	...
49	Central Provinces and Berar	...	...	...	...	...	...	...	...	...
50	Coorg	...	...	...	...	...	...	...	...	...
51	Madras	10,237	8,545	1,692	4,827	4,065	762	55	51	4
	Ganjam	*182*	*163*	*19*	*1,055*	*1,055*	...	...	...	...
	Vizagapatam ...	*457*	*369*	*88*	*415*	*360*	*55*	*1*	*1*	...
	Godavery	*221*	*172*	*49*	*358*	*260*	*98*	...	...	...
	Tanjore	*143*	*68*	*75*	*20*	*14*	*6*	*1*	*1*	...
52	North-West Frontier Province.	...	...	...	...	...	...	...	...	...
53	Punjab	484	432	52	473	427	46	14	11	3
54	United Provinces of Agra and Oudh.	463	399	64	1,939	1,482	457	21	21	...
	Fyzabad	*108*	*72*	*36*	*563*	*450*	*113*	...	...	...
	(ii) States and Agencies ...	150	127	23	69	36	33	2	2	...
55	Baroda	...	...	...	...	...	...	...	...	...
56	Bengal States	...	...	...	...	...	...	...	...	...
57	Bombay States	...	...	...	...	...	...	...	...	...
58	Central India Agency ...	...	...	...	8	...	8	...	...	...
59	Central Provinces States ...	...	...	...	...	...	...	...	...	...
60	Hyderabad	38	38	...	...	...	...	...	...	...
61	Kashmir	...	...	...	...	...	...	...	...	...
62	Madras States	...	...	...	...	...	...	...	...	...
	Cochin	...	...	...	...	...	...	...	...	...
	Travancore	...	...	...	...	...	...	...	...	...
63	Mysore	58	50	8	...	...	...	2	2	...
64	North-West Frontier (Agencies and Tribal Areas).	...	..	...	...	...	...	...	...	...
65	Punjab States	...	...	...	...	...	...	...	...	...
66	Rajputana Agency ...	54	39	15	61	36	25	...	...	...
67	United Provinces States ...	...	...	...	...	...	...	...	...	...
	(c) French and Portuguese Settlements.	...	...	...	...	...	...	...	...	...
	(d) India (unspecified) ...	15	15	...	61	61	...	...	...	...
	B. Born in other Asiatic Countries	2,625	2,377	248	2,112	1,933	179	78	54	24
68	Afghanistan	...	...	...	...	...	...	...	...	...
69	Arabia	...	...	...	12	9	3	...	...	...
70	Armenia	...	...	...	...	...	...	...	...	...
71	Bhûtan	...	...	...	...	...	...	...	...	...
72	Ceylon	...	...	...	...	...	...	...	...	...
73	China	2,612	2,367	245	1,795	1,645	150	4	4	...
74	French Indo-China ...	...	...	...	...	...	...	...	...	...
75	Hongkong	...	...	...	...	...	...	...	...	...
76	Japan	1	...	1	10	...	10	...	...	...
77	Maldives	...	...	...	...	...	...	...	...	...
78	Mongolia	...	...	...	...	...	...	...	...	...
79	Nepal	...	...	...	...	...	...	...	...	...
80	Persia	...	...	...	39	39	...	15	8	7
81	Russian Turkistan ...	...	...	...	...	...	...	...	...	...
82	Siam	...	...	...	...	...	...	...	...	...
83	Straits Settlements and Malaya.	12	10	2	245	229	16	59	42	17
					11	11	...	...	...	...
84	Turkey in Asia	...	...	...	...	...	...	...	...	...
85	Asia (unspecified)	...	...	...	...	...	...	...	...	...

Birth-Place.

STATE WHERE ENUMERATED.

Thatôn.			Amherst.			Tavoy.			Mergui.			
Persons.	Males.	Females.	Persons.	Males.	Females.	Persons.	Males.	Females.	Persons.	Males.	Females.	Serial No.
53	54	55	56	57	58	59	60	61	62	63	64	
17,569	14,627	2,942	22,157	20,033	2,124	934	884	50	3,770	3,602	168	
...	...	...	3,259	3,175	84	60	59	1	61	60	1	
...	...	...	3,259	3,175	84	60	59	1	61	60	1	42
...	...	...	*2,794*	*2,713*	*81*	*59*	*58*	*1*	*61*	*60*	*1*	
...	...	...	...	...	...	...	...	...	...	...	...	43
17,561	14,622	2,939	18,804	16,773	2,031	854	805	49	3,706	3,539	167	
17,515	14,584	2,931	18,743	16,729	2,014	854	805	49	3,634	3,467	167	
...	...	...	3	3	...	...	...	...	...	...	...	44
...	...	...	...	...	...	...	...	...	...	...	...	45
...	...	...	...	...	...	...	...	...	...	...	...	46
4,275	3,787	488	1,656	1,446	210	342	323	19	546	489	57	47
386	339	47	1,634	1,500	134	21	19	2	17	13	4	48
53	49	4	20	18	2	...	...	...	2	2	...	49
...	...	...	...	...	...	...	...	...	...	...	...	50
11,847	9,557	2,290	12,361	10,774	1,587	391	366	25	2,971	2,870	101	51
...	...	...	*127*	*64*	*63*	...	...	...	*1*	*1*	...	
...	...	...	*1,256*	*801*	*455*	...	...	...	*570*	*556*	*14*	
...	...	...	*642*	*419*	*223*	...	...	...	*46*	*43*	*3*	
...	...	...	*309*	*191*	*118*	...	...	...	...	...	...	
...	...	...	194	194	...	...	...	...	11	11	...	52
513	456	57	332	306	26	72	70	2	73	69	4	53
441	396	45	2,543	2,488	55	28	27	1	14	13	1	54
...	...	...	*43*	*32*	*11*	*9*	*9*	...	*3*	*2*	*1*	
46	38	8	61	44	17	...	...	...	72	72	...	
...	...	...	1	1	...	...	...	...	...	...	...	55
...	...	...	...	...	...	...	...	...	...	...	...	56
...	...	...	24	20	4	...	...	...	...	...	...	57
...	...	...	...	...	...	...	...	...	1	1	...	58
...	...	...	...	...	...	...	...	...	...	...	...	59
...	...	...	20	8	12	...	...	...	13	13	...	60
...	...	...	...	...	...	...	...	...	43	43	...	61
...	...	...	2	2	...	...	...	...	...	...	...	62
...	...	...	...	...	...	...	...	...	...	...	...	
...	...	...	2	2	...	...	...	...	...	...	...	
35	31	4	1	...	1	...	...	...	1	1	...	63
...	...	...	...	...	...	...	...	...	...	...	...	64
...	...	...	2	2	...	...	...	...	...	...	...	65
11	7	4	11	11	...	...	...	...	14	14	...	66
...	...	...	...	...	...	...	...	...	...	...	...	67
...	...	...	57	52	5	...	...	...	...	...	...	
8	5	3	37	33	4	20	20	...	3	3	...	
2,447	2,041	406	4,168	3,326	842	928	906	22	1,866	1,665	201	
...	...	...	...	...	...	...	...	...	...	...	...	68
...	...	...	7	7	...	1	1	...	...	...	...	69
...	...	...	...	...	...	...	...	...	...	...	...	70
4	4	...	...	...	...	...	...	...	...	...	...	71
10	8	2	5	3	2	3	3	...	1	1	...	72
1,861	1,619	242	2,466	2,147	319	882	864	18	1,577	1,463	114	73
...	...	...	...	...	...	...	...	...	...	...	...	74
...	...	...	...	...	...	...	...	...	...	...	...	75
...	...	...	23	1	22	...	...	...	61	42	19	76
...	...	...	...	...	...	...	...	...	...	...	...	77
...	...	...	...	...	...	...	...	...	...	...	...	78
15	11	4	...	...	...	26	26	...	13	12	1	79
...	...	...	...	...	...	...	...	...	...	...	...	80
...	...	...	...	...	...	...	...	...	...	...	...	81
557	399	158	1,636	1,144	492	15	11	4	187	122	65	82
...	...	...	21	16	5	1	1	...	27	25	2	83
...	...	...	9	7	2	...	...	...	...	...	...	84
...	...	...	1	1	...	...	...	...	...	...	...	85

PROVINCE, DISTRICT, OR

Serial No.	District, State, Province, or Country where born.	THAYETMYO.			PAKÔKKU.			MINBU.		
		Persons.	Males.	Females.	Persons.	Males.	Females.	Persons.	Males.	Females.
	1	65	66	67	68	69	70	71	72	73
	A. BORN IN INDIA.									
	II. Beyond Burma	2,194	1,832	362	1,677	1,499	178	3.223	3,010	213
	(a) Contiguous Province ...	...	...	...	237	224	13	77	68	9
	Eastern Bengal and Assam—									
42	(i) British Territory ...	...	...	...	236	223	13	77	68	9
	Chittagong	...	...	...	*220*	*212*	*8*	*44*	*42*	*2*
43	(ii) States of Eastern Bengal and Assam.	...	...	...	1	1	...	...	...	...
	(b) Non-Contiguous Provinces	2,189	1,831	358	1,408	1,247	161	3,145	2,941	204
	(i) British Territory ...	2,126	1,791	335	1,383	1,228	155	2,965	2,763	202
44	Ajmer-Merwara	...	...	...	3	3	...	...	...	...
45	Andamans and Nicobars ...	...	...	...	1	...	1	...	...	...
46	Baluchistan	...	...	...	...	...	...	20	20	...
47	Bengal	600	523	77	349	307	42	857	843	14
48	Bombay (including Aden)...	104	80	24	43	39	4	76	67	9
49	Central Provinces and Berar	...	...	...	3	3	...	3	3	...
50	Coorg	...	...	...	1	1	...	...	...	...
51	Madras	1,041	857	184	496	461	35	1,388	1,314	74
	Ganjam	...	...	...	...	...	...	...	...	...
	Visagapatam ...	...	...	...	...	...	...	*4*	*4*	...
	Godavery	...	...	...	*2*	*2*	...	*2*	*2*	...
	Tanjore	...	...	...	...	...	...	*1*	*1*	...
52	North-West Frontier Province.	3	3	...	4	2	2	24	21	3
53	Punjab	162	132	30	242	197	45	386	309	77
54	United Provinces of Agra and Oudh.	216	196	20	241	215	26	211	186	25
	Fysabad	...	...	...	*48*	*43*	*5*	*8*	*8*	...
	(ii) States and Agencies ...	63	40	23	25	19	6	180	178	2
55	Baroda	...	...	...	...	...	...	...	...	...
56	Bengal States	...	...	...	...	...	...	...	...	...
57	Bombay States	...	...	...	...	...	...	...	...	...
58	Central India Agency ...	...	...	...	...	...	...	...	...	...
59	Central Provinces States ...	...	...	...	21	19	2	...	...	...
60	Hyderabad	19	12	7	...	...	...	...	...	...
61	Kashmir	...	...	...	...	...	...	...	...	...
62	Madras States	...	...	...	...	...	...	...	...	...
	Cochin	...	...	...	...	...	...	...	...	...
	Travancore	...	...	...	...	...	...	...	...	...
63	Mysore	23	15	8	3	...	3	...	...	...
64	North-West Frontier (Agencies and Tribal Areas).	...	...	...	...	...	...	...	...	...
65	Punjab States	...	...	...	1	...	1	24	24	
66	Rajputana Agency ...	21	13	8	...	...	...	156	154	2
67	United Provinces States ...	...	...	...	...	...	...	...	...	...
	(c) French and Portuguese Settlements.	...	...	...	...	...	...	...	...	...
	(d) India (unspecified) ...	5	1	4	32	28	4	1	1	...
	B. Born in other Asiatic Countries	249	219	30	224	197	27	329	310	19
68	Afghanistan...	1	1	...	...	...	...	1	1	...
69	Arabia	8	...	8	20	20	...	...	...	...
70	Armenia	...	...	...	...	...	...	...	...	...
71	Bhūtan	...	...	...	...	...	...	...	...	...
72	Ceylon	...	...	...	5	4	1	3	3	...
73	China	222	205	17	185	164	21	323	304	19
74	French Indo-China ...	...	...	...	...	...	...	...	...	...
75	Hongkong	...	...	...	...	...	...	...	...	...
76	Japan	2	...	2	...	...	...	...	...	...
77	Maldives	...	...	...	...	...	...	...	...	...
78	Mongolia	...	...	...	...	...	...	...	...	...
79	Nepal	9	7	2	...	...	...	2	2	...
80	Persia	...	...	...	14	9	5	...	...	...
81	Russian Turkistan	...	...	...	...	...	...	...	...	...
82	Siam	1	1	...	...	...	...	...	...	...
83	Straits Settlements and Malaya.	6	5	1	...	...	...	...	...	...
84	Turkey in Asia	...	...	...	...	...	...	...	...	...
85	Asia (unspecified)	...	...	...	...	...	...	...	...	...

Birth-Place.

STATE WHERE ENUMERATED.

Magwe.			Mandalay (including City.)			Mandalay City.			Bhamo.			
Persons.	Males.	Females.	Persons.	Males.	Females.	Persons.	Males.	Females.	Persons.	Males.	Females.	Serial No.
74	75	76	77	78	79	80	81	82	83	84	85	
8,808	8,407	401	18,886	15.283	3,158	11,148	9,254	1,894	8.910	8,533	877	
283	274	9	449	380	69	346	332	14	124	124	...	
283	274	9	447	380	67	346	332	14	124	124	...	42
283	*274*	*9*	*425*	*379*	*46*	*346*	*332*	*14*	*73*	*73*	...	
...	...	...	2	...	2	...	...	...	...	...	...	43
3,525	3,133	392	17,483	14,510	2,973	10,633	8,806	1,827	3,777	3,402	375	
3,479	3,101	378	16,560	13,718	2,842	9,744	8,032	1,712	3,580	3,221	359	
...	...	...	...	...	...	...	...	...	...	...	...	44
...	...	...	...	...	...	...	...	...	1	...	1	45
...	...	...	...	...	...	...	...	...	...	...	...	46
812	732	80	3,094	2,535	559	2,028	1,617	411	664	634	30	47
104	90	14	1,308	1,145	163	969	856	113	71	63	8	48
1	...	1	17	14	3	...	...	...	21	...	21	49
...	...	...	...	...	...	...	...	...	...	...	...	50
1,550	1,393	157	5,434	4,099	1,335	3,416	2,645	771	279	204	75	51
694	*682*	*12*	*348*	*346*	*2*	*17*	*17*	...	...	...	...	
108	*98*	*10*	*78*	*62*	*16*	...	...	...	...	...	...	
...	...	...	*36*	*5*	*31*	7	*5*	2	...	...	...	
...	...	...	*1*	...	*1*	...	...	...	...	...	...	
...	...	...	86	82	4	...	...	...	176	176	...	52
472	384	88	4,189	3,631	558	2,789	2,412	377	2,115	1,943	172	53
540	502	38	2 432	2,212	220	542	502	40	253	201	52	54
127	*118*	*9*	*480*	*394*	*86*	*17*	...	*17*	*36*	*36*	...	
46	32	14	923	792	131	889	774	115	197	181	16	
...	...	...	...	...	...	...	...	...	1	1	...	55
...	...	...	...	...	...	...	...	...	...	...	..	56
...	...	...	...	...	...	...	...	...	...	...	...	57
...	...	...	...	...	...	...	...	...	...	...	...	58
...	...	...	...	...	...	...	...	...	...	...	...	59
3	2	1	19	9	10	...	...	...	1	1	...	60
...	...	...	10	9	1	...	...	...	...	...	...	61
...	...	...	...	...	...	...	...	...	...	...	...	62
...	...	...	...	...	...	...	...	...	...	...	...	
...	...	...	...	...	...	...	...	...	...	...	...	
3	3	...	255	235	20	253	235	18	1	...	1	63
...	...	...	...	...	...	...	...	...	...	...	...	64
30	26	4	13	7	6	13	7	6	184	169	15	65
10	1	9	38	30	8	35	30	5	10	10	...	66
...	...	...	588	502	86	588	502	86	...	...	...	67
...	...	...	...	...	...	2	2	...	...	...	...	
...	...	...	454	343	111	167	114	53	9	7	2	
247	240	7	2,197	1,870	827	1.161	1,040	121	7,988	4,397	8,601	
...	...	...	...	...	...	...	...	...	...	...	...	68
...	...	...	1	...	1	...	...	...	2	2	...	69
...	...	...	...	...	...	...	...	...	..	...	...	70
...	...	...	...	...	...	...	...	...	...	...	...	71
6	5	1	...	...	...	6	6	...	352	352	...	72
240	235	5	1,282	1,149	133	1,140	1,024	116	7,511	3,913	3,598	73
...	...	...	...	...	...	...	...	...	...	...	...	74
...	...	...	...	...	...	...	...	...	...	...	...	75
1	...	1	21	16	5	5	...	5	102	102	...	76
...	...	...	...	...	...	...	...	...	...	...	...	77
...	...	...	...	...	...	...	...	...	...	...	...	78
...	...	...	878	694	184	...	...	...	28	26	2	79
...	...	...	1	1	...	...	...	...	...	...	...	80
...	...	...	...	...	...	...	...	...	...	...	...	81
...	...	...	...	...	...	...	...	...	3	2	1	82
...	...	...	10	6	4	6	6	...	...	...	...	83
...	...	...	...	...	...	...	...	...	...	...	...	84
...	...	...	4	4	...	4	4	...	...	...	...	85

PROVINCE, DISTRICT, OR

Serial No.	District, State, Province, or Country where born.	Myitkyina. Persons.	Myitkyina. Males.	Myitkyina. Females.	Katha. Persons.	Katha. Males.	Katha. Females.	Ruby Mines. Persons.	Ruby Mines. Males.	Ruby Mines. Females.
	1	86	87	88	89	90	91	92	93	94
	A. BORN IN INDIA.									
	II. Beyond Burma	**4,746**	**4,372**	**374**	**1,793**	**1,653**	**140**	**2,120**	**1,880**	**240**
	(a) Contiguous Province ...	**456**	**415**	**41**	**135**	**126**	**9**	**174**	**172**	**2**
	Eastern Bengal and Assam—									
42	(i) British Territory ...	448	415	33	120	113	7	173	171	2
	Chittagong	*303*	*281*	*22*	*95*	*92*	*3*	*117*	*115*	*2*
43	(ii) States of Eastern Bengal and Assam.	8	...	8	15	13	2	1	1	...
	(b) Non-Contiguous Provinces	**4,267**	**3,951**	**316**	**1,649**	**1,518**	**131**	**1,944**	**1,706**	**238**
	(i) British Territory ...	**4,094**	**3,835**	**259**	**1,575**	**1,450**	**125**	**1,914**	**1,682**	**232**
44	Ajmer-Merwara	...	...	...	...	...	...	...	...	...
45	Andamans and Nicobars ...	...	...	...	...	...	...	...	...	...
46	Baluchistan	...	...	...	...	...	...	...	...	...
47	Bengal	673	543	130	512	472	40	362	269	93
48	Bombay (including Aden)	108	100	8	40	33	7	57	53	4
49	Central Provinces and Berar	5	5	...	...	...	...	1	1	...
50	Coorg	...	...	...	..	...	...	...	...	...
51	Madras	376	362	14	511	477	34	266	239	27
	Ganjam	*117*	*117*	...	*110*	*110*	...	...	...	...
	Visagapatam ..	...	...	...	...	...	...	...	...	...
	Godavery	...	...	...	...	...	...	...	...	...
	Tanjore	...	...	...	*4*	*4*	...	...	...	...
52	North-West Frontier Province.	15	15	...	...	...	...	9	9	...
53	Punjab	1,792	1,748	44	263	251	12	732	689	43
54	United Provinces of Agra and Oudh.	1,125	1,062	63	249	217	32	487	422	65
	Fysabad	*178*	*163*	*15*	*63*	*55*	*8*	*75*	*65*	*10*
	(ii) States and Agencies ...	**173**	**116**	**57**	**74**	**68**	**6**	**30**	**24**	**6**
55	Baroda	...	...	...	...	...	...	...	...	...
56	Bengal States	...	...	...	...	...	...	...	...	...
57	Bombay States	...	...	...	...	...	...	...	...	...
58	Central India Agency ...	...	...	...	5	5	...	...	...	...
59	Central Provinces State ...	...	...	...	13	13	...	...	...	...
60	Hyderabad	2	2	...	24	20	4	1	1	...
61	Kashmir	...	...	...	...	...	...	...	...	...
62	Madras States	...	...	...	...	...	...	...	...	...
	Cochin	...	...	...	...	...	...	...	...	...
	Travancore	...	...	...	...	...	...	...	...	..
63	Mysore	5	5	...	7	7	...	...	...	...
64	North-West Frontier (Agencies and Tribal areas).	...	...	...	...	...	...	...	...	...
65	Punjab States	104	67	37	14	14	...	29	23	6
66	Rajputana Agency ...	62	42	20	11	9	2	...	...	...
67	United Provinces States ...	...	...	...	...	...	...	...	...	...
	(c) French and Portuguese Settlements.	...	...	...	...	...	...	...	...	...
	(d) India (unspecified) ...	**23**	**6**	**17**	**9**	**9**	...	**2**	**2**	...
	B. Born in other Asiatic Countries	**5,744**	**4,139**	**1,605**	**710**	**525**	**185**	**4,651**	**3,867**	**784**
68	Afghanistan	...	...	...	...	...	...	...	...	...
69	Arabia	...	...	...	...	...	...	...	...	...
70	Armenia	...	...	...	...	...	...	...	...	...
71	Bhūtan	...	...	...	...	...	...	...	...	...
72	Ceylon	2	2	...	9	6	3	1	1	...
73	China	3,677	2,585	1,092	673	494	179	4,115	3,452	663
74	French Indo-China ...	...	...	...	...	...	...	...	...	...
75	Hongkong	...	...	...	...	...	...	...	...	...
76	Japan	...	...	...	...	...	...	...	...	...
77	Maldives	...	...	...	...	...	...	...	...	...
78	Mongolia	...	...	...	...	...	...	...	...	...
79	Nepal	2,047	1,552	495	27	24	3	526	407	119
80	Persia	...	...	...	...	...	...	...	...	...
81	Russian Turkistan	...	...	...	...	...	...	...	...	...
82	Siam	11	...	11	1	1	...	...	...	...
83	Straits Settlements and Malaya.	7	...	7	...	...	...	9	7	2
84	Turkey in Asia	...	...	...	...	...	...	...	...	...
85	Asia (unspecified)	...	...	...	...	...	...	...	...	...

Birth-Place.

STATE WHERE ENUMERATED.

Shwebo.			Sagaing.			Lower Chindwin.			Upper Chindwin.			
Persons.	Males.	Females.	Persons.	Males.	Females.	Persons.	Males.	Females.	Persons.	Males.	Females.	Serial No.
95	96	97	98	99	100	101	102	103	104	105	106	
2,458	**2,059**	**899**	**762**	**1,502**	**260**	**1,523**	**1,305**	**218**	**2,721**	**2,260**	**461**	
54	**54**	...	**226**	**197**	**29**	**154**	**145**	**9**	**657**	**551**	**106**	
54	54	...	208	189	19	94	85	9	161	161	...	42
52	*52*	...	*208*	*189*	*19*	*81*	*77*	*4*	*154*	*154*	...	
...	...	...	18	8	10	60	60	...	496	390	106	43
2,323	**1,961**	**362**	**1,495**	**1,266**	**229**	**1,368**	**1,159**	**209**	**2,064**	**1,709**	**355**	
1,504	**1,319**	**185**	**1,487**	**1,260**	**227**	**1,340**	**1,134**	**206**	**2062**	**1,707**	**355**	
..	...	...	...	...	...	1	1	...	...	...	...	44
1	1	...	...	...	...	...	...	...	...	...	...	45
...	...	...	...	...	...	3	2	1	...	...	...	46
651	505	146	422	394	28	208	195	13	531	357	177	47
25	25	...	105	84	21	52	46	6	227	205	22	48
...	...	...	...	...	...	2	2	...	18	13	5	49
...	...	...	...	...	...	...	...	...	...	...	...	50
21	21	...	453	348	105	165	132	33	125	111	14	51
...	...	...	*9*	*9*	...	*7*	*7*	...	...	...	...	
...	...	...	*22*	*22*	...	...	...	...	...	...	...	
21	*21*	...	*2*	*2*	...	*2*	*2*	...	...	...	...	
...	...	...	...	...	...	*4*	*4*	...	...	...	...	
...	...	...	...	...	...	5	2	3	...	...	...	52
616	578	38	159	129	30	570	460	110	696	628	68	53
190	189	1	348	305	43	334	294	40	465	393	72	54
14	*14*	...	*124*	*124*	...	*55*	*51*	*4*	*206*	*165*	*41*	
819	642	177	8	6	2	28	25	3	2	2	...	
...	...	...	...	...	...	...	...	...	...	...	...	55
...	...	...	...	...	...	...	...	...	...	...	...	56
...	...	...	...	...	...	...	...	...	...	...	...	57
...	...	...	...	...	...	...	...	...	...	...	...	58
40	40	...	...	...	...	...	...	...	...	...	...	59
2	2	...	3	2	1	4	4	...	...	...	..	60
...	...	...	...	...	...	...	...	...	...	...	...	61
693	516	177	...	...	...	...	...	...	...	...	...	62
...	...	...	...	...	...	...	...	...	...	...	...	
...	...	...	...	...	...	...	...	...	...	...	...	
81	81	...	...	...	...	2	...	2	...	...	...	63
...	...	...	...	...	...	...	...	...	...	...	...	64
...	...	...	...	...	...	7	6	1	2	2	...	65
3	3	...	5	4	1	15	15	...	...	...	...	66
...	...	...	...	...	...	...	...	...	...	..	...	67
...	...	...	3	1	2	...	...	...	...	...	...	
81	**44**	**37**	**38**	**38**	...	**1**	**1**	...	...	...	...	
209	**198**	**16**	**77**	**69**	**8**	**102**	**82**	**20**	**808**	**217**	**91**	
31	31	...	...	...	...	1	1	...	...	...	...	68
...	...	...	...	...	...	1	1	...	...	...	...	69
...	...	...	...	...	...	...	...	...	...	...	...	70
...	...	...	...	...	...	...	...	...	...	...	...	71
1	1	...	3	3	...	1	1	...	...	...	...	72
174	158	16	72	65	7	92	76	16	164	105	59	73
...	...	...	...	...	...	...	...	...	...	...	...	74
...	...	...	...	...	...	...	...	...	...	...	...	75
...	...	...	...	...	...	...	...	...	...	...	...	76
...	...	...	...	...	...	...	...	...	...	...	...	77
...	...	...	...	...	...	...	...	...	...	...	...	78
...	...	...	1	1	...	3	2	1	142	110	32	79
1	1	...	1	...	1	...	...	...	...	...	...	80
...	...	...	...	...	...	...	...	...	...	...	...	81
...	...	...	...	...	...	3	...	3	2	2	...	82
2	2	...	...	...	...	...	...	...	...	...	...	83
...	...	...	...	...	...	1	1	...	...	...	...	84
...	...	...	...	...	...	...	...	...	...	...	...	85

Serial No.	District, State, Province, or Country where born.	PROVINCE, DISTRICT, OR								
		KYAUKSÈ.			MEIKTILA.			YAMÈTHIN.		
		Persons.	Males.	Females.	Persons.	Males.	Females.	Persons.	Males.	Females.
	1	107	108	109	110	111	112	113	114	115
	A. BORN IN INDIA.									
	II. Beyond Burma	1,066	908	168	4,544	4,001	548	4,816	8,924	892
	(a) Contiguous Province ... Eastern Bengal and Assam—	1	...	1	65	63	2	144	134	10
42	(i) British Territory ...	1	...	1	65	63	2	144	134	10
	Chittagong	*1*	...	*1*	*56*	*54*	*2*	*114*	*113*	*1*
43	(ii) States of Eastern Bengal and Assam.	...	...	...	...	...	...	...	...	...
	(b) Non-Contiguous Provinces	954	813	141	4,106	3,581	525	4,543	3,678	865
	(i) British Territory ...	954	813	141	3,952	3,442	510	4,326	3,487	839
44	Ajmer-Merwara	...	...	...	...	...	...	...	...	...
45	Andamans and Nicobars ...	...	...	...	...	...	...	1	...	1
46	Baluchistan	...	...	...	...	...	...	...	...	...
47	Bengal	416	358	58	506	460	46	1,044	852	192
48	Bombay (including Aden)...	2	...	2	390	344	46	122	97	25
49	Central Provinces and Berar	...	...	...	19	19	...	5	5	...
50	Coorg	...	...	...	...	...	...	...	...	...
51	Madras	223	171	52	871	713	158	1,812	1,478	334
	Ganjam	...	...	...	...	...	...	*304*	*286*	*18*
	Visagapatam ...	...	...	...	...	...	...	*444*	*352*	*92*
	Godavery	...	...	...	*20*	*20*	...	*2*	...	*2*
	Tanjore	...	...	...	*6*	*6*	...	...	...	...
52	North-West Frontier Province.	...	...	...	...	...	...	...	...	...
53	Punjab	36	31	5	1,240	1,097	143	524	395	129
54	United Provinces of Agra and Oudh.	277	253	24	926	809	117	818	660	158
	Fysabad	*136*	*123*	*13*	*228*	*202*	*26*	*233*	*196*	*37*
	(ii) States and Agencies ...	...	...	...	154	139	15	217	191	26
55	Baroda	...	...	...	...	...	...	...	...	...
56	Bengal States	...	...	...	...	...	...	...	...	...
57	Bombay States	...	...	...	...	...	...	...	...	...
58	Central India Agency ...	...	...	...	25	25	...	...	...	...
59	Central Provinces States ...	...	...	...	...	...	...	...	...	...
60	Hyderabad	...	...	...	28	15	13	94	84	10
61	Kashmir	...	...	...	...	...	...	...	...	...
62	Madras States	...	...	...	20	20	...	...	...	...
	Cochin	...	...	...	*6*	*6*	...	...	...	...
	Travancore	...	...	...	*4*	*4*	...	...	...	...
63	Mysore	...	...	...	...	...	...	3	3	...
64	North-West Frontier (Agencies and Tribal Areas).	...	...	...	...	...	...	...	...	...
65	Punjab States	...	...	...	...	...	...	35	27	8
66	Rajputana Agency ...	...	...	...	81	79	2	85	77	8
67	United Provinces States ...	...	...	...	...	...	...	...	...	...
	(c) French and Portuguese Settlements.	...	...	...	...	...	...	2	2	...
	(d) India (unspecified) ...	111	90	21	373	357	16	127	110	17
	B. Born in other Asiatic Countries	124	128	1	415	400	15	1,078	1,027	46
68	Afghanistan	...	...	...	...	...	...	...	...	...
69	Arabia	...	...	...	2	2	...	...	...	...
70	Armenia	...	...	...	...	...	...	...	...	...
71	Bhûtan	...	...	...	...	...	...	...	...	...
72	Ceylon	...	...	...	...	...	...	13	10	3
73	China	124	123	1	337	324	13	779	746	33
74	French Indo-China ...	...	...	...	...	...	...	...	...	...
75	Hongkong	...	...	...	...	...	...	...	...	...
76	Japan	...	...	...	...	...	...	5	...	5
77	Maldives	...	...	...	...	...	...	...	...	...
78	Mongolia	...	...	...	...	...	...	...	...	...
79	Nepal	...	...	...	76	74	2	41	37	4
80	Persia	...	...	...	...	...	...	1	1	...
81	Russian Turkistan ..	...	...	...	...	...	...	...	...	...
82	Siam	...	...	...	...	...	...	1	1	...
83	Straits Settlements and Malaya.	...	...	...	...	...	...	231	230	1
84	Turkey in Asia	...	...	...	...	...	...	2	2	...
85	Asia (unspecified)	...	...	...	...	...	...	...	...	...

Birth-Place.

STATE WHERE ENUMERATED.

Myingyan.			Northern Shan States.			Southern Shan States.			Pakôkku Hill Tracts.			Chin Hills.			
Persons.	Males.	Females.	Persons.	Males.	Females.	Persons.	Males.	Females.	Persons.	Males.	Females	Persons.	Males.	Females.	Serial No.
116	117	118	119	120	121	122	123	124	125	126	127	128	129	130	
2,051	1,917	134	2,625	2,398	227	2,944	2,555	389	41	32	9	1,005	797	208	
340	340	...	76	63	13	23	22	1	2	2	...	13	9	4	
340	340	...	64	59	5	23	22	1	1	1	...	12	9	3	42
340	*340*	...	*42*	*41*	*1*	*18*	*18*	...	*1*	*1*	...	*2*	*2*	...	
...	...	...	12	4	8	...	...	...	1	1	...	1	...	1	43
1,678	1,544	134	2,499	2,292	207	2,890	2,503	387	39	30	9	953	749	204	
1,590	1,467	123	2,315	2,109	206	2,857	2,472	385	36	27	9	865	669	196	
...	...	...	2	2	...	...	...	...	...	...	...	...	...	...	44
...	...	...	...	...	...	..	...	...	...	...	...	...	...	...	45
...	...	...	...	...	...	..	...	...	...	...	...	...	...	...	46
559	535	24	487	457	30	702	630	72	16	8	8	69	41	28	47
125	111	14	118	102	16	113	97	16	...	...	...	13	13	...	48
...	...	...	13	5	8	32	22	10	...	...	...	34	23	11	49
...	...	...	...	...	...	...	...	...	...	...	...	...	...	...	50
381	336	45	571	553	18	413	379	34	1	1	...	255	191	64	51
...	...	...	*236*	*236*	...	*101*	*101*	...	...	...	...	...	...	...	
...	...	...	*12*	*12*	...	...	...	...	...	...	...	..	...	...	
15	*15*	...	*15*	*15*	...	...	...	...	...	..	...	...	...	...	
...	...	..	*2*	*1*	*1*	...	...	...	...	...	...	...	...	...	
...	...	...	9	8	1	17	17	...	...	...	...	2	...	2	52
135	111	24	658	587	71	1,027	880	147	19	18	1	308	253	55	53
390	374	16	457	395	62	553	447	106	...	...	...	184	148	36	54
119	*109*	*10*	*66*	*66*	...	*28*	*28*	...	...	...	...	...	...	...	
88	77	11	184	183	1	33	31	2	3	3	..	88	80	8	
...	...	...	8	8	...	...	...	...	...	...	...	...	...	...	55
11	...	11	...	...	...	...	...	...	...	...	..	...	...	..	56
...	...	...	...	...	...	...	...	...	..	...	...	...	...	...	57
...	...	...	133	133	...	...	...	...	1	1	...	...	...	...	58
...	...	...	...	...	...	...	...	...	1	1	...	...	...	...	59
...	...	...	7	7	...	7	5	2	...	...	...	...	...	...	60
...	...	..	...	...	...	...	...	...	...	...	...	...	...	...	61
...	...	...	1	1	...	...	...	...	...	...	...	...	...	...	62
...	...	...	...	...	...	...	...	...	...	...	...	...	...	...	
...	...	...	...	...	...	...	...	...	...	...	...	...	...	...	
...	...	...	1	1	...	11	11	...	...	...	...	80	80	...	63
...	...	...	1	1	...	...	...	...	...	...	...	...	...	...	64
...	...	...	10	10	...	15	15	...	1	1	...	8	...	8	65
...	...	...	23	22	1	...	...	...	...	...	...	...	...	...	66
77	77	...	...	...	..	...	..	...	...	...	...	...	...	...	67
...	...	...	...	...	...	1	1	...	...	...	...	...	...	...	
33	33	...	50	43	7	30	29	1	...	...	...	39	39	...	
225	202	23	10,403	6,680	3,723	5,217	4,004	1,213	98	80	18	423	324	99	
...	...	...	1	1	...	16	16	...	...	...	...	...	...	...	68
...	...	...	...	..	...	...	...	...	...	...	...	...	...	...	69
...	...	...	...	...	...	...	...	...	...	...	...	...	...	...	70
...	...	...	...	...	...	...	...	...	...	...	...	...	...	...	71
2	2	...	10	6	4	2	2	...	...	...	...	...	...	...	72
223	200	23	9,861	6,231	3,630	3,326	2,685	641	...	...	...	...	...	...	73
...	...	...	...	...	...	1	...	1	...	...	...	...	...	...	74
...	...	...	...	...	...	...	...	...	...	...	...	..	...	...	75
...	...	...	1	1	...	...	...	...	...	...	...	...	...	...	76
..	...	...	...	...	...	...	...	...	...	...	...	...	...	...	77
...	...	...	529	440	89	710	618	92	98	80	18	...	...	...	78
...	...	...	...	...	...	3	3	...	...	...	...	423	324	99	79
...	...	...	..	...	...	...	...	...	..	...	...	...	...	...	80
..	...	...	...	...	...	...	...	...	...	...	...	...	...	...	81
...	...	...	...	...	...	1,157	679	478	...	...	...	...	...	...	82
...	...	...	1	1	...	2	1	1	...	...	...	...	...	...	83
...	...	..	...	...	...	...	...	...	...	...	...	...	...	...	84
...	...	...	...	...	...	...	...	...	...	...	...	...	...	...	85

Serial No.	District, State, Province, or Country where born.	PROVINCE, DISTRICT, OR								
		WHOLE PROVINCE.			AKYAB.			NORTHERN ARAKAN.		
		Persons.	Males.	Females.	Persons.	Males.	Females.	Persons.	Males.	Females.
	1	2	3	4	5	6	7	8	9	10
	C. Born in Europe ...	8,337	7,060	1,277	150	132	18	5	4	1
86	United Kingdom ...	7,354	6,279	1,075	141	125	16	5	4	1
	England and Wales	*5,105*	*4,326*	*779*	*118*	*102*	*16*	*4*	*4*	...
	Scotland	*1,040*	*907*	*133*	*23*	*23*	...	*1*	...	*1*
	Ireland	*1,209*	*1,046*	*163*	...	...	...	...	...	...
87	Austria-Hungary ...	137	123	14	...	...	...	...	...	...
88	Belgium	15	12	3	...	...	...	...	...	...
89	Denmark	4	4	...	...	...	...	...	...	...
90	France	211	113	98	...	...	...	...	...	...
91	Germany	214	184	30	7	7	...	...	...	...
92	Gibraltar	13	8	5	...	...	...	...	...	...
93	Greece	71	70	1	...	...	...	...	...	...
94	Holland	59	55	4	...	...	...	...	...	...
95	Italy	33	24	9	...	...	...	...	...	...
96	Malta	3	3	...	...	...	...	...	...	...
97	Norway	17	17	..	...	...	...	...	..	...
98	Sweden	44	44	...	...	...	...	...	...	...
99	Portugal	6	6	...	...	...	...	...	...	...
100	Russia	31	17	14	...	...	...	...	...	...
101	Spain	16	14	2	...	...	...	...	...	...
102	Switzerland	7	4	3	...	...	...	...	...	...
103	Europe (unspecified)	102	83	19	2	...	2	...	...	...
	D. Born in Africa ...	53	42	11	...	...	...	...	...	...
104	Cape Colony ...	15	13	2	...	...	...	...	...	...
105	Egypt	1	1	...	...	...	...	...	...	...
106	Mauritius ...	1	1	...	...	...	...	...	...	...
107	Africa (unspecified) ...	36	27	9	...	...	...	...	...	...
	E. Born in America ...	403	277	126	...	...	...	...	...	...
108	Canada	2	2	...	...	...	...	...	...	...
109	Newfoundland ...	1	1	...	...	...	...	...	...	...
110	United States ...	21	20	1	...	...	...	...	...	...
111	America (unspecified)	379	254	125	...	...	...	...	...	...
	F. Born in Australasia ...	205	173	32	...	...	...	...	...	...
112	Australia ...	149	119	30	...	...	...	...	...	...
113	Java	2	...	2	...	...	...	...	...	...
114	New Zealand ...	7	7	...	...	...	...	...	...	...
115	Philippines ...	47	47	...	...	...	...	...	...	..
	Not enumerated by Birth-place.	59,006	29,534	29,472	...	...	...	...	...	...
	Total Population ...	12,115,217	6 183 494	5,931,723	529,943	289,474	240,469	22,234	11,405	10,829

Birth-Place.

STATE WHERE ENUMERATED.

Kyaukpyu.			Sandoway.			City of Rangoon.			Hanthawaddy.			
Persons.	Males.	Females.	Persons.	Males.	Females.	Persons.	Males.	Females.	Persons.	Males.	Females.	Serial No.
11	12	13	14	15	16	17	18	19	20	21	22	
2	**1**	**1**	**3**	**3**	...	**3,914**	**3,321**	**593**	**452**	**401**	**51**	
2	1	1	3	3	...	3,336	2,814	522	430	388	42	86
1	*1*	...	*1*	*1*	..	*2,543*	*2,183*	*360*	*336*	*297*	*39*	
...	...	...	...	...	...	*580*	*494*	*86*	*89*	*86*	*3*	
1	...	*1*	*2*	*2*	...	*213*	*137*	*76*	*5*	*5*	...	
...	...	...	...	...	...	112	111	1	1	1	...	87
...	...	...	...	...	...	10	9	1	...	...	...	88
...	...	...	...	...	...	4	4	...	...	...	...	89
...	...	...	...	...	...	64	47	17	12	4	8	90
...	...	...	...	...	...	153	135	18	3	3	...	91
...	...	...	...	...	...	13	8	5	...	...	...	92
...	...	...	...	...	...	46	45	1	...	...	...	93
...	...	...	...	...	...	57	53	4	2	2	...	94
...	...	...	...	...	...	19	14	5	...	...	...	95
...	...	...	...	...	...	...	...	...	2	2	...	96
...	...	...	...	...	...	9	9	...	...	...	...	97
...	...	...	...	...	...	17	17	...	...	...	...	98
...	...	...	...	...	...	1	1	...	...	...	...	99
...	...	...	...	...	...	30	16	14	...	...	...	100
...	...	...	...	...	...	4	2	2	...	...	...	101
...	...	...	...	...	...	2	1	1	...	...	...	102
...	...	...	...	...	...	37	35	2	2	1	1	103
...	...	...	...	...	...	**36**	**28**	**8**	...	...	...	
...	...	...	...	...	...	11	11	...	...	...	...	104
...	...	...	...	...	...	...	...	...	...	...	...	105
...	...	...	...	...	...	...	...	...	...	...	...	106
...	...	...	...	...	...	25	17	8	...	...	...	107
...	...	...	...	...	...	**154**	**91**	**63**	**11**	**7**	**4**	
...	...	...	...	...	...	...	...	...	...	...	...	108
...	...	...	...	...	...	...	...	...	...	...	...	109
...	...	...	...	...	...	...	...	...	...	...	...	110
...	...	...	...	...	...	154	91	63	11	7	4	111
...	...	...	...	...	...	**87**	**59**	**28**	**4**	**1**	**3**	
...	...	...	...	...	...	85	59	26	3	...	3	112
...	...	...	...	...	...	2	...	2	...	...	...	113
...	...	...	...	...	...	...	...	...	1	1	...	114
...	...	...	...	...	...	...	...	...	...	...	...	115
...	...	...	...	...	...	...	...	...	...	...	...	
184,916	**89,571**	**95,345**	**102,803**	**51,475**	**51,328**	**293,316**	**208,111**	**85,205**	**539,109**	**295,886**	**243,223**	

Serial No.	District, State, Province, or Country where born.	Tharrawaddy.			Pegu.			Prome.		
		Persons.	Males.	Females.	Persons.	Males.	Females.	Persons.	Males.	Females.
	1	23	24	25	26	27	28	29	30	31
	O. Born in Europe ...	16	11	5	34	28	6	48	36	12
86	United Kingdom ...	12	7	5	34	28	6	45	34	11
	England and Wales	11	6	5	29	24	5	30	23	7
	Scotland	1	1	...	3	3	...	13	10	3
	Ireland	...	...	...	2	1	1	2	1	1
87	Austria-Hungary ...	...	...	...	...	...	...	1	...	1
88	Belgium	...	...	...	...	...	...	...	...	...
89	Denmark	...	...	...	...	...	...	...	...	...
90	France	3	3	...	...	...	...	...	...	...
91	Germany	...	...	...	...	...	...	...	...	...
92	Gibraltar	...	...	...	...	...	...	...	...	...
93	Greece	...	...	...	...	...	...	...	...	...
94	Holland	...	...	...	...	...	...	...	...	...
95	Italy	1	1	...	...	...	...	...	...	...
96	Malta	...	...	...	...	...	...	...	...	...
97	Norway	...	...	...	...	...	...	...	...	...
98	Sweden	...	...	...	...	...	...	...	...	...
99	Portugal	...	...	...	...	...	...	2	2	...
100	Russia	...	...	...	...	...	...	...	...	...
101	Spain	...	...	...	...	...	...	...	...	...
102	Switzerland	...	...	...	...	...	...	...	...	...
103	Europe (unspecified)	...	...	...	...	...	...	...	...	...
	D. Born in Africa ...	...	...	...	1	1	...	...	...	...
104	Cape Colony	...	...	...	1	1	...	...	...	...
105	Egypt	...	...	...	...	...	...	...	...	...
106	Mauritius	...	...	...	...	...	...	...	...	...
107	Africa (unspecified)...	...	...	...	...	...	...	...	...	...
	E. Born in America ...	5	2	3	7	2	5	2	1	1
108	Canada	...	...	...	...	...	...	...	...	...
109	Newfoundland ...	...	...	...	...	...	...	...	...	...
110	United States ...	...	...	...	...	...	...	...	...	...
111	America (unspecified)	5	2	3	7	2	5	2	1	1
	F. Born in Australasia ...	...	...	...	2	2	...	...	...	...
112	Australia	...	...	...	2	2	...	...	...	...
113	Java	...	...	...	...	...	...	...	...	...
114	New Zealand ...	...	...	...	...	...	...	...	...	...
115	Philippines	...	...	...	...	...	...	...	...	...
	Not enumerated by Birth-place.	...	...	...	...	...	...	...	...	...
	Total Population ...	433,320	216,442	216,878	429,121	229,540	199,581	378,871	186,213	192,658

Birth-Place.

STATE WHERE ENUMERATED.

Bassein.			Henzada.			Myaungmya.			Ma-ubin.			
Persons.	Males.	Females.	Persons.	Males.	Females.	Persons.	Males.	Females.	Persons.	Males.	Females.	Serial No.
32	33	34	35	36	37	38	39	40	41	42	43	
270	201	69	33	27	6	16	10	6	21	16	5	
176	146	30	19	15	4	10	6	4	19	15	4	86
132	*107*	*5*	*12*	*9*	*3*	*6*	*3*	*3*	*10*	*6*	*4*	
43	*39*	*4*	*4*	*4*	...	*4*	*3*	*1*	*7*	*7*	...	
1	...	*1*	*3*	*2*	*1*	...	...	...	*2*	*2*	...	
...	...	...	1	...	1	...	...	...	...	...	...	87
...	...	...	...	...	...	...	...	...	...	...	...	88
...	...	...	...	...	...	...	...	...	...	...	...	89
40	1	39	9	9	...	4	4	...	1	1	...	90
23	23	...	3	3	...	...	...	...	...	...	...	91
...	...	...	...	...	...	...	...	...	...	...	...	92
10	10	...	...	...	...	...	...	...	...	...	...	93
...	...	...	...	...	...	...	...	...	...	...	...	94
5	5	...	...	...	...	...	...	...	...	...	...	95
...	...	...	...	...	...	...	...	...	...	...	...	96
8	8	...	...	...	...	...	...	...	...	...	...	97
...	...	...	...	...	...	...	...	...	...	...	...	98
...	...	...	...	...	...	...	...	...	...	...	...	99
...	...	...	...	...	...	...	...	...	...	...	...	100
8	8	...	...	...	...	...	...	...	...	...	...	101
...	...	...	...	...	...	...	...	...	...	...	...	102
...	...	...	1	...	1	2	...	2	1	...	1	103
...	...	...	...	...	...	...	...	...	1	...	1	
...	...	...	...	...	...	...	...	...	...	...	...	104
...	...	...	...	...	...	...	...	...	...	...	...	105
...	...	...	...	...	...	...	...	...	...	...	...	106
...	...	...	...	...	...	...	...	...	1	...	1	107
7	5	2	9	3	6	...	...	...	6	6	...	
...	...	...	...	...	...	...	...	...	...	...	...	108
...	...	...	...	...	...	...	...	...	...	...	...	109
...	...	...	...	...	...	...	...	...	...	...	...	110
7	5	2	9	3	6	...	...	...	6	6	...	111
21	21	...	2	2	...	...	...	...	...	...	...	
21	21	...	2	2	...	...	...	...	...	...	...	112
...	...	...	...	...	...	...	...	...	...	...	...	113
...	...	...	...	...	...	...	...	...	...	...	...	114
...	...	...	...	...	...	...	...	...	...	...	...	115
...	...	...	...	...	...	...	...	...	...	...	...	
440,988	226,773	214,215	532,357	264,319	268,038	334,852	176,465	158,387	305,073	155,715	149,358	

Serial No.	District, State, Province, or Country where born.	PROVINCE, DISTRICT, OR — PYAPÔN. Persons.	Males.	Females.	TOUNGOO. Persons.	Males.	Females.	SALWEEN. Persons.	Males.	Females.
	1	44	45	46	47	48	49	50	51	52
	C. Born in Europe ...	24	19	5	42	16	26	7	7	...
86	United Kingdom ...	24	19	5	38	16	22	6	6	...
	England and Wales	7	5	2	36	16	20	2	2	...
	Scotland	17	14	3	2	...	2	3	3	...
	Ireland	...	...	...	...	...	...	1	1	...
87	Austria-Hungary ..	...	...	...	...	...	...	...	...	...
88	Belgium	...	...	...	...	...	...	...	...	...
89	Denmark	...	...	...	...	...	...	...	...	...
90	France	...	...	...	...	...	...	...	...	...
91	Germany	...	...	...	...	...	...	...	...	...
92	Gibraltar	...	...	...	...	...	...	...	...	...
93	Greece	...	...	...	...	...	...	...	...	...
94	Holland	...	...	...	...	...	...	...	...	...
95	Italy	...	...	...	4	...	4	...	...	...
96	Malta	...	...	...	...	...	...	...	...	...
97	Norway	...	...	...	...	...	...	...	...	...
98	Sweden	...	...	...	...	...	...	...	...	...
99	Portugal	...	...	...	...	...	...	...	...	...
100	Russia	...	...	...	...	...	...	...	...	...
101	Spain	...	...	...	...	...	...	...	...	...
102	Switzerland	...	...	...	...	...	...	...	...	...
103	Europe (unspecified)	...	...	...	...	...	...	1	1	...
	D. Born in Africa ...	...	...	...	...	...	...	...	...	...
104	Cape Colony	...	...	...	...	...	...	...	...	...
105	Egypt	...	...	...	...	...	...	...	...	...
106	Mauritius	...	...	...	...	...	...	...	...	...
107	Africa (unspecified) ...	...	...	...	...	...	...	...	...	...
	E. Born in America ...	...	...	...	8	...	8	...	...	...
108	Canada	...	...	...	...	...	...	...	...	...
109	Newfoundland ...	...	...	...	...	...	...	...	...	...
110	United States ...	...	...	...	...	...	...	...	...	...
111	America (unspecified)	...	...	...	8	...	8	...	...	...
	F. Born in Australasia ...	...	...	...	...	...	...	...	...	...
112	Australia	...	...	...	...	...	...	...	...	...
113	Java	...	...	...	...	...	...	...	...	...
114	New Zealand... ...	...	...	...	...	...	...	...	...	...
115	Philippines	...	...	...	...	...	...	...	...	...
	Not enumerated by Birth-place.	...	...	...	...	...	...	...	...	...
	Total Population ...	256,215	139,641	116,574	351,076	181,488	169,588	46,608	24,741	21,867

Birth-Place.

STATE WHERE ENUMERATED.

Thatôn.			Amherst.			Tavoy.			Mergui.			
Persons.	Males.	Females.	Persons.	Males.	Females.	Persons.	Males.	Females.	Persons.	Males.	Females.	Serial No.
53	54	55	56	57	58	59	60	61	62	63	64	
6	5	1	180	131	49	38	3	5	38	38	5	
3	2	1	92	57	35	35	31	4	36	31	5	86
1	*1*	...	*59*	*26*	*33*	*32*	*28*	*4*	*31*	27	*4*	
2	*1*	*1*	*25*	*23*	*2*	*2*	*2*	...	*5*	*4*	*1*	
...	...	...	*8*	*8*	...	*1*	*1*	...	...	...	...	
...	...	...	...	...	...	...	...	...	...	...	...	87
...	...	...	...	...	...	...	...	...	...	...	...	88
...	...	...	...	...	...	...	...	...	...	...	...	89
3	3	...	16	7	9	1	1	...	1	1	...	90
...	...	...	11	11	...	1	1	...	1	1	...	91
...	...	...	...	...	...	...	...	...	...	...	...	92
...	...	...	14	14	...	...	...	...	...	...	...	93
...	...	...	...	...	...	...	...	...	...	...	...	94
...	...	...	...	...	...	...	...	...	...	...	...	95
...	...	...	...	...	...	...	...	...	...	...	...	96
...	...	...	...	...	...	...	...	...	...	...	...	97
...	...	...	26	26	...	...	...	...	...	...	...	98
...	...	...	...	...	...	...	...	...	...	...	...	99
...	...	...	1	1	...	...	...	...	...	...	...	100
...	...	...	4	4	...	...	...	...	...	...	...	101
...	...	...	5	3	2	...	...	...	...	...	...	102
...	...	...	11	8	3	1	...	1	...	...	...	103
...	...	...	1	...	1	...	...	...	...	...	...	
...	...	...	1	...	1	...	...	...	...	...	...	104
...	...	...	...	...	...	...	...	...	...	...	...	105
...	...	...	...	...	...	...	...	...	...	...	...	106
...	...	...	...	...	...	...	...	...	...	...	...	107
...	...	...	18	8	5	2	2	...	2	2	...	
...	...	...	...	...	...	...	...	...	...	...	...	108
...	...	...	...	...	...	...	...	...	...	...	...	109
...	...	...	...	...	...	...	...	...	2	2	...	110
...	...	...	13	8	5	2	2	...	...	...	...	111
...	...	...	20	19	1	3	3	...	46	46	...	
...	...	...	[illegible]	19	1	3	3	...	...	...	...	112
...	...	...	...	...	...	...	...	...	...	...	...	113
...	...	...	...	...	...	...	...	...	...	...	...	114
...	...	...	...	...	...	...	...	...	46	46	...	115
...	...	...	...	...	...	...	...	...	...	...	...	
416,975	217,770	199,205	367,918	198,430	169,488	135,293	68,667	66,626	111,424	59,530	51,894	

Serial No.	District, State, Province, or Country where born.	Thayetmyo.			Pakôkku.			Minbu.		
		Persons.	Males.	Females.	Persons.	Males.	Females.	Persons.	Males.	Females.
	1	65	66	67	68	69	70	71	72	73
	C. Born in Europe ..	**139**	**134**	**5**	**40**	**31**	**9**	**18**	**14**	**4**
86	United Kingdom ...	137	132	5	40	31	9	17	14	3
	England and Wales	*125*	*120*	*5*	*33*	*25*	*8*	*16*	*13*	*3*
	Scotland	*2*	*2*	...	*5*	*5*	...	...	...	...
	Ireland	*10*	*10*	...	*2*	*1*	*1*	*1*	*1*	...
87	Austria-Hungary ...	...	...	...	...	...	...	...	...	...
88	Belgium	...	...	...	...	...	...	...	...	...
89	Denmark	...	...	...	...	...	...	...	...	...
90	France	1	1	...	...	...	...	...	...	...
91	Germany	...	...	...	...	...	...	1	...	1
92	Gibraltar	...	...	...	...	...	...	...	...	...
93	Greece	...	...	...	...	...	...	...	...	...
94	Holland	...	...	...	...	...	...	...	...	...
95	Italy	...	...	...	...	...	...	...	...	...
96	Malta	...	...	...	...	...	...	...	...	...
97	Norway	...	...	...	...	...	...	...	...	...
98	Sweden	...	...	...	...	...	...	...	...	...
99	Portugal	...	...	...	...	...	...	...	...	...
100	Russia	...	...	...	...	...	...	...	...	...
101	Spain	...	...	...	...	...	...	...	...	...
102	Switzerland	...	...	...	...	...	...	...	...	...
103	Europe (unspecified)	1	1	...	...	...	...	...	...	...
	D. Born in Africa ...	...	...	...	...	...	...	...	...	...
104	Cape Colony	...	...	...	...	...	...	...	...	...
105	Egypt	...	...	...	...	...	...	...	...	...
106	Mauritius	...	...	...	...	...	...	...	...	...
107	Africa (unspecified) ...	...	...	...	...	...	...	...	...	...
	E. Born in America ...	**8**	**7**	**1**	**13**	**12**	**1**	...	...	...
108	Canada	...	...	...	...	...	...	...	...	...
109	Newfoundland ...	1	1	...	...	...	...	...	...	...
110	United States ...	2	1	1	12	12	...	...	...	...
111	America (unspecified)	5	5	...	1	...	1	...	...	...
	F. Born in Australasia ...	...	...	...	...	...	...	**1**	**1**	...
112	Australia	...	...	...	...	...	...	...	...	...
113	Java	...	...	...	...	...	...	...	...	...
114	New Zealand... ...	...	...	...	...	...	...	1	1	...
115	Philippines	...	...	...	...	...	...	...	...	...
	Not enumerated by Birth-place.	...	...	...	...	...	...	...	...	...
	Total Population ...	**248,275**	**122,231**	**126,044**	**409,909**	**196,159**	**213,750**	**263,939**	**128,837**	**135,102**

Birth-Place.

STATE WHERE ENUMERATED.

Magwe.			Mandalay (including City).			Mandalay City.			Bhamo.			
Persons.	Males.	Females.	Persons.	Males.	Females.	Persons.	Males.	Females.	Persons.	Males.	Females.	Serial No.
74	75	76	77	78	79	80	81	82	83	84	85	
46	41	5	1,527	1,283	244	554	451	103	256	230	26	
46	41	5	1,453	1,249	204	489	423	66	244	226	18	86
34	*29*	*5*	*436*	*317*	*119*	*147*	*112*	*35*	*220*	*205*	*15*	
11	*11*	...	*111*	*92*	*19*	*86*	*78*	*8*	*12*	*12*	...	
1	*1*	...	*906*	*840*	*66*	*256*	*233*	*23*	*12*	*9*	*3*	
...	...	...	18	10	8	15	7	8	...	...	...	87
...	...	...	...	...	...	...	...	...	...	...	...	88
...	...	...	...	...	...	...	...	...	...	...	...	89
...	...	...	46	21	25	40	18	22	1	1	...	90
...	...	...	7	...	7	7	...	7	4	...	4	91
...	...	...	...	...	...	...	...	...	...	...	...	92
...	...	...	...	...	...	...	...	...	...	...	...	93
...	...	...	...	...	...	...	...	...	...	...	...	94
...	...	...	...	...	...	...	...	...	...	...	...	95
...	...	...	...	...	...	...	...	...	...	...	...	96
...	...	...	...	...	...	...	...	...	...	...	...	97
...	...	...	...	...	...	...	...	...	...	...	...	98
...	...	...	3	3	...	3	3	...	...	...	...	99
...	...	...	...	...	...	...	...	...	...	...	...	100
...	...	...	...	...	...	...	...	...	...	...	...	101
...	...	...	...	...	...	...	...	...	...	...	...	102
...	...	...	...	...	...	...	...	...	7	3	4	103
...	...	...	...	...	...	...	...	...	1	...	1	
...	...	...	...	...	...	...	...	...	1	...	1	104
...	...	...	...	...	...	...	...	...	...	...	...	105
...	...	...	...	...	...	...	...	...	...	...	...	106
...	...	...	...	...	...	...	...	...	...	...	...	107
91	85	6	7	2	5	...	...	...	8	6	2	
...	...	...	...	...	...	...	...	...	1	1	...	108
...	...	...	...	...	...	...	...	...	...	...	...	109
3	3	...	...	...	...	...	...	...	...	...	...	110
88	82	6	7	2	5	...	...	...	7	5	2	111
1	1	...	...	...	...	...	...	...	1	1	...	
1	1	...	...	...	...	...	...	...	...	...	...	112
...	...	...	...	...	...	...	...	...	...	...	...	113
...	...	...	...	...	...	...	...	...	1	1	...	114
...	...	...	...	...	...	...	...	...	...	...	...	115
...	...	...	...	...	...	...	...	...	...	...	...	
316,909	156,387	160,522	340,770	170,750	170,020	138,299	69,718	68,581	107,811	55,528	52,283	

PROVINCE, DISTRICT, OR

Serial No.	District, State, Province, or Country where born.	Myitkyina.			Katha.			Ruby Mines.		
		Persons.	Males.	Females.	Persons.	Males.	Females.	Persons.	Males.	Females.
	1	86	87	88	89	90	91	92	93	94
	C. Born in Europe ...	**76**	**67**	**9**	**39**	**33**	**6**	**40**	**31**	**9**
86	United Kingdom ...	55	49	6	38	33	5	40	31	9
	England and Wales	*36*	*30*	*6*	*31*	*27*	*4*	*36*	*28*	*8*
	Scotland	*9*	*9*	...	*7*	*6*	*1*	*4*	*3*	*1*
	Ireland	*10*	*10*	...	...	...	...	...	...	...
87	Austria-Hungary ...	2	...	2	...	...	...	...	...	...
88	Belgium	1	...	1	...	...	...	...	...	...
89	Denmark	...	...	...	...	...	...	...	...	...
90	France	...	...	...	...	...	...	...	...	...
91	Germany	...	...	...	...	...	...	...	...	...
92	Gibraltar	...	...	...	...	...	...	...	...	...
93	Greece	...	...	...	...	...	...	...	...	...
94	Holland	...	...	...	...	...	...	...	...	...
95	Italy	...	...	...	...	...	...	...	...	...
96	Malta	...	...	...	...	...	...	...	...	...
97	Norway	...	...	...	...	...	...	...	...	...
98	Sweden	...	...	...	...	...	...	...	...	...
99	Portugal	...	...	...	...	...	...	...	...	...
100	Russia	...	...	...	...	...	...	...	...	...
101	Spain	...	...	...	...	...	...	...	...	...
102	Switzerland	...	...	...	...	...	...	...	...	...
103	Europe (unspecified)	18	18	...	1	...	1	...	...	...
	D. Born in Africa ...	...	...	...	**9**	**9**	...	**1**	**1**	...
104	Cape Colony	...	...	...	...	...	...	...	...	...
105	Egypt	...	...	...	1	1	...	...	...	...
106	Mauritius	...	...	...	...	...	...	...	...	...
107	Africa (unspecified)...	...	...	...	8	8	...	1	1	...
	E. Born in America ...	**2**	**2**	...	**6**	**2**	**4**	...	...	...
108	Canada	...	...	...	...	...	...	...	...	...
109	Newfoundland ...	...	...	...	...	...	...	...	...	...
110	United States ...	...	...	...	...	...	...	...	...	...
111	America (unspecified)	2	2	...	6	2	4	...	...	...
	F. Born in Australasia ...	**6**	**6**	...	**1**	**1**	...	...	...	...
112	Australia	5	5	...	...	...	...	...	...	...
113	Java	...	...	...	...	...	...	...	...	...
114	New Zealand ...	1	1	...	1	1	...	...	...	...
115	Philippines	...	...	...	...	...	...	...	...	...
	Not enumerated by Birth-place.	...	...	...	...	...	...	...	...	...
	Total Population ...	**85,577**	**47,863**	**37,714**	**198,193**	**98,148**	**100,045**	**100,618**	**54,487**	**46,131**

Birth-Place.

STATE WHERE ENUMERATED.

Shwebo.			Sagaing.			Lower Chindwin.			Upper Chindwin.			
Persons.	Males.	Females.	Persons.	Males.	Females.	Persons.	Males.	Females.	Persons.	Males.	Females.	
95	96	97	98	99	100	101	102	103	104	105	106	Serial No.
529	492	37	20	18	2	15	7	8	18	18	...	
526	489	37	19	17	2	15	7	8	18	18	...	86
513	*480*	*33*	*19*	*17*	*2*	*11*	*5*	*6*	*18*	*18*	...	
8	*6*	*2*	...	...	...	...	...	...	...	...	...	
5	*3*	*2*	...	...	...	*4*	*2*	*2*	...	...	...	
...	...	...	...	...	...	...	...	...	...	...	...	87
...	...	...	1	1	...	...	...	...	...	...	...	88
3	3	...	...	...	...	...	...	...	...	...	...	89
...	...	...	...	...	...	...	...	...	...	...	...	90
...	...	...	...	...	...	...	...	...	...	...	...	91
...	...	...	...	...	...	...	...	...	...	...	...	92
...	...	...	...	...	...	...	...	...	...	...	...	93
...	...	...	...	...	...	...	...	...	...	...	...	94
...	...	...	...	...	...	...	...	...	...	...	...	95
...	...	...	...	...	...	...	...	...	...	...	...	96
...	...	...	...	...	...	...	...	...	...	...	...	97
...	...	...	...	...	...	...	...	...	...	...	...	98
...	...	...	...	...	...	...	...	...	...	...	...	99
...	...	...	...	...	...	...	...	...	...	...	...	100
...	...	...	...	...	...	...	...	...	...	...	...	101
...	...	...	...	...	...	...	...	...	...	...	...	102
...	...	...	...	...	...	...	...	...	...	...	...	103
1	1	...	...	...	...	...	...	...	...	...	...	
...	...	...	...	...	...	...	...	...	...	...	...	104
...	...	...	...	...	...	...	...	...	...	...	...	105
...	...	...	...	...	...	...	...	...	...	...	...	106
1	1	...	...	...	...	...	...	...	...	...	...	107
1	...	1	...	...	...	...	...	...	...	...	...	
...	...	...	...	...	...	...	...	...	...	...	...	108
...	...	...	...	...	...	...	...	...	...	...	...	109
...	...	...	...	...	...	...	...	...	...	...	...	110
1	...	1	...	...	...	...	...	...	...	...	...	111
2	2	...	...	...	...	...	...	...	...	...	...	
...	...	...	...	...	...	...	...	...	...	...	...	112
...	...	...	...	...	...	...	...	...	...	...	...	113
2	2	...	...	...	...	...	...	...	...	...	...	114
...	...	...	...	...	...	...	...	...	...	...	...	115
...	...	...	...	...	...	...	...	...	...	...	...	
356,363	168,070	188,293	312,111	147,816	164,295	316,175	141,262	174,913	170,622	86,141	84,481	

IMPERIAL TABLE XI.—

PROVINCE, DISTRICT, OR

Serial No.	District, State, Province, or Country where born.	Kyaukse. Persons.	Kyaukse. Males.	Kyaukse. Females.	Meiktila. Persons.	Meiktila. Males.	Meiktila. Females.	Yamèthin. Persons.	Yamèthin. Males.	Yamèthin. Females.
	1	107	108	109	110	111	112	113	114	115
	C. Born in Europe ...	15	8	7	79	70	9	55	47	8
86	United Kingdom ...	11	5	6	77	70	7	46	38	8
	England and Wales	*6*	*4*	*2*	*56*	*51*	*5*	*35*	*29*	*6*
	Scotland	...	...	...	*20*	*19*	*1*	*7*	*6*	*1*
	Ireland	*5*	*1*	*4*	*1*	...	*1*	*4*	*3*	*1*
87	Austria-Hungary ...	1	...	1	...	...	...	...	...	...
88	Belgium	...	...	...	1	...	1	2	2	...
89	Denmark	...	...	...	...	...	...	...	...	...
90	France	3	3	...	...	...	...	2	2	...
91	Germany	...	...	...	...	...	...	...	...	...
92	Gibraltar	...	...	...	...	...	...	...	...	...
93	Greece	...	...	...	...	...	...	...	...	...
94	Holland	...	...	...	...	...	...	...	...	...
95	Italy	...	...	...	...	...	...	1	1	...
96	Malta	...	...	...	...	...	...	...	...	...
97	Norway	...	...	...	...	...	...	...	...	...
98	Sweden	...	...	...	...	...	...	...	...	...
99	Portugal	...	...	...	...	...	...	...	...	...
100	Russia	...	...	...	...	...	...	...	...	...
101	Spain	...	...	...	...	...	...	...	...	...
102	Switzerland	...	...	...	...	...	...	...	...	...
103	Europe (unspecified)	...	...	...	1	...	1	4	4	...
	D. Born in Africa ...	...	...	...	...	...	...	...	...	...
104	Cape Colony ...	...	...	...	...	...	...	...	...	...
105	Egypt	...	...	...	...	...	...	...	...	...
106	Mauritius	...	...	...	...	...	...	...	...	...
107	Africa (unspecified)	...	...	...	...	...	...	...	...	...
	E. Born in America ...	2	2	...	1	1	...	3	2	1
108	Canada	...	...	...	...	...	...	1	1	...
109	Newfoundland ...	...	...	...	...	...	...	...	...	...
110	United States ...	2	2	...	...	...	...	...	...	...
111	America (unspecified)	...	...	...	1	1	...	2	1	1
	F. Born in Australasia...	...	...	...	...	...	...	1	1	...
112	Australia	...	...	...	...	...	...	1	1	...
113	Java ...	...	...	...	...	...	...	...	...	...
114	New Zealand ...	...	...	...	...	...	...	...	...	...
115	Philippines ...	...	...	...	...	...	...	...	...	...
	Not enumerated by Birth-place.	...	...	...	...	...	...	...	...	...
	Total Population ...	141,426	68,868	72,558	279,822	134,170	145,652	307,419	153,223	154,196

Birth-Place.

STATE WHERE ENUMERATED.

Myingyan.			Northern Shan States.			Southern Shan States.			Pakokku Hill Tracts.			Chin Hills.			
Persons.	Males.	Females.	Persons.	Males.	Females.	Persons.	Males.	Females.	Persons.	Males.	Females.	Persons.	Males.	Females.	Serial No.
116	117	118	119	120	121	122	123	124	125	126	127	128	129	130	
81	29	2	20	18	2	64	47	17	1	1	...	10	6	4	
29	27	2	16	14	2	50	33	17	1	1	...	10	6	4	86
12	*11*	*1*	*16*	*14*	2	*40*	*25*	*15*	*1*	*1*	...	*10*	*6*	*4*	
16	*15*	*1*	...	...	...	*4*	*4*	...	...	...	...	...	...	...	
1	*1*	...	...	...	...	*6*	*4*	*2*	...	...	...	...	...	...	
...	...	...	1	1	...	...	...	...	...	...	...	...	...	...	87
...	...	...	...	...	...	...	...	...	...	...	...	...	...	...	88
...	...	...	...	...	...	...	...	...	...	...	...	...	...	...	89
1	1	...	...	...	...	...	...	...	...	...	...	...	...	...	90
...	...	...	...	...	...	...	...	...	...	...	...	...	...	...	91
...	...	...	...	...	...	...	...	...	...	...	...	...	...	...	92
...	...	...	1	1	...	...	...	...	...	...	...	...	...	...	93
...	...	...	...	...	...	...	...	...	...	...	...	...	...	...	94
...	...	...	...	...	...	3	3	...	...	...	...	...	...	...	95
...	...	...	1	1	...	...	...	...	...	...	...	...	...	...	96
...	...	...	...	...	...	...	...	...	...	...	...	...	...	...	97
...	...	...	1	1	...	...	...	...	...	...	...	...	...	...	98
...	...	...	...	...	...	...	...	...	...	...	...	...	...	...	99
...	...	...	...	...	...	...	...	...	...	...	...	...	...	...	100
...	...	...	...	...	...	...	...	...	...	...	...	...	...	...	101
...	...	...	...	...	...	...	...	...	...	...	...	...	...	...	102
1	1	...	...	...	...	11	11	...	...	...	...	...	...	...	103
...	...	...	1	1	...	1	1	...	...	...	...	...	...	...	
...	...	...	1	1	...	...	...	...	...	...	...	...	...	...	104
...	...	...	...	...	...	...	...	...	...	...	...	...	...	...	105
...	...	...	...	...	...	1	1	...	...	...	...	...	...	...	106
...	...	...	...	...	...	...	...	...	...	...	...	...	...	...	107
28	20	8	2	2	...	9	5	4	...	...	...	1	...	1	
...	...	...	...	...	...	...	...	...	...	...	...	...	...	...	108
...	...	...	...	...	...	...	...	...	...	...	...	...	...	...	109
...	...	...	...	...	...	...	...	...	...	...	...	...	...	...	110
23	20	3	2	2	...	9	5	4	...	...	...	1	...	1	111
...	...	...	4	4	...	8	8	...	...	...	...	...	...	...	
...	...	...	4	4	...	2	2	...	...	...	...	...	...	...	112
...	...	...	...	...	...	...	...	...	...	...	...	...	...	...	113
...	...	...	...	...	...	...	...	...	...	...	...	...	...	...	114
...	...	...	...	...	...	1	1	...	...	...	...	...	...	...	115
...	...	...	44,166	22,450	21,716	5,717	2,606	8,111	9,123	4,478	4,645	...	...	...	
441,905	211,119	230,786	458,952	230,545	228,407	900,202	448,705	451,497	26,251	12,967	13,284	119,556	58,562	60,994	

IMPERIAL TABLES XII & XIIA.

Infirmities.

NOTE 1.—The following is the arrangement of these Tables :—

Table XII, Part I, Distribution by Age.

Table XII, Part II, Distribution by Districts.

Table XIIA, Distribution by Selected Tribes and Races.

NOTE 2.—No record of the Infirmities was taken in the Pakôkku Hill Tracts, or in the estimated areas of Karenni, West Manglün and Kokang. Particulars for the inhabitants of these areas are, therefore, omitted from the Infirmity Tables. This accounts for the differences in the figures for the Shan, Karen, Chin, Wa-Palaung and Chinese Races, given in columns 2, 3 and 4 of this Table and as given in Table XIII.

Imperial Table XII.—*Infirmities.*

PART I.—DISTRIBUTION BY AGE.

Age.	Population afflicted.			Insane.			Deaf Mutes.			Blind.			Lepers.		
	Persons.	Males.	Females.	Persons.	Males.	Females.	Persons.	Males.	Females.	Persons.	Males.	Females.	Persons.	Males.	Females.
1	2	3	4	5	6	7	8	9	10	11	12	13	14	15	16
0—1	36	18	18	4	2	2	4	4	...	25	11	14	3	1	2
1—2	60	30	30	7	3	4	17	9	8	36	18	18	...	...	...
2—3	133	73	60	18	8	10	65	35	30	45	27	18	5	3	2
3—4	221	112	109	48	22	26	103	55	48	67	34	33	3	1	2
4—5	294	148	146	61	30	31	132	71	61	89	41	48	12	6	6
Total 0—5	*744*	*381*	*363*	*138*	*65*	*73*	*321*	*174*	*147*	*262*	*131*	*131*	*23*	*11*	*12*
5—10	1,809	1,022	787	335	168	167	880	512	368	513	296	217	81	46	35
10—15	2,687	1,527	1,160	586	322	264	1,185	676	509	655	370	285	261	159	102
15—20	3,519	2,018	1,501	922	532	390	1,287	701	586	777	444	333	533	341	192
20—25	4,160	2,287	1,873	1,170	667	503	1,339	669	670	950	497	453	701	454	247
25—30	3,379	2,034	1,345	1,030	602	428	749	441	308	795	420	375	805	571	234
30—35	3,941	2,337	1,604	1,179	671	508	796	449	347	990	511	479	976	706	270
35—40	3,003	1,859	1,144	881	534	347	407	220	187	892	473	419	823	632	191
40—45	3,338	1,966	1,372	977	557	420	454	266	188	1,155	591	564	752	552	200
45—50	2,473	1,383	1,090	596	300	296	238	114	124	1,074	563	511	565	406	159
50—55	2,730	1,460	1,270	589	294	295	249	134	115	1,342	663	679	550	369	181
55—60	2,159	985	1,174	339	143	196	174	90	84	1,326	562	764	320	190	130
60—65	2,778	1,327	1,451	365	166	199	169	101	68	1,919	858	1,061	325	202	123
65—70	1,993	897	1,096	202	91	111	136	78	58	1,512	638	874	143	90	53
70 and over	3,406	1,376	2,030	273	108	165	180	106	74	2,773	1,049	1,724	180	113	67
Total ...	***42,119***	***22,859***	***19,260***	***9,582***	***5,220***	***4,862***	***8,564***	***4,731***	***3,833***	***16,935***	***8,066***	***8,869***	***7,038***	***4,842***	***2,196***

IMPERIAL TABLE XII.—*Infirmities.*

PART II.—DISTRIBUTION BY DISTRICTS.

Serial No.	District or State.	Population Afflicted.			Insane.			Deaf Mutes.			Blind.			Lepers.		
		Persons.	Males.	Females.	Persons.	Males.	Females.	Persons.	Males.	Females.	Persons.	Males.	Females.	Persons.	Males.	Females.
	1	2	3	4	5	6	7	8	9	10	11	12	13	14	15	16
	Provincial Total ...	**42,119**	**22,859**	**19,260**	**9,582**	**5,220**	**4,362**	**8,564**	**4,731**	**3,833**	**16,935**	**8,066**	**8,869**	**7,038**	**4,842**	**2,196**
	Burma Proper ...	**31,451**	**17,502**	**13,949**	**6,525**	**3,711**	**2,814**	**5,474**	**3,134**	**2,340**	**13,465**	**6,469**	**6,996**	**5,987**	**4,188**	**1,799**
	Arakan Division ...	***1,539***	***911***	***628***	***685***	***371***	***264***	***358***	***218***	***140***	***381***	***219***	***162***	***165***	***103***	***62***
1	Akyab ...	882	521	361	388	226	162	208	130	78	206	122	84	80	43	37
2	Northern Arakan	111	65	46	29	13	16	8	4	4	30	18	12	44	30	14
3	Kyaukpyu ..	368	219	149	152	94	58	82	50	32	100	51	49	34	24	10
4	Sandoway ...	178	106	72	66	38	28	60	34	26	45	28	17	7	6	1
	Pegu Division ...	***4,648***	***2,988***	***1,660***	***1,306***	***911***	***395***	***644***	***387***	***257***	***1,572***	***842***	***730***	***1,121***	***843***	***278***
5	City of Rangoon	862	690	172	569	471	98	60	42	18	101	59	42	132	118	14
6	Hanthawaddy ...	1,161	731	430	199	116	83	226	133	93	372	212	160	364	270	94
7	Tharrawaddy ...	772	416	356	144	74	70	120	73	47	361	169	192	147	100	47
8	Pegu	894	589	305	168	101	67	101	62	39	327	199	128	298	227	71
9	Prome	954	557	397	226	149	77	137	77	60	411	203	208	180	128	52
	Irrawaddy Division	***3,662***	***2,289***	***1,373***	***703***	***425***	***278***	***595***	***359***	***236***	***1,163***	***618***	***545***	***1,201***	***887***	***314***
10	Bassein ...	664	407	257	152	92	60	98	55	43	187	97	90	227	163	64
11	Henzada ...	1,212	756	456	231	140	91	207	123	84	422	227	195	352	266	86
12	Myaungmya ...	518	344	174	98	66	32	68	46	22	157	81	76	195	151	44
13	Ma-ubin ...	776	488	288	153	83	70	113	68	45	211	120	91	299	217	82
14	Pyapôn ...	492	294	198	69	44	25	109	67	42	186	93	93	128	90	38
	Tenasserim Division	***2,697***	***1,661***	***1,036***	***727***	***417***	***310***	***625***	***406***	***219***	***959***	***538***	***421***	***386***	***300***	***86***
15	Toungoo ...	841	479	362	188	106	82	174	112	62	395	202	193	84	59	25
16	Salween ...	75	42	33	28	14	14	23	15	8	15	6	9	9	7	2
17	Thatôn ...	701	463	238	190	117	73	153	101	52	231	140	91	127	105	22
18	Amherst ...	583	388	195	165	94	71	142	90	52	158	105	53	118	99	19
19	Tavoy ...	313	182	131	103	53	50	82	55	27	99	54	45	29	20	9
20	Mergui ...	184	107	77	53	33	20	51	33	18	61	31	30	19	10	9
	Magwe Division ...	***4,492***	***2,385***	***2,107***	***846***	***496***	***350***	***744***	***412***	***332***	***2,151***	***965***	***1,186***	***751***	***512***	***239***
21	Thayetmyo ...	773	459	314	158	101	57	109	67	42	352	175	177	154	116	38
22	Pakôkku ...	1,610	810	800	298	155	143	351	187	164	807	374	433	154	94	60
23	Minbu ...	1,194	656	538	258	168	90	144	75	69	533	233	300	259	180	79
24	Magwe ...	915	460	455	132	72	60	140	83	57	459	183	276	184	122	62
	Mandalay Division...	***4,393***	***2,308***	***2,085***	***760***	***375***	***385***	***1,234***	***646***	***588***	***1,706***	***852***	***854***	***693***	***435***	***258***
25	Mandalay (including City).	1,562	842	720	238	118	120	100	52	48	807	410	397	417	262	155
	Mandalay City ...	*803*	*481*	*322*	*80*	*45*	*35*	*49*	*34*	*15*	*297*	*153*	*144*	*377*	*249*	*128*
26	Bhamo ...	813	402	411	97	39	58	511	254	257	166	83	83	39	26	13
27	Myitkyina ...	710	396	314	142	79	63	406	232	174	135	70	65	27	15	12
28	Katha ...	853	434	419	144	69	75	128	60	68	424	210	214	157	95	62
29	Ruby Mines ...	455	234	221	139	70	69	89	48	41	174	79	95	53	37	16
	Sagaing Division ...	***6,322***	***3,046***	***3,276***	***995***	***460***	***535***	***876***	***470***	***406***	***3,406***	***1,452***	***1,954***	***1,045***	***664***	***381***
30	Shwebo ...	1,389	636	753	197	79	118	166	96	70	850	349	501	176	112	64
31	Sagaing ...	1,790	879	911	242	114	128	137	77	60	944	402	542	467	286	181
32	Lower Chindwin	1,727	828	899	196	95	101	154	83	71	1,071	447	624	306	203	103
33	Upper Chindwin	1,416	703	713	360	172	188	419	214	205	541	254	287	96	63	33
	Meiktila Division ...	***3,703***	***1,919***	***1,784***	***553***	***256***	***297***	***398***	***236***	***162***	***2,127***	***983***	***1,144***	***625***	***444***	***181***
34	Kyauksè ...	779	421	358	123	58	65	49	30	19	495	247	248	112	86	26
35	Meiktila ...	860	423	437	140	65	75	90	45	45	480	213	267	150	100	50
36	Yamèthin ...	901	472	429	133	62	71	121	79	42	526	245	281	121	86	35
37	Myingyan ...	1,163	603	560	157	71	86	138	82	56	626	278	348	242	172	70
	Specially Administered Territories.	**10,668**	**5,357**	**5,311**	**3,057**	**1,509**	**1,548**	**3,090**	**1,597**	**1,493**	**3,470**	**1,597**	**1,873**	**1,051**	**654**	**397**
38	Northern Shan States.	4,074	2,030	2,044	717	374	343	1,605	811	794	1,542	722	820	210	123	87
39	Southern Shan States.	4,315	2,132	2,183	891	426	465	1,005	519	486	1,807	817	990	612	370	242
*																
41	Chin Hills ...	2,279	1,195	1,084	1,449	709	740	480	267	213	121	58	63	229	161	68

* No record of the Infirmities was taken in the Pakôkku Hill Tracts. (Serial No. 40).

IMPERIAL TABLE XIIA.—*Infirmities by selected Tribes and Races.*

Tribe or Race.	POPULATION DEALT WITH.			INSANE.			DEAF MUTES.			BLIND.			LEPERS.		
	Persons.	Males.	Females.	Persons.	Males.	Females.	Persons.	Males.	Females.	Persons.	Males.	Females.	Persons.	Males.	Females.
1	2	3	4	5	6	7	8	9	10	11	12	13	14	15	16
Burmese ...	7,479,433	3,650,902	3,828,531	4,812	2,746	2,066	3,508	2,012	1,496	11,399	5,590	5,809	4,963	3,427	1,536
Arakanese ...	344,123	177,089	167,034	209	125	84	101	56	45	102	68	34	20	6	14
Intha ...	52,685	25,771	26,914	94	45	49	42	23	19	129	51	78	122	82	40
Kadu ...	11,196	5,600	5,596	20	1	19	33	14	19	60	27	33	34	20	14
Taungyo ...	19,656	9,271	10,385	31	4	27	6	3	3	25	11	14	24	15	9
Danu ...	70,947	35,264	35,683	48	29	19	56	35	21	135	58	77	11	6	5
Kachin ...	162,368	80,764	81,604	379	176	203	1,630	839	791	381	226	155	59	35	24
Chin ...	243,066	119,373	123,693	1,558	792	766	613	343	270	214	107	107	301	218	83
Shan ...	941,724	465,609	476,115	1,207	637	570	1,412	742	670	2,881	1,436	1,445	762	409	353
Taungthu ...	183,054	91,597	91,457	154	32	122	108	25	83	178	48	130	43	33	10
Karen ...	903,626	450,971	452,655	421	245	176	360	227	133	395	192	203	367	279	88
Talaing ...	320,629	159,235	161,394	109	75	34	110	76	34	110	71	39	86	68	18
Wa-Palaung	150,375	74,600	75,775	177	79	98	323	146	177	295	137	158	41	20	21
Chinese ...	104,641	79,830	24,811	24	17	7	154	78	76	50	29	21	33	32	1

IMPERIAL TABLE XIII.

Caste, Tribe, Race, or Nationality.

NOTE I.—The scheme of classification adopted in this table is as follows :—

	Pages.	Columns.
Indigenous tribes and races ...	142, 143	2 to 27
Non-indigenous Buddhist and Animist races.	144	28 to 31
Hindu castes	144, 145	32 to 55
Musalman tribes	146	56 to 61
Other races	146, 147	62 to 83

NOTE II.—Minor and localised tribes and races have been grouped into composite columns. An analysis of the entries in all such columns is given below and on page 148. The figures include the inhabitants of the estimated areas for which a racial analysis has been effected.

NOTE III.—The grouping of the Kachin-Burma Hybrid tribes and tribes of the Lolo Group in columns 10 and 11, and of the Salôns with the Mōn Khmĕr tribes in columns 26 and 27 has no ethnical significance. It was dictated by considerations of space. Separation has been effected in the table given below.

NOTE IV.—A complete analysis of columns 22 and 23 has not been attempted, as the large number of unspecified Karens makes any comparison between the Sgau and Pwo Karens impossible. An analysis of other Karen tribes is given on page 148.

NOTE V.—Details are given for eleven Hindu castes only. Owing to the difficulty of translating caste names into Burmese, the figures for the less known castes are unreliable. The majority of them are also numerically insignificant. An analysis of the figures in columns 54 and 55 shows—

	Males.	Females.
Other Castes returned ...	114,759	28,272
Castes not returned	79,170	20,537
TOTAL ...	193,929	48,809

NOTE VI.—A statement explaining the discrepancies between racial and religious classification in Tables VI and XIII is given on page 148.

Analysis of the Races and Tribes included in columns {10, 11 / 18, 19 / 26, 27} of this Table.

Columns.	Race.	Southern Shan States.		Northern Shan States.		Ruby Mines.		Myitkyina.		Bhamo.		Mergui.		Other Districts.		Total.	
		Males.	Females.	Males.	Females.	Males.	Females.	Males.	Females.	Males.	Females.	Males.	Females.	Males.	Females.	Males.	Females.
10—11	——	31,352	28,581	1,943	1,867	965	1,315	4,410	4,046	1,528	1,491	...	...	97	...	40,285	37,300
	Kachin-Burma Hybrids.	72	3	114	105	196	96	3,582	3,802	1,068	1,032	...	...	97	...	5,129	5,038
	Lashi	...	...	...	...	...	...	1,132	1,242	291	243	...	...	...	...	1,423	1,485
	Tsi	...	...	...	...	122	83	1,044	1,254	212	288	...	...	...	...	1,378	1,625
	Maingtha	72	3	6	4	74	13	68	19	45	...	...	...	97	...	362	39
	Maru	...	...	108	101	...	...	1,338	1,287	520	501	...	...	...	...	1,966	1,889
	Lolo Group	31,280	28,578	1,829	1,762	769	1,219	828	244	450	459	...	...	...	...	35,156	32,262
	Lolo (Myen) ...	...	...	166	173	...	...	...	...	...	...	...	...	...	...	166	173
	Lisu	705	607	1,643	1,563	769	1,219	828	244	450	459	...	...	...	...	4,395	4,092
	Lahu (Muhso) ..	9,180	8,877	20	26	...	...	...	...	...	...	...	...	...	...	9,200	8,903
	Kwi (Lahu Hsi) ...	832	2,357	...	...	...	...	...	...	...	...	...	...	...	...	832	2,357
	Akha (Kaw) ...	17,685	15,496	...	...	...	...	...	...	...	...	...	...	...	...	17,685	15,496
	Akō	2,878	1,241	...	...	...	...	...	...	...	...	...	...	...	...	2,878	1,241
18—19	Other Shan Tribes ..	30,190	29,723	...	...	...	...	...	...	...	...	5,068	4,557	1	2	[illegible]	[illegible]
	Khün	21,663	20,703	...	...	...	...	...	...	...	...	...	...	...	...	21,663	20,703
	Lü	8,426	8,905	...	...	...	...	...	...	...	...	...	...	...	...	8,426	8,905
	Daye	87	114	...	...	...	...	...	...	...	...	...	...	...	...	87	114
	Siamese	14	1	...	...	...	...	...	...	...	...	5,068	4,557	1	2	5,083	4,560
26—27	——	28,573	27,089	47,648	46,746	10,586	10,600	...	...	1,273	1,154	1,000	964	55	28	89,035	86,581
	Mōn Khmĕr Tribes...	28,573	27,089	47,648	46,746	10,586	10,600	...	...	1,273	1,154	...	...	55	28	88,035	85,617
	Palaung	18,085	17,676	43,985	43,172	10,360	10,600	...	...	78	100	...	...	55	28	72,563	71,576
	Palè	...	...	35	33	...	...	...	...	...	...	...	...	...	...	35	33
	Yin (Riang) ..	3,941	3,864	53	70	...	...	...	...	...	...	...	...	...	...	3,994	3,934
	Wa	2,984	2,931	3,198	3,196	226	...	...	...	1,095	1,054	...	...	...	...	7,503	7,181
	Ea (In)	1,563	1,795	97	...	...	...	...	...	...	...	...	...	...	...	1,660	1,795
	Pyin	155	120	...	...	...	...	...	...	...	...	...	...	...	...	155	120
	Lamet	231	...	...	...	...	...	...	...	...	...	...	...	...	...	231	...
	Danaw	1,201	523	...	...	...	...	...	...	...	...	...	...	...	...	1,201	523
	Yao	362	150	...	...	...	...	...	...	...	...	...	...	...	...	362	150
	Miao	51	40	280	275	...	...	...	...	...	...	...	...	...	...	331	315
	Salôn (Mawken) ...	...	...	...	...	...	...	...	...	...	...	1,000	964	...	...	1,000	964

INDIGENOUS TRIBES

Serial No.	District or State.	BURMESE.						KACHIN AND LOLO GROUPS.			
		BURMESE.		ARAKANESE.		OTHER BURMESE TRIBES.		KACHINS.		LOLO GROUP AND KACHIN-BURMA HYBRIDS.	
		Males.	Females.	Males.	Females.	Males.	Females.	Males.	Females.	Males.	Females.
	1	2	3	4	5	6	7	8	9	10	11
	Provincial Total ...	3,650,902	3,828,531	177,089	167,034	80,224	82,647	80,764	81,604	40,285	37,300
	Burma Proper ...	3,641,067	3,819,744	177,086	167,030	11,869	12,206	43,943	42,585	6,990	6,852
	Arakan Division ...	102,879	116,598	175,609	162,447	2,536	2,678	...	...	...	...
1	Akyab ...	44,205	47,980	110,450	98,982	247	360	...	...	...	...
2	Northern Arakan ..	115	9	106	51	2,289	2,318	...	...	...	...
3	Kyaukpyu ...	27,972	39,404	50,990	47,349	...	...	...	...	...	...
4	Sandoway ...	30,587	29,205	14,063	16,065	...	...	...	...	...	...
	Pegu Division ..	740,091	744,238	269	86	826	811	11	...	...	...
5	City of Rangoon ...	44,401	43,573	220	69	1	...	8	...	...	...
6	Hanthawaddy ...	193,059	184,730	7	12	127	156	1	...	...	...
7	Tharrawaddy ...	191,164	199,552	2	1	...	...	...	...	...	...
8	Pegu ...	141,787	134,969	37	4	698	655	2	...	...	...
9	Prome ...	169,680	181,414	3	...	...	...	...	...	...	...
	Irrawaddy Division ...	708,753	700,485	768	4,075	4	...	2	...	...	...
10	Bassein ...	158,520	151,938	423	3,973	...	...	...	...	...	...
11	Henzada ...	226,392	236,500	19	21	...	...	2	...	...	...
12	Myaungmya ..	110,204	108,562	291	79	...	...	...	...	...	...
13	Ma-ubin ...	103,363	101,791	...	2	...	...	...	...	...	...
14	Pyapôn ...	110,274	100,685	35	...	4	...	...	...	...	...
	Tenasserim Division ...	284,221	280,470	6	3	391	150	...	...	...	...
15	Toungoo ..	114,256	114,586	...	2	38	44	...	...	...	...
16	Salween ...	886	517	4	1	...	...	...	...	...	...
17	Thatôn ...	43,802	42,382	...	...	151	62	...	...	...	...
18	Amherst ...	31,384	29,491	...	...	202	44	...	...	...	...
19	Tavoy ...	59,629	60,270	...	...	...	...	...	...	...	...
20	Mergui ...	34,264	33,224	2	...	...	...	...	...	...	...
	Magwe Division ...	559,256	600,212	3	1	...	21	...	...	...	...
21	Thayetmyo ...	107,979	113,398	...	...	...	...	...	...	...	...
22	Pakokku ...	187,117	206,203	...	...	...	...	...	...	...	...
23	Minbu ..	113,297	122,122	...	...	...	21	...	...	...	...
24	Magwe ...	150,863	158,489	3	1	...	...	...	...	...	...
	Mandalay Division ...	217,915	225,298	391	406	7,118	7,041	43,675	42,490	6,910	6,852
25	Mandalay (including City).	136,352	148,681	384	400	1,333	1,269	38	3	...	...
	Mandalay City ...	*51,579*	*57,661*	*370*	*400*	...	...	*38*	*1*	...	...
26	Bhamo ...	12,868	11,932	...	...	234	63	18,749	19,622	1,518	1,491
27	Myitkyina ..	4,124	2,909	3	3	521	333	16,562	16,472	4,410	4,046
28	Katha ...	44,668	44,734	4	1	4,900	5,254	2,763	2,869	17	...
29	Ruby Mines ..	19,903	17,042	...	2	130	122	5,563	3,524	965	1,315
	Sagaing Division ...	488,009	565,033	14	...	467	406	237	78	...	...
30	Shwebo ...	161,029	184,056	...	...	65	23	18	1	...	...
31	Sagaing ...	144,608	162,564	...	...	...	...	...	...	...	...
32	Lower Chindwin ...	139,484	174,415	...	...	...	...	...	...	...	...
33	Upper Chindwin ...	42,888	43,998	14	...	402	383	219	77	...	...
	Meiktila Division ...	539,943	587,410	26	12	527	1,099	18	17	80	...
34	Kyauksè ...	65,171	69,703	...	...	290	267	...	...	...	...
35	Meiktila ...	127,752	142,931	13	...	44	631	...	...	80	...
36	Yamèthin ...	139,273	144,630	3	...	192	201	18	17	...	...
37	Myingyan ..	207,747	230,145	10	12	1	...	...	...	...	...
	Specially Administered Territories.	9,835	8,787	3	4	68,355	70,441	36,821	39,019	33,295	30,448
38	Northern Shan States	3,492	2,914	3	4	5,589	5,097	34,938	38,640	1,943	1,867
39	Southern Shan States	6,296	5,844	...	...	62,666	65,344	1,883	379	31,352	28,581
40	Pakôkku Hill Tracts ...	20	12	...	...	...	...	...	...	...	...
41	Chin Hills ...	27	17	...	...	...	...	...	...	...	...

Tribe, Race, or Nationality.

AND RACES.

CHIN.				SHAN.				KAREN.				MÖN KHMĔR AND OTHERS.				
Chins (unspecified).		Other Chin Tribes.		Shans (unspecified).		Other Shan Tribes.		Taungthu.		Other Karens.		Talaings.		Wa-Palaung, Miao-Yao and Salôns.		
Males.	Females.	Males.	Females.	Males.	Females.	Males.	Females.	Males.	Females.	Males.	Females.	Males.	Females.	Males.	Females.	Serial No.
12	13	14	15	16	17	18	19	20	21	22	23	24	25	26	27	
65,113	66,210	86,052	89,101	460,444	466,435	35,259	34,282	91,597	91,457	458,161	461,480	159,235	161,394	89,055	86,581	
62,247	63,172	18,954	18,472	159,954	158,168	5,069	4,559	28,077	29,250	427,320	422,212	159,114	161,374	12,834	12,746	
22,598	21,706	14,593	14,236	59	29	...	...	2	1	12	45	...	...	...	...	
9,536	9,545	7,258	7,042	33	26	...	...	1	...	4	27	...	...	...	...	1
1,204	1,156	7,260	7,108	...	..	...	...	...	...	...	...	...	...	...	...	2
7,752	7,034	75	86	10	2	...	...	1	1	4	1	...	...	...	...	3
4,106	3,971	...	...	16	1	...	...	...	...	4	17	...	...	...	...	4
7,369	7,236	...	...	14,591	15,266	1	2	943	774	61,025	61,371	29,482	31,317	...	...	
...	...	...	...	268	323	...	...	1	...	801	488	326	314	...	...	5
47	132	...	...	6,690	7,391	...	...	82	76	25,578	26,492	5,575	5,760	...	...	6
752	770	...	...	1,977	2,029	...	...	...	...	11,635	11,725	2	12	...	...	7
814	449	...	...	5,147	5,008	1	...	860	698	20,801	20,212	23,579	25,230	...	...	8
5,756	5,885	...	...	509	521	...	2	...	...	2,210	2,454	...	1	...	...	9
2,877	3,201	...	...	1,621	1,408	...	...	...	...	170,840	174,646	5,642	7,546	...	...	
284	255	...	...	215	129	...	...	...	...	47,670	50,236	497	2,374	...	...	10
2,584	2,909	...	...	541	566	...	...	...	...	23,354	24,748	590	634	...	...	11
6	5	...	...	267	111	...	...	...	...	50,564	46,807	568	400	...	...	12
...	9	...	...	79	123	...	...	...	...	41,407	44,753	361	592	...	...	13
3	23	...	...	519	479	...	...	...	...	7,845	8,102	3,626	3,546	...	...	14
120	76	...	...	22,283	19,572	5,068	4,557	27,048	28,383	193,047	184,016	123,941	122,489	1,020	969	
69	76	...	...	8,676	8,188	...	...	3,097	3,011	38,099	36,312	275	232	...	5	15
26	...	...	...	2,297	1,471	...	...	12	8	20,885	19,744	18	12	...	...	16
1	...	...	...	4,056	3,822	...	...	22,242	23,863	83,654	79,961	40,926	39,997	...	...	17
24	...	...	...	7,230	6,083	...	...	1,687	1,501	36,498	34,685	82,458	82,012	...	...	18
...	...	...	...	24	8	...	...	2	...	5,690	5,346	189	176	...	...	19
...	...	...	...	...	...	5,068	4,557	8	...	8,221	7,968	75	60	1,020	964	20
26,985	28,029	3,517	3,428	32	221	...	...	...	...	36	46	4	...	14	16	
10,740	11,068	...	...	10	13	...	...	...	...	12	21	...	...	...	...	21
3,682	3,521	3,517	3,428	...	160	...	...	...	...	1	1	...	...	...	...	22
11,458	12,297	...	...	11	25	...	...	...	...	12	17	4	...	14	16	23
1,105	1,143	...	...	11	23	...	...	...	...	11	7	...	...	...	...	24
509	1,309	162	202	81,363	82,422	...	...	14	4	297	172	35	20	11,759	11,757	
9	9	...	...	2,835	2,634	...	...	...	...	41	41	12	6	...	3	25
9	...	...	...	137	203	...	...	...	...	32	28	5	...	...	3	
...	...	...	...	13,103	13,621	...	...	...	...	55	65	...	...	1,173	1,154	26
...	...	...	...	11,832	10,035	...	...	...	...	8	6	10	...	...	...	27
...	...	162	202	48,971	46,286	..	...	...	...	137	46	6	7	...	...	28
500	1,300	...	...	11,222	9,846	...	...	14	4	56	13	8	7	10,586	10,600	29
1,116	975	682	606	38,947	38,389	...	...	...	...	203	61	2	2	...	...	
...	...	...	...	639	589	...	...	...	...	115	48	1	2	...	...	30
...	...	...	...	1	12	...	...	...	...	2	3	...	...	...	...	31
...	...	...	...	7	4	...	...	...	...	86	10	...	...	...	...	32
1,116	975	682	606	38,300	37,784	...	...	...	...	...	...	1	...	...	...	33
672	640	...	...	1,068	861	...	...	70	88	1,860	1,856	8	...	42	4	
...	...	...	...	44	40	...	...	...	...	...	1	...	...	...	...	34
...	...	...	...	81	78	...	...	10	29	5	4	...	...	2	...	35
661	639	...	...	817	736	...	...	57	59	1,835	1,847	8	...	38	4	36
11	1	...	...	126	7	...	...	3	...	20	4	...	...	...	...	37
2,866	3,038	67,098	70,629	300,490	308,267	30,190	29,723	63,520	62,207	30,841	39,268	121	20	76,221	73,835	
...	...	...	...	113,652	116,730	...	...	...	199	419	114	8	4	47,648	46,746	38
...	..	...	...	186,836	191,537	30,190	29,723	63,520	62,007	30,416	39,146	113	16	28,573	27,089	39
2	...	12,817	13,234	...	...	...	...	...	1	...	...	...	...	...	...	40
2,864	3,038	54,281	57,405	2	...	...	...	...	...	6	8	...	...	...	...	41

Serial No.	District or State.	NON-INDIGENOUS BUDDHIST AND ANIMIST RACES. Chinese. Males.	Chinese. Females.	Other Asiatic Races. Males.	Other Asiatic Races. Females.	HINDU Brahman. Males.	Brahman. Females.	Chatri. Males.	Chatri. Females.	Chetty. Males.	Chetty. Females.	Kapu. Males.	Kapu. Females.
	1	28	29	30	31	32	33	34	35	36	37	38	39
	Provincial Total ...	89,345	33,489	288	378	16,551	4,619	9,296	1,646	12,663	1,703	12,588	2,376
	Burma Proper ...	66,669	17,093	288	378	16,288	4,594	8,939	1,582	12,636	1,703	12,547	2,369
	Arakan Division ...	607	80	1	15	762	154	370	99	140	20	139	14
1	Akyab	458	63	1	15	586	92	136	...	137	20	103	...
2	Northern Arakan ...	...	...	...	...	116	59	198	94	...	...	34	14
3	Kyaukpyu ...	59	15	...	...	32	2	...	...	3	...	1	...
4	Sandoway	90	2	...	...	28	1	36	5	...	...	1	...
	Pegu Division ...	25,568	5,396	186	236	8,591	1,420	4,636	819	8,450	1,084	8,541	1,722
5	City of Rangoon ...	12,941	3,114	184	217	5,699	937	3,796	657	6,886	805	6,337	1,162
6	Hanthawaddy ...	5,045	777	...	...	1,900	238	403	89	574	56	1,500	400
7	Tharrawaddy ...	1,902	231	...	...	216	29	126	18	245	30	103	31
8	Pegu	4,464	1,045	2	12	533	123	182	30	460	72	390	99
9	Prome	1,216	229	...	7	243	93	129	25	285	121	211	30
	Irrawaddy Division ...	12,230	1,405	2	44	1,297	135	1,021	59	1,582	206	1,399	148
10	Bassein	2,504	254	...	27	274	22	163	5	107	24	346	23
11	Henzada	1,719	282	...	...	360	77	427	26	400	32	260	25
12	Myaungmya ...	3,075	256	1	12	239	6	139	17	330	47	429	36
13	Ma-ubin	1,950	182	1	5	212	9	196	6	289	13	106	18
14	Pyapon	2,982	431	...	...	212	21	96	5	456	90	258	46
	Tenasserim Division ...	13,403	2,505	95	58	1,141	301	427	67	1,489	200	2,234	431
15	Toungoo	2,154	346	...	8	434	172	...	...	191	35	117	36
16	Salween	18	6	...	...	19	15	...	...	...	...	2	...
17	Thatôn	3,089	870	...	...	201	24	51	19	268	39	119	48
18	Amherst	4,678	925	...	22	430	81	326	33	856	115	1,374	346
19	Tavoy	1,320	126	..	...	48	9	2	...	6	...	24	...
20	Mergui	2,144	232	95	28	9	...	48	15	168	11	598	1
	Magwe Division ...	983	81	...	3	517	114	226	31	152	27	46	9
21	Thayetmyo ...	220	17	...	2	133	23	66	17	47	9	21	9
22	Pakôkku	...	...	...	...	106	20	59	4	28	...	25	...
23	Minbu	408	40	...	...	145	23	74	3	29	5	...	...
24	Magwe	355	24	...	1	131	48	27	7	48	13	...	...
	Mandalay Division .	11,578	7,382	4	16	3,006	2,150	1,674	424	409	108	204	27
25	Mandalay (including City).	1,461	251	...	16	2,088	1,946	684	243	221	86	56	21
	Mandalay City .	*1,285*	*200*	...	...	*1,219*	*1,233*	*298*	*115*	*185*	*88*	*30*	*14*
26	Bhamo	3,355	3,458	4	...	124	40	54	16	20	1	5	2
27	Myitkyina ...	3,918	1,985	...	...	371	60	594	113	36	20	43	4
28	Katha	379	63	...	...	70	15	79	7	21	...	...	...
29	Ruby Mines ...	2,465	1,625	...	...	353	89	263	45	111	1	...	...
	Sagaing Division ...	541	114	...	...	341	172	319	53	231	25	4	1
30	Shwebo	192	27	...	...	57	19	122	4	143	17	...	...
31	Sagaing ...	141	15	...	...	151	118	26	8	71	8	...	...
32	Lower Chindwin ...	146	22	...	...	54	14	50	26	17	...	1	...
33	Upper Chindwin ...	62	50	...	...	79	21	121	15	...	...	3	1
	Meiktila Division ...	1,759	130	...	6	633	148	266	30	183	33	80	17
34	Kyauksè	124	1	...	...	28	13	56	9	19	1	4	6
35	Meiktila	498	18	...	...	317	76	153	20	66	16	8	1
36	Yamèthin ...	863	58	...	5	190	43	31	1	66	11	30	10
37	Myingyan ..	274	53	...	1	98	16	26	...	32	5	38	...
	Specially Administered Territories.	22,676	16,396	...	...	263	25	357	64	27	...	41	7
38	Northern Shan States ...	19,613	15,440	...	...	78	9	140	25	1	...	6	7
39	Southern Shan States ...	3,063	956	...	...	159	4	167	15	26	...	35	...
40	Pakôkku Hill Tracts ...	...	...	...	...	2	1	...	...	...	...	...	...
41	Chin Hills	...	...	...	...	24	11	50	24	...	...	...	..

Caste, Tribe, Race, or Nationality.

CASTES.

Mala.		Manipuri.		Padiyachi.		Pali.		Sudra.		Uriya.		Vellala.		Other Hindu Castes and Castes not returned.		
Males.	Females.	Males.	Females.	Males.	Females.	Males.	Females.	Males.	Females.	Males.	Females.	Males.	Females.	Males.	Females.	Serial No.
40	41	42	43	44	45	46	47	48	49	50	51	52	53	54	55	
18,106	3,142	1,626	1,727	8,085	3,723	4,527	1,334	21,350	5,456	9,810	601	4,119	1,893	193,929	48,809	
18,065	3,138	1,620	1,725	8,074	3,722	4,515	1,329	21,308	5,451	9,235	597	4,087	1,893	189,386	47,485	
98	11	143	...	16	...	16	...	1,733	54	984	21	69	...	10,285	869	
65	5	143	...	...	...	16	...	1,668	53	878	17	69	...	9,617	849	1
31	6	...	...	5	...	...	...	...	...	7	3	...	...	...	...	2
2	...	...	...	11	...	...	...	2	...	37	1	...	...	484	15	3
...	...	...	...	...	...	...	...	63	1	62	...	...	...	184	5	4
14,403	2,424	114	66	3,427	1,794	3,119	735	16,082	4,243	3,556	297	3,201	1,722	95,627	26,322	
11,373	1,405	1	...	448	164	2,069	315	13,888	3,688	488	71	2,632	1,489	35,411	8,629	5
911	176	4	5	2,418	1,051	703	282	553	43	1,950	134	464	155	33,571	9,557	6
248	68	5	...	27	9	39	5	6	...	116	4	29	40	4,965	1,047	7
1,817	771	104	45	490	547	303	132	1,635	512	775	85	69	35	18,599	6,542	8
54	4	...	16	44	23	5	1	...	...	227	3	7	3	3,081	547	9
1,243	158	153	129	1,277	277	480	167	642	60	2,523	70	559	4	24,337	4,180	
96	11	3	...	43	12	18	...	139	49	120	16	39	4	9,123	1,185	10
340	24	150	129	500	...	125	31	200	...	1,600	19	...	...	1,750	325	11
301	16	...	...	253	27	...	...	...	...	296	...	...	...	3,499	493	12
32	...	...	...	79	...	...	...	196	7	232	24	...	..	3,433	540	13
474	107	...	...	602	238	337	136	107	4	275	11	520	...	6,532	1,637	14
1,636	452	...	...	3,191	1,560	772	357	1,101	771	789	26	118	105	31,909	10,295	
243	40	...	...	256	88	...	...	751	622	363	...	...	...	7,715	3,157	15
...	...	...	...	...	..	5	1	...	...	...	...	...	...	205	27	16
769	319	...	...	1,561	786	271	118	3	2	223	7	18	17	8,647	3,295	17
605	92	...	...	1,354	682	496	238	269	143	153	18	100	88	12,439	3,626	18
6	...	...	...	7	3	...	...	...	...	8	1	...	...	680	48	19
13	1	...	...	13	1	...	...	78	4	42	...	...	...	2,223	142	20
331	5	...	...	12	1	7	1	1,044	46	144	12	7	8	4,934	965	
7	3	...	..	12	1	...	..	48	33	89	12	6	5	1,174	469	21
1	2	...	...	...	...	...	...	2	...	3	...	1	...	791	128	22
...	...	...	...	...	...	...	..	989	10	42	...	...	...	1,170	161	23
323	...	...	...	...	...	7	1	5	3	10	...	...	3	1,799	207	24
119	20	1,108	1,453	65	39	77	65	445	188	588	54	114	44	12,830	2,738	
50	20	1,087	1,448	57	29	71	62	360	171	330	38	57	36	6,131	779	25
31	*17*	*225*	*332*	*40*	*18*	*45*	*45*	*128*	*34*	*57*	*26*	*6*	...	*3,005*	*698*	
5	...	...	...	...	...	6	2	...	...	32	2	...	...	1,158	185	26
...	...	9	1	...	...	...	...	81	10	149	7	...	2	3,334	1,358	27
...	...	12	4	8	10	...	...	4	1	74	6	57	6	943	118	28
64	...	...	...	...	...	...	1	...	6	3	1	...	...	1,264	304	29
8	3	97	77	59	31	4	2	175	52	151	70	3	4	3,715	1,034	
...	...	...	...	51	27	...	...	...	...	..	...	...	...	1,468	397	30
...	3	2	3	...	...	...	...	159	50	92	63	..	...	727	291	31
8	...	3	3	...	1	4	1	4	2	34	...	3	4	451	104	32
...	...	92	71	8	3	...	1	12	...	25	7	...	...	1,069	242	33
227	65	5	...	27	20	40	2	86	37	500	47	16	6	5,749	1,082	
3	...	5	...	...	...	...	...	12	13	65	5	6	1	484	85	34
3	1	...	...	11	6	16	...	45	12	90	1	10	5	1,755	319	35
179	64	...	...	16	14	4	2	19	12	231	41	...	...	2,302	500	36
42	...	...	...	...	...	20	...	10	...	114	...	...	...	1,208	178	37
41	4	6	2	11	1	12	5	42	5	575	4	32	...	4,543	1,324	
10	4	2	2	6	1	5	5	20	4	285	2	13	...	1,684	298	38
31	...	4	...	5	...	7	...	20	1	290	2	19	...	1,875	622	39
...	...	...	...	...	...	...	...	2	...	...	...	...	...	111	35	40
...	...	...	...	...	...	...	...	...	...	...	...	...	...	873	369	41

Serial No.	District or State.	MUSALMAN TRIBES. Shaik. Males.	Shaik. Females.	Zerbadi. Males.	Zerbadi. Females.	Other Musalman Tribes. Males.	Other Musalman Tribes. Females.	European British Subjects. Males.	European British Subjects. Females.	Other Europeans. Males.	Other Europeans. Females.	Americans. Males.	Americans. Females.
	1	56	57	58	59	60	61	62	63	64	65	66	67
	Provincial Total ...	**152,412**	**85,156**	**28,047**	**31,682**	**87,765**	**32,228**	**8,904**	**2,924**	**711**	**246**	**263**	**122**
	Burma Proper ...	**151,988**	**84,944**	**27,955**	**31,605**	**86,974**	**32,050**	**8,795**	**2,888**	**701**	**246**	**256**	**117**
	Arakan Division ...	**86,383**	**65,510**	**2,430**	**2,480**	**18,965**	**10,714**	**195**	**61**	**9**	**5**	...	...
1	Akyab	85,803	65,234	180	125	17,433	9,872	177	48	8	4	...	...
2	Northern Arakan ...	36	8	...	...	...	...	4	1	...	...	...	...
3	Kyaukpyu ...	450	260	477	452	1,195	712	1	3	...	1	...	...
4	Sandoway ...	94	8	1,773	1,903	337	130	13	9	1	...	...	...
	Pegu Division ...	**37,814**	**6,911**	**3,547**	**4,303**	**26,297**	**6,672**	**4,623**	**1,589**	**392**	**123**	**97**	**64**
5	City of Rangoon ...	31,163	5,171	1,648	2,051	12,267	2,030	3,866	1,206	356	86	75	53
6	Hanthawaddy ...	3,291	719	786	820	7,876	2,619	595	196	21	34	16	
7	Tharrawaddy ...	839	250	271	376	1,580	568	31	14	2	...	3	4
8	Pegu	1,620	389	438	556	3,497	1,101	77	55	12	2	...	5
9	Prome	901	382	404	500	1,077	294	54	28	1	1	3	2
	Irrawaddy Division ...	**4,131**	**712**	**3,075**	**3,733**	**10,861**	**2,511**	**357**	**137**	**94**	**42**	**9**	**6**
10	Bassein	619	110	1,410	1,515	3,657	803	242	90	74	42	5	2
11	Henzada	784	278	423	453	1,768	828	57	30	14	...	4	4
12	Myaungmya ...	2,328	292	491	803	2,873	314	17	7	3	...	...	...
13	Ma-ubin	...	...	645	834	22	238	20	6	3	...	...	...
14	Pyapôn	400	32	106	128	2,541	328	21	4	...	...	...	...
	Tenasserim Division	**9,902**	**4,289**	**5,948**	**7,017**	**16,214**	**7,648**	**435**	**290**	**154**	**51**	**15**	**22**
15	Toungoo	1,583	949	367	402	2,183	856	163	135	10	6	5	15
16	Salween	45	13	37	26	267	20	11	1	...	...	2	4
17	Thatón	1,845	314	1,253	1,290	3,780	1,762	4	4	9	...	...	...
18	Amherst	5,932	2,787	1,709	2,621	6,916	2,717	112	125	92	10	8	3
19	Tavoy	214	120	262	300	401	206	83	1	3	...	...	...
20	Mergui	273	106	2,320	2,378	2,667	2,087	62	24	40	35	...	...
	Magwe Division ...	**947**	**314**	**729**	**820**	**2,374**	**519**	**272**	**68**	**9**	**2**	**99**	**6**
21	Thayetmyo ...	429	230	365	439	567	134	166	15	2	2	4	1
22	Pakôkku	163	13	47	88	471	112	38	24	5	...	14	1
23	Minbu	204	33	247	175	321	45	18	9	1	...	...	...
24	Magwe	151	38	70	118	1,015	228	50	20	1	...	81	4
	Mandalay Division ...	**4,949**	**1,880**	**5,682**	**6,352**	**7,848**	**2,922**	**1,916**	**553**	**29**	**15**	**17**	**15**
25	Mandalay (including City).	3,526	1,628	5,119	5,904	4,694	2,333	1,418	473	25	13	12	8
	Mandalay City ...	*2,790*	*1,431*	*3,294*	*4,029*	*2,774*	*984*	*577*	*315*	*25*	*13*	*3*	*6*
26	Bhamo	464	55	130	141	1,335	257	266	36	2	...	3	3
27	Myitkyina ...	491	78	147	149	988	44	99	17	1	2	...	...
28	Katha	137	78	172	115	429	176	59	8	1	...	2	4
29	Ruby Mines ...	331	41	114	43	402	112	74	19	...	...	...	...
	Sagaing Division ...	**2,920**	**2,156**	**1,848**	**1,886**	**1,905**	**320**	**635**	**96**	**5**	**3**	**5**	**4**
30	Shwebo	2,123	1,981	744	824	557	97	560	63	5	...	...	...
31	Sagaing	411	105	887	886	385	61	35	17	...	3	5	3
32	Lower Chindwin ...	169	19	114	108	330	50	21	15	...	...	...	...
33	Upper Chindwin ...	217	51	103	68	633	112	19	1	...	...	...	1
	Meiktila Division ...	**4,942**	**3,172**	**4,696**	**5,014**	**2,510**	**744**	**362**	**94**	**9**	**5**	**14**	...
34	Kyauksè	833	235	1,180	1,820	463	307	16	14	4	1	2	...
35	Meiktila	912	530	607	600	1,221	140	224	41	...	1	...	...
36	Yamèthin ...	2,938	2,339	2,615	2,428	319	229	77	22	2	1	...	...
37	Myingyan ...	259	68	294	166	507	63	45	17	3	2	12	...
	Specially Administered Territories.	**424**	**212**	**92**	**77**	**791**	**178**	**109**	**36**	**10**	...	**7**	**5**
38	Northern Shan States	330	71	90	77	497	117	29	6	8	...	1	...
39	Southern Shan States	21	111	...	...	254	47	69	26	2	...	6	4
40	Pakôkku Hill Tracts	...	...	...	...	5	1	2	...	...	...	...	...
41	Chin Hills ...	73	30	2	...	35	13	9	4	...	...	...	1

Caste, Tribe, Race, or Nationality.

OTHER RACES.																
Armenians.		Anglo-Indians.		Christians. Race not returned.		Indian Christians.		Sikh.		Jain.		Parsi.		Jew.		
Males.	Females.	Males.	Females.	Males.	Females.	Males.	Females.	Males.	Females.	Males.	Females.	Males.	Females.	Males.	Females.	Serial No.
68	69	70	71	72	73	74	75	76	77	78	79	80	81	82	83	
146	127	6,039	5,067	290	162	15,857	7,232	5,527	1,166	416	79	195	105	559	465	
146	127	5,989	5,042	258	159	15,092	7,194	5,210	1,091	416	79	195	105	559	465	
...	...	208	93	...	...	115	14	39	4	11	6	...	...	19	7	
...	...	88	80	...	...	111	13	33	4	11	6	...	...	19	7	1
...	...	...	1	...	...	...	1	...	...	...	...	...	...	...	...	2
...	...	9	7	...	...	4	...	...	...	...	...	...	...	...	...	3
...	...	11	5	...	...	...	...	6	...	...	...	...	...	...	...	4
122	99	3,689	3,054	84	33	6,905	4,479	1,691	334	294	41	140	88	388	374	
120	99	3,152	2,679	84	33	5,346	3,577	1,095	168	258	38	121	75	381	369	5
2	...	354	257	...	...	1,240	705	495	146	35	3	11	11	2	1	6
...	...	51	34	...	...	71	21	23	4	1	...	6	2	5	4	7
...	...	110	65	...	...	183	125	54	14	...	...	...	...	...	...	8
...	...	22	19	...	...	65	51	24	2	...	...	2	...	...	...	9
3	3	106	78	32	7	4,696	870	170	21	75	13	18	15	34	21	
2	3	28	25	...	...	119	65	3	...	4	...	12	10	14	13	10
...	...	28	27	32	7	64	47	14	...	11	3	1	...	6	4	11
...	...	27	16	...	...	242	76	2	...	15	3	5	2	...	...	12
...	...	14	5	...	...	3,053	200	...	...	19	1	...	...	3	...	13
1	...	9	5	...	...	1,218	482	151	21	26	6	...	3	11	4	14
2	...	884	825	...	...	1,445	657	86	11	29	14	8	2	54	29	
...	...	156	115	...	...	188	129	77	11	5	...	2	1	15	9	15
...	...	...	...	...	...	2	1	...	...	...	...	...	...	...	...	16
2	...	97	52	...	...	719	152	4	...	2	...	3	...	...	...	17
...	...	590	627	...	...	448	338	5	...	22	14	3	1	30	20	18
...	...	14	7	...	...	42	5	...	...	...	...	...	...	3	...	19
...	...	27	24	...	...	46	32	...	...	...	...	...	...	6	...	20
...	...	89	63	...	...	289	175	533	153	5	4	3	...	15	17	
...	...	18	17	...	...	90	87	12	6	1	...	1	...	10	13	21
...	...	17	7	...	...	38	19	31	19	...	...	2	...	...	...	22
...	...	18	17	...	...	49	17	326	66	...	...	...	...	...	...	23
...	...	36	22	...	...	112	52	164	62	4	4	...	...	5	4	24
22	17	781	664	5	3	1,048	736	2,146	340	2	...	26	...	47	16	
11	17	687	596	...	2	916	669	611	169	2	...	26	...	47	16	25
4	*9*	*379*	*260*	...	...	*916*	*583*	*572*	*157*	...	...	*26*	...	*32*	...	
...	...	12	12	...	...	37	21	816	104	...	...	...	...	...	...	26
...	...	20	13	5	1	44	17	663	29	...	...	...	...	...	...	27
...	...	32	19	...	...	39	22	2	...	...	...	...	...	...	...	28
...	...	30	24	...	...	12	7	54	38	...	...	...	...	...	...	29
7	3	140	94	...	...	226	145	271	85	...	1	...	...	2	1	
1	...	37	40	...	...	126	72	17	5	...	1	...	...	...	...	30
6	3	57	42	...	...	50	37	...	...	...	...	...	...	...	...	31
...	...	15	10	...	...	34	35	227	70	...	...	...	...	...	...	32
...	...	31	2	...	...	16	1	27	10	...	...	...	...	2	1	33
1	5	192	171	137	116	368	118	274	143	...	...	...	...	...	...	
...	...	23	17	...	...	21	9	15	10	...	...	...	...	...	...	34
...	...	45	38	137	116	7	4	58	33	...	...	...	...	...	...	35
1	5	104	103	...	...	145	79	188	96	...	...	...	...	...	...	36
...	...	20	13	...	...	195	26	13	4	...	...	...	...	...	...	37
...	...	50	25	32	3	765	38	317	75	...	...	...	...	...	...	
...	...	18	14	...	...	17	10	...	...	...	...	...	...	...	...	38
...	...	26	10	32	3	738	26	11	4	...	...	...	...	...	...	39
...	...	...	...	...	...	4	...	2	...	...	...	...	...	...	...	40
...	...	6	1	...	...	6	2	304	71	...	...	...	...	...	...	41

Analysis of the Races and Tribes included in columns 6 and 7 of this Table.

Other Burmese Tribes.	District.	NUMBER OF PERSONS. Males. Column 6.	Females. Column 7.
Taungyo ..	——	9,271	10,385
	Southern Shan States.	9,236	10,296
	Other districts ...	35	89
Intha ...	——	25,771	26,914
	Southern Shan States.	25,769	26,904
	Other districts ...	2	10
Danu ...	——	35,264	35,683
	Northern Shan States.	5,588	5,069
	Southern Shan States.	27,661	28,144
	Meiktila	35	591
	Yamèthin ...	167	179
	Mandalay (including city).	1,310	1,269
	Kyauksè ...	290	267
	Ruby Mines ...	95	113
	Other districts ...	118	51
Hpôn ...	Myitkyina ...	176	202
Tavoyan ...	——	397	126
	Thatòn	148	62
	Amherst	202	44
	Other districts ...	47	20
Kadu ..	——	5,600	5,596
	Katha	4,900	5,254
	Myitkyina ...	313	112
	Bhamo	161	63
	Upper Chindwin ...	121	137
	Other districts ...	105	30
Chaungtha	——	1,194	1,312
	Northern Arakan	1,056	1,038
	Akyab	138	274
Mrö ...	——	1,342	1,366
	Northern Arakan	1,233	1,280
	Akyab	109	86
Taman ...	——	281	246
Yabein ...	——	775	774
	Pegu	648	631
	Hanthawaddy ...	127	143
Yaw ...	——	53	43
	Myitkyina ...	32	19
	Other districts ..	21	24
Total ...	......	80,124	82,647

Analysis of Karen Tribes entered in columns 22 and 23 (other than Sgau-Karen, Pwo-Karen and Karen unspecified).

Tribe.	District.	NUMBER OF PERSONS. Males. Column 22.	Females. Column 23.
Karenni ...	——	9,252	9,756
	Southern Shan States.	8,678	9,322
	Amherst	260	126
	Toungoo	167	188
	Other districts ...	147	120
Karennet ...	Southern Shan States.	1,791	1,930
Karenbyu ...		446	344
Zayein ...		2,559	2,422
Sinsin ...		156	377
Brè ...		3,149	3,762
Manö ...		221	1,224
Padaung ...		4,106	4,410
Yinbaw ...		467	444
Total ...	......	22,147	24,669

Analysis of the Races and Tribes included in columns 14 and 15 of this Table.

Other Chin Tribes.	District.	NUMBER OF PERSONS. Males. Column 14.	Females. Column 15.
Taungtha ...	——	8,888	8,574
	Akyab	5,371	5,146
	Pakôkku	3,517	3,428
Khami	——	8,243	8,129
	Akyab	1,346	1,381
	Northern Arakan ...	6,897	6,748
Anu	——	235	244
	Northern Arakan ...	235	239
	Upper Chindwin ...	...	5
Chaw ...	Northern Arakan ...	128	121
Daingnet ...	Akyab ...	496	458
M'haing ...		8	15
Thet ...		37	42
Yindu ...	Pakôkku Hill Tracts.	2,138	2,210
Chinbòk ...		8,916	9,263
Chinbōn ...		818	782
Baungshe ...	——	7,056	7,160
	Pakôkku Hill Tracts.	945	979
	Chin Hills	6,111	6,181
Siyin ...	Chin Hills	1,526	1,582
Yoe ...		1,890	2,028
Klang ...		3,385	3,341
Shisho ...		15	4
Kamhon ...		5,389	5,493
Yaun ...		7,007	6,561
Seintaung ...		3,900	4,018
Wi ...		422	410
Lamban ...		2,057	2,406
Kadoe ...		497	512
Whamah ...		1,570	1,813
Yokwa ...		1,239	1,610
Tashon ...		2,840	3,303
Haka ...		62	62
Ngawn ...		1,839	1,992
Sokte ...		5,616	5,752
Yakaw ...		4,227	4,722
Laiyo ...		3,028	3,375
Kwangli ...		1,661	2,040
Hawchit ...	Upper Chindwin	10	10
Naga ...		672	591
Sitton ...	Kyaukpyu	75	86
Kyunakya ...	Katha	162	202
Total ...	.....	86,052	89,111

Racial and Religious discrepancies Explained.

It is difficult to exhibit an agreement between the figures in Tables VI and XIII owing to tribal and racial limits not coinciding with religious divisions. Apparent discrepancies are to be found as indicated in the following statement:—

Race and Religion.	Table.	Columns.	Males.	Females.
Buddhist and Animist Races.	XIII	2 to 31	5,563,713	5,687,933
	VI	5 to 10	5,481,602	5,604,450
		Discrepancy	+ 82,111	+ 83,483
Mahomedan Tribes.	XIII	56 to 61	268,224	149,366
	VI	15 & 16	271,428	149,349
		Discrepancy	—3,204	—283
Christian Races	XIII	62 to 75	32,210	15,880
	VI	18 & 19	111,033	99,048
		Discrepancy	—78,823	—83,168
Confucian, Secularist, etc.	XIII	......	...	...
	VI	33 to 37	84	32
		Discrepancy	—84	—32
		Total Discrepancy...	*Nil*	*Nil*

Analysis of Races included in columns {30, 31 / 60, 61 / 62, 63 / 64, 65} of this Table.

Other Asiatic Races.	NUMBER OF PERSONS. Males. Column 30.	Females. Column 31.
Japanese	180	362
Phillipino ...	6	...
Singalese	46	3
Manilla	3	3
Corean	2	...
Malaysian races ...	51	10
Total ...	288	378

Other Musalman Tribes.	NUMBER OF PERSONS. Males. Column 60.	Females. Column 61.
Saiyed	5,398	1,473
Pathan	6,967	1,074
Malay	2,265	1,974
Other and unspecified Musalman Tribes.	73,135	27,707
Total ...	87,765	32,228

European British Subjects.	NUMBER OF PERSONS. Males. Column 62.	Females. Column 63.
English	6,567	2,549
Scotch	907	133
Welsh	14	4
Irish	1,214	190
Canadian	3	8
Australian ...	115	23
Mauritian ...	1	...
British	83	17
Total ...	8,904	2,924

Other Europeans.	NUMBER OF PERSONS. Males. Column 64.	Females. Column 65.
Greek	54	4
Italian	21	13
French	94	98
Spanish	9	4
Portuguese ...	85	65
Finn	2	...
Russian	8	10
Hungarian ...	...	1
Norwegian ...	15	...
Dutch	32	3
Swedish	26	2
Danish	5	...
German	144	26
Austrian	26	2
Belgian	2	...
Goanese	182	18
Swiss	1	...
Maltese	5	...
Total ...	711	246

With the above exceptions the corresponding columns of the two Imperial Tables agree with each other. The respective plus and minus discrepancies of 82,111 males and 83,483 females can be shewn as follows:—

		Males.	Females.
(i) Buddhist and Animist races entering other religions	......	83,892	85,092
(ii) Mahomedan race (Zerbadi) entering Buddhist religion ...	......	1,781	1,609
	Discrepancy	+82,111	+83,483

Particulars of the entries under (i) above are given in the following statement:—

Race.	Religion. Mahomedan. Males.	Mahomedan. Females.	Christian. Males.	Christian. Females.	Confucian. Males.	Confucian. Females.	Secularist, etc. Males.	Secularist, etc. Females.
Burmese	...	...	9,152	8,294	...	...	27	18
Arakanese... ...	3,558	1,117	125	97	...	...	...	...
Kachins	...	...	924	943	...	...	...	...
Chins	...	...	119	101	...	...	...	...
Shans	...	...	4,793	4,837	...	...	...	...
Karens	...	...	62,564	67,707	...	...	...	...
Talaings	...	...	897	1,014	...	...	...	...
Chinese	1,427	775	249	175	57	14	...	...
Total ...	4,985	1,892	78,823	83,168	57	14	27	18

IMPERIAL TABLE XIV.

Civil Condition by Age for Selected Races.

NOTE.—The entries in this table are not exhaustive for the populations of the ten selected tribes and races. During the process of sorting, every individual who obviously belonged to one of the ten categories was included. But there were many members who were enumerated as belonging to sub-tribes or subdivisions of the main categories and whose exact tribal classification was not determined until the process of tabulation was commenced. It was then impossible without a disproportionate amount of labour to commence sorting afresh for those who had been thereby excluded. This table therefore comprises all the members of the ten selected tribes and races who were enumerated either under their general tribal or racial names, or under their more easily identified subdivisions. The figures for the Talaing, Arakanese, Kachin, Danu, and Taungthu agree with those given for these races in Table XIII, showing that the analysis in this table is comprehensive for these races. It is not comprehensive for the Karen, Shan, Chin, Wa-Palaung, and Chinese races.

Tribe or Race.	Locality.	Sex.	Population dealt with.	Unmarried.						
				Total.	0—5	5—12	12—15	15—20	20—40	40 and over.
1	2	3	4	5	6	7	8	9	10	11
Talaing ...	Amherst and Thatôn Districts principally, but extending westwards into Pegu, Hanthawaddy, and Pyapôn Districts.	Male ...	159,235	96,572	25,053	31,388	11,650	13,946	12,381	2,154
		Female ...	161,394	93,093	25,680	32,607	11,326	14,001	7,643	1,836
Karen ...	Tenasserim Division, the Southern Shan States and the rural portions of the Deltaic Plain Districts.	Male ...	450,971	266,240	63,494	85,476	30,439	38,654	41,692	6,485
		Female ...	452,655	253,384	66,453	86,186	30,400	35,191	28,411	6,743
Arakanese ...	Arakan Division and Bassein District.	Male ...	177,089	88,312	19,167	28,210	12,373	15,434	9,795	3,333
		Female ...	167,034	78,130	18,982	28,300	10,813	10,647	6,227	3,161
Shan ...	Northern and Southern Shan States, the Northern Hill Districts and the Eastern Districts of the Deltaic Plain.	Male ...	465,609	248,014	58,576	75,063	29,227	37,009	36,079	12,060
		Female ...	476,115	216,439	55,979	72,677	26,766	30,151	17,669	13,197
Chin ...	The Arakan Division, the Chin Hills, the Pakôkku Hill Tracts and the Western portions of the Pakôkku, Minbu, Thayetmyo, Prome and Henzada Districts.	Male ...	119,373	66,955	16,463	21,475	7,660	10,542	9,348	1,467
		Female ...	123,693	61,200	18,165	21,579	5,933	8,037	6,122	1,364
Kachin ...	The Northern Hill Districts and the Northern Shan States.	Male ...	80,764	46,061	6,071	12,793	6,606	8,037	10,087	2,467
		Female ...	81,604	40,657	7,011	11,168	4,908	6,339	9,090	2,141
Wa-Palaung ...	The Northern and Southern Shan States and the specially administered areas attached to the Ruby Mines District.	Male ...	74,600	41,369	9,564	9,211	4,962	6,383	6,733	4,516
		Female ...	75,775	37,123	9,279	10,949	4,165	6,249	3,839	2,642
Danu ...	The Northern and Southern Shan States and Mandalay District.	Male ...	35,264	19,643	4,505	5,787	2,697	2,946	2,820	888
		Female ...	35,683	18,809	4,856	6,474	2,745	2,526	1,663	545
Taungthu ...	Southern Shan States and Thatôn District.	Male ...	91,597	52,661	16,506	16,500	5,959	6,796	5,555	1,345
		Female ...	91,457	49,221	12,889	15,160	8,575	6,793	4,636	1,168
Chinese ...	Distributed all over Burma, but principally in the Deltaic Plains, the Tenasserim Coast, the Northern and Southern Shan States, and the Districts of Myitkyina, Bhamo and Ruby Mines.	Male ...	79,830	46,529	5,296	7,970	3,193	5,687	19,875	4,508
		Female ...	24,811	12,418	2,990	3,662	1,627	1,985	1,444	710

by age for selected Races.

Married.							Widowed.						
Total.	0—5	5—12	12—15	15—20	20—40	40 and over.	Total.	0—5	5—12	12—15	15—20	20—40	40 and over.
12	13	14	15	16	17	18	19	20	21	22	23	24	25
57,310	...	...	12	701	32,326	24,271	5,353	...	...	...	17	1,466	3,870
58,376	...	51	54	3,177	37,109	17,985	9,925	...	...	...	129	2,241	7,555
165,951	...	...	186	2,497	91,854	71,414	18,780	...	...	1	150	5,033	13,596
163,894	...	353	299	8,976	105,682	48,584	35,377	...	4	2	509	8,129	26,733
70,248	...	...	85	10,328	32,612	27,223	18,529	...	...	...	1,324	8,192	9,013
66,851	...	...	12	6,905	40,499	19,435	22,053	...	...	...	843	7,439	13,771
182,552	...	1	385	9,257	88,942	83,967	35,043	...	...	2	3,888	11,983	19,170
194,429	...	6	585	18,674	103,885	71,279	65,247	...	...	46	3,582	19,650	41,969
47,165	...	...	13	761	25,487	20,904	5,253	...	...	...	53	1,851	3,349
50,035	...	1	50	3,454	32,191	14,339	12,458	...	...	1	133	2,645	9,679
31,421	...	...	...	2,316	14,805	14,300	3,282	...	...	4	56	1,323	1,899
30,393	...	...	52	5,134	15,669	9,538	10,554	...	...	...	176	2,858	7,520
28,153	...	1	1	3,033	12,873	12,245	5,078	...	...	...	225	2,127	2,726
30,602	...	...	169	2,349	17,140	10,944	8,050	..	...	...	399	1,865	5,786
12,694	...	1	...	670	5,917	6,106	2,927	...	...	...	82	1,106	1,739
13,706	...	3	66	912	7,520	5,205	3,168	...	...	27	28	806	2,307
33,311	...	...	25	1,653	16,091	15,542	5,625	...	...	...	354	1,928	3,343
32,826	...	18	25	4,708	17,863	10,212	9,410	...	...	...	421	2,583	6,406
29,716	...	1	9	1,159	17,061	11,486	3,585	...	...	...	115	1,228	2,242
9,927	..	9	43	816	6,123	2,936	2,466	...	...	...	30	567	1,869

IMPERIAL TABLE XV. A-I.

Occupation or means of livelihood.
General Table, Provincial and City Summary.

NOTE I.—Table XV comprises the following Sections :—

Section.	Nature of Table.	Page.
XV. A-I	General Table, Provincial and City Summary ...	153 to 164
XV. A-II	General Table, by Districts	165 to 230
XV. B(i)	Subsidiary occupations of agriculturists (actual workers only). (i) Rent Receivers ...	231 and 233
XV. B(ii)	Subsidiary occupations of agriculturists (actual workers only). (ii) Rent Payers ...	234 and 235
XV. B(iii)	Subsidiary occupations of agriculturists (actual workers only). (iii) Field Labourers ...	236 and 237
XV. C	Mixed occupations (not prepared for Burma) ...	...
XV. D	Distribution by Religion	239 to 244
XV. E-I	Industrial Statistics I. Provincial Summary	245 to 249
XV. E-II	Industrial Statistics II. Distribution by Districts ...	251 to 255
XV. E-III	Industrial Statistics III. Ownerships of Factories ...	256
XV. E-IV	Industrial Statistics IV. Caste or Race of factory managers	256

NOTE II.—The scheme of occupational classification adopted is radically different from that of the Census of 1901. It is given in full detail in columns I to IV of this section and in an abbreviated form on the title page of Section XV. A-II. It is based on the system of Monsieur Bertillon, specially devised to secure sufficient uniformity of arrangement to facilitate the international comparison of industrial statistics, while permitting sufficient elasticity for the treatment of the peculiar conditions of each country. This object is achieved by a fourfold division of occupations into Classes, Sub-Classes, Orders and Groups, the first three being uniform for all nations adopting the system, the fourth being specially adapted to the industrial conditions under immediate consideration.

NOTE III.—This section gives the classification of occupations for
- The Province.
- Burma Proper.
- Specially Administered Territories.
- The City of Rangoon.
- The City of Mandalay.

NOTE IV.—Records of occupation were not taken for the Pakôkku Hill Tracts, nor for the estimated areas of Kokang, West Manglün and the Brè Tract of Karenni. The populations of these areas are therefore omitted from all sections of Table XV. Details of the omitted populations will be found on page 23 of this Volume.

NOTE V.—The division of Group 2 into Sub-Groups 2(*a*), 2(*b*), and 2(*c*) has been suggested by agricultural and administrative conditions in Burma.

Class.	Sub-class.	Serial No.	ORDER AND GROUP. Description.	PROVINCIAL TOTAL. Total Workers and Dependents.	ACTUAL WORKERS. Total. Males.	Total. Females.	Partially Agriculturists. Males.	Partially Agriculturists. Females.	Dependents	BURMA PROPER. Total Workers and Dependents.	ACTUAL WORKERS. Total. Males.	Total. Females.	Partially Agriculturists. Males.	Partially Agriculturists. Females.	Dependents.
1	2	3	4	5	6	7	8	9	10	11	12	13	14	15	16
			All Industries ...	12,039,083	3,823,666	2,913,743	58,882	48,954	5,311,674	10,610,256	3,359,096	2,493,098	43,168	38,524	4,758,062
A			**Production of Raw Materials**	8,639,688	2,622,348	2,153,325	9,122	10,040	3,864,015	7,548,110	2,277,191	1,827,678	6,589	5,941	3,443,241
	I		EXPLOITATION OF THE SURFACE OF THE EARTH.	8,624,395	2,615,932	2,150,953	9,051	9,972	3,857,510	7,534,644	2,271,921	1,825,338	6,518	5,873	3,437,385
	II		EXTRACTION OF MINERALS ...	15,293	6,416	2,372	71	68	6,505	13,466	5,270	2,340	71	68	5,856
B			**Preparation and supply of Material substances.**	2,403,804	746,832	632,683	31,995	33,805	1,024,289	2,159,077	676,876	549,677	24,017	28,046	932,524
	III		INDUSTRY	806,431	249,433	220,310	9,620	12,901	336,688	713,768	231,194	177,377	7,418	10,952	305,197
	IV		TRANSPORT	393,652	181,734	43,944	8,110	4,024	167,974	364,297	171,009	37,928	6,692	3,735	155,360
	V		TRADE	1,203,721	315,665	368,429	14,265	16,880	519,627	1,081,012	274,673	334,372	9,907	13,359	471,967
C			**Public Administration and Liberal Arts.**	445,846	200,019	29,839	10,942	1,535	215,988	392,776	174,275	25,686	8,107	1,405	192,825
	VI		PUBLIC FORCE	79,495	40,188	1,717	2,569	188	37,590	72,819	36,879	1,661	1,965	175	34,279
	VII		PUBLIC ADMINISTRATION ...	103,108	36,238	4,394	4,944	549	62,476	80,375	30,255	3,390	3,430	504	55,730
	VIII		PROFESSIONS AND LIBERAL ARTS ...	256,276	121,417	23,235	3,361	787	111,624	224,325	105,405	20,190	2,661	715	98,730
	IX		PERSONS LIVING ON THEIR INCOME ...	6,967	2,176	493	68	11	4,238	6,257	1,736	445	51	11	4,076
D			**Miscellaneous ... ...**	549,745	244,467	97,896	6,823	3,574	207,382	510,293	230,754	90,057	4,455	3,122	189,482
	X		DOMESTIC SERVICE	85,771	47,816	10,987	750	383	26,968	70,015	45,423	9,757	570	215	23,835
	XI		INSUFFICIENTLY DESCRIBED OCCUPATIONS.	429,399	180,246	76,922	5,771	3,018	172,231	400,003	170,033	71,204	3,671	2,743	158,766
	XII		UNPRODUCTIVE	34,575	16,405	9,987	302	173	8,183	31,275	15,298	9,096	214	164	6,831
A.—PRODUCTION OF RAW MATERIALS.	I.—EXPLOITATION OF THE SURFACE OF THE EARTH.	1	PASTURE AND AGRICULTURE ...	8,472,391	2,567,202	2,123,276	6,989	8,760	3,781,913	7,388,274	2,224,908	1,798,787	4,661	4,773	3,364,579
		1(a)	ORDINARY CULTIVATION ...	8,083,712	2,434,999	2,024,772	26	...	3,623,941	7,083,161	2,118,545	1,724,606	15	...	3,240,010
		1	Income from Rent of Agricultural Land.	220,485	59,921	68,997	1	...	91,567	182,835	48,108	54,084	1	...	80,643
		2	Ordinary cultivators ...	6,225,154	1,858,632	1,559,824	12	...	2,796,698	5,294,320	1,567,540	1,288,518	12	...	2,438,262
			(a) Cultivating their own land ...	3,810,610	1,140,684	980,589	10	...	1,689,337	3,274,909	974,041	818,505	10	...	1,482,363
			(b) Tenants ...	1,599,331	460,354	369,597	...	...	769,380	1,542,972	441,141	353,942	...	...	747,889
			(c) *Taungya* cultivators ...	805,213	257,594	209,638	2	...	337,981	476,439	152,358	116,071	2	...	208,010
		3	Agents, managers of landed estates, clerks, rent collectors, etc.	123	31	7	...	...	85	123	31	7	...	...	85
		4	Farm servants and field labourers ...	1,647,950	516,415	395,944	13	...	735,591	1,605,883	502,866	381,997	2	...	721,020
		1(b)	GROWERS OF SPECIAL PRODUCTS AND MARKET GARDENING.	238,511	68,447	68,274	4,338	6,628	101,790	178,797	51,511	48,119	2,856	3,036	79,167
		5	Tea, coffee, cinchona, indigo and rubber plantations.	6,217	3,848	189	...	6	2,180	6,203	3,848	175	...	...	2,180
		6	Fruit, flower, vegetable, betel, vine, areca nut, etc., growers.	232,294	64,599	68,085	4,338	6,622	99,610	172,594	47,663	47,944	2,856	3,036	76,987
		1(c)	FORESTRY	42,765	12,507	10,599	511	586	19,659	40,504	11,824	10,171	455	548	18,509
		7	Forest officers, rangers, guards, etc.	5,116	1,626	134	42	6	3,356	4,817	1,478	130	23	6	3,209
		8	Wood cutters; firewood, lac, cutch and rubber collectors, and charcoal burners.	37,649	10,881	10,465	469	580	16,303	35,687	10,346	10,041	432	542	15,300
		1(d)	RAISING OF FARM STOCK ...	105,944	50,884	19,109	2,031	1,539	35,951	84,353	42,663	15,369	1,312	1,182	26,321
		9	Cattle and buffalo breeders and keepers.	2,645	1,333	276	130	15	1,036	1,985	970	204	36	12	811
		10	Sheep, goat and pig breeders ...	12,232	3,667	2,526	303	280	6,030	9,439	2,689	2,071	146	131	4,679
		11	Breeders of other animals (horses, mules, etc.)	35	...	11	...	...	24	35	...	11	...	...	24
		12	Herdsmen, shepherds, goatherds, etc.	91,032	45,884	16,296	1,658	1,244	28,852	72,894	39,004	13,083	1,130	1,049	20,807
		1(e) 13	RAISING OF SMALL ANIMALS (birds, bees, silkworms, etc.).	1,459	365	522	23	7	572	1,459	365	522	23	7	572
		2	FISHING AND HUNTING ...	152,004	48,730	27,677	2,062	1,212	75,597	146,370	47,013	26,551	1,857	1,100	72,806
		14	Fishing	151,601	48,475	27,676	2,060	1,212	75,450	146,272	46,965	26,550	1,857	1,100	72,757
		15	Hunting	403	255	1	2	...	147	98	48	1	...	...	49
	II.—EXTRACTION OF MINERALS.	3	MINES	8,173	4,682	639	8	23	2,852	6,346	3,536	607	8	23	2,203
		16	Coal mines and petroleum wells ...	3,319	1,879	250	8	1	1,190	3,319	1,879	250	8	1	1,190
		17	Mines and metallic minerals (gold, iron, etc.).	4,854	2,803	389	...	22	1,662	3,027	1,657	357	...	22	1,013
		4 18	QUARRIES OF HARD ROCKS.—Other minerals (jade, rubies, limestone, etc.)	3,896	781	1,267	29	21	1,848	3,896	781	1,267	29	21	1,848
		5	SALT, ETC.	3,224	953	466	34	24	1,805	3,224	953	466	34	24	1,805
		19	Rock, sea and marsh salt ...	3,224	953	466	34	24	1,805	3,224	953	466	34	24	1,805
		20	Extraction of saltpetre, alum and other substances soluble in water.	...	...	...	...	...	...	...	...	...	...	...	...

Provincial and City Summary.

SPECIALLY ADMINISTERED TERRITORIES.						CITY OF RANGOON.						CITY OF MANDALAY.						
Total Workers and Dependents.	ACTUAL WORKERS.				Dependents.	Total Workers and Dependents.	ACTUAL WORKERS.				Dependents.	Total Workers and Dependents.	ACTUAL WORKERS.				Dependents.	
	TOTAL.		PARTIALLY AGRICULTURISTS.				TOTAL.		PARTIALLY AGRICULTURISTS.				TOTAL.		PARTIALLY AGRICULTURISTS.			
	Males.	Females.	Males.	Females.			Males.	Females.	Males.	Females.			Males.	Females.	Males.	Females.		
17	18	19	20	21	22	23	24	25	26	27	28	29	30	31	32	33	34	
1,428,827	454,570	416,045	15,714	10,440	553,612	293,316	169,249	17,557	732	273	106,510	138,299	46,676	32,822	17	40	58,801	
1,091,578	345,157	325,647	2,533	4,099	420,774	9,151	4,434	688	3	263	4,029	7,729	2,398	1,831	...	...	3,500	A
1,089,751	344,011	325,615	2,533	4,099	420,125	9,139	4,428	688	3	263	4,023	7,714	2,395	1,830	...	...	3,489	I
1,827	1,146	32	...	...	649	12	6	...	...	...	6	15	3	1	...	...	11	II
244,727	69,956	83,005	7,978	5,759	91,765	174,103	95,117	12,645	452	10	66,341	90,151	25,379	25,578	17	40	39,194	B
92,663	18,239	42,933	2,202	1,949	31,491	79,988	45,257	5,696	26	2	29,035	36,705	10,953	10,441	17	40	15,311	III
29,385	10,725	6,016	1,418	289	12,614	30,908	23,514	136	327	...	7,258	10,964	4,645	853	...	...	5,465	IV
122,709	40,992	34,057	4,358	3,521	47,660	63,207	26,346	6,813	99	8	30,048	42,482	9,781	14,284	...	...	18,417	V
53,070	25,744	4,153	2,835	130	23,173	33,379	15,917	1,288	214	...	16,174	15,734	8,832	683	...	...	6,229	C
6,676	3,309	56	604	13	3,311	6,529	4,702	5	188	...	1,822	5,150	3,261	9	...	...	1,879	VI
13,733	5,983	1,004	1,514	45	6,746	12,014	5,638	77	10	...	6,299	2,337	1,163	72	...	...	1,102	VII
31,951	16,012	3,045	700	72	12,894	13,555	5,275	1,154	14	...	7,126	7,721	4,322	525	...	...	2,874	VIII
710	440	48	17	...	222	1,281	301	52	2	...	927	526	85	77	...	...	364	IX
39,452	13,713	7,839	2,368	452	17,900	76,683	53,781	2,936	63	...	19,966	24,685	10,067	4,730	...	...	9,888	D
6,756	2,393	1,230	180	168	3,133	23,015	16,613	1,339	37	...	5,063	4,746	2,480	471	...	...	1,795	X
29,396	10,213	5,718	2,100	275	13,465	49,120	33,939	672	25	...	14,503	18,978	7,181	3,975	...	...	7,822	XI
3,300	1,107	891	88	9	1,302	4,548	3,229	985	1	...	394	961	406	284	...	...	271	XII
1,084,117	342,294	324,489	2,328	3,087	417,334	8,355	3,837	674	2	263	3,844	6,919	2,144	1,729	...	...	3,046	I
1,000,551	316,454	300,166	11	...	383,931	5,362	1,791	562	1	...	3,009	4,061	1,624	1,066	...	...	2,271	I(a)
37,650	11,813	14,913	...	...	10,924	1,934	433	278	1	...	1,223	532	142	108	...	...	282	1
920,834	291,092	271,306	...	...	358,436	2,732	1,083	246	...	...	1,403	3,418	1,121	687	...	...	1,610	2
535,701	166,643	162,084	...	...	206,974	1,722	680	199	...	...	843	2,335	803	492	...	...	1,040	
50,359	19,213	15,655	...	...	21,491	1,002	399	46	...	...	557	807	235	147	...	...	425	
328,774	165,236	93,567	...	...	129,971	8	4	1	...	...	3	276	83	48	...	...	145	
...	...	...	...	...	...	56	10	7	...	...	39	...	...	...	...	...	...	3
42,067	13,549	13,947	11	...	14,571	640	265	31	...	...	344	1,011	361	271	...	...	379	4
89,714	16,936	20,155	1,482	3,592	22,623	2,481	1,718	105	...	263	658	556	172	184	...	...	200	I(b)
14	...	14	...	6	...	...	...	...	...	...	...	...	...	...	...	...	...	5
59,700	16,936	20,141	1,482	3,586	22,623	2,481	1,718	105	...	263	658	556	172	184	...	...	200	6
2,261	683	428	56	38	1,150	224	126	...	...	...	98	439	124	133	..	...	182	I(c)
299	148	4	19	..	147	101	50	...	...	...	51	54	7	22	...	...	25	7
1,962	535	424	37	38	1,003	123	76	...	...	...	47	385	117	111	...	...	157	8
21,591	8,221	3,740	779	357	9,630	265	188	7	1	...	70	543	208	70	...	..	265	I(d)
660	363	72	94	3	225	6	2	2	...	...	2	79	21	5	...	...	55	9
2,793	978	455	157	159	1,360	3	2	...	...	...	1	144	27	38	...	...	79	10
...	...	...	...	...	...	...	...	...	...	...	...	32	...	11	...	...	21	11
18,138	6,831	2,213	528	195	8,045	256	184	5	1	...	67	288	160	16	...	...	112	12
...	...	...	...	...	...	23	14	...	...	...	9	420	16	276	...	...	128	I(e) 13
5,634	1,717	1,126	205	112	2,791	784	591	14	1	...	179	795	251	101	...	...	443	II
5,329	1,510	1,126	203	112	2,693	782	589	14	1	...	179	795	251	101	...	...	448	14
305	207	...	2	...	98	2	2	...	...	...	...	...	...	...	...	...	...	15
1,827	1,146	22	...	...	649	8	2	...	...	...	6	11	3	1	...	...	7	III
...	...	...	...	...	...	4	...	...	..	...	4	...	...	...	...	...	...	16
1,827	1,146	32	...	...	649	4	2	...	...	...	2	11	3	1	...	...	7	17
...	...	...	...	...	...	4	4	...	...	...	...	4	...	...	...	...	4	IV 18
...	...	...	...	...	...	...	...	...	...	...	...	...	...	...	...	...	...	V
...	...	...	...	...	...	...	...	...	...	...	...	...	...	...	...	...	...	19
...	...	...	...	...	...	...	...	...	...	...	...	...	...	...	...	...	...	20

Class.	Sub-class.	Serial No.	ORDER AND GROUP. Description.	PROVINCIAL TOTAL. Total Workers and Dependents.	PROVINCIAL TOTAL. Actual Workers. Total. Males.	PROVINCIAL TOTAL. Actual Workers. Total. Females.	PROVINCIAL TOTAL. Actual Workers. Partially Agriculturists. Males.	PROVINCIAL TOTAL. Actual Workers. Partially Agriculturists. Females.	PROVINCIAL TOTAL. Dependents.	BURMA PROPER. Total Workers and Dependents.	BURMA PROPER. Actual Workers. Total. Males.	BURMA PROPER. Actual Workers. Total. Females.	BURMA PROPER. Actual Workers. Partially Agriculturists. Males.	BURMA PROPER. Actual Workers. Partially Agriculturists. Females.	BURMA PROPER. Dependents.
1	2	3	4	5	6	7	8	9	10	11	12	13	14	15	16
B.—PREPARATION AND SUPPLY OF MATERIAL SUBSTANCES.	III.—INDUSTRY.	VI	TEXTILES	155,050	9,123	103,316	147	5,850	42,611	107,075	8,139	68,858	117	4,519	30,078
		21	Cotton ginning, cleaning and pressing	2,282	373	514	95	72	1,395	1,671	373	316	95	72	982
		22	Cotton spinning, sizing and weaving	132,737	5,219	91,766	48	5,143	35,752	85,649	4,265	57,714	18	3,879	23,075
		23	Jute spinning, pressing and weaving	...	...	...	...	...	...	...	...	...	...	...	...
		24	Rope, twine and string	1,241	418	379	3	22	444	1,210	411	367	3	22	432
		25	Other fibres (cocoanut, aloes, flax, hemp, straw, etc.).	15	10	4	...	...	1	15	10	4	...	...	1
		26	Wool carders and spinners, weavers of woollen blankets carpets, etc.	46	23	1	...	...	22	46	23	1	...	...	22
		27	Silk spinners and weavers ...	18,621	3,047	10,616	1	613	4,958	18,376	3,029	10,420	1	546	4,927
		28	Hair, camel and horse hair bristles work, brush makers, etc.	...	...	...	...	...	...	...	...	...	...	...	...
		29	Persons occupied with feathers ...	...	...	...	...	...	...	...	...	...	...	...	...
		30	Dyeing, bleaching, printing preparation and sponging of textiles.	62	28	4	...	...	30	62	28	4	...	...	30
		31	Other (lace, crape, embroideries, fringes, etc.) and insufficiently described textile industries.	46	5	32	...	...	9	46	5	32	...	...	9
		VII	HIDES, SKINS AND HARD MATERIALS FROM THE ANIMAL KINGDOM.	624	232	59	2	...	333	503	183	59	2	..	261
		32	Tanners, curriers, leather dressers, leather dyers, etc.	161	88	22	..	...	51	161	88	22	...	...	51
		33	Makers of leather articles, such as trunks, water-bags, etc.	207	72	34	2	...	101	112	23	34	2	...	55
		34	Furriers	5	1	..	...	...	4	5	1	...	...	...	4
		35	Bone, ivory, horn, shell, etc., workers.	251	71	3	...	...	177	225	71	3	...	...	151
		VIII	WOOD	191,686	68,469	26,958	3,579	1,704	96,259	179,646	63,517	25,123	2,782	1,593	91,006
		36	Sawyers, carpenters, turners and joiners, etc.	143,719	54,281	11,827	3,058	1,065	77,611	134,779	50,329	10,729	2,397	965	73,721
		37	Basketmakers and other industries of wooden material, inlcuding leaves.	47,967	14,188	15,151	521	639	18,648	44,867	13,188	14,394	385	628	17,285
		IX	METALS	34,912	14,036	2,151	370	227	18,725	31,891	12,250	1,969	238	227	17,672
		38	Forging and rolling of iron and other metals.	483	33	143	...	...	307	483	33	143	...	...	307
		39	Plough and agricultural implement makers.	3	3	...	...	...	...	3	3	...	...	...	...
		40	Makers of arms, guns, etc. ..	67	22	...	1	...	45	66	21	...	1	...	45
		41	Other workers in iron and makers of implements and tools, principally or exclusively of iron.	29,040	11,859	1,498	356	212	15,683	26,338	10,289	1,330	227	212	14,719
		42	Workers in brass, copper and bell metal	554	137	10	...	...	407	554	137	10	...	...	407
		43	Workers in other metals (tin, zinc, lead, quick silver, etc.).	4,759	1,982	500	13	15	2,277	4,441	1,767	486	10	15	2,188
		44	Workers in mints, die-sinkers, etc. ...	6	.	...	...	...	6	6	...	...	...	...	6
		X	CERAMICS	18,821	4,656	6,087	132	154	7,478	16,836	4,514	6,292	133	128	6,030
		45	Makers of glass and crystal ware ...	192	85	18	...	...	91	192	83	18		...	91
		46	Makers of porcelain	12	3	...	...	...	9	9	3	...	...	...	6
		47	Potters and earthen pipe and bowl makers.	15,323	3,001	6,147	127	151	6,175	13,416	2,889	5,752	118	125	4,775
		48	Brick and tile makers	3,242	1,564	476	25	3	1,202	3,167	1,534	476	15	3	1,157
		49	Others (mosaic, talc, mica, alabaster, etc., workers).	52	5	46	...	...	1	52	5	46	...	...	1
		XI	CHEMICAL PRODUCTS PROPERLY SO CALLED AND ANALOGOUS.	10,560	4,502	1,990	31	71	4,068	10,050	4,474	1,715	21	28	3,861
		50	Manufacture of matches and explosive materials.	1	1	...	...	...	...	1	1	...	...	...	...
		51	Manufacture of ærated and mineral waters.	132	70	3	...	...	59	109	52	1	...	...	56
		52	Manufacture of dyes, paint and ink	4	3	...	...	...	1	4	3	...	...	...	1
		53	Manufacture and refining of vegetable and mineral oils.	9,110	4,041	1,542	16	59	3,527	9,016	4,041	1,490	16	27	3,485
		54	Manufacture of paper, cardboard and papier maché.	108	...	56	...	9	112	...	...	...	...	...	...
		55	Others (soap, candles, lac, cutch, perfumes and miscellaneous drugs).	1,145	387	389	15	3	369	920	377	224	5	1	319
		XII	FOOD INDUSTRIES	178,255	59,889	44,845	2,842	3,633	73,521	165,440	55,322	41,932	2,280	3,317	68,186
		56	Rice pounders and huskers, and flour grinders.	110,623	43,020	28,745	1,256	3,083	38,858	100,700	39,446	26,625	765	2,926	34,629
		57	Bakers and biscuit makers ...	1,234	904	76	2	..	254	1,234	904	76	2	...	254
		58	Grain parchers, etc.	94	31	...	...	...	63	94	31	...		...	63
		59	Butchers	6,897	1,890	1,612	77	160	3,395	4,985	1,334	1,145	18	1	2,506
		60	Fish curers	20	...	13	...	...	7	20	...	13	...	...	7
		61	Butter, cheese and ghee makers ...	...	...	...	...	...	...	...	...	...	...	...	...
		62	Makers of sugar, molasses and *gur* ...	8,298	684	5,378	40	308	2,236	8,288	684	5,378	40	308	2,226
		63	Sweetmeat makers, preparers of jams and condiments, etc.	2,113	532	742	9	15	839	1,962	427	741	9	15	794
		64	Brewers and distillers	653	365	16	3	...	272	628	365	...	3	...	263
		65	Toddy drawers	35,152	11,301	904	1,433	17	22,947	34,720	10,960	904	1,421	17	22,847
		66	Manufacturers of tobacco, opium and *ganja.*	13,171	1,162	7,359	22	50	4,650	12,809	1,162	7,050	22	50	4,597

Provincial and City Summary.

SPECIALLY ADMINISTERED TERRITORIES.						CITY OF RANGOON.						CITY OF MANDALAY.						
Total Workers and Dependents.	ACTUAL WORKERS. Total.		Partially Agriculturists.		Dependents.	Total Workers and Dependents.	ACTUAL WORKERS. Total.		Partially Agriculturists.		Dependents.	Total Workers and Dependents.	ACTUAL WORKERS. Total.		Partially Agriculturists.		Dependents.	
	Males.	Females.	Males.	Females.			Males.	Females.	Males.	Females.			Males.	Females.	Males.	Females.		
17	18	19	20	21	22	23	24	25	26	27	28	29	30	31	32	33	34	
47,975	984	34,458	30	1,331	12,533	214	108	25	...	...	81	8,510	1,503	5,504	...	...	1,503	VI
611	...	198	...	...	413	...	...	...	...	...	...	32	...	13	...	...	19	21
47,088	959	34,052	30	1,264	12,077	23	5	10	...	...	8	4,825	506	3,485	...	...	834	22
...	...	...	...	...	...	...	...	...	...	...	...	...	...	...	...	...	...	23
31	7	12	...	...	12	55	38	...	...	...	17	90	...	62	...	...	28	24
...	[illegible]	...	...	...	...	10	10	...	...	...	...	...	...	...	...	...	...	25
...	...	...	...	...	...	46	23	1	...	...	22	...	...	...	...	...	...	26
245	18	196	...	67	31	...	...	...	...	...	...	3,562	997	1,943	...	...	622	27
...	...	...	...	...	...	...	...	...	...	...	...	...	...	...	...	...	...	28
...	...	...	...	...	...	...	...	...	...	...	...	...	...	...	...	...	...	29
...	...	...	...	...	...	62	28	4	...	...	30	...	...	...	...	...	...	30
...	...	...	...	...	...	18	4	10	...	...	4	1	...	1	...	...	...	31
121	49	...	...	...	72	56	24	5	...	...	27	286	112	32	...	...	142	VII
...	...	...	...	...	...	17	11	...	...	...	6	119	77	...	...	...	42	32
95	49	...	...	...	46	13	...	2	...	...	11	55	...	32	...	...	23	33
...	...	...	...	...	...	5	1	...	...	...	4	...	...	...	...	...	...	34
36	...	...	...	...	26	21	12	3	...	...	6	112	35	...	...	...	77	35
12,040	4,952	1,835	797	111	5,253	14,206	6,615	146	6	...	7,445	7,448	2,639	1,218	...	...	3,591	VIII
8,940	3,952	1,098	661	100	3,890	13,938	6,533	126	6	...	7,279	5,733	2,338	453	...	...	2,947	36
3,100	1,000	737	136	11	1,363	268	82	20	...	...	166	1,715	306	765	...	...	644	37
3,021	1,786	182	132	...	1,053	3,720	1,920	7	2	...	1,793	1,823	717	56	...	...	1,050	IX
...	..	...	...	...	...	...	...	...	...	...	...	48	24	...	...	...	24	38
...	...	...	...	...	...	3	3	...	...	...	..	...	...	...	...	...	...	39
1	1	...	...	...	...	39	5	...	...	...	34	...	...	...	...	...	...	40
2,702	1,370	168	129	...	964	2,533	1,372	4	2	...	1,157	1,439	593	32	...	...	814	41
...	...	...	...	...	...	230	104	...	...	...	126	10	10	...	...	...	...	42
318	215	14	3	...	89	915	436	3	..	...	476	326	90	24	...	...	212	43
...	...	...	...	...	...	...	...	..	...	...	...	...	...	...	...	...	...	44
1,985	142	395	19	26	1,448	620	437	14	2	...	169	475	170	158	...	...	147	X
...	...	...	...	...	...	...	...	...	...	...	...	51	28	...	...	...	23	45
3	...	...	...	...	3	1	1	...	...	...	...	...	...	...	...	...	...	46
1,907	112	395	9	26	1,400	147	113	8	...	...	26	172	43	80	...	...	49	47
75	30	...	10	...	45	472	323	6	2	...	143	252	99	78	...	...	73	48
...	...	...	...	...	...	...	...	...	...	...	...	...	...	...	...	...	...	49
510	28	275	10	43	207	711	600	1	...	...	110	258	14	138	...	...	106	XI
...	...	...	...	...	...	1	1	...	...	...	...	...	...	...	...	...	...	50
23	18	2	...	...	3	13	9	...	...	...	4	17	14	...	...	...	3	51
...	...	...	...	...	...	1	...	...	...	...	1	...	...	...	...	..	...	52
94	...	52	...	32	42	509	442	...	...	...	67	...	...	...	...	...	...	53
168	...	56	...	9	112	...	...	...	...	...	...	...	...	...	..	...	...	54
225	10	165	10	2	50	187	148	1	...	...	38	241	...	138		...	103	55
12,815	4,567	2,913	562	316	5,335	31,097	19,479	3,368	5	1	8,250	3,327	1,074	852	...	...	1,401	XII
9,923	3,574	2,120	491	157	4,229	25,606	17,631	1,611	3	1	6,364	2,110	780	566	...	...	764	56
...	...	...	...	...	...	1,146	873	51	2	...	222	...	...	...	...	...	...	57
...	...	...	...	...	...	26	...	...	..	...	26	43	26	...	...	...	17	58
1,912	556	467	59	159	88)	1,043	441	82	..	...	520	455	60	129	...	...	269	59
...	...	...	...	...	...	...	...	...	...	...	...	...	...	...	...	...	...	60
.	...	...	...	...	...	...	...	...	...	...	...	...	...	...	...	...	...	61
10	...	...	...	...	10	...	...	...	...	...	...	5	...	4	..	...	1	62
151	105	1	...	...	45	185	97	2	...	...	26	160	35	57	...	...	68	63
25	...	16	...	...	9	...	...	...	...	...	...	..	...	..	..	...	...	64
432	332	...	12	...	100	52	41	1	...	...	10	...	...	...	...	...	...	65
362	...	309	...	...	55	3,099	396	1,621	...	...	1,082	551	173	96	..	...	282	66

Class.	Sub-class.	Serial No.	Description.	PROVINCIAL TOTAL. Total Workers and Dependents.	Actual Workers. Total. Males.	Actual Workers. Total. Females.	Partially Agriculturists. Males.	Partially Agriculturists. Females.	Dependents.	BURMA PROPER. Total Workers and Dependents.	Actual Workers. Total. Males.	Actual Workers. Total. Females.	Partially Agriculturists. Males.	Partially Agriculturists. Females.	Dependents.
1	2	3	4	5	6	7	8	9	10	11	12	13	14	15	16
B.—PREPARATION AND SUPPLY OF MATERIAL SUBSTANCES.	III.—INDUSTRY—concluded.	XIII	INDUSTRIES OF DRESS AND THE TOILET ..	116,056	45,886	23,830	1,419	729	46,340	107,457	42,495	21,543	989	656	43,419
		67	Hat, cap and turban makers ...	364	167	117	12	10	80	123	56	43	2	...	24
		68	Tailors, milliners, dress makers and darners, embroiderers on linen.	60,870	25,083	10,702	1,082	240	25,085	56,923	22,858	9,975	758	230	24,090
		69	Shoe, boot and sandal makers ...	11,972	5,093	1,939	39	38	4,940	11,245	4,897	1,750	25	28	4,598
		70	Other industries pertaining to dress-gloves, socks, gaiters, belts, buttons, umbrellas, canes, etc.	1,607	470	225	4	...	912	1,480	431	175	1	...	874
		71	Washing, cleaning and dyeing ...	23,742	9,706	4,949	164	218	9,087	21,478	9,268	3,934	144	206	8,276
		72	Barbers, hairdressers and wig makers.	4,877	2,660	1,265	12	17	952	4,739	2,619	1,255	6	17	865
		73	Other industries connected with the toilet (tattooers, shampooers, bath-houses, etc).	12,624	2,707	4,633	106	206	5,284	11,469	2,366	4,411	53	175	4,692
		XIV	FURNITURE INDUSTRIES	1,862	1,513	69	56	40	280	1,852	1,513	69	56	40	270
		74	Cabinet makers, carriage painters, etc.	1,820	1,494	67	39	40	259	1,810	1,494	67	39	40	249
		75	Upholsterers, tent-makers, etc. ...	42	19	2	17	...	21	42	19	2	17	...	21
		XV	BUILDING INDUSTRIES	24,257	9,780	3,041	177	65	10,536	23,520	9,456	3,806	151	65	10,258
		76	Lime burners, cement workers ...	1,167	394	207	...	...	566	1,167	304	207	...	...	566
		77	Excavators, plinth builders and well sinkers.	269	204	2	...	...	63	244	186	2	...	...	56
		78	Stone and marble workers, masons and bricklayers, *pucca* house builders.	13,003	6,030	997	140	47	5,976	12,494	5,816	883	119	47	5,795
		79	Others (thatchers, building contractors, house painters, tilers, plumbers, locksmiths, etc.)	9,818	3,152	2,735	37	18	3,931	9,615	3,060	2,714	32	18	3,841
		XVI	CONSTRUCTION OF MEANS OF TRANSPORT.	2,187	1,154	58	51	30	975	1,803	958	19	42	...	816
		80	Cart, carriage, palki, etc., makers and wheelwrights.	1,198	507	10	32	...	681	861	328	10	23	...	529
		81	Saddlers, harness-makers, whip and lashmakers.	144	81	...	4	...	63	144	81	...	4	...	63
		82	Ship and boat builders	845	566	48	15	30	231	798	565	9	15	...	224
		XVII 83	PRODUCTION AND TRANSMISSION OF PHYSICAL FORCES. (Gas works, electric light and ice factories).	180	72	...	1	...	108	180	72	...	1	...	108
		XVIII	INDUSTRIES OF LUXURY AND THOSE PERTAINING TO LITERATURE AND THE ARTS AND SCIENCES.	58,878	23,454	4,802	652	318	30,622	55,375	21,840	4,483	514	300	29,052
		84	Printers, lithographers, engravers, etc.	2,981	1,343	29	2	...	1,609	2,972	1,340	29	2	...	1,603
		85	Newspaper and magazine managers and editors, journalists, etc.	114	47	...	...	...	67	114	47	...	...	...	67
		86	Bookbinders and stitchers, envelope makers, etc.	861	563	15	2	1	283	841	558	5	2	...	278
		87	Makers of musical instruments ...	307	15	249	...	9	43	32	15	...	...	...	17
		88	Makers of watches and clocks and optical, photographic and surgical instruments.	1,045	415	12	9	...	618	956	395	8	3	...	553
		89	Workers in precious stones and metals, enamellers, imitation jewellery-makers, gilders, etc.	50,232	19,851	4,055	623	300	26,326	47,394	18,291	3,999	491	292	25,104
		90	Makers of bangles, rosaries, bead and other necklaces, spangles, lingams and sacred threads.	1,297	168	404	1	8	725	1,030	142	404	1	8	484
		91	Toy, kite, cage, fishing tackle, etc., makers, taxidermists, etc.	1,566	792	28	...	...	746	1,566	792	28	...	...	746
		92	Others, including managers, persons other than performers employed in theatres and other places of public entertainment, employés of public societies, race course service, huntsmen, etc.	475	260	10	15	...	205	470	260	10	15	...	200
		XIX 93	INDUSTRIES CONCERNED WITH REFUSE MATTER. (Sweepers, scavengers, dust and sweeping contractors).	13,103	6,667	1,604	141	80	4,832	12,140	6,451	1,509	92	79	4,180
	IV.—TRANSPORT.	XX	TRANSPORT BY WATER	131,071	65,770	9,546	2,290	384	55,755	127,840	64,725	8,698	2,190	360	54,417
		94	Harbour works, dockyards and pilots	695	449	19	...	...	227	695	449	19	...	...	227
		95	Shipowners and their employés, ship brokers, ships' officers, engineers, mariners and firemen.	11,539	10,349	45	284	1	1,145	11,474	10,322	45	284	1	1,107
		96	Persons employed on the maintenance of streams, rivers and canals (including construction).	66	32	2	...	1	32	66	32	2	...	1	32
		97	Boat owners, boat men and tow men	118,771	54,940	9,480	2,006	382	54,351	115,605	53,922	8,632	1,906	358	53,051
		XXI	TRANSPORT BY ROAD	230,168	96,076	33,439	5,544	3,580	100,653	204,621	86,584	28,285	4,239	3,315	89,752
		98	Persons employed on the construction and maintenance of roads and bridges.	91,541	42,516	16,960	2,654	2,014	32,065	82,333	38,438	15,148	2,081	1,881	28,747
		99	Cart owners and drivers, coach-men, stable boys, tramway, mail carriage, etc., managers and employés (excluding private servants).	132,099	49,851	16,227	2,827	1,551	66,021	116,123	44,614	12,903	2,107	1,419	58,606
		100	Palki, etc., bearers and owners ...	149	137	4	...	...	8	149	137	4	...	...	8
		101	Pack elephant, camel, mule, ass and bullock owners and drivers.	6,304	3,517	248	37	15	2,539	5,941	3,340	230	25	15	2,371
		102	Porters and messengers	75	55	...	26	...	20	75	55	...	26	...	20
		XXII	TRANSPORT BY RAIL	27,686	17,665	717	258	30	9,304	27,348	17,584	711	246	30	9,053
		103	Railway employés of all kinds other than construction coolies.	22,633	14,754	614	247	30	7,265	22,486	14,695	613	236	30	7,178
		104	Labourers employed on railway construction.	5,053	2,911	103	11	..	2,033	4,862	2,889	98	10	...	1,875
		XXIII 105	POST OFFICE, TELEGRAPH AND TELEPHONE SERVICES.	4,727	2,223	242	18	30	2,262	4,488	2,116	234	17	30	2,138

Provincial and City Summary.

SPECIALLY ADMINISTERED TERRITORIES.						CITY OF RANGOON.						CITY OF MANDALAY.						
Total Workers and Dependents.	ACTUAL WORKERS. Total.		Partially Agriculturists.		Dependents.	Total Workers and Dependents.	ACTUAL WORKERS. Total.		Partially Agriculturists.		Dependents.	Total Workers and Dependents.	ACTUAL WORKERS. Total.		Partially Agriculturists.		Dependents.	
	Males.	Females.	Males.	Females.			Males.	Females.	Males.	Females.			Males.	Females.	Males.	Females.		
17	18	19	20	21	22	23	24	25	26	27	28	29	30	31	32	33	34	
8,599	3,391	2,257	490	73	2,921	13,670	7,689	1,814	4	1	4,167	8,680	2,381	1,682	...	...	4,617	XIII
241	111	74	20	10	56	52	17	26	...	...	9	...	...	...	...	...	...	67
3,947	2,225	727	324	10	995	5,668	2,969	1,181	3	1	1,518	2,592	466	15	...	...	2,111	68
727	196	189	14	10	342	2,280	1,230	106	...	...	944	2,461	824	746	...	...	891	69
127	39	50	3	...	38	316	122	58	...	...	136	838	222	59	...	...	557	70
2,264	438	1,015	20	12	811	3,690	2,048	379	...	...	1,263	1,541	516	470	...	...	855	71
138	41	10	6	...	87	1,456	1,241	22	1	...	193	138	108	7	...	...	23	72
1,155	341	222	53	31	592	208	62	42	...	...	104	1,110	245	385	...	...	480	73
10	...	...	...	...	10	389	228	...	...	...	161	70	...	53	17	40	17	XIV
10	...	...	...	...	10	389	228	...	...	...	161	53	...	53	...	40	...	74
...	...	...	...	...	...	...	...	...	...	...	...	17	...	...	17	...	17	75
737	324	135	26	...	278	2,991	1,870	2	...	...	1,119	1,493	514	182	...	...	797	XV
...	...	...	...	...	...	9	9	...	...	...	...	...	...	...	...	...	...	76
25	18	...	...	...	7	113	107	...	...	...	26	...	...	...	...	...	...	77
509	214	114	21	...	181	1,128	842	...	...	...	286	1,276	424	176	...	...	676	78
203	92	21	5	...	90	1,731	912	2	...	...	817	217	90	6	...	...	121	79
384	186	39	9	30	159	677	394	...	...	...	283	158	91	3	...	...	64	XVI
337	185	...	9	...	152	290	89	...	...	...	201	85	51	...	...	...	34	80
...	...	...	...	...	...	29	13	...	...	...	16	70	40	...	...	...	30	81
47	1	39	...	30	7	358	292	...	...	...	66	3	...	3	...	...	...	82
...	...	...	...	...	...	161	61	...	1	...	100	...	...	...	...	...	...	XVII 83
3,503	1,614	319	138	18	1,570	8,569	4,003	84	6	...	4,482	3,294	1,238	482	...	...	1,524	XVIII
9	3	...	...	...	6	2,378	1,166	2	2	...	1,410	40	11	10	...	...	19	84
...	...	...	...	...	...	98	37	...	...	...	61	15	9	...	...	...	6	85
20	5	10	...	1	5	757	516	...	2	...	241	13	11	...	...	...	2	86
275	...	249	...	9	26	13	8	...	...	...	5	6	2	...	...	...	4	87
89	20	4	6	...	65	307	121	1	...	...	185	64	16	1	...	...	47	88
2,838	1,360	56	132	8	1,222	4,408	1,056	69	2	...	2,383	2,523	1,192	231	...	...	1,200	89
267	26	...	...	...	241	31	2	6	...	...	23	532	46	240	...	...	246	90
...	...	...	...	...	...	31	26	1	...	...	7	...	...	...	...	...	...	91
5	...	...	...	...	5	348	171	5	...	...	167	1	1	...	...	...	...	92
953	216	95	49	1	632	2,907	1,829	290	...	...	848	883	450	81	...	...	351	XIX 93
3,231	1,045	848	100	24	1,338	16,586	13,614	48	300	...	2,924	760	358	30	...	...	372	XX
...	...	...	...	...	...	126	58	...	...	...	58	68	13	7	...	...	48	94
65	27	...	...	...	38	9,741	8,974	5	268	...	762	59	13	10	...	...	36	95
...	...	...	...	...	...	7	3	...	...	...	4	...	...	...	...	...	...	96
3,166	1,018	848	100	24	1,300	6,722	4,579	43	32	...	2,100	641	332	22	...	...	288	97
25,547	9,492	5,154	1,305	265	10,901	8,024	6,138	44	22	...	1,842	9,003	3,499	794	...	...	4,713	XXI
9,208	4,078	1,812	573	133	3,318	1,960	1,157	23	...	...	180	1,415	433	312	...	...	670	98
15,976	5,237	3,324	720	132	7,415	6,477	4,804	21	22	...	1,652	7,414	2,900	482	...	...	4,032	99
...	...	...	...	...	...	140	137	...	...	...	3	...	...	...	...	...	...	100
363	177	18	12	...	168	36	29	...	...	...	7	177	166	...	...	...	11	101
...	...	...	...	...	...	11	11	...	...	...	...	...	...	...	...	...	...	102
338	81	6	12	...	251	5,643	3,468	21	4	...	2,154	746	558	16	...	...	172	XXII
147	59	1	11	...	87	5,636	3,463	22	4	...	2,152	590	450	15	...	...	124	103
191	22	5	1	...	164	7	5	...	...	...	2	156	108	...	...	...	48	104
290	107	8	1	...	124	655	294	23	1	...	338	443	290	4	...	...	209	XXIII 105

Class.	Sub-class.	Serial No.	Description.	PROVINCIAL TOTAL. Total Workers and Dependents.	PROVINCIAL TOTAL. Actual Workers. Total. Males.	Total. Females.	Partially Agriculturists. Males.	Partially Agriculturists. Females.	Dependents.	BURMA PROPER. Total Workers and Dependents.	BURMA PROPER. Actual Workers. Total. Males.	Total. Females.	Partially Agriculturists. Males.	Partially Agriculturists. Females.	Dependents.
1	2	3	4	5	6	7	8	9	10	11	12	13	14	15	16
B.—PREPARATION AND SUPPLY OF MATERIAL SUBSTANCES.	V.—TRADE.	XXIV-106	BANKS, ESTABLISHMENTS OF CREDIT, EXCHANGE AND INSURANCE. (Bank managers, money lenders, exchange and insurance agents, money changers and brokers and their employés.)	17,345	6,758	2,346	565	133	8,241	16,663	6,329	2,285	543	131	8,049
		XXV-107	BROKERAGE, COMMISSION AND EXPORT. Brokers, commission (agents, commercial travellers, warehouse owners and employés.)	21,415	7,608	1,423	69	49	12,384	20,995	7,590	1,423	68	40	11,982
		XXVI-108	TRADE IN TEXTILES. (Trade in piece-goods, wool, cotton, silk, hair and other textiles.)	74,875	21,006	22,811	1,330	1,274	31,058	61,872	17,294	18,382	570	1,059	26,196
		XXVII-109	TRADE IN SKINS, LEATHER AND FURS. (Trade in skins, leather, furs, feathers, horns, etc.)	1,481	525	130	5	15	826	1,225	337	118	5	12	770
		XXVIII-110	TRADE IN WOOD. [Trade in wood (not firewood), cork, bark, etc.]	21,988	7,979	2,480	203	205	11,529	20,010	7,562	2,398	192	203	10,050
		XXIX-111	TRADE IN METALS. (Machinery, knife, tool, etc., sellers.)	1,644	444	528	72	...	672	1,337	259	528	5	...	550
		XXX-112	TRADE IN POTTERY	10,386	2,425	3,784	246	238	4,177	9,035	2,237	3,211	200	130	3,587
		XXXI-113	TRADE IN CHEMICAL PRODUCTS. (Drugs, dyes, paints, petroleum, explosives, etc.)	2,903	1,025	404	10	32	1,474	2,866	1,011	400	9	32	1,455
		XXXII	HOTELS, CAFES, RESTAURANTS, ETC. ...	21,651	9,335	3,445	864	212	8,871	19,310	8,306	2,938	690	183	8,066
		114	Vendors of wine, liquors, aerated waters, etc.	14,474	6,501	1,990	732	168	5,983	12,741	5,727	1,612	561	13[illegible]	5,402
		115	Owners and managers of hotels, cook-shops, *sarais*, etc., and their employés.	7,177	2,834	1,455	132	44	2,888	6,569	2,579	1,326	129	44	2,664
		XXXIII	OTHER TRADE IN FOOD STUFFS ...	513,911	113,579	169,795	5,208	8,204	230,537	459,263	98,832	154,066	2,695	6,334	206,365
		116	Fish dealers	107,111	22,420	38,655	1,155	2,502	46,0[illegible]6	98,314	20,323	35,988	1,025	2,098	42,003
		117	Grocers and sellers of vegetable oil, salt and other condiments.	55,978	9,398	9,630	15[illegible]	564	16,950	31,465	8,571	8,344	107	243	14,550
		118	Sellers of milk, butter, ghee, poultry, eggs, etc.	10,378	4,456	1,837	85	54	4,085	9,591	4,097	1,772	61	54	3,722
		119	Sellers of sweetmeats, sugar, *gur* and molasses.	108,839	17,902	38,634	31	82	52,303	104,853	17,236	37,504	26	82	50,113
		120	Cardamom, betel-leaf, vegetables, fruit and areca nut sellers.	117,309	25,849	41,063	1,730	2,698	49,497	95,155	20,566	35,196	1,067	1,942	39,393
		121	Grain and pulse dealers ...	105,332	27,908	26,805	1,615	1,681	50,529	94,300	23,172	24,120	1,075	1,465	47,008
		122	Tobacco, opium, *ganja*, etc., sellers	22,362	3,906	10,336	188	420	8,120	20,459	3,365	9,528	185	303	7,566
		123	Dealers in sheep, goats and pigs ...	1,058	173	89	55	35	796	155	58	16	...	3	81
		124	Dealers in hay, grass and fodder ...	5,544	1,567	1,756	190	168	2,221	4,971	1,444	1,598	149	139	1,929
		XXXIV-125	TRADE IN CLOTHING AND TOILET ARTICLES. (Clothing, hats, umbrellas, socks, ready-made shoes, perfumes, etc.)	6,531	2,813	1,103	158	16	2,615	5,031	1,980	996	30	16	2,055
		XXXV	TRADE IN FURNITURE	13,496	4,487	3,445	128	183	5,564	11,999	3,770	3,386	108	183	4,843
		126	Trade in furniture, carpets, curtains and bedding.	7,137	1,905	2,277	85	57	2,955	6,390	1,594	2,218	65	57	2,578
		127	Hardware, cooking utensils, porcelain, crockery, glassware, bottles, articles for gardening, the cellar, etc.	6,359	2,582	1,168	43	126	2,609	5,609	2,176	1,168	43	126	2,265
		XXXVI-128	TRADE IN BUILDING MATERIALS. (Stones, bricks, plaster, cement, sand tiles, thatch, etc.)	3,057	891	1,180	36	46	986	2,411	539	1,042	32	41	830
		XXXVII-129	TRADE IN MEANS OF TRANSPORT. [Dealers and hirers of elephants, camels, horses, cattle, asses, mules, etc., sellers (not makers) of carriages, saddlery, etc.]	15,661	6,226	2,371	379	139	7,064	12,556	4,487	1,948	143	131	6,121
		XXXVIII-130	TRADE IN FUEL. (Dealers in firewood, charcoal, coal, cowdung, etc.)	10,753	3,738	2,224	130	214	4,791	9,002	3,057	1,675	90	58	4,270
		XXXIX	TRADE IN ARTICLES OF LUXURY AND THOSE PERTAINING TO LETTERS AND THE ARTS AND SCIENCES.	10,961	3,883	1,488	106	191	5,590	9,915	3,615	1,272	97	44	5,028
		131	Dealers in precious stones, jewellery (real and imitation), clocks, optical instruments, etc.	8,591	3,154	1,001	94	25	4,436	8,298	2,962	996	90	25	4,340
		132	Dealers in common bangles, bead necklaces, fans, small articles, toys, hunting and fishing tackle, flowers, etc.	1,150	236	246	7	72	668	775	236	176	7	19	363
		133	Publishers, booksellers, stationers, dealers in music, pictures, musical instruments and curiosities.	1,220	493	241	5	54	486	842	417	100	...	...	325
		XL-134	TRADE IN REFUSE MATTER. (Dealers in rags, stable refuse, etc.)	94	27	6	...	...	61	90	27	6	...	..	57
		XLI	TRADE OF OTHER SORTS	455,569	122,916	149,466	4,766	5,729	183,187	417,432	107,441	138,298	3,430	4,753	171,693
		135	Shop-keepers otherwise unspecified	450,939	121,031	149,010	4,737	5,703	180,898	413,093	105,693	137,850	3,420	4,727	169,550
		136	Itinerant traders, pedlars, hawkers, etc.	456	260	28	...	...	168	456	260	28	...	...	168
		137	Conjurors, acrobats, fortune-tellers, reciters, exhibitors of curiosities and wild animals.	3,816	1,447	422	16	26	1,947	3,553	1,336	414	9	26	1,803
		138	Other trades (including farmers of pounds, tolls and markets.)	358	178	6	13	...	174	330	152	6	1	...	172

Provincial and City Summary.

	SPECIALLY ADMINISTERED TERRITORIES.						CITY OF RANGOON.						CITY OF MANDALAY.					
	Total Workers and Dependents.	ACTUAL WORKERS. Total.		Partially Agriculturists.		Dependents.	Total Workers and Dependents.	ACTUAL WORKERS. Total.		Partially Agriculturists.		Dependents.	Total Workers and Dependents.	ACTUAL WORKERS. Total.		Partially Agriculturists.		Dependents.
		Males.	Females.	Males.	Females.			Males.	Females.	Males.	Females.			Males.	Females.	Males.	Females.	
	17	18	19	20	21	22	23	24	25	26	27	28	29	30	31	32	33	34
XXIV-106	682	429	61	22	2	192	2,286	834	160	6	5	1,292	369	94	28	...	...	247
XXV-107	420	18	...	1	...	402	5,857	2,764	77	5	...	3,016	948	367	26	...	...	555
XXVI-108	13,003	3,712	4,429	760	215	4,862	5,216	2,436	438	17	...	2,342	3,291	811	1,112	...	...	1,368
XXVII-109	256	188	12	...	3	56	228	86	1	...	...	141	121	69	...	...	...	52
XXVIII-110	1,978	417	82	11	2	1,479	3,212	2,074	33	22	...	1,105	960	375	137	...	...	448
XXIX-111	307	185	...	67	...	122	240	139	7	...	...	94	...	...	...	...	...	...
XXX-112	1,351	188	573	46	108	590	52	27	11	...	...	14	24	17	...	...	...	7
XXXI-113	37	14	4	1	...	19	351	192	28	1	...	131	87	41	...	...	...	46
XXXII	2,341	1,029	507	174	29	805	3,167	1,787	202	7	...	1,178	1,222	298	351	...	...	573
114	1,733	774	378	171	29	581	2,019	716	12	7	...	1,291	422	106	102	...	...	214
115	608	255	129	3	...	224	2,148	1,071	190	...	...	887	800	192	249	...	...	359
XXXIII	54,648	14,747	15,729	1,513	1,870	24,172	27,485	9,599	4,152	19	1	13,734	18,277	2,761	8,079	...	...	7,437
116	8,797	2,097	2,667	130	404	4,033	2,325	636	576	...	...	1,113	2,078	241	999	...	...	838
117	4,513	827	1,286	52	321	2,400	2,829	1,550	240	2	...	1,039	1,296	335	322	...	...	639
118	787	359	65	24	...	363	1,705	1,160	94	...	...	451	827	201	254	...	...	372
119	3,986	666	1,130	5	...	2,190	1,826	848	354	1	...	624	3,695	936	1,421	...	...	1,338
120	22,154	5,283	6,767	663	756	10,104	4,843	1,204	1,690	1	1	1,949	4,082	404	1,935	...	...	1,743
121	11,032	4,736	2,775	540	216	3,521	11,341	3,280	529	15	...	7,532	3,788	537	1,585	...	...	1,666
122	1,903	541	808	3	112	554	2,064	505	659	...	...	899	2,178	101	1,429	...	...	648
123	903	115	73	55	32	715	42	22	3	...	...	17	...	...	...	...	...	...
124	573	123	158	41	29	292	510	393	7	...	...	110	333	6	134	...	...	193
XXXIV-125	1,500	833	107	128	...	560	389	167	42	...	...	180	2,246	942	491	...	...	813
XXXV	1,477	717	39	20	...	721	970	375	15	...	...	580	303	134	42	...	...	127
126	747	311	59	20	...	377	251	79	13	...	...	159	344	97	42	...	...	205
127	750	406	...	...	...	344	719	296	2	...	...	421	59	37	...	...	...	22
XXXVI-128	646	352	138	4	5	156	112	60	2	...	...	50	15	...	7	...	...	8
XXXVII-129	3,105	1,739	423	236	8	943	479	268	2	...	...	209	712	117	103	...	...	492
XXXVIII-130	1,751	681	549	30	156	521	704	309	87	...	...	308	853	180	239	...	...	434
XXXIX	1,046	268	216	9	147	562	1,270	502	178	...	...	590	2,685	871	570	...	...	1,244
131	293	192	5	4	...	96	642	281	38	...	...	323	2,257	696	510	...	...	1,051
132	375	...	70	...	53	305	366	74	127	...	...	165	137	53	8	...	...	76
133	378	76	141	5	94	161	262	147	13	...	...	102	291	122	52	...	...	117
XL-134	4	...	...	...	...	4	38	21	6	...	...	11	5	...	...	...	...	5
XLI	38,137	15,475	11,168	1,336	976	11,494	11,151	4,706	1,372	22	2	5,073	10,364	2,704	3,099	...	...	4,561
135	37,846	15,338	11,160	1,317	976	11,348	10,410	4,335	1,348	22	2	4,727	9,847	2,481	3,065	...	...	4,301
136	...	...	...	...	...	...	437	260	19	...	...	158	...	...	...	...	...	...
137	263	111	8	7	...	144	242	97	4	...	...	141	508	215	34	...	...	259
138	28	26	...	12	...	2	62	14	1	...	...	47	9	8	...	...	...	1

Class.	Sub-class.	Serial No.	ORDER AND GROUP. Description.	PROVINCIAL TOTAL. Total Workers and Dependents.	Actual Workers. Total. Males.	Actual Workers. Total. Females.	Partially Agriculturists. Males.	Partially Agriculturists. Females.	Dependents.	BURMA PROPER. Total Workers and Dependents.	Actual Workers. Total. Males.	Actual Workers. Total. Females.	Partially Agriculturists. Males.	Partially Agriculturists. Females.	Dependents.
1	2	3	4	5	6	7	8	9	10	11	12	13	14	15	16
C.—PUBLIC ADMINISTRATION AND LIBERAL ARTS.	VI.—PUBLIC FORCE.	XLII 139	ARMY	24,984	18,717	68	1,954	...	6,199	22,247	17,162	49	1,460	...	5,036
		140	Army (Native States)	...	...	...	...	...	...	...	...	...	...	...	...
		XLIII 141	NAVY	28	11	...	...	...	17	27	11	...	...	...	26
		XLIV	POLICE	54,483	21,460	1,649	615	188	31,374	50,545	19,706	1,612	505	175	29,227
		142	Police	54,266	21,390	1,647	596	188	31,229	50,442	19,679	1,612	499	175	29,151
		143	Village Watchmen	217	70	2	19	...	145	103	27	...	6	...	76
	VII.—PUBLIC ADMINISTRATION.	XLV	PUBLIC ADMINISTRATION	103,108	36,238	4,394	4,944	549	62,476	89,375	30,255	3,390	3,430	504	55,730
		144	Service of the State	34,294	13,021	898	786	150	20,375	31,835	11,697	863	204	149	19,275
		145	Service of Native and Foreign States	2,976	1,324	360	114	...	1,292	69	19	2	...	...	48
		146	Municipal and other local (not village) service.	4,174	2,445	60	50	1	1,669	4,086	2,397	54	50	...	1,635
		147	Village officials and servants other than watchmen.	61,664	19,448	3,076	3,994	398	39,140	53,385	16,142	2,471	3,176	355	34,722
	VIII.—PROFESSIONS AND LIBERAL ARTS.	XLVI	RELIGION	140,834	79,102	11,087	1,277	137	50,645	116,263	65,343	8,930	734	102	41,990
		148	Priests, ministers, etc. ...	128,642	77,008	5,799	1,273	72	45,835	104,993	63,285	4,050	731	46	37,656
		149	Religious mendicants, inmates of monasteries, etc.	11,638	1,925	5,270	2	65	4,443	10,770	1,909	4,860	2	56	4,001
		150	Catechists, readers, church and mission service.	434	113	17	2	...	304	380	93	17	1	...	270
		151	Temple, burial or burning ground service, pilgrim conductors, circumcisers.	120	56	1	...	...	63	120	56	1	...	...	63
		XLVII	LAW	8,306	2,874	393	52	1	5,039	8,229	2,827	390	52	1	5,012
		152	Lawyers of all kinds, including Kazis, law agents and mukhtiars.	6,079	1,553	353	34	1	4,173	6,006	1,510	350	34	1	4,146
		153	Lawyers' clerks, petition-writers, etc.	2,227	1,321	40	18	...	866	2,223	1,317	40	18	...	866
		XLVIII	MEDICINE	52,172	18,769	6,341	1,535	382	27,062	48,599	17,557	6,142	1,433	379	24,900
		154	Medical practitioners of all kinds, including dentists, oculists and veterinary surgeons.	49,582	18,120	5,434	1,519	382	26,028	46,069	16,927	5,251	1,417	379	23,891
		155	Midwives, vaccinators, compounders, nurses, masseurs, etc.	2,590	649	907	16	...	1,034	2,530	630	891	16	...	1,009
		XLIX 156	INSTRUCTION. (Professors and teachers of all kinds, and clerks and servants connected with education.)	26,939	9,818	2,776	302	190	14,345	25,344	9,262	2,628	263	190	13,454
		L	LETTERS AND ARTS AND SCIENCES ...	28,025	10,854	2,638	195	77	14,533	25,830	10,416	2,100	179	43	13,374
		157	Public scribes, stenographers, etc. ...	1,866	787	40	...	...	1,039	1,843	787	35	...	...	1,021
		158	Architects, surveyors, engineers, and their employés.	3,998	1,577	107	52	7	2,314	3,850	1,457	107	42	7	2,236
		159	Others (authors, photographers, artists, sculptors astronomers, meteorologists, botanists, astrologers, etc.).	5,666	1,842	524	23	10	3,301	5,327	1,643	519	19	10	3,165
		160	Music composers and masters, players on all kinds of musical instruments (not military), singers, actors, and dancers.	16,495	6,649	1,967	120	60	7,879	14,870	6,529	1,439	118	26	6,902
	IX.—PERSONS LIVING ON THEIR INCOME.	LI 161	PERSONS LIVING PRINCIPALLY ON THEIR INCOME. Proprietors (other than of agricultural land), fund and scholarship-holders and pensioners.	6,967	2,176	493	68	11	4,298	6,257	1,736	445	51	11	4,076
D.—MISCELLANEOUS.	X.—DOMESTIC SERVICE.	LII	DOMESTIC SERVICE	85,771	47,816	10,987	750	383	26,968	79,015	45,423	9,757	570	215	23,835
		162	Cooks, water carriers, doorkeepers, watchmen and other indoor servants.	82,197	45,153	10,862	745	360	26,182	75,483	42,771	9,632	565	192	23,080
		163	Private grooms, coachmen, dog boys, etc.	3,574	2,663	125	5	23	786	3,532	2,652	125	5	23	755
	XI.—INSUFFICIENTLY DESCRIBED OCCUPATIONS.	LIII	GENERAL TERMS WHICH DO NOT INDICATE A DEFINITE OCCUPATION.	489,399	180,246	76,922	5,771	3,028	172,231	400,003	170,035	71,204	3,671	2,743	158,766
		164	Manufacturers, businessmen and contractors otherwise unspecified.	10,852	3,816	222	73	18	6,814	8,793	3,574	223	40	17	5,006
		165	Cashiers, accountants, book-keepers, clerks and other employés in unspecified offices, warehouses and shops.	58,873	22,562	2,136	361	287	34,175	53,252	21,047	1,869	246	278	30,336
		166	Mechanics otherwise unspecified ..	8,240	4,617	244	4	4	3,379	8,223	4,613	242	4	4	3,368
		167	Labourers and workmen otherwise unspecified.	351,434	149,251	74,320	5,333	2,709	127,863	329,735	140,799	68,880	3,381	2,444	120,056
	XII.—UNPRODUCTIVE.	LIV 168	INMATES OF JAILS, ASYLUMS AND HOSPITALS.	8,500	8,052	44	2	...	404	8,481	8,052	44	2	...	385
		LV 169	BEGGARS, VAGRANTS, PROSTITUTES (procurers, receivers of stolen goods, cattle poisoners, etc.).	26,075	8,353	9,943	300	173	7,779	22,794	7,246	9,052	212	164	6,496

Provincial and City Summary.

SPECIALLY ADMINISTERED TERRITORIES. Total Workers and Dependents.	Actual Workers. Total. Males.	Actual Workers. Total. Females.	Actual Workers. Partially Agriculturists. Males.	Actual Workers. Partially Agriculturists. Females.	Dependents.	CITY OF RANGOON. Total Workers and Dependents.	Actual Workers. Total. Males.	Actual Workers. Total. Females.	Actual Workers. Partially Agriculturists. Males.	Actual Workers. Partially Agriculturists. Females.	Dependents.	CITY OF MANDALAY. Total Workers and Dependents.	Actual Workers. Total. Males.	Actual Workers. Total. Females.	Actual Workers. Partially Agriculturists. Males.	Actual Workers. Partially Agriculturists. Females.	Dependents.	
17	18	19	20	21	22	23	24	25	26	27	28	29	30	31	32	33	34	
2,737	1,555	19	494	...	1,163	4,245	3,522	3	185	...	720	3,073	2,316	8	...	...	849	XLII 139
...	...	...	...	...	...	...	...	...	...	...	...	...	...	...	...	...	...	140
1	...	...	...	...	1	27	11	...	...	...	16	...	...	...	...	...	...	XLIII 141
3,938	1,754	37	110	13	2,147	2,257	1,169	2	3	...	1,086	2,077	1,046	1	...	...	1,030	XLIV
3,824	1,711	35	97	13	2,078	2,245	1,169	2	3	...	1,074	2,077	1,046	1	...	...	1,030	142
114	43	2	13	...	69	12	...	...	...	...	12	...	...	...	...	...	...	143
13,733	5,983	1,004	1,514	45	6,746	12,014	5,638	77	10	...	6,299	2,337	1,163	72	...	...	1,102	XLV
2,459	1,324	35	582	1	1,100	8,833	3,606	42	4	...	5,185	1,357	479	67	...	...	793	144
2,907	1,305	358	114	...	1,244	6	3	...	...	...	3	...	...	...	...	...	...	145
88	48	6	...	1	34	3,126	2,012	35	6	...	1,079	78	37	1	...	...	40	146
8,279	3,306	605	818	43	4,368	49	17	...	...	...	36	902	629	4	...	...	269	147
24,571	13,759	2,157	543	35	8,655	4,773	2,297	375	...	...	2,101	4,115	3109	250	...	...	756	XLVI
23,649	13,723	1,747	542	26	8,179	4,055	2,065	397	...	...	1,691	3,437	2,963	2	...	...	472	148
868	16	410	...	9	442	547	178	61	...	...	308	535	122	248	...	...	165	149
54	20	...	1	...	34	103	25	14	...	...	64	133	16	...	...	...	117	150
...	...	...	...	...	...	68	29	1	...	...	38	10	8	...	...	...	2	151
77	47	3	...	...	27	1,214	361	2	4	...	851	225	60	8	...	...	157	XLVII
73	42	3	...	...	27	571	139	...	4	...	432	185	44	6	...	...	135	152
4	4	...	...	...	...	643	222	2	...	...	410	40	16	2	...	...	22	153
3,573	1,212	199	102	3	2,162	2,932	932	399	6	...	1,601	1,388	476	118	...	...	794	XLVIII
3,513	1,193	183	102	3	2,137	2,211	812	22	5	...	1,377	1,258	472	64	...	...	722	154
60	19	16	...	...	25	721	120	377	1	...	224	130	4	54	...	...	72	155
1,595	556	148	39	...	891	1,936	574	207	1	...	1,155	855	251	84	...	...	530	XLIX 156
2,135	438	538	16	34	1,159	2,700	1,111	171	3	...	1,418	1,128	426	65	...	...	637	L
23	...	5	...	...	18	119	49	25	...	...	45	135	46	...	...	...	89	157
148	120	...	10	...	28	768	294	1	3	...	473	133	50	1	...	...	82	158
339	198	5	4	...	136	392	166	1	...	...	225	382	176	8	...	...	198	159
1,625	120	528	2	34	977	1,421	602	144	...	...	675	478	154	36	...	...	268	160
710	440	48	17	...	222	1,281	302	52	2	...	927	526	85	77	...	...	364	LI 161
6,756	2,393	1,230	180	168	3,133	23,015	16,613	1,339	37	...	5,063	4,746	2,480	471	...	...	1,795	LII
6,714	2,382	1,230	180	168	3,102	21,189	15,069	1,332	34	...	4,788	4,377	2,258	465	...	...	1,654	162
42	11	...	...	...	31	1,826	1,544	7	3	...	275	369	222	6	...	...	141	163
29,396	10,213	5,718	2,100	275	13,465	49,120	33,939	672	25	...	14,509	18,978	7,181	3,975	...	...	7,822	LIII
2,059	242	9	33	1	1,808	2,031	687	2	6	...	1,342	272	79	4	...	...	189	164
5,621	1,515	267	115	9	3,839	16,569	7,668	119	11	...	8,842	2,504	859	39	...	...	1,606	165
17	4	2	...	...	11	3,202	1,715	6	3	...	1,381	329	68	2	...	...	259	166
21,699	8,452	5,440	1,952	265	7,807	27,418	23,929	545	5	...	2,944	15,873	6,175	3,930	...	...	5,768	167
19	...	...	...	...	19	2,759	2,719	2	1	...	38	90	80	...	...	...	10	LIV 168
3,281	1,107	891	88	9	1,283	1,789	510	923	...	...	356	871	326	284	...	...	262	LV 169

IMPERIAL TABLE XV-AII.

Occupation or means of livelihood. General Table by Districts.

NOTE I.—The following statement gives in an abbreviated form the scheme of occupational classification adopted. The full scheme is given in the first four columns of Table XV —A-I and XV—D.

Class.	Sub-class.	Order. Number.	Order. Designation.	Group.	Page.	Column.
A Production of Raw Materials.	I. Exploitation of the surface of the earth.	I	Pasture and Agriculture	1 to 13	166 to 171	1 to 93
		II	Fishing and Hunting	14 & 15	172 & 173	94 to 111
	II. Extraction of minerals.	III	Mines	16 & 17	173 & 174	112 to 129
		IV	Quarries of hard rocks	18	174	130 to 135
		V	Salt, etc., ...	19 & 20	174	136 to 141
B Preparation and supply of Material Substances.	III. Industry.	VI	Textiles	21 to 31	174 to 177	142 to 171
		VII	Hides, skins, and hard materials from the Animal Kingdom.	32 to 35	177	172 to 183
		VIII	Wood	36 & 37	178 & 179	184 to 201
		IX	Metals	38 to 44	179 to 181	202 to 231
		X	Ceramics	45 to 49	181 & 182	232 to 255
		XI	Chemical products—property so called, and analogous.	50 to 55	183 & 184	256 to 279
		XII	Food industries	56 to 66	185 to 187	280 to 327
		XIII	Industries of dress and the toilet ...	67 to 73	187 to 189	328 to 363
		XIV	Furniture industries	74 & 75	190	364 to 375
		XV	Building industries	76 to 79	191 & 192	376 to 399
		XVI	Construction of means of transport ...	80 to 82	192 & 193	400 to 417
		XVII	Production and transmission of physical forces, heat light, electricity, motive powers, etc.	83	193	418 to 423
		XVIII	Industries of luxury, and those pertaining to Literature and the Arts and Sciences.	84 to 92	194 to 196	424 to 459
		XIX	Industries pertaining to refuse matter ...	93	196	460 to 465
	IV. Transport	XX	Transport by water	94 to 97	197	466 to 483
		XXI	Transport by road	98 to 102	198 & 199	484 to 507
		XXII	Transport by rail	103 & 104	199 & 200	508 to 525
		XXIII	Post Office, Telegraph and Telephone Services.	105	201	526 to 531
	V. Trade.	XXIV	Banks, establishments of credit exchange and insurance.	106	201	532 to 537
		XXV	Brokerage, commission and export ...	107	201	538 to 543
		XXVI	Trade in textiles	108	202	544 to 549
		XXVII	Trade in skins, leathers and furs ...	109	202	550 to 555
		XXVIII	Trade in wood	110	203	556 to 561
		XXIX	Trade in metals	111	203	562 to 567
		XXX	Trade in pottery	112	203	568 to 573
		XXXI	Trade in chemical products	113	204	574 to 579
		XXXII	Hotels, cafès, restaurants, etc. ...	114 & 115	204 & 205	580 to 597
		XXXIII	Other trade in food-stuffs	116 to 124	205 to 209	598 to 657
		XXXIV	Trade in clothing and toilet articles ...	125	209	658 to 663
		XXXV	Trade in furniture	126 & 127	210 & 211	664 to 681
		XXXVI	Trade in building materials	128	211	682 to 687
		XXXVII	Trade in means of transport ...	129	211	688 to 693
		XXXVIII	Trade in fuel	130	212	694 to 699
		XXXIX	Trade in articles of luxury and those pertaining to Literature and the Arts and Sciences.	131 to 133	212 & 213	700 to 723
		XL	Trade in refuse matter	134	214	724 to 729
		XLI	Trade of other sorts	135 to 138	214 & 215	730 to 747
C Public Administration and Liberal Arts.	VI. Public Force.	XLII	Army	139 & 140	215	748 to 753
		XLIII	Navy	141	216	754 to 759
		XLIV	Police	142 & 143	216 & 217	760 to 771
	VII. Public Administration.	XLV	Public Administration	144 to 147	217 & 218	772 to 801
	VIII. Professions and Liberal Arts.	XLVI	Religion	148 to 151	219 & 220	802 to 819
		XLVII	Law	152 & 153	220 & 221	820 to 837
		XLVIII	Medicine	154 & 155	221 & 222	838 to 855
		XLIX	Instruction	156	223	856 to 861
		L	Literature and the Arts and Sciences ...	157 to 160	223 & 224	862 to 891
	IX. Persons living on their income.	LI	Persons living principally on their income	161	225	892 to 897
D Miscellaneous	X. Domestic service.	LII	Domestic service	162 & 163	225 & 226	898 to 915
	XI. Insufficiently described occupations.	LIII	General terms which do not indicate a definite occupation.	164 to 167	227 & 228	916 to 945
	XII. Unproductive.	LIV	Inmates of Jails, Asylums and Hospitals.	168	229	946 to 951
		LV	Beggars, Vagrants, Prostitutes ...	169	229	952 to 957

NOTE II.—No persons have been recorded as coming under Groups 20, 23, 28, 29, 61, and 140, which have therefore been omitted from the Table.

NOTE III.—The numbers of persons entered under Groups 3, 5, 11, 25, 26, 30, 31, 32, 33, 34, 39, 40, 44, 46, 49, 50, 52, 54, 58, 60, 64, 67, 70, 75, 77, 81, 84, 86, 88, 92, 96, 100, 102, 134, 136, 138, 141, 145, and 151, are so small that they have been omitted from the Group columns of this part of Table XV. A Provincial and City summary for these omitted Groups is given in Table XV—A-I, and an Analysis by Religion in Table XV—D. They have also been included in the figures for the 55 Orders of occupations given in this Table.

Serial No.	District or State.	Order 1.—Pasture and Agriculture. Total Workers and Dependents.	Workers. Males.	Workers. Females.	Dependents.	Sub-Order 1(a), Ordinary Cultivation. Total Workers and Dependents.	Workers. Males.	Workers. Females.	Dependents.	Group 1, Income from Rent of Agricultural Land. Total Workers and Dependents.	Workers. Males.	Workers. Females.	Dependents.	Group 2, Total Workers and Dependents.
	1	2	3	4	5	6	7	8	9	10	11	12	13	14
	Provincial Total ...	8,472,391	2,567,202	2,123,276	3,781,913	8,083,712	2,434,999	2,024,772	3,623,941	220,485	59,921	68,997	91,567	6,225,154
	Burma Proper ...	7,388,274	2,224,908	1,798,787	3,364,579	7,083,161	2,118,545	1,724,606	3,240,010	182,835	48,108	54,084	80,643	5,294,320
	Arakan Division ...	638,143	198,132	145,521	294,490	619,154	190,057	141,040	288,057	17,626	4,873	4,324	8,429	479,777
1	Akyab ...	392,319	126,922	86,986	178,411	378,378	121,068	83,809	173,501	12,397	3,659	2,495	6,243	261,545
2	Northern Arakan ...	21,081	7,081	6,856	7,144	21,069	7,073	6,854	7,142	...	...	...	...	21,067
3	Kyaukpyu ...	141,688	39,746	29,931	72,011	139,116	38,907	29,159	71,050	2,500	534	862	1,104	122,908
4	Sandoway ...	83,055	24,383	21,748	36,924	80,591	23,099	21,218	36,364	2,729	680	957	1,082	74,257
	Pegu Division ...	1,315,891	390,896	273,711	651,284	1,252,615	365,197	261,609	625,709	27,564	6,902	7,740	12,922	717,213
5	City of Rangoon ...	8,355	3,837	674	3,844	5,361	1,791	562	3,009	1,934	433	278	1,223	2,752
6	Hanthawaddy ...	373,736	108,510	49,319	215,948	351,688	99,100	46,015	206,573	5,235	1,242	1,011	2,982	151,808
7	Tharrawaddy ...	340,917	101,428	94,778	144,711	325,194	95,361	91,355	138,478	5,775	1,605	1,789	2,381	193,722
8	Pegu ...	318,729	94,214	48,495	176,020	309,148	90,263	47,097	171,788	6,402	1,785	1,202	3,415	161,433
9	Prome ...	274,104	82,898	80,445	110,761	261,223	78,782	76,580	105,861	8,218	1,837	3,460	2,921	207,518
	Irrawaddy Division ...	1,374,287	429,134	342,116	603,037	1,304,481	404,182	324,442	575,857	29,441	8,079	7,932	13,430	797,747
10	Bassein ...	331,232	101,109	82,882	147,241	310,437	93,962	77,627	138,848	6,992	2,416	1,174	3,402	179,498
11	Henzada ...	402,934	120,906	122,443	159,585	373,088	109,976	113,958	149,154	9,994	2,814	3,539	3,641	228,800
12	Myaungmya ...	250,765	80,470	56,257	114,038	243,484	77,879	54,690	110,915	4,458	1,072	1,343	2,043	167,268
13	Ma-ubin ...	204,256	65,509	50,443	88,304	196,365	62,766	48,581	85,018	3,063	867	862	1,334	128,106
14	Pyapôn ...	185,100	61,140	30,091	93,869	181,107	59,599	29,586	91,922	4,934	910	1,014	3,010	94,075
	Tenasserim Division ...	1,066,263	309,552	213,327	543,384	1,013,657	291,514	203,593	518,550	18,305	4,794	4,055	9,456	765,469
15	Toungoo ...	264,853	72,870	52,256	139,727	251,708	68,873	49,287	133,548	4,875	1,258	992	2,625	185,555
16	Salween ...	42,617	12,155	6,582	23,880	41,806	11,856	6,451	23,499	165	44	34	87	32,399
17	Thatôn ...	335,362	99,723	65,433	170,206	321,274	95,088	63,206	162,980	5,883	1,631	1,036	3,216	224,604
18	Amherst ...	258,280	77,121	53,350	127,809	244,729	72,260	51,102	121,367	5,473	1,395	1,422	2,656	183,035
19	Tavoy ...	93,320	25,298	18,678	49,344	88,947	23,947	17,745	47,257	1,526	361	431	734	74,984
20	Mergui ...	71,831	22,385	17,028	32,418	65,191	19,490	15,802	29,899	383	105	140	138	57,892
	Magwe Division ...	915,896	260,822	238,406	416,668	898,299	254,643	233,774	409,882	17,772	4,225	6,277	7,270	825,213
21	Thayetmyo ...	190,202	52,388	41,497	96,317	186,924	51,467	40,785	94,672	3,637	767	1,266	1,604	172,211
22	Pakôkku ...	291,582	81,565	77,145	132,872	286,275	79,584	75,650	131,041	4,674	1,076	1,674	1,924	269,112
23	Minbu ...	189,311	57,022	47,796	84,493	182,979	54,651	46,101	82,227	3,942	955	1,336	1,651	166,835
24	Magwe ...	244,801	69,847	71,968	102,986	242,121	68,941	71,238	101,942	5,519	1,427	2,001	2,091	217,055
	Mandalay Division ...	475,915	152,859	131,987	191,069	451,174	145,385	125,140	180,649	26,887	9,662	8,653	8,572	372,461
25	Mandalay (including City).	124,341	36,451	32,305	55,585	114,836	33,255	29,395	52,186	3,905	465	1,997	1,443	87,386
	Mandalay City ...	*6,919*	*2,144*	*1,729*	*3,046*	*4,961*	*1,624*	*1,066*	*2,271*	*532*	*142*	*108*	*282*	*3,418*
26	Bhamo ...	79,875	23,633	25,168	31,074	75,644	22,052	24,159	29,433	13,236	4,309	6,143	2,784	54,621
27	Myitkyina ...	64,318	25,637	22,621	16,060	62,634	24,929	22,480	15,225	502	258	5	239	59,716
28	Katha ...	156,309	46,167	39,407	70,735	152,674	45,303	38,438	68,933	7,159	3,286	331	3,542	132,439
29	Ruby Mines ...	51,072	20,971	12,486	17,615	45,386	19,846	10,668	14,872	2,085	1,344	177	564	38,299
	Sagaing Division ...	805,393	237,611	243,587	324,195	774,910	229,719	233,161	312,030	24,459	6,296	9,272	8,891	672,990
30	Shwebo ...	270,466	86,899	84,125	99,442	265,365	85,667	82,386	97,312	7,583	2,879	2,440	2,264	239,311
31	Sagaing ...	222,288	60,509	66,381	95,398	213,815	57,783	63,220	92,812	9,304	1,151	4,263	3,890	171,195
32	Lower Chindwin ...	192,726	55,914	56,317	80,495	185,297	54,230	53,543	77,524	5,818	1,414	2,184	2,220	165,348
33	Upper Chindwin ...	119,913	34,283	36,764	48,860	110,433	31,039	34,012	44,382	1,754	852	385	517	97,136
	Meiktila Division ...	796,486	245,902	210,132	340,452	768,871	237,748	201,847	329,276	20,781	3,277	5,831	11,673	662,450
34	Kyauksè ...	83,305	28,125	22,218	32,962	79,168	26,564	21,296	31,308	1,557	364	616	577	58,780
35	Meiktila ...	178,655	62,244	47,309	69,102	170,708	60,680	44,297	65,731	5,387	907	706	3,774	145,690
36	Yamèthin ...	234,031	68,486	44,494	121,021	227,594	66,265	43,313	118,016	8,165	850	1,655	5,660	192,652
37	Myingyan ...	300,525	87,047	96,111	117,367	291,401	84,239	92,941	114,221	5,672	1,156	2,854	1,662	266,328
	Specially Administered Territories.	1,084,117	342,294	324,489	417,334	1,000,551	316,454	300,166	383,931	37,650	11,813	14,913	10,924	920,834
38	Northern Shan States	334,649	107,971	98,146	128,532	299,470	97,003	88,117	114,350	19,982	6,820	9,795	3,367	268,516
39	Southern Shan States	632,464	199,049	189,658	243,757	584,182	184,229	175,365	224,588	17,450	4,886	5,053	7,511	535,681
40	Chin Hills ...	117,004	35,274	36,685	45,045	116,892	35,222	36,684	44,993	218	107	65	46	116,637

Occupations. Details by Districts.

Ordinary Cultivators — Workers — Males	Ordinary Cultivators — Workers — Females	Ordinary Cultivators — Dependents	Sub-group 2(a), Cultivating Owners — Total Workers and Dependents	Sub-group 2(a) — Workers — Males	Sub-group 2(a) — Workers — Females	Sub-group 2(a) — Dependents	Sub-group 2(b), Cultivating Tenants — Total Workers and Dependents	Sub-group 2(b) — Workers — Males	Sub-group 2(b) — Workers — Females	Sub-group 2(b) — Dependents	Sub-group 2(c), *Taungya* Cultivators — Total Workers and Dependents	Sub-group 2(c) — Workers — Males	Sub-group 2(c) — Workers — Females	Sub-group 2(c) — Dependents	Group 4, Farm Servants and Field Labourers — Total Workers and Dependents	Group 4 — Workers — Males	Group 4 — Workers — Females	Group 4 — Dependents	Serial No.
15	16	17	18	19	20	21	22	23	24	25	26	27	28	29	30	31	32	33	
1,858,632	**1,559,824**	**2,796,698**	**3,810,610**	**1,140,684**	**980,589**	**1,689,337**	**1,599,331**	**460,354**	**369,597**	**769,380**	**805,212**	**257,594**	**309,638**	**237,981**	**1,647,950**	**516,415**	**395,944**	**735,591**	
1,567,540	**1,288,518**	**2,438,262**	**3,274,909**	**974,041**	**818,505**	**1,482,363**	**1,542,972**	**441,141**	**353,942**	**747,889**	**476,439**	**152,358**	**116,071**	**208,010**	**1,605,882**	**502,866**	**381,997**	**721,000**	
139,155	**106,545**	**234,077**	**272,317**	**75,453**	**60,050**	**136,814**	**143,241**	**40,126**	**32,834**	**70,281**	**64,219**	**23,576**	**13,662**	**26,982**	**181,751**	**46,029**	**30,172**	**45,551**	
76,622	56,613	128,310	145,866	40,215	32,903	72,748	86,007	26,476	15,348	44,185	29,670	9,031	8,362	11,577	104,436	40,787	24,701	38,948	1
7,072	6,853	7,142	171	68	24	79	9,727	10	6,422	3,295	11,169	6,904	407	3,768	2	1	1	..	2
34,127	23,978	64,803	82,078	22,711	15,750	43,577	26,278	7,593	5,622	13,063	14,552	3,823	2,566	8,163	13,708	4,246	4,319	5,143	3
21,334	19,101	33,822	44,202	12,459	11,333	20,410	21,227	6,047	5,448	9,738	8,828	2,828	2,326	3,674	3,605	995	1,150	1,460	4
206,094	**158,705**	**352,414**	**423,717**	**122,039**	**102,625**	**199,053**	**262,134**	**73,334**	**48,274**	**140,526**	**31,362**	**10,781**	**7,806**	**12,825**	**507,772**	**152,290**	**95,157**	**260,326**	
1,083	246	1,403	1,722	680	199	843	1,002	399	46	557	8	4	1	3	640	265	31	344	5
39,160	22,594	90,054	63,813	17,011	11,386	35,336	85,427	21,284	10,796	53,347	2,568	785	412	1,371	104,644	58,697	22,410	113,537	6
57,028	52,874	83,820	125,724	36,358	35,164	54,202	61,473	18,619	15,988	26,866	6,525	2,051	1,722	2,752	125,695	36,728	36,692	52,275	7
44,336	25,014	92,083	83,377	22,023	13,144	47,610	73,816	20,182	10,888	42,746	4,240	1,531	982	1,727	141,307	44,142	20,881	76,284	8
64,487	57,977	85,054	149,081	45,287	42,732	61,062	40,416	12,850	10,556	17,010	18,021	6,350	4,689	6,982	45,487	12,458	15,143	17,886	9
245,900	**191,724**	**360,123**	**462,114**	**144,274**	**113,919**	**203,921**	**305,765**	**91,409**	**71,600**	**142,756**	**29,868**	**10,217**	**6,205**	**13,446**	**477,270**	**150,197**	**124,786**	**200,287**	
53,120	38,923	87,455	116,192	35,215	24,883	56,094	56,110	14,758	12,650	28,702	7,196	3,147	1,390	2,659	123,947	38,426	37,530	47,991	10
68,475	67,771	92,554	150,798	45,705	45,411	59,682	70,236	20,599	19,946	29,691	7,766	2,171	2,414	3,181	134,294	38,687	42,648	52,959	11
52,330	39,014	75,924	83,466	25,774	19,668	38,024	78,965	24,503	18,657	35,835	4,837	2,053	689	2,095	71,735	24,471	14,333	32,931	12
43,225	29,719	55,161	70,730	24,507	17,480	28,743	47,739	15,987	10,595	21,157	9,637	2,732	1,644	5,261	65,196	18,673	18,000	28,523	13
28,749	16,297	49,029	40,928	13,073	6,477	21,378	52,715	15,562	9,752	27,401	432	124	68	250	82,098	29,940	12,275	39,883	14
215,470	**160,097**	**389,902**	**425,782**	**123,454**	**96,736**	**215,592**	**165,503**	**45,685**	**28,099**	**91,729**	**164,184**	**46,332**	**35,262**	**82,991**	**229,872**	**71,242**	**39,441**	**129,289**	
50,762	34,688	100,105	77,539	21,966	13,986	41,587	58,474	15,270	9,641	33,563	49,542	13,526	11,061	24,955	61,271	16,849	13,607	30,815	15
10,872	6,139	22,388	11,393	2,605	1,283	7,415	935	286	90	559	27,071	7,891	4,766	14,414	2,242	940	278	1,024	16
63,506	49,520	111,578	153,235	44,008	36,781	72,447	40,350	10,976	6,705	22,669	31,018	8,522	6,034	16,462	90,787	29,951	12,650	48,186	17
52,455	40,057	90,583	112,039	31,587	24,734	55,778	41,786	12,439	7,919	21,028	23,610	8,489	7,404	13,717	56,217	18,406	9,623	28,188	18
20,778	15,939	38,257	42,031	11,705	10,448	19,878	18,070	4,643	2,406	11,021	14,883	4,430	3,085	7,368	12,439	2,808	1,375	8,256	19
17,097	13,754	27,041	39,544	11,553	9,504	18,487	6,283	2,071	1,338	2,879	12,060	3,473	2,912	5,675	6,916	2,288	1,908	2,720	20
235,499	**201,260**	**388,454**	**535,829**	**153,892**	**130,173**	**249,764**	**231,511**	**64,445**	**56,503**	**110,563**	**57,873**	**17,162**	**12,584**	**28,127**	**55,301**	**14,916**	**26,237**	**14,248**	
48,083	33,374	90,754	110,883	30,919	22,031	57,933	31,316	28,880	5,800	16,627	30,012	8,284	5,534	16,194	11,076	2,617	6,145	2,314	21
75,492	69,858	123,762	168,438	48,687	43,220	76,531	96,220	75,298	25,816	45,106	4,454	1,507	822	2,125	12,476	3,013	4,118	5,345	22
50,525	39,489	76,821	91,562	27,668	22,196	41,598	63,602	18,998	14,426	30,178	11,671	3,859	2,867	4,945	12,202	3,171	5,276	3,755	23
61,399	58,539	97,117	164,946	46,618	44,726	73,602	40,373	11,269	10,452	18,652	11,736	3,512	3,361	4,863	19,547	6,115	10,698	2,734	24
117,747	**100,591**	**154,123**	**228,924**	**68,256**	**58,983**	**101,685**	**60,070**	**15,529**	**14,263**	**30,278**	**83,467**	**33,962**	**27,345**	**22,160**	**51,826**	**17,976**	**15,896**	**17,954**	
24,811	21,978	40,597	63,285	18,250	15,888	29,147	20,672	5,592	5,403	9,677	3,429	969	687	1,773	23,545	7,979	5,420	10,146	25
1,121	*687*	*1,610*	*2,335*	*803*	*492*	*1,040*	*807*	*235*	*147*	*425*	*276*	*83*	*48*	*145*	*1,011*	*361*	*271*	*379*	
14,748	14,500	25,373	33,959	10,075	9,306	14,578	15,457	3,529	3,568	8,360	5,205	1,144	1,626	2,435	7,787	2,975	3,516	1,276	26
23,873	21,549	14,294	14,512	4,346	4,707	5,459	5,268	1,558	528	3,182	39,936	17,969	16,314	5,655	2,416	798	926	692	27
38,029	33,321	61,087	108,161	31,300	27,059	49,802	9,818	2,189	2,280	5,349	14,460	4,540	3,984	5,936	15,076	3,988	4,784	4,304	28
16,286	9,241	12,772	9,007	4,285	2,023	2,699	8,855	2,661	2,484	3,710	20,437	9,340	4,734	6,363	5,002	2,216	1,250	1,536	29
202,433	**196,497**	**274,060**	**438,669**	**140,034**	**123,689**	**174,946**	**213,338**	**56,610**	**64,887**	**91,841**	**20,983**	**5,789**	**7,921**	**7,273**	**77,459**	**20,989**	**27,392**	**29,078**	
77,488	73,461	88,362	188,850	65,037	54,926	68,887	47,209	11,694	16,953	18,562	3,252	757	1,582	913	18,471	5,300	6,485	6,686	30
48,231	47,729	75,235	98,976	30,515	28,125	40,336	64,212	16,766	15,490	31,956	8,007	950	4,124	2,943	33,316	8,401	11,228	13,687	31
48,822	46,091	70,435	81,763	25,942	19,519	36,302	32,945	22,779	26,375	33,791	640	101	197	342	14,129	3,993	5,268	4,868	32
27,892	29,216	40,028	69,080	18,540	21,119	29,421	18,972	5,371	6,059	7,552	9,084	3,981	2,028	3,075	11,543	3,295	4,412	3,837	33
205,242	**172,099**	**285,109**	**477,557**	**146,629**	**130,320**	**200,588**	**161,410**	**54,008**	**37,482**	**69,928**	**24,483**	**4,600**	**5,287**	**14,396**	**84,631**	**29,227**	**20,927**	**30,487**	
19,572	15,053	24,155	39,436	13,458	9,837	16,141	17,966	5,909	4,497	7,560	1,378	205	719	454	18,889	6,637	5,627	6,575	34
50,520	39,232	55,938	116,260	37,608	34,677	43,885	22,756	11,254	3,399	8,103	6,674	1,568	1,156	3,950	19,631	9,253	4,359	6,019	35
56,939	36,119	99,594	120,128	38,669	26,082	64,437	48,916	15,861	7,227	25,828	14,608	2,409	2,870	9,329	26,772	8,476	5,539	12,757	36
78,211	82,695	105,422	192,735	56,814	59,794	76,125	71,772	20,979	22,359	28,434	1,823	418	542	663	19,399	4,871	7,392	7,136	37
291,092	**271,306**	**358,436**	**525,701**	**166,643**	**162,084**	**206,974**	**56,359**	**19,213**	**15,655**	**21,491**	**328,774**	**105,236**	**92,567**	**129,971**	**42,067**	**12,849**	**12,947**	**16,571**	
86,318	76,600	105,598	126,940	38,848	42,487	45,605	18,281	6,593	4,453	7,235	123,295	40,877	20,560	52,758	10,972	3,865	1,722	5,385	38
169,665	158,088	207,928	292,196	92,697	82,994	116,505	38,016	12,612	11,189	14,215	205,469	64,356	63,905	77,208	31,051	9,678	12,224	9,249	39
35,109	36,618	44,910	116,565	35,098	36,603	44,864	62	8	13	41	10	3	2	5	44	6	1	37	40

Serial No.	DISTRICT OR STATE.	SUB-ORDER I (b)—GROWERS OF SPECIAL PRODUCTS AND MARKET GARDENING. Total Workers and Dependents.	Actual Workers. Total. Males.	Actual Workers. Total. Females.	Actual Workers. Partially Agriculturist. Males.	Actual Workers. Partially Agriculturist. Females.	Dependents.	GROUP 6, FRUIT, FLOWER, VEGETABLE, BETEL, VINE, AND ARECA NUT, GROWERS. Total Workers and Dependents.	Actual Workers. Total. Males.	Actual Workers. Total. Females.	Actual Workers. Partially Agriculturists. Males.	Actual Workers. Partially Agriculturists. Females.	Dependents.
	1	34	35	36	37	38	39	40	41	42	43	44	45
	Provincial Total ...	238,511	68,447	68,274	4,338	6,628	101,790	232,294	64,599	68,085	4,438	6,622	99,610
	Burma Proper ...	178,797	51,511	48,119	2,856	3,036	79,167	172,594	47,663	47,944	2,856	3,036	76,987
	Arakan Division ...	10,263	3,489	2,770	64	28	3,904	10,263	3,489	2,770	64	28	3,904
1	Akyab	7,283	2,700	1,831	54	28	2,752	7,283	2,700	1,821	54	28	2,752
2	Northern Arakan ...	7	4	1	...	...	2	7	4	1	...	...	2
3	Kyaukpyu ...	1,687	402	575	10	...	710	1,687	402	575	10	...	710
4	Sandoway ...	1,186	383	363	...	...	440	1,186	383	363	...	...	440
	Pegu Division ...	39,073	12,408	9,494	291	526	17,171	37,436	11,535	9,466	291	526	16,435
5	City of Rangoon ...	2,481	1,718	105	...	263	658	2,481	1,718	105	...	263	658
6	Hanthawaddy ...	12,247	3,891	2,527	82	75	5,829	10,614	3,018	2,499	82	75	5,097
7	Tharrawaddy ...	11,837	3,383	3,080	84	108	5,374	11,837	3,383	3,080	84	108	5,374
8	Pegu	2,591	519	723	12	5	1,349	2,591	519	723	12	5	1,349
9	Prome	9,917	2,897	3,059	113	75	3,961	9,913	2,897	3,059	113	75	3,957
	Irrawaddy Division ...	47,635	14,357	13,412	610	860	19,866	47,569	14,302	13,412	610	860	19,855
10	Bassein	14,332	3,633	4,314	100	34	6,385	14,332	3,633	4,314	100	34	6,385
11	Henzada ...	20,718	6,790	5,967	378	646	7,961	20,718	6,790	5,967	378	646	7,961
12	Myaungmya ...	5,361	1,700	1,354	64	41	2,307	5,361	1,700	1,354	64	41	2,307
13	Ma-ubin	6,163	1,924	1,604	51	139	2,635	6,097	1,869	1,604	51	139	2,614
14	Pyapôn	1,061	310	173	17	...	578	1,061	310	173	17	...	578
	Tenasserim Division ...	38,408	11,424	8,219	736	382	18,765	33,982	8,514	8,072	736	382	17,327
15	Toungoo	8,837	2,116	2,407	364	293	4,314	8,837	2,116	2,407	364	293	4,314
16	Salween	557	193	127	...	21	237	557	193	127	...	21	237
17	Thatôn	10,092	2,925	1,755	131	20	5,412	10,091	2,925	1,754	131	20	5,412
18	Amherst	9,706	2,947	1,927	182	31	4,832	8,845	2,553	1,875	182	31	4,417
19	Tavoy	3,157	709	829	48	17	1,619	3,157	709	829	48	17	1,619
20	Mergui	6,059	2,534	1,174	11	...	2,351	2,436	18	1,080	11	...	1,338
	Magwe Division ...	7,158	1,712	2,030	58	12	3,426	7,144	1,703	2,030	58	12	3,411
21	Thayetmyo ...	1,525	392	277	6	...	856	1,517	388	277	6	..	852
22	Pakôkku	1,350	316	484	7	1	550	1,350	316	484	7	1	550
23	Minbu	3,014	675	874	40	6	1,465	3,014	675	874	40	6	1,465
24	Magwe	1,269	329	395	5	5	545	1,263	324	395	5	5	544
	Mandalay Division ...	13,333	3,531	3,895	409	430	5,907	13,332	3,530	3,895	409	420	5,907
25	Mandalay (including City).	4,991	1,774	1,536	105	78	1,681	4,991	1,774	1,536	105	78	1,681
	Mandalay City ...	*556*	*172*	*184*	...	...	*200*	*556*	*172*	*184*	...	...	*200*
26	Bhamo	2,260	514	702	194	82	1,044	2,260	514	702	194	82	1,044
27	Myitkyina ...	895	278	79	13	1	538	895	278	79	13	1	538
28	Katha	1,689	308	515	36	43	866	1,688	307	515	36	43	866
29	Ruby Mines ...	3,498	657	1,063	61	216	1,778	3,498	657	1,063	61	216	1,778
	Sagaing Division ...	11,925	2,368	4,370	435	388	5,177	11,925	2,368	4,370	435	388	5,177
30	Shwebo	1,173	190	306	35	28	677	1,173	190	306	35	28	677
31	Sagaing	2,925	715	1,390	63	253	820	2,925	715	1,390	63	253	820
32	Lower Chindwin ...	1,523	319	459	63	55	745	1,523	319	459	63	55	745
33	Upper Chindwin ...	6,294	1,144	2,215	274	52	2,935	6,294	1,144	2,215	274	52	2,935
	Meiktila Division ...	11,112	2,222	3,909	253	420	4,961	11,112	2,222	3,909	253	420	4,961
34	Kyauksè	2,190	592	633	144	72	965	2,190	592	633	144	72	965
35	Meiktila	3,070	343	1,421	20	292	1,306	3,070	343	1,421	20	292	1,306
36	Yamèthin ...	2,714	734	522	60	23	1,458	2,714	734	522	60	23	1,458
37	Myingyan ...	3,138	553	1,353	29	33	1,232	3,138	553	1,353	29	33	1,232
	Specially Administered Territories.	59,714	16,936	20,155	1,482	3,592	21,623	59,700	16,936	20,141	1,482	3,586	21,623
38	Northern Shan States	30,568	8,885	9,257	334	1,100	12,426	30,568	8,885	9,257	334	1,100	12,426
39	Southern Shan States	29,118	8,035	10,897	1,148	2,492	10,186	29,104	8,035	10,883	1,148	2,486	10,186
40	Chin Hills ...	28	16	1	...	...	11	28	16	1	...	...	11

Occupations. Details by Districts.

SUB-ORDER I (c)—FORESTRY.						GROUP 7, FOREST OFFICERS, RANGERS, GUARDS, ETC.						GROUP 8, WOODCUTTERS, FIREWOOD, LAC, CUTCH AND RUBBER COLLECTORS, AND CHARCOAL BURNERS.						
Total Workers and Dependents.	Actual Workers. Total.		Actual Workers. Partially Agriculturist.		Dependents.	Total Workers and Dependents.	Actual Workers. Total.		Actual Workers. Partially Agriculturist.		Dependents.	Total Workers and Dependents.	Actual Workers. Total.		Actual Workers. Partially Agriculturist.		Dependents.	
	Males.	Females.	Males.	Females.			Males.	Females.	Males.	Females.			Males.	Females.	Males.	Females.		Serial No.
46	47	48	49	50	51	52	53	54	55	56	57	58	59	60	61	62	63	
42,765	12,507	10,599	511	586	19,659	5,116	1,626	134	42	6	3,256	37,649	10,881	10,465	469	580	16,403	
40,504	11,824	10,171	455	548	18,509	4,817	1,478	130	23	6	3,209	35,687	10,346	10,041	432	542	15,300	
834	207	221	12	8	406	173	49	32	...	5	92	661	158	189	12	3	314	
517	125	128	...	3	264	94	34	...	...	...	60	423	91	128	...	3	204	1
2	2	...	...	...	...	2	2	...	...	...	...	...	...	...	...	...	...	2
276	71	90	12	5	115	54	8	31	...	5	15	222	63	59	12	...	100	3
39	9	3	...	...	27	33	5	1	...	...	17	16	4	2	...	...	10	4
6,933	2,020	1,181	23	25	3,742	947	292	42	3	1	623	5,986	1,728	1,139	20	24	3,119	
224	126	...	...	...	98	101	50	...	...	...	51	123	76	...	...	...	47	5
1,371	405	160	9	...	806	181	40	...	1	...	141	1,190	365	160	8	...	665	6
1,007	398	125	4	15	484	341	95	33	1	1	213	666	303	92	3	14	271	7
2,951	816	371	6	3	1,764	199	71	2	1	...	126	2,752	745	369	5	3	1,638	8
1,380	265	525	4	7	590	125	36	7	...	...	82	1,255	229	518	4	7	508	9
11,383	3,706	2,961	111	172	4,726	207	37	13	...	...	157	11,176	3,669	2,948	111	172	4,569	
3,081	1,437	391	38	2	1,253	62	3	8	...	...	51	3,019	1,434	383	38	2	1,202	10
5,328	1,265	2,150	41	126	1,913	103	23	3	...	...	77	5,225	1,242	2,147	41	126	1,836	11
843	399	68	...	4	376	30	10	2	...	...	18	813	389	66	...	4	358	12
405	128	100	32	40	177	1	1	...	...	...	...	404	127	100	32	40	177	13
1,726	477	252	...	...	997	11	...	...	...	...	11	1,715	477	252	...	...	986	14
5,532	1,708	588	32	28	3,036	1,381	407	20	5	...	964	4,151	1,301	568	27	28	2,072	
2,391	726	320	21	24	1,345	609	85	2	1	...	528	1,782	641	318	20	24	823	15
140	30	...	...	...	110	69	12	...	...	...	57	71	18	...	...	...	53	16
943	221	59	5	...	663	212	84	7	...	...	121	731	137	52	5	...	542	17
1,587	526	176	6	4	885	418	196	1	4	...	221	1,169	330	175	2	4	664	18
172	34	6	...	...	132	57	23	...	...	...	34	115	11	6	...	...	98	19
399	171	27	...	...	101	16	7	...	...	...	9	283	164	27	...	...	92	20
2,591	806	514	6	11	1,272	598	172	6	1	...	410	1,993	634	508	5	11	862	
656	229	118	...	...	309	112	14	2	...	...	96	544	215	116	...	...	213	21
989	343	174	...	...	472	173	57	...	...	...	116	816	286	174	...	...	356	22
562	159	128	5	3	275	162	55	...	...	...	107	400	104	128	5	3	168	23
384	75	94	1	8	215	151	46	4	1	...	101	233	29	90	...	8	114	24
4,806	1,458	1,605	135	84	1,743	543	186	25	...	...	332	4,263	1,272	1,580	135	84	1,411	
2,061	337	874	83	60	850	69	7	22	...	...	40	1,992	330	852	83	60	810	25
439	*124*	*133*	...	...	*182*	*54*	*7*	*22*	...	...	*25*	*385*	*117*	*111*	...	...	*157*	
1,284	789	233	12	...	268	80	39	1	...	...	40	1,204	744	232	12	...	228	26
60	23	...	...	...	37	50	14	...	...	...	36	10	9	...	...	...	1	27
672	195	136	...	6	341	212	73	2	...	...	137	460	122	134	...	6	204	28
729	120	362	40	18	247	132	53	...	...	...	79	597	67	362	40	18	168	29
5,364	1,076	2,272	56	161	2,016	565	177	1	7	...	387	4,799	899	2,271	49	161	1,629	
690	145	319	...	4	226	39	19	...	...	...	20	651	126	319	...	4	206	30
1,376	357	567	13	90	452	154	11	...	2	...	143	1,222	346	567	11	90	309	31
2,061	213	1,133	2	61	715	86	42	1	1	...	43	1,975	171	1,132	1	61	672	32
1,237	361	253	41	6	623	286	105	...	4	...	181	951	256	253	37	6	442	33
3,061	853	829	80	59	1,279	403	158	1	7	...	244	2,658	695	828	73	59	1,035	
106	27	3	6	...	76	29	18	...	6	...	11	77	9	3	...	...	65	34
665	77	226	26	15	362	26	12	...	...	...	14	639	65	226	26	15	348	35
1,572	611	332	38	...	629	328	108	1	1	...	219	1,244	503	331	37	...	410	36
718	138	268	10	44	312	20	20	...	...	...	...	698	118	268	10	44	312	37
2,261	683	428	56	38	1,150	299	148	4	19	...	147	1,962	535	424	37	38	1,003	
461	279	35	13	...	147	38	1	4	...	...	33	423	278	31	13	...	114	38
1,800	404	393	43	38	1,003	261	147	...	19	...	114	1,539	257	393	24	38	889	39
...	...	...	...	...	...	...	...	...	...	...	...	...	...	...	...	...	...	40

Serial No.	DISTRICT OR STATE.	SUB-ORDER 1 (d)—RAISING OF FARM STOCK. Total Workers and Dependents.	Actual Workers. Total. Males.	Actual Workers. Total. Females.	Actual Workers. Partially Agriculturist. Males.	Actual Workers. Partially Agriculturist. Females.	Dependents.	GROUP 9, CATTLE AND BUFFALO BREEDERS AND KEEPERS. Total Workers and Dependents.	Actual Workers. Total. Males.	Actual Workers. Total. Females.	Actual Workers. Partially Agriculturist. Males.	Actual Workers. Partially Agriculturist. Females.	Dependents.
	1	64	65	66	67	68	69	70	71	72	73	74	75
	Provincial Total ...	1,05,944	50,884	19,109	2,091	1,539	35,951	2,645	1,333	276	130	15	1,036
	Burma Proper ...	84,353	42,663	15,369	1,312	1,182	26,321	1,985	970	204	36	12	811
	Arakan Division ...	7,992	4,379	1,490	48	4	2,123	22	1	12	...	4	9
1	Akyab ...	6,141	3,029	1,218	46	...	1,894	...	...	...	...	...	...
2	Northern Arakan ...	3	2	1	...	...	...	...	...	...	...	...	...
3	Kyaukpyu ...	609	366	107	2	4	136	22	1	12	...	4	9
4	Sandoway ...	1,239	982	164	...	...	93	...	...	...	...	...	...
	Pegu Division ..	16,321	10,850	1,190	95	42	4,281	798	561	14	9	1	223
5	City of Rangoon ...	265	188	7	1	...	70	6	2	2	...	...	2
6	Hanthawaddy ...	8,009	4,903	507	61	27	2,599	508	333	3	9	...	172
7	Tharrawaddy ...	2,878	2,286	217	10	12	375	147	125	2	...	1	20
8	Pegu	5,710	2,519	260	18	3	931	89	54	7	...	...	28
9	Prome	1,459	954	199	5	...	306	48	47	...	...	...	1
	Irrawaddy Division ...	10,788	6,889	1,301	75	37	2,598	73	45	...	2	...	28
10	Bassein	3,382	2,077	550	26	5	755	5	4	...	...	...	1
11	Henzada ...	3,800	2,875	368	34	25	557	54	32	...	...	...	22
12	Myaungmya ...	1,077	492	145	2	...	440	1	1	...	...	...	...
13	Ma-ubin ...	1,323	691	158	12	7	474	13	8	...	2	...	5
14	Pyapôn	1,206	754	80	1	...	372	...	...	...	...	...	...
	Tenasserim Division ...	8,588	4,893	928	111	13	2,777	54	15	4	...	...	35
15	Toungoo ...	1,857	1,144	236	20	5	477	...	...	...	...	...	...
16	Salween ...	114	76	4	...	...	34	...	...	...	...	...	...
17	Thatôn	3,035	1,487	410	23	1	1,138	54	15	4	...	...	35
18	Amherst ...	2,258	1,388	145	46	7	785	...	...	...	...	...	...
19	Tavoy	1,042	608	98	22	..	336	...	...	...	...	...	...
20	Mergui	282	190	25	...	...	67	...	...	...	...	...	...
	Magwe Division ...	7,844	3,659	2,088	95	13	2,097	302	67	74	1	1	162
21	Thayetmyo ..	1,097	300	317	2	...	480	227	56	40	...	...	131
22	Pakôkku ...	2,967	1,321	837	2	1	809	22	1	10	...	...	11
23	Minbu	2,756	1,537	693	72	9	526	14	...	10	...	1	4
24	Magwe	1,024	501	241	19	3	282	39	10	14	1	...	15
	Mandalay Division ...	6,182	2,469	1,071	261	67	2,642	84	21	5	...	...	58
25	Mandalay (including City).	2,033	1,069	224	48	18	740	81	21	5	...	...	55
	Mandalay City ...	*543*	*208*	70	...	...	*265*	79	*21*	5	...	...	53
26	Bhamo	687	284	74	35	11	329	...	...	...	...	...	...
27	Myitkyina ...	729	407	62	100	1	260	5	...	...	...	...	3
28	Katha	1,274	361	315	38	12	595	...	...	...	...	...	...
29	Ruby Mines ...	1,459	348	393	40	25	718	...	...	...	...	...	...
	Sagaing Division ...	13,202	4,445	3,784	263	428	4,972	88	...	53	...	5	35
30	Shwebo	3,238	897	1,114	12	33	1,227	...	...	...	...	...	...
31	Sagaing	4,172	1,654	1,204	75	249	1,314	28	...	11	...	2	17
32	Lower Chindwin ...	3,845	1,158	1,182	58	127	1,511	...	...	...	...	...	...
33	Upper Chindwin ...	1,946	742	284	118	19	920	60	...	42	...	3	18
	Meiktila Division ...	13,437	5,079	3,527	364	578	4,831	564	260	42	24	1	262
34	Kyauksè ...	1,841	942	286	86	26	613	...	...	...	...	...	...
35	Meiktila ...	4,212	1,144	1,365	88	498	1,703	564	260	42	24	1	262
36	Yamèthin ..	2,116	876	327	45	4	913	...	...	...	...	...	...
37	Myingyan ...	5,268	2,117	1,549	145	50	1,602	...	...	...	...	...	...
	Specially Administered Territories.	21,591	8,221	3,740	779	357	9,630	660	363	72	94	3	225
38	Northern Shan States	4,150	1,804	737	279	186	1,609	408	335	...	94	..	73
39	Southern Shan States	17,364	6,381	3,003	500	171	7,980	252	28	72	...	3	152
40	Chin Hills ...	77	36	...	...	...	41	...	...	...	...	..	...

Occupations. Details by Districts.

GROUP 10, SHEEP, GOAT AND PIG BREEDERS.						GROUP 12, HERDSMEN, SHEPHERDS, GOATHERDS, ETC.						SUB-ORDER I (e)—RAISING OF SMALL ANIMALS. GROUP 13, RAISING OF POULTRY, BEES, SILKWORMS, ETC.						
Total Workers and Dependents.	ACTUAL WORKERS.				Dependents.	Total Workers and Dependents.	ACTUAL WORKERS.				Dependents.	Total Workers and Dependents	ACTUAL WORKERS.				Dependents.	Serial No.
	Total.		Partially Agriculturist.				Total.		Partially Agriculturist.				Total.		Partially Agriculturist.			
	Males.	Females.	Males.	Females.			Males.	Females.	Males.	Females.			Males.	Females.	Males.	Females.		
76	77	78	79	80	81	82	83	84	85	86	87	88	89	90	91	92	93	
12,232	2,667	2,526	303	280	6,039	91,032	45,884	16,296	1,658	1,244	28,852	1,450	355	522	23	7	572	
9,439	2,689	2,071	146	121	4,679	72,894	39,004	13,083	1,130	1,049	20,807	1,450	365	522	23	7	572	
426	85	122	...	...	219	7,544	4,293	1,356	48	...	1,895	...	...	...	...	...	...	
405	85	104	...	...	216	5,736	2,944	1,114	46	...	1,678	...	...	...	...	...	...	1
...	...	...	...	...	...	3	2	1	...	...	...	...	...	...	...	...	...	2
19	...	16	...	...	3	568	365	79	2	...	124	...	...	...	...	...	...	3
2	...	2	...	...	...	1,237	982	162	...	...	93	...	...	...	...	...	...	4
1,341	427	118	...	...	796	14,182	9,862	1,058	86	41	3,262	949	331	237	23	7	381	
3	2	...	...	...	1	256	184	5	1	...	67	23	14	...	...	...	9	5
877	301	66	...	...	510	6,624	4,269	438	52	27	1,917	471	220	110	6	2	141	6
82	25	8	...	...	49	2,649	2,136	207	10	11	306	1	...	1	...	...	...	7
156	33	18	...	...	105	3,465	2,432	235	18	3	798	329	97	44	17	5	188	8
223	66	26	...	...	131	1,188	841	173	5	...	174	125	...	82	...	...	43	9
931	273	163	...	3	495	9,784	6,571	1,138	73	34	2,075	...	...	...	...	...	...	
406	126	50	...	...	230	2,971	1,947	500	26	5	524	...	...	...	...	...	...	10
221	44	76	...	3	101	3,525	2,799	292	34	22	434	...	...	...	...	...	...	11
117	24	21	...	...	62	959	457	124	2	...	378	...	...	...	...	...	...	12
128	65	5	...	...	58	1,182	618	153	10	7	411	...	...	...	...	...	...	13
59	4	11	...	...	44	1,147	750	69	1	...	328	...	...	...	...	...	...	14
1,025	239	262	1	2	525	7,529	4,539	753	110	11	2,227	78	13	9	...	...	56	
143	22	43	...	...	78	1,714	1,122	193	20	5	399	60	11	6	...	...	43	15
...	...	...	...	...	...	114	76	4	...	...	34	...	...	...	...	...	...	16
281	108	39	1	1	134	2,700	1,364	367	22	...	969	18	2	3	...	...	13	17
384	155	31	...	1	198	1,874	1,233	114	46	6	527	...	...	...	...	...	...	18
177	43	45	...	...	89	865	565	53	21	...	247	...	...	...	...	...	...	19
30	11	3	...	...	16	252	179	22	...	...	51	...	...	...	...	...	...	20
980	236	262	2	...	484	6,560	3,356	1,752	92	12	1,452	4	2	...	...	...	2	
30	4	12	...	...	14	840	240	265	2	...	335	...	...	...	...	...	...	21
675	132	187	1	...	356	2,270	1,188	640	1	1	442	1	1	...	...	...	...	22
154	76	28	...	...	50	2,588	1,461	655	72	8	472	...	...	...	...	...	...	23
123	24	35	1	...	64	862	467	192	17	3	203	3	1	...	...	...	2	24
594	299	77	24	6	218	5,472	2,249	978	237	61	2,245	420	16	276	...	...	128	
184	26	66	...	6	92	1,736	1,029	142	48	12	572	420	16	276	...	...	128	25
144	*27*	*38*	...	...	*79*	*288*	*160*	*16*	...	...	*112*	*420*	*16*	*276*	...	...	*123*	
114	55	...	14	...	59	573	229	74	21	11	270	...	...	...	...	...	...	26
6	...	...	...	...	6	720	407	62	100	1	251	...	...	...	...	...	...	27
58	18	11	...	...	29	1,216	343	307	38	12	566	...	...	...	...	...	...	28
232	100	...	10	...	132	1,227	248	393	30	25	586	...	...	...	...	...	...	29
2,023	727	999	52	110	1,307	10,090	3,728	2,732	211	323	3,620	3	3	...	...	...	...	
204	43	72	...	3	89	3,094	854	1,042	12	30	1,138	...	...	...	...	...	...	30
1,218	409	293	25	27	416	3,026	1,245	900	50	220	881	...	...	...	...	...	...	31
1,607	242	617	27	80	748	2,238	910	565	31	47	763	...	...	...	...	...	...	32
94	25	17	...	...	54	1,792	719	225	118	16	848	3	3	...	...	...	...	33
1,227	423	259	67	...	545	11,743	4,406	2,326	273	577	4,021	5	...	...	...	...	5	
71	29	9	6	...	33	1,770	913	277	80	26	580	...	...	...	...	...	...	34
422	196	53	35	...	173	3,223	688	1,270	29	497	1,265	...	...	...	...	...	...	35
262	59	41	...	...	162	1,854	817	286	45	4	751	5	...	...	...	...	5	36
378	129	66	26	...	177	4,896	1,988	1,483	119	50	1,425	...	...	...	...	...	...	37
2,793	978	455	157	159	2,360	18,138	6,880	3,213	528	195	8,045	...	...	...	...	...	...	
1,834	668	367	129	158	799	1,908	801	370	56	28	737	...	...	...	...	...	...	38
959	310	88	28	1	561	16,153	6,043	2,843	472	167	7,267	...	...	...	...	...	...	39
...	...	...	...	...	...	77	36	...	...	...	41	...	...	...	...	...	...	40

Serial No.	DISTRICT OR STATE.	ORDER II, FISHING AND HUNTING. Total Workers and Dependents.	Actual Workers. Total. Males.	Actual Workers. Total. Females.	Actual Workers. Partially Agriculturist. Males.	Actual Workers. Partially Agriculturist. Females.	Dependents.	GROUP 14, FISHING. Total Workers and Dependents.	Actual Workers. Total. Males.	Actual Workers. Total. Females.	Actual Workers. Partially Agriculturist. Males.	Actual Workers. Partially Agriculturist. Females.	Dependents.
	1	94	95	96	97	98	99	100	101	102	103	104	105
	Provincial Total ...	152,004	48,730	27,677	2,062	1,212	75,597	151,601	48,475	27,676	2,060	1,212	75,450
	Burma Proper ...	146,370	47,013	26,551	1,857	1,100	72,806	146,272	46,965	26,550	1,857	1,100	72,757
	Arakan Division ...	11,785	3,800	2,649	30	3	5,336	11,782	3,800	2,649	30	3	5,333
1	Akyab ...	5,531	1,807	1,893	14	3	1,831	5,528	1,807	1,893	14	3	1,828
2	Northern Arakan ...	2	2	...	...	...	...	2	2	...	...	...	...
3	Kyaukpyu ...	4,267	1,288	610	16	...	2,369	4,267	1,288	610	16	...	2,369
4	Sandoway ...	1,985	703	146	...	...	1,136	1,985	703	146	...	...	1,136
	Pegu Division ...	25,015	7,850	5,527	130	134	11,638	24,988	7,834	5,527	130	134	11,627
5	City of Rangoon ...	784	591	14	1	...	179	782	589	14	1	...	179
6	Hanthawaddy ...	5,854	1,889	818	39	16	3,147	5,838	1,878	818	39	16	3,142
7	Tharrawaddy ..	9,278	2,646	2,360	65	83	4,272	9,278	2,646	2,360	65	83	4,272
8	Pegu ...	5,076	1,823	742	21	1	2,511	5,067	1,820	742	21	1	2,505
9	Prome ...	4,023	901	1,593	4	34	1,529	4,023	901	1,593	4	34	1,529
	Irrawaddy Division ...	46,542	14,952	7,808	317	459	23,782	46,516	14,945	7,808	317	459	23,763
10	Bassein ...	6,532	2,287	1,174	18	10	3,071	6,532	2,287	1,174	18	10	3,071
11	Henzada ...	6,684	2,267	985	60	79	3,431	6,684	2,267	985	60	79	3,432
12	Myaungmya ...	6,841	2,275	1,077	136	6	3,480	6,829	2,275	1,077	136	6	3,477
13	Ma-ubin ...	19,017	5,728	3,984	67	364	9,305	19,017	5,728	3,984	67	364	9,305
14	Pyapôn ...	7,468	2,395	588	36	...	4,485	7,454	2,388	588	36	...	4,478
	Tenasserim Division ...	24,680	8,414	3,685	259	26	12,581	24,661	8,403	3,685	259	26	12,573
15	Toungoo ...	1,644	589	212	8	4	843	1,638	586	212	8	4	840
16	Salween ..	36	24	...	...	...	12	36	24	...	...	...	12
17	Thatôn ...	1,610	565	248	6	1	797	1,608	563	248	6	1	797
18	Amherst ...	2,663	1,114	167	75	11	1,382	2,657	1,111	167	75	11	1,379
19	Tavoy ...	4,774	1,334	568	165	6	2,872	4,769	1,331	568	165	6	2,870
20	Mergui ...	13,953	4,788	2,490	5	4	6,675	13,953	4,788	2,490	5	4	6,675
	Magwe Division ...	8,085	2,467	1,412	41	12	4,206	8,080	2,466	1,412	41	12	4,202
21	Thayetmyo ...	2,283	716	295	...	2	1,272	2,282	715	295	...	2	1,272
22	Pakôkku ...	1,776	546	358	1	...	872	1,776	546	358	1	...	872
23	Minbu ...	2,713	818	495	25	1	2,400	2,710	818	495	25	1	1,397
24	Magwe ...	1,313	387	264	15	9	662	1,312	387	264	15	9	661
	Mandalay Division ...	13,416	4,558	1,924	409	79	6,934	13,412	4,556	1,924	409	79	6,932
25	Mandalay (including City).	6,642	2,083	1,006	257	44	3,553	6,642	2,083	1,006	257	44	3,553
	Mandalay City ...	*795*	*251*	*101*	...	...	*443*	*795*	*251*	*101*	...	...	*443*
26	Bhamo ...	1,056	757	66	36	...	233	1,056	757	66	36	...	233
27	Myitkyina ...	865	362	137	8	1	366	865	362	137	8	1	366
28	Katha ...	3,045	808	356	31	15	1,881	3,042	807	356	31	15	1,879
29	Ruby Mines ...	1,808	548	359	77	19	901	1,807	547	359	77	19	901
	Sagaing Division ...	9,991	3,285	2,174	546	316	4,532	9,989	3,284	2,173	546	316	4,532
30	Shwebo ...	1,681	324	476	43	46	1,081	1,881	324	476	43	46	1,081
31	Sagaing ...	3,297	1,342	590	131	114	1,365	3,295	1,341	589	131	114	1,365
32	Lower Chindwin ...	2,731	692	842	111	152	1,198	2,732	692	842	111	152	1,198
33	Upper Chindwin ...	2,081	987	266	261	4	888	2,081	927	266	261	4	888
	Meiktila Division ...	6,856	1,687	1,372	125	71	3,797	6,844	1,677	1,372	125	71	3,795
34	Kyauksè ...	903	184	306	37	14	413	903	184	306	37	14	413
35	Meiktila ...	2,243	305	572	15	51	1,366	2,243	305	572	15	51	1,366
36	Yamèthin ...	637	249	104	19	2	344	683	247	104	19	2	332
37	Myingyan ...	3,023	949	390	54	4	1,684	3,015	941	390	54	4	1,684
	Specially Administered Territories.	5,634	1,717	1,126	205	112	2,791	5,329	1,510	1,126	203	112	2,693
38	Northern Shan States	1,086	495	183	...	29	408	901	391	183	...	29	327
39	Southern Shan States	4,541	1,216	943	205	83	2,382	4,421	1,113	943	203	83	2,365
40	Chin Hills ...	7	6	...	...	...	1	7	6	...	...	...	1

Occupations. Details by Districts.

	GROUP 15, HUNTING.						ORDER III, MINES.						GROUP 16, COAL MINES AND PETROLEUM WELLS.						
	Total Workers and Dependents.	ACTUAL WORKERS. Total. Males.	ACTUAL WORKERS. Total. Females.	ACTUAL WORKERS. Partially Agriculturist. Males.	ACTUAL WORKERS. Partially Agriculturist. Females.	Dependents.	Total workers and Dependents.	ACTUAL WORKERS. Total. Males.	ACTUAL WORKERS. Total. Females.	ACTUAL WORKERS. Partially Agriculturist. Males.	ACTUAL WORKERS. Partially Agriculturist. Females.	Dependents.	Total Workers and Dependents.	ACTUAL WORKERS. Total. Males.	ACTUAL WORKERS. Total. Females.	ACTUAL WORKERS. Partially Agriculturist. Males.	ACTUAL WORKERS. Partially Agriculturist. Females.	Dependents.	Serial No.
	106	107	108	109	110	111	112	113	114	115	116	117	118	119	120	121	122	123	
	403	255	1	2	...	147	9,173	4,682	639	8	23	2,852	3,319	1,879	250	8	1	1,190	
	98	48	1	...	...	49	6,346	3,536	607	8	23	2,203	3,319	1,879	250	8	1	1,190	
	3	...	...	...	...	3	4	1	...	...	...	3	4	1	...	...	...	3	
	3	...	...	...	...	3	...	...	...	...	...	...	...	...	...	...	...	...	1
	...	...	...	...	...	...	...	...	...	...	...	...	...	...	...	...	...	...	2
	...	...	...	...	...	...	4	1	...	...	...	3	4	1	...	...	...	3	3
	...	...	...	...	...	...	...	...	...	...	...	...	...	...	...	...	...	...	4
	27	16	...	...	...	11	68	38	...	...	...	30	4	...	...	...	...	4	
	2	2	...	...	...	...	8	2	...	...	...	6	4	...	...	...	...	4	5
	16	11	...	...	...	5	9	8	...	...	...	1	...	...	...	...	...	...	6
	...	...	...	...	...	...	...	...	...	...	...	...	...	...	...	...	...	...	7
	9	3	...	...	...	6	1	1	...	...	...	...	...	...	...	...	...	...	8
	...	...	...	...	...	...	50	27	...	...	...	23	...	...	...	...	...	...	9
	26	7	...	...	...	19	27	11	...	...	...	16	23	11	...	...	...	12	
	...	...	...	...	...	...	...	...	...	...	...	...	...	...	...	...	...	...	10
	...	...	...	...	...	...	...	...	...	...	...	...	...	...	...	...	...	...	11
	12	...	...	...	...	12	27	11	...	...	...	16	23	11	...	...	...	12	12
	...	...	...	...	...	...	...	...	...	...	...	...	...	...	...	...	...	...	13
	14	7	...	...	...	7	...	...	...	...	...	...	...	...	...	...	...	...	14
	19	11	...	...	...	8	2,403	1,579	58	...	...	766	...	...	...	...	...	...	
	6	3	...	...	...	3	5	1	...	...	...	4	...	...	...	...	...	...	15
	...	...	...	...	...	...	...	...	...	...	...	...	...	...	...	...	...	...	16
	2	2	...	...	...	...	...	...	...	...	...	...	...	...	...	...	...	...	17
	6	3	...	...	...	3	35	14	...	...	...	21	...	...	...	...	...	...	18
	5	3	...	...	...	2	2,106	1,416	45	...	...	645	...	...	...	...	...	...	19
	...	...	...	...	...	...	257	148	13	...	...	96	...	...	...	...	...	...	20
	5	1	...	...	...	4	3,168	1,769	252	...	1	1,147	3,146	1,758	250	...	1	1,138	
	1	1	...	...	...	...	31	20	2	...	...	9	26	19	...	...	...	7	21
	...	...	...	...	...	...	1	...	...	...	...	1	...	...	...	...	...	...	22
	3	...	...	...	...	3	16	10	...	...	...	6	...	...	...	...	...	...	23
	1	...	...	...	...	1	3,120	1,739	250	...	1	1,131	3,120	1,739	250	...	1	1,131	24
	4	2	...	...	...	2	12	4	1	...	...	7	...	...	...	...	...	...	
	...	...	...	...	...	...	11	3	1	...	...	7	...	...	...	...	...	...	25
	...	...	...	...	...	...	*11*	*3*	*1*	...	...	7	...	...	...	...	...	...	
	...	...	...	...	...	...	...	...	...	...	...	...	...	...	...	...	...	...	26
	...	...	...	...	...	...	1	1	...	...	...	...	...	...	...	...	...	...	27
	3	1	...	...	...	2	...	...	...	...	...	...	...	...	...	...	...	...	28
	1	1	...	...	...	...	...	...	...	...	...	...	...	...	...	...	...	...	29
	2	1	1	...	...	...	481	5	294	...	22	182	...	...	...	...	...	...	
	...	...	...	...	...	...	...	...	...	...	...	...	...	...	...	...	...	...	30
	2	1	1	...	...	...	78	...	67	...	21	11	...	...	...	...	...	...	31
	...	...	...	...	...	...	4	4	...	...	...	...	...	...	...	...	...	...	32
	...	...	...	...	...	...	399	1	227	...	1	171	...	...	...	...	...	...	33
	12	10	...	...	...	2	183	129	2	8	...	52	142	109	...	8	...	33	
	...	...	...	...	...	...	142	109	...	8	...	33	142	109	...	8	...	33	34
	...	...	...	...	...	...	2	2	...	...	...	...	...	...	...	...	...	...	35
	4	2	...	...	...	2	...	...	...	...	...	...	...	...	...	...	...	...	36
	8	8	...	...	...	...	39	18	2	...	...	19	...	...	...	...	...	...	37
	305	207	...	2	...	98	2,827	1,146	32	...	...	649	...	...	...	...	...	...	
	185	104	...	...	...	81	2,549	963	29	...	...	557	...	...	...	...	...	...	38
	120	103	...	2	...	17	278	183	3	...	...	92	...	...	...	...	...	...	39
	...	...	...	...	...	...	...	...	...	...	...	...	...	...	...	...	...	...	40

Serial No.	DISTRICT OR STATE.	GROUP 17—MINES AND METALLIC MINERALS. Total Workers and Dependents.	GROUP 17 ACTUAL WORKERS. Total. Males.	GROUP 17 ACTUAL WORKERS. Total. Females.	GROUP 17 ACTUAL WORKERS. Partially Agriculturist. Males.	GROUP 17 ACTUAL WORKERS. Partially Agriculturist. Females.	GROUP 17 Dependents.	ORDER IV (GROUP 18)—OTHER MINERALS. Total Workers and Dependents.	GROUP 18 ACTUAL WORKERS. Total. Males.	GROUP 18 ACTUAL WORKERS. Total. Females.	GROUP 18 ACTUAL WORKERS. Partially Agriculturist. Males.	GROUP 18 ACTUAL WORKERS. Partially Agriculturist. Females.	GROUP 18 Dependents.
	1	124	125	126	127	128	129	130	131	132	133	134	135
	Provincial Total ...	4,854	2,803	389	...	22	1,662	3,896	781	1,267	29	21	1,848
	Burma Proper ...	3,027	1,657	357	...	22	1,013	3,896	781	1,267	29	21	1,848
	Arakan Division ...	...	...	...	...	...	...	...	...	...	...	...	...
1	Akyab	...	...	...	...	...	...	...	...	...	...	...	...
2	Northern Arakan ...	...	...	...	...	...	...	...	...	...	...	...	...
3	Kyaukpyu ...	...	...	...	...	...	...	...	...	...	...	...	...
4	Sandoway ...	...	...	...	...	...	...	...	...	...	...	...	...
	Pegu Division ...	64	38	...	...	...	26	23	15	...	...	...	8
5	City of Rangoon ...	4	2	...	...	...	2	4	4	...	...	...	...
6	Hanthawaddy ...	9	8	...	...	...	1	19	11	...	...	...	8
7	Tharrawaddy ...	...	...	...	...	...	...	...	...	...	...	...	...
8	Pegu	1	1	...	...	...	...	...	...	...	...	...	...
9	Prome	50	27	...	...	...	23	...	...	...	...	...	..
	Irrawaddy Division ...	4	..	...	...	...	4	2	...	...	...	...	2
10	Bassein	...	...	...	...	...	...	2	...	...	...	...	2
11	Henzada ...	...	...	...	...	...	...	...	...	...	...	...	...
12	Myaungmya ...	4	...	...	...	...	4	...	...	...	...	...	...
13	Ma-ubin	...	...	...	...	...	...	...	...	...	...	...	...
14	Pyapôn	...	...	...	...	...	...	...	...	...	...	...	...
	Tenasserim Division	2,403	1,579	58	...	...	766	2	1	...	...	...	1
15	Toungoo ...	5	1	...	...	...	4	...	...	...	...	...	...
16	Salween	...	...	...	...	...	...	...	...	...	...	...	...
17	Thatòn	...	...	...	...	...	...	2	1	...	...	...	1
18	Amherst	35	14	...	...	...	21	...	...	...	...	...	...
19	Tavoy	2,106	1,416	45	...	...	645	...	...	...	...	...	...
20	Mergui	257	148	13	...	...	96	...	...	...	...	...	...
	Magwe Division ...	22	11	2	...	...	9	4	1	...	...	...	3
21	Thayetmyo ...	5	1	2	...	...	2	4	1	...	...	...	3
22	Pakôkku ...	1	...	...	...	...	1	...	...	...	...	...	...
23	Minbu	16	10	...	...	...	6	...	...	...	...	...	...
24	Magwe	...	...	...	...	...	...	...	...	...	...	...	...
	Mandalay Division ...	12	4	1	...	...	7	3,860	759	1,267	27	21	1,834
25	Mandalay (including City).	11	3	1	...	...	7	4	...	...	...	...	4
	Mandalay City ...	*11*	*3*	*1*	...	...	*7*	*4*	...	...	...	...	*4*
26	Bhamo	...	...	...	...	...	...	...	...	...	...	...	...
27	Myitkyina ...	1	1	...	...	...	...	4	4	...	...	...	...
28	Katha	...	...	...	...	...	...	...	...	...	...	...	...
29	Ruby Mines ...	...	...	...	...	...	...	3,852	755	1,267	27	21	1,830
	Sagaing Division ...	481	5	294	...	22	182	1	1	...	...	...	...
30	Shwebo	...	...	...	...	...	...	...	...	...	...	...	...
31	Sagaing	78	...	67	...	21	11	...	...	...	...	...	...
32	Lower Chindwin ...	4	4	...	...	...	...	...	...	...	...	...	...
33	Upper Chindwin ...	399	1	227	...	1	171	1	1	...	...	...	...
	Meiktila Division ...	41	20	2	...	...	19	4	4	...	2	...	...
34	Kyauksè	...	...	...	...	...	...	...	...	...	...	...	...
35	Meiktila	2	2	...	...	...	...	...	...	...	...	...	...
36	Yamèthin ..	...	...	...	...	...	...	4	4	...	2	...	...
37	Myingyan ...	39	18	2	...	...	19	...	...	...	...	...	...
	Specially Administered Territories.	1,827	1,146	32	...	...	649	...	...	...	...	...	...
38	Northern Shan States	1,549	963	29	...	...	557	...	...	...	...	...	...
39	Southern Shan Staest	278	183	3	...	...	92	...	...	...	...	...	...
40	Chin Hills ...	...	...	...	...	...	...	...	...	...	...	...	...

Occupations. Details by Districts.

ORDER V (GROUP 19)—ROCK, SEA, AND MARSH SALT. Total Workers and Dependents.	Actual Workers. Total. Males.	Actual Workers. Total. Females.	Actual Workers. Partially Agriculturist. Males.	Actual Workers. Partially Agriculturist. Females.	Dependents.	ORDER VI—TEXTILES. Total Workers and Dependents.	Actual Workers. Total. Males.	Actual Workers. Total. Females.	Actual Workers. Partially Agriculturist. Males.	Actual Workers. Partially Agriculturist. Females.	Dependents.	GROUP 21—COTTON GINNING, CLEANING, AND PRESSING. Total Workers and Dependents.	Actual Workers. Total. Males.	Actual Workers. Total. Females.	Actual Workers. Partially Agriculturist. Males.	Actual Workers. Partially Agriculturist. Females.	Dependents.	Serial No.
136	137	138	139	140	141	142	143	144	145	146	147	148	149	150	151	152	153	
3,224	953	466	34	24	1,805	155,050	9,123	103,316	147	5,850	42,611	2,282	273	514	95	72	1,296	
3,224	953	466	34	24	1,805	107,075	8,139	68,858	117	4,519	20,078	1,671	273	316	95	72	982	
887	320	129	1	...	448	2,733	936	1,731	...	9	1,066	..	...	...	...	...	...	
9	4	...	...	...	5	2,646	901	1,003	...	4	742	...	...	...	...	...	...	1
...	...	...	...	...	...	...	...	...	...	...	...	...	...	...	...	...	...	2
868	314	117	1	...	437	928	35	596	...	5	297	...	...	...	...	...	...	3
10	2	2	...	...	6	159	...	132	...	...	27	...	...	...	...	...	...	4
259	96	26	1	4	137	10,265	647	7,089	17	71	2,529	1	1	...	...	...	...	
...	...	...	...	...	...	814	108	25	...	...	81	...	...	...	...	...	...	5
259	96	26	1	4	137	2,436	111	1,851	2	12	474	...	...	...	...	...	...	6
...	...	...	...	...	...	693	63	514	...	17	121	...	...	...	...	...	...	7
...	...	...	...	...	...	614	...	493	...	16	121	...	...	...	...	...	...	8
...	...	...	...	...	..	6,303	365	4,206	15	26	1,732	1	1	..	...	...	...	9
1,380	346	193	32	20	841	4,773	188	3,213	...	121	1,372	...	...	...	...	...	...	
585	142	76	22	8	367	807	...	590	...	12	217	...	...	...	...	...	...	10
...	...	...	...	...	...	2,357	105	1,386	..	53	866	...	...	...	...	...	...	11
795	204	117	10	12	474	689	58	529	...	27	182	...	...	...	...	...	...	12
...	...	...	...	...	...	528	53	396	...	29	93	...	...	...	...	...	...	13
...	...	...	...	...	...	398	12	312	...	...	74	...	...	...	...	...	...	14
640	182	89	...	...	369	11,745	670	8,621	1	109	2,454	11	10	...	...	...	1	
...	...	...	...	...	...	1,218	103	788	1	5	327	1	1	...	...	...	...	15
...	...	...	...	...	...	29	...	29	...	...	...	...	...	...	...	...	...	16
179	68	29	...	...	82	2,709	232	2,101	...	3	376	7	7	...	...	...	...	17
194	3	42	...	...	149	2,507	64	1,856	...	24	587	...	...	...	...	...	...	18
218	80	18	...	...	120	5,166	269	3,752	...	77	1,145	..	...	...	...	...	...	19
49	31	...	...	...	18	116	2	95	...	...	19	3	2	...	..	...	1	20
34	...	29	...	...	5	23,028	673	15,572	2	275	6,783	33	7	16	...	...	20	
...	...	...	...	...	...	1,487	67	1,043	...	5	377	2	...	1	..	...	1	21
34	...	29	...	...	5	15,906	332	10,897	...	30	4,677	25	5	15	...	...	5	22
...	...	...	...	...	...	4,147	183	2,766	1	201	1,198	3	1	...	...	...	2	23
...	..	...	...	...	...	1,488	91	866	1	39	531	3	1	...	...	...	2	24
...	...	...	...	...	...	26,384	2,203	10,625	...	641	3,566	32	...	13	...	...	19	
...	...	...	...	...	...	15,178	2,164	9,784	...	582	3,230	32	...	13	...	...	19	25
...	...	...	...	...	...	*8,510*	*1,503*	*5,504*	...	...	*1,503*	*32*	...	*13*	...	...	*19*	
...	...	...	...	...	...	445	...	333	...	36	112	...	...	...	...	...	...	26
...	...	...	...	...	...	118	20	65	...	...	33	...	...	...	...	...	...	27
...	..	...	...	...	...	207	3	145	...	5	59	...	...	...	...	...	...	28
...	...	...	...	...	...	436	16	288	...	21	132	..	...	...	...	...	...	29
26	4	10	...	...	2	21,669	1,843	12,470	2	2,640	7,254	3	3	...	...	...	...	
...	...	...	...	...	...	2,837	247	1,615	1	233	975	...	...	...	...	...	...	30
...	...	...	...	...	...	5,136	1,303	2,436	...	170	1,397	...	...	...	...	...	...	31
4	4	...	...	...	...	12,980	221	7,991	1	2,182	4,768	3	3	...	...	...	...	32
12	...	10	..	...	2	716	72	430	...	57	814	...	...	...	...	...	...	33
8	5	...	...	...	3	15,478	979	9,845	95	648	4,954	1,591	352	287	95	72	952	
...	...	...	...	...	...	1,518	229	957	...	103	332	...	...	...	...	...	...	34
...	...	...	...	...	...	3,695	124	2,524	...	207	1,047	...	...	...	...	...	...	35
8	5	...	...	...	3	1,433	183	827	...	22	423	...	...	...	...	...	...	36
...	...	...	...	...	...	8,832	443	5,237	95	316	5,152	1,591	352	287	95	72	952	37
...	...	...	...	...	...	47,975	984	34,458	30	1,331	12,533	621	...	198	...	...	423	
...	...	...	...	...	...	2,182	...	1,504	...	332	678	16	...	15	...	...	1	38
...	...	..	...	...	...	45,793	984	32,954	30	999	11,855	595	...	183	...	...	418	39
...	...	...	...	...	...	...	...	...	...	...	...	...	...	...	...	...	...	40

Serial No.	DISTRICT OR STATE.	GROUP 22, COTTON SPINNING, SIZING AND WEAVING. Total Workers and Dependents.	Actual Workers. Total. Males.	Actual Workers. Total. Females.	Actual Workers. Partially Agriculturist. Males.	Actual Workers. Partially Agriculturist. Females.	Dependents.	GROUP 24, ROPE, TWINE AND STRING. Total Workers and Dependents.	Actual Workers. Total. Males.	Actual Workers. Total. Females.	Actual Workers. Partially Agriculturist. Males.	Actual Workers. Partially Agriculturist. Females.	Dependents.
	1	154	155	156	157	158	159	160	161	162	163	164	165
	Provincial Total ...	132,737	5,119	91,766	48	5,143	35,782	1,241	418	379	3	22	444
	Burma Proper ...	856,49	4,160	57,714	18	3,879	23,675	1,210	411	367	3	22	432
	Arakan Division ...	3,176	545	1,720	...	9	911	76	38	4	...	...	34
1	Akyab ...	2,101	513	986	...	4	602	68	38	1	...	...	29
2	Northern Arakan ...	...	...	...	...	...	...	...	...	...	...	...	...
3	Kyaukpyu ...	918	32	594	...	5	292	7	...	2	...	...	5
4	Sandoway ...	157	...	130	...	...	27	1	...	1	...	...	...
	Pegu Division ...	6,988	142	5,319	15	60	1,527	357	94	139	2	...	124
5	City of Rangoon ...	23	5	10	...	...	8	55	38	...	...	...	17
6	Hanthawaddy ...	2,274	88	1,764	...	12	422	135	22	73	2	...	42
7	Tharrawaddy ...	629	29	511	...	17	89	66	34	...	...	...	32
8	Pegu ...	614	...	493	...	26	121	...	...	...	...	...	...
9	Prome ...	3,448	20	2,541	15	15	887	101	...	68	...	...	33
	Irrawaddy Division ...	4,010	109	2,856	...	113	1,045	117	79	...	...	...	38
10	Bassein ...	805	...	588	...	10	217	...	...	...	...	...	...
11	Henzada ...	1,598	26	1,033	...	47	539	117	79	...	...	...	38
12	Myaungmya ...	687	38	527	...	27	122	...	...	...	...	...	...
13	Ma-ubin ...	522	33	396	...	29	93	...	...	...	...	...	...
14	Pyapôn ...	398	12	312	...	...	74	...	...	...	...	...	...
	Tenasserim Division ...	9,315	348	7,253	...	32	1,714	126	63	1	...	...	62
15	Toungoo ...	1,141	77	785	..	5	279	34	7	1	...	...	26
16	Salween ...	29	...	29	...	...	...	...	...	...	...	...	...
17	Thatôn ...	2,620	177	2,101	...	3	342	82	48	...	...	...	34
18	Amherst ...	2,490	54	1,855	...	24	581	10	8	...	...	...	2
19	Tavoy ...	2,922	40	2,388	...	...	494	...	...	...	...	...	...
20	Mergui ...	113	...	95	...	...	18	...	...	...	...	...	...
	Magwe Division ...	22,614	622	15,325	2	272	6,667	57	27	8	...	3	22
21	Thayetmyo ...	1,477	64	1,039	...	2	374	8	3	3	...	3	2
22	Pakôkku ...	15,829	312	10,868	...	30	4,649	32	15	4	...	...	13
23	Minbu ...	3,832	156	2,552	1	201	1,124	11	9	1	...	...	1
24	Magwe ...	1,476	90	866	1	39	520	6	...	...	...	...	6
	Mandalay Division ...	6,358	594	4,539	...	289	1,225	90	...	62	...	...	28
25	Mandalay (including City).	5,152	555	3,708	...	227	889	90	...	62	...	...	28
	Mandalay City ...	4,825	506	3,485	...	...	834	90	...	62	...	...	28
26	Bhamo ...	445	...	333	...	36	112	...	...	...	...	...	...
27	Myitkyina ...	118	20	65	...	...	33	...	...	...	...	...	...
28	Katha ...	207	3	145	...	5	59	...	...	...	...	...	...
29	Ruby Mines ...	436	16	288	...	21	132	...	...	...	...	...	...
	Sagaing Division ...	20,464	1,489	12,038	1	2,580	6,937	188	33	101	1	19	54
30	Shwebo ...	2,163	173	1,241	...	184	749	159	27	81	1	8	51
31	Sagaing ...	4,603	1,020	2,377	...	157	1,206	29	6	20	...	11	3
32	Lower Chindwin ...	12,977	218	7,991	1	2,182	4,768	...	...	...	...	...	...
33	Upper Chindwin ...	725	72	439	...	57	214	...	...	...	...	...	...
	Meiktila Division ...	12,724	411	8,674	...	524	3,639	199	77	52	...	...	70
34	Kyauksè ...	730	126	475	...	54	129	...	...	...	...	...	...
35	Meiktila ...	3,695	124	2,524	...	207	1,047	...	...	...	...	...	...
36	Yamèthin ...	1,192	85	777	...	19	330	141	77	...	...	...	64
37	Myingyan ...	7,107	76	4,898	...	244	2,133	58	...	52	...	...	6
	Specially Administered Territories.	47,088	959	34,052	30	1,264	12,077	31	7	12	...	...	12
38	Northern Shan States	1,077	...	1,315	...	265	662	2	...	1	...	...	1
39	Southern Shan States	45,111	959	32,737	30	999	11,415	29	7	11	...	...	11
40	Chin Hills ...	...	...	...	...	...	...	...	...	...	...	...	...

Occupations. Details by Districts.

GROUP 27, SILK SPINNERS AND WEAVERS.						ORDER VII.—HIDES, SKINS, AND HARD MATERIALS FROM THE ANIMAL KINGDOM.						GROUP 35. BONE, IVORY, HORN AND SHELL WORKERS.						
Total Workers and Dependents.	Actual Workers. Total. Males.	Actual Workers. Total. Females.	Actual Workers. Partially Agriculturist. Males.	Actual Workers. Partially Agriculturist. Females.	Dependents.	Total Workers and Dependents.	Actual Workers. Total. Males.	Actual Workers. Total. Females.	Actual Workers. Partially Agriculturist. Males.	Actual Workers. Partially Agriculturist. Females.	Dependents.	Total Workers and Dependents.	Actual Workers. Total. Males.	Actual Workers. Total. Females.	Actual Workers. Partially Agriculturist. Males.	Actual Workers. Partially Agriculturist. Females.	Dependents.	Serial No.
166	167	168	169	170	171	172	173	174	175	176	177	178	179	180	181	182	183	
18,621	3,047	10,616	1	613	4,958	624	232	59	2	...	333	251	71	3	...	...	177	
18,376	3,029	10,420	1	546	4,927	503	183	59	2	...	261	225	71	3	...	...	151	
480	353	16	...	...	111	...	...	...	...	...	...	...	...	...	...	...	...	
477	350	16	...	...	111	...	...	...	...	...	...	...	...	...	...	...	...	1
...	...	...	...	...	...	...	...	...	...	...	...	...	...	...	...	...	...	2
3	3	...	...	...	...	...	...	...	...	...	...	...	...	...	...	...	...	3
...	...	...	...	...	...	...	...	...	...	...	...	...	...	...	...	...	...	4
2,760	344	1,598	...	11	818	56	24	5	...	...	27	21	12	3	...	...	6	
...	...	...	...	...	...	56	24	5	...	...	27	21	12	3	...	...	6	5
7	...	1	...	...	6	...	...	...	...	...	...	...	...	...	...	...	...	6
...	...	...	...	...	...	...	...	...	...	...	...	...	...	...	...	...	...	7
...	...	...	...	...	...	...	...	...	...	...	...	...	...	...	...	...	...	8
2,753	344	1,597	...	11	812	...	...	...	...	...	...	...	...	...	...	...	...	9
644	...	356	...	8	288	25	...	22	...	...	3	...	...	...	...	...	...	
2	...	2	...	2	...	...	...	...	...	...	...	...	...	...	...	...	...	10
640	...	352	...	6	288	...	...	...	...	...	...	...	...	...	...	...	...	11
2	...	2	...	...	...	25	...	22	...	...	3	...	...	...	...	...	...	12
...	...	...	...	...	...	...	...	...	...	...	...	...	...	...	...	...	...	13
...	...	...	...	...	...	...	...	...	...	...	...	...	...	...	...	...	...	14
2,289	249	1,364	1	77	676	78	22	...	...	...	56	78	22	...	...	...	56	
39	18	...	1	...	21	...	...	...	...	...	...	...	...	...	...	...	...	15
...	...	...	...	...	...	...	...	...	...	...	...	...	...	...	...	...	...	16
...	...	...	...	...	...	...	...	...	...	...	...	...	...	...	...	...	...	17
6	2	...	...	...	4	64	22	...	...	...	42	64	22	...	...	...	42	18
2,244	229	1,364	...	77	651	14	...	...	...	...	14	14	...	...	...	...	14	19
...	...	...	...	...	...	...	...	...	...	...	...	...	...	...	...	...	...	20
324	17	223	...	...	84	12	7	...	...	...	5	...	...	...	...	...	...	
...	...	...	...	...	...	...	...	...	...	...	...	...	...	...	...	...	...	21
20	...	10	...	...	10	12	7	...	...	...	5	...	...	...	...	...	...	22
301	17	213	...	...	71	...	...	...	...	...	...	...	...	...	...	...	...	23
3	...	...	...	...	3	...	...	...	...	...	...	...	...	...	...	...	...	24
9,903	1,609	6,000	...	355	2,294	295	114	32	...	...	149	121	37	...	...	...	84	
9,903	1,609	6,000	...	355	2,294	295	114	32	...	...	149	121	37	...	...	...	84	25
3,562	*997*	*1,943*	...	...	*622*	*286*	*112*	*32*	...	...	*142*	*112*	*35*	...	...	...	*77*	
...	...	...	...	...	...	...	...	...	...	...	...	...	...	...	...	...	...	26
...	...	...	...	...	...	...	...	...	...	...	...	...	...	...	...	...	...	27
...	...	...	...	...	...	...	...	...	...	...	...	...	...	...	...	...	...	28
...	...	...	...	...	...	...	...	...	...	...	...	...	...	...	...	...	...	29
1,012	318	331	...	43	363	37	16	...	2	...	21	5	...	...	...	...	5	
515	47	293	...	41	175	...	...	...	...	...	...	...	...	...	...	...	...	30
497	271	38	...	2	188	...	...	...	...	...	...	...	...	...	...	...	...	31
...	...	...	...	...	...	37	16	...	2	...	21	5	...	...	...	...	5	32
...	...	...	...	...	...	...	...	...	...	...	...	...	...	...	...	...	...	33
964	139	532	...	52	293	...	...	...	...	...	...	...	...	...	...	...	...	
788	103	482	...	49	203	...	...	...	...	...	...	...	...	...	...	...	...	34
...	...	...	...	...	...	...	...	...	...	...	...	...	...	...	...	...	...	35
100	21	50	...	3	29	...	...	...	...	...	...	...	...	...	...	...	...	36
76	15	...	...	...	61	...	...	...	...	...	...	...	...	...	...	...	...	37
245	18	196	...	67	31	121	49	...	...	...	72	26	...	...	...	...	26	
187	...	173	...	67	14	26	...	...	...	...	26	26	...	...	...	...	26	38
58	18	23	...	...	17	95	49	...	...	...	46	...	...	...	...	...	...	39
...	...	...	...	...	...	...	...	...	...	...	...	...	...	...	...	...	...	40

Serial No.	DISTRICT OR STATE.	ORDER VIII.—WOOD. Total Workers and Dependents.	ORDER VIII.—WOOD. Actual Workers. Total. Males.	ORDER VIII.—WOOD. Actual Workers. Total. Females.	ORDER VIII.—WOOD. Actual Workers. Partially Agriculturist. Males.	ORDER VIII.—WOOD. Actual Workers. Partially Agriculturist. Females.	ORDER VIII.—WOOD. Dependents.	GROUP 36, SAWYERS, CARPENTERS, TURNERS, AND JOINERS. Total Workers and Dependents.	GROUP 36. Actual Workers. Total. Males.	GROUP 36. Actual Workers. Total. Females.	GROUP 36. Actual Workers. Partially Agriculturist. Males.	GROUP 36. Actual Workers. Partially Agriculturist. Females.	GROUP 36. Dependents.
	1	184	185	186	187	188	189	190	191	192	193	194	195
	Provincial Total ...	191,686	68,469	26,958	3,579	1,704	96,259	143,719	54,281	11,827	3,058	1,065	77,611
	Burma Proper ...	179,646	63,517	25,123	2,782	1,593	91,006	134,779	50,329	10,729	2,397	965	73,721
	Arakan Division ...	11,459	4,500	1,492	31	52	5,467	8,956	3,399	913	25	43	4,644
1	Akyab ..	8,808	3,544	1,177	22	...	4,087	6,742	2,541	745	22	...	3,456
2	Northern Arakan ...	19	19	...	...	...	...	19	19	...	...	...	...
3	Kyaukpyu ...	1,304	456	271	9	52	577	988	384	161	3	43	443
4	Sandoway ...	1,328	481	44	...	...	803	1,207	455	7	..	...	745
	Pegu Division ...	35,317	14,525	2,772	195	34	18,030	28,465	12,406	748	128	6	15,311
5	City of Rangoon ...	14,205	6,615	146	6	...	7,445	13,938	6,533	126	6	...	7,279
6	Hanthawaddy ...	7,579	2,665	1,001	50	1	3,912	5,023	1,910	196	33	1	2,917
7	Tharrawaddy ...	3,771	1,449	506	38	29	1,726	2,418	1,050	128	30	4	1,240
8	Pegu ...	5,268	1,941	599	37	2	2,728	3,783	1,483	173	36	...	2,132
9	Prome ...	4,493	1,845	429	28	2	2,219	3,298	1,130	125	23	1	1,745
	Irrawaddy Division ...	28,541	10,026	3,887	280	261	14,628	18,922	7,330	803	201	47	10,789
10	Bassein ...	6,163	2,445	442	50	3	3,276	5,102	2,076	217	49	2	2,809
11	Henzada ...	9,229	3,176	1,635	159	214	4,418	4,979	1,944	227	85	41	2,808
12	Myaungmya ...	4,837	1,902	495	20	1	2,440	3,656	1,607	191	20	1	1,858
13	Ma-ubin ...	4,744	1,381	1,103	87	43	2,260	2,180	854	42	53	3	1,284
14	Pyapôn ...	3,568	1,122	212	14	...	2,234	3,005	849	126	14	...	2,030
	Tenasserim Division ...	21,196	7,688	1,746	824	205	11,762	16,824	6,454	287	776	9	10,083
15	Toungoo ...	4,907	2,010	377	58	89	2,520	3,562	1,523	25	34	...	2,014
16	Salween ...	176	77	11	1	1	88	175	76	11	1	1	88
17	Thatôn ...	5,402	1,733	419	48	...	3,250	3,843	1,250	57	29	...	2,536
18	Amherst ...	6,646	2,078	394	39	15	4,174	5,960	1,903	132	35	8	3,925
19	Tavoy ...	2,162	1,171	280	672	...	711	1,677	1,110	17	672	...	550
20	Mergui ...	1,903	619	265	6	...	1,019	1,607	592	45	5	...	970
	Magwe Division ...	17,206	6,696	1,261	56	15	9,289	12,872	5,041	512	44	14	7,319
21	Thayetmyo ...	3,662	1,508	217	6	1	1,937	2,705	1,013	173	5	1	1,519
22	Pakôkku ...	6,887	2,712	437	8	1	3,738	5,420	2,218	143	7	1	3,059
23	Minbu ...	3,608	1,418	313	25	11	1,877	2,552	998	82	18	10	1,472
24	Magwe ...	3,049	1,018	291	17	2	1,737	2,195	812	114	14	2	1,269
	Mandalay Division ...	16,710	6,700	2,268	293	162	7,742	13,844	6,127	1,003	374	85	6,714
25	Mandalay (including City).	9,863	3,403	1,690	41	63	4,770	7,384	2,957	562	25	2	3,865
	Mandalay City ...	*7,448*	*2,639*	*1,218*	...	...	*3,591*	*5,733*	*2,333*	*453*	...	...	*2,947*
26	Bhamo ...	1,514	669	29	175	2	816	1,487	661	17	175	2	809
27	Myitkyina ...	514	236	25	2	...	253	508	232	25	2	...	251
28	Katha ...	1,942	746	85	30	4	1,111	1,778	668	56	27	3	1,054
29	Ruby Mines ...	2,877	1,646	439	145	93	792	2,687	1,609	343	145	78	735
	Sagaing Division ...	22,913	6,053	4,728	586	284	12,132	16,994	4,585	2,298	535	201	10,111
30	Shwebo ...	4,047	613	709	34	21	2,725	3,685	497	609	28	21	2,579
31	Sagaing ...	6,934	2,020	1,446	102	141	3,468	5,323	1,422	858	97	104	3,043
32	Lower Chindwin ...	8,873	2,205	2,394	140	122	4,274	5,075	1,489	696	105	76	2,890
33	Upper Chindwin ...	3,059	1,215	179	310	...	1,665	2,911	1,177	135	305	...	1,599
	Meiktila Division ...	26,304	7,379	6,969	453	680	11,956	17,902	4,987	4,165	314	560	8,750
34	Kyauksè ...	3,253	912	998	145	74	1,353	2,444	703	619	97	45	1,122
35	Meiktila ..	4,061	1,075	1,784	71	502	2,102	3,885	842	1,387	41	482	1,656
36	Yamèthin ...	4,618	1,675	455	106	5	2,488	3,248	1,183	136	90	5	1,929
37	Myingyan ...	13,462	3,717	3,732	131	99	6,013	8,325	2,259	2,013	86	28	4,043
	Specially Administered Territories.	12,040	4,952	1,835	797	111	5,253	8,940	3,952	1,098	661	100	3,890
38	Northern Shan States	3,328	1,458	656	76	66	1,214	2,287	1,073	348	55	60	866
39	Southern Shan States	8,665	3,466	1,179	721	45	4,023	6,611	2,853	750	606	40	3,008
40	Chin Hills ...	44	28	...	...	...	16	42	26	..	...	...	16

Occupations. Details by Districts.

GROUP 37, BASKET MAKERS, AND INDUSTRIES CONCERNED WITH WOODY MATERIALS, SUCH AS LEAVES, REEDS, ETC.						ORDER IX.—METALS.						GROUP 38, FORGING AND ROLLING OF IRON AND OTHER METALS.						
Total Workers and Dependents.	ACTUAL WORKERS.				Dependents.	Total Workers and Dependents.	ACTUAL WORKERS.				Dependents.	Total Workers and Dependents.	ACTUAL WORKERS.				Dependents.	Serial No.
	Total.		Partially Agriculturist.				Total.		Partially Agriculturist.				Total.		Partially Agriculturist.			
	Males.	Females.	Males.	Females.			Males.	Females.	Males.	Females.			Males.	Females.	Males.	Females.		
196	197	198	199	200	201	202	203	204	205	206	207	208	209	210	211	212	213	
47,967	14,188	15,131	521	639	18,648	34,912	14,036	2,151	370	227	18,725	483	33	142	—	...	307	
44,867	13,188	14,394	385	628	17,285	31,891	12,290	1,969	238	227	17,672	483	33	143	—	...	307	
2,503	1,101	579	6	9	823	1,571	708	117	...	...	746	...	...	...	...	...	...	
2,066	1,003	432	...	...	631	1,232	526	113	...	...	593	...	...	...	...	...	...	1
...	...	...	...	...	...	12	12	...	...	...	...	...	...	...	...	...	...	2
316	72	110	6	9	134	256	140	1	...	...	115	...	...	...	...	...	...	3
121	26	37	...	...	58	71	30	3	...	...	38	...	...	...	...	...	...	4
6,852	2,109	2,024	31	28	2,719	9,242	3,919	577	28	16	4,746	...	...	...	...	...	...	
268	82	20	...	...	166	3,720	1,920	7	2	...	1,793	...	...	...	...	...	...	5
2,556	755	806	17	...	995	1,663	667	13	11	...	983	...	...	...	...	...	...	6
1,353	399	468	8	25	486	1,607	436	450	4	16	721	...	...	...	...	...	...	7
1,680	458	426	1	2	596	1,116	394	10	5	...	712	...	...	...	...	...	...	8
1,395	415	304	5	1	476	1,136	502	97	6	...	537	...	...	...	...	...	...	9
9,629	2,696	3,084	79	214	3,839	4,493	1,783	268	28	8	2,442	...	...	...	...	...	...	
1,061	369	225	1	1	467	1,076	399	21	1	...	696	...	...	...	...	...	...	10
4,250	1,232	1,408	74	173	1,610	1,301	550	90	16	8	661	...	...	...	...	...	...	11
1,281	295	304	...	...	582	990	373	93	5	...	524	...	...	...	...	...	...	12
2,564	587	1,061	4	40	976	729	337	20	6	...	372	...	...	...	...	...	...	13
563	273	86	...	...	204	397	124	44	...	...	229	...	...	...	...	...	...	14
4,372	1,234	1,459	48	96	1,679	4,715	1,798	74	14	...	2,843	16	...	...	...	...	16	
1,345	487	352	24	89	506	930	310	4	4	...	616	...	...	...	...	...	...	15
1	1	...	...	...	..	49	27	...	...	...	22	...	...	...	...	...	...	16
1,559	483	362	19	...	714	1,432	523	16	5	...	893	...	...	...	...	...	...	17
686	175	262	4	7	249	1,769	744	43	3	...	983	...	...	...	...	...	...	18
485	61	263	...	...	161	261	114	2	1	...	145	...	...	...	...	...	...	19
296	27	220	1	...	49	274	80	10	1	...	184	16	...	...	...	...	16	20
4,334	1,615	749	12	1	1,970	3,194	1,084	276	14	...	1,836	389	...	143	...	...	246	
957	495	44	1	..	418	1,008	222	152	2	...	634	389	...	143	...	...	246	21
1,467	494	294	1	...	679	790	288	81	...	...	481	...	...	...	...	...	...	22
1,056	420	231	7	1	405	866	355	79	12	...	438	...	...	...	...	...	...	23
854	206	180	3	...	408	530	219	22	...	...	289	...	...	...	...	...	...	24
2,866	573	1,265	19	77	1,028	2,761	1,167	101	66	9	1,493	78	33	...	...	...	45	
2,479	446	1,128	16	61	905	2,138	867	83	18	9	1,188	48	24	...	...	...	24	25
1,715	306	765	...	...	644	1823	717	56	...	...	1,050	48	24	...	...	...	24	
37	8	12	...	...	7	83	60	...	...	...	23	...	...	...	...	...	...	26
6	4	...	...	...	2	161	108	...	10	...	53	...	...	...	...	...	...	27
164	78	29	3	1	57	201	50	12	...	...	139	30	9	...	...	...	21	28
190	37	96	...	15	57	178	82	6	38	...	90	...	...	...	...	...	...	29
5,919	1,468	2,430	51	83	2,081	3,080	842	354	11	123	1,884	...	...	...	...	...	...	
362	116	100	6	...	146	652	214	50	...	...	388	...	...	...	...	...	...	30
1,611	398	588	5	37	425	829	269	43	...	14	527	...	...	...	...	...	...	31
3,798	716	1,698	35	46	1,384	1,428	281	261	8	109	886	...	...	...	...	...	...	32
148	38	44	5	...	66	171	78	...	3	...	93	...	...	...	...	...	...	33
8,402	2,392	2,804	139	120	3,206	2,835	949	204	77	71	1,682	...	...	...	...	...	...	
819	209	379	48	39	231	339	153	52	39	3	134	...	...	...	...	...	...	34
1,076	233	397	30	30	446	543	153	79	36	17	312	...	...	...	...	...	...	35
1,370	492	319	16	...	559	928	286	61	17	51	581	...	...	...	...	...	...	36
5,137	1,458	1,709	45	71	1,970	1,025	357	12	5	...	656	...	...	...	...	...	...	37
3,100	1,000	737	136	11	1,363	3,021	1,786	182	132	...	1,053	...	...	...	...	...	...	
1,041	385	308	21	6	348	715	489	...	10	...	226	...	...	...	...	...	...	38
2,057	613	429	115	5	1,015	2,296	1,295	182	122	...	819	...	...	...	...	...	...	39
2	2	...	...	...	...	10	2	...	...	...	8	...	...	...	...	...	...	40

Serial No.	DISTRICT OR STATE.	GROUP 41, OTHER WORKERS IN IRON, AND MAKERS OF TOOLS PRINCIPALLY OR EXCLUSIVELY OF IRON.						GROUP 42, WORKERS IN BRASS, COPPER, AND BELL METAL.					
		Total Workers and Dependents.	ACTUAL WORKERS.				Dependents.	Total Workers and Dependents.	ACTUAL WORKERS.				Dependents.
			TOTAL.		PARTIALLY AGRICULTURIST.				TOTAL.		PARTIALLY AGRICULTURIST.		
			Males.	Females.	Males.	Females.			Males.	Females.	Males.	Females.	
	1	214	215	216	217	218	219	220	221	222	223	224	225
	Provincial Total ...	29,040	11,859	1,498	356	212	15,683	554	137	10	...	...	407
	Burma Proper ...	26,338	10,289	1,330	227	212	14,719	554	137	10	...	...	407
	Arakan Division ...	1,361	539	117	...	...	705	...	...	...	...	...	...
1	Akyab	1,041	368	113	...	...	560	...	...	...	...	...	...
2	Northern Arakan ...	12	12	...	...	...	...	...	...	...	...	...	...
3	Kyaukpyu ...	244	135	1	...	...	108	...	...	...	...	...	...
4	Sandoway	64	24	3	...	...	37	...	...	...	...	...	...
	Pegu Division ...	6,771	3,097	139	23	1	3,535	238	107	...	...	...	131
5	City of Rangoon ...	2,533	1,372	4	2	...	1,157	230	104	...	...	...	126
6	Hanthawaddy .	1,514	607	12	11	...	895	4	1	...	...	...	3
7	Tharrawaddy ...	774	330	25	4	1	419	...	...	...	...	...	...
8	Pegu	940	337	10	5	...	593	4	2	...	...	...	2
9	Prome	1,010	451	88	1	...	471	...	...	...	...	...	...
	Irrawaddy Division ...	4,093	1,557	266	28	8	2,270	...	...	...	...	...	...
10	Bassein	1,048	388	21	1	...	639	...	...	...	...	...	...
11	Henzada	1,265	531	88	16	8	646	...	...	...	...	...	...
12	Myaungmya ...	841	298	93	5	...	450	...	...	...	...	...	...
13	Ma-ubin	651	280	20	6	...	351	...	...	...	...	...	...
14	Pyapôn	288	60	44	...	...	184	...	...	...	...	...	...
	Tenasserim Division ...	4,050	1,533	64	12	...	2,453	53	4	...	...	...	49
15	Toungoo	844	286	4	2	...	554	1	1	...	...	...	...
16	Salween	44	27	...	...	...	17	...	...	...	...	...	...
17	Thatôn	1,251	442	13	5	...	796	...	...	...	...	...	...
18	Amherst	1,522	633	40	3	...	849	52	3	...	...	...	49
19	Tavoy	206	89	2	1	...	115	...	...	...	...	...	...
20	Mergui	183	56	5	1	...	122	...	...	...	...	...	...
	Magwe Division ...	2,548	980	122	14	...	1,446	23	21	...	...	...	22
21	Thayetmyo ...	587	217	9	2	...	361	...	...	...	...	...	...
22	Pakokku	701	262	19	...	...	420	...	...	...	...	...	...
23	Minbu	773	299	73	12	...	401	23	11	...	...	...	22
24	Magwe	487	202	21	...	...	264	...	...	...	...	...	...
	Mandalay Division ...	2,259	1,009	77	65	9	1,173	16	15	...	...	...	1
25	Mandalay (including City).	1,734	733	59	17	9	942	10	10	...	...	...	...
	Mandalay City ...	*1,439*	*593*	*32*	...	...	*814*	*10*	*10*	...	...	...	...
26	Bhamo	72	58	...	...	...	14	...	...	...	...	...	...
27	Myitkyina ...	159	106	...	10	...	53	...	...	...	...	...	...
28	Katha	126	37	12	...	...	77	...	...	...	...	...	...
29	Ruby Mines ...	168	75	6	38	...	87	6	5	...	...	...	1
	Sagaing Division ...	2,622	720	342	11	123	1,560	224	...	10	...	...	214
30	Shwebo	611	205	50	...	...	356	...	...	...	...	...	...
31	Sagaing	749	220	43	...	14	486	...	...	...	...	...	...
32	Lower Chindwin ...	1,143	249	249	8	109	645	224	...	10	...	...	214
33	Upper Chindwin ...	119	46	...	3	...	73	...	...	...	...	...	...
	Meiktila Division ...	2,634	854	203	74	71	1,577	...	...	...	...	...	...
34	Kyaukse	321	143	52	28	3	126	...	...	...	...	...	...
35	Meiktila	441	95	79	24	17	267	...	...	...	...	...	...
36	Yamèthin ...	892	275	60	17	51	557	...	...	...	...	...	...
37	Myingyan ...	980	341	12	5	...	627	...	...	...	...	...	...
	Specially Administered Territories.	2,702	1,570	168	129	...	964	...	...	...	...	...	...
38	Northern Shan States	628	437	...	10	...	191	...	...	...	...	...	...
39	Southern Shan States	2,064	1,131	168	119	...	765	...	...	...	...	...	...
40	Chin Hills ...	10	2	...	...	...	8	...	...	...	...	...	...

Occupations. Details by Districts.

GROUP 43. WORKERS IN OTHER METALS.						ORDER X.—CERAMICS.						GROUP 45. MAKERS OF GLASS AND CRYSTAL WARE.						
Total Workers and Dependents.	ACTUAL WORKERS.				Dependents.	Total Workers and Dependents.	ACTUAL WORKERS.				Dependents.	Total Workers and Dependents.	ACTUAL WORKERS.				Dependents.	
	Total.		Partially Agriculturist.				Total.		Partially Agriculturist.				Total.		Partially Agriculturist.			
	Males.	Females.	Males.	Females.			Males.	Females.	Males.	Females.			Males.	Females.	Males.	Females.		Serial No.
226	227	228	229	230	231	232	233	234	235	236	237	238	239	240	241	242	243	
4,759	1,982	500	13	15	2,277	18,821	4,656	6,687	253	154	7,478	192	83	18	...	...	92	
4,441	1,767	486	10	15	2,188	16,836	4,524	6,292	133	128	6,030	192	83	18	...	...	92	
220	169	...	...	...	41	1,886	178	793	1	5	915	4	...	1	...	...	3	
191	158	...	...	...	33	1,486	112	657	...	5	717	...	...	...	...	...	...	1
...	...	...	...	...	...	...	...	...	...	...	...	...	...	...	...	...	...	2
12	5	...	...	...	7	335	52	106	1	...	177	4	...	1	...	...	3	3
7	6	...	...	...	1	65	14	30	...	...	21	...	...	...	...	...	...	4
2,191	707	438	5	15	1,046	4,002	1,420	1,236	6	32	1,456	41	19	...	...	...	22	
915	436	3	...	...	476	620	437	14	2	...	169	...	...	...	...	...	...	5
145	59	1	...	...	85	709	351	66	3	3	292	4	1	...	...	...	3	6
835	106	425	...	15	302	532	158	197	1	21	177	8	4	...	...	...	4	7
172	55	...	...	...	117	1,042	254	288	...	8	500	26	11	...	...	...	15	8
126	51	9	5	...	66	1,099	210	571	...	...	318	3	3	...	...	...	...	9
400	226	2	...	...	172	3,129	723	1,397	95	42	1,019	30	15	2	...	...	13	
28	11	...	...	...	17	1,358	58	865	...	...	435	9	9	...	...	...	...	10
36	19	2	...	...	15	1,172	424	352	92	38	396	7	...	...	...	...	7	11
149	75	...	...	...	74	264	74	91	...	...	99	10	5	2	...	...	5	12
78	37	...	...	...	21	282	139	71	3	4	72	...	...	...	...	...	...	13
109	64	...	...	...	45	53	18	18	...	...	17	4	3	...	...	...	1	14
596	261	10	2	...	305	2,056	403	833	4	1	800	40	14	1	...	...	25	
85	23	...	2	...	62	409	77	166	1	...	166	2	...	...	...	...	2	15
5	...	...	...	...	5	4	2	...	...	...	2	5	1	...	...	...	2	16
181	81	3	...	...	97	714	70	486	...	...	158	34	12	1	...	...	21	17
195	103	2	...	...	85	789	239	115	...	1	435	...	...	...	...	...	...	18
55	25	...	...	...	30	62	...	49	...	...	13	...	...	...	...	...	...	19
75	24	5	...	...	46	78	15	17	5	...	46	1	1	...	...	...	...	20
228	93	9	...	...	126	1,298	259	509	12	1	520	26	7	14	...	...	5	
26	5	...	...	...	21	258	62	95	...	...	101	...	...	...	...	...	...	21
89	26	2	...	...	61	133	20	63	...	...	44	7	4	2	...	...	1	22
70	45	6	...	...	19	621	105	255	10	...	261	7	3	2	...	...	2	23
43	17	1	...	...	25	286	72	110	2	1	104	12	...	10	...	...	2	24
408	110	24	1	...	274	843	230	380	2	7	233	51	28	...	...	...	23	
346	100	24	1	...	222	841	230	379	2	7	232	51	28	...	...	...	23	25
326	*90*	*24*	...	...	*212*	*475*	*170*	*158*	...	...	*147*	*51*	*28*	...	...	...	*23*	
11	2	...	...	...	9	2	...	1	...	...	1	...	...	...	...	...	...	26
2	2	...	...	...	...	...	...	...	...	...	...	...	...	...	...	...	...	27
45	4	...	-	...	41	...	...	...	...	...	...	...	...	...	...	...	...	28
4	2	...	...	...	2	...	...	...	...	...	...	...	...	...	...	...	...	29
234	122	2	...	...	110	2,479	967	799	4	24	713	...	...	...	...	...	...	
41	9	...	...	...	32	1,440	734	219	...	11	487	...	...	...	...	...	...	30
80	49	...	...	...	31	492	100	305	2	...	87	...	...	...	...	...	...	31
61	32	2	...	...	27	428	131	211	2	13	86	...	...	...	...	...	...	32
52	32	...	...	...	20	119	2	64	...	...	53	...	...	...	...	...	...	33
174	79	1	2	...	94	1,143	354	485	9	16	364	...	...	...	...	...	...	
8	6	...	...	...	2	401	11	397	5	15	93	...	...	...	...	...	...	34
85	46	...	2	...	39	152	121	...	...	...	31	...	...	...	...	...	...	35
36	11	1	...	...	24	60	10	13	1	1	37	...	...	...	...	...	...	36
45	16	...	...	...	29	530	212	115	3	...	203	...	...	...	...	...	...	37
328	225	14	3	...	89	1,985	142	395	19	26	1,448	...	...	...	...	...	...	
87	52	...	...	...	35	95	3	81	...	5	71	...	...	...	...	...	...	38
251	163	14	3	...	54	1,890	139	374	19	23	1,377	...	...	...	...	...	...	39
...	...	...	...	...	...	...	...	...	...	...	...	...	...	...	...	...	...	40

Serial No.	DISTRICT OR STATE.	GROUP 47, POTTERS AND EARTHEN PIPE AND BOWL MAKERS. Total Workers and Dependents.	Actual Workers. Total. Males.	Actual Workers. Total. Females.	Actual Workers. Partially Agriculturist. Males.	Actual Workers. Partially Agriculturist. Females.	Dependents.	GROUP 48, BRICK AND TILE MAKERS. Total Workers and Dependents.	Actual Workers. Total. Males.	Actual Workers. Total. Females.	Actual Workers. Partially Agriculturist. Males.	Actual Workers. Partially Agriculturist. Females.	Dependents.
	1	244	245	246	247	248	249	250	251	252	253	254	255
	Provincial Total ...	15,323	3,001	6,147	127	151	6,175	3,242	1,564	475	25	3	1,202
	Burma Proper ...	13,416	2,889	5,752	118	125	4,775	3,167	1,534	476	15	3	1,157
	Arakan Division ...	1,716	158	744	1	5	814	160	15	48	...	...	97
1	Akyab	1,486	112	657	...	5	717	...	...	...	...	...	...
2	Northern Arakan ...	...	...	...	...	...	...	...	...	...	...	...	...
3	Kyaukpyu ...	200	45	65	1	...	90	131	7	40	...	...	84
4	Sandoway ...	30	1	22	...	...	7	29	8	8	...	...	13
	Pegu Division ...	2,752	685	1,038	2	32	1,029	1,205	705	98	4	...	402
5	City of Rangoon ...	117	113	8	...	...	26	472	323	6	2	...	143
6	Hanthawaddy ...	282	138	13	2	3	131	420	212	53	1	...	155
7	Tharrawaddy ...	397	81	189	...	21	127	127	73	8	1	...	46
8	Pegu	906	178	271	...	8	457	110	65	17	...	...	28
9	Prome	1,020	175	557	...	...	288	76	32	14	...	...	30
	Irrawaddy Division ...	2,660	460	1,318	95	42	882	439	238	77	...	...	124
10	Bassein	1,311	22	860	...	...	429	38	27	5	...	...	6
11	Henzada	1,044	382	316	92	38	346	121	42	36	...	...	43
12	Myaungmya ...	145	20	88	...	...	37	109	51	1	...	...	57
13	Ma-ubin	122	32	36	3	4	54	160	107	35	...	...	18
14	Pyapôn	38	4	18	...	...	16	11	11	...	...	...	...
	Tenasserim Division ...	1,588	196	810	4	1	582	428	193	22	...	...	213
15	Toungoo	389	73	166	1	...	150	18	4	...	...	...	14
16	Salween	1	1	...	...	...	...	...	...	...	...	...	...
17	Thatôn	601	27	481	...	...	93	79	31	4	...	...	44
18	Amherst	462	84	97	...	1	281	327	155	18	...	...	154
19	Tavoy	62	...	49	...	...	13	...	...	...	[illegible]	...	...
20	Mergui	73	11	17	3	...	45	4	3	...	...	...	1
	Magwe Division ...	957	125	454	10	1	378	315	127	61	2	...	127
21	Thayetmyo ...	149	10	81	...	...	58	109	52	14	...	...	43
22	Pakôkku	41	5	24	...	...	12	85	11	43	...	...	31
23	Minbu	572	84	251	10	...	237	42	18	2	...	...	22
24	Magwe	195	26	98	...	1	71	79	46	2	2	...	31
	Mandalay Division ...	538	101	302	...	7	135	254	101	78	2	...	75
25	Mandalay (including City).	536	101	301	...	7	134	254	101	78	2	...	75
	Mandalay City ...	*172*	*43*	*80*	...	...	*49*	*252*	*99*	*78*	...	..	*75*
26	Bhamo	2	...	1	...	...	1	...	...	...	...	...	...
27	Myitkyina ...	...	...	...	...	...	...	...	...	...	...	...	...
28	Katha	...	...	...	...	...	...	...	...	...	...	...	...
29	Ruby Mines ...	...	...	...	...	...	...	...	...	...	...	...	...
	Sagaing Division ...	2,121	815	676	2	24	630	307	150	77	2	...	80
30	Shwebo	1,350	708	173	...	11	469	44	26	...	...	...	18
31	Sagaing	487	95	305	2	...	87	5	5	...	...	...	...
32	Lower Chindwin ...	274	12	195	...	13	67	154	119	16	2	...	19
33	Upper Chindwin ...	10	...	3	...	...	7	104	...	61	...	...	43
	Meiktila Division ...	1,084	349	420	4	13	325	59	5	15	5	3	39
34	Kyauksè	386	6	295	...	13	85	15	5	2	5	2	8
35	Meiktila	152	121	...	...	...	31	...	...	...	...	...	...
36	Yamèthin ...	16	10	...	1	...	6	44	...	13	...	1	31
37	Myingyan ...	530	212	115	3	...	203	...	...	...	...	...	...
	Specially Administered Territories.	1,907	112	395	9	26	1,400	75	30	..	10	...	45
38	Northern Shan States	92	3	21	...	3	68	...	...	...	...	...	...
39	Southern Shan States	1,815	109	374	9	23	1,332	75	30	...	10	...	45
40	Chin Hills ...	...	...	...	...	...	...	...	...	...	...	...	...

Occupations. Details by Districts.

ORDER XI.—CHEMICAL AND ANALOGOUS PRODUCTS.						GROUP 51, MANUFACTURE OF ÆRATED AND MINERAL WATERS.						GROUP 53, MANUFACTURE AND REFINING OF VEGETABLE AND MINERAL OILS.						
Total Workers and Dependents.	Actual Workers. Total. Males.	Actual Workers. Total. Females.	Actual Workers. Partially Agriculturist. Males.	Actual Workers. Partially Agriculturist. Females.	Dependents.	Total Workers and Dependents.	Actual Workers. Total. Males.	Actual Workers. Total. Females.	Actual Workers. Partially Agriculturist. Males.	Actual Workers. Partially Agriculturist. Females.	Dependents.	Total Workers and Dependents.	Actual Workers. Total. Males.	Actual Workers. Total. Females.	Actual Workers. Partially Agriculturist. Males.	Actual Workers. Partially Agriculturist. Females.	Dependents.	Serial No.
256	257	258	259	260	261	262	263	264	265	266	267	268	269	270	271	272	273	
10,560	4,502	1,990	31	71	4,068	132	70	3	...	...	59	9,110	4,041	1,542	16	59	3,527	
10,050	4,474	1,715	21	28	3,861	109	52	1	...	...	56	9,016	4,041	1,490	16	27	3,485	
52	16	17	1	2	19	1	1	...	...	...	...	42	15	15	1	2	12	
10	8	...	...	...	2	...	...	...	...	...	...	10	8	...	...	...	2	1
...	...	...	...	...	...	...	...	...	...	...	...	...	...	...	...	...	...	2
41	7	17	1	2	17	...	...	...	...	...	...	32	7	15	1	2	10	3
1	1	...	...	...	...	1	1	...	...	...	...	...	...	...	...	...	...	4
7,727	3,841	948	1	2	2,938	23	13	...	...	...	10	7,497	3,674	945	1	2	2,878	
711	600	1	...	...	110	13	9	...	...	...	4	509	442	...	...	...	67	5
6,801	3,180	886	...	...	2,735	...	...	...	...	...	...	6,801	3,180	886	...	...	2,735	6
95	46	10	1	2	39	...	...	...	...	...	...	89	46	10	1	2	33	7
12	1	3	...	...	8	...	...	...	...	...	...	4	...	1	...	...	3	8
108	14	48	...	...	46	10	4	...	...	...	6	94	6	48	...	...	40	9
43	26	5	...	...	12	24	19	...	...	...	5	19	7	5	...	...	7	
2	...	1	...	...	1	...	...	...	...	...	...	2	...	1	...	...	1	10
34	19	4	...	...	11	24	19	...	...	...	5	10	...	4	...	...	6	11
...	...	...	...	...	...	...	...	...	...	...	...	...	...	...	...	...	...	12
...	...	...	...	...	...	...	...	...	...	...	...	...	...	...	...	...	...	13
7	7	...	...	...	...	...	...	...	...	...	...	7	7	...	...	...	...	14
520	127	117	12	8	276	7	...	1	...	...	6	506	127	114	12	8	265	
257	46	85	12	8	126	1	...	...	...	...	1	256	46	85	12	8	125	15
...	...	...	...	...	...	...	...	...	...	...	...	...	...	...	...	...	...	16
120	20	14	...	...	86	6	...	1	...	...	5	109	20	13	...	...	76	17
32	13	...	...	...	19	...	...	...	...	...	...	32	13	...	...	...	19	18
50	27	...	...	...	23	...	...	...	...	...	...	50	27	...	...	...	23	19
61	21	18	...	...	22	...	...	...	...	...	...	59	21	16	...	...	22	20
555	201	151	1	1	203	...	...	...	...	...	...	520	200	144	1	1	176	
111	44	6	...	...	61	...	...	...	...	...	...	86	44	...	...	...	42	21
8	1	4	...	...	3	...	...	...	...	...	...	6	...	4	...	...	2	22
369	98	140	1	1	131	...	...	...	...	...	...	369	95	140	1	1	131	23
67	58	1	...	...	8	...	...	...	...	...	...	59	58	...	...	...	1	24
294	18	138	...	...	138	49	14	...	...	...	35	4	4	...	...	...	...	
262	18	138	...	...	106	17	14	...	...	...	3	4	4	...	...	...	...	25
258	*14*	*138*	...	...	*106*	*17*	*14*	...	...	...	*3*	...	...	...	...	...	...	
...	...	...	...	...	...	...	...	...	...	...	...	...	...	...	...	...	...	26
...	...	...	...	...	...	...	...	...	...	...	...	...	...	...	...	...	...	27
32	...	...	...	...	32	32	...	...	...	...	32	...	...	...	...	...	...	28
..	...	...	...	...	...	...	...	...	...	...	...	...	...	...	...	...	...	29
449	239	71	6	1	139	5	5	...	...	...	...	23	11	...	1	...	12	
54	...	54	...	...	...	...	...	...	...	...	...	...	...	...	...	...	...	30
22	...	11	...	...	11	...	...	...	...	...	...	...	...	...	...	...	...	31
167	88	6	2	1	73	5	5	...	...	...	...	6	3	...	...	...	3	32
206	151	...	4	...	55	...	...	...	...	...	...	17	8	...	1	...	9	33
420	6	268	...	14	136	...	...	...	...	...	...	405	3	267	...	14	135	
...	...	...	...	...	...	...	...	...	...	...	...	...	...	...	...	...	...	34
402	...	267	...	14	135	...	...	...	...	...	...	402	...	267	...	14	135	35
3	3	...	...	...	...	...	...	...	...	...	...	...	...	...	...	...	...	36
5	3	1	...	...	1	...	...	...	...	...	...	3	3	...	...	...	...	37
510	28	275	10	43	207	23	18	2	...	...	3	94	...	52	...	32	42	
32	18	2	...	...	12	23	18	2	...	...	3	9	...	...	...	...	9	38
478	10	273	10	43	195	...	...	...	...	...	...	85	...	52	...	32	33	39
...	...	...	...	...	...	...	...	...	...	...	...	...	...	...	...	...	...	40

Serial No.	DISTRICT OR STATE.	GROUP 55, MANUFACTURE OF SOAP, CANDLES, LAC, CUTCH, PERFUMES AND MISCELLANEOUS DRUGS. Total Workers and Dependents.	Actual Workers. Total. Males.	Actual Workers. Total. Females.	Actual Workers. Partially Agriculturist. Males.	Actual Workers. Partially Agriculturist. Females.	Dependents.	ORDER XII.—FOOD INDUSTRIES. Total Workers and Dependents.	Actual Workers. Total. Males.	Actual Workers. Total. Females.	Actual Workers. Partially Agriculturist. Males.	Actual Workers. Partially Agriculturist. Females.	Dependents.
	1	274	275	276	277	278	279	280	281	282	283	284	285
	Provincial Total ...	1,145	387	389	15	3	369	178,255	59,889	44,845	2,842	3,533	73,521
	Burma Proper ...	920	377	224	5	1	319	165,440	55,322	41,932	2,280	3,317	68,186
	Arakan Division ...	9	...	2	...	...	7	9,397	3,781	2,125	4	11	3,491
1	Akyab ...	...	...	...	...	...	...	7,963	3,541	1,471	2	7	2,951
2	Northern Arakan ...	...	...	...	...	...	...	...	...	...	...	...	...
3	Kyaukpyu ...	9	...	2	...	...	7	892	138	440	2	4	314
4	Sandoway ...	...	...	...	...	...	...	542	102	214	...	...	226
	Pegu Division ...	205	153	3	...	...	49	47,380	24,180	8,111	56	24	14,989
5	City of Rangoon ...	187	148	1	...	...	38	31,097	19,479	3,358	5	1	8,250
6	Hanthawaddy ...	...	...	...	...	...	...	6,049	2,014	1,265	6	3	2,770
7	Tharrawaddy ...	6	...	...	...	...	6	1,302	479	266	7	3	557
8	Pegu ...	8	1	2	...	...	5	2,457	482	1,088	7	16	887
9	Prome ...	4	4	...	...	...	...	6,475	1,826	2,124	31	1	2,525
	Irrawaddy Division ...	...	...	...	...	...	...	12,033	4,692	3,258	68	77	4,083
10	Bassein ...	...	...	...	...	...	...	3,526	2,181	587	47	3	818
11	Henzada ...	...	...	...	...	...	...	2,345	593	699	11	34	1,053
12	Myaungmya ...	...	...	...	...	...	...	2,013	817	390	2	10	806
13	Ma-ubin ...	...	...	...	...	...	...	2,486	392	1,246	8	30	848
14	Pyapôn ...	...	...	...	...	...	...	1,663	709	396	...	...	558
	Tenasserim Division ...	7	...	2	...	...	5	9,806	3,192	2,272	15	204	4,342
15	Toungoo ...	...	...	...	...	...	...	1,[illegible]81	533	473	2	11	915
16	Salween ...	...	...	...	...	...	...	19	6	1	...	...	12
17	Thatôn ...	5	...	...	...	...	5	1,044	270	252	...	17	522
18	Amherst ...	...	...	...	...	...	...	5,170	1,912	1,124	7	176	2,134
19	Tavoy ...	...	...	...	...	...	...	1,092	362	210	5	...	520
20	Mergui ...	2	...	2	...	...	...	560	109	212	1	...	239
	Magwe Division ...	35	1	7	...	...	27	18,202	3,635	4,789	121	281	9,778
21	Thayetmyo ...	25	...	6	...	...	19	1,592	358	503	...	82	731
22	Pakôkku ...	2	1	...	...	...	1	8,425	1,424	1,871	18	15	5,130
23	Minbu ...	...	...	...	...	...	...	4,716	870	1,735	97	183	2,111
24	Magwe ...	8	...	1	...	...	7	3,469	983	680	6	1	1,806
	Mandalay Division ...	241	...	138	...	...	103	10,521	2,600	3,100	159	263	4,821
25	Mandalay (including City.)	241	...	138	...	...	103	7,575	1,807	2,361	45	197	3,407
	Mandalay City ...	*241*	...	*138*	...	...	*103*	*3,327*	*1,074*	*852*	...	...	*1,401*
26	Bhamo ...	...	...	...	...	...	...	913	217	235	33	...	461
27	Myitkyina ...	...	...	...	...	...	...	240	78	66	5	...	96
28	Katha ...	...	...	...	...	...	...	734	181	243	6	46	310
29	Ruby Mines ...	...	...	...	...	...	...	1,059	317	195	70	20	547
	Sagaing Division ...	421	223	71	5	1	127	25,089	4,398	10,359	345	1,[illegible]54	10,332
30	Shwebo ...	54	...	54	...	...	...	6,161	821	2,459	30	274	2,881
31	Sagaing ...	22	...	11	...	...	11	5,667	1,239	1,782	45	271	2,646
32	Lower Chindwin ...	156	80	6	2	1	70	11,011	1,493	5,415	105	763	4,103
33	Upper Chindwin ...	189	143	...	3	...	46	2,250	845	703	165	46	702
	Meiktila Division ...	2	...	1	...	...	1	33,022	8,744	7,918	1,512	1,203	16,350
34	Kyauksè ...	...	...	...	...	...	...	6,499	1,190	3,395	159	839	1,914
35	Meiktila ...	...	...	...	...	...	...	3,451	809	1,055	47	117	1,587
36	Yamèthin ...	...	...	...	...	...	...	2,573	541	782	13	59	1,250
37	Myingyan ...	2	...	1	...	...	1	20,489	6,204	2,686	1,293	85	11,599
	Specially Administered Territories.	225	10	165	10	2	50	12,815	4,567	2,913	562	316	5,335
38	Northern Shan States	...	...	...	...	...	...	3,823	1,727	637	147	155	1,459
39	Southern Shan States	225	10	165	10	2	50	8,963	2,831	2,276	415	161	3,866
40	Chin Hills ...	...	...	...	...	...	...	29	19	...	...	...	10

Occupations. Details by Districts.

GROUP 56, RICE POUNDERS AND HUSKERS AND FLOUR GRINDERS. Total Workers and Dependents.	Actual Workers. Total. Males.	Actual Workers. Total. Females.	Partially Agriculturist. Males.	Partially Agriculturist. Females.	Dependents.	GROUP 57, BAKERS AND BISCUIT MAKERS. Total Workers and Dependents.	Actual Workers. Total. Males.	Actual Workers. Total. Females.	Partially Agriculturists. Males.	Partially Agriculturists. Females.	Dependents.	GROUP 59, BUTCHERS. Total Workers and Dependents.	Actual Workers. Total. Males.	Actual Workers. Total. Females.	Partially Agriculturist. Males.	Partially Agriculturist. Females.	Dependents.	Serial No.
286	287	288	289	290	291	292	293	294	295	296	297	298	299	300	301	302	303	
110,623	43,020	28,745	1,256	2,083	38,858	1,234	904	76	2	...	254	6,897	1,890	1,612	77	160	3,395	
100,700	39,446	26,625	765	2,926	34,629	1,234	904	76	2	...	254	4,985	1,334	1,145	28	1	2,506	
8,873	3,694	1,932	2	11	3,247	6	4	...	...	...	2	22	6	2	...	...	14	
7,737	3,515	1,371	2	7	2,851	6	4	...	...	...	2	2	1	1	...	...	...	1
...	...	...	...	...	...	...	...	...	...	...	...	...	...	...	...	...	...	2
637	78	373	...	4	186	...	...	...	...	...	...	15	4	1	...	...	10	3
499	101	188	...	...	210	...	...	...	...	...	...	5	1	...	...	...	4	4
24,519	11,043	3,192	26	17	10,284	1,175	899	51	2	...	225	2,161	564	604	...	...	993	
15,606	7,631	1,611	3	1	6,364	1,146	873	51	2	...	222	1,043	441	82	...	...	520	5
4,955	1,958	593	5	2	2,404	...	...	...	...	...	...	531	19	326	...	...	186	6
840	335	158	7	3	347	10	9	...	...	...	1	36	...	9	...	...	27	7
1,108	388	253	7	10	467	19	17	...	...	...	2	98	44	10	...	...	44	8
2,010	731	577	4	1	702	...	...	...	...	...	...	453	60	177	...	...	216	9
7,566	4,116	1,159	64	49	2,291	1	1	...	...	...	...	122	43	9	...	...	70	
3,343	2,121	475	47	3	747	...	...	...	...	...	...	33	10	...	...	...	23	10
723	225	203	7	34	295	...	...	...	...	...	...	21	3	7	...	...	11	11
1,693	768	264	2	10	661	1	1	...	...	...	...	20	...	1	...	...	19	12
758	313	143	8	2	302	...	...	...	...	...	...	14	10	...	...	...	4	13
1,049	689	74	...	...	286	...	...	...	...	...	...	34	20	1	...	...	13	14
6,547	2,639	1,277	14	176	2,631	...	...	...	...	...	...	325	103	35	...	...	187	
906	218	269	2	1	419	...	...	...	...	...	...	230	78	33	...	...	119	15
10	2	1	...	...	7	...	...	...	...	...	...	1	1	...	...	...	...	16
514	185	97	...	1	232	...	...	...	...	...	...	82	22	2	...	...	58	17
3,807	1,814	631	7	174	1,362	...	...	...	...	...	...	...	...	...	...	...	...	18
988	341	176	5	...	471	...	...	...	...	...	...	8	...	...	...	...	8	19
322	79	103	...	...	140	...	...	...	...	...	...	4	2	...	...	...	2	20
6,982	1,170	3,323	60	269	2,489	...	...	...	...	...	...	503	110	131	...	...	262	
744	164	342	...	82	238	...	...	...	...	...	...	110	21	35	...	...	54	21
2,888	563	1,274	2	8	1,051	...	...	...	...	...	...	75	25	20	...	...	30	22
2,785	382	1,439	56	178	964	...	...	...	...	...	...	140	17	27	...	...	96	23
565	61	268	2	1	236	...	...	...	...	...	...	178	47	49	...	...	82	24
8,445	2,065	2,546	151	263	3,834	1	...	1	...	...	...	1,138	283	296	7	...	559	
5,755	1,310	1,966	38	197	2,479	...	...	...	...	...	...	964	256	192	7	...	516	25
3,110	*1,780*	*566*	...	...	*764*	...	...	...	...	...	...	*458*	*60*	*129*	...	...	*269*	
692	190	81	32	...	421	...	...	...	...	...	...	42	18	...	...	...	24	26
240	78	66	5	...	96	...	...	...	...	...	...	...	...	...	...	...	...	27
714	181	238	6	46	295	1	...	1	...	...	...	19	...	4	...	...	15	28
1,044	306	195	70	20	543	...	...	...	...	...	...	13	9	...	...	...	4	29
14,101	2,292	6,885	230	1,088	4,924	51	...	24	...	...	27	548	121	144	5	1	283	
3,103	593	1,446	23	159	1,064	...	...	...	...	...	...	221	69	52	...	...	100	30
3,069	488	1,423	30	230	1,158	...	...	...	...	...	...	103	25	40	...	...	38	31
5,844	421	3,324	40	653	2,099	51	...	24	...	...	27	108	7	42	...	1	59	32
2,085	790	692	137	46	603	...	...	...	...	...	...	116	20	10	5	...	86	33
13,667	2,427	6,311	228	1,053	4,929	...	...	...	...	...	...	266	104	24	6	...	138	
5,303	899	2,959	118	804	1,445	...	...	...	...	...	...	3	...	2	...	...	1	34
2,659	354	1,033	36	115	1,272	...	...	...	...	...	...	155	82	3	5	...	70	35
2,283	488	754	12	59	1,041	...	...	...	...	...	...	108	22	19	1	...	67	36
3,422	686	1,565	52	75	1,171	...	...	...	...	...	...	...	...	...	...	...	...	37
9,923	3,574	2,120	491	157	4,229	...	...	...	...	...	...	1,912	556	467	59	159	889	
2,285	1,194	294	88	47	797	...	...	...	...	...	...	1,431	463	342	59	108	626	38
7,619	2,361	1,826	403	110	3,432	...	...	...	...	...	...	481	91	125	...	51	263	39
19	19	...	...	...	...	...	...	...	...	...	...	...	...	...	...	...	...	40

IMPERIAL TABLE XV-AII.—

Serial No.	District or State.	Groups 62, Makers of sugar, molasses and gur. — Total Workers and Dependents.	Actual Workers. Total. Males.	Actual Workers. Total. Females.	Partially Agriculturist. Males.	Partially Agriculturist. Females.	Dependents.	Group 63, Sweetmeat makers and preparers of jams and condiments. — Total Workers and Dependents.	Actual Workers. Total. Males.	Actual Workers. Total. Females.	Partially Agriculturist. Males.	Partially Agriculturist. Females.	Dependents.
	1	304	305	306	307	308	309	310	311	312	313	314	315
	Provincial Total ...	8,298	684	5,378	40	308	2,236	2,113	532	742	9	15	839
	Burma Proper ...	8,288	684	5,378	40	308	2,226	1,962	427	741	9	15	794
	Arakan Division ...	47	21	2	...	...	24	111	23	...	2	...	88
1	Akyab	...	...	...	...	...	...	80	...	...	...	...	80
2	Northern Arakan ...	...	...	...	...	...	...	...	...	...	...	...	...
3	Kyaukpyu ...	47	21	2	...	...	24	31	23	...	2	...	8
4	Sandoway ...	...	...	...	...	...	...	...	...	...	...	...	...
	Pegu Division ...	281	27	122	...	...	132	802	124	405	1	5	273
5	City of Rangoon ...	...	...	...	...	...	...	125	97	2	...	...	26
6	Hanthawaddy ...	65	3	...	...	...	62	44	18	6	1	...	20
7	Tharrawaddy ...	4	...	1	...	...	3	20	9	...	...	...	11
8	Pegu	...	...	...	...	...	...	526	...	346	...	5	180
9	Prome	212	24	121	...	...	67	87	...	51	...	...	36
	Irrawaddy Division ...	288	31	170	1	...	85	342	45	143	...	...	154
10	Bassein	5	...	3	...	...	2	42	33	...	...	...	9
11	Henzada... ...	283	31	169	1	...	83	...	...	...	...	...	...
12	Myaungmya ...	...	...	...	...	...	...	39	...	23	...	...	16
13	Ma-ubin	...	...	...	...	...	...	46	12	8	...	...	26
14	Pyapôn	...	...	...	...	...	...	215	...	112	...	...	103
	Tenasserim Division	261	103	27	1	...	131	182	52	59	...	20	71
15	Toungoo... ...	50	20	7	...	...	23	131	45	45	...	10	41
16	Salween	...	...	...	...	...	...	...	...	...	...	...	...
17	Thatôn	37	3	4	...	...	30	28	3	10	...	...	15
18	Amherst	99	48	12	...	...	39	...	...	...	...	...	...
19	Tavoy	29	13	3	...	...	13	23	4	4	...	...	15
20	Mergui	46	19	1	1	...	26	...	...	...	...	...	...
	Magwe Division ...	929	39	761	...	12	129	192	86	30	...	...	76
21	Thayetmyo ...	22	...	9	...	...	13	2	...	...	...	...	2
22	Pakôkku ...	542	20	489	...	7	33	...	...	...	...	...	...
23	Minbu	222	11	177	...	5	34	...	...	...	...	...	...
24	Magwe	143	8	86	...	...	49	190	86	30	...	...	74
	Mandalay Division ...	5	...	4	...	...	1	259	44	103	1	...	112
25	Mandalay (including City).	5	...	4	...	...	1	250	35	103	...	...	112
	Mandalay City ...	*5*	...	*4*	...	...	*1*	*160*	*35*	*57*	...	...	*68*
26	Bhamo	...	...	...	...	...	...	9	9	...	1	...	...
27	Myitkyina ...	...	...	...	...	...	...	...	...	...	...	...	...
28	Katha	...	...	...	...	...	...	...	...	...	...	...	...
29	Ruby Mines ...	...	...	...	...	...	...	...	...	...	...	...	...
	Sagaing Division ...	4,465	352	2,959	26	263	1,154	19	10	1	3	...	8
30	Shwebo	1,591	61	921	7	114	609	...	...	...	...	...	...
31	Sagaing	378	88	157	7	41	133	...	...	...	...	...	...
32	Lower Chindwin ...	2,496	203	1881	12	108	412	...	...	...	...	...	...
33	Upper Chindwin ...	...	...	...	...	...	...	19	10	1	3	...	8
	Meiktila Division ...	2,012	111	1,331	12	33	570	55	43	...	2	...	12
34	Kyauksè	356	22	273	8	33	61	...	...	...	...	...	...
35	Meiktila	104	49	...	4	...	55	55	43	...	2	...	12
36	Yamèthin ...	29	4	5	...	...	20	...	...	...	...	...	...
37	Myingyan ...	1,523	36	1,053	...	...	434	...	...	...	...	...	...
	Specially Administered Territories.	10	...	...	...	...	10	151	105	1	...	...	45
38	Northern Shan States	...	...	...	...	...	...	1	...	1	...	...	...
39	Southern Shan States	...	...	...	...	...	...	150	105	...	...	...	45
40	Chin Hills ...	10	...	...	...	...	10	...	...	...	...	...	...

Occupations. Details by Districts.

GROUP 65, TODDY DRAWERS.						GROUP 66, MANUFACTURERS OF TOBACCO, OPIUM AND GANJA.						ORDER XIII, INDUSTRIES OF DRESS AND THE TOILET.						
Total Workers and Dependents.	Actual Workers. Total.		Actual Workers. Partially Agriculturist.		Dependents.	Total Workers and Dependents.	Actual Workers. Total.		Actual Workers. Partially Agriculturists.		Dependents.	Total Workers and Dependents.	Actual Workers. Total.		Actual Workers. Partially Agriculturist.		Dependents.	
	Males.	Females.	Males.	Females.			Males.	Females.	Males.	Females.			Males.	Females.	Males.	Females.		Serial No.
316	317	318	319	320	321	322	323	324	325	326	327	328	329	330	331	332	333	
35,152	11,301	904	1,433	17	22,947	13,171	1,162	7,359	22	50	4,650	116,056	45,886	23,830	1,429	729	46,340	
34,780	10,969	904	1,421	17	22,847	12,809	1,162	7,050	22	50	4,597	107,457	42,495	21,543	989	656	43,419	
16	...	7	...	...	9	322	33	182	...	..	107	4,950	2,333	762	4	...	1,855	
...	...	...	...	...	...	138	21	99	...	...	18	3,651	1,915	293	1	...	1,443	1
...	...	...	...	...	...	...	...	...	...	...	...	20	16	4	...	...	...	2
2	...	...	...	...	2	160	12	64	...	...	84	431	229	55	3	...	147	3
14	...	7	...	...	7	24	...	19	...	...	5	848	173	410	...	...	265	4
2,317	1,124	88	27	...	1,105	6,088	499	3,638	...	2	1,951	28,036	14,779	4,342	19	35	8,915	
52	41	1	...	...	10	3,099	396	1,621	...	...	1,082	13,670	7,689	1,814	4	1	4,167	5
6	4	...	...	...	2	437	12	329	...	1	96	5,347	3,543	601	...	3	1,203	6
227	103	16	...	...	108	165	23	82	...	...	60	2,636	931	541	6	16	1,164	7
6	5	...	...	...	1	700	28	479	...	1	193	2,752	981	762	5	11	1,009	8
2,026	971	71	27	...	984	1,687	40	1,127	...	...	520	3,631	1,635	624	4	4	1,372	9
972	353	2	3	...	617	2,741	102	1,773	...	28	866	14,511	7,135	1,479	66	32	5,897	
29	12	...	...	...	17	73	4	49	...	...	20	3,691	1,989	274	10	2	1,428	10
900	331	2	3	...	567	418	3	318	...	...	97	3,915	1,701	588	29	19	1,626	11
43	10	...	...	...	33	217	38	102	...	...	77	1,894	830	144	2	5	920	12
...	...	...	...	...	...	1,668	57	1,095	...	28	516	3,176	1,771	221	12	5	1,184	13
...	...	...	...	...	...	365	...	209	...	...	156	1,835	844	252	13	...	739	14
453	138	49	...	..	266	2,038	157	825	...	18	1,056	9,288	2,816	2,199	43	17	4,273	
232	83	2	...	...	147	372	89	117	...	...	165	1,858	672	394	1	1	792	15
...	...	...	...	...	...	8	3	...	...	...	5	57	18	7	...	...	32	16
144	50	2	...	...	92	239	7	137	...	16	95	1,840	421	328	6	...	1,091	17
26	3	6	...	...	17	1,238	47	475	...	2	716	2,952	1,253	542	32	...	1,157	18
10	2	...	...	...	8	34	2	27	...	...	5	1,373	274	383	4	16	716	19
41	...	39	...	...	2	147	9	69	...	...	69	1,178	178	545	...	...	455	20
9,106	2,114	323	61	...	6,669	381	58	219	...	...	104	7,487	3,044	2,066	62	11	2,377	
580	161	22	...	...	397	134	12	95	...	...	27	1,541	509	223	...	...	809	21
4,798	749	80	16	...	3,969	47	14	8	...	...	25	2,792	1,058	1,344	1	2	390	22
1,485	460	18	41	...	1,007	84	...	74	...	...	10	1,917	900	374	49	7	643	23
2,243	744	203	4	...	1,296	116	32	42	...	...	42	1,237	567	125	12	2	545	24
2	2	...	...	...	...	728	180	250	...	...	298	15,708	4,264	3,227	291	76	8,217	
...	...	...	...	...	...	558	180	96	...	...	282	11,416	2,885	2,042	172	46	6,489	25
...	...	...	...	...	...	*551*	*173*	*96*	...	...	*282*	*8,680*	*2,381*	*1,682*	...	...	*4,617*	
...	...	...	...	...	...	170	...	154	...	...	16	1,064	400	184	17	8	480	26
...	...	...	...	...	...	...	...	...	...	...	...	384	176	37	24	...	171	27
...	...	...	...	...	...	...	...	...	...	...	...	1,059	258	384	19	2	417	28
2	2	...	..	..	...	...	..	...	...	...	...	1,785	545	580	59	20	660	29
5,669	1,580	244	60	...	3,845	236	43	102	21	2	91	12,789	4,029	3,363	288	267	5,397	
1,139	96	...	...	...	1,043	107	2	40	...	1	65	2,884	1,068	609	21	67	1,207	30
2,117	638	162	8	...	1,317	...	...	...	...	...	...	2,767	1,038	490	101	51	1,239	31
2,413	846	82	52	...	1,485	99	16	62	1	1	21	5,302	1,355	1,737	87	117	2,210	32
...	...	...	...	...	...	30	25	...	20	...	5	1,836	568	527	79	32	741	33
16,185	5,658	191	1,270	17	10,336	275	90	61	1	...	124	14,688	4,095	4,105	216	219	6,488	
822	257	161	32	2	404	15	12	...	1	...	3	2,261	675	790	75	71	796	34
476	281	17	...	2	178	2	...	2	...	...	...	4,843	1,250	1,255	67	216	2,338	35
143	27	...	...	...	116	110	...	4	...	...	6	2,968	595	1,265	26	28	1,108	36
14,744	5,093	13	1,238	13	9,638	248	78	55	...	...	115	4,616	1,575	785	48	24	2,256	37
432	332	...	12	...	100	362	...	309	...	...	53	8,599	3,391	2,287	430	73	2,921	
104	70	...	...	...	34	...	...	...	...	...	...	3,387	967	1,043	81	36	1,377	38
328	262	...	12	...	66	362	...	309	...	...	53	5,175	2,407	1,237	349	37	1,531	39
...	...	...	...	...	...	...	...	...	...	...	...	37	17	7	...	...	13	40

Serial No.	District or State.	Group 68, Tailors, Milliners, Dress-makers and Embroiderers. Total Workers and Dependents.	Actual Workers. Total. Males.	Total. Females.	Partially Agriculturist. Males.	Partially Agriculturist. Females.	Dependents.	Group 69, Shoe, Boot and Sandal Makers. Total Workers and Dependents.	Actual Workers. Total. Males.	Total. Females.	Partially Agriculturist. Males.	Partially Agriculturist. Females.	Dependents.
	1	334	335	336	337	338	339	340	341	342	343	344	345
	Provincial Total ...	60,870	25,083	10,702	1,082	240	25,085	11,972	5,093	1,939	29	28	4,940
	Burma Proper ...	56,923	22,858	9,975	758	230	24,090	11,245	4,897	1,750	25	28	4,598
	Arakan Division ...	3,264	1,349	533	4	...	1,382	42	32	...	...	...	10
1	Akyab	2,097	1,003	85	1	...	1,009	28	21	...	...	...	7
2	Northern Arakan ...	16	12	4	...	...	...	...	...	...	...	...	...
3	Kyaukpyu ...	350	181	38	3	...	131	8	7	...	...	...	1
4	Sandoway ...	801	153	406	...	...	242	6	4	...	...	...	2
	Pegu Division ...	15,124	7,683	2,970	12	32	4,471	3,265	1,772	183	1	...	1,310
5	City of Rangoon ...	5,668	2,969	1,181	3	1	1,518	2,280	1,230	106	...	...	944
6	Hanthawaddy ...	4,021	2,955	369	...	2	697	140	44	17	...	...	79
7	Tharrawaddy ...	1,927	527	471	5	15	929	103	59	1	...	...	43
8	Pegu	1,466	325	605	1	11	536	108	70	3	1	...	35
9	Prome	2,042	907	344	3	4	791	634	369	56	...	...	209
	Irrawaddy Division ...	10,446	4,949	938	66	24	4,559	547	260	26	...	...	261
10	Bassein	2,807	1,481	180	10	1	1,146	165	105	2	...	...	58
11	Henzada	2,979	1,272	451	29	15	1,256	245	112	2	...	...	131
12	Myaungmya ..	1,451	665	47	2	3	739	39	11	5	...	...	23
13	Ma-ubin	2,096	1,045	134	12	5	917	50	10	12	...	...	28
14	Pyapôn	1,113	486	126	13	...	501	48	22	5	...	...	21
	Tenasserim Division ...	5,712	1,161	1,664	34	16	2,887	520	240	63	...	...	217
15	Toungoo	1,120	312	290	...	...	518	164	99	6	...	...	59
16	Salween	46	11	6	...	...	29	...	...	...	...	...	...
17	Thatôn	1,002	52	241	...	...	709	86	34	2	...	...	50
18	Amherst	1,433	515	294	30	...	624	200	83	35	...	...	82
19	Tavoy	1,176	191	343	4	16	642	36	19	...	...	...	17
20	Mergui	935	80	490	...	...	365	34	5	20	...	...	9
	Magwe Division ...	4,527	1,828	1,401	20	10	1,298	755	418	33	...	...	304
21	Thayetmyo ...	766	219	65	...	...	482	201	69	19	...	...	113
22	Pakôkku	2,021	794	1,119	1	2	108	176	104	1	...	...	71
23	Minbu	991	475	177	7	6	339	351	232	8	...	...	111
24	Magwe	749	340	40	12	2	369	27	13	5	...	...	9
	Mandalay Division ...	6,816	1,561	702	232	34	4,553	2,792	951	830	4	12	1,011
25	Mandalay (including City).	4,102	595	15	157	11	3,492	2,719	893	828	3	12	998
	Mandalay City ...	*2,592*	*456*	*15*	...	...	*2,111*	*2,461*	*824*	*746*	...	...	*891*
26	Bhamo	801	262	153	10	5	386	7	6	...	1	...	1
27	Myitkyina ...	158	78	22	20	...	58	6	6	...	...	...	...
28	Katha	576	197	68	19	...	311	4	...	2	...	...	2
29	Ruby Mines ...	1,179	429	444	26	18	306	56	46	...	...	...	10
	Sagaing Division ...	5,051	1,802	1,099	221	86	2,150	2,325	876	461	8	15	988
30	Shwebo	928	347	176	20	6	405	731	394	27	...	1	310
31	Sagaing	780	210	107	84	2	463	655	394	39	5	12	222
32	Lower Chindwin ...	1,851	821	303	54	46	722	926	81	395	3	2	450
33	Upper Chindwin ...	1,492	424	503	63	32	560	13	7	...	...	...	6
	Meiktila Division ...	5,983	2,525	668	169	28	2,790	999	348	154	12	1	497
34	Kyaukse	557	220	107	55	9	230	152	79	17	4	1	56
35	Meiktila	1,624	644	238	53	5	741	326	35	78	2	...	213
36	Yamèthin ...	1,314	348	73	16	1	893	180	131	18	5	...	31
37	Myingyan ...	2,488	1,313	250	45	13	925	341	103	41	1	...	197
	Specially Administered Territories.	3,947	2,225	727	324	10	995	727	196	189	14	10	342
38	Northern Shan States	2,076	592	708	59	6	776	202	108	1	...	...	93
39	Southern Shan States	1,847	1,624	13	265	4	210	524	88	188	14	10	248
40	Chin Hills ...	24	9	6	...	...	9	1	...	...	...	...	1

Occupations. Details by Districts.

GROUP 71, WASHING, DYEING AND CLEANING.						GROUP 72, BARBERS, HAIR DRESSERS AND WIGMAKERS.						GROUP 73, OTHER INDUSTRIES CONNECTED WITH THE TOILET (TATTOOERS, SHAMPOOERS), ETC.						
Total Workers and Dependents.	ACTUAL WORKERS.				Dependents.	Total Workers and Dependents.	ACTUAL WORKERS.				Dependents.	Total Workers and Dependents.	ACTUAL WORKERS.				Dependents.	Serial No.
	TOTAL.		PARTIALLY AGRICULTURIST.				TOTAL.		PARTIALLY AGRICULTURIST.				TOTAL.		PARTIALLY AGRICULTURIST.			
	Males.	Females.	Males.	Females.			Males.	Females.	Males.	Females.			Males.	Females.	Males.	Females.		
346	347	348	349	350	351	352	353	354	355	356	357	358	359	360	361	362	363	
23,742	9,706	4,949	164	218	9,087	4,877	2,660	1,265	12	17	952	12,624	2,707	4,633	106	206	5,284	
21,478	9,268	3,934	144	206	8,276	4,739	2,619	1,255	6	17	865	11,469	2,366	4,411	53	175	4,692	
1,323	787	214	...	...	322	238	125	7	...	...	106	65	31	8	...	...	26	
1,266	752	201	...	...	313	230	118	7	...	...	105	30	21	...	...	...	9	1
3	3	...	...	...	...	1	1	...	...	...	...	...	...	...	...	...	...	2
38	22	12	...	...	4	6	6	...	...	...	...	19	4	5	...	...	10	3
16	10	1	...	...	5	1	...	...	...	...	1	16	6	3	...	...	7	4
6,219	3,380	716	1	2	2,123	1,850	1,503	30	1	...	317	1,123	253	355	2	1	515	
3,690	2,048	379	...	...	1,263	1,456	1,241	22	1	...	193	208	62	42	...	...	104	5
826	448	124	...	2	254	83	28	2	...	...	53	276	67	89	...	...	120	6
362	241	22	...	...	99	76	67	...	...	...	9	155	25	47	1	1	83	7
792	406	89	1	...	297	180	122	6	...	...	52	171	33	59	...	...	79	8
549	237	102	...	...	210	55	45	...	...	...	10	313	66	118	1	...	129	9
2,081	1,282	214	...	3	585	277	216	1	...	...	60	1,079	408	293	...	4	378	
482	302	70	...	1	110	98	78	1	...	...	19	99	22	20	...	...	57	10
385	228	43	...	2	114	59	45	...	...	...	14	222	33	86	...	2	103	11
146	72	20	...	...	54	43	26	...	...	...	17	204	53	72	...	2	79	12
727	507	40	...	...	180	26	24	...	...	...	2	272	180	35	...	...	57	13
341	173	41	...	...	127	51	43	...	...	...	8	282	120	80	...	...	82	14
2,017	911	319	2	...	787	459	348	9	2	1	102	526	140	135	5	...	251	
353	165	35	...	...	153	64	49	5	...	1	10	154	44	58	1	...	52	15
4	3	1	...	...	...	2	2	...	...	...	...	5	2	...	...	...	3	16
477	219	59	...	...	199	102	70	1	2	...	31	150	36	25	4	...	89	17
951	411	183	2	...	357	253	201	2	...	...	50	140	40	28	...	...	72	18
97	50	19	...	...	28	8	5	1	...	...	2	33	9	11	...	...	13	19
135	63	22	...	...	50	30	21	...	...	...	9	44	9	13	...	...	22	20
856	452	72	41	...	332	156	124	2	...	...	30	1,105	218	520	1	1	367	
269	142	21	...	...	106	45	33	...	...	...	12	177	42	81	...	...	54	21
140	63	17	...	...	60	19	16	...	...	...	3	436	91	207	...	...	138	22
214	117	15	41	...	82	33	26	...	...	...	7	328	50	174	1	1	104	23
233	130	19	...	...	84	59	49	2	...	...	8	164	35	58	...	...	71	24
2,991	945	774	43	6	1,272	521	253	68	2	...	200	1,723	329	778	10	24	616	
1,919	643	570	1	...	706	447	221	67	1	...	159	1,387	308	503	10	23	576	25
1,541	516	470	...	...	555	138	108	7	...	...	23	1,110	245	385	...	...	480	
237	122	28	6	3	87	5	5	...	...	...	...	14	5	3	...	...	6	26
152	69	14	3	...	69	61	20	...	1	...	41	7	3	1	...	...	3	27
133	41	26	...	1	66	8	7	1	...	...	...	315	13	271	...	1	31	28
550	70	136	33	2	344	...	...	...	...	...	...	...	...	...	...	...	...	29
1,796	634	389	41	90	773	33	19	3	...	...	11	3,564	687	1,410	18	76	1,467	
593	208	176	...	56	209	3	...	3	...	...	...	613	109	227	1	4	277	30
543	167	132	8	29	244	9	4	...	...	...	5	780	263	212	4	17	305	31
396	139	76	17	14	181	11	9	...	...	...	2	2,114	304	957	13	55	853	32
264	120	5	16	...	139	10	6	...	...	...	4	57	11	14	...	...	32	33
4,195	877	1,236	16	105	2,082	1,205	31	1,135	1	16	39	2,284	300	912	17	69	1,072	
1,121	276	492	3	33	353	13	4	2	...	...	7	397	83	172	12	28	142	34
1,925	382	634	9	70	909	33	23	...	...	...	10	934	165	315	3	41	454	35
242	99	10	4	1	133	1,154	2	1,133	1	16	19	78	15	31	...	...	32	36
907	120	100	...	1	687	5	2	...	...	...	3	875	37	394	2	...	444	37
2,264	438	1,015	20	12	811	138	41	10	6	...	87	1,155	341	222	53	31	592	
447	43	169	...	...	235	94	19	9	6	...	66	372	107	92	16	30	173	38
1,806	387	846	20	12	573	43	22	...	...	...	21	783	234	130	37	1	419	39
11	8	...	...	...	3	1	...	1	...	...	...	...	...	...	...	...	...	40

	DISTRICT OR STATE.	ORDER XIV.—FURNITURE INDUSTRIES.					
		Total Workers and Dependents.	ACTUAL WORKERS.				Dependents.
			TOTAL.		PARTIALLY AGRICULTURIST.		
			Males.	Females.	Males.	Females.	
	1	364	365	366	367	368	369
Serial No.							
	Provincial Total ...	1,862	1,523	69	56	40	280
	Burma Proper ...	1,852	1,513	69	56	40	270
	Arakan Division ...	...	...	...	...	...	...
1	Akyab ...	...	...	...	...	...	...
2	Northern Arakan ...	...	...	...	...	...	...
3	Kyaukpyu ...	...	...	...	...	...	...
4	Sandoway ...	...	...	...	...	...	...
	Pegu Division ...	1,583	1,382	...	...	...	200
5	City of Rangoon ...	389	228	...	...	...	161
6	Hanthawaddy ...	1,189	1,154	...	...	...	35
7	Tharrawaddy ...	...	...	...	...	...	...
8	Pegu ...	5	1	...	...	...	4
9	Prome ...	...	...	...	...	...	...
	Irrawaddy Division ...	26	18	...	...	...	8
10	Bassein ...	26	18	...	...	...	8
11	Henzada ...	...	...	...	...	...	...
12	Myaungmya ...	...	...	...	...	...	...
13	Ma-ubin ...	...	...	...	...	...	...
14	Pyapôn ...	...	...	...	...	...	...
	Tenasserim Division ...	26	2	12	...	...	12
15	Toungoo ...	25	2	12	...	...	11
16	Salween ...	...	...	...	...	...	...
17	Thatôn ...	...	...	...	...	...	...
18	Amherst ...	...	...	...	...	...	...
19	Tavoy ...	...	...	...	...	...	...
20	Mergui ...	1	...	...	...	...	1
	Magwe Division ...	36	9	2	...	...	25
21	Thayetmyo ...	24	...	1	...	...	23
22	Pakôkku ...	1	1	...	...	...	...
23	Minbu ...	9	8	...	...	...	1
24	Magwe ...	2	...	1	...	...	1
	Mandalay Division ...	87	17	53	17	40	17
25	Mandalay (including City).	87	17	53	17	40	17
	Mandalay City ...	70	...	53	17	40	17
26	Bhamo ...	...	...	...	...	...	...
27	Myitkyina ...	...	...	...	...	...	...
28	Katha ...	...	...	...	...	...	...
29	Ruby Mines ...	...	...	...	...	...	...
	Sagaing Division ...	77	77	...	38	...	...
30	Shwebo ...	77	77	...	38	...	...
31	Sagaing ...	...	...	...	...	...	...
32	Lower Chindwin ...	...	...	...	...	...	...
33	Upper Chindwin ...	...	...	...	...	...	...
	Meiktila Division ...	17	7	2	1	...	8
34	Kyauksè ...	2	...	2	...	...	...
35	Meiktila ...	15	7	...	1	...	8
36	Yamèthin ...	...	...	...	...	...	...
37	Myingyan ...	...	...	...	...	...	...
	Specially Administered Territories.	10	...	...	...	...	10
38	Northern Shan States	...	...	...	...	...	...
39	Southern Shan States	10	...	...	...	...	10
40	Chin Hills ...	...	...	...	...	...	...

	DISTRICT OR STATE.	GROUP 74. CABINET MAKERS, CARRIAGE PAINTERS, ETC.					
		Total Workers and Dependents.	ACTUAL WORKERS.				Dependents.
			TOTAL.		PARTIALLY AGRICULTURIST.		
			Males.	Females.	Males.	Females.	
	1	370	371	372	373	374	375
Serial No.							
	Provincial Total ...	1,820	1,494	67	39	40	259
	Burma Proper ...	1,810	1,494	67	39	40	249
	Arakan Division ...	...	...	...	...	...	...
1	Akyab ...	...	...	...	...	...	...
2	Northern Arakan ...	...	...	...	...	...	...
3	Kyaukpyu ...	...	...	...	...	...	...
4	Sandoway ...	...	...	...	...	...	...
	Pegu Division ...	1,578	1,382	...	...	...	196
5	City of Rangoon ...	389	228	...	...	...	161
6	Hanthawaddy ...	1,189	1,154	...	...	...	35
7	Tharrawaddy ...	...	...	...	...	...	...
8	Pegu ...	...	...	...	...	...	...
9	Prome ...	...	...	...	...	...	...
	Irrawaddy Division ...	26	18	...	...	...	8
10	Bassein ...	26	18	...	...	...	8
11	Henzada ...	...	...	...	...	...	...
12	Myaungmya ...	...	...	...	...	...	...
13	Ma-ubin ...	...	...	...	...	...	...
14	Pyapôn ...	...	...	...	...	...	...
	Tenasserim Division ...	26	2	12	...	...	12
15	Toungoo ...	25	2	12	...	...	11
16	Salween ...	...	...	...	...	...	...
17	Thatôn ...	...	...	...	...	...	...
18	Amherst ...	...	...	...	...	...	...
19	Tavoy ...	...	...	...	...	...	...
20	Mergui ...	1	...	...	...	...	1
	Magwe Division ...	35	8	2	...	...	25
21	Thayetmyo ...	24	...	1	...	...	23
22	Pakôkku ...	...	...	...	...	...	...
23	Minbu ...	9	8	...	...	...	1
24	Magwe ...	2	...	1	...	...	1
	Mandalay Division ...	53	...	53	...	40	...
25	Mandalay (including City).	53	...	53	...	40	...
	Mandalay City ...	53	...	53	...	40	...
26	Bhamo ...	...	...	...	...	...	...
27	Myitkyina ...	...	...	...	...	...	...
28	Katha ...	...	...	...	...	...	...
29	Ruby Mines ...	...	...	...	...	...	...
	Sagaing Division ...	77	77	...	38	...	...
30	Shwebo ...	77	77	...	38	...	...
31	Sagaing ...	...	...	...	...	...	...
32	Lower Chindwin ...	...	...	...	...	...	...
33	Upper Chindwin ...	...	...	...	...	...	...
	Meiktila Division ...	15	7	...	1	...	8
34	Kyauksè ...	...	...	...	...	...	...
35	Meiktila ...	...	...	...	...	...	...
36	Yamèthin ...	15	7	...	1	...	8
37	Myingyan ...	...	...	...	...	...	...
	Specially Administered Territories.	10	...	...	...	...	10
38	Northern Shan States	...	...	...	...	...	...
39	Southern Shan States	10	...	...	...	...	10
40	Chin Hills ...	...	...	...	...	...	...

Occupations. Details by Districts.

ORDER XV.—BUILDING INDUSTRIES.						GROUP 76, LIME-BURNERS, CEMENT WORKERS, ETC.						GROUP 78, STONE AND MARBLE WORKERS, MASONS AND BRICK-LAYERS.						
Total Workers and Dependents.	ACTUAL WORKERS.				Dependents.	Total Workers and Dependents.	ACTUAL WORKERS.				Dependents.	Total Workers and Dependents.	ACTUAL WORKERS.				Dependents.	
	TOTAL.		PARTIALLY AGRICULTURIST.				TOTAL.		PARTIALLY AGRICULTURIST.				TOTAL.		PARTIALLY AGRICULTURIST.			
	Males.	Females.	Males.	Females.			Males.	Females.	Males.	Females.			Males.	Females.	Males.	Females.		Serial No.
376	377	378	379	380	381	382	383	384	385	386	387	388	389	390	391	392	393	
24,257	9,780	2,941	177	65	10,526	1,167	294	207	...	...	566	13,008	6,020	997	140	47	5,976	
22,520	9,456	2,806	151	65	10,258	1,167	294	207	...	...	566	12,494	5,816	883	119	47	5,795	
1,895	944	223	...	2	728	...	...	...	...	...	...	500	250	36	...	...	214	
1,463	833	72	...	3	558	...	...	...	...	...	...	450	219	30	...	...	201	1
...	...	...	...	...	...	...	...	...	...	...	...	...	...	...	...	...	...	2
95	23	40	...	...	32	...	...	...	...	...	...	42	15	6	...	...	21	3
337	88	111	...	...	138	...	...	...	...	...	...	28	16	...	...	...	12	4
6,868	2,244	959	20	5	3,665	9	9	...	...	...	...	3,232	1,871	109	15	4	1,252	
2,991	1,870	2	...	...	1,119	9	9	...	...	...	...	1,128	842	...	...	...	286	5
2,403	652	862	4	1	889	...	...	...	...	...	...	740	367	26	...	...	347	6
426	201	41	10	4	184	...	...	...	...	...	...	400	190	37	10	4	173	7
495	260	17	2	...	218	...	...	...	...	...	...	483	253	17	2	...	213	8
553	261	37	4	...	255	...	...	...	...	...	...	481	219	29	3	...	233	9
3,339	1,140	580	17	32	1,619	96	4	35	...	...	57	1,938	846	151	17	26	941	
517	184	130	2	6	203	...	...	...	...	...	...	339	139	30	2	...	170	10
962	371	103	14	26	488	...	...	...	...	...	...	926	367	98	14	26	461	11
1,003	348	200	1	...	455	96	4	35	...	...	57	429	196	17	1	...	216	12
251	159	6	...	...	86	...	...	...	...	...	...	152	95	6	...	...	51	13
606	78	141	...	...	387	...	...	...	...	...	...	92	49	...	...	...	43	14
4,582	1,417	1,184	54	...	1,981	654	282	118	...	...	254	1,585	656	130	50	...	799	
386	195	14	50	...	177	13	6	...	...	...	7	326	165	12	50	...	149	15
2	1	...	...	...	1	...	...	...	...	...	...	2	1	...	...	...	1	16
1,731	618	332	2	...	781	641	276	118	...	...	247	642	250	55	...	...	337	17
1,299	285	406	2	...	608	...	...	...	...	...	...	337	150	13	...	...	174	18
955	212	414	...	...	329	...	...	...	...	...	...	208	65	49	...	...	94	19
209	106	18	...	...	85	...	...	...	...	...	...	70	25	1	...	...	44	20
2,183	735	423	20	8	1,025	335	91	33	...	...	211	1,164	512	51	...	...	601	
540	179	28	...	...	333	320	91	21	...	...	208	203	85	6	...	...	112	21
442	180	67	...	...	195	...	...	...	...	...	...	362	180	11	...	...	171	22
765	172	286	20	8	307	1	...	...	...	...	1	337	132	6	...	...	199	23
436	204	42	...	...	190	14	...	12	...	...	2	262	115	28	...	...	119	24
1,934	739	196	2	...	999	12	8	...	...	...	4	1,593	573	189	1	...	831	
1,619	560	196	1	...	863	12	8	...	...	...	4	1,369	456	189	...	...	724	25
1,493	*514*	*182*	...	...	*797*	...	...	...	...	...	...	*1,276*	*424*	*176*	...	...	*676*	
44	18	...	1	...	26	...	...	...	...	...	...	44	18	...	1	...	26	26
36	12	...	...	...	24	...	...	...	...	...	...	36	12	...	...	...	24	27
43	31	...	...	...	12	...	...	...	...	...	...	12	9	...	...	...	3	28
192	118	...	...	...	74	...	...	...	...	...	...	132	78	...	...	...	54	29
1,406	621	114	11	17	671	...	...	...	...	...	...	1,259	559	114	9	17	586	
342	161	12	1	...	169	...	...	...	...	...	...	298	140	12	1	...	146	30
142	88	...	2	...	54	...	...	...	...	...	...	133	82	...	1	...	51	31
890	344	102	8	17	444	...	...	...	...	...	...	800	311	102	7	17	387	32
32	28	...	...	...	4	...	...	...	...	...	...	28	26	...	...	...	2	33
1,353	616	127	27	...	610	61	...	21	...	...	40	1,203	549	103	27	...	551	
189	120	12	10	...	57	16	...	9	...	...	7	162	114	...	10	...	48	34
269	122	33	...	...	114	...	...	...	...	...	...	262	115	33	...	...	114	35
562	249	48	16	...	265	45	...	12	...	...	33	446	195	36	16	...	215	36
333	125	34	1	...	174	...	...	...	...	...	...	333	125	34	1	...	174	37
737	324	135	26	...	278	...	...	...	...	...	...	509	214	114	21	...	181	
162	69	15	11	...	78	...	...	...	...	...	...	92	40	3	11	...	49	38
575	255	120	15	...	200	...	...	...	...	...	...	417	174	111	10	...	132	39
...	...	...	...	...	...	...	...	...	...	...	...	...	...	...	...	...	...	40

Serial No.	DISTRICT OR STATE.	GROUP 79.—OTHERS (THATCHERS, BUILDING CONTRACTORS, HOUSE PAINTERS, TILERS, PLUMBERS, LOCKSMITHS, ETC). Total Workers and Dependents.	Actual Workers. Total. Males.	Actual Workers. Total. Females.	Actual Workers. Partially Agriculturist. Males.	Actual Workers. Partially Agriculturist. Females.	Dependents.	ORDER XVI.—CONSTRUCTION OF MEANS OF TRANSPORT. Total Workers and Dependents.	Actual Workers. Total. Males.	Actual Workers. Total. Females.	Actual Workers. Partially Agriculturist. Males.	Actual Workers. Partially Agriculturist. Females.	Dependents.
	1	394	395	396	397	398	399	400	401	402	403	404	405
	Provincial Total ...	9,818	3,152	2,735	37	18	3,931	2,187	1,154	58	51	30	975
	Burma Proper ...	9,615	3,060	2,714	32	18	3,841	1,803	968	19	42	...	816
	Arakan Division ...	1,369	688	187	...	2	494	18	7	6	...	...	5
1	Akyab ...	1,013	614	42	...	3	357	9	...	6	...	...	3
2	Northern Arakan	...	...	...	...	...	...	...	...	...	...	...	...
3	Kyaukpyu	53	8	34	...	...	11	9	7	...	...	...	2
4	Sandoway	303	66	111	...	...	126	...	...	...		...	...
	Pegu Division	3,504	1,257	850	5	1	1,397	756	413	...	...	...	343
5	City of Rangoon	1,731	912	2	...	...	817	677	394	...	...	...	283
6	Hanthawaddy	1,663	285	836	4	1	542	22	6	...	...	...	16
7	Tharrawaddy	26	11	4	...	...	11	26	7	...	...	...	19
8	Pegu ...	12	7	...	...	...	5	10	1	...	...	...	9
9	Prome ...	72	42	8	1	...	22	21	5	...	...	...	16
	Irrawaddy Division ...	1,302	290	392	...	6	620	153	92	...	13	...	61
10	Bassein ...	175	45	98	...	6	32	1	1	...	...	...	...
11	Henzada	36	4	5	...	...	27	149	91	...	13	...	58
12	Myaungmya	478	148	148	...	...	182	3	...	...	...	...	3
13	Ma-ubin	99	64	...	...	...	35	...	...	...	...	...	...
14	Pyapôn ...	514	29	141	...	...	344	...	...	...	...	...	...
	Tenasserim Division ...	2,343	479	926	4	...	938	111	35	...	...	...	76
15	Toungoo	47	24	2	...	...	21	24	...	...	...	...	24
16	Salween ...	...	...	...	...	...	...	...	...	...	...	...	...
17	Thaton ...	448	92	159	2	...	197	45	24	...	...	...	21
18	Amherst	962	135	393	2	...	434	35	7	...	...	...	28
19	Tavoy ...	747	147	365	...	...	235	...	...	...	...	...	...
20	Mergui ...	139	81	17	...	...	41	7	4	...	...	...	3
	Magwe Division ...	579	66	239	20	8	274	14	1	1	...	...	12
21	Thayetmyo	17	3	1	...	...	13	...	...	...	...	...	...
22	Pakôkku	80	...	56	...	...	24	...	...	...	...	...	...
23	Minbu ...	426	40	280	20	8	106	1	1	...	...	...	...
24	Magwe ...	56	23	2	...	...	31	13	...	1	...	...	12
	Mandalay Division ...	329	158	7	1	...	164	255	109	9	1	...	137
25	Mandalay (including City).	238	96	7	1	...	135	174	99	3	...	...	72
	Mandalay City ...	*217*	*90*	*6*	...	...	*121*	*158*	*91*	*3*	...	...	*64*
26	Bhamo ...	...	...	...	...	...	...	4	...	...	...	...	4
27	Myitkyina	...	...	...	...	...	...	...	...	...	...	...	...
28	Katha ...	31	22	...	...	...	9	77	10	6	1	...	61
29	Ruby Mines	60	40	...	...	...	20						
	Sagaing Division ...	107	62	...	2	...	45	15	1	3	...	...	11
30	Shwebo ...	44	21	...	...	...	23	1	1	...	...	...	...
31	Sagaing	9	6	...	1	...	3	2	...	...	...	...	2
32	Lower Chindwin	50	35	...	1	...	17	12	...	3	...	...	9
33	Upper Chindwin	4	2	...	...	...	2	...	...	...	...	...	...
	Meiktila Division ...	82	60	2	...	...	19	481	310	...	28	...	171
34	Kyauksè ...	11	6	3	...	...	2	154	97	...	16	...	57
35	Meiktila	...	...	...	...	...	...	...	...	...	...	...	...
36	Yamèthin	71	54	...	...	...	17	327	213	...	12	...	114
37	Myingyan	...	...	...	...	...	...	...	...	...	...	...	...
	Specially Administered Territories.	203	92	21	5	...	90	384	186	39	9	30	159
38	Northern Shan States	45	11	12	...	...	22	30	24	...	9	...	6
39	Southern Shan States	158	81	9	5	...	68	346	161	39	...	30	146
40	Chin Hills ...	...	...	...	...	...	...	8	1	...	...	...	7

Occupations. Details by Districts.

GROUP 80.—CART AND CARRIAGE MAKERS AND WHEELWRIGHTS.						GROUP 82.—SHIP AND BOAT BUILDERS.						ORDER XVII (GROUP 83). PRODUCTION AND TRANSMISSION OF PHYSICAL FORCES (GAS, ELECTRIC LIGHT, ICE, ETC.)						
Total Workers and Dependents.	ACTUAL WORKERS.				Dependents.	Total Workers and Dependents.	ACTUAL WORKERS.				Dependents.	Total Workers and Dependents.	ACTUAL WORKERS.				Dependents.	
	Total.		Partially Agriculturist.				Total.		Partially Agriculturist.				Total.		Partially Agriculturist.			
	Males.	Females.	Males.	Females.			Males.	Females.	Males.	Females.			Males.	Females.	Males.	Females.		Serial No.
406	407	408	409	410	411	412	413	414	415	416	417	418	419	420	421	422	423	
1,198	507	10	32	...	681	845	565	48	15	20	231	180	72	...	1	...	108	
861	322	10	23	...	529	798	565	9	15	...	224	180	72	...	1	...	108	
...	...	...	...	...	...	18	7	6	...	...	5	...	...	...	...	...	...	
...	...	...	...	...	...	9	...	6	...	...	3	...	...	...	...	...	...	1
...	...	...	...	...	...	...	...	...	...	...	...	...	...	...	...	...	...	2
...	...	...	...	...	...	9	7	...	...	...	2	...	...	...	...	...	...	3
...	...	...	...	...	...	...	...	...	...	...	...	...	...	...	...	...	...	4
359	108	...	...	...	261	358	292	...	...	...	66	162	62	...	1	...	100	
290	89	...	...	...	201	358	292	...	...	...	66	161	61	...	1	...	100	5
12	6	...	...	...	16	...	...	...	...	...	...	...	...	...	...	...	...	6
26	7	...	...	...	19	...	...	...	...	...	...	...	...	...	...	...	...	7
10	1	...	...	...	9	...	...	...	...	...	...	1	1	...	...	...	...	8
21	5	...	...	...	16	...	...	...	...	...	...	...	...	...	...	...	...	9
...	...	...	...	...	...	152	91	...	13	...	61	...	...	...	...	...	...	
...	...	...	...	...	...	...	...	...	...	...	...	...	...	...	...	...	...	10
...	...	...	...	...	...	149	91	...	13	...	58	...	...	...	...	...	...	11
...	...	...	...	...	...	3	...	...	...	...	3	...	...	...	...	...	...	12
...	...	...	...	...	...	...	...	...	...	...	...	...	...	...	...	...	...	13
...	...	...	...	...	...	...	...	...	...	...	...	...	...	...	...	...	...	14
93	26	...	...	...	67	18	9	...	...	...	9	5	4	...	...	...	1	
19	...	...	...	...	19	5	...	...	...	...	5	...	...	...	...	...	...	15
...	...	...	...	...	...	...	...	...	...	...	...	...	...	...	...	...	...	16
39	19	...	...	...	20	6	5	...	...	...	1	...	...	...	...	...	...	17
35	7	...	...	...	28	...	...	...	...	...	...	5	4	...	...	...	1	18
...	...	...	...	...	...	...	...	...	...	...	...	...	...	...	...	...	...	19
...	...	...	...	...	...	7	4	...	...	...	3	...	...	...	...	...	...	20
14	1	1	...	...	12	...	...	...	...	...	...	...	...	...	...	...	...	
...	...	...	...	...	...	...	...	...	...	...	...	...	...	...	...	...	...	21
...	...	...	...	...	...	...	...	...	...	...	...	...	...	...	...	...	...	22
1	1	...	...	...	...	...	...	...	...	...	...	...	...	...	...	...	...	23
13	...	1	...	...	12	...	...	...	...	...	...	...	...	...	...	...	...	24
182	69	6	1	...	107	3	...	3	...	...	...	2	...	...	...	...	2	
101	59	...	...	...	42	3	...	3	...	...	...	...	...	...	...	...	...	25
85	*51*	...	...	...	*34*	*3*	...	*3*	...	...	...	...	...	...	...	...	...	
4	...	...	...	...	4	...	...	...	...	...	...	...	...	...	...	...	...	26
...	...	...	...	...	...	...	...	...	...	...	...	...	...	...	...	...	...	27
...	...	...	...	...	...	...	...	...	...	...	...	...	...	...	...	...	...	28
77	10	6	1	...	61	...	...	...	...	...	...	2	...	...	...	...	2	29
13	1	3	...	...	9	2	...	...	...	...	2	11	6	...	...	...	5	
1	1	...	...	...	...	...	...	...	...	...	...	10	6	...	...	...	4	30
...	...	...	...	...	...	2	...	...	...	...	2	1	...	...	...	...	1	31
12	...	3	...	...	9	...	...	...	...	...	...	...	...	...	...	...	...	32
...	...	...	...	...	...	...	...	...	...	...	...	...	...	...	...	...	...	33
190	117	...	22	...	73	247	166	...	2	...	81	...	...	...	...	...	...	
110	70	...	12	...	40	...	...	...	...	...	...	...	...	...	...	...	...	34
...	...	...	...	...	...	...	...	...	...	...	...	...	...	...	...	...	...	35
80	47	...	10	...	33	247	166	...	2	...	81	...	...	...	...	...	...	36
...	...	...	...	...	...	...	...	...	...	...	...	...	...	...	...	...	...	37
337	185	...	9	...	152	47	1	39	...	30	7	...	...	...	...	...	...	
30	24	...	9	...	6	...	...	...	...	...	...	...	...	...	...	...	...	38
307	161	...	...	...	146	39	...	39	...	30	...	...	...	...	...	...	...	39
...	...	...	...	...	...	8	1	...	...	...	7	...	...	...	...	...	...	40

Serial No.	DISTRICT OR STATE.	ORDER XVIII.—INDUSTRIES OF LUXURY AND THOSE PERTAINING TO LITERATURE AND THE ARTS AND SCIENCES.						GROUP 84, PRINTERS, LITHOGRAPHERS, ENGRAVERS, ETC.					
		Total Workers and Dependents.	ACTUAL WORKERS. Total.		Partially Agriculturist.		Dependents.	Total Workers and Dependents.	ACTUAL WORKERS. Total.		Partially Agriculturist.		Dependents.
			Males.	Females.	Males.	Females.			Males.	Females.	Males.	Females.	
	1	424	425	426	427	428	429	430	431	432	433	434	435
	Provincial Total ...	58,878	23,454	4,802	652	318	30,622	2,981	1,343	29	2	...	1,609
	Burma Proper ...	55,375	21,840	4,483	514	300	29,052	2,972	1,340	29	2	...	1,603
	Arakan Division ...	4,850	2,033	899	7	17	1,918	...	...	...	...	...	...
1	Akyab	3,841	1,693	765	1	11	1,383	...	...	...	...	...	...
2	Northern Arakan ...	11	4	...	1	...	7	...	...	...	...	...	...
3	Kyaukpyu ...	752	235	134	6	6	383	...	...	...	...	...	...
4	Sandoway ...	246	101	...	..	...	145	...	...	...	...	...	...
	Pegu Division ...	16,421	7,265	312	22	...	8,844	2,758	1,268	2	2	...	1,488
5	City of Rangoon ...	8,569	4,003	84	6	...	4,482	2,578	1,166	2	2	..	1,410
6	Hanthawaddy ...	2,657	1,102	79	8	...	1,476	25	18	...	...	...	7
7	Tharrawaddy ...	1,369	523	89	3	...	757	6	...	...	...	...	6
8	Pegu	2,009	792	23	3	...	1,194	17	11	...	...	...	6
9	Prome	1,817	845	37	2	...	935	132	73	...	...	...	59
	Irrawaddy Division ...	7,745	3,170	184	40	22	4,291	22	6	..	...	...	16
10	Bassein	1,372	504	25	16	...	843	...	...	...	...	...	...
11	Henzada	2,418	976	166	13	15	1,276	22	6	...	...	...	16
12	Myaungmya ...	1,253	466	53	2	...	734	...	.	...	...	...	...
13	Ma-ubin	1,336	517	21	9	7	798	...	...	...	...	...	...
14	Pyapôn	1,366	707	19	...	...	640	...	...	...	...	...	...
	Tenasserim Division ...	6,285	2,291	156	21	...	3,838	74	30	1	...	...	43
15	Toungoo	1,436	579	8	3	...	849	8	...	...	...	...	8
16	Salween	47	20	...	...	...	27	...	...	...	...	...	...
17	Thatôn	1,691	592	33	7	...	1,066	4	1	...	...	...	3
18	Amherst	2,153	856	40	9	...	1,257	62	29	1	...	...	32
19	Tavoy	460	198	...	1	...	262	...	...	...	...	...	...
20	Mergui	498	46	75	1	...	377	...	...	...	...	...	...
	Magwe Division ...	4,392	1,715	435	30	...	2,242	19	6	...	...	...	13
21	Thayetmyo ...	973	372	107	2	...	494	...	..	...	..	...	...
22	Pakôkku	1,152	467	36	..	...	649	6	2	...	...	...	4
23	Minbu	1,328	481	230	22	...	617	5	2	...	...	...	3
24	Magwe	939	395	62	6	...	482	8	2	...	...	...	6
	Mandalay Division ...	5,707	2,296	597	145	29	2,814	94	30	22	...	...	42
25	Mandalay (including City).	4,009	1,515	524	8	6	1,970	71	21	12	...	...	38
	Mandalay City ...	*3,294*	*1,288*	*482*	...	...	*1,524*	*40*	*11*	*10*	...	...	*19*
26	Bhamo	217	114	3	1	...	100	3	1	...	...	...	2
27	Myitkyina	96	25	...	1	...	71	...	...	...	...	...	...
28	Katha	700	259	...	2	...	441	...	...	...	...	...	...
29	Ruby Mines ...	685	383	70	133	23	232	20	8	10	...	...	2
	Sagaing Division ...	4,036	1,282	731	78	37	2,023	5	...	4	...	...	1
30	Shwebo	1,090	344	143	30	...	603	...	...	...	...	...	...
31	Sagaing	1,240	254	426	2	37	560	5	...	4	...	...	1
32	Lower Chindwin ...	998	344	152	7	...	502	...	...	...	...	...	...
33	Upper Chindwin ...	708	340	10	39	...	358	...	...	...	...	...	...
	Meiktila Division ...	5,939	1,788	1,069	171	195	3,082	...	...	...	...	...	...
34	Kyauksè	891	404	83	107	2	404	...	...	...	...	...	...
35	Meiktila ..	2,790	601	881	32	164	1,308	...	...	...	...	...	...
36	Yamèthin ...	1,103	362	103	28	29	638	...	...	...	...	...	...
37	Myingyan ...	1,155	421	2	4	...	732	...	...	...	...	..	...
	Specially Administered Territories.	3,503	1,614	319	138	18	1,570	9	3	...	...	...	6
38	Northern Shan States	572	227	4	10	...	341	...	...	...	...	...	...
39	Southern Shan States	2,921	1,383	315	128	18	1,223	9	3	...	...	...	6
40	Chin Hills ...	10	4	...	...	...	6	...	...	..	...	...	...

Occupations. Details by Districts.

GROUP 88, MAKERS OF WATCHES, CLOCKS, OPTICAL, PHOTOGRAPHIC, AND SURGICAL INSTRUMENTS.						GROUP 89, WORKERS IN PRECIOUS STONES, AND METALS, ENAMELLERS, IMITATION JEWELLERY MAKERS, GUILDERS, ETC.						GROUP 90, MAKERS OF BANGLES, ROSARIES, BEAD AND OTHER NECKLACES, SPANGLES AND SACRED THREADS.						
Total Workers and Dependents.	ACTUAL WORKERS. Total. Males.	ACTUAL WORKERS. Total. Females.	ACTUAL WORKERS. Partially Agriculturist. Males.	ACTUAL WORKERS. Partially Agriculturist. Females.	Dependents.	Total Workers and Dependents.	ACTUAL WORKERS. Total. Males.	ACTUAL WORKERS. Total. Females.	ACTUAL WORKERS. Partially Agriculturist. Males.	ACTUAL WORKERS. Partially Agriculturist. Females.	Dependents.	Total Workers and Dependents.	ACTUAL WORKERS. Total. Males.	ACTUAL WORKERS. Total. Females.	ACTUAL WORKERS. Partially Agriculturist. Males.	ACTUAL WORKERS. Partially Agriculturist. Females.	Dependents.	Serial No.
436	437	438	439	440	441	442	443	444	445	446	447	448	449	450	451	452	453	454
1,045	415	12	9	...	618	50,232	19,851	4,055	623	300	26,326	1,257	168	404	1	8	725	
956	395	8	3	...	553	47,354	18,251	2,999	491	252	25,104	1,030	142	404	1	8	484	
5	1	...	...	...	4	3,657	1,405	733	7	10	1,519	165	2	144	...	7	19	
...	...	...	...	...	...	2,721	1,094	600	1	4	1,027	158	...	143	...	7	15	1
...	...	...	...	...	...	11	4	...	...	...	7	...	...	...	...	...	...	2
...	...	...	...	...	..	750	235	133	6	6	382	2	...	1	...	...	1	3
5	1	...	...	...	4	185	72	...	...	...	113	5	2	...	...	...	3	4
406	160	2	1	...	244	11,708	5,025	285	16	...	6,353	141	30	16	1	...	95	
307	121	1	...	...	185	4,408	1,956	69	2	...	2,383	31	2	6	...	...	23	5
25	6	...	...	...	19	2,564	1,059	79	7	...	1,426	37	19	...	1	...	18	6
7	...	1	...	...	6	1,345	517	87	3	...	741	...	...	...	...	...	...	7
40	21	...	1	...	19	1,802	743	23	2	...	1,036	...	...	...	...	...	...	8
27	12	..	...	..	15	1,584	750	27	2	...	807	73	9	10	...	...	54	9
28	8	...	...	...	20	7,551	3,139	273	40	22	4,139	19	...	1	...	..	18	
3	...	...	...	...	3	1,351	504	25	16	...	822	18	...	...	...	...	18	10
9	2	...	...	...	7	2,381	968	160	13	15	1,253	1	...	1	...	...	..	11
8	5	...	...	...	3	1,150	460	48	2	...	642	..	...	...	...	...	...	12
...	...	...	..	...	...	1,336	517	21	9	7	798	...	...	...	...	...	...	13
8	1	...	...	...	7	1,333	690	19	...	...	624	...	...	...	...	...	...	14
291	69	2	...	...	220	5,946	2,158	152	21	...	3,636	60	29	1	...	...	30	
32	8	...	...	...	14	1,388	564	8	3	...	816	16	5	...	...	...	11	15
...	...	...	...	...	...	47	20	...	...	...	27	...	...	...	...	...	...	16
35	9	...	...	...	16	1,618	558	33	7	...	1,027	40	24	...	...	...	16	17
114	48	...	...	...	66	1,965	776	38	9	...	1,151	4	...	1	...	...	3	18
26	4	...	.	...	22	434	194	...	1	...	240	...	...	...	...	...	...	19
4	...	2	...	...	2	494	46	73	1	...	375	...	...	...	...	...	...	20
55	32	2	...	...	21	4,288	1,666	428	30	...	2,194	12	5	1	...	...	6	
13	3	...	..	..	10	956	368	107	2	...	481	...	...	...	...	...	...	21
7	4	2	...	...	1	1,133	458	34	...	...	641	5	2	...	...	...	3	22
20	11	...	...	...	9	1,294	464	230	22	...	600	...	...	...	...	...	...	23
15	14	...	...	...	1	905	376	57	6	...	472	7	3	1	...	...	...	24
86	20	1	...	...	65	4,820	2,157	334	145	29	2,329	532	46	240	...	...	246	
69	16	1	...	...	52	3,162	1,389	271	8	6	1,502	533	46	240	...	...	246	25
64	*16*	*1*	...	...	*47*	*2,683*	*1,192*	*231*	...	...	*1,200*	*532*	*46*	*240*	...	...	*246*	
2	2	...	...	...	...	212	111	3	1	...	98	...	...	...	...	...	...	26
15	2	...	...	...	13	81	23	...	1	...	58	...	...	...	...	...	...	27
...	...	...	...	...	...	700	259	...	2	...	441	...	...	...	...	..	...	28
...	...	...	...	...	...	665	375	60	133	23	330		...	...	...	...	...	29
141	81	1	1	...	59	2,788	1,114	726	62	27	1,948	1	1	...	...	...	...	
...	...	...	...	..	...	1,001	269	143	15	...	580	...	...	...	...	...	...	30
4	2	...	..	...	2	1,231	252	422	2	37	557	...	...	...	...	...	...	31
132	77	1	1	...	54	854	256	151	6	...	447	...	...	...	...	...	...	32
5	2	...	...	...	3	732	337	10	39	...	355	1	1	...	...	...	...	33
44	24	...	1	...	20	5,631	1,607	1,066	270	294	2,936	100	29	1	...	1	70	
...	...	...	...	...	...	690	293	82	107	1	315	44	4	1	...	1	39	34
43	23	...	...	...	20	2,746	578	881	32	164	1,287	...	...	...	...	...	...	35
1	1	...	1	...	...	1,046	336	103	27	29	607	56	25	...	...	...	31	36
...	...	...	...	...	...	1,149	420	2	4	...	727	...	...	...	...	...	...	37
89	20	4	6	...	65	2,838	1,560	56	132	8	1,222	267	26	...	...	...	241	
89	30	4	6	...	65	483	207	...	4	...	276	...	...	...	...	...	...	38
...	...	...	...	...	...	2,345	1,349	56	128	8	940	257	26	...	...	...	241	39
...	...	...	...	...	...	10	4	...	...	...	6	..	...	...	...	...	...	40

Serial No.	District or State.	Group 91, Toy, Kite, Cage, and Fishing Tackle Makers, Taxidermists, etc. — Total Workers and Dependents.	Actual Workers. Total. Males.	Actual Workers. Total. Females.	Actual Workers. Partially Agriculturist. Males.	Actual Workers. Partially Agriculturist. Females.	Dependents.	Order XIX—(Group 93), Industries concerned with Refuse Matter (Sweepers, Scavengers, Dust Collectors, etc.) — Total Workers and Dependents.	Actual Workers. Total. Males.	Actual Workers. Total. Females.	Actual Workers. Partially Agriculturist. Males.	Actual Workers. Partially Agriculturist. Females.	Dependents.
	1	454	455	456	457	458	459	460	461	462	463	464	465
	Provincial Total ...	1,566	792	28	...	...	746	13,103	6,667	1,604	141	80	4,832
	Burma Proper ...	1,566	792	28	...	...	746	12,140	6,451	1,509	92	79	4,180
	Arakan Division ..	1,002	624	22	...	...	356	1,328	831	172	...	...	325
1	Akyab	962	599	22	...	...	341	1,294	817	167	...	...	310
2	Northern Arakan ...	...	...	...	...	...	...	7	6	1	...	...	...
3	Kyaukpyu ...	...	...	...	...	...	...	9	1	4	...	...	4
4	Sandoway ...	40	25	...	...	..	15	18	7	..	...	..	11
	Pegu Division ...	180	41	1	...	...	138	4,174	2,807	281	...	...	1,085
5	City of Rangoon ...	34	26	1	...	...	7	2,707	1,829	230	...	...	848
6	Hanthawaddy ...	...	...	...	...	...	...	373	325	13	...	...	35
7	Tharrawaddy ...	...	...	...	...	...	...	252	190	8	...	...	54
8	Pegu	146	15		...	...	131	272	196	22	...	...	54
9	Prome	...	...	...	.	...	...	370	267	9	...	...	94
	Irrawaddy Division ...	95	1	5	...	...	89	664	461	22	...	...	181
10	Bassein... ..	...	...	...	...	...	...	106	71	2	...	...	33
11	Henzada ..	..	...	...	...	...	...	212	158	2	...	...	52
12	Myaungmya ...	95	1	5	...	...	89	105	62	2	...	...	41
13	Ma-ubin ...	...	...	..	...	...	...	130	94	10	...	...	26
14	Pyapôn	...	...	...	...	...	...	111	76	6	..	...	29
	Tenasserim Division ...	...	...	...	...	...	...	712	407	78	...	...	227
15	Toungoo	...	...	...	...	...	...	194	106	27	...	...	61
16	Salween	...	..	...	...	...	...	1	...	1	...	...	...
17	Thatôn	...	...	...	...	...	...	29	7	3	...	...	19
18	Amherst	...	...	...	...	...		380	198	39	...	...	143
19	Tavoy	...	...	...	...	...	...	70	65	3	...	...	2
20	Mergui	...	...	...	...	...	...	38	31	5	...	...	2
	Magwe Division ..	...	...	...	...	...	...	1,095	362	117	...	...	616
21	Thayetmyo ..	...	...	...	...	...	...	205	84	31	...	...	90
22	Pakôkku	...	...	...	...	...	...	429	99	23	...	...	307
23	Minbu	...	...	..	...	...	...	259	108	53	...	...	98
24	Magwe	...	...	...	...	...	...	202	71	10	...	...	121
	Mandalay Division ...	124	12	...	...	...	112	1,746	1,039	107	42	...	600
25	Mandalay (including City).	124	12	...	...	...	112	1,296	709	93	22	...	494
	Mandalay City ...	...	...	...	..	...	...	883	450	81	...	...	352
26	Bhamo	...	...	...	...	...	...	154	126	4	13	...	24
27	Myitkyina ...	...	...	...	...	...	...	146	102	8	5	...	36
28	Katha	...	...	..	...	..	...	112	64	2	...	...	46
29	Ruby Mines ...	...	...	...	...	...	...	38	38	...	2	...	...
	Sagaing Division ...	10	9	...	...	...	1	720	337	100	50	4	283
30	Shwebo	...	...	..	...	...	...	305	129	72	...	2	104
31	Sagaing	...	...	...	...	...	...	203	70	25	2	2	108
32	Lower Chindwin ...	10	9	...	...	...	1	114	59	1	...	...	54
33	Upper Chindwin ..	...	...	...	...	..	..	98	79	2	48	...	17
	Meiktila Division ...	155	105	...	...	...	50	1,701	207	631	...	75	863
34	Kyauksè	155	105	...	...	...	50	242	83	29	...	12	130
35	Meiktila ..	...	...	...	...	...	...	1,061	35	516	...	63	510
36	Yamèthin ..	...	...	...	...	...	...	119	35	10	...	...	74
37	Myingyan ...	...	..	...	...	...	...	279	54	76	...	...	149
	Specially Administered Territories.	...	...	...	...	...	...	963	216	95	49	1	652
38	Northern Shan States	...	...	...	...	...	...	104	43	15	8	...	46
39	Southern Shan States	...	...	...	...	...	...	799	149	79	41	1	571
40	Chin Hills ...	...	...	...	...	...	...	60	24	1	...	...	53

Occupations. Details by Districts.

ORDER XX—TRANSPORT BY WATER.						GROUP 95, SHIP OWNERS, AND THEIR EMPLOYEES, SHIP BROKERS, SHIP'S OFFICERS, ENGINEERS, MARINERS, AND FIREMEN.						GROUP 97, BOAT OWNERS, BOATMEN, AND TOWMEN.						
Total Workers and Dependents.	ACTUAL WORKERS.				Dependents.	Total Workers and Dependents.	ACTUAL WORKERS.				Dependents.	Total Workers and Dependents.	ACTUAL WORKERS.				Dependents.	
	Total.		Partially Agriculturist.				Total.		Partially Agriculturist.				Total.		Partially Agriculturist.			
	Males.	Females.	Males.	Females.			Males.	Females.	Males.	Females.			Males.	Females.	Males.	Females.		Serial No.
465	467	468	469	470	471	472	473	474	475	476	477	478	479	480	481	482	483	
131,071	65,770	9,546	2,290	384	55,755	11,539	10,349	45	284	1	1,143	118,771	54,940	9,480	2,006	380	54,351	
127,840	64,725	8,698	2,190	360	54,417	11,474	10,322	45	284	1	1,107	115,605	53,922	8,632	1,906	358	53,051	
13,827	8,377	1,235	563	42	4,215	905	806	24	..	...	95	12,900	7,569	1,211	563	42	4,120	
11,251	7,375	992	543	24	2,884	819	793	...	...	...	26	10,430	6,580	992	543	24	2,858	1
29	29	...	...	...	...	...	...	...	...	...	...	29	29	...	...	...	...	2
1,430	526	186	20	18	718	10	9	...	...	...	1	1,420	517	186	20	18	717	3
1,117	447	57	...	...	613	96	4	24	..	...	63	1,021	443	33	...	...	545	4
41,208	24,088	1,178	500	8	15,942	9,790	9,016	5	268	...	769	31,249	14,981	1,171	232	7	15,097	
16,586	13,614	48	300	...	2,924	9,741	8,974	5	268	...	762	6,722	4,579	43	32	...	2,100	5
14,423	5,574	721	51	4	8,128	17	15	...	...	...	2	14,402	5,559	721	51	4	8,122	6
1,766	626	210	11	2	930	...	...	...	...	...	...	1,735	598	210	11	2	927	7
6,672	3,494	80	134	2	3,098	32	27	...	...	...	5	6,630	3,466	78	134	1	3,086	8
1,761	780	119	4	...	862	—	...	...	...	...	–	1,760	779	119	4	...	862	9
23,111	12,007	1,588	233	53	9,516	17	5	...	...	...	12	22,889	11,839	1,576	233	53	9,474	
4,453	2,121	220	28	...	2,112	2	2	...	...	...	...	4,449	2,119	220	28	...	2,110	10
4,891	2,012	278	93	30	2,601	6	...	...	...	...	6	4,815	1,977	266	93	30	2,572	11
3,199	2,115	246	54	12	838	9	3	...	...	...	6	3,190	2,112	246	54	12	832	12
3,516	1,955	175	30	11	1,386	...	...	...	...	...	...	3,446	1,890	175	30	11	1,381	13
7,052	3,804	669	28	...	2,579	...	...	...	...	...	...	6,989	3,741	669	28	...	2,579	14
13,114	6,639	322	89	5	6,153	440	286	6	...	1	148	12,634	6,338	316	89	4	5,980	
1,328	517	82	8	3	729	...	...	...	...	...	...	1,328	517	82	8	3	729	15
155	131	4	...	...	20	...	...	...	...	...	...	155	131	4	...	...	20	16
2,715	1,345	51	21	...	1,319	47	20	...	...	...	27	2,668	1,325	51	21	...	1,292	17
6,819	3,629	109	50	1	3,081	116	1	6	...	1	109	6,667	3,617	103	50	...	2,947	18
904	423	23	7	1	548	27	27	...	...	...	...	[illegible]	[illegible]	23	7	1	548	19
1,103	594	53	3	...	456	250	238	...	...	...	12	853	356	53	3	...	444	20
10,603	4,175	597	75	6	5,831	131	123	...	16	...	8	10,446	4,045	597	59	6	5,804	
3,236	1,329	244	2	...	1,653	57	55	...	...	...	1	3,165	1,271	244	2	...	1,650	21
4,608	1,533	194	6	...	2,881	27	27	...	...	...	...	4,579	1,504	194	6	...	2,881	22
1,823	890	57	48	2	876	45	38	...	16	...	7	1,772	852	57	32	2	863	23
936	423	102	19	4	411	2	2	...	...	...	...	930	418	102	19	4	410	24
8,478	3,149	756	146	16	4,573	120	65	10	.	...	45	8,286	3,068	739	146	16	4,479	
5,098	1,793	506	48	12	2,799	59	13	10	...	...	36	4,970	1,767	489	48	12	2,714	25
769	*358*	*39*	—	...	*372*	*59*	*13*	*10*	...	..	*36*	*642*	*332*	*22*	...	...	*288*	
910	459	71	38	...	380	41	33	...	...	...	9	869	427	71	38	...	371	26
312	194	6	40	...	112	6	6	...	...	...	...	306	188	6	40	...	112	27
1,566	533	148	20	4	885	1	1	...	...	...	...	1,562	529	148	20	4	885	28
592	170	25	...	...	397	13	13	...	...	...	—	579	157	25	...	...	397	29
11,154	4,291	1,692	470	135	5,171	20	13	...	...	...	7	11,032	4,189	1,692	470	135	5,151	
1,441	443	360	23	37	638	...	...	...	...	...	...	1,435	438	360	23	37	637	30
2,981	1,344	399	99	38	1,238	1	1	...	...	...	...	2,973	1,342	399	99	38	1,232	31
3,970	1,349	704	182	58	1,917	15	12	...	...	...	3	3,946	1,332	704	182	58	1,910	32
2,762	1,153	229	166	2	1,378	4	...	...	...	...	4	2,678	1,077	229	166	2	1,372	33
6,245	1,999	1,330	114	95	3,016	31	8	...	...	...	23	6,169	1,893	1,330	114	95	2,946	
973	294	238	34	18	441	...	..	...	...	...	...	973	294	238	34	18	441	34
1,806	308	693	9	61	805	...	...	...	...	...	...	1,806	308	693	9	61	805	35
585	72	160	...	5	353	...	...	...	...	...	...	585	72	160	...	5	353	36
2,981	1,325	239	71	11	1,417	31	8	...	...	...	23	2,805	1,219	239	71	11	1,347	37
3,231	1,045	848	100	24	1,338	65	27	...	...	...	38	3,166	1,018	848	100	24	1,300	
182	75	9	...	2	98	2	2	...	...	..	...	180	73	9	...	2	98	38
3,042	970	839	100	22	1,233	63	25	...	...	...	38	2,979	945	839	100	22	1,195	39
7	...	...	...	...	7	...	...	...	...	...	...	7	...	..	...	...	7	40

Serial No.	DISTRICT OR STATE.	ORDER XXI—TRANSPORT BY ROAD.						GROUP 98, CONSTRUCTION AND MAINTENANCE OF ROADS AND BRIDGES.					
		Total Workers and Dependents.	ACTUAL WORKERS. Total.		ACTUAL WORKERS. Partially Agriculturist.		Dependents.	Total Workers and Dependents.	ACTUAL WORKERS. Total.		ACTUAL WORKERS. Partially Agriculturist.		Dependents.
			Males.	Females.	Males.	Females.			Males.	Females.	Males.	Females.	
	1	484	485	486	487	488	489	490	491	492	493	494	495
	Provincial Total ...	230,168	96,076	33,439	5,544	3,580	100,653	91,541	42,516	16,960	2,654	2,014	32,065
	Burma Proper ...	204,621	86,584	28,285	4,239	3,315	89,752	82,333	38,438	15,148	2,081	1,881	28,747
	Arakan Division ...	11,934	6,642	1,534	79	3	3,758	7,393	4,856	614	75	1	1,923
1	Akyab ...	10,409	5,866	1,383	67	...	3,160	6,302	4,228	496	65	...	1,578
2	Northern Arakan ...	7	2	...	...	...	5	...	...	...	...	...	...
3	Kyaukpyu ...	955	507	107	12	3	341	785	457	93	10	1	235
4	Sandoway ...	563	267	44	...	...	252	306	171	25	...	...	110
	Pegu Division ...	37,856	19,158	2,496	413	76	16,202	11,190	6,260	1,001	222	34	3,929
5	City of Rangoon ...	8,024	6,138	44	22	...	1,842	1,360	1,157	23	...	...	180
6	Hanthawaddy ...	7,638	2,048	556	67	14	4,134	2,253	1,183	345	12	9	1,725
7	Tharrawaddy ...	7,275	3,277	640	36	36	3,358	1,545	1,075	97	...	8	373
8	Pegu ...	8,293	4,074	609	244	26	3,610	3,032	1,047	181	201	17	904
9	Prome ...	6,626	2,721	647	44	...	3,258	2,000	898	355	9	...	747
	Irrawaddy Division ...	16,187	8,821	1,105	225	192	6,261	6,283	4,207	520	114	59	1,556
10	Bassein ...	3,625	2,210	197	38	20	1,218	1,325	937	89	11	19	299
11	Henzada ...	7,144	3,564	463	69	30	3,112	1,905	1,363	168	2	21	369
12	Myaungmya ...	1,328	879	50	8	...	399	876	596	20	8	...	260
13	Maubin ...	2,614	1,282	246	17	136	1,086	842	518	99	...	13	225
14	Pyapôn ...	1,476	886	144	93	6	446	1,335	788	144	93	6	403
	Tenasserim Division ...	23,223	11,380	851	381	21	10,992	7,554	4,751	476	237	11	2,327
15	Toungoo ...	6,321	2,905	163	57	5	3,253	851	690	12	...	...	149
16	Salween ...	166	107	20	...	...	39	64	39	10	...	...	15
17	Thatôn ...	6,017	2,919	267	139	5	2,831	2,119	1,497	203	101	5	719
18	Amherst ...	7,482	3,900	343	168	11	3,239	2,772	1,816	216	121	6	740
19	Tavoy ..	2,474	1,124	43	27	...	1,307	946	388	27	15	...	531
20	Mergui ...	763	425	15	...	...	323	502	321	8	...	...	173
	Magwe Division ...	22,483	8,308	2,624	169	35	11,551	10,771	4,454	1,800	84	32	4,527
21	Thayetmyo ...	2,658	806	331	...	1	1,521	1,289	463	164	...	...	662
22	Pakôkku ...	5,543	2,049	510	10	6	2,984	2,191	867	311	7	6	1,013
23	Minbu ...	5,943	2,626	683	126	15	2,634	3,528	1,780	576	65	14	1,172
24	Magwe ...	8,339	2,837	1,100	33	13	4,412	3,763	1,344	749	12	12	1,670
	Mandalay Division ...	30,731	14,646	3,758	1,153	121	12,327	11,899	6,300	1,958	362	50	3,641
25	Mandalay (including City).	14,761	6,055	1,730	188	59	6,976	3,390	1,287	782	42	25	1,321
	Mandalay City ...	*9,006*	*3,499*	*794*	...	...	*4,713*	*1,415*	*433*	*312*	...	...	*670*
26	Bhamo ..	2,404	1,246	361	381	1	797	626	182	339	21	...	105
27	Myitkyina ...	3,134	2,578	91	162	...	465	2,547	2,212	60	156	...	275
28	Katha ...	3,435	1,164	852	47	8	1,419	854	257	407	25	3	190
29	Ruby Mines ...	6,997	3,603	724	375	53	2,670	4,482	2,362	370	118	22	1,750
	Sagaing Division ...	26,233	7,818	7,361	937	1,774	11,054	11,914	3,371	4,175	523	1,271	4,368
30	Shwebo ...	8,532	2,003	3,239	139	1,239	3,290	5,014	1,095	2,203	95	983	1,716
31	Sagaing ...	7,553	1,633	2,212	200	271	3,708	2,708	835	942	126	214	931
32	Lower Chindwin ...	6,904	1,816	1,858	258	264	3,230	3,285	782	1,001	164	74	1,502
33	Upper Chindwin .	3,244	2,366	52	330	...	826	907	659	29	148	...	219
	Meiktila Division ...	35,974	9,811	8,556	882	1,093	17,607	15,329	4,239	4,604	454	423	6,486
34	Kyauksè ...	7,439	2,420	1,631	333	237	3,388	4,395	1,425	1,300	214	219	1,670
35	Meiktila ...	9,639	1,658	3,546	254	748	4,435	4,003	842	1,407	157	112	1,754
36	Yamèthin ...	7,152	2,243	846	136	49	4,063	2,016	458	513	25	39	1,045
37	Myingyan ...	11,744	3,490	2,533	129	68	5,721	4,915	1,514	1,384	58	63	2,017
	Specially Administered Territories.	25,547	9,492	5,154	1,305	265	10,901	9,208	4,078	1,812	573	133	3,318
38	**Northern Shan States**	5,761	2,761	989	282	71	2,011	1,746	1,068	186	112	29	492
39	**Southern Shan States**	19,733	6,712	4,161	1,023	194	8,860	7,410	2,992	1,632	461	104	2,796
40	**Chin Hills** ...	53	19	4	...	...	30	52	18	4	...	...	30

Occupations. Details by Districts.

GROUP 99, CART OWNERS AND DRIVERS, COACHMEN, STABLE BOYS, TRAMWAY AND MAIL CARRIAGE MANAGERS AND EMPLOYES.						GROUP 101, PACK ELEPHANT, CAMEL, MULE, ASS, AND BULLOCK OWNERS, AND DRIVERS.						ORDER XXII, TRANSPORT BY RAIL.						
Total Workers and Dependents.	ACTUAL WORKERS.				Dependents.	Total Workers and Dependents.	ACTUAL WORKERS.				Dependents.	Total Workers and Dependents.	ACTUAL WORKERS.				Dependents.	
	TOTAL.		PARTIALLY AGRICULTURIST.				TOTAL.		PARTIALLY AGRICULTURIST.				TOTAL.		PARTIALLY AGRICULTURIST.			
	Males.	Females.	Males.	Females.			Males.	Females.	Males.	Females.			Males.	Females.	Males.	Females.		Serial No.
496	497	498	499	500	501	502	503	504	505	506	507	508	509	510	511	512	513	
132,099	49,851	16,227	2,827	1,551	66,021	6,304	3,517	248	37	15	2,539	27,686	17,665	717	258	30	9,304	
116,123	44,614	12,903	2,107	1,419	58,606	5,941	3,340	230	25	15	2,371	27,348	17,584	711	246	30	9,053	
4,501	1,758	920	4	2	1,823	40	28	...	..	...	12	83	36	...	...	...	47	
4,094	1,627	887	2	...	1,580	13	11	..	...	...	2	12	4	...	...	...	8	1
..	...	...	...	...	...	7	2	...	...	...	5	...	...	...	...	...	...	2
152	36	14	2	2	102	18	14	...	...	...	4	71	32	..	...	...	39	3
255	95	19	...	...	141	2	1	...	...	...	1	...	...	...	...	...	...	4
26,249	12,584	1,489	191	42	12,176	256	165	89	...	...	89	15,701	10,282	46	36	...	5,373	
6,477	4,804	21	21	...	1,652	36	29	...	...	...	7	5,643	3,468	21	4	...	2,154	5
4,379	1,761	211	55	5	2,407	6	4	...	...	...	2	4,033	1,989	5	27	...	2,039	6
5,638	2,148	537	35	28	2,953	83	54	2	...	...	27	1,270	854	...	...	...	416	7
5,174	2,057	428	43	9	2,689	85	69	...	...	...	17	4,691	3,948	14	5	...	729	8
4,581	1,814	292	35	...	2,475	45	9	..	...	...	36	64	23	6	...	...	35	9
9,422	4,160	585	111	133	4,677	482	454	...	...	...	28	1,331	972	5	5	...	354	
1,963	951	108	27	1	904	337	322	...	...	...	15	235	135	...	...	...	80	10
5,191	2,161	300	67	9	2,730	48	35	...	...	...	13	1,063	815	5	5	...	243	11
355	186	30	...	...	139	97	97	...	...	...	...	2	2	...	...	...	...	12
1,772	764	147	17	123	861	...	...	...	...	...	...	...	...	...	...	...	...	13
141	98	...	...	...	43	...	...	...	...	...	...	1	...	...	...	...	1	14
14,903	6,218	372	144	10	8,333	746	411	3	...	...	332	2,740	1,796	67	7	18	877	
4,918	1,941	149	57	5	2,828	552	274	2	...	...	276	1,610	980	64	...	18	576	15
80	58	10	...	...	12	22	10	...	...	...	12	17	11	...	...	...	6	16
3,561	1,392	64	23	...	2,105	37	30	...	...	...	7	1,092	799	3	3	...	290	17
4,615	2,018	127	47	5	2,470	93	66	...	...	...	29	5	4	...	4	...	1	18
1,502	719	15	12	...	768	26	17	1	...	...	8	2	2	...	...	...	..	19
247	90	7	...	...	150	14	14	...	...	...	...	4	...	...	...	...	4	20
10,898	3,505	820	59	3	6,573	751	306	4	...	...	441	86	34	18	...	...	34	
1,255	279	167	...	1	809	114	64	...	...	...	50	25	16	1	...	..	8	21
2,818	965	199	3	...	1,654	530	216	...	...	...	314	11	4	...	...	...	7	22
2,333	795	107	35	1	1,431	23	9	...	...	...	14	32	3	17	...	...	12	23
4,492	1,466	347	21	1	2,679	84	17	4	...	...	63	18	11	...	...	...	7	24
16,990	7,255	1,656	783	71	8,081	1,840	1,091	144	8	...	605	2,864	1,952	125	8	3	787	
10,961	4,600	811	146	34	5,550	410	168	137	...	...	105	2,312	1,671	16	5	...	625	25
7,414	*2,900*	*482*	...	...	*4,032*	*177*	*166*	..	...	...	*11*	*746*	*558*	*16*	...	...	*172*	
1,365	732	22	354	1	611	413	332	...	6	...	81	24	...	12	...	...	12	26
452	262	31	4	...	159	135	104	...	2	...	31	23	20	...	...	...	3	27
1,730	442	441	22	5	856	842	465	4	...	...	373	486	259	97	3	3	130	28
2,475	1,219	351	257	31	905	40	22	3	...	...	15	19	2	...	...	..	17	29
13,080	3,821	2,111	390	488	6,148	1,239	626	75	24	15	538	1,675	1,018	62	10	7	595	
5,452	882	1,036	44	256	1,534	66	26	...	...	...	40	721	444	5	...	...	272	30
4,845	798	1,270	74	57	2,777	...	...	...	...	...	...	777	469	24	...	7	284	31
3,135	865	782	104	175	1,488	484	169	75	...	15	240	113	67	18	...	...	28	32
1,648	1,276	23	168	...	349	689	431	...	24	...	258	64	38	15	10	...	11	33
20,058	5,313	3,950	425	670	10,795	587	259	2	3	...	326	2,898	1,494	388	180	2	1,016	
3,043	924	331	119	18	1,718	1	1	...	...	...	...	181	68	7	...	...	106	34
5,636	816	2,139	127	636	2,681	...	...	...	...	...	...	1,462	1,130	47	175	..	295	35
4,567	1,527	331	128	11	2,709	569	258	2	3	...	309	985	249	236	5	2	500	36
6,812	1,976	1,149	71	5	3,687	17	...	...	...	...	17	270	57	98	...	...	115	37
15,976	5,237	2,324	780	132	7,415	363	177	18	10	—	168	338	81	6	12	...	251	
3,973	1,676	803	170	42	1,514	22	17	...	...	...	5	336	80	6	12	...	250	38
11,982	3,560	2,521	550	90	5,901	341	160	18	12	...	163	...	...	...	...	...	...	39
1	1	...	...	...	...	...	...	...	...	...	...	2	1	...	...	...	1	40

Serial No.	DISTRICT OR STATE.	GROUP 103, RAILWAY EMPLOYES OF ALL KINDS OTHER THAN CONSTRUCTION COOLIES.						GROUP 104, LABOURERS EMPLOYED ON RAILWAY CONSTRUCTION.					
		Total Workers and Dependents.	ACTUAL WORKERS.				Dependents.	Total Workers and Dependents.	ACTUAL WORKERS.				Dependents.
			TOTAL.		PARTIALLY AGRICULTURIST.				TOTAL.		PARTIALLY AGRICULTURIST.		
			Males.	Females.	Males.	Females.			Males.	Females.	Males.	Females.	
	1	514	515	516	517	518	519	520	521	522	523	524	525
	Provincial Total ...	22,633	14,754	614	247	30	7,265	5,053	2,911	103	11	...	2,039
	Burma Proper ...	22,486	14,695	613	236	30	7,178	4,862	2,889	98	10	...	1,875
	Arakan Division ...	83	36	...	...	...	47	...	...	...	...	...	...
1	Akyab ...	12	4	...	...	...	8	...	...	...	...	...	...
2	Northern Arakan ...	...	...	...	...	...	...	...	...	...	...	...	...
3	Kyaukpyu ...	71	32	...	...	...	39	...	...	...	...	...	...
4	Sandoway ...	...	...	...	...	...	...	...	...	...	...	...	...
	Pegu Division ...	12,995	8,505	26	35	...	4,064	2,706	1,377	20	1	...	1,309
5	City of Rangoon ...	5,636	3,463	21	4	...	2,152	7	5	...	...	...	2
6	Hanthawaddy ...	2,309	1,202	5	27	...	1,042	1,724	727	...	...	...	927
7	Tharrawaddy ...	700	420	...	...	...	280	570	434	...	...	...	136
8	Pegu ...	4,308	3,740	...	4	...	568	383	208	14	1	...	161
9	Prome ...	42	20	...	...	...	22	22	3	6	...	...	13
	Irrawaddy Division ...	598	394	5	...	...	199	703	578	...	5	...	125
10	Bassein ...	70	18	...	...	...	52	165	137	...	...	...	28
11	Henzada ...	525	374	5	...	...	146	538	441	...	5	...	97
12	Myaungmya ...	2	2	...	...	...	...	...	...	...	...	...	...
13	Ma-ubin ...	...	...	...	...	...	...	...	...	...	...	...	...
14	Pyapôn ...	1	...	...	...	...	1	...	...	...	...	...	...
	Tenasserim Division ...	2,031	1,239	67	7	18	725	709	557	...	...	...	152
15	Toungoo ...	924	447	64	...	18	483	626	533	...	...	...	93
16	Salween ...	17	11	...	...	...	6	...	...	...	...	...	...
17	Thatôn ...	1,009	775	3	3	...	231	83	24	...	...	...	59
18	Amherst ...	5	4	...	4	...	1	...	...	...	...	...	...
19	Tavoy ...	2	2	...	...	...	...	...	...	...	...	...	...
20	Mergui ...	4	...	...	...	...	4	...	...	...	...	...	...
	Magwe Division ...	75	31	15	...	...	29	11	3	3	...	...	5
21	Thayetmyo ...	25	16	1	...	...	8	...	...	...	...	...	...
22	Pakôkku ...	11	4	...	...	...	7	...	...	...	...	...	...
23	Minbu ...	27	3	14	...	...	10	5	...	3	...	...	2
24	Magwe ...	12	8	...	...	...	4	6	3	...	...	...	3
	Mandalay Division ...	2,452	1,683	125	6	2	644	412	269	...	2	...	143
25	Mandalay (including City).	1,930	1,402	16	3	...	512	382	269	...	2	...	113
	Mandalay City ...	*590*	*450*	*16*	...	...	*124*	*156*	*108*	...	...	...	*48*
26	Bhamo ...	24	...	12	...	...	12	...	...	...	...	...	...
27	Myitkyina ...	23	20	...	...		3	...	...	...	...	...	...
28	Katha ...	472	259	97	3	3	116	14	...	...	...	...	14
29	Ruby Mines ...	3	2	...	...	...	1	16	...	...	...	...	16
	Sagaing Division ...	1,638	992	62	10	7	584	37	26	...	...	...	11
30	Shwebo ...	692	425	5	...	...	262	29	19	...	...	...	10
31	Sagaing ...	776	469	24	...	7	283	1	...	...	...	...	1
32	Lower Chindwin ...	112	66	18	...	...	28	1	1	...	...	...	...
33	Upper Chindwin ...	58	32	15	10	...	11	6	6	...	...	...	...
	Meiktila Division ...	2,614	1,415	313	178	2	886	284	79	75	2	...	130
34	Kyauksè ...	177	68	3	...	...	106	4	...	4	...	...	...
35	Meiktila ...	1,414	1,085	47	175	...	282	48	35	...	...	...	13
36	Yamèthin ...	756	206	165	3	2	385	229	43	71	2	...	115
37	Myingyan ...	267	56	98	...	...	113	3	1	...	...	...	2
	Specially Administered Territories.	147	59	1	11	...	87	191	22	5	1	...	164
38	**Northern Shan States**	145	58	1	11	...	86	191	22	5	1	...	164
39	**Southern Shan States**	...	...	...	...	...	...	...	...	...	...	...	...
40	**Chin Hills** ...	2	1	...	...	...	1	...	...	...	...	...	...

Occupations. Details by Districts.

ORDER XXIII.—(GROUP 105), POST OFFICE, TELEGRAPH AND TELEPHONE SERVICES.						ORDER XXIV.—(GROUP 106), BANKS, ESTABLISHMENTS OF CREDIT, EXCHANGE, AND INSURANCE.						ORDER XXV.—(GROUP 107), BROKERAGE, COMMISSION, AND EXPORT; COMMERCIAL TRAVELLERS, WAREHOUSE OWNERS AND EMPLOYÉS.						
Total Workers and Dependents.	Actual Workers. Total. Males.	Actual Workers. Total. Females.	Actual Workers. Partially Agriculturist. Males.	Actual Workers. Partially Agriculturist. Females.	Dependents.	Total Workers and Dependents.	Actual Workers. Total. Males.	Actual Workers. Total. Females.	Actual Workers. Partially Agriculturist. Males.	Actual Workers. Partially Agriculturist. Females.	Dependents.	Total Workers and Dependents.	Actual Workers. Total. Males.	Actual Workers. Total. Females.	Actual Workers. Partially Agriculturist. Males.	Actual Workers. Partially Agriculturist. Females.	Dependents.	Serial No.
526	527	528	529	530	531	532	533	534	535	536	537	538	539	540	541	542	543	
4,727	2,223	242	18	30	2,262	17,345	6,758	2,346	565	133	8,241	21,415	7,608	1,423	69	49	12,384	
4,488	2,116	234	17	30	2,138	16,663	6,329	2,285	543	131	8,049	20,995	7,590	1,423	68	49	11,982	
631	312	53	...	8	266	1,454	512	167	4	3	775	1,045	471	194	2	5	380	
503	280	...	...	...	223	1,178	433	112	1	3	633	858	451	86	...	...	321	1
2	2	...	...	...	..	...	...	...	...	...	...	...	...	...	...	...	...	2
95	11	53	--	8	31	146	44	28	3	...	74	123	13	80	2	5	30	3
31	19	...	...	...	12	130	35	27	...	...	68	64	7	28	...	...	29	4
1,130	574	23	1	...	533	4,504	1,679	465	58	26	2,360	8,388	3,688	189	5	...	4,511	
655	294	23	1	...	338	2,286	834	160	6	5	1,292	5,857	2,764	77	5	...	3,016	5
122	59	...	...	...	63	704	178	83	12	11	443	916	212	88	...	...	616	6
64	31	...	...	...	33	424	168	104	2	6	152	415	184	11	...	...	220	7
171	126	...	...	...	45	550	263	51	36	4	236	436	178	11	...	...	247	8
118	64	...	...	...	54	540	236	67	2	...	237	764	350	2	...	...	412	9
349	211	2	...	...	136	3,398	1,632	453	47	19	1,313	4,220	1,177	317	11	8	2,726	
161	120	2	...	...	39	776	373	121	37	7	282	787	209	60	...	...	518	10
82	43	...	...	...	39	521	180	129	6	6	212	1,693	564	96	10	6	1,033	11
43	18	...	...	...	25	414	155	58	1	1	201	485	114	85	...	...	286	12
46	18	...	...	...	28	514	104	76	3	5	334	628	108	33	1	2	487	13
17	12	...	...	...	5	1,173	820	69	...	...	284	627	182	43	.	...	402	14
495	242	2	...	...	251	1,560	504	206	22	10	850	1,828	650	54	7	...	1,124	
59	28	2	...	...	29	454	144	63	2	...	247	784	364	26	4	...	394	15
3	...	...	...	...	3	7	2	...	...	...	5	7	3	...	...	...	4	16
145	70	...	...	...	75	301	130	21	18	...	150	383	154	6	2	...	223	17
232	117	...	...	...	115	602	177	84	2	9	341	562	93	18	1	...	451	18
28	12	...	...	...	16	113	30	18	...	...	65	31	15	...	...	...	16	19
28	15	...	...	...	13	83	21	20	...	1	42	61	21	4	...	...	36	20
392	160	26	...	...	206	1,073	388	181	25	2	504	1,844	697	128	8	...	1,019	
45	19	2	...	...	24	239	78	32	2	..	129	395	169	13	...	...	213	21
171	61	8	...	...	102	242	71	46	1	...	125	583	206	43	...	...	334	22
88	27	15	...	...	46	258	108	58	18	1	92	456	207	6	...	...	243	23
88	53	1	...	...	34	334	131	45	4	1	158	410	115	56	8	...	239	24
693	358	31	...	2	304	1,689	898	131	341	11	660	1,530	380	161	...	8	989	
493	266	4	...	...	223	556	142	65	...	2	349	1,061	374	26	...	...	661	25
443	230	4	...	...	209	369	94	28	...	...	247	948	367	26	...	...	555	
24	14	...	...	...	10	838	687	...	341	...	151	...	...	...	...	...	...	26
42	20	...	...	...	22	36	21	1	...	...	14	2	...	...	...	...	2	27
80	24	27	...	2	29	85	28	23	...	4	34	451	6	135	...	8	310	28
54	34	...	...	...	20	174	20	42	...	5	112	16	...	...	...	...	16	29
438	155	16	15	...	267	1,249	329	288	12	40	632	658	149	192	9	...	316	
46	12	16	...	...	18	316	66	91	1	6	159	20	1	16	...	...	3	30
72	22	...	2	...	50	485	91	116	4	13	278	233	103	...	9	...	130	31
167	85	...	13	...	82	291	108	59	7	17	124	397	45	177	...	...	175	32
153	36	...	...	...	117	157	64	22	...	4	71	8	...	...	...	...	8	33
360	104	81	1	20	175	1,736	387	394	34	20	955	1,482	378	197	26	28	907	
59	17	20	...	20	22	285	60	67	4	2	158	177	66	3	9	...	108	34
59	28	...	...	...	31	306	107	7	10	...	192	74	16	36	...	...	22	35
163	20	61	...	...	82	419	59	119	...	6	241	552	29	88	1	25	435	36
79	39	...	1	...	40	726	161	201	20	12	364	679	267	70	16	3	342	37
239	107	8	1	...	124	682	429	61	22	2	192	420	18	...	1	...	402	
70	49	.	---	...	21	12	10	...	1	...	2	84	4	...	1	...	80	38
155	53	5	1	...	97	662	414	61	21	2	187	335	13	...	...	...	322	39
14	5	3	...	...	6	8	5	...	...	...	3	1	1	--	...	...	...	40

Serial No.	DISTRICT OR STATE.	ORDER XXVI.—(GROUP 108), TRADE IN PIECE-GOODS, WOOL, COTTON, SILK, HAIR, AND OTHER TEXTILES.						ORDER XXVII.—(GROUP 109), TRADE IN SKINS, LEATHERS, FURS, FEATHERS, HORNS, ETC.					
		Total Workers and Dependents.	ACTUAL WORKERS.				Dependents.	Total Workers and Dependents.	ACTUAL WORKERS.				Dependents.
			Total.		Partially Agriculturist.				Total.		Partially Agriculturist.		
			Males.	Females.	Males.	Females.			Males.	Females.	Males.	Females.	
	1	544	545	546	547	548	549	550	551	552	553	554	555
	Provincial Total ...	**74,875**	**21,006**	**22,811**	**1,330**	**1,274**	**31,058**	**1,481**	**525**	**130**	**5**	**15**	**826**
	Burma Proper ...	**61,872**	**17,294**	**18,382**	**570**	**1,059**	**26,196**	**1,225**	**337**	**118**	**5**	**12**	**770**
	Arakan Division ...	**5,015**	**1,442**	**1,761**	**8**	**14**	**1,812**	...	...	...	...	...	...
1	Akyab	3,751	1,028	1,411	3	11	1,312	...	...	...	...	...	...
2	Northern Arakan ...	61	50	3	...	...	8	...	...	...	...	...	...
3	Kyaukpyu ...	739	195	242	5	3	302	...	...	...	...	...	...
4	Sandoway ...	464	169	105	...	...	190	...	...	...	...	...	...
	Pegu Division ...	**11,362**	**4,208**	**2,301**	**30**	**16**	**4,860**	**282**	**111**	**4**	...	...	**167**
5	City of Rangoon ...	5,216	2,436	438	17	...	2,342	228	86	1	...	...	141
6	Hanthawaddy ...	1,265	331	465	3	5	466	33	20	2	...	...	11
7	Tharrawaddy ...	1,406	349	430	...	9	617	2	1	...	...	...	1
8	Pegu	1,193	448	253	5	2	492	17	3	1	...	...	13
9	Prome	2,282	634	715	5	...	933	2	1	...	...	...	1
	Irrawaddy Division ...	**8,115**	**2,774**	**1,987**	**56**	**43**	**3,354**	**38**	**9**	**2**	...	...	**27**
10	Bassein	1,960	841	391	26	4	728	...	...	...	...	...	...
11	Henzada ...	2,722	635	861	16	38	1,226	38	9	2	...	...	27
12	Myaungmya ...	920	518	93	...	...	309	...	...	...	...	...	...
13	Ma-ubin ...	1,750	410	523	12	1	808	...	...	...	...	...	...
14	Pyapôn ...	763	361	119	2	...	283	...	...	...	...	...	...
	Tenasserim Division ...	**5,211**	**1,546**	**1,258**	**9**	**20**	**2,407**	**192**	**22**	...	...	...	**170**
15	Toungoo ...	1,077	307	259	5	...	511	179	13	...	...	...	166
16	Salween ...	49	42	2	...	...	5	...	...	...	...	...	...
17	Thatôn ...	1,368	569	309	1	4	490	1	1	...	...	...	...
18	Amherst ...	1,743	468	358	...	13	917	12	8	...	...	...	4
19	Tavoy	505	81	212	3	3	212	...	...	...	...	...	...
20	Mergui	469	79	118	...	...	272	...	...	...	...	...	...
	Magwe Division ...	**6,060**	**1,269**	**2,330**	**8**	**33**	**2,461**	**160**	**38**	**42**	**1**	...	**80**
21	Thayetmyo ...	720	128	216	...	1	376	21	9	2	...	...	10
22	Pakôkku ...	3,364	652	1,364	3	8	1,348	45	7	12	...	...	26
23	Minbu ...	1,178	252	494	3	24	432	28	15	...	...	...	13
24	Magwe ...	798	237	256	2	...	305	66	7	28	1	...	31
	Mandalay Division ...	**7,596**	**2,084**	**2,502**	**160**	**52**	**3,010**	**121**	**69**	...	...	...	**52**
25	Mandalay (including City).	4,707	1,177	1,720	10	16	1,810	121	69	...	...	...	52
	Mandalay City ...	*3,291*	*811*	*1,112*	...	...	*1,368*	*121*	*69*	...	...	...	*52*
26	Bhamo ...	604	90	188	8	1	317	...	...	...	...	...	...
27	Myitkyina ...	309	142	37	19	...	130	...	...	...	...	...	...
28	Katha ...	801	261	234	16	4	306	...	...	...	...	...	...
29	Ruby Mines ...	1,175	405	323	107	31	447	...	...	...	...	...	...
	Sagaing Division ...	**10,645**	**2,384**	**3,559**	**222**	**761**	**4,702**	**206**	**67**	**35**	**4**	**1**	**104**
30	Shwebo ...	3,101	375	1,232	12	142	1,494	17	7	...	...	...	10
31	Sagaing ...	3,055	632	1,240	41	503	1,183	12	2	1	...	1	9
32	Lower Chindwin ...	2,955	625	905	25	109	1,425	177	58	34	4	...	85
33	Upper Chindwin ...	1,534	752	182	144	7	600	...	...	...	...	...	...
	Meiktila Division ...	**7,868**	**1,594**	**2,684**	**77**	**120**	**3,590**	**226**	**21**	**35**	...	**11**	**170**
34	Kyauksè ..	760	172	220	16	3	368	3	1	..	...	...	2
35	Meiktila ...	3,281	502	1,096	46	73	1,683	34	1	14	...	11	19
36	Yamèthin ...	1,378	431	328	9	16	619	165	12	21	...	...	132
37	Myingyan ...	2,449	489	1,040	6	28	920	24	7	...	...	...	17
	Specially Administered Territories.	**13,003**	**3,712**	**4,429**	**760**	**215**	**4,862**	**256**	**188**	**12**	...	**3**	**56**
38	Northern Shan States	2,701	1,280	553	144	117	868	2	2	...	...	...	...
39	Southern Shan States	10,237	2,405	3,876	616	98	3,956	254	186	12	...	3	56
40	Chin Hills ...	65	27	...	...	...	38	...	...	...	...	...	...

Occupations. Details by Districts.

ORDER XXVIII.—(GROUP 110), TRADE IN WOOD, CORK, BARK, ETC.						ORDER XXIX.—(GROUP 111), TRADE IN METALS, MACHINERY; KNIFE AND TOOL SELLERS.						ORDER XXX.—(GROUP 112), TRADE IN POTTERY.						
Total Workers and Dependents.	Actual Workers.				Dependents.	Total Workers and Dependents.	Actual Workers.				Dependents.	Total Workers and Dependents.	Actual Workers.				Dependents.	
	Total.		Partially Agriculturist.				Total.		Partially Agriculturist.				Total.		Partially Agriculturist.			
	Males.	Females.	Males.	Females.			Males.	Females.	Males.	Females.			Males.	Females.	Males.	Females.		Serial No.
556	557	558	559	560	561	562	563	564	565	566	567	568	569	570	571	572	573	
21,988	7,979	2,480	203	205	11,529	1,644	444	528	72	...	672	10,386	2,425	3,784	246	238	4,277	
20,010	7,562	2,398	192	203	10,050	1,337	259	528	5	...	550	9,035	2,237	3,211	200	130	3,587	
652	364	30	20	...	258	805	...	493	...	...	312	516	91	170	...	8	255	
454	274	13	...	...	167	805	...	493	...	...	312	132	35	28	...	...	69	1
16	7	...	...	...	9	...	...	...	...	...	...	...	...	...	...	...	...	2
124	62	13	20	...	49	...	...	...	...	...	...	364	47	139	...	8	178	3
58	21	4	...	...	33	-	...	...	...	...	...	20	9	3	...	...	8	4
5,485	2,904	241	30	6	2,240	311	178	9	...	...	184	1,576	263	640	9	2	673	
3,212	2,074	53	22	...	1,105	240	139	7	...	...	94	52	27	11	...	...	14	5
491	196	32	...		263	50	30	2	...	...	18	885	105	403	9	...	377	6
259	54	75	...	6	130	...	...	...	...	...	...	87	19	37	...	3	31	7
867	313	62	8	...	492	6	5	..	...	...	3	164	40	46	...	...	78	8
656	267	139	...	...	250	15	6	...	...	...	9	388	72	143	...	...	173	9
1,095	179	365	1	...	551	29	15	2	...	...	12	1,549	618	297	...	2	634	
603	13	314	...	...	276	1	1	...	...	...	..	916	557	20	...	...	339	10
66	16	16	...	...	34	28	14	2	...	...	12	483	15	221	...	3	247	11
365	150	27	1	...	188	...	...	...	...	...	...	57	9	24	...	...	24	12
...	...	...	...	..	...	...	...	..	...	...	...	40	37	...	...	...	3	13
61	...	8	...	...	53	...	..	...	...	...	...	53	...	32	...	...	21	14
4,012	1,245	231	5	3	2,537	83	28	18	...	...	37	259	71	70	3	...	118	
898	282	49	2	...	567	9	1	3	...	...	5	88	41	6	3	...	41	15
...	...	...	...	...	...	...	...	...	...	...	...	...	...	...	...	...	...	16
633	272	33	1	...	328	...	...	...	...	...	...	97	16	44	..	...	37	17
2,415	683	121	1	3	1,611	30	5	14	...	...	11	72	14	19	...	...	39	18
50	3	28	...	...	19	3	...	1	...	...	2	2	...	1	...	...	1	19
17	5	...	1	...	12	41	22	...	...	...	19	...	...	...	...	...	...	20
768	220	148	19	...	408	38	15	5	...	...	18	506	95	248	...	4	163	
128	1	21	...	...	96	...	...	...	...	...	...	47	19	7	...	...	21	21
240	50	47	...	...	143	29	10	2	...	...	17	201	32	111	...	...	58	22
276	108	45	17	...	123	2	...	2	...	...	...	127	15	62	...	4	50	23
134	53	35	2	...	46	7	5	1	...	..	1	131	29	68	...	..	34	24
2,207	977	534	59	148	1,696	...	...	...	...	...	...	876	95	506	15	...	275	
1,582	661	230	52	26	691	...	...	...	...	...	...	580	60	337	15	...	183	25
960	375	137	...	...	448	...	...	...	...	...	...	24	17	...	...	...	7	
401	105	128	7	76	168	...	...	...	...	...	...	80	28	18	...	...	34	26
37	18	...	...	...	19	...	...	...	...	...	...	...	...	...	...	...	...	27
783	137	27	...	...	619	...	...	...	...	...	...	183	...	144	...	...	39	28
404	56	149	...	46	199	...	...	...	...	...	...	33	7	7	...	...	19	29
2,815	1,288	464	46	38	1,263	19	11	1	5	...	7	1,452	539	354	156	14	559	
239	130	16	...	2	93	...	...	...	...	...	...	490	67	204	...	...	219	30
307	133	98	1	13	76	...	...	...	...	...	...	34	26	...	...	...	8	31
1,709	720	291	24	21	692	18	10	1	5	...	7	468	126	150	6	14	192	32
560	199	59	21	2	302	1	1	...	...	...	...	460	320	...	150	...	140	33
1,975	493	285	10	8	1,297	52	12	...	...	...	40	2,302	465	926	17	98	920	
1,069	294	161	9	...	614	...	...	...	...	...	...	233	154	1	2	...	78	34
168	45	...	...	...	123	46	12	...	...	...	34	35	20	...	...	...	15	35
502	103	64	3	8	335	...	...	...	...	...	...	357	103	53	...	...	201	36
236	51	60	...	...	125	6	...	...	...	...	6	1,676	188	872	15	98	616	37
1,978	417	80	11	2	1,479	307	185	...	67	...	122	1,351	188	573	46	108	390	
316	237	22	10	...	57	119	26	...	...	...	93	151	17	59	...	...	75	38
1,662	180	60	1	2	1,423	188	159	...	67	...	29	1,200	171	514	46	108	515	39
...	...	...	...	...	...	...	...	...	...	...	...	...	...	...	...	...	...	40

Serial No.	DISTRICT OR STATE.	ORDER.—XXXI (GROUP 113), TRADE IN CHEMICAL PRODUCTS (DRUGS, DYES, PAINTS, PETROLEUM, EXPLOSIVES, ETC.) — Total Workers and Dependents.	Actual Workers. Total. Males.	Actual Workers. Total. Females.	Actual Workers. Partially Agriculturist. Males.	Actual Workers. Partially Agriculturist. Females.	Dependents.	ORDER XXXII.—HOTELS, CAFES, RESTAURANTS, ETC. — Total Workers and Dependents.	Actual Workers. Total. Males.	Actual Workers. Total. Females.	Actual Workers. Partially Agriculturist. Males.	Actual Workers. Partially Agriculturist. Females.	Dependents.
	1	574	575	576	577	578	579	580	581	582	583	584	585
	Provincial Total ...	2,903	1,025	404	10	32	1,474	21,651	9,335	3,445	864	212	8,871
	Burma Proper ...	2,866	1,011	400	9	32	1,455	19,310	8,306	2,938	690	183	8,066
	Arakan Division ...	33	3	15	...	...	15	268	154	13	...	...	101
1	Akyab	...	...	...	...	...	...	177	117	4	...	...	56
2	Northern Arakan ...	...	...	...	...	...	...	24	15	...	...	...	9
3	Kyaukpyu ...	5	2	2	...	...	1	20	6	1	...	...	13
4	Sandoway ...	28	1	13	...	...	14	47	16	8	...	...	23
	Pegu Division ...	884	500	50	2	...	334	5,327	2,614	564	12	23	2,149
5	City of Rangoon ...	351	192	28	1	...	131	3,167	1,787	202	7	...	1,178
6	Hanthawaddy ...	283	184	1	1	...	98	779	208	183	5	23	382
7	Tharrawaddy ...	20	2	6	...	...	12	193	94	18	...	...	81
8	Pegu	24	7	9	...	...	8	770	417	68	...	...	285
9	Prome	206	115	6	...	...	85	418	108	87	1	...	223
	Irrawaddy Division ...	333	113	69	...	26	151	1,502	894	70	...	...	528
10	Bassein	7	2	...	...	...	5	632	446	33	...	...	153
11	Henzada	27	19	2	...	...	6	362	178	27	...	...	157
12	Myaungmya ...	19	8	...	...	...	11	246	151	5	...	...	90
13	Ma-ubin	278	84	67	...	26	127	239	119	1	...	...	119
14	Pyapôn	2	...	...	...	...	2	23	...	4	...	...	19
	Tenasserim Division ...	286	77	86	...	...	123	2,641	632	239	3	...	770
15	Toungoo	146	17	74	...	...	55	197	100	11	...	...	86
16	Salween	...	...	...	...	...	...	...	...	...	...	...	...
17	Thatôn	37	25	1	...	...	11	404	236	31	1	...	237
18	Amherst	96	33	11	...	...	52	635	247	44	2	...	344
19	Tavoy	4	...	...	...	...	4	35	14	1	...	...	20
20	Mergui	3	2	...	...	...	1	280	35	152	...	...	93
	Magwe Division ...	784	105	129	...	1	550	839	316	198	1	...	325
21	Thayetmyo ...	39	1	5	...	...	33	51	3	17	...	...	31
22	Pakôkku	96	41	6	...	...	49	129	61	12	...	...	56
23	Minbu	248	50	65	...	1	133	378	199	83	...	...	96
24	Magwe	401	13	53	...	...	335	281	53	86	1	...	142
	Mandalay Division ...	87	41	...	...	...	46	2,352	703	560	101	1	1,089
25	Mandalay (including City).	87	41	...	...	...	46	1,233	399	354	...	...	580
	Mandalay City ...	*87*	*41*	...	...	...	*46*	*1,222*	*298*	*351*	...	...	*573*
26	Bhamo	...	...	...	...	...	...	69	21	2	1	...	46
27	Myitkyina ...	...	...	...	...	...	...	54	52	...	...	...	2
28	Katha	...	...	...	...	...	...	341	65	121	...	...	155
29	Ruby Mines ...	...	...	...	...	...	...	655	266	83	100	1	306
	Sagaing Division ...	411	158	42	7	5	211	3,408	1,098	960	19	159	1,350
30	Shwebo	5	2	...	...	...	3	522	342	58	2	26	122
31	Sagaing	191	58	25	3	5	108	1,662	641	230	7	83	791
32	Lower Chindwin ...	215	98	17	4	...	100	1,028	79	618	6	45	331
33	Upper Chindwin ...	...	...	...	...	...	...	196	36	54	4	5	106
	Meiktila Division ...	48	14	9	...	...	25	2,973	1,895	334	553	...	1,744
34	Kyauksè	...	...	...	...	...	...	229	113	21	2	...	95
35	Meiktila	4	...	...	...	...	4	964	467	47	45	...	450
36	Yamèthin... ...	...	...	...	...	...	...	475	148	64	11	...	263
37	Myingyan ...	44	14	9	...	...	21	2,305	1,167	202	425	...	936
	Specially Administered Territories.	37	14	4	1	...	19	2,341	1,029	507	174	29	805
38	Northern Shan States	3	2	...	...	...	1	1,566	729	247	169	10	590
39	Southern Shan States	34	12	4	1	...	18	756	293	257	5	19	206
40	Chin Hills ...	...	...	...	...	...	...	19	7	3	...	...	9

Occupations. Details by Districts.

GROUP 114, VENDORS OF WINES, LIQUORS, AERATED WATERS, ETC.						GROUP 115, OWNERS AND MANAGERS OF HOTELS, COOKSHOPS, ETC., AND THEIR EMPLOYÉS.						ORDER XXXIII.—OTHER TRADE IN FOODSTUFFS.						
Total Workers and Dependents.	ACTUAL WORKERS.				Dependents.	Total Workers and Dependents.	ACTUAL WORKERS.				Dependents.	Total Workers and Dependents.	ACTUAL WORKERS.				Dependents.	
	TOTAL.		PARTIALLY AGRICULTURIST.				TOTAL.		PARTIALLY AGRICULTURIST.				TOTAL.		PARTIALLY AGRICULTURIST.			
	Males.	Females.	Males.	Females.			Males.	Females.	Males.	Females.			Males.	Females.	Males.	Females.		Serial No.
586	587	588	589	590	591	592	593	594	595	596	597	598	599	600	601	602	603	
14,474	6,501	1,990	732	168	5,983	7,177	2,834	1,455	132	44	2,888	512,911	112,579	169,795	5,208	8,204	230,537	
12,741	5,727	1,612	561	139	5,402	6,569	2,579	1,326	129	44	2,664	459,263	98,832	154,066	3,695	6,334	206,365	
222	132	11	...	...	79	46	22	2	...	...	22	30,086	8,080	8,378	83	56	13,628	
163	114	2	...	...	47	14	3	2	...	...	9	22,063	6,866	5,009	59	56	10,188	1
...	...	...	...	...	...	24	15	...	...	...	9	35	12	4	...	...	19	2
20	6	1	...	...	13	...	...	...	...	...	...	4,638	751	1,835	24	...	2,052	3
39	12	8	...	...	19	8	4	...	...	...	4	3,350	451	1,530	...	...	1,369	4
2,510	1,235	273	13	23	1,002	2,817	1,379	291	...	...	1,147	94,686	22,702	27,020	137	273	44,964	
1,019	716	12	7	...	291	2,148	1,071	190	...	...	887	27,485	9,599	4,152	19	1	13,734	5
681	160	178	5	23	343	98	48	11	...	...	39	21,876	4,356	7,127	8	36	10,393	6
159	86	7	...	...	66	34	8	11	...	...	15	15,771	2,882	5,959	21	168	6,930	7
307	183	10	...	...	114	463	234	58	...	...	171	14,497	3,172	4,032	43	61	7,293	8
344	90	66	1	...	188	74	18	21	...	...	35	15,057	2,693	5,780	46	7	6,614	9
1,119	703	51	...	...	365	383	191	19	...	...	173	94,351	20,240	31,155	253	998	42,956	
618	442	29	...	...	147	14	4	4	...	...	6	20,618	5,306	6,510	53	16	8,802	10
274	130	17	...	...	127	88	48	10	...	...	30	24,173	4,432	9,395	124	824	10,346	11
152	101	1	...	...	50	94	50	4	...	...	40	18,684	4,181	5,650	18	52	8,853	12
52	30	...	...	...	22	187	89	1	...	...	97	19,470	4,048	6,162	46	106	9,260	13
23	...	4	...	...	19	...	...	...	...	...	...	11,406	2,273	3,438	12	...	5,695	14
1,158	409	198	3	...	551	483	223	41	...	...	219	44,509	8,995	14,684	293	87	20,830	
91	44	4	...	...	43	106	56	7	...	...	43	16,023	3,916	4,160	248	38	7,947	15
...	...	...	...	...	...	...	...	...	...	...	...	155	30	48	...	...	77	16
190	101	3	1	...	86	304	135	28	...	...	141	9,005	1,694	3,303	12	4	4,008	17
603	240	39	2	...	324	32	7	5	...	...	20	13,234	2,504	4,553	12	36	6,177	18
14	2	1	...	...	11	21	12	...	...	...	9	3,338	481	1,336	20	9	1,521	19
260	22	151	...	...	87	20	13	1	...	...	6	2,754	370	1,284	1	...	1,100	20
676	280	138	...	...	258	163	36	60	1	...	67	38,601	6,671	15,958	84	237	15,992	
17	3	...	...	...	14	34	...	17	...	...	17	8,491	1,329	3,589	2	13	3,573	21
109	50	9	...	...	50	20	11	3	...	...	6	9,590	1,711	3,901	16	1	3,978	22
359	198	70	...	...	91	19	1	13	...	...	5	11,742	1,620	5,574	47	186	4,548	23
191	29	59	...	...	103	90	24	27	1	...	39	8,798	2,011	2,894	19	37	3,893	24
1,138	276	303	1	1	559	1,214	427	257	100	...	530	47,715	9,522	18,337	779	568	19,856	
426	106	105	...	...	215	807	193	249	...	...	365	30,861	5,364	12,951	258	289	12,546	25
422	*106*	*102*	...	...	*214*	*800*	*192*	*249*	...	...	*359*	*18,277*	*2,761*	*8,079*	...	...	*7,437*	
58	21	1	1	...	36	11	...	1	...	...	10	3,233	1,066	890	164	6	1,277	26
54	52	...	...	...	2	...	...	...	...	...	...	1,575	345	361	17	2	869	27
338	64	119	...	...	155	3	1	2	...	...	...	4,880	1,030	1,942	75	33	1,908	28
262	33	78	...	1	151	393	233	5	100	...	155	7,166	1,717	2,193	265	238	3,256	29
2,302	1,008	305	10	115	989	1,106	90	655	9	44	361	55,708	10,482	21,230	1,052	3,153	23,996	
492	327	56	2	24	109	30	15	2	...	2	13	11,845	1,680	4,822	76	904	5,343	30
1,633	628	226	6	83	779	29	13	4	1	...	12	15,141	3,073	5,684	179	795	6,384	31
109	37	23	...	8	49	919	42	595	6	37	282	19,671	3,289	8,473	253	1,391	7,909	32
68	16	...	2	...	52	128	20	54	2	5	54	9,051	2,440	2,251	544	63	4,360	33
3,616	1,684	333	534	...	1,599	357	211	1	19	...	145	53,587	12,140	17,304	1,014	962	24,143	
225	110	21	2	...	94	4	3	...	...	...	1	8,210	2,151	2,862	96	119	3,197	34
738	337	46	32	...	355	226	130	1	13	...	95	17,002	3,862	4,717	557	519	8,423	35
358	79	64	5	...	215	117	69	...	6	...	48	12,942	3,309	3,527	188	123	6,105	36
2,295	1,158	202	495	...	935	10	9	...	...	...	1	15,434	2,818	6,198	173	201	6,418	37
1,733	774	378	171	29	581	608	255	129	3	...	224	54,648	14,747	15,729	2,113	1,870	24,172	
1,266	709	122	169	10	435	300	20	125	...	...	155	18,810	3,962	5,611	810	847	9,237	38
448	58	253	2	19	137	308	235	4	3	...	69	35,738	10,731	10,114	1,303	1,023	14,893	39
19	7	3	...	...	9	...	...	...	...	...	...	100	54	4	...	...	42	40

Serial No.	District or State.	Group 116, Fish Dealers. Total Workers and Dependents.	Actual Workers. Total. Males.	Actual Workers. Total. Females.	Partially Agriculturist. Males.	Partially Agriculturist. Females.	Dependents.	Group 117, Grocers and Sellers of Vegetable Oils, Salt, and other Condiments. Total Workers and Dependents.	Actual Workers. Total. Males.	Actual Workers. Total. Females.	Partially Agriculturist. Males.	Partially Agriculturist. Females.	Dependents.
	1	604	605	606	607	608	609	610	611	612	613	614	615
	Provincial Total ..	107,111	22,420	38,655	1,155	2,502	46,036	35,978	9,398	9,630	159	564	16,950
	Burma Proper ..	58,314	20,383	35,988	1,025	2,098	42,003	31,465	8,571	8,344	107	243	14,550
	Arakan Division ..	7,660	2,224	2,102	35	3	3,334	1,269	393	410	...	...	466
1	Akyab	5,088	1,703	1,081	19	3	2,304	731	325	80	...	...	326
2	Northern Arakan ...	21	8	4	...	...	9	...	...	...	...	...	...
3	Kyaukpyu ...	1,379	343	449	16	...	587	470	42	318	...	...	110
4	Sandoway ...	1,172	170	568	...	...	434	68	26	12	...	...	30
	Pegu Division ...	16,863	3,044	6,198	12	84	7,621	6,090	2,517	1,166	4	1	2,407
5	City of Rangoon ...	2,325	636	576	...	...	1,113	2,829	1,550	240	2	...	1,059
6	Hanthawaddy ...	3,055	471	1,149	1	24	1,435	1,325	410	390	...	...	525
7	Tharrawaddy ...	5,144	840	2,133	4	48	2,171	958	222	291	...	...	445
8	Pegu	3,025	542	955	4	12	1,528	391	117	79	2	...	195
9	Prome	3,314	555	1,385	3	...	1,374	587	218	166	...	1	203
	Irrawaddy Division ...	19,234	4,496	5,897	111	225	8,841	9,550	2,277	2,521	...	36	4,752
10	Bassein	3,615	956	1,077	17	4	1,582	1,910	453	482	...	...	975
11	Henzada ...	5,254	1,021	2,057	57	141	2,176	2,127	422	675	...	33	1,030
12	Myaungmya ...	2,604	754	671	2	11	1,179	3,055	723	805	...	3	1,527
13	Ma-ubin ...	5,961	1,409	1,625	31	69	2,927	1,526	394	422	...	...	710
14	Pyapôn	1,800	355	467	4	...	977	932	285	137	...	...	510
	Tenasserim Division ...	6,260	1,078	2,218	30	15	2,964	2,256	538	454	...	...	1,264
15	Toungoo ...	1,525	284	499	12	...	742	642	184	123	...	...	335
16	Salween ...	15	7	2	...	...	6	...	...	...	...	...	...
17	Thatôn	1,503	317	564	5	...	622	419	75	134	...	...	210
18	Amherst ...	1,613	236	596	1	6	781	956	237	126	...	...	593
19	Tavoy	1,003	130	333	11	9	540	124	30	39	...	...	55
20	Mergui	601	104	224	1	...	273	115	12	32	...	...	71
	Magwe Division ...	11,013	1,809	5,013	18	46	4,191	1,729	421	420	...	...	888
21	Thayetmyo ...	2,545	322	1,214	2	5	1,009	222	24	76	...	...	122
22	Pakokku ...	3,005	488	1,386	2	...	1,131	517	88	127	...	...	302
23	Minbu	3,027	438	1,541	4	24	1,048	517	107	129	...	...	281
24	Magwe	2,436	561	872	10	17	1,003	473	202	88	...	...	183
	Mandalay Division ...	10,022	1,900	4,102	94	131	4,020	2,614	752	673	...	5	1,189
25	Mandalay (including City).	5,288	758	2,533	32	88	1,997	1,917	624	455	...	5	838
	Mandalay City ...	*2,078*	*241*	*999*	..	...	*838*	*1,296*	*335*	*322*	...	...	*639*
26	Bhamo	1,050	364	280	24	...	406	175	29	25	...	...	121
27	Myitkyina ..	418	96	83	8	...	234	43	10	13	...	...	20
28	Katha	1,038	347	322	10	17	369	330	62	145	...	..	123
29	Ruby Mines ...	2,228	335	879	20	26	1,014	149	27	35	...	...	87
	Sagaing Division ...	14,728	2,988	6,005	356	1,430	5,735	4,984	886	1,896	12	193	2,202
30	Shwebo	3,322	387	1,550	19	454	1,376	1,141	234	394	...	10	513
31	Sagaing	3,545	680	1,178	72	236	1,387	714	112	288	...	24	314
32	Lower Chindwin ...	6,146	1,086	2,842	123	723	2,218	2,137	323	970	2	159	844
33	Upper Chindwin ...	1,715	535	426	142	17	754	992	217	244	10	...	531
	Meiktila Division ...	12,534	2,784	4,453	369	164	5,297	2,973	787	804	91	8	1,382
34	Kyaukse	1,068	240	442	24	15	386	749	172	247	2	...	330
35	Meiktila	4,588	1,167	1,254	271	75	2,167	598	152	107	6	...	339
36	Yamèthin ...	1,713	545	395	28	5	773	621	124	185	31	...	312
37	Myingyan ...	5,165	832	2,362	46	69	1,971	1,005	339	265	52	8	401
	Specially Administered Territories.	8,797	2,097	2,667	130	404	4,033	4,513	827	1,286	52	321	2,400
38	Northern Shan States	2,428	445	803	2	301	1,180	1,078	367	275	...	...	436
39	Southern Shan States	6,361	1,647	1,864	128	103	2,850	3,435	460	1,011	52	321	1,964
40	Chin Hills ...	8	5	...	...	...	3	...	...	...	...	...	...

Occupations. Details by Districts.

GROUP 118, SELLERS OF MILK, BUTTER, GHEE, POULTRY, EGGS, ETC.						GROUP 119, SELLERS OF SWEETMEATS, SUGAR, MOLASSES, AND GUR.						GROUP 120, CARDAMOM, BETEL-LEAF, VEGETABLES, FRUIT, AND ARECA-NUT SELLERS.						
Total Workers and Dependents.	ACTUAL WORKERS.				Dependents.	Total Workers and Dependents.	ACTUAL WORKERS.				Dependents.	Total Workers and Dependents.	ACTUAL WORKERS.				Dependents.	
	TOTAL.		PARTIALLY AGRICULTURIST.				TOTAL.		PARTIALLY AGRICULTURIST.				TOTAL.		PARTIALLY AGRICULTURIST.			
	Males.	Females.	Males.	Females.			Males.	Females.	Males.	Females.			Males.	Females.	Males.	Females.		Serial No.
615	617	618	619	620	621	622	623	624	625	626	627	628	629	630	631	632	633	
10,378	4,456	1,837	85	54	4,085	108,839	17,902	38,634	31	82	52,303	117,309	25,849	41,963	1,730	2,698	49,497	
9,591	4,097	1,772	61	54	3,722	104,853	17,236	37,504	26	82	50,113	95,155	20,566	35,156	1,067	1,942	39,392	
90	41	12	...	...	37	6,921	1,308	2,017	1	...	3,596	9,483	3,038	2,269	30	19	4,276	
...	...	...	...	...	...	4,909	1,145	1,237	1	...	2,527	7,642	2,799	1,421	28	19	3,422	1
...	...	...	...	...	...	...	...	...	...	...	...	...	...	...	...	...	...	2
47	20	7	...	...	20	1,323	125	476	...	...	722	860	117	363	2	...	380	3
43	21	5	...	...	17	689	38	304	...	...	347	981	122	485	...	...	374	4
2,692	1,598	205	...	...	889	20,217	3,750	7,195	1	21	9,272	17,982	3,449	6,973	35	113	7,560	
1,705	1,160	94	...	...	451	1,826	848	354	1	...	624	4,843	1,204	1,690	1	1	1,949	5
465	218	12	...	...	235	7,705	1,234	3,016	...	...	3,455	4,145	627	1,586	4	9	1,932	6
68	2	24	...	...	42	3,686	613	1,441	...	21	1,632	2,171	438	863	3	55	870	7
328	162	45	...	...	121	2,544	417	842	...	...	1,285	3,914	788	1,375	25	42	1,751	8
126	56	30	...	...	40	4,456	638	1,542	...	...	2,276	2,909	392	1,459	2	6	1,058	9
657	364	87	...	1	206	32,314	4,814	12,909	...	1	14,591	14,159	3,199	5,079	29	367	5,881	
76	50	4	...	...	22	7,743	1,327	2,089	...	...	3,427	3,106	1,304	819	11	4	983	10
280	156	52	...	...	72	6,321	932	2,516	...	1	2,873	4,214	520	2,132	9	347	1,562	11
130	69	6	...	...	55	7,333	1,153	2,738	...	...	3,442	1,925	348	757	2	6	820	12
42	...	15	...	1	27	6,667	1,038	2,795	...	...	2,834	2,797	521	717	5	10	1,559	13
129	89	10	...	...	30	4,250	364	1,871	...	...	2,015	2,117	506	634	2	...	957	14
927	450	144	...	8	333	8,833	1,631	2,977	2	...	4,225	13,294	2,692	5,025	237	46	5,477	
363	171	43	...	8	149	3,711	631	1,144	...	...	1,936	5,332	1,713	1,186	224	15	2,433	15
22	8	...	...	...	14	83	4	37	...	...	42	21	7	5	...	...	9	16
272	114	61	...	...	97	1,219	222	475	...	...	522	2,920	433	1,220	6	4	1,267	17
215	134	27	...	...	54	2,294	614	727	2	...	953	2,878	289	1,376	5	27	1,215	18
25	12	3	...	...	10	1,065	126	417	...	...	522	854	109	463	2	...	276	19
30	11	10	...	...	9	461	34	177	...	...	250	1,189	141	769	...	...	279	20
433	189	47	...	...	197	7,720	1,125	2,874	...	4	3,721	8,371	1,408	3,760	13	48	3,203	
171	71	19	...	...	81	2,312	432	884	...	...	1,006	1,083	156	516	...	7	411	21
16	3	2	...	...	11	1,564	217	632	...	...	715	2,250	500	879	9	1	871	22
81	40	6	...	...	35	2,120	173	831	...	4	1,116	2,616	324	1,454	1	29	838	23
165	75	20	...	...	70	1,714	303	527	...	...	884	2,422	428	911	3	11	1,083	24
1,743	601	367	32	2	775	9,174	1,944	3,076	2	28	4,154	9,390	1,767	3,840	201	208	3,783	
956	242	274	...	1	440	6,930	1,535	2,324	...	23	3,071	6,491	906	3,037	44	40	2,548	25
827	*201*	*254*	...	...	*372*	*3,695*	*936*	*1,421*	...	...	*1,338*	*4,082*	*404*	*1,935*	...	...	*1,743*	
53	29	2	12	...	22	347	52	139	...	...	156	340	155	92	5	...	93	26
94	12	30	...	...	52	404	57	117	...	...	230	154	48	42	1	...	64	27
218	126	19	19	...	73	707	112	273	2	...	322	573	180	184	24	15	209	28
422	192	42	1	1	188	786	188	223	...	5	375	1,832	478	485	127	153	869	29
1,186	448	279	6	...	459	9,434	986	3,321	15	8	5,127	9,279	1,602	4,155	224	737	2,822	
167	105	2	1	...	60	1,725	216	573	...	2	936	2,721	328	1,137	11	272	1,256	30
335	52	150	...	...	133	3,916	293	1,587	2	...	2,036	2,764	436	1,516	22	323	812	31
185	79	15	2	...	91	2,407	324	635	12	6	1,448	2,323	303	1,162	28	125	858	32
499	212	112	4	...	175	1,386	153	526	1	...	707	1,471	535	340	163	17	596	33
1,863	406	681	23	42	826	10,250	1,688	3,125	5	20	5,427	13,297	3,420	4,095	298	404	5,791	
62	37	...	...	...	25	2,091	441	623	...	5	1,027	1,614	311	666	21	60	637	34
1,185	276	400	14	29	509	2,448	376	745	5	...	1,327	4,371	1,224	974	148	234	2,173	35
540	65	225	2	14	250	2,908	447	935	...	15	1,526	3,960	1,207	805	88	21	1,768	36
76	28	6	7	...	42	2,803	424	832	...	...	1,547	3,352	579	1,560	41	89	1,213	37
787	359	65	24	...	363	3,986	666	1,130	5	...	2,190	22,154	5,283	6,767	663	756	10,104	
573	231	49	13	...	293	956	233	297	...	...	426	10,801	1,226	3,746	59	518	5,829	38
135	92	12	11	...	31	3,026	429	833	5	...	1,764	11,353	4,057	3,021	604	238	4,275	39
79	36	4	...	...	39	4	4	...	...	...	...	...	...	...	...	...	...	40

Serial No.	DISTRICT OR STATE.	GROUP 121, GRAIN AND PULSE DEALERS.						GROUP 122, TOBACCO, OPIUM, AND GANJA SELLERS.					
		Total Workers and Dependents.	ACTUAL WORKERS.				Dependents	Total Workers and Dependents.	ACTUAL WORKERS.				Dependents.
			TOTAL.		PARTIALLY AGRICULTURIST.				TOTAL.		PARTIALLY AGRICULTURIST.		
			Males.	Females.	Males.	Females.			Males.	Females.	Males.	Females.	
	1	634	635	636	637	638	639	640	641	642	643	644	645
	Provincial Total ...	105,332	27,908	26,895	1,615	1,681	50,529	22,362	3,906	10,336	188	420	8,120
	Burma Proper ...	94,300	23,172	24,120	1,075	1,465	47,008	20,459	3,365	9,528	185	308	7,566
	Arakan Division ...	3,608	939	1,220	12	34	1,449	1,044	126	348	5	...	570
1	Akyab	2,864	807	944	11	34	1,113	829	87	246	...	...	496
2	Northern Arakan ...	...	...	...	...	...	...	14	4	...	...	...	10
3	Kyaukpyu	437	63	183	1	...	191	111	30	39	5	...	42
4	Sandoway ...	307	69	93	...	...	145	90	5	63	...	...	22
	Pegu Division ...	25,522	7,055	3,239	85	39	15,228	4,550	772	2,033	...	15	1,745
5	City of Rangoon ...	11,341	3,280	529	15	...	7,532	2,064	506	659	...	...	899
6	Hanthawaddy	4,306	1,306	455	3	2	2,545	767	44	519	...	1	204
7	Tharrawaddy ...	3,101	714	812	14	30	1,575	643	53	395	...	14	195
8	Pegu	3,770	1,043	525	12	7	2,195	462	69	210	...	...	183
9	Prome	3,004	706	918	41	...	1,380	614	100	250	...	...	264
	Irrawaddy Division ...	16,506	4,804	3,717	112	230	7,985	1,920	272	941	1	138	697
10	Bassein ...	3,591	1,144	869	25	8	1,578	577	72	270	...	...	235
11	Henzada ..	5,257	1,332	1,477	58	166	2,448	707	43	482	...	136	182
12	Myaungmya ...	3,390	1,099	600	13	32	1,691	247	35	73	1	...	139
13	Ma-ubin	2,144	579	484	10	24	1,081	325	99	104	...	2	122
14	Pyapôn	2,124	650	287	6	...	1,187	54	23	12	...	...	19
	Tenasserim Division...	9,269	2,085	1,901	21	15	5,283	3,537	363	1,958	3	1	1,216
15	Toungoo	3,849	857	904	9	13	2,088	551	53	257	3	...	241
16	Salween	12	4	4	...	...	4	2	...	...	...	...	2
17	Thatôn	2,112	477	530	1	...	1,105	538	46	318	...	...	174
18	Amherst	2,695	619	320	4	2	1,756	2,421	250	1,379	...	1	793
19	Tavoy	249	64	71	7	...	114	18	10	4	...	...	4
20	Mergui	352	64	72	...	...	216	6	4	...	...	...	2
	Magwe Division ...	8,050	1,583	3,115	53	139	3,352	815	40	536	...	...	282
21	Thayetmyo ...	1,679	311	586	...	1	782	345	...	248	...	...	97
22	Pakôkku	1,964	379	725	5	...	860	156	13	92	...	...	51
23	Minbu	3,146	483	1,496	42	129	1,167	120	13	74	...	...	33
24	Magwe	1,261	410	308	6	9	543	194	14	122	...	...	58
	Mandalay Division ...	9,407	1,753	3,496	223	68	4,158	5,168	429	1,833	103	24	906
25	Mandalay (including City).	5,182	859	2,096	73	9	2,227	2,416	107	1,589	...	22	780
	Mandalay City ...	*3,788*	*537*	*1,585*	...	...	*1,666*	*2,178*	*101*	*1,429*	...	...	648
26	Bhamo	1,127	336	351	103	6	440	85	63	1	...	...	21
27	Myitkyina ...	384	98	67	8	...	219	78	24	4	...	2	50
28	Katha	1,214	167	457	20	...	590	344	35	235	...	...	74
29	Ruby Mines ...	1,500	293	525	14	53	682	245	200	4	103	...	41
	Sagaing Division ...	12,507	2,783	4,113	375	663	5,611	2,801	600	1,075	63	87	1,226
30	Shwebo	2,463	387	921	41	161	1,085	303	21	166	4	5	116
31	Sagaing	3,293	1,044	872	81	196	1,383	562	155	93	2	16	314
32	Lower Chindwin ...	3,921	609	1,699	52	295	1,613	1,772	379	764	33	48	629
33	Upper Chindwin ...	2,824	743	551	201	11	1,530	164	45	52	23	18	67
	Meiktila Division ...	9,451	2,170	3,319	194	277	3,942	2,634	763	804	10	43	1,067
34	Kyauksè ...	1,852	352	874	44	39	625	774	598	10	5	...	166
35	Meiktila	2,991	473	1,157	85	152	1,361	318	76	66	5	29	176
36	Yamèthin ...	2,288	749	639	38	67	1,000	834	77	311	...	1	446
37	Myingyan ...	2,300	596	749	27	19	955	708	12	417	...	13	279
	Specially Administered Territories.	11,032	4,736	2,775	540	216	3,521	1,903	541	808	3	112	554
38	Northern Shan States	2,073	1,183	308	135	22	582	788	261	131	...	6	395
39	Southern Shan States	8,950	3,544	2,467	404	194	2,939	1,115	280	677	3	106	158
40	Chin Hills ...	9	9	...	...	...	...	...	...	...	...	...	...

Occupations. Details by Districts.

GROUP 123, DEALERS IN SHEEP, GOATS, AND PIGS.						GROUP 124, DEALERS IN HAY, GRASS, AND FODDER.						ORDER XXXIV—(GROUP 125), TRADE IN CLOTHING AND TOILET ARTICLES.						
Total Workers and Dependents.	ACTUAL WORKERS.				Dependents.	Total Workers and Dependents.	ACTUAL WORKERS.				Dependents.	Total Workers and Dependents.	ACTUAL WORKERS.				Dependents.	Serial No.
	TOTAL.		PARTIALLY AGRICULTURIST.				TOTAL.		PARTIALLY AGRICULTURIST.				TOTAL.		PARTIALLY AGRICULTURIST.			
	Males.	Females.	Males.	Females.			Males.	Females.	Males.	Females.			Males.	Females.	Males.	Females.		
646	647	648	649	650	651	652	653	654	655	656	657	658	659	660	661	662	663	
1,058	172	89	55	25	796	5,944	1,967	1,756	190	168	2,221	6,531	2,813	1,103	158	26	2,615	
155	58	16	...	3	81	4,971	1,444	1,598	149	139	1,929	5,031	1,980	996	30	26	2,055	
...	...	...	...	...	...	11	11	...	...	...	...	53	30	2	...	...	21	
...	...	...	...	...	...	...	...	...	...	...	...	1	1	...	...	...	...	1
...	...	...	...	...	...	...	...	...	...	...	...	...	...	...	...	...	...	2
...	...	...	...	...	...	11	11	...	...	...	...	47	26	2	...	...	19	3
...	...	...	...	...	...	...	...	...	...	...	...	5	3	...	...	...	2	4
91	38	4	...	...	49	679	479	7	...	...	193	722	270	101	...	1	351	
42	22	3	...	...	17	510	393	7	...	...	110	389	167	42	...	...	180	5
...	...	...	...	...	...	108	46	...	...	...	62	23	2	3	...	...	18	6
...	...	...	...	...	...	...	...	...	...	...	...	74	12	24	...	1	38	7
49	16	1	...	...	32	14	12	...	...	...	2	76	18	18	...	...	40	8
...	...	...	...	...	...	47	28	...	...	...	19	160	71	14	...	...	75	9
3	...	1	...	...	2	18	14	3	...	...	1	162	72	22	...	...	68	
...	...	...	...	...	...	...	...	...	...	...	...	64	41	2	...	...	21	10
3	...	1	...	...	2	10	6	3	...	...	1	53	20	7	...	...	26	11
...	...	...	...	...	...	...	...	...	...	...	...	19	...	12	...	...	6	12
...	...	...	...	...	...	8	8	...	...	...	...	14	6	...	...	...	8	13
...	...	...	...	...	...	...	...	...	...	...	...	12	5	...	...	...	7	14
6	...	1	...	...	5	227	158	6	...	2	63	124	32	26	...	...	66	
...	...	...	...	...	...	50	23	4	...	2	23	15	5	1	...	...	7	15
...	...	...	...	...	...	...	...	...	...	...	...	...	...	...	...	...	...	16
6	...	1	...	...	5	16	10	...	...	...	6	40	9	8	...	...	23	17
...	...	...	...	...	...	161	125	2	...	...	34	40	6	10	...	...	24	18
...	...	...	...	...	...	...	...	...	...	...	...	20	11	8	...	...	7	19
...	...	...	...	...	...	...	...	...	...	...	...	1	1	...	...	...	...	20
29	11	3	...	...	15	471	95	190	...	...	186	298	90	62	...	...	146	
...	...	...	...	...	...	134	23	46	...	...	65	17	2	9	...	...	6	21
5	1	1	...	...	3	113	28	57	...	...	34	141	1	33	...	...	107	22
...	...	...	...	...	...	115	48	43	...	...	30	35	6	16	...	...	13	23
24	10	2	...	...	12	109	8	44	...	...	57	105	81	4	...	...	20	24
...	...	...	...	...	...	2,197	276	950	124	102	871	2,252	942	494	...	...	816	
...	...	...	...	...	...	1,681	333	643	109	101	705	2,252	942	494	...	...	816	25
...	...	...	...	...	...	*333*	*6*	*134*	...	...	*193*	*2,246*	*942*	*491*	...	...	*813*	
...	...	...	...	...	...	56	38	...	15	...	18	...	...	...	...	...	...	26
...	...	...	...	...	...	...	...	...	...	...	...	...	...	...	...	...	...	27
...	...	...	...	...	...	456	1	307	...	1	148	...	...	...	...	...	...	28
...	...	...	...	...	...	4	4	...	...	...	...	...	...	...	...	...	...	29
1	1	...	...	...	...	788	188	386	1	35	214	1,281	404	275	26	15	512	
1	1	...	...	...	...	2	1	...	...	...	1	93	18	19	5	2	56	30
...	...	...	...	...	...	6	1	...	...	...	5	123	21	44	...	9	58	31
...	...	...	...	...	...	780	186	386	1	35	208	1,065	455	212	21	4	398	32
...	...	...	...	...	...	...	...	...	...	...	...	...	...	...	...	...	...	33
25	8	7	...	3	10	580	123	56	24	...	401	149	50	24	4	...	75	
...	...	...	...	...	...	...	...	...	...	...	...	18	...	5	...	...	13	34
...	...	...	...	...	...	503	118	14	23	...	371	74	31	...	2	...	43	35
...	...	...	...	...	...	77	5	42	1	...	30	28	19	...	2	...	9	36
25	8	7	...	3	10	...	...	...	...	...	...	29	...	19	...	...	10	37
903	115	73	55	32	715	573	123	158	41	29	292	1,500	833	107	128	...	560	
...	...	...	...	...	...	113	16	2	...	...	95	491	377	52	107	...	62	38
903	115	73	55	32	715	460	107	156	41	29	197	1,009	456	55	21	...	498	39
...	...	...	...	...	...	...	...	...	...	...	...	...	...	...	...	...	...	40

Serial No.	District or State.	Order XXXV—Trade in Furniture. Total Workers and Dependents.	Actual Workers. Total. Males.	Actual Workers. Total. Females.	Actual Workers. Partially Agriculturist. Males.	Actual Workers. Partially Agriculturist. Females.	Dependents.	Group 126, Trade in Furniture, Carpets, Curtains, and Bedding. Total Workers and Dependents.	Actual Workers. Total. Males.	Actual Workers. Total. Females.	Actual Workers. Partially Agriculturist. Males.	Actual Workers. Partially Agriculturist. Females.	Dependents.
	1	664	665	666	667	668	669	670	671	672	673	674	675
	Provincial Total ...	13,496	4,487	3,445	128	183	5,564	7,137	1,905	2,227	85	57	2,955
	Burma Proper ...	11,999	3,770	3,386	108	183	4,843	6,390	1,594	2,218	65	57	2,578
	Arakan Division ..	89	63	6	...	...	20	85	63	6	...	...	16
1	Akyab ...	43	34	5	...	...	4	43	34	5	...	...	4
2	Northern Arakan ...	...	...	...	...	...	...	...	...	...	...	...	...
3	Kyaukpyu ...	2	...	1	...	...	1	2	...	1	...	...	1
4	Sandoway ...	44	29	...	...	...	15	40	29	...	...	...	11
	Pegu Division ...	2,718	1,363	150	...	...	1,205	798	306	145	...	...	347
5	City of Rangoon ...	970	375	15	...	...	580	251	79	13	...	...	159
6	Hanthawaddy ...	355	156	94	...	...	105	348	153	94	...	...	101
7	Tharrawaddy ...	...	...	...	...	...	...	...	...	...	...	...	...
8	Pegu ...	166	57	38	...	...	71	166	57	38	...	...	71
9	Prome ...	1,227	775	3	...	...	449	33	17	...	...	...	16
	Irrawaddy Division ...	1,547	154	923	...	34	470	1,508	149	917	...	34	442
10	Bassein ...	115	1	58	...	...	56	85	...	55	...	...	30
11	Henzada ...	366	69	161	...	2	136	362	69	158	...	2	135
12	Myaungmya ...	89	31	46	...	...	12	84	27	46	...	...	11
13	Ma-ubin ...	975	53	656	...	32	266	975	53	656	...	32	266
14	Pyapôn ...	2	...	2	...	...	...	2	...	2	...	...	...
	Tenasserim Division ...	220	54	22	...	...	144	146	46	19	...	...	81
15	Toungoo ...	18	4	4	...	...	10	18	4	4	...	...	10
16	Salween ...	...	...	...	...	...	...	...	...	...	...	...	...
17	Thatôn ...	35	8	4	...	...	23	10	4	3	...	...	3
18	Amherst ...	130	41	8	...	...	81	81	37	6	...	...	38
19	Tavoy ..	...	...	...	...	...	...	...	...	...	...	...	...
20	Mergui ...	37	1	6	...	...	30	37	1	6	...	...	30
	Magwe Division ...	828	107	274	...	52	447	729	94	213	...	...	422
21	Thayetmyo ...	38	...	...	...	...	38	38	...	...	...	...	38
22	Pakôkku ...	161	16	52	...	...	93	149	9	52	...	...	88
23	Minbu ...	328	56	100	...	52	172	257	52	45	...	...	160
24	Magwe ...	301	35	122	...	...	144	285	33	116	...	...	136
	Mandalay Division ...	647	221	230	...	2	196	321	130	54	...	...	137
25	Mandalay (including City).	303	134	42	...	...	127	244	97	42	...	...	105
	Mandalay City ...	*303*	*134*	*42*	...	...	*127*	*244*	97	*42*	...	...	*105*
26	Bhamo ...	110	50	46	...	...	14	...	...	...	...	...	...
27	Myitkyina ...	3	1	...	...	...	2	...	...	...	...	...	...
28	Katha ...	217	50	140	...	2	47	66	30	10	...	...	26
29	Ruby Mines ...	14	6	2	...	...	6	11	3	2	...	...	6
	Sagaing Division ...	2,757	1,000	765	69	73	992	1,803	615	574	46	23	614
30	Shwebo ...	293	93	50	...	...	150	165	37	38	...	...	90
31	Sagaing ...	1,233	326	501	15	20	406	744	71	491	...	19	182
32	Lower Chindwin ...	994	484	176	14	49	334	657	410	7	6	...	240
33	Upper Chindwin ...	237	97	38	40	4	102	237	97	38	40	4	102
	Meiktila Division ...	3,193	808	1,016	39	22	1,369	1,000	191	290	19	...	519
34	Kyauksè ...	277	68	83	11	...	126	277	68	83	11	...	126
35	Meiktila ...	60	...	60	...	...	...	60	...	60	...	...	...
36	Yamèthin ...	769	123	185	8	...	461	615	123	128	8	...	364
37	Myingyan ...	2,087	617	688	20	22	782	48	...	19	...	...	29
	Specially Administered Territories.	1,497	727	59	20	...	721	747	311	59	20	...	377
38	Northern Shan States	1,040	565	4	19	...	471	328	161	4	19	...	163
39	Southern Shan States	457	152	55	1	...	250	419	150	55	1	...	214
40	Chin Hills ...	...	...	...	...	...	...	...	...	...	...	...	...

Occupations. Details by Districts.

GROUP 127, TRADE IN HARDWARE, COOKING UTENSILS, PORCELAIN, CROCKERY, GLASSWARE, BOTTLES, GARDENING AND CELLAR REQUISITES.						ORDER XXXVI—(GROUP 128), TRADE IN BUILDING MATERIALS.						ORDER XXXVII—(GROUP 129), TRADE IN MEANS OF TRANSPORT.						
Total Workers and Dependents.	Actual Workers. Total. Males.	Actual Workers. Total. Females.	Actual Workers. Partially Agriculturist. Males.	Actual Workers. Partially Agriculturist. Females.	Dependents.	Total Workers and Dependents.	Actual Workers. Total. Males.	Actual Workers. Total. Females.	Actual Workers. Partially Agriculturist. Males.	Actual Workers. Partially Agriculturist. Females.	Dependents.	Total Workers and Dependents.	Actual Workers. Total. Males.	Actual Workers. Total. Females.	Actual Workers. Partially Agriculturist. Males.	Actual Workers. Partially Agriculturist. Females.	Dependents.	Serial No.
676	677	678	679	680	681	682	683	684	685	686	687	688	689	690	691	692	693	
6,359	2,582	1,268	43	126	2,609	3,057	891	1,180	36	46	986	15,661	6,226	2,371	379	139	7,064	
5,609	2,176	1,268	43	126	2,265	2,411	539	1,042	32	41	830	12,556	4,487	1,948	143	131	6,121	
4	...	...	...	...	4	3	2	...	...	...	1	843	254	160	...	1	409	
...	...	...	...	...	...	...	...	...	...	...	...	690	232	112	...	...	356	1
...	...	...	...	...	...	...	...	...	...	...	...	...	...	...	...	...	...	2
...	...	...	...	...	...	1	...	...	...	...	1	99	11	42	...	1	46	3
4	...	...	...	...	4	2	2	...	...	...	...	54	21	6	...	...	27	4
1,900	1,057	5	...	...	858	831	161	320	...	3	350	2,693	1,125	318	6	15	1,250	
719	296	2	...	...	421	112	60	2	...	...	50	479	268	2	...	...	209	5
7	3	...	...	...	4	28	3	1	...	...	24	669	263	93	3	...	313	6
...	...	...	...	...	...	620	78	299	...	3	243	563	184	103	1	10	276	7
..	...	...	...	...	...	63	17	18	...	...	28	670	316	69	2	2	285	8
1,194	758	5	...	...	433	8	3	...	...	...	5	312	94	51	...	3	167	9
39	5	6	...	...	28	288	79	53	14	1	156	1,564	416	397	14	27	751	
30	1	3	...	...	26	36	16	10	14	...	10	234	42	103	...	...	89	10
4	...	3	...	...	1	9	...	4	...	...	5	973	254	212	14	22	507	11
5	4	...	..	...	1	67	...	4	...	1	63	93	30	28	...	...	35	12
...	...	...	...	...	...	128	38	35	...	...	55	264	90	54	...	5	120	13
...	...	...	...	...	...	48	25	...	...	...	23	...	...	...	...	...	...	14
74	8	3	...	...	63	129	36	12	1	...	81	1,728	729	161	6	1	838	
...	...	...	...	...	...	7	...	...	...	...	7	920	320	126	5	1	474	15
...	...	...	...	...	...	...	...	...	...	...	...	40	23	...	...	...	17	16
25	4	1	...	...	20	62	24	5	1	...	33	268	116	25	1	...	127	17
49	4	2	...	...	43	60	12	7	...	...	41	435	239	7	...	...	189	18
...	...	...	...	...	...	...	...	...	...	...	...	65	31	3	...	...	32	19
...	...	...	...	...	...	...	...	...	...	...	...	...	...	...	...	...	...	20
99	13	61	...	52	25	277	13	195	...	...	69	625	218	72	...	...	325	
...	...	...	...	...	...	1	1	...	...	...	...	243	65	42	...	...	136	21
12	7	...	...	...	5	3	...	2	...	...	1	149	71	8	...	...	70	22
71	4	55	...	52	12	209	2	182	...	...	35	86	35	12	...	...	39	23
16	2	6	...	...	8	64	10	11	...	...	43	137	47	10	...	...	80	24
326	91	176	...	2	59	37	20	7	8	...	10	1,289	551	139	41	1	699	
59	37	...	...	...	22	37	20	7	8	...	10	909	271	104	1	...	534	25
59	*37*	...	...	...	*22*	*15*	...	*7*	...	...	*8*	*772*	*777*	*703*	...	...	*492*	
110	50	46	...	...	14	...	...	...	...	...	...	276	190	20	38	1	66	26
3	1	...	...	...	2	...	...	...	...	...	...	47	23	10	...	...	14	27
151	...	130	...	2	21	...	...	...	...	...	...	49	25	5	2	...	19	28
3	3	...	...	...	...	...	...	...	...	...	...	108	42	...	...	...	66	29
954	385	191	23	50	378	494	210	183	7	3	101	1,647	564	235	23	8	848	
128	56	12	...	...	60	...	...	...	...	...	...	122	83	...	6	...	39	30
489	255	10	15	1	224	217	164	24	3	...	29	636	189	128	2	4	339	31
337	74	169	8	49	94	269	41	159	3	3	69	793	285	80	14	...	428	32
...	...	...	...	...	...	8	5	...	1	...	3	76	7	27	1	4	42	33
2,193	617	726	20	22	850	352	18	272	2	34	62	2,077	620	466	52	78	982	
...	...	...	...	...	...	241	4	222	...	34	15	76	5	30	...	21	41	34
...	..	...	...	...	...	...	...	...	...	...	...	1,144	71	430	1	57	643	35
154	...	57	...	...	97	31	14	...	2	...	17	382	192	6	21	...	184	36
2,039	617	669	20	22	753	80	...	50	..	...	30	535	352	...	31	...	273	37
750	406	...	...	...	344	646	352	138	4	5	156	3,105	1,739	423	236	8	943	
712	404	...	...	...	308	3	...	1	...	...	2	1,414	819	262	143	6	333	38
38	2	...	...	...	36	643	352	137	4	5	154	1,691	920	161	93	2	610	39
...	...	...	...	...	...	...	...	...	...	...	...	...	...	...	...	...	...	40

Serial No.	District or State.	ORDER XXXVIII—(GROUP 130), TRADE IN FUEL (FIREWOOD, COAL, CHARCOAL, COWDUNG, ETC.): Total Workers and Dependents.	Actual Workers. Total. Males.	Actual Workers. Total. Females.	Actual Workers. Partially Agriculturist. Males.	Actual Workers. Partially Agriculturist. Females.	Dependents.	ORDER XXXIX—TRADE IN ARTICLES OF LUXURY AND THOSE PERTAINING TO LETTERS, AND THE ARTS AND SCIENCES: Total Workers and Dependents.	Actual Workers. Total. Males.	Actual Workers. Total. Females.	Actual Workers. Partially Agriculturist. Males.	Actual Workers. Partially Agriculturist. Females.	Dependents.
	1	694	695	696	697	698	699	700	701	702	703	704	705
	Provincial Total	10,753	3,728	2,224	120	214	4,791	10,961	3,883	1,488	106	191	5,590
	Burma Proper	9,002	3,057	1,675	90	58	4,270	9,915	3,615	1,272	97	44	5,028
	Arakan Division	248	96	51	...	...	101	49	28	1	...	...	20
1	Akyab	186	61	51	...	...	74	43	24	...	...	...	19
2	Northern Arakan	...	...	...	...	...	...	...	...	...	...	...	...
3	Kyaukpyu	11	6	...	...	...	5	6	4	1	...	...	1
4	Sandoway	51	29	...	...	...	22	...	...	...	...	...	...
	Pegu Division	3,405	1,268	447	12	2	1,690	2,010	769	235	7	...	1,006
5	City of Rangoon	704	309	87	...	...	308	1,270	502	178	...	...	590
6	Hanthawaddy	793	263	96	1	...	434	255	112	10	7	...	133
7	Tharrawaddy	72	21	22	...	...	29	45	16	12	...	...	17
8	Pegu	1,487	655	149	11	2	683	136	49	9	...	...	78
9	Prome	349	20	93	...	...	236	304	90	26	...	...	188
	Irrawaddy Division	1,103	400	169	3	1	534	272	143	20	3	...	109
10	Bassein	41	15	13	...	...	13	58	30	7	...	...	21
11	Henzada	124	30	52	3	1	42	34	12	3	...	...	19
12	Myaungmya	344	120	72	...	...	152	30	10	6	...	...	14
13	Ma-ubin	103	29	17	...	...	57	56	33	...	3	...	23
14	Pyapôn	491	206	15	...	...	270	94	58	4	...	...	32
	Tenasserim Division	748	207	137	8	1	404	549	205	62	2	...	280
15	Toungoo	140	4	63	...	1	73	96	21	24	...	...	51
16	Salween	...	...	...	...	...	...	...	...	...	...	...	...
17	Thatôn	217	122	6	8	...	89	136	59	12	...	...	65
18	Amherst	301	48	66	...	...	187	292	109	26	2	...	157
19	Tavoy	86	33	...	...	...	53	18	16	...	...	...	2
20	Mergui	4	...	2	...	...	2	7	...	...	...	...	7
	Magwe Division	212	31	63	...	...	118	293	104	43	...	...	146
21	Thayetmyo	105	3	34	...	...	68	86	52	...	...	...	34
22	Pakôkku	28	6	8	...	...	14	23	5	2	...	...	16
23	Minbu	39	8	11	...	...	20	128	28	30	...	...	70
24	Magwe	40	14	10	...	...	16	56	19	11	...	...	26
	Mandalay Division	1,791	647	383	21	12	761	5,768	2,055	770	68	...	2,943
25	Mandalay (including City).	1,307	487	274	4	12	636	2,696	878	570	...	...	1,248
	Mandalay City	*853*	*180*	*239*	...	...	*434*	*2,685*	*871*	*570*	...	...	*1,244*
26	Bhamo	141	56	44	14	...	41	181	106	31	10	...	44
27	Myitkyina	83	...	29	...	...	54	779	549	25	58	...	205
28	Katha	26	16	2	1	...	8	32	11	...	...	...	21
29	Ruby Mines	144	88	34	2	...	22	2,080	511	144	...	...	1,425
	Sagaing Division	901	247	291	16	42	363	682	250	97	15	19	335
30	Shwebo	552	189	133	13	...	230	333	87	62	...	...	184
31	Sagaing	150	...	110	...	32	40	35	6	4	...	...	25
32	Lower Chindwin	123	19	43	5	10	61	298	150	30	14	19	118
33	Upper Chindwin	76	39	5	...	...	32	16	7	1	1	...	8
	Meiktila Division	594	161	134	30	...	299	292	61	44	2	25	187
34	Kyauksè	353	134	38	30	...	183	22	7	1	...	...	14
35	Meiktila	13	4	...	...	...	9	184	29	33	2	25	122
36	Yamèthin	64	23	8	...	...	33	5	...	...	...	...	5
37	Myingyan	162	...	88	...	...	74	81	25	10	...	...	46
	Specially Administered Territories.	1,751	681	549	30	156	521	1,046	268	216	9	147	562
38	Northern Shan States	1,084	584	170	17	35	330	53	16	13	...	...	24
39	Southern Shan States	667	97	379	13	121	191	993	252	203	9	147	538
40	Chin Hills	...	...	...	...	...	...	...	...	...	...	...	...

GROUP 131, DEALERS IN PRECIOUS STONES, JEWELLERY, CLOCKS, OPTICAL INSTRUMENTS, ETC.						GROUP 132, DEALERS IN COMMON BANGLES, BEAD NECKLACES, FANS, TOYS, FLOWERS, HUNTING AND FISHING TACKLE.						GROUP 133, PUBLISHERS, BOOKSELLERS, STATIONERS, DEALERS IN MUSIC, PICTURES, MUSICAL INSTRUMENTS, AND CURIOS.						
Total Workers and Dependents.	Actual Workers. Total. Males.	Actual Workers. Total. Females.	Partially Agriculturist. Males.	Partially Agriculturist. Females.	Dependents.	Total Workers and Dependents.	Actual Workers. Total. Males.	Actual Workers. Total. Females.	Partially Agriculturist. Males.	Partially Agriculturist. Females.	Dependents.	Total Workers and dependents.	Actual Workers. Total. Males.	Actual Workers. Total. Females.	Partially Agriculturist. Males.	Partially Agriculturist. Females.	Dependents.	Serial No.
706	707	708	709	710	711	712	713	714	715	716	717	718	719	720	721	722	723	
8,591	2,154	1,001	94	25	4,436	1,150	236	246	7	72	668	1,220	493	241	5	94	486	
8,298	2,962	996	90	25	4,340	775	236	176	7	19	263	842	417	200	...	...	225	
40	22	...	...	...	18	7	4	1	...	...	2	2	2	...	...	...	...	
40	22	...	...	...	18	3	2	...	...	...	1	...	...	...	...	...	...	1
...	...	...	...	...	...	...	...	...	...	...	...	...	...	...	...	...	...	2
...	...	...	...	...	...	4	2	1	...	...	1	2	2	...	...	...	...	3
...	...	...	...	...	...	...	...	...	...	...	...	...	...	...	...	...	...	4
2,157	452	76	...	...	609	522	139	139	7	...	244	331	178	20	...	...	133	
642	281	38	...	...	323	366	74	127	...	...	165	262	147	13	...	...	102	5
116	45	8	...	...	63	123	59	2	7	...	62	16	8	...	...	...	8	6
24	10	3	...	...	11	4	...	4	...	...	...	17	6	5	...	...	6	7
128	44	9	...	...	75	6	3	...	...	...	3	2	2	...	...	...	...	8
247	72	18	...	...	157	23	3	6	...	...	14	34	15	2	...	...	17	9
206	106	15	2	...	85	41	21	4	...	...	16	25	16	1	...	...	8	
47	24	3	...	...	20	5	...	4	...	...	1	6	6	...	...	...	...	10
24	4	3	...	...	17	...	...	...	...	...	...	10	8	...	...	...	2	11
30	10	6	...	...	14	...	...	...	...	...	...	...	...	...	...	...	...	12
20	12	...	3	...	8	36	21	...	...	...	15	...	...	...	...	...	...	13
85	56	3	...	...	26	...	...	...	...	...	...	9	2	1	...	...	6	14
518	194	62	2	...	262	2	2	...	...	...	...	29	9	...	...	...	20	
90	18	24	...	...	48	...	...	...	...	...	...	6	3	...	...	...	3	15
...	...	...	...	...	...	...	...	...	...	...	...	...	...	...	...	...	...	16
121	52	12	...	...	57	2	2	...	...	...	...	13	5	...	...	...	8	17
289	108	26	2	...	155	...	...	...	...	...	...	3	1	...	...	...	2	18
18	16	...	...	...	2	...	...	...	...	...	...	...	...	...	...	...	...	19
...	...	...	...	...	...	...	...	...	...	...	...	7	...	...	...	...	7	20
246	88	36	...	...	122	15	10	1	...	...	4	32	6	6	...	...	20	
86	52	...	...	...	34	...	...	...	...	...	...	...	...	...	...	...	...	21
11	2	...	...	...	9	2	...	...	...	...	2	10	3	2	...	...	3	22
100	16	28	...	...	56	13	10	1	...	...	2	15	2	1	...	...	12	23
49	18	8	...	...	23	...	...	...	...	...	...	7	1	3	...	...	3	24
5,220	1,792	695	68	...	2,733	144	60	8	...	...	76	404	203	67	...	...	124	
2,257	696	510	...	...	1,051	144	60	8	...	...	76	295	122	52	...	...	121	25
2,257	*696*	*510*	...	...	*1,051*	*137*	*53*	*8*	...	...	*76*	*291*	*122*	*52*	...	...	*117*	
73	25	16	10	...	32	...	...	...	...	...	...	108	81	15	...	...	12	26
778	549	85	58	...	204	...	...	...	...	...	...	1	...	...	...	...	1	27
82	11	...	...	...	21	...	...	...	...	...	...	...	...	...	...	...	...	28
2,080	511	144	...	...	1,425	...	...	...	...	...	...	...	...	...	...	...	...	29
620	247	68	15	...	305	44	...	23	...	19	21	18	3	6	...	...	9	
300	86	56	...	...	158	18	...	...	...	...	18	15	1	6	...	...	8	30
35	6	4	...	...	25	...	...	...	...	...	...	...	...	...	...	...	...	31
269	148	7	14	...	114	26	...	23	...	...	3	3	2	...	...	...	1	32
16	7	1	1	...	8	...	...	...	...	...	...	...	...	...	...	...	...	33
291	61	44	2	25	186	...	...	...	...	...	...	2	...	...	...	...	2	
22	7	1	...	...	14	...	...	...	...	...	...	...	...	...	...	...	...	34
184	29	33	2	25	122	...	...	...	...	...	...	...	...	...	...	...	...	35
4	...	...	...	...	4	...	...	...	...	...	...	1	...	...	...	...	2	36
81	25	10	...	...	46	...	...	...	...	...	...	...	...	...	...	...	...	37
293	192	5	4	...	96	375	...	70	...	53	305	378	76	141	5	94	161	
...	...	...	...	...	...	...	...	...	...	...	...	53	16	13	...	...	24	38
293	192	5	4	...	96	375	...	70	...	53	305	325	60	128	5	94	137	39
...	...	...	...	...	...	...	...	...	...	...	...	...	...	...	...	...	...	40

Serial No.	DISTRICT OR STATE.	ORDER XL, (GROUP 134). TRADE IN REFUSE MATTER. Total Workers and Dependents.	ACTUAL WORKERS. Total. Males.	Total. Females.	Partially Agriculturist. Males.	Partially Agriculturist. Females.	Dependents.	ORDER XLI, TRADE OF OTHER SORTS. Total Workers and Dependents.	ACTUAL WORKERS. Total. Males.	Total. Females.	Partially Agriculturist. Males.	Partially Agriculturist. Females.	Dependents.
	1	724	725	726	727	728	729	730	731	732	733	734	735
	Provincial Total ...	94	27	6	...	...	61	455,569	122,916	149,466	4,766	5,729	83,187
	Burma Proper ...	90	27	6	...	...	57	417,432	107,441	138,298	3,430	4,753	171,693
	Arakan Division ...	...	...	...	...	...	...	22,529	7,033	6,999	68	74	8,497
1	Akyab ...	...	...	...	...	...	...	14,292	5,068	4,127	35	47	5,097
2	Northern Arakan ...	...	...	...	...	...	...	189	115	15	..	...	59
3	Kyaukpyu ...	...	...	...	...	...	...	5,604	1,362	1,791	33	27	2,451
4	Sandoway ...	...	...	...	...	...	..	2,444	488	1,066	...	...	890
	Pegu Division ...	81	27	6	...	...	48	97,857	26,509	30,518	354	426	40,830
5	City of Rangoon ...	38	21	6	...	...	11	11,151	4,705	1,372	22	2	5,073
6	Hanthawaddy ...	43	6	...	...	...	37	27,192	7,955	7,153	38	106	12,084
7	Tharrawaddy ...	...	...	...	...	...	...	17,983	4,427	6,648	202	187	6,908
8	Pegu ...	...	...	...	...	...	...	21,098	5,263	7,182	48	95	9,656
9	Prome ...	...	...	...	...	...	...	19,433	4,161	8,163	44	26	7,109
	Irrawaddy Division ...	3	...	...	...	...	3	107,109	28,625	35,256	788	1,807	43,228
10	Bassein ...	...	...	...	...	...	...	26,257	6,233	9,701	155	97	10,323
11	Henzada ...	...	...	...	...	...	...	24,899	5,297	9,991	109	644	9,611
12	Myaungmya ...	3	...	...	...	...	3	22,978	6,701	6,973	247	266	9,304
13	Ma-ubin ...	...	...	...	...	...	...	19,137	5,841	5,340	179	500	7,956
14	Pyapôn ...	...	...	...	...	...	...	13,838	4,553	3,251	98	...	6,034
	Tenasserim Division ...	1	...	...	...	..	1	59,273	13,313	19,656	181	188	26,304
15	Toungoo ...	...	...	...	...	...	...	16,194	3,613	5,301	61	71	7,280
16	Salween ...	...	...	...	...	...	...	1,156	403	210	...	...	543
17	Thatôn ...	1	...	...	...	...	1	19,203	4,604	6,567	27	22	8,032
18	Amherst ...	...	...	...	...	...	...	12,209	2,814	3,568	78	32	5,827
19	Tavoy ...	...	...	...	...	...	...	5,269	775	2,347	13	63	2,147
20	Mergui ...	...	...	...	...	...	...	5,242	1,104	1,663	8	...	2,475
	Magwe Division ...	...	...	...	...	...	...	46,794	10,111	16,912	144	204	19,771
21	Thayetmyo ...	...	...	...	...	...	...	9,269	1,688	3,647	7	15	3,934
22	Pakôkku ...	...	...	...	...	...	...	19,251	3,885	6,031	38	34	8,735
23	Minbu ...	..	...	...	...	...	...	9,659	2,280	4,117	40	117	3,256
24	Magwe ...	...	...	...	...	...	...	8,615	2,252	2,517	59	38	3,846
	Mandalay Division ...	5	...	...	...	...	5	30,631	8,149	9,396	638	272	13,086
25	Mandalay (including City).	5	...	...	...	...	5	15,389	3,397	5,724	160	121	6,268
	Mandalay City ...	5	...	...	...	...	5	10,364	2,704	3,099	...	...	4,561
26	Bhamo ...	...	...	..	...	...	...	3,065	672	653	50	11	1,740
27	Myitkyina ...	...	...	...	...	...	...	1,941	840	347	225	13	754
28	Katha ...	...	...	...	...	...	...	5,074	1,436	1,529	115	71	2,109
29	Ruby Mines ...	...	...	...	...	...	...	5,162	1,804	1,143	85	57	2,215
	Sagaing Division ...	...	...	...	...	...	...	25,118	7,861	8,034	700	983	9,223
30	Shwebo ...	...	...	...	...	...	...	9,677	1,825	2,719	45	298	5,133
31	Sagaing ...	...	...	...	...	...	...	4,154	2,569	1,027	107	263	558
32	Lower Chindwin ...	...	...	...	...	...	...	6,650	1,429	3,147	120	380	2,074
33	Upper Chindwin ...	...	...	...	...	...	...	4,687	2,038	1,141	428	42	1,458
	Meiktila Division ...	...	...	...	...	...	...	28,121	5,840	11,507	557	1,208	10,754
34	Kyauksè ...	...	...	...	...	...	...	4,258	821	1,950	100	282	1,487
35	Meiktila ...	...	...	...	...	...	...	9,146	1,806	3,969	292	685	3,371
36	Yamèthin ...	...	...	...	...	...	...	7,526	1,313	2,783	68	72	3,430
37	Myingyan ...	...	...	...	...	...	...	7,191	1,900	2,825	97	69	2,466
	Specially Administered Territories.	4	..	...	...	...	4	38,137	15,475	11,168	1,336	976	11,494
38	Northern Shan States	...	...	...	...	...	...	7,195	2,650	2,009	174	243	2,536
39	Southern Shan States	4	...	...	...	...	4	30,716	12,656	9,155	1,162	733	8,905
40	Chin Hills ...	...	...	...	...	...	...	226	163	4	...	...	83

Occupations. Details by Districts.

GROUP 135, SHOPKEEPERS OTHERWISE UNSPECIFIED.						GROUP 137, CONJURORS, ACROBATS, FORTUNE-TELLERS, RECITERS, EXHIBITORS OF ANIMALS AND CURIOSITIES.						ORDER XLII—(GROUP 139), ARMY.						
Total Workers and Dependents.	ACTUAL WORKERS.				Dependents.	Total Workers and Dependents.	ACTUAL WORKERS.				Dependents.	Total Workers and Dependents.	ACTUAL WORKERS.				Dependents.	
	TOTAL.		PARTIALLY AGRICULTURIST.				TOTAL.		PARTIALLY AGRICULTURIST.				TOTAL.		PARTIALLY AGRICULTURIST.			
	Males.	Females.	Males.	Females.			Males.	Females.	Males.	Females.			Males.	Females.	Males.	Females.		Serial No.
736	737	738	739	740	741	742	743	744	745	746	747	748	749	750	751	752	753	
450,939	121,031	149,010	4,737	5,703	180,898	3,816	1,447	422	16	26	1,947	24,984	18,717	68	1,954	...	6,199	
423,093	105,693	137,850	3,420	4,727	169,550	3,553	1,336	414	9	26	1,803	22,247	17,162	49	1,460	...	5,036	
22,322	7,008	6,950	68	69	8,364	206	24	49	...	5	133	337	192	1	...	...	144	
14,181	5,052	4,123	35	47	5,006	110	15	4	...	...	91	16	11	1	...	...	4	1
189	115	15	...	...	59	...	...	...	...	...	...	299	162	...	...	...	137	2
5,518	1,357	1,749	33	22	2,412	86	5	42	...	5	39	6	4	...	...	...	2	3
2,434	484	1,063	...	...	887	10	4	3	...	...	3	16	15	...	...	...	1	4
96,751	25,973	30,461	354	416	40,317	562	239	37	...	...	286	5,019	4,216	6	185	...	797	
10,410	4,335	1,348	22	2	4,727	242	97	4	...	..	141	4,245	3,522	3	185	...	720	5
27,123	7,934	7,146	38	106	12,043	57	16	7	...	...	34	423	376	...	...	...	47	6
17,924	4,393	6,643	202	187	6,888	53	31	5	...	...	17	129	107	3	...	...	19	7
21,950	5,180	7,175	48	95	9,595	121	65	7	...	...	49	203	192	...	...	...	11	8
19,344	4,131	8,149	44	26	7,064	89	30	14	...	...	45	19	19	...	...	...	...	9
106,756	28,445	35,243	785	1,507	43,068	330	173	9	3	...	148	467	401	...	..	...	66	
26,197	6,203	9,701	154	97	10,293	58	30	...	1	...	28	117	109	...	...	...	8	10
24,793	5,263	9,982	107	644	9,542	98	27	9	2	...	62	53	51	...	...	...	2	11
22,915	6,681	6,969	247	266	9,265	50	14	...	...	...	36	109	94	..	...	...	15	12
19,050	5,765	5,340	179	500	7,945	87	76	...	...	...	11	36	4	...	...	...	32	13
13,801	4,527	3,251	98	...	6,025	37	26	...	...	...	11	152	143	...	...	...	9	14
58,720	13,093	19,629	177	187	26,008	499	213	18	4	1	268	669	507	5	...	...	157	
16,034	3,570	5,287	58	70	7,177	130	40	5	3	1	85	270	200	2	...	...	68	15
1,156	403	210	...	...	543	...	...	...	...	...	...	3	...	...	...	...	3	16
19,029	4,503	6,557	26	22	7,069	163	98	10	1	...	55	227	164	...	...	...	65	17
12,037	2,746	3,568	78	32	5,723	169	67	...	...	...	102	103	93	...	...	...	10	18
5,254	768	2,347	13	63	2,139	15	7	...	...	...	8	14	...	3	...	...	11	19
5,220	1,103	1,660	2	...	2,457	22	1	3	...	...	18	52	50	...	...	..	2	20
46,375	9,949	16,889	143	204	19,537	357	151	22	...	...	184	753	547	8	...	...	198	
9,228	1,677	3,646	7	15	3,905	28	10	1	...	...	17	289	226	6	...	...	57	21
19,046	3,791	6,625	38	34	8,630	203	93	6	...	...	104	203	144	...	...	...	59	22
9,568	2,247	4,112	40	117	3,209	70	34	5	...	...	31	84	66	...	...	...	18	23
8,533	2,234	2,506	58	38	3,793	56	14	10	...	...	32	177	111	2	...	...	64	24
29,837	7,827	9,350	638	272	12,660	779	314	46	...	1	419	11,278	8,461	21	1,262	...	2,796	
14,642	3,086	5,685	160	121	5,871	735	303	39	...	...	393	5,258	3,950	8	658	...	1,300	25
9,847	*2,481*	*3,065*	...	...	*4,301*	*508*	*215*	*34*	...		*259*	*3,073*	*2,216*	*8*	...	...	*849*	
3,033	665	646	50	10	1,722	32	7	7	...	1	18	1,610	1,189	10	390	...	411	26
1,937	840	347	228	13	750	4	...	..	...	...	4	3,758	2,816	1	214	...	941	27
5,066	1,432	1,529	115	71	2,105	8	4	...	...	...	4	310	274	2	...	...	34	28
5,159	1,804	1,143	85	57	2,212	...	...	...	...	...	...	342	232	...	...	...	110	29
24,455	7,704	7,813	698	964	8,938	656	155	221	2	19	280	3,095	2,429	...	13	...	676	
9,460	1,779	2,669	45	298	5,012	217	46	50	...	...	121	1,155	998	...	...	...	157	30
4,061	2,529	1,023	107	263	509	93	40	4	...	...	49	473	429	...	...	...	44	31
6,359	1,397	2,980	120	361	1,982	284	30	167	...	19	87	821	510	...	13	...	312	32
4,575	1,999	1,141	426	42	1,435	62	39	...	2	...	23	645	482	...	...	...	163	33
27,867	5,694	11,515	557	1,108	10,658	164	67	12	...	...	85	629	419	8	...	...	202	
4,239	815	1,945	100	282	1,479	17	6	5	...	...	6	31	16	3	...	...	12	34
9,095	1,783	3,969	292	685	3,343	51	23	...	...	...	28	526	338	1	...	...	137	35
7,453	1,274	2,783	68	72	3,306	71	38	...	...	...	33	71	15	4	...	...	52	36
7,080	1,822	2,818	97	63	2,440	25	...	7	...	...	18	1	...	...	...	.	1	37
37,846	15,338	11,160	1,317	976	11,248	263	111	8	7	...	144	2,727	1,555	19	494	...	1,163	
7,163	2,649	2,001	174	243	2,512	32	1	7	...	...	24	893	733	...	470	...	160	38
30,457	12,520	9,154	1,143	733	8,783	231	110	1	7	...	120	1,269	501	..	24	...	769	39
226	169	4	...	...	53	...	...	...	...	...	...	575	322	19	...	..	234	40

Serial No.	DISTRICT OR STATE.	ORDER XLIII—(GROUP 141), NAVY. Total Workers and Dependents.	Actual Workers. Total. Males.	Actual Workers. Total. Females.	Actual Workers. Partially Agriculturist. Males.	Actual Workers. Partially Agriculturist. Females.	Dependents.	ORDER XLIV—POLICE AND VILLAGE WATCHMEN. Total Workers and Dependents.	Actual Workers. Total. Males.	Actual Workers. Total. Females.	Actual Workers. Partially Agriculturist. Males.	Actual Workers. Partially Agriculturist. Females.	Dependents.
	1	754	755	756	757	758	759	760	761	762	763	764	765
	Provincial Total ...	28	11	...	...	...	17	54,483	21,460	1,649	615	188	31,374
	Burma Proper ...	27	11	...	...	...	16	50,545	19,706	1,612	505	175	29,227
	Arakan Division ...	...	...	...	...	...	...	4,123	1,387	553	...	17	2,183
1	Akyab ...	...	...	...	...	...	...	1,948	689	361	...	1	898
2	Northern Arakan ...	...	...	...	...	...	...	254	88	...	...	...	166
3	Kyaukpyu ...	...	...	...	...	...	...	1,089	366	192	...	16	531
4	Sandoway ...	...	...	...	...	...	...	832	244	...	...	...	588
	Pegu Division ...	27	11	...	...	...	16	10,329	4,530	83	4	...	5,716
5	City of Rangoon ...	27	11	...	...	...	16	2,257	1,169	2	3	...	1,086
6	Hanthawaddy ...	...	...	...	...	...	...	1,765	546	9	...	...	1,210
7	Tharrawaddy ...	...	...	...	...	...	...	2,139	806	40	...	...	1,293
8	Pegu ...	...	...	...	...	...	...	1,879	848	2	...	...	1,029
9	Prome ...	...	...	...	...	...	...	2,289	1,161	30	1	..	1,098
	Irrawaddy Division ...	...	...	...	...	...	...	5,538	2,175	56	1	7	3,307
10	Bassein ...	...	...	...	...	...	...	1,196	437	12	...	...	747
11	Henzada ...	...	...	...	...	...	...	1,741	759	37	1	7	945
12	Myaungmya ...	...	...	...	...	...	...	824	333	2	...	...	489
13	Ma-ubin ...	...	...	...	...	...	...	1,020	260	...	...	...	760
14	Pyapôn ...	...	...	...	...	...	...	757	386	5	...	...	366
	Tenasserim Division ...	...	...	...	...	...	...	5,740	2,285	21	6	...	3,434
15	Toungoo ...	...	...	...	...	...	...	1,122	325	5	1	...	792
16	Salween ...	...	...	...	...	...	...	308	191	...	...	...	117
17	Thatôn ...	...	...	...	...	...	...	1,229	451	...	1	...	778
18	Amherst ...	...	...	...	...	...	...	1,722	621	16	3	...	1,085
19	Tavoy ...	...	...	...	...	...	...	595	324	...	...	...	271
20	Mergui ...	...	...	...	...	...	...	764	373	...	1	...	391
	Magwe Division ...	...	...	...	...	...	...	6,030	1,905	113	19	...	4,012
21	Thayetmyo ...	...	...	...	...	...	...	1,448	420	...	...	...	1,028
22	Pakokku ...	...	...	...	...	...	...	1,978	581	...	...	...	1,397
23	Minbu ...	...	...	...	...	...	...	1,237	400	101	18	...	736
24	Magwe ...	...	...	...	...	...	...	1,367	504	12	1	...	851
	Mandalay Division ...	...	...	...	...	...	...	8,321	4,087	80	439	15	4,154
25	Mandalay (including City).	...	...	...	...	...	...	4,991	2,638	14	393	...	2,339
	Mandalay City ...	...	...	...	...	...	...	*2,077*	*1,046*	*1*	...	...	*1,030*
26	Bhamo ...	...	...	...	...	...	...	520	245	5	2	...	270
27	Myitkyina ..	...	...	...	...	...	...	767	321	...	27	...	446
28	Katha ...	...	...	...	...	...	...	869	300	...	1	...	569
29	Ruby Mines ...	...	...	...	...	...	...	1,174	583	61	16	15	530
	Sagaing Division ...	...	...	...	...	...	...	4,807	1,434	404	8	97	2,969
30	Shwebo ...	...	...	...	...	...	...	1,910	565	152	...	...	1,193
31	Sagaing ...	...	...	...	...	...	...	716	183	59	...	26	474
32	Lower Chindwin ...	...	...	...	...	...	...	1,292	346	143	6	71	803
33	Upper Chindwin ...	...	...	...	...	...	...	889	340	50	2	...	499
	Meiktila Division ...	...	...	...	...	...	...	5,657	1,903	302	28	39	3,452
34	Kyaukse ...	...	...	...	...	...	...	692	245	44	7	...	403
35	Meiktila ...	...	...	...	...	...	...	1,664	588	180	...	34	896
36	Yamèthin ...	...	...	...	...	...	...	1,562	426	78	6	5	1,058
37	Myingyan ...	...	...	...	...	...	...	1,709	644	...	15	...	1,065
	Specially Administered Territories.	1	...	...	...	...	1	3,938	1,754	37	120	13	2,147
38	Northern Shan States	...	...	...	...	...	...	1,520	678	11	17	2	831
39	Southern Shan States	1	...	...	...	...	1	2,043	856	26	93	11	1,161
40	Chin Hills ...	...	...	...	...	...	...	375	220	...	...	...	155

Occupations. Details by Districts.

GROUP 142—POLICE.						ORDER XLV—PUBLIC ADMINISTRATION.						GROUP 144—SERVICE OF THE STATE.						
Total Workers and Dependents.	Actual Workers. Total. Males.	Actual Workers. Total. Females.	Actual Workers. Partially Agriculturist. Males.	Actual Workers. Partially Agriculturist. Females.	Dependents.	Total Workers and Dependents.	Actual Workers. Total. Males.	Actual Workers. Total. Females.	Actual Workers. Partially Agriculturist. Males.	Actual Workers. Partially Agriculturist. Females.	Dependents.	Total Workers and Dependents.	Actual Workers. Total. Males.	Actual Workers. Total. Females.	Actual Workers. Partially Agriculturist. Males.	Actual Workers. Partially Agriculturist. Females.	Dependents.	Serial No.
766	767	768	769	770	771	772	773	774	775	776	777	778	779	780	781	782	783	
54,266	21,390	1,647	596	188	31,229	103,108	36,238	4,394	4,944	549	62,476	34,294	13,021	898	786	150	20,375	
50,442	19,679	1,612	499	175	29,151	89,275	30,255	3,290	3,430	504	55,730	31,835	11,697	863	204	149	19,275	
4,121	1,386	553	...	17	2,180	4,920	1,776	472	102	20	2,672	1,909	796	118	36	12	995	
1,948	689	361	...	1	898	2,870	1,170	225	58	...	1,475	1,255	602	86	30	...	567	1
254	88	...	...	...	166	11	5	...	...	...	6	11	5	...	...	...	6	2
1,089	366	192	...	16	531	1,040	245	222	44	20	573	290	43	32	6	12	215	3
830	243	...	...	...	587	999	356	25	...	...	618	353	146	...	...	...	207	4
10,316	4,529	83	4	...	5,704	24,694	9,318	225	615	11	15,041	12,755	4,886	52	12	...	7,817	
2,245	1,169	2	3	...	1,074	12,014	5,638	77	10	...	6,299	8,833	3,606	42	4	...	5,185	5
1,765	546	9	...	...	1,210	4,507	1,321	13	229	1	3,173	1,395	468	3	2	...	924	6
2,139	805	40	...	...	1,293	2,301	766	42	108	2	1,493	550	181	2	...	...	367	7
1,878	847	2	...	...	1,029	3,440	956	132	167	1	2,352	1,110	444	...	5	...	666	8
2,289	1,161	30	1	...	1,098	2,432	637	71	101	7	1,724	867	187	5	1	...	675	9
5,538	2,175	56	1	7	2,307	10,387	2,480	320	241	54	6,587	2,830	1,226	26	...	...	1,468	
1,196	437	12	...	...	747	2,156	732	31	55	6	1,393	508	104	1	...	...	313	10
1,741	759	37	1	7	945	2,868	857	126	154	27	1,885	806	247	9	...	...	550	11
824	333	2	...	...	489	2,470	673	79	17	20	1,718	621	290	3	...	...	328	12
1,020	260	...	...	...	760	1,493	735	13	15	1	745	550	392	7	...	...	151	13
757	386	5	...	...	366	1,400	483	71	...	...	846	345	213	6	...	...	126	14
5,680	2,272	21	6	...	2,387	11,005	2,249	213	334	6	7,543	5,070	1,641	136	11	...	3,293	
1,122	325	5	1	...	792	2,594	769	45	165	2	1,780	704	266	3	6	...	435	15
308	191	...	...	...	117	114	41	1	...	...	72	33	10	..	...	...	23	16
1,169	438	...	1	...	731	2,625	642	31	85	...	1,952	1,069	229	22	1	...	818	17
1,782	681	16	3	...	1,085	3,990	1,293	129	51	4	2,568	2,531	915	106	...	...	1,510	18
595	324	...	...	...	271	838	294	5	12	...	539	320	117	5	...	...	198	19
764	373	...	1	...	391	844	210	2	21	...	632	413	104	...	4	...	309	20
6,030	1,905	123	19	...	4,022	10,988	3,277	86	430	...	7,625	2,992	901	15	27	...	2,077	
1,448	420	...	...	...	1,028	2,722	803	11	89	...	1,908	871	330	...	...	...	541	21
1,978	581	...	...	...	1,397	3,388	923	16	91	...	2,449	385	80	1	1	...	304	22
1,237	400	101	18	...	736	2,377	665	6	70	...	1,706	1,041	304	...	25	...	737	23
1,367	504	22	1	...	851	2,501	886	53	180	...	1,562	696	187	14	1	...	495	24
8,321	4,084	80	437	15	4,147	9,447	3,780	474	578	91	5,193	3,281	1,241	129	86	...	1,911	
4,981	2,635	14	391	...	2,332	4,636	2,008	212	117	4	2,422	2,457	885	111	7	...	1,461	25
2,077	*1,046*	*1*	...	...	*1,030*	*2,337*	*1,163*	*72*	...	...	*1,102*	*1,357*	*497*	*67*	..	...	*793*	
520	245	5	2	...	270	963	434	16	68	...	513	242	64	7	1	...	171	26
767	321	...	27	...	446	861	341	8	58	...	512	243	118	8	27	...	117	27
869	300	...	1	...	569	1,733	582	44	129	13	1,107	180	71	3	1	...	106	28
1,174	583	61	16	15	530	1,254	481	194	206	74	639	159	103	...	50	...	56	29
4,789	1,425	404	4	97	2,960	7,707	2,292	548	454	175	4,868	1,711	546	286	18	130	879	
1,910	565	152	...	...	1,193	1,997	597	53	64	...	1,347	456	142	5	...	...	309	30
716	183	59	...	26	474	1,525	552	122	62	12	851	182	96	...	...	...	86	31
1,277	837	143	2	71	797	2,088	617	359	142	163	1,112	712	193	277	15	130	242	32
886	340	50	2	...	496	2,097	585	14	186	...	1,558	361	115	4	3	...	242	33
5,657	1,903	302	28	29	3,452	10,227	3,084	940	676	147	6,201	1,286	350	202	14	7	825	
692	245	44	7	...	403	1,815	898	119	224	29	798	249	82	29	1	2	138	34
1,064	588	180	...	34	296	2,690	604	537	74	51	1,549	283	123	...	...	...	160	35
1,592	426	78	6	5	1,088	2,924	803	285	120	67	1,836	473	76	71	2	3	326	36
1,709	644	...	15	...	1,065	2,798	779	1	258	...	2,018	281	69	1	11	...	211	37
3,804	1,711	25	97	13	2,078	13,733	5,983	1,004	1,514	45	6,746	2,459	1,324	35	580	1	1,100	
1,516	678	11	17	2	827	3,055	838	406	85	1	1,811	205	81	3	...	...	121	38
1,933	813	24	80	11	1,096	10,224	5,000	596	1,350	44	4,628	2,216	1,222	32	582	1	962	39
375	220	...	...	...	155	454	145	2	79	...	307	38	21	...	...	...	17	40

Serial No.	DISTRICT OR STATE.	GROUP 145, SERVICE OF FOREIGN AND NATIVE STATES. Total Workers and Dependents.	Actual Workers. Total. Males.	Actual Workers. Total. Females.	Actual Workers. Partially Agriculturist. Males.	Actual Workers. Partially Agriculturist. Females.	Dependents.	GROUP 146, MUNICIPAL AND LOCAL SERVICE OTHER THAN VILLAGE OFFICIALS. Total Workers and Dependents.	Actual Workers. Total. Males.	Actual Workers. Total. Females.	Actual Workers. Partially Agriculturist. Males.	Actual Workers. Partially Agriculturist. Females.	Dependents.
	1	784	785	786	787	788	789	790	791	792	793	794	795
	Provincial Total ...	2,976	1,324	360	114	...	1,292	4,174	2,445	60	50	1	1,669
	Burma Proper ...	69	19	2	...	...	48	4,086	2,397	54	50	...	1,625
	Arakan Division ...	7	6	...	...	...	1	22	6	...	...	...	16
1	Akyab ...	7	6	...	...	...	1	2	...	...	...	...	2
2	Northern Arakan ...	...	...	...	...	...	...	...	...	...	...	...	...
3	Kyaukpyu ...	...	...	...	...	...	...	8	3	...	...	...	5
4	Sandoway ...	...	...	...	...	...	...	12	3	...	...	...	9
	Pegu Division ...	7	4	...	...	...	3	3,543	2,211	36	50	...	1,296
5	City of Rangoon ...	6	3	...	...	...	3	3,126	2,012	35	6	...	1,079
6	Hanthawaddy ...	1	1	...	...	...	...	250	116	...	44	...	134
7	Tharrawaddy ...	...	...	...	...	...	...	81	62	...	...	...	19
8	Pegu ...	...	...	...	...	...	...	52	14	1	...	...	37
9	Prome ...	...	...	...	...	...	...	34	7	...	...	...	27
	Irrawaddy Division ...	2	...	...	...	...	2	89	20	17	...	...	52
10	Bassein ...	2	...	...	...	...	2	21	9	...	...	...	12
11	Henzada ...	...	...	...	...	...	...	34	10	...	...	...	24
12	Myaungmya ...	...	...	...	...	...	...	18	1	13	...	...	4
13	Ma-ubin ...	...	...	...	...	...	...	...	...	...	...	...	...
14	Pyapôn ...	...	...	...	...	...	...	16	...	4	...	...	12
	Tenasserim Division	1	1	...	...	...	...	220	88	...	...	...	132
15	Toungoo ...	...	...	...	...	...	...	12	6	...	...	...	6
16	Salween ...	1	1	...	...	...	...	...	...	...	...	...	...
17	Thatôn ...	...	...	...	...	...	...	34	8	...	...	...	26
18	Amherst ...	...	...	...	...	...	...	172	73	...	...	...	99
19	Tavoy ...	...	...	...	...	...	...	...	...	...	...	...	...
20	Mergui ...	...	...	...	...	...	...	2	1	...	...	...	1
	Magwe Division ...	6	1	...	...	...	5	105	28	...	...	...	77
21	Thayetmyo ...	...	...	...	...	...	...	36	6	...	...	...	30
22	Pakôkku ...	1	...	...	...	...	1	14	3	...	...	...	11
23	Minbu ...	5	1	...	...	...	4	28	8	...	...	...	20
24	Magwe ...	...	...	...	...	...	...	27	11	...	...	...	16
	Mandalay Division ...	2	...	...	...	...	2	83	39	1	...	...	43
25	Mandalay (including City).	...	...	...	...	...	...	82	38	1	...	...	43
	Mandalay City ...	...	...	...	...	...	...	78	37	1	...	...	40
26	Bhamo ...	...	...	...	...	...	...	1	1	...	...	...	...
27	Myitkyina ...	2	...	...	...	...	2	...	...	...	...	...	...
28	Katha ...	...	...	...	...	...	...	...	...	...	...	...	...
29	Ruby Mines ...	...	...	...	...	...	...	...	...	...	...	...	...
	Sagaing Division ...	35	...	2	...	...	33	19	2	...	...	...	17
30	Shwebo ...	...	...	...	...	...	...	...	...	...	...	...	...
31	Sagaing ...	...	...	...	...	...	...	1	...	...	...	...	1
32	Lower Chindwin ...	...	...	...	...	...	...	12	...	...	...	...	12
33	Upper Chindwin ...	35	...	2	...	...	33	6	2	...	...	...	4
	Meiktila Division ...	9	7	...	...	...	2	5	3	...	...	...	2
34	Kyauksè ...	9	7	...	...	...	2	...	...	...	...	...	...
35	Meiktila ...	...	...	...	...	...	...	...	...	...	...	...	...
36	Yamèthin ...	...	...	...	...	...	...	2	2	...	...	...	...
37	Myingyan ...	...	...	...	...	...	...	3	1	...	...	...	2
	Specially Administered Territories.	2,907	1,305	358	114	...	1,244	88	48	6	...	1	24
38	Northern Shan States	565	23	137	3	...	405	65	39	3	...	1	23
39	Southern Shan States	2,337	1,281	221	111	...	835	23	9	3	...	...	11
40	Chin Hills ...	5	1	...	...	...	4	...	...	...	...	...	...

Occupation. Details by Districts.

GROUP 147, VILLAGE OFFICIALS AND SERVANTS OTHER THAN WATCHMEN.						ORDER XLVI—RELIGION.						GROUP 148, PRIESTS, MINISTERS, ETC.						
Total Workers and Dependents.	ACTUAL WORKERS.				Dependents.	Total Workers and Dependents.	ACTUAL WORKERS.				Dependents.	Total Workers and Dependents.	ACTUAL WORKERS.				Dependents.	
	TOTAL.		PARTIALLY AGRICULTURIST.				TOTAL.		PARTIALLY AGRICULTURIST				TOTAL.		PARTIALLY AGRICULTURIST.			
	Males.	Females.	Males.	Females.			Males.	Females.	Males.	Females.			Males.	Females.	Males.	Females.		Serial No.
796	797	798	799	800	801	802	803	804	805	806	807	808	809	810	811	812	813	
61,664	**19,448**	**2,076**	**2,924**	**298**	**39,140**	**140,834**	**79,102**	**11,087**	**1,277**	**127**	**50,648**	**128,642**	**77,008**	**5,799**	**1,272**	**72**	**46,835**	
52,385	**26,142**	**2,471**	**3,176**	**255**	**24,772**	**116,263**	**65,343**	**8,930**	**734**	**102**	**41,990**	**104,993**	**62,286**	**4,052**	**731**	**46**	**37,656**	
2,982	**968**	**354**	**66**	**8**	**1,660**	**5,085**	**2,397**	**549**	**2**	**21**	**2,139**	**4,551**	**2,285**	**404**	**2**	**21**	**1,922**	
1,606	562	139	28	...	905	3,529	1,567	475	2	21	1,487	3,135	1,420	403	2	21	1,312	1
...	...	...	...	...	...	10	6	...	...	...	4	10	6	...	...	...	4	2
742	199	190	38	8	353	1,012	523	46	...	...	442	946	523	1	...	...	422	3
634	207	25	...	...	402	535	301	28	...	...	206	460	286	...	...	...	174	4
8,289	**2,217**	**247**	**522**	**11**	**5,825**	**17,826**	**9,434**	**1,592**	**7**	**2**	**6,800**	**15,298**	**8,821**	**582**	**4**	...	**5,895**	
49	17	...	...	...	32	4,773	2,297	375	...	...	2,101	4,055	2,065	299	...	...	1,691	5
2,861	736	10	183	1	2,115	3,775	2,301	307	2	...	1,167	3,082	2,038	32	...	...	1,012	6
1,670	523	40	108	2	1,107	2,814	1,394	481	...	...	939	2,165	1,366	48	...	...	751	7
2,278	498	131	162	1	1,649	3,256	1,941	251	3	...	1,064	2,964	1,853	131	2	...	980	8
1,531	443	66	100	7	1,022	3,208	1,501	198	2	2	1,509	3,032	1,499	72	2	...	1,461	9
7,466	**2,124**	**277**	**241**	**54**	**5,065**	**10,804**	**6,687**	**676**	**25**	**15**	**3,441**	**9,972**	**6,641**	**125**	**25**	...	**3,207**	
1,685	529	30	55	6	1,066	1,839	934	216	...	...	689	1,531	900	20	...	...	611	10
2,028	600	117	154	27	1,311	3,963	2,574	215	13	15	1,174	3,662	2,571	11	13	...	1,080	11
1,831	382	63	17	20	1,386	1,629	1,027	54	8	...	548	1,565	1,027	14	8	...	524	12
943	343	6	15	1	594	1,712	1,090	121	4	...	501	1,665	1,090	85	4	...	492	13
1,039	270	61	...	...	708	1,661	1,062	70	...	...	529	1,550	1,053	7	...	...	490	14
5,714	**1,519**	**77**	**288**	**6**	**4,118**	**11,461**	**6,632**	**776**	**42**	**4**	**4,053**	**10,442**	**6,447**	**271**	**42**	**4**	**3,722**	
1,878	497	42	159	2	1,339	2,821	1,446	129	28	3	1,246	2,482	1,357	43	28	3	1,082	15
80	30	1	...	...	49	199	100	8	...	...	91	196	100	8	...	...	88	16
1,522	405	9	84	...	1,108	3,106	2,001	248	...	...	857	2,814	1,972	20	...	...	822	17
1,287	305	23	51	4	959	3,319	2,165	208	9	1	946	3,202	2,165	132	9	1	905	18
518	177	...	12	...	341	1,392	631	90	5	...	671	1,265	622	...	5	...	643	19
429	105	2	17	...	322	624	289	93	...	...	242	482	231	68	...	...	183	20
7,884	**2,347**	**71**	**408**	...	**5,466**	**14,778**	**8,361**	**484**	**1**	...	**5,933**	**12,802**	**7,842**	**43**	**1**	...	**5,018**	
1,815	467	11	87	...	1,337	3,072	1,103	108	...	...	1,861	1,642	521	24	...	...	1,027	21
2,988	840	15	90	...	2,133	4,818	2,658	134	1	...	2,029	4,647	2,651	...	1	...	1,996	22
1,303	352	6	45	...	945	3,392	2,196	192	...	...	1,004	3,166	2,194	2	...	...	970	23
1,778	683	39	179	...	1,051	3,496	2,407	50	...	...	1,039	3,448	2,406	17	...	...	1,025	24
6,081	**2,500**	**344**	**492**	**91**	**3,237**	**15,687**	**8,515**	**1,428**	**52**	**13**	**5,744**	**14,456**	**8,369**	**788**	**52**	**12**	**5,299**	
2,097	1,079	100	120	4	918	8,036	5,563	715	34	1	1,758	7,358	5,417	467	34	1	1,474	25
902	*629*	*4*	...	...	*269*	*4115*	*3,109*	*250*	...	...	*756*	*3,437*	*2,963*	*2*	...	...	*472*	
720	369	9	67	...	342	997	400	122	7	...	477	919	400	64	7	...	455	26
616	223	...	31	...	393	535	206	9	3	...	320	518	206	9	3	...	303	27
1,553	511	41	128	13	1,001	4,726	1,775	339	...	12	2,612	4,315	1,775	58	...	12	2,482	28
1,095	318	194	156	74	583	1,391	571	233	9	...	587	1,346	571	190	9	...	585	29
5,942	**1,742**	**260**	**436**	**65**	**3,939**	**22,534**	**12,980**	**1,587**	**343**	**18**	**7,967**	**21,212**	**12,798**	**866**	**343**	...	**7,654**	
1,541	455	48	64	...	1,038	6,216	2,961	407	56	16	2,848	5,938	2,960	259	56	...	2,719	30
1,342	456	122	62	12	764	6,928	4,404	584	27	...	1,940	6,679	4,388	430	27	...	1,861	31
1,364	424	82	127	33	858	5,889	3,900	379	178	2	1,610	5,345	3,730	107	178	...	1,508	32
1,695	408	8	183	...	1,279	3,501	1,715	217	82	...	1,569	3,351	1,715	70	82	...	1,566	33
8,927	**2,724**	**841**	**662**	**140**	**5,362**	**18,088**	**10,337**	**1,848**	**261**	**29**	**5,903**	**16,098**	**10,137**	**963**	**261**	**8**	**4,998**	
1,557	809	90	223	27	658	2,582	1,516	584	42	7	482	2,493	1,516	513	42	7	464	34
2,407	481	537	74	51	1,389	4,970	2,373	679	41	21	1,918	3,532	2,373	129	41	...	1,030	35
2,449	725	214	118	62	1,510	3,551	2,482	307	30	1	762	3,166	2,282	153	30	1	731	36
2,514	709	...	247	...	1,805	6,985	3,966	278	148	...	2,741	6,867	3,966	168	148	...	2,733	37
8,279	**3,306**	**605**	**818**	**43**	**4,368**	**24,571**	**12,759**	**2,157**	**543**	**35**	**8,655**	**23,649**	**12,723**	**1,747**	**542**	**26**	**8,179**	
2,220	695	263	82	...	1,262	6,292	3,959	798	37	15	1,535	6,174	3,057	694	37	15	1,521	38
5,648	2,488	340	657	43	2,820	18,253	9,786	1,358	506	20	7,109	17,449	9,750	1,052	505	11	6,647	39
411	123	2	79	...	286	26	14	1	...	...	11	26	14	1	...	...	11	40

Serial No.	DISTRICT OR STATE.	GROUP 149, RELIGIOUS MENDICANTS, INMATES OF MONASTERIES, ETC. — Total Workers and Dependents.	Actual Workers — Total — Males.	Actual Workers — Total — Females.	Actual Workers — Partially Agriculturist — Males.	Actual Workers — Partially Agriculturist — Females.	Dependents.	ORDER XLVII—LAW. — Total Workers and Dependents.	Actual Workers — Total — Males.	Actual Workers — Total — Females.	Actual Workers — Partially Agriculturist — Males.	Actual Workers — Partially Agriculturist — Females.	Dependents.
	1	814	815	816	817	818	819	820	821	822	823	824	825
	Provincial Total ...	11,638	1,925	5,270	2	65	4,443	8,306	2,874	393	52	1	5,039
	Burma Proper ...	10,770	1,909	4,860	2	56	4,001	8,229	2,827	390	52	1	5,012
	Arakan Division ...	506	148	145	...	...	213	530	105	192	1	...	233
1	Akyab ...	394	147	72	...	...	175	377	87	162	...	...	128
2	Northern Arakan ...	...	...	...	...	...	...	...	...	...	...	...	...
3	Kyaukpyu ...	65	...	45	...	...	20	90	8	30	1	...	52
4	Sandoway ...	47	1	28	...	...	18	63	10	...	...	...	53
	Pegu Division ...	2,263	517	995	2	2	751	2,360	664	3	7	...	1,693
5	City of Rangoon ...	547	178	61	...	...	308	1,214	361	2	4	...	851
6	Hanthawaddy ...	693	263	275	2	...	155	377	48	...	1	...	329
7	Tharrawaddy ...	648	27	413	...	...	208	199	51	...	2	...	148
8	Pegu ...	208	49	120	...	...	39	233	81	...	...	...	152
9	Prome ...	167	...	126	...	2	41	337	123	1	...	...	213
	Irrawaddy Division ...	824	43	541	...	15	240	972	277	55	16	...	640
10	Bassein ...	308	34	196	...	...	78	236	71	11	4	...	154
11	Henzada ...	304	...	204	...	15	90	233	36	36	...	...	161
12	Myaungmya ...	64	...	40	...	...	24	221	92	...	11	...	129
13	Ma-ubin ...	47	...	38	...	...	9	109	41	5	1	...	63
14	Pyapôn ...	111	9	63	...	...	39	173	37	3	...	...	133
	Tenasserim Division ...	1,012	185	505	...	...	322	872	192	12	3	1	668
15	Toungoo ...	339	89	86	...	...	164	195	54	9	2	1	132
16	Salween ...	3	...	...	...	...	3	5	1	...	...	...	4
17	Thatôn ...	284	29	228	...	...	27	216	47	...	...	...	169
18	Amherst ...	117	...	76	...	...	41	395	81	3	1	...	311
19	Tavoy ...	127	9	90	...	...	28	24	5	...	...	...	19
20	Mergui ...	142	58	25	...	...	59	37	4	...	...	...	33
	Magwe Division ...	1,844	507	441	...	...	896	792	246	43	1	...	503
21	Thayetmyo ...	1,402	501	84	...	...	817	92	23	...	...	...	69
22	Pakôkku ...	170	3	134	...	...	33	149	33	2	...	...	114
23	Minbu ...	226	2	190	...	...	34	351	130	39	1	...	182
24	Magwe ...	46	1	33	...	...	12	200	60	2	...	...	138
	Mandalay Division ...	1,070	122	627	...	...	321	419	104	22	...	...	293
25	Mandalay (including City).	535	122	248	...	...	165	334	84	22	...	...	228
	Mandalay City ...	*535*	*122*	*248*	...	...	*165*	*225*	*60*	*8*	...	...	*157*
26	Bhamo ...	62	...	55	...	...	7	11	5	...	...	...	6
27	Myitkyina ...	17	...	...	...	...	17	20	4	...	...	...	16
28	Katha ...	411	...	281	...	...	130	48	8	...	...	...	40
29	Ruby Mines ...	45	...	43	...	...	2	6	3	...	...	...	3
	Sagaing Division ...	1,221	187	721	...	18	323	344	82	18	...	...	244
30	Shwebo ...	278	1	148	...	16	129	128	46	...	...	...	82
31	Sagaing ...	249	16	154	...	...	79	59	17	...	...	...	42
32	Lower Chindwin ...	544	170	272	...	2	102	103	13	6	...	...	84
33	Upper Chindwin ...	150	...	147	...	...	3	54	6	12	...	...	36
	Meiktila Division ...	2,030	200	885	...	21	945	1,940	1,157	45	24	...	738
34	Kyauksè ...	89	...	71	...	...	18	77	27	...	...	...	50
35	Meiktila ...	1,438	...	550	...	21	888	1,210	1,011	...	22	...	199
36	Yamèthin ...	385	200	154	...	...	31	348	63	45	1	...	240
37	Myingyan ...	118	...	110	...	...	8	305	56	...	1	...	249
	Specially Administered Territories.	868	16	410	...	9	442	77	47	3	...	...	27
38	Northern Shan States	118	...	104	...	...	14	32	27	3	...	...	2
39	Southern Shan States	750	16	306	...	9	428	35	10	...	...	...	25
40	Chin Hills ..	...	...	...	...	...	...	10	10	...	...	...	...

Occupations. Details by Districts.

GROUP 152, LAWYERS, LAW AGENTS, AND MUKHTIARS.						GROUP 153, LAWYERS, CLERKS, PETITION WRITERS, ETC.						ORDER XLVIII—MEDICINE.						
Total Workers and Dependents.	ACTUAL WORKERS.				Dependents.	Total Workers and Dependents.	ACTUAL WORKERS.				Dependents.	Total Workers and Dependents.	ACTUAL WORKERS.				Dependents.	Serial No.
	TOTAL.		PARTIALLY AGRICULTURIST.				TOTAL.		PARTIALLY AGRICULTURIST.				TOTAL.		PARTIALLY AGRICULTURIST.			
	Males.	Females.	Males.	Females.			Males.	Females.	Males.	Females.			Males.	Females.	Males.	Females.		
826	827	828	829	830	831	832	833	834	835	836	837	838	839	840	841	842	843	
6,079	1,553	353	34	1	4,172	2,207	1,281	40	18	...	866	52,172	18,769	6,241	1,535	382	27,062	
6,006	1,510	350	34	1	4,146	2,223	1,317	40	18	...	866	48,899	17,557	6,142	1,433	379	24,900	
521	103	192	1	...	226	9	2	...	...	...	7	2,488	1,503	345	21	8	1,620	
377	87	162	...	...	128	...	...	...	...	...	...	2,120	1,058	261	2	...	801	1
...	...	...	..	...	...	...	...	...	...	...	...	22	9	...	...	...	13	2
90	8	30	1	...	52	...	...	...	...	...	...	803	285	63	19	8	455	3
54	8	...	...	...	46	9	2	...	...	...	7	543	171	21	...	...	351	4
1,612	406	1	7	...	1,205	748	258	2	...	...	488	11,832	4,793	895	831	5	6,144	
571	139	...	4	...	432	643	222	2	...	...	419	2,932	932	399	6	...	1,601	5
351	43	...	1	...	308	26	5	...	...	...	21	2,516	1,014	147	23	...	1,355	6
176	49	...	2	...	127	23	2	...	...	...	21	2,245	1,308	125	771	5	812	7
179	52	...	...	...	127	54	29	...	...	...	25	2,524	907	63	20	...	1,564	8
335	123	1	...	..	211	2	...	...	...	...	2	1,615	632	161	11	...	822	9
909	270	19	16	...	600	62	7	36	...	...	20	8,634	3,009	1,342	70	41	4,282	
231	66	11	4	...	154	5	5	...	...	...	...	1,494	415	170	16	1	909	10
178	36	...	...	...	142	55	...	36	...	...	19	2,520	951	231	44	33	1,338	11
218	90	...	11	...	128	3	2	...	...	...	1	1,389	565	97	4	1	737	12
109	41	5	1	...	63	...	...	...	...	...	...	1,274	511	101	6	6	662	13
173	37	3	...	...	133	...	...	...	..	...	...	1,957	567	743	...	...	647	14
656	118	12	3	1	306	216	74	...	..	...	142	6,195	2,164	270	33	...	2,761	
171	40	9	2	1	122	24	14	...	...	...	10	2,204	735	55	22	...	1,414	15
5	1	...	...	...	4	...	...	...	...	...	...	72	32	...	...	...	40	16
166	33	...	...	...	133	50	14	...	...	...	36	1,613	606	54	5	...	953	17
253	35	3	1	...	215	142	46	...	...	...	96	1,465	510	103	6	...	852	18
24	5	...	...	...	19	...	...	...	...	...	...	500	165	35	...	...	300	19
37	4	...	...	...	33	...	...	...	...	...	...	341	116	23	...	...	202	20
712	219	43	1	...	451	79	27	...	...	...	52	2,901	1,376	161	27	...	2,364	
92	23	...	...	...	69	...	...	...	...	...	...	608	203	25	3	...	380	21
140	31	2	...	...	107	9	2	...	...	...	7	1,113	386	22	3	...	705	22
290	110	39	1	...	141	61	20	...	...	...	41	1,177	418	59	16	...	700	23
191	55	2	...	...	134	9	5	...	...	...	4	1,003	369	55	5	...	579	24
379	88	20	...	...	271	40	16	2	...	...	22	2,681	1,375	384	51	26	1,922	
294	68	20	...	...	206	40	16	2	...	...	22	2,059	708	211	16	9	1,140	25
185	*44*	*6*	...	...	*135*	*40*	*16*	*2*	...	...	*22*	*1,388*	*476*	*118*	—	...	*794*	
11	5	...	...	...	6	...	...	...	...	...	...	263	129	28	12	...	106	26
20	4	...	...	...	16	...	...	...	...	...	...	197	83	...	2	...	114	27
48	8	...	...	..	40	...	...	...	...	...	...	815	329	47	12	1	439	28
6	3	...	...	...	3	...	..	...	...	...	...	347	126	98	9	16	123	29
230	79	18	...	...	233	14	3	...	...	...	11	5,180	1,226	1,746	124	239	2,218	
128	46	...	...	...	82	...	...	...	...	...	...	1,964	349	1,130	3	...	485	30
59	17	...	...	...	42	...	...	...	...	...	...	807	221	130	2	8	456	31
89	10	6	...	...	73	14	3	...	...	...	11	1,457	368	452	78	231	637	32
54	6	12	...	...	36	...	...	...	...	...	...	952	278	34	41	...	640	33
886	227	45	6	...	614	1,054	930	...	18	...	124	5,688	2,101	999	276	60	2,588	
77	27	...	...	...	50	...	...	...	...	...	...	972	459	151	153	...	362	34
184	91	...	4	...	93	1,026	920	...	18	...	106	2,295	945	494	96	51	856	35
320	53	45	1	...	222	28	10	...	...	...	18	1,352	347	215	13	4	790	36
305	56	...	1	...	249	...	...	...	...	...	..	1,089	350	139	14	5	580	37
72	42	3	...	...	27	4	4	...	...	...	...	2,572	1,212	199	102	3	2,260	
32	27	3	...	...	2	...	...	...	...	...	...	802	293	29	24	...	480	38
31	6	...	...	...	25	4	4	...	...	...	...	2,720	901	170	78	3	1,649	39
10	10	...	...	...	...	...	...	...	...	...	...	51	18	...	...	...	33	40

Serial No.	DISTRICT OR STATE.	GROUP 154. MEDICAL PRACTITIONERS, DENTISTS, OCCULISTS, VETERINARY SURGEONS.						GROUP 155. MIDWIVES, VACCINATORS, COMPOUNDERS, NURSES, MASSEURS, ETC.					
		Total Workers and Dependents.	ACTUAL WORKERS.				Dependents.	Total Workers and Dependents.	ACTUAL WORKERS.				Dependents.
			TOTAL.		PARTIALLY AGRICULTURIST.				TOTAL.		PARTIALLY AGRICULTURIST.		
			Males.	Females.	Males.	Females.			Males.	Females.	Males.	Females.	
	1	844	845	846	847	848	849	850	851	852	853	854	855
	Provincial Total ...	49,582	18,120	5,434	1,519	382	26,028	2,590	649	907	16	...	1,034
	Burma Proper ...	46,069	16,927	5,251	1,417	379	23,891	2,530	630	891	16	...	1,009
	Arakan Division ...	3,464	1,516	335	21	8	1,613	24	7	10	...	...	7
1	Akyab ...	2,117	1,057	261	2	...	799	3	1	...	...	...	2
2	Northern Arakan ...	22	9	...	...	...	13	...	...	...	...	...	...
3	Kyaukpyu ...	787	279	55	19	8	453	16	6	8	...	...	2
4	Sandoway ...	538	171	19	...	...	348	5	...	2	...	...	3
	Pegu Division ...	10,873	4,604	454	830	5	5,815	959	189	441	1	...	329
5	City of Rangoon ...	2,211	812	22	5	...	1,377	721	120	377	1	...	224
6	Hanthawaddy ...	2,442	1,008	111	23	...	1,323	74	6	36	...	...	32
7	Tharrawaddy ...	2,190	1,281	119	771	5	790	55	27	6	...	...	22
8	Pegu ...	2,454	877	50	20	...	1,527	70	30	13	...	...	27
9	Prome ...	1,576	626	152	11	...	798	39	6	9	...	...	24
	Irrawaddy Division ...	8,412	2,944	1,299	70	41	4,169	222	65	43	...	...	114
10	Bassein ...	1,451	411	160	16	1	880	43	4	10	...	...	29
11	Henzada ...	2,469	947	208	44	33	1,314	51	4	23	...	...	24
12	Myaungmya ...	1,306	513	94	4	1	699	83	52	3	...	...	28
13	Ma-ubin ...	1,248	511	100	6	6	637	26	...	1	...	...	25
14	Pyapôn ...	1,938	562	737	...	...	639	19	5	6	...	...	8
	Tenasserim Division ...	5,946	2,144	181	33	...	3,621	249	20	89	...	...	140
15	Toungoo ...	2,156	730	46	22	...	1,380	48	5	9	...	...	34
16	Salween ...	66	51	...	...	...	35	6	1	...	...	...	5
17	Thatôn ...	1,573	603	35	5	...	935	40	3	19	...	...	18
18	Amherst ...	1,363	506	64	6	...	793	102	4	39	...	...	59
19	Tavoy ...	472	161	25	...	...	286	28	4	10	...	...	14
20	Mergui ...	316	113	11	...	...	192	25	3	12	...	...	10
	Magwe Division ...	3,779	1,339	128	27	...	2,312	122	37	33	...	...	52
21	Thayetmyo ...	599	199	21	3	...	379	9	4	4	...	...	1
22	Pakôkku ...	1,100	379	19	3	...	702	13	7	3	...	...	3
23	Minbu ...	1,118	402	40	16	...	676	59	16	19	...	...	24
24	Magwe ...	962	359	48	5	...	555	41	10	7	...	...	24
	Mandalay Division ...	3,353	1,328	240	51	26	1,785	328	47	144	...	...	137
25	Mandalay (including City).	1,889	704	136	16	9	1,049	170	4	75	...	...	91
	Mandalay City ...	*1,258*	*472*	*64*	...	...	*722*	*130*	*4*	*54*	...	...	*72*
26	Bhamo ...	217	109	10	12	...	98	46	20	18	...	...	8
27	Myitkyina ...	193	83	...	2	...	110	4	...	...	...	...	4
28	Katha ...	765	207	45	12	1	413	50	22	2	...	...	26
29	Ruby Mines ...	289	125	49	9	16	115	58	1	49	...	...	8
	Sagaing Division ...	4,912	1,178	1,660	124	239	2,074	268	38	86	...	..	144
30	Shwebo ...	1,845	347	1,082	3	...	416	119	2	48	...	...	69
31	Sagaing ...	784	214	120	2	8	450	23	7	10	...	...	6
32	Lower Chindwin ...	1,377	351	433	78	231	593	80	17	19	...	...	44
33	Upper Chindwin ...	906	266	25	41	...	615	46	12	9	...	...	25
	Meiktila Division ...	5,230	1,874	954	261	60	2,502	358	227	45	15	...	86
34	Kyauksè ...	883	484	115	140	...	334	89	25	36	13	...	28
35	Meiktila ...	2,047	745	489	94	51	813	248	200	5	2	...	43
36	Yamèthin ...	1,335	345	211	13	4	779	17	2	4	...	...	11
37	Myingyan ...	1,065	350	139	14	5	576	4	...	...	...	...	4
	Specially Administered Territories.	3,513	1,193	183	102	3	2,137	60	19	16	...	...	25
38	Northern Shan States	792	287	28	24	...	477	10	6	1	...	...	3
39	Southern Shan States	2,674	888	155	78	3	1,631	46	13	15	...	...	18
40	Chin Hills ...	47	18	...	...	...	29	4	...	...	...	...	4

Occupations. Details by Districts.

ORDER XLIX—(GROUP 156), INSTRUCTION—PROFESSORS, TEACHERS, AND EDUCATIONAL CLERKS AND SERVANTS.						ORDER L—LETTERS, AND ARTS AND SCIENCES.						GROUP 157, PUBLIC SCRIBES, STENOGRAPHERS, ETC.						
Total Workers and Dependents.	ACTUAL WORKERS. Total. Males.	ACTUAL WORKERS. Total. Females.	ACTUAL WORKERS. Partially Agriculturist. Males.	ACTUAL WORKERS. Partially Agriculturist. Females.	Dependents.	Total Workers and Dependents.	ACTUAL WORKERS. Total. Males.	ACTUAL WORKERS. Total. Females.	ACTUAL WORKERS. Partially Agriculturist. Males.	ACTUAL WORKERS. Partially Agriculturist. Females.	Dependents.	Total Workers and Dependents.	ACTUAL WORKERS. Total. Males.	ACTUAL WORKERS. Total. Females.	ACTUAL WORKERS. Partially Agriculturist. Males.	ACTUAL WORKERS. Partially Agriculturist. Females.	Dependents.	Serial No.
856	857	858	859	860	861	862	863	864	865	866	867	868	869	870	871	872	873	
26,939	9,818	2,776	302	190	14,345	28,025	10,854	2,638	195	77	14,533	1,866	787	40	...	...	1,039	
25,344	9,262	2,628	263	190	13,454	25,890	10,416	2,100	179	43	13,374	1,843	787	35	...	...	1,021	
1,452	460	293	...	...	700	2,446	752	442	5	15	1,252	179	87	...	...	...	52	
1,092	322	278	...	...	492	1,661	515	277	...	...	869	32	25	...	...	...	7	1
8	3	...	...	...	5	23	1	...	...	...	22	23	1	...	...	...	22	2
136	62	5	...	...	69	555	165	158	5	15	232	120	57	...	...	...	63	3
217	73	10	...	...	134	207	71	7	...	...	129	4	4	...	...	...	...	4
6,474	2,358	489	20	2	3,607	6,663	2,976	360	11	1	3,327	379	[illegible]	31	...	...	156	
1,936	574	207	1	...	1,111	2,700	1,111	171	3	...	1,418	119	49	25	...	...	45	5
1,741	659	94	3	...	968	1,252	601	35	1	...	616	193	128	6	...	...	69	6
1,028	388	73	2	2	567	664	341	30	3	1	293	7	2	...	...	...	5	7
1,081	430	83	...	...	568	812	419	41	1	...	352	52	18	...	...	...	34	8
688	307	32	4	...	349	1,235	504	83	2	...	648	8	5	...	...	...	3	9
4,669	1,848	436	10	9	2,385	3,997	1,492	385	10	4	2,120	113	30	...	...	...	81	
1,357	468	89	2	...	800	861	301	104	3	...	456	42	...	...	...	...	42	10
1,331	618	141	5	4	572	1,898	652	157	6	2	1,089	3	...	...	...	...	3	11
816	303	71	1	2	442	517	206	94	1	2	217	68	30	...	...	...	36	12
779	264	97	2	3	418	249	116	17	...	...	116	...	...	...	...	...	...	13
386	195	38	...	...	153	472	217	13	...	...	242	...	...	...	...	...	...	14
4,896	2,026	366	21	4	2,474	2,681	1,157	221	4	2	1,303	327	[illegible]	...	...	...	134	
1,147	373	91	14	4	683	487	288	14	...	...	185	166	141	...	...	...	25	15
20	7	...	...	...	13	6	6	...	...	...	...	1	1	...	...	...	...	16
808	345	78	4	...	385	795	353	38	2	...	404	83	41	...	...	...	42	17
1,689	596	156	1	...	937	1,152	409	140	2	2	603	61	5	...	...	...	56	18
494	316	23	1	...	155	156	63	26	...	...	67	14	3	...	...	...	11	19
698	379	18	1	...	301	85	38	3	...	...	44	2	2	...	...	...	...	20
1,401	673	55	...	...	673	3,293	1,376	158	26	...	1,759	179	[illegible]	3	...	...	123	
317	138	13	...	...	166	605	254	10	...	...	341	5	1	...	...	...	4	21
357	179	16	...	...	162	942	348	64	...	...	530	99	10	3	...	...	86	22
390	173	9	...	...	208	962	420	44	7	...	498	54	22	...	...	...	22	23
337	183	17	...	...	157	784	351	40	19	...	390	21	80	...	...	...	11	24
1,862	681	284	86	...	898	1,968	736	111	...	...	1,181	272	[illegible]	1	...	...	269	
1,158	340	147	2	...	671	1,366	532	82	...	...	752	181	66	...	...	...	115	25
865	251	84	...	...	530	1,128	426	65	...	...	637	135	46	...	...	...	89	
182	80	12	4	...	90	413	137	...	...	...	276	68	25	...	...	...	33	26
59	18	2	...	...	39	36	19	1	...	...	16	3	...	...	...	...	3	27
209	45	121	...	...	45	143	47	28	...	...	68	20	1	1	...	...	18	28
255	200	2	80	...	53	10	1	...	...	...	9	...	...	...	...	...	...	29
1,555	489	128	6	1	938	2,450	929	146	61	14	1,285	214	76	...	...	...	138	
725	193	46	2	1	486	667	150	61	1	2	456	89	...	...	...	...	89	30
304	98	30	1	...	176	657	277	19	6	3	361	37	22	...	...	...	15	31
310	125	31	3	...	154	855	396	40	47	9	419	74	46	...	...	...	28	32
216	73	21	...	...	122	271	96	26	7	...	149	14	8	...	...	...	6	33
3,073	737	577	130	174	1,759	2,392	1,008	277	62	7	1,107	180	52	...	...	...	128	
278	56	23	2	...	199	506	219	129	24	2	158	19	14	...	...	...	5	34
1,970	426	461	109	164	1,083	209	79	40	...	3	90	14	3	...	...	...	11	35
301	79	34	2	10	188	228	101	33	...	...	94	61	31	...	...	...	30	36
524	176	59	17	...	289	1,449	609	75	38	2	765	86	4	...	...	...	82	37
1,595	556	148	39	...	891	2,135	438	538	16	34	1,159	23	...	5	...	...	18	
816	326	8	15	...	482	324	198	10	...	...	116	3	...	...	...	...	3	38
749	212	140	24	...	397	1,810	239	528	16	34	1,043	20	...	5	...	...	15	39
30	18	...	...	...	12	1	1	...	...	...	...	...	...	...	...	...	...	40

Serial No.	DISTRICT OR STATE.	GROUP 158, ARCHITECTS, SURVEYORS, ENGINEERS AND THEIR EMPLOYES. Total Workers and Dependents.	Actual Workers. Total. Males.	Actual Workers. Total. Females.	Actual Workers. Partially Agriculturist. Males.	Actual Workers. Partially Agriculturist. Females.	Dependents.	GROUP 159, OTHERS (AUTHORS, ARTISTS, SCULPTORS, PHOTOGRAPHERS, ASTRONOMERS, ETC). Total Workers and Dependents.	Actual Workers. Total. Males.	Actual Workers. Total. Females.	Actual Workers. Partially Agriculturist. Males.	Actual Workers. Partially Agriculturist. Females.	Dependents.
	1	874	875	876	877	878	879	880	881	882	883	884	885
	Provincial Total ...	3,998	1,577	107	52	7	2,314	5,666	1,841	524	23	10	3,301
	Burma Proper ...	3,850	1,457	107	42	7	2,286	5,327	1,643	519	19	10	3,165
	Arakan Division ...	179	77	11	...	4	91	495	31	247	...	1	217
1	Akyab	84	51	...	...	...	33	435	5	232	...	...	198
2	Northern Arakan ...	...	...	...	...	...	...	...	...	...	...	...	...
3	Kyaukpyu ...	37	9	11	...	4	17	28	10	15	...	1	3
4	Sandoway ...	58	17	...	...	...	41	32	16	...	...	...	16
	Pegu Division ..	1,428	557	6	5	...	865	1,031	480	23	...	...	528
5	City of Rangoon ...	768	294	1	3	...	473	392	166	1	...	...	225
6	Hanthawaddy ..	333	140	4	1	...	189	318	177	3	...	...	138
7	Tharrawaddy ...	19	10	...	...	...	9	28	12	...	...	...	16
8	Pegu	295	109	1	1	...	185	98	50	...	...	...	48
9	Prome	13	4	...	...	...	9	195	75	19	...	...	101
	Irrawaddy Division ...	410	153	6	1	...	251	919	217	110	2	...	592
10	Bassein	67	41	...	...	...	26	174	68	...	2	...	106
11	Henzada ...	41	1	3	...	...	37	510	42	92	...	...	376
12	Myaungmya ...	76	31	3	1	...	42	146	65	18	...	...	63
13	Ma-ubin	27	9	...	...	...	18	12	6	...	...	...	6
14	Pyapón	199	71	...	...	...	128	77	36	...	...	...	41
	Tenasserim Division ...	562	197	26	2	...	339	386	130	30	2	...	216
15	Toungoo ...	32	13	...	...	...	19	30	9	...	...	...	21
16	Salween ...	1	1	...	...	...	...	4	4	...	...	...	...
17	Thatôn ...	262	90	...	...	...	172	129	47	1	2	...	81
18	Amherst ..	234	73	26	2	...	135	123	37	20	...	...	66
19	Tavoy	17	8	...	...	...	9	56	22	6	...	...	28
20	Mergui	16	12	...	...	...	4	44	11	3	...	...	30
	Magwe Division ...	305	121	2	6	...	182	820	326	33	6	...	461
21	Thayetmyo ...	40	13	...	...	...	27	164	92	2	...	...	70
22	Pakôkku ...	34	16	...	...	...	18	158	52	11	...	...	95
23	Minbu	142	61	2	4	...	79	333	107	17	1	...	209
24	Magwe	89	31	...	2	...	58	165	75	3	5	...	87
	Mandalay Division ...	322	127	1	...	...	194	644	232	13	...	...	399
25	Mandalay (including City).	147	55	1	...	...	91	452	209	12	...	...	231
	Mandalay City ...	*133*	*50*	*1*	...	...	*82*	*382*	*176*	*8*	...	..	*198*
26	Bhamo	144	63	...	...	...	81	178	17	...	..	...	161
27	Myitkyina ...	...	...	...	...	...	...	7	6	...	...	...	1
28	Katha	27	8	...	...	...	19	1	...	1	...	...	...
29	Ruby Mines ...	4	1	...	...	...	3	6	...	...	...	...	6
	Sagaing Division ...	453	192	14	28	...	247	609	141	63	8	9	405
30	Shwebo	89	6	13	...	...	70	238	31	21	...	...	186
31	Sagaing	150	87	...	2	...	63	175	15	12	...	3	148
32	Lower Chindwin ...	171	97	1	26	...	73	142	84	14	6	6	44
33	Upper Chindwin ...	43	2	...	...	...	41	54	11	16	2	...	27
	Meiktila Division ...	191	33	41	...	3	117	423	86	...	1	...	337
34	Kyauksè ...	19	...	...	...	...	19	3	2	...	...	...	1
35	Meiktila ...	105	27	26	...	3	52	2	2	...	...	...	...
36	Yamèthin ...	40	6	15	...	...	19	26	23	...	...	...	3
37	Myingyan ...	27	...	...	...	...	27	392	59	...	1	...	333
	Specially Administered Territories	148	120	...	10	...	28	339	198	5	4	...	136
38	**Northern Shan States** ...	...	...	...	...	...	...	237	148	1	...	...	88
39	**Southern Shan States** ...	148	120	...	10	...	28	101	49	4	4	...	48
40	**Chin Hills**	...	...	...	...	...	...	1	1	...	...	...	...

*Occupations. **Details by Districts.***

GROUP 160, MUSIC COMPOSERS AND MASTERS, AND PLAYERS, SINGERS, ACTORS, DANCERS.						ORDER LI.—(GROUP 161), PERSONS LIVING PRINCIPALLY ON THEIR INCOME (OTHER THAN AGRICULTURAL LAND OWNERS).						ORDER LII.—DOMESTIC SERVICE.						
Total Workers and Dependents.	ACTUAL WORKERS.				Dependents.	Total Workers and Dependents.	ACTUAL WORKERS.				Dependents.	Total Workers and Dependents.	ACTUAL WORKERS.				Dependents.	
	Total.		Partially Agriculturist.				Total.		Partially Agriculturist.				Total.		Partially Agriculturist.			
	Males.	Females.	Males.	Females.			Males.	Females.	Males.	Females.			Males.	Females.	Males.	Females.		Serial No.
886	887	888	889	890	891	892	893	894	895	896	897	898	899	900	901	902	903	
16,495	6,649	1,967	120	60	7,879	6,967	2,176	492	68	11	4,298	85,771	47,816	10,987	750	283	26,968	
14,870	6,529	1,439	118	26	6,902	6,257	1,736	445	51	11	4,076	79,023	45,432	9,757	570	225	23,835	
1,593	557	184	5	10	852	313	68	32	2	...	213	4,791	2,352	783	1	18	1,656	
1,110	434	45	...	...	631	144	20	27	...	...	97	3,385	1,852	423	...	...	1,110	1
...	...	...	...	...	...	8	3	...	...	...	5	71	58	3	...	...	10	2
370	89	132	5	10	149	42	17	...	2	...	25	810	250	203	1	18	357	3
113	34	7	...	...	72	119	28	5	...	...	86	525	192	154	...	...	179	4
3,825	1,747	300	6	1	1,778	2,482	686	182	3	...	1,614	31,976	22,042	2,350	62	23	7,584	
1,421	602	144	...	...	675	1,281	302	52	2	...	927	23,015	16,613	1,339	37	...	5,063	5
408	166	22	...	...	220	731	203	103	1	...	425	3,493	1,913	367	2	...	1,213	6
610	317	30	3	1	263	59	19	7	...	...	33	1,407	916	144	1	4	347	7
367	242	40	...	...	85	107	22	12	...	...	73	2,270	1,580	246	22	8	444	8
1,019	420	64	3	...	535	305	140	9	...	...	156	1,791	1,020	254	...	11	517	9
2,555	1,090	269	7	4	1,196	465	99	59	5	2	307	5,804	2,610	903	18	37	2,291	
578	192	104	1	...	282	56	28	3	4	...	25	1,048	611	175	5	...	262	10
1,344	609	62	6	2	673	125	22	17	1	2	86	2,046	1,033	534	2	33	479	11
227	78	73	..	2	76	68	16	8	...	...	44	865	656	66	...	4	143	12
210	101	17	...	...	92	87	33	2	...	...	52	865	520	83	...	...	262	13
196	110	13	...	...	73	129	...	29	...	...	100	1,000	790	65	11	...	145	14
1,406	637	165	...	2	604	1,308	291	29	2	...	888	6,927	2,898	974	9	20	2,065	
259	125	14	...	...	120	260	67	7	2	...	186	1,549	920	177	1	14	452	15
...	...	...	...	...	...	...	...	...	...	...	...	61	36	6	...	...	19	16
321	175	37	...	...	109	154	34	5	...	..	115	1,060	624	111	...	...	325	17
734	294	94	...	2	346	552	59	16	1	...	477	2,940	1,827	271	...	6	842	18
69	30	20	...	...	19	65	29	...	...	...	36	1,036	363	314	8	...	359	19
23	13	...	...	...	10	277	202	2	...	...	74	291	128	95	...	...	68	20
1,989	876	120	14	...	993	323	92	22	5	5	210	6,466	2,860	1,370	2	4	2,236	
396	148	8	...	...	240	182	49	1	3	...	132	1,355	682	133	...	1	550	21
651	270	50	...	...	331	16	3	3	...	...	10	2,132	746	682	...	...	704	22
433	220	25	2	...	188	73	17	16	...	5	40	1,135	336	380	...	3	419	23
509	238	37	12	...	234	52	22	2	2	...	28	1,844	1,096	185	3	...	563	24
730	275	96	...	...	359	976	249	102	25	4	624	10,622	5,766	1,019	264	6	3,838	
586	202	69	...	...	315	742	139	99	3	4	504	7,125	3,708	718	52	4	2,699	25
478	*154*	*56*	...	...	*368*	*526*	*85*	*77*	...	...	*364*	*4,746*	*2,480*	*471*	...	...	*1,795*	
23	22	...	...	...	1	2	...	1	...	...	1	863	661	29	202	...	173	26
26	13	1	...	...	12	140	35	...	12	...	105	725	448	29	4	...	248	27
95	38	26	...	...	31	31	19	3	1	...	9	1,114	493	210	3	2	411	28
...	...	...	...	...	...	61	56	...	9	...	5	796	456	33	3	...	307	29
1,174	520	60	25	5	595	170	45	13	2	...	112	5,795	2,119	1,059	139	63	2,617	
251	113	27	1	2	111	85	13	10	...	...	62	1,976	579	370	1	14	1,027	30
295	153	7	4	...	135	11	5	1	1	...	5	1,654	491	429	24	26	734	31
468	169	25	15	3	274	49	17	1	2	...	31	1,127	542	170	32	4	415	32
160	75	10	5	...	75	25	10	1	...	...	14	1,038	507	90	82	19	441	33
1,898	837	236	61	4	825	219	107	4	5	...	108	6,603	2,776	1,279	74	44	2,548	
465	203	129	24	2	133	23	7	1	1	...	15	1,076	595	104	55	5	377	34
88	47	14	..	...	27	137	81	...	2	...	56	1,966	537	520	3	33	909	35
101	41	18	...	...	42	35	12	3	...	...	20	1,632	898	165	12	5	569	36
944	546	75	37	2	323	24	7	...	2	...	17	1,929	746	490	4	1	693	37
1,625	120	528	2	34	977	710	440	48	27	...	222	6,756	2,392	1,230	180	168	3,132	
84	50	9	...	...	25	246	149	20	7	...	77	1,067	523	141	30	18	403	38
1,541	70	519	2	34	952	464	291	28	10	...	148	5,455	1,737	1,085	138	150	2,633	39
...	...	...	...	...	...	...	...	...	...	...	...	234	133	4	12	...	97	40

Serial No.	DISTRICT OR STATE.	GROUP 162, COOKS, WATER CARRIERS, DOOR-KEEPERS, WATCHMEN AND OTHER INDOOR SERVANTS.						GROUP 163, PRIVATE GROOMS, COACHMEN, DOG-BOYS, ETC.					
		Total Workers and Dependents.	ACTUAL WORKERS.				Dependents.	Total Workers and Dependents.	ACTUAL WORKERS.				Dependents.
			TOTAL.		PARTIALLY AGRICULTURIST.				TOTAL.		PARTIALLY AGRICULTURIST.		
			Males.	Females.	Males.	Females.			Males.	Females.	Males.	Females.	
	1	904	905	906	907	908	909	910	911	912	913	914	915
	Provincial Total ...	**82,197**	**45,153**	**10,862**	**745**	**360**	**26,182**	**3,574**	**2,663**	**125**	**5**	**23**	**786**
	Burma Proper ...	**75,483**	**42,771**	**9,632**	**365**	**192**	**23,080**	**3,532**	**2,652**	**125**	**5**	**23**	**755**
	Arakan Division ...	**4,774**	**2,350**	**783**	**1**	**18**	**1,641**	**17**	**2**	...	...	...	**15**
1	Akyab ...	3,385	1,852	423	...	...	1,110	...	...	...	...	...	...
2	Northern Arakan ...	71	58	3	...	...	10	...	...	...	...	...	...
3	Kyaukpyu ...	801	250	203	1	18	348	9	...	...	...	...	9
4	Sandoway ...	517	190	154	...	...	173	8	2	...	...	...	6
	Pegu Division ...	**29,863**	**20,333**	**2,290**	**59**	**12**	**7,240**	**2,113**	**1,709**	**60**	**3**	**11**	**344**
5	City of Rangoon ...	21,180	15,069	1,332	34	...	4,788	1,826	1,544	7	3	...	275
6	Hanthawaddy ...	3,485	1,906	367	2	...	1,212	8	7	...	...	...	1
7	Tharrawaddy ...	1,295	828	144	1	4	323	112	88	...	...	...	24
8	Pegu ...	2,251	1,567	245	22	8	430	10	13	1	...	...	5
9	Prome ...	1,643	963	202	...	...	478	148	57	52	...	11	39
	Irrawaddy Division ...	**5,781**	**3,571**	**923**	**18**	**27**	**1,287**	**43**	**39**	...	...	...	**4**
10	Bassein ...	1,048	611	175	5	...	262	...	...	...	...	...	...
11	Henzada ...	2,013	1,002	534	2	33	477	33	31	...	...	...	2
12	Myaungmya ...	862	654	66	...	4	142	3	2	...	...	...	1
13	Ma-ubin ...	865	520	83	...	...	262	...	...	...	...	...	...
14	Pyapon ...	993	784	65	11	...	144	7	6	...	...	...	1
	Tenasserim Division ...	**6,605**	**3,658**	**942**	**9**	**8**	**2,005**	**332**	**240**	**32**	...	**12**	**60**
15	Toungoo ...	1,417	840	150	1	2	418	132	71	27	...	12	34
16	Salween ...	61	36	6	...	...	19	...	...	...	...	...	...
17	Thatôn ...	1,038	609	111	...	...	318	22	15	...	...	...	7
18	Amherst ...	2,770	1,681	266	...	6	823	170	146	5	...	...	19
19	Tavoy ...	1,032	359	314	8	...	359	4	4	...	...	...	...
20	Mergui ...	287	124	95	...	...	68	4	4	...	...	...	...
	Magwe Division ...	**6,162**	**2,689**	**1,344**	**3**	**4**	**2,129**	**304**	**171**	**26**	...	...	**107**
21	Thayetmyo ...	1,307	655	123	...	1	529	48	27	...	...	...	21
22	Pakôkku ...	2,103	726	682	...	...	695	29	20	...	...	...	9
23	Minbu ...	1,051	332	361	...	3	358	84	4	19	...	...	61
24	Magwe ...	1,701	976	178	3	...	547	143	120	7	...	...	16
	Mandalay Division ...	**10,045**	**5,397**	**1,013**	**262**	**6**	**3,635**	**578**	**369**	**6**	**2**	...	**203**
25	Mandalay (including City).	6,658	3,415	712	52	4	2,531	467	293	6	...	...	168
	Mandalay City ...	*4,377*	*2,258*	*465*	...	...	*1,654*	*369*	*222*	*6*	...	...	*141*
26	Bhamo ...	862	661	29	202	...	172	1	...	...	...	...	1
27	Myitkyina ...	701	427	19	2	...	245	24	21	...	2	...	3
28	Katha ...	1,108	487	210	3	2	411	6	6	...	...	...	...
29	Ruby Mines ...	716	407	33	3	...	276	80	49	...	...	...	31
	Sagaing Division ...	**5,691**	**2,032**	**1,058**	**130**	**63**	**2,601**	**104**	**87**	**1**	...	...	**26**
30	Shwebo ...	1,976	579	370	1	14	1,027	...	...	...	...	...	...
31	Sagaing ...	1,653	491	429	24	26	733	1	...	...	...	...	1
32	Lower Chindwin ...	1,058	484	170	32	4	404	69	58	...	...	...	11
33	Upper Chindwin ...	1,004	478	89	82	19	437	34	29	1	...	...	4
	Meiktila Division ...	**6,562**	**2,741**	**1,279**	**74**	**44**	**2,542**	**41**	**35**	...	...	...	**6**
34	Kyauksè ...	1,068	593	104	55	5	371	8	2	...	...	...	6
35	Meiktila ...	1,940	511	520	3	33	909	26	26	...	...	...	...
36	Yamèthin ...	1,632	898	165	12	5	569	...	...	...	...	...	...
37	Myingyan ...	1,922	739	490	4	1	693	7	7	...	...	...	...
	Specially Administered Territories.	**6,714**	**2,382**	**1,230**	**180**	**168**	**3,102**	**42**	**11**	...	...	...	**31**
38	Northern Shan States	1,030	512	141	30	18	377	37	11	...	...	...	26
39	Southern Shan States	5,450	1,737	1,085	138	150	2,628	5	...	...	...	...	5
40	Chin Hills ...	234	133	4	12	...	97	...	...	...	...	...	...

ORDER LIII.—GENERAL TERMS NOT INDICATING A DEFINITE OCCUPATION.						GROUP 164, MANUFACTURERS, BUSINESS MEN AND CONTRACTORS, OTHERWISE UNSPECIFIED.						GROUP 165, CASHIERS, ACCOUNTANTS, BOOK-KEEPERS, CLERKS, EMPLOYES IN UNSPECIFIED OFFICES, WAREHOUSES, AND SHOPS.						
Total Workers and Dependents.	ACTUAL WORKERS. Total.		Partially Agriculturist.		Dependents.	Total Workers and Dependents.	ACTUAL WORKERS. Total.		Partially Agriculturist.		Dependents.	Total Workers and Dependents.	ACTUAL WORKERS. Total.		Partially Agriculturist.		Dependents.	Serial No.
	Males.	Females.	Males.	Females.			Males.	Females.	Males.	Females.			Males.	Females.	Males.	Females.		
916	917	918	919	920	921	922	923	924	925	926	927	928	929	930	931	932	933	
429,399	180,246	76,922	5,771	3,028	172,231	10,852	2,816	222	73	18	6,814	58,873	22,562	2,136	361	287	24,175	
400,003	170,033	71,204	3,671	2,743	158,766	8,793	2,574	213	40	17	5,006	53,252	21,047	1,869	246	278	30,336	
27,998	10,024	7,882	139	32	10,089	659	501	...	1	...	158	2,299	794	191	18	15	1,214	
13,678	7,224	1,226	64	4	5,228	573	476	...	1	...	97	1,353	587	94	...	4	672	1
...	...	...	...	...	...	...	...	...	...	...	...	...	...	...	...	...	...	2
12,752	2,282	6,431	75	28	4,039	17	3	...	..	...	14	600	136	97	18	11	367	3
1,565	518	225	...	...	822	69	22	...	...	...	47	246	71	...	...	...	175	4
95,549	52,129	8,481	126	51	34,939	3,489	1,450	47	6	...	1,990	22,562	10,004	134	20	1	12,425	
49,120	33,939	672	25	...	14,509	2,031	687	2	6	...	1,342	16,569	7,608	119	11	...	8,842	5
17,890	6,788	2,089	39	8	9,013	475	199	39	...	...	257	3,015	1,132	...	7	...	1,883	6
8,981	2,748	2,540	6	14	3,673	111	50	2	...	...	59	1,362	534	11	...	1	817	7
10,066	4,711	1,241	35	25	4,114	250	97	2	...	...	151	762	277	...	2	...	485	8
9,492	3,943	1,939	21	4	3,610	602	417	2	...	...	183	855	453	4	...	...	398	9
45,188	22,064	5,953	265	204	17,171	626	283	10	...	...	333	5,478	2,192	58	5	...	3,207	
11,736	6,613	1,292	19	7	3,831	241	111	5	...	...	125	1,301	457	25	...	...	819	10
11,043	4,589	2,022	119	106	4,432	236	107	...	...	...	129	1,015	393	14	2	...	608	11
3,840	2,220	356	6	22	1,264	81	39	...	...	...	42	951	367	2	...	...	582	12
10,345	4,664	1,436	61	69	4,245	9	2	...	...	...	7	1,345	502	2	3	...	841	13
8,224	3,978	847	60	...	3,399	59	24	5	...	...	30	866	474	15	...	...	377	14
48,495	24,095	5,899	180	160	18,501	775	247	17	1	4	521	5,898	2,359	47	7	...	3,490	
11,144	5,261	1,480	46	118	4,403	231	64	15	...	4	152	1,537	442	6	1	...	1,089	15
1,006	470	76	...	...	440	12	2	...	...	...	10	95	37	1	...	...	57	16
8,847	3,975	1,043	39	1	3,831	164	57	1	...	...	106	731	302	3	...	...	426	17
17,315	9,539	1,484	87	39	6,292	310	106	1	1	...	203	2,466	1,198	9	6	...	1,259	18
4,984	1,402	1,441	8	2	2,141	30	7	...	...	...	23	590	206	5	...	...	379	19
5,197	3,428	375	...	...	1,394	28	11	...	...	...	17	479	174	25	...	...	282	20
45,780	13,605	11,220	124	118	20,973	[illegible]	133	17	1	...	333	2,582	1,126	8	11	...	1,449	
6,841	1,986	1,516	1	2	3,339	117	27	2	...	...	88	571	262	...	1	...	309	21
37,782	5,148	3,639	98	14	8,995	100	30	1	...	..	69	1,040	429	1	3	...	610	22
7,577	2,600	1,828	21	67	3,149	155	49	...	...	...	106	435	173	4	7	...	258	23
13,520	3,891	4,139	14	35	5,490	111	27	14	1	...	70	537	262	3	...	...	272	24
48,928	19,109	10,418	1,117	226	19,401	1,027	320	40	6	9	667	5,387	1,894	140	63	20	3,353	
30,746	11,229	7,219	187	162	12,298	493	149	20	3	...	324	3,322	1,130	61	...	...	2,131	25
18,978	*7,181*	*3,975*	...	...	*7,822*	*272*	*79*	*4*	...	...	*189*	*2,504*	*859*	*39*	...	...	*1,606*	
4,141	1,324	551	113	1	2,266	182	67	1	1	...	114	553	217	2	6	...	334	26
3,190	2,157	182	767	...	871	189	47	...	...	...	142	386	124	...	...	...	262	27
5,024	1,777	807	74	40	2,440	117	29	19	1	9	69	574	205	7	...	...	362	28
5,827	2,642	1,659	76	23	1,526	36	18	...	1	...	18	552	218	70	57	20	264	29
38,170	13,660	8,664	900	971	15,846	681	202	61	8	4	429	3,386	941	436	26	122	2,009	
8,223	2,803	2,149	150	81	3,271	279	88	50	...	...	141	998	393	27	5	...	578	30
9,694	3,904	1,762	145	346	4,028	166	41	1	2	...	124	572	236	...	6	...	336	31
14,673	4,674	3,865	294	520	6,134	102	27	...	1	...	75	1,234	109	409	3	126	716	32
5,580	2,279	888	311	24	2,413	134	45	10	5	4	79	582	203	...	12	...	379	33
49,068	15,327	12,785	710	981	21,846	1,063	449	21	17	...	592	5,758	1,736	855	96	116	3,167	
7,642	3,051	1,429	363	84	3,162	305	189	3	14	...	113	300	136	5	6	...	159	34
11,883	2,696	3,903	142	645	5,284	338	122	6	...	...	210	2,259	483	573	57	95	1,203	35
10,803	2,644	1,460	111	43	5,609	386	131	10	3	...	245	1,471	567	131	11	21	773	36
19,630	8,936	5,993	94	209	7,701	34	7	2	...	...	25	1,728	550	146	22	...	1,032	37
29,396	10,213	5,718	2,100	275	13,465	2,059	242	9	33	1	1,808	5,621	1,515	267	115	9	3,820	
5,739	2,250	1,571	222	37	1,918	339	116	7	28	1	216	1,614	923	104	52	...	587	38
23,561	7,931	4,137	1,878	238	11,493	1,703	122	2	5	...	1,579	3,082	583	160	63	9	3,239	39
96	32	10	...	...	54	17	4	...	...	...	13	25	9	3	...	...	13	40

Serial No.	DISTRICT OR STATE.	GROUP 166, MECHANICS OTHERWISE UNSPECIFIED.						GROUP 167, LABOURERS AND WORKMEN OTHERWISE UNSPECIFIED.					
		Total Workers and Dependents.	ACTUAL WORKERS. Total.		ACTUAL WORKERS. Partially Agriculturist.		Dependents.	Total Workers and Dependents.	ACTUAL WORKERS. Total.		ACTUAL WORKERS. Partially Agriculturist.		Dependents.
			Males.	Females.	Males.	Females.			Males.	Females	Males.	Females.	
	1	934	935	936	937	938	939	940	941	942	943	944	945
	Provincial Total ...	8,240	4,617	244	4	4	3,379	351,434	149,251	74,320	5,333	2,709	127,863
	Burma Proper ...	8,223	4,613	242	4	4	3,368	329,735	140,799	68,880	3,381	2,444	120,056
	Arakan Division ...	257	193	20	...	2	44	24,880	8,536	7,671	120	15	8,673
1	Akyab	224	184	2	...	...	38	11,528	5,977	1,130	63	...	4,421
2	Northern Arakan ...	...	...	...	...	...	...	...	...	...	...	...	...
3	Kyaukpyu ...	25	3	18	...	2	4	12,110	2,140	6,316	57	15	3,654
4	Sandoway ...	8	6	...	...	...	2	1,242	419	225	...	...	598
	Pegu Division ...	4,658	2,400	122	3	2	2,136	64,839	38,275	8,178	97	48	18,386
5	City of Rangoon ...	3,102	1,715	6	3	...	1,381	27,418	23,929	545	5	...	2,944
6	Hanthawaddy ...	1,283	550	91	...	...	642	15,097	4,907	1,959	32	8	6,231
7	Tharrawaddy ...	125	37	25	...	2	63	7,383	2,127	2,502	6	11	2,754
8	Pegu	69	32	...	...	...	37	8,985	4,305	1,239	53	25	3,441
9	Prome	79	66	...	...	...	13	7,956	3,007	1,933	21	4	3,016
	Irrawaddy Division ...	932	571	88	...	...	273	38,152	19,017	5,797	260	204	13,338
10	Bassein	338	176	7	...	...	155	9,856	5,869	1,255	19	7	2,732
11	Henzada	65	38	...	...	...	27	9,727	4,051	2,008	117	106	3,668
12	Myaungmya ...	137	119	...	...	...	18	2,671	1,695	354	6	22	622
13	Ma-ubin	40	24	...	...	...	16	8,951	4,136	1,434	58	69	3,381
14	Pyapôn	352	214	81	...	...	57	6,947	3,266	746	60	...	2,935
	Tenasserim Division ...	944	495	7	...	...	442	40,878	20,994	5,828	172	156	14,056
15	Toungoo	70	7	7	...	...	56	9,306	4,748	1,452	45	114	3,106
16	Salween	1	1	...	...	...	...	898	450	75	...	...	373
17	Thatôn	105	66	...	...	...	39	7,849	3,550	1,039	39	1	3,260
18	Amherst	673	349	...	...	...	324	13,866	7,886	1,474	80	39	4,506
19	Tavoy	66	52	...	...	...	14	4,298	1,137	1,436	8	2	1,725
20	Mergui	29	20	...	...	...	9	4,661	3,223	352	...	...	1,086
	Magwe Division ...	621	514	2	...	...	105	42,033	11,852	11,095	122	118	19,086
21	Thayetmyo ...	32	21	...	...	...	11	6,121	1,676	1,514	...	2	2,931
22	Pakôkku	137	96	1	...	...	40	16,505	4,593	3,636	95	14	8,276
23	Minbu	67	47	...	...	...	20	6,920	2,331	1,824	14	67	2,765
24	Magwe	385	350	1	...	...	34	12,487	3,252	4,121	13	35	5,114
	Mandalay Division ...	675	346	3	...	...	326	41,849	16,559	10,235	1,148	197	15,055
25	Mandalay (including City).	334	71	2	...	...	261	26,597	9,879	7,136	184	162	9,582
	Mandalay City ...	*320*	*68*	*2*	...	...	*259*	*15,873*	*6,175*	*3,930*	...	...	*5,768*
26	Bhamo	42	31	...	...	...	11	3,364	1,009	548	106	1	1,807
27	Myitkyina ...	229	217	...	...	...	12	2,386	1,749	182	767	...	455
28	Katha	8	7	...	...	...	1	4,325	1,536	781	73	31	2,008
29	Ruby Mines ...	62	20	1	...	...	41	5,177	2,386	1,588	18	3	1,203
	Sagaing Division ...	27	25	...	...	...	2	34,076	12,493	8,167	866	841	13,416
30	Shwebo	...	...	...	...	...	...	6,946	2,322	2,072	145	81	2,552
31	Sagaing	5	4	...	...	...	1	8,951	3,623	1,761	137	346	3,567
32	Lower Chindwin ...	15	14	...	...	...	1	13,322	4,524	3,456	290	394	5,342
33	Upper Chindwin ...	7	7	...	...	...	...	4,857	2,024	878	294	20	1,955
	Meiktila Division ...	109	69	...	1	...	40	43,028	13,073	11,909	596	865	18,046
34	Kyauksè	6	2	...	...	...	4	7,031	2,724	1,421	343	84	2,886
35	Meiktila	24	16	...	...	...	8	9,262	2,075	3,324	85	550	3,863
36	Yamèthin ...	13	10	...	1	...	3	8,933	2,936	1,319	96	22	4,678
37	Myingyan ...	66	41	...	...	...	25	17,802	5,338	5,845	72	209	6,619
	Specially Administered Territories.	17	4	2	...	...	11	21,699	8,452	5,440	1,952	265	7,807
38	Northern Shan States	12	4	2	...	...	6	3,774	1,207	1,458	142	36	1,109
39	Southern Shan States	2	...	...	...	...	2	17,874	7,226	3,975	1,810	229	6,673
40	Chin Hills ...	3	...	...	...	...	3	51	19	7	...	...	25

Occupations. Details by Districts.

Order LIV.—(Group 168), Inmates of Jails, Hospitals and Asylums.						Order LV.—(Group 169), Beggars, Vagrants, Prostitutes, Receivers of Stolen Goods, etc.						
Total Workers and Dependents.	Actual Workers.				Dependents.	Total Workers and dependents.	Actual Workers.				Dependents.	Serial No.
	Total.		Partially Agriculturist.				Total.		Partially Agriculturist.			
	Males.	Females.	Males.	Females.			Males.	Females.	Males.	Females.		
946	947	948	949	950	951	952	953	954	955	956	957	
8,500	8,052	44	2	...	404	26,075	8,353	9,943	300	173	7,779	
8,481	8,052	44	2	...	385	22,794	7,246	9,052	212	164	6,496	
920	815	15	...	...	80	1,384	377	511	...	...	496	
782	687	15	...	...	80	1,231	317	463	...	...	451	1
...	...	...	...	...	...	13	8	4	...	...	1	2
128	128	...	...	...	...	95	32	28	...	..	35	3
...	...	...	...	...	...	45	20	16	...	...	9	4
2,978	2,925	7	1	...	46	3,265	1,100	1,334	1	...	831	
2,759	2,719	2	1	...	38	1,789	510	923	...	...	356	5
211	205	...	...	...	6	417	170	91	...	...	156	6
...	...	...	...	...	...	136	45	47	...	...	44	7
...	...	...	...	...	...	344	139	99	1	...	106	8
8	1	5	...	...	2	579	236	174	...	...	169	9
1,524	1,450	7	...	...	67	1,677	903	387	2	4	387	
71	70	1	...	...	...	246	63	77	1	...	101	10
280	207	6	...	...	67	793	614	106	...	4	73	11
964	964	...	...	...	...	251	84	68	...	...	99	12
209	209	...	...	...	...	194	77	72	...	...	45	13
...	...	...	...	...	...	193	60	64	1	...	69	14
547	393	2	...	...	152	1,499	566	345	2	...	588	
151	151	...	...	...	...	494	148	154	2	...	192	15
3	1	...	...	...	2	19	9	...	...	...	10	16
...	...	...	...	...	...	133	59	36	...	...	38	17
59	31	...	...	...	28	808	337	133	...	...	338	18
60	36	...	...	...	24	15	4	6	...	...	5	19
274	174	2	...	...	98	30	9	16	...	...	5	20
1,138	1,126	1	...	...	11	3,986	1,246	1,639	...	...	1,101	
886	885	1	...	...	...	93	34	43	...	...	16	21
...	...	...	...	...	...	2,053	731	801	...	...	521	22
...	...	...	...	...	...	1,475	405	672	...	...	398	23
252	241	...	...	...	11	365	76	123	...	...	166	24
104	90	...	...	...	14	2,765	793	1,228	3	2	744	
90	80	...	...	...	10	2,038	567	941	1	2	530	25
90	*80*	...	...	...	*10*	*871*	*326*	*284*	...	...	*261*	
3	2	...	...	...	1	110	72	20	2	...	18	26
...	...	...	...	...	...	29	10	3	...	...	16	27
8	6	...	...	...	2	290	85	108	...	...	97	28
3	2	...	...	...	1	298	59	156	...	...	85	29
17	17	...	1	...	...	3,884	1,231	1,769	171	87	884	
16	16	...	...	...	...	689	243	261	13	...	185	30
...	...	...	...	...	...	1,114	388	473	4	3	253	31
1	1	...	1	...	...	2,568	472	748	130	84	348	32
...	...	...	...	...	...	513	128	287	24	...	98	33
1,263	1,236	12	...	...	15	4,334	1,030	1,839	33	71	1,465	
28	16	...	...	...	12	730	280	324	...	...	126	34
3	3	...	...	...	...	1,731	330	602	32	59	799	35
5	1	1	...	...	3	749	191	324	...	12	234	36
1,227	1,216	11	...	...	...	1,124	229	589	1	...	306	37
19	...	...	...	...	19	3,281	1,107	891	88	9	1,283	
19	...	...	...	...	19	848	272	320	6	...	256	38
...	...	...	...	...	...	2,433	835	571	82	9	1,027	39
...	...	...	...	...	...	...	...	...	...	...	...	40

IMPERIAL TABLE XV-B.

Occupations or Means of Livelihood.

IMPERIAL TABLE XV.—B-I.—*Subsidiary Occupations*

Serial No.	District or State.	Total number of Rent Receivers (Actual Workers).		Number of Actual Workers who returned subsidiary occupations.		DETAILS OF							
						Rent Payers' Cultivators.		Agricultural Labourers.		Cart Owners and Cartmen.		Money Lenders and Grain Dealers.	
		M.	F.	M.	F.	M.	F.	M.	F.	M.	F.	M.	F.
	1	2	3	4	5	6	7	8	9	10	11	12	13
	Provincial Total ...	**59,921**	**68,997**	**7,470**	**6,418**	**2,187**	**1,984**	**480**	**247**	**635**	...	**563**	**477**
	Burma Proper ...	**48,108**	**54,084**	**4,690**	**3,477**	**1,068**	**712**	**202**	**224**	**562**	...	**492**	**288**
	Arakan Division ...	*4,873*	*4,324*	*339*	*242*	*149*	*91*	*20*	*20*	...	...	*22*	*24*
1	Akyab ...	3,659	2,495	257	170	117	52	17	16	...	...	12	18
2	Northern Arakan	...	...	...	...	...	...	...	...	...	...	...	...
3	Kyaukpyu ...	534	862	34	21	1	2	2	4	...	...	7	4
4	Sandoway ...	680	967	48	51	31	37	1	...	...	...	3	2
	Pegu Division ...	*6,902*	*7,740*	*581*	*340*	*90*	*26*	*9*	*31*	*110*	...	*110*	*40*
5	City of Rangoon	433	278	27	3	4	...	...	...	...	...	7	2
6	Hanthawaddy ...	1,242	1,011	161	79	41	6	3	3	...	...	38	17
7	Tharrawaddy ...	1,605	1,789	85	74	8	9	3	13	...	...	28	7
8	Pegu ...	1,785	1,202	181	80	19	7	...	2	57	...	29	6
9	Prome ..	1,837	3,460	127	104	18	4	3	13	53	...	8	8
	Irrawaddy Division	*8,079*	*7,932*	*885*	*716*	*186*	*174*	*57*	*48*	*50*	...	*90*	*62*
10	Bassein ...	2,416	1,174	193	162	46	9	6	11	17	...	28	15
11	Henzada ...	2,814	3,539	280	297	94	90	10	28	33	...	21	20
12	Myaungmya ...	1,072	1,343	42	74	3	1	...	2	...	...	4	16
13	Ma-ubin ...	867	862	225	118	31	71	40	2	...	...	16	3
14	Pyapôn ...	910	1,014	145	65	12	3	1	...	...	...	21	8
	Tenasserim Division	*4,794*	*4,055*	*556*	*331*	*116*	*66*	*12*	*12*	*130*	...	*55*	*80*
15	Toungoo ...	1,258	992	128	78	37	25	1	5	36	...	16	12
16	Salween ...	44	34	...	3	...	...	...	...	...	...	...	...
17	Thatôn ...	1,631	1,036	182	71	45	5	4	5	73	...	7	...
18	Amherst ...	1,395	1,422	226	163	32	33	5	2	21	...	29	16
19	Tavoy ...	361	431	18	16	2	3	2	...	...	...	2	2
20	Mergui ...	105	140	2	..	...	...	...	...	...	...	1	...
	Magwe Division ...	*4,225*	*6,277*	*827*	*256*	*26*	*16*	*11*	*21*	*78*	...	*48*	*83*
21	Thayetmyo ...	767	1,266	58	41	7	8	1	...	...	...	3	21
22	Pakôkku ...	1,076	1,674	36	46	6	2	...	2	...	...	8	2
23	Minbu ...	955	1,336	59	45	2	...	2	...	...	...	16	3
24	Magwe ...	1,427	2,001	174	124	11	6	8	19	73	...	21	7
	Mandalay Division	*9,662*	*8,653*	*699*	*204*	*131*	*18*	*62*	*17*	*39*	...	*18*	*6*
25	Mandalay (including City).	465	1,997	56	13	1	1	1	1	...	...	13	2
	Mandalay City ...	*142*	*108*	...	...	...	...	...	...	...	...	...	...
26	Bhamo ...	4,309	6,143	99	107	18	11	10	7	17	...	5	...
27	Myitkyina ...	258	5	9	1	3	...	2	1	...	...	...	...
28	Katha ...	3,286	331	35	22	16	6	15	7	...	..	...	1
29	Ruby Mines ...	1,344	177	500	61	93	...	34	1	22	...	...	3
	Sagaing Division ...	*6,296*	*9,272*	*950*	*983*	*322*	*233*	*15*	*63*	*160*	...	*101*	*62*
30	Shwebo ...	2,879	2,440	229	298	57	88	14	35	35	...	38	19
31	Sagaing ...	1,151	4,263	70	497	5	131	...	4	..	...	11	21
32	Lower Chindwin	1,414	2,184	216	172	17	9	1	21	67	...	47	21
33	Upper Chindwin	852	385	435	16	243	5	...	3	58	...	5	1
	Meiktila Division ...	*8,277*	*6,831*	*853*	*405*	*48*	*88*	*16*	*17*	...	...	*48*	*81*
34	Kyauksè ...	364	616	63	39	5	2	3	6	...	...	6	6
35	Meiktila ...	907	706	89	86	16	16	1	1	...	...	9	2
36	Yamèthin ...	850	1,655	86	170	6	51	5	4	...	...	9	14
37	Myingyan ...	1,156	2,854	115	110	21	19	7	6	...	...	24	9
	Specially Administered Territories.	**11,813**	**14,918**	**2,780**	**2,941**	**1,119**	**1,272**	**278**	**23**	**78**	...	**71**	**189**
38	N. Shan States ...	6,820	9,795	1,955	1,226	1,015	373	232	...	73	...	24	100
39	S. Shan States ...	4,886	5,053	825	1,715	104	899	46	23	...	...	47	89
40	Pakôkku Hill Tracts.	..	...	...	...	...	...	...	...	...	...	...	..
41	Chin Hills ...	107	65	...	...	...	...	...	...	...	...	...	...

of Agricultural Rent Receivers (Actual workers only).

SUBSIDIARY OCCUPATIONS RETURNED.

Other Traders of all kinds.		Fishermen, Boat Owners and Boatmen.		Cattle Breeders, Owners, Dealers, Milkmen, and Butchers.		Clerks of all kinds (not Government).		School Masters, Teachers, and Lawyers.		Doctors.		Goldsmiths, Jewellers, Pearl Fishers, etc.		Other Occupations.		Serial No.
M.	F.	M.	F.	M.	F.	M.	F.	M.	F.	M.	F.	M.	F.	M.	F.	
14	15	16	17	18	19	20	21	22	23	24	25	26	27	28	29	
832	1,032	326	316	90	123	232	259	123	374	61	8	90	39	1,851	1,559	
528	661	274	160	52	113	146	74	92	29	50	6	68	22	1,156	1,188	
15	*86*	*40*	*11*	*16*	*8*	*13*	*2*	*2*	*6*	*8*	...	*7*	*8*	*52*	*46*	
10	32	36	10	16	...	11	1	1	6	...	...	6	3	31	32	1
...	...	...	...	...	...	...	...	...	...	...	...	...	...	...	..	2
5	3	4	1	...	3	2	1	1	...	3	...	1	...	8	3	3
...	1	...	...	...	...	...	...	...	...	...	...	...	...	13	11	4
80	*48*	*48*	*7*	*2*	*28*	*7*	*2*	*8*	*1*	*10*	*2*	*2*	...	*116*	*160*	
7	...	...	...	..	...	4	...	...	...	...	...	...	...	5	1	5
38	8	25	1	...	...	...	...	...	...	2	1	1	...	13	43	6
9	13	1	2	...	..	...	2	1	1	1	1	...	...	34	26	7
25	19	5	1	2	...	3	...	2	...	7	...	1	...	31	45	8
1	8	12	3	...	23	...	...	...	...	...	...	...	...	32	45	9
171	*112*	*69*	*48*	*5*	*14*	*5*	*1*	*14*	*1*	*18*	...	*24*	*6*	*206*	*260*	
27	29	3	13	1	13	4	...	8	1	3	...	23	5	27	66	10
64	10	10	7	3	1	...	...	...	...	10	..	...	1	35	140	11
7	35	3	2	1	...	...	...	...	...	...	...	...	...	24	18	12
12	5	31	17	...	...	...	...	4	...	...	...	...	...	91	20	13
61	33	12	4	...	...	1	1	2	...	5	...	1	...	29	16	14
84	*60*	*23*	*8*	*7*	*7*	*2*	...	...	...	*2*	...	*4*	...	*121*	*148*	
10	6	2	...	...	1	...	...	...	...	2	...	...	...	24	29	15
...	...	...	...	...	...	...	...	...	...	...	...	...	...	...	3	16
...	2	12	...	1	...	...	...	...	...	...	...	2	...	38	59	17
73	52	6	1	6	3	2	...	...	...	...	...	2	...	50	56	18
1	...	3	7	...	3	...	...	...	...	...	...	...	...	8	1	19
...	...	...	...	...	...	...	...	...	...	...	...	...	...	1	...	20
22	*9*	*8*	*9*	*1*	*1*	*6*	...	*1*	...	*8*	*1*	*5*	...	*128*	*166*	
...	...	3	...	...	...	...	...	...	...	...	...	...	...	44	12	21
7	6	...	3	...	...	2	...	...	...	...	...	1	...	12	31	22
10	2	3	1	...	1	...	...	...	...	...	...	...	...	26	38	23
5	1	2	5	1	...	4	...	1	...	3	1	4	...	41	85	24
74	*27*	*58*	*21*	*6*	*2*	*16*	*1*	*81*	*1*	*1*	*1*	*16*	...	*248*	*110*	
6	6	3	1	6	...	...	1	...	1	1	...	...	...	25	...	25
...	...	...	...	...	...	...	...	...	...	...	...	...	...	...	...	
2	3	5	...	...	...	1	...	5	...	...	...	...	...	36	86	26
...	...	...	...	...	...	...	...	...	...	...	...	...	...	4	...	27
3	3	...	...	...	2	...	...	1	...	...	1	...	...	...	2	28
63	15	50	20	...	...	15	...	25	...	...	...	15	...	183	22	29
58	*287*	*22*	*54*	*5*	*68*	*74*	*80*	*88*	*12*	*8*	*1*	*9*	*12*	*148*	*221*	
26	38	10	32	2	3	10	14	3	6	1	...	...	8	33	55	30
17	193	7	14	3	20	...	9	...	...	...	...	1	3	26	102	31
6	6	5	7	...	35	12	7	...	6	4	1	8	1	49	58	32
4	...	...	1	...	...	52	...	30	...	3	...	...	..	40	6	33
29	*182*	*21*	*7*	*10*	*5*	*28*	*88*	*8*	*8*	*5*	*1*	*2*	*1*	*148*	*77*	
6	8	3	...	4	...	9	9	5	4	1	1	2	...	19	3	34
...	15	18	...	2	...	10	24	...	3	2	...	...	1	31	24	35
8	68	...	...	...	1	3	2	2	1	...	...	...	...	53	29	36
15	41	...	7	4	4	1	3	1	...	2	...	...	...	40	21	37
804	871	52	156	88	10	86	185	81	845	11	2	22	17	695	871	
193	139	15	50	24	...	6	110	19	333	10	2	12	...	332	119	38
111	232	37	106	14	10	80	75	12	12	1	...	10	17	363	252	39
...	...	...	...	...	...	...	...	...	...	...	...	...	...	...	...	40
...	...	...	...	...	..	...	...	...	...	...	...	...	...	...	...	41

Serial No.	District or State.	Total number of Rent Payers (Actual Workers).		Number of Actual Workers who returned subsidiary occupation.		DETAILS OF									
						Rent Receivers.		Field Labourers.		General Labourers		Money Lenders and Grain Dealers.		Other Traders of all kinds.	
		M.	F.	M.	F.	M.	F.	M.	F.	M.	F.	M.	F.	M.	F.
	1	2	3	4	5	6	7	8	9	10	11	12	13	14	15
	Provincial Total ...	1,858,632	1,559,824	170,219	104,491	5,488	2,336	62,414	33,545	24,368	11,397	2,810	1,519	10,044	8,015
	Burma Proper ...	1,567,540	1,288,518	139,623	75,175	2,602	1,235	51,336	24,475	20,855	7,517	2,211	1,118	6,492	5,442
	Arakan Division ...	*139,155*	*106,545*	*4,571*	*2,492*	*59*	*42*	*1,341*	*424*	*545*	*423*	*56*	*63*	*297*	*485*
1	Akyab ...	76,622	56,613	2,119	1,187	16	28	804	150	228	202	37	50	29	227
2	Northern Arakan	7,072	6,853	33	...	...	...	...	...	...	...	...	...	13	...
3	Kyaukpyu ...	34,127	23,978	1,275	639	22	4	319	61	128	119	15	11	255	158
4	Sandoway ...	21,334	19,101	1,144	666	21	10	218	213	189	102	4	2	...	100
	Pegu Division ...	*206,094*	*158,705*	*16,063*	*6,476*	*82*	*45*	*6,970*	*2,329*	*1,417*	*849*	*228*	*124*	*368*	*682*
5	City of Rangoon	1,083	246	75	6	30	...	...	...	2	...	...	...	9	...
6	Hanthawaddy ...	39,160	22,594	2,491	750	12	15	673	139	252	211	63	10	56	127
7	Tharrawaddy ...	57,028	52,874	3,767	1,827	13	10	1,743	511	239	323	54	14	95	244
8	Pegu ...	44,336	25,014	5,310	1,756	12	18	2,347	754	378	208	79	17	161	176
9	Prome ...	64,487	57,977	4,420	2,137	15	2	2,207	925	546	107	32	83	47	85
	Irrawaddy Division	*245,900*	*191,724*	*13,829*	*9,560*	*292*	*89*	*5,788*	*3,819*	*1,921*	*647*	*144*	*98*	*363*	*963*
10	Bassein ...	53,120	38,923	979	908	20	21	207	37	244	6	32	38	75	175
11	Henzada ...	68,475	67,771	7,726	4,945	36	37	4,081	2,892	1,068	379	24	31	26	225
12	Myaungmya ...	52,330	39,014	1,873	958	20	5	527	144	176	12	51	20	46	293
13	Ma-ubin ...	43,226	29,719	1,824	2,346	188	26	648	746	318	250	5	4	42	101
14	Pyapôn ...	28,749	16,297	1,427	403	28	...	325	...	115	...	32	5	174	169
	Tenasserim Division	*215,470*	*160,097*	*18,226*	*7,980*	*63*	*31*	*5,707*	*2,438*	*4,873*	*592*	*196*	*131*	*782*	*704*
15	Toungoo ...	50,762	34,688	3,676	1,431	19	7	1,056	375	904	110	33	92	69	182
16	Salween ...	10,872	6,139	118	46	1	3	6	...	7	...	...	...	...	...
17	Thatôn ...	63,506	49,520	4,392	1,908	7	4	1,691	427	1,139	152	16	8	52	113
18	Amherst ...	52,455	40,057	8,598	3,927	18	15	2,476	1,552	2,688	325	134	31	566	364
19	Tavoy ...	20,778	15,939	1,140	615	18	2	438	83	127	5	10	...	9	45
20	Mergui ...	17,097	13,754	302	53	...	...	40	1	8	...	3	...	86	...
	Magwe Division ...	*235,499*	*201,260*	*15,744*	*7,347*	*53*	*27*	*5,472*	*1,664*	*3,288*	*627*	*243*	*25*	*723*	*801*
21	Thayetmyo ...	48,083	33,374	1,640	796	3	...	810	21	32	4	3	15	17	1
22	Pakôkku ...	75,492	69,858	2,649	1,587	1	...	979	38	447	51	15	2	160	159
23	Minbu ...	50,525	39,489	6,064	2,985	8	13	2,280	947	856	156	124	3	370	106
24	Magwe ...	61,399	58,539	5,391	1,979	41	14	1,403	658	1,953	416	101	5	176	35
	Mandalay Division	*117,747*	*100,591*	*16,605*	*8,950*	*523*	*303*	*3,639*	*2,847*	*3,336*	*887*	*139*	*125*	*1,882*	*628*
25	Mandalay (including City).	24,811	21,978	4,202	1,340	14	2	866	397	836	195	23	5	988	123
	Mandalay City ...	1,121	687	...	...	...	...	...	...	...	...	...	...	...	...
26	Bhamo ...	14,748	14,500	1,532	1,158	8	37	666	27	139	32	5	97	56	107
27	Myitkyina ...	23,873	21,549	1,644	495	...	...	17	12	201	85	4	...	91	23
28	Katha ...	38,029	33,323	5,777	3,852	463	182	1,729	1,822	1,235	381	106	23	125	185
29	Ruby Mines ...	16,286	9,241	3,350	2,105	38	82	361	89	925	144	1	...	122	190
	Sagaing Division ...	*202,433*	*196,497*	*37,843*	*21,295*	*650*	*281*	*17,015*	*10,477*	*3,472*	*2,285*	*868*	*182*	*1,214*	*723*
30	Shwebo ...	77,488	73,461	16,909	7,977	173	160	8,978	4,606	1,033	687	120	31	153	171
31	Sagaing ...	48,231	47,729	5,642	4,554	348	27	732	1,667	666	959	420	87	730	205
32	Lower Chindwin	48,822	46,091	8,171	6,907	18	38	3,408	3,875	861	583	306	31	294	187
33	Upper Chindwin	27,892	29,216	7,121	1,857	111	6	3,897	329	912	56	22	33	37	160
	Meiktila Division ...	*205,242*	*173,099*	*16,842*	*11,075*	*880*	*467*	*5,404*	*977*	*2,003*	*1,257*	*337*	*365*	*1,363*	*1,006*
34	Kyauksè ...	19,572	15,053	2,513	2,234	66	43	179	318	170	302	57	17	504	168
35	Meiktila ...	50,520	39,232	2,380	1,870	289	82	66	43	83	34	41	59	189	70
36	Yamèthin ...	56,939	36,119	5,668	2,519	508	203	2,385	37	456	309	180	22	406	329
37	Myingyan ...	78,211	82,695	6,281	4,452	17	139	2,774	579	1,294	612	59	267	264	439
	Specially Administered Territories.	291,092	271,306	30,596	29,316	2,886	1,101	11,078	9,070	3,513	3,880	599	406	3,552	2,578
38	N. Shan States ...	86,318	76,600	10,721	10,996	1,412	966	3,920	3,147	1,114	764	103	116	1,870	1,215
39	S. Shan States ...	169,665	158,088	19,864	18,320	1,474	135	7,158	5,923	2,399	3,116	496	290	1,682	1,358
40	Pakôkku Hill Tracts.	...	...	...	...	...	...	...	...	...	...	...	...	...	...
41	Chin Hills ...	35,109	36,618	11	...	...	...	...	...	...	...	...	...	...	...

of Agricultural Rent Payers (Actual workers only).

SUBSIDIARY OCCUPATIONS RETURNED.

Fishermen, Boat Owners and Boatmen.		Cartmen and Transport Workers.		Cattle Breeders, Owners and Dealers, and Milkmen and Butchers.		Village Watchmen.		Weavers.		Potters.		Oil Pressers.		Blacksmiths, Tinsmiths, Carpenters.		Other Occupations.		Serial No.
M.	F.	M.	F.	M.	F.	M.	F.	M.	F.	M.	F.	M.	F.	M.	F.	M.	F.	
16	17	18	19	20	21	22	23	24	25	26	27	28	29	30	31	32	33	
9,511	2,535	4,410	...	6,737	2,135	1,243	909	1,509	12,357	754	1,246	2,259	555	3,949	1,064	34,723	26,878	
8,699	2,306	3,916	...	5,119	1,530	930	295	1,085	6,714	632	1,055	1,717	362	2,852	728	31,177	22,403	
835	*133*	...	...	*226*	*42*	*31*	*22*	*15*	*39*	*45*	*21*	*19*	*20*	*81*	*53*	*1,021*	*725*	
298	61	...	...	111	15	18	12	13	1	33	8	15	8	59	42	458	383	1
11	...	...	...	4	...	...	...	...	...	...	...	...	...	...	...	5	...	2
171	26	...	...	111	27	12	10	2	38	12	13	3	11	20	11	205	150	3
355	46	...	...	...	...	1	...	...	...	...	...	1	1	2	...	353	192	4
941	*474*	*944*	...	*117*	*10*	*47*	*7*	*49*	*534*	*101*	*61*	*77*	*2*	*229*	*9*	*4,493*	*1,400*	
...	...	...	...	...	...	1	...	...	...	...	...	...	...	1	...	32	6	5
231	31	237	...	34	...	5	...	13	67	3	2	...	...	39	3	873	145	6
286	249	157	...	4	...	9	3	21	105	48	15	14	2	51	5	1,033	346	7
292	28	233	...	76	8	8	...	1	33	5	5	45	...	50	1	1,623	508	8
132	166	317	...	3	2	24	4	14	329	45	39	18	...	88	...	932	395	9
1,805	*533*	*381*	...	*140*	*36*	*50*	*20*	*114*	*501*	*43*	*35*	*20*	*30*	*475*	*32*	*2,293*	*2,757*	
173	40	73	...	12	10	3	12	7	99	...	1	...	...	18	2	115	467	10
503	233	283	...	13	21	11	4	25	339	4	34	19	30	361	15	1,272	705	11
529	137	25	...	61	4	2	...	36	29	39	...	1	...	51	11	309	303	12
257	98	...	...	...	...	...	...	19	25	...	...	...	...	24	3	323	1,093	13
343	25	...	...	54	1	34	4	27	9	...	...	...	...	21	1	274	189	14
1,334	*164*	*525*	...	*860*	*117*	*54*	*21*	*104*	*934*	*26*	*76*	*12*	*16*	*299*	*6*	*3,391*	*2,750*	
383	76	132	...	41	6	1	...	24	38	13	23	3	16	52	...	946	506	15
...	...	...	...	...	1	...	...	...	...	...	...	...	...	...	...	104	42	16
237	15	223	...	99	72	3	...	19	580	2	34	1	...	62	...	841	503	17
510	36	147	...	624	18	48	2	57	130	10	19	7	...	169	3	1,144	1,432	18
158	35	23	...	96	20	2	19	4	186	1	...	...	...	1	3	253	222	19
46	2	...	...	...	...	...	...	...	...	...	...	1	...	15	...	103	45	20
687	*129*	*449*	...	*54*	*426*	*19*	...	*255*	*2137*	*58*	*86*	*343*	*19*	*303*	*1*	*3,797*	*1,905*	
115	1	118	...	2	...	...	...	1	102	...	...	8	...	8	...	523	652	21
120	16	134	...	2	...	6	...	85	1,133	2	5	...	...	103	...	595	183	22
308	74	85	...	38	421	10	...	73	650	5	14	326	14	80	1	1,501	586	23
144	38	112	..	12	5	3	...	96	252	51	67	9	5	112	...	1,178	484	24
948	*207*	*624*	...	*1,162*	*172*	*447*	*24*	*42*	*409*	*79*	*42*	*257*	*11*	*337*	*5*	*3,590*	*3,840*	
315	47	165	...	721	24	3	3	11	77	...	12	26	9	61	4	173	442	25
...	...	...	...	...	...	...	...	...	...	...	...	...	...	...	...	...	...	
158	...	273	...	31	17	1	...	3	48	5	6	15	...	15	...	157	787	26
79	8	...	...	10	...	6	1	...	10	6	...	7	...	43	...	1,180	356	27
345	148	115	...	340	104	323	...	15	109	68	24	205	2	110	1	598	871	28
51	4	71	...	60	27	114	20	13	165	..	...	4	..	108	...	1,482	1,384	29
1,604	*341*	*590*	...	*724*	*424*	*98*	*145*	*215*	*1,127*	*141*	*471*	*603*	*215*	*576*	*152*	*10,073*	*4,522*	
120	92	182	...	483	212	60	86	40	217	58	208	44	51	139	81	5,326	1,375	30
447	151	103	...	58	35	21	20	28	107	14	6	417	59	47	53	1,611	1,178	31
506	63	78	...	161	174	9	37	136	346	69	246	131	85	284	17	1,910	1,225	32
531	35	227	...	22	3	8	2	11	457	...	11	11	20	106	1	1,226	744	33
545	*325*	*403*	...	*1,836*	*303*	*184*	*56*	*291*	*1,033*	*139*	*263*	*386*	*49*	*552*	*470*	*2,519*	*4,504*	
33	16	...	...	288	8	36	10	142	231	19	201	38	19	239	231	742	670	34
126	114	...	...	117	71	85	43	15	32	15	21	77	23	81	44	1,196	1,234	35
53	118	186	...	895	84	27	1	65	166	4	3	87	...	104	2	312	1,245	36
333	77	217	...	536	140	36	2	69	604	101	38	184	7	128	193	269	1,355	37
812	229	494	...	1,618	605	313	614	424	5,643	122	191	542	193	1,097	336	3,546	4,475	
274	20	102	...	154	456	199	507	162	1,989	6	22	111	86	364	176	930	1,532	38
538	209	392	...	1,464	149	114	107	262	3,654	116	169	431	107	733	160	2,605	2,943	39
...	...	...	...	...	...	...	...	...	...	...	...	...	...	...	...	...	...	40
...	...	...	...	...	...	...	...	...	...	...	...	...	...	...	...	11	...	41

IMPERIAL TABLE XV.—B-III.—*Subsidiary Occupations*

Serial No.	District or State.	Total number of Agricultural Labourers (Actual Workers).		Number of Actual Workers who returned subsidiary occupations.		DETAILS OF							
						Rent Receivers.		Rent Payers.		General Labourers.		Rice Pounders, and Rice Mill Coolies.	
		M.	F.	M.	F.	M.	F.	M.	F.	M.	F.	M.	F.
	1	2	3	4	5	6	7	8	9	10	11	12	13
	Provincial Total ...	**516,415**	**395,944**	**45,922**	**26,915**	**1,052**	**450**	**5,989**	**4,069**	**6.654**	**4,149**	**10,895**	**2,872**
	Burma Proper ...	**502,866**	**381,997**	**44,040**	**26,013**	**835**	**422**	**5,439**	**3,939**	**6,454**	**4,132**	**10,803**	**2,811**
	Arakan Division ...	***46,029***	***30,171***	***1,674***	***1,013***	***4***	***8***	***142***	***226***	***24***	***58***	***498***	***140***
1	Akyab ...	40,787	24,701	1,529	764	2	6	128	205	24	53	498	107
2	Northern Arakan	1	1	...	...	...	...	...	...	...	...	...	...
3	Kyaukpyu ...	4,246	4,319	128	191	2	2	14	19	...	5	...	32
4	Sandoway ...	995	1,150	17	58	...	...	...	2	...	...	...	1
	Pegu Division ...	***152,290***	***95,157***	***13,681***	***6,034***	***11***	***7***	***705***	***1,546***	***2,001***	***741***	***5,316***	***790***
5	City of Rangoon	265	31	4	...	...	...	...	...	...	...	...	...
6	Hanthawaddy ...	58,697	22,410	4,114	1,038	5	...	107	232	209	127	1,820	216
7	Tharrawaddy ...	36,728	36,692	2,810	2,102	...	7	182	445	308	183	1,214	299
8	Pegu ...	44,142	20,881	5,872	2,108	2	...	320	718	1,379	312	2,106	220
9	Prome ...	12,458	15,143	881	786	4	...	96	151	105	119	175	55
	Irrawaddy Division	***150,197***	***124,786***	***9,473***	***7,897***	***161***	***47***	***1,446***	***1,062***	***1,200***	***1,889***	***2,291***	***822***
10	Bassein ...	38,426	37,530	908	1,078	7	7	77	37	27	...	334	297
11	Henzada ...	38,687	42,648	4,181	3,859	42	17	1,015	409	1,068	1,534	834	353
12	Myaungmya ...	24,471	14,333	745	524	...	...	15	95	7	145	209	...
13	Ma-ubin ...	18,673	18,000	1,450	1,459	108	23	127	521	35	200	501	110
14	Pyapôn ...	29,940	12,275	2,189	477	4	...	212	...	63	10	413	62
	Tenasserim Division	***71,242***	***39,441***	***9,178***	***8,170***	***13***	***5***	***856***	***328***	***1,663***	***357***	***2,495***	***849***
15	Toungoo ...	16,849	13,607	1,659	1,001	2	...	294	214	419	203	359	31
16	Salween ...	940	278	12	...	...	...	1	...	2	...	...	...
17	Thatôn ...	29,951	12,650	3,227	1,026	2	...	253	38	832	1	601	6
18	Amherst ...	18,406	9,623	3,679	1,080	9	5	260	75	292	146	1,335	312
19	Tavoy ...	2,808	1,375	576	60	...	...	47	1	117	7	200	...
20	Mergui ...	2,288	1,908	25	3	...	...	1	...	1	...	...	...
	Magwe Division ...	***14,916***	***26,237***	***517***	***871***	***8***	***4***	***13***	***4***	***30***	***133***	***15***	***9***
21	Thayetmyo ...	2,617	6,145	59	54	2	...	5	...	...	...	...	2
22	Pakôkku ...	3,013	4,118	96	119	...	...	1	...	10	32	1	...
23	Minbu ...	3,171	5,276	240	449	...	1	5	1	7	6	14	7
24	Magwe ...	6,115	10,698	122	249	1	3	2	3	13	95	...	...
	Mandalay Division ...	***17,976***	***15,896***	***2,871***	***1,139***	***131***	***47***	***1,124***	***63***	***400***	***190***	***29***	***108***
25	Mandalay (including City).	7,979	5,420	502	457	2	3	20	16	262	176	25	68
	Mandalay City ...	*301*	*871*	...	...	...	...	...	...	...	...	...	...
26	Bhamo ...	2,995	3,516	166	303	10	20	19	19	7	...	1	2
27	Myitkyina ...	798	926	169	47	3	...	5	4	29	5	...	...
28	Katha ...	3,988	4,784	1,635	155	100	24	1,064	20	40	1	...	16
29	Ruby Mines ...	2,216	1,250	399	177	16	...	16	4	62	8	3	17
	Sagaing Division ...	***20,989***	***27,392***	***3,247***	***3,378***	***197***	***97***	***638***	***558***	***418***	***646***	***39***	***286***
30	Shwebo ...	5,300	6,485	873	1,020	45	44	108	167	102	208	17	67
31	Sagaing ...	8,401	11,228	749	1,036	6	15	115	304	154	274	11	76
32	Lower Chindwin	3,993	5,268	549	921	...	33	107	60	63	160	2	26
33	Upper Chindwin	3,293	4,411	1,076	401	146	5	308	27	99	4	9	117
	Meiktila Division ...	***29,227***	***22,917***	***3,399***	***3,011***	***315***	***207***	***515***	***152***	***718***	***118***	***121***	***312***
34	Kyauksè ...	6,627	5,627	1,039	1,626	233	126	85	49	31	...	45	246
35	Meiktila ...	9,253	4,359	1,358	512	62	46	198	57	481	20	22	24
36	Yamèthin ...	8,476	5,539	644	482	20	29	174	26	126	65	44	24
37	Myingyan ...	4,871	7,392	358	391	...	6	58	20	80	33	10	18
	Specially Administered Territories.	**13,549**	**13,947**	**1,882**	**902**	**217**	**28**	**550**	**130**	**200**	**17**	**92**	**61**
38	N. Shan States ...	3,865	1,722	697	165	43	23	358	21	76	10	37	6
39	S. Shan States ...	9,678	12,224	1,185	737	174	5	192	109	124	7	55	55
40	Pakôkku Hill Tracts.	...	...	...	...	...	...	...	...	...	...	...	...
41	Chin Hills ...	6	1	...	...	...	...	...	...	...	...	...	...

of Agricultural Labourers (Actual workers only).

SUBSIDIARY OCCUPATIONS RETURNED.

Other Traders of all kinds.		Fishermen, Boat Owners, and Boatmen.		Cartmen and Transport Workers.		Cattle Breeders, Owners and Dealers, and Milkmen and Butchers.		Village Watchmen.		Weavers.		Potters.		Blacksmiths, Tinsmiths, Carpenters.		Other Occupations.		Serial No.
M.	F.	M.	F.	M.	F.	M.	F.	M.	F.	M.	F.	M.	F.	M.	F.	M.	F.	
14	15	16	17	18	19	20	21	22	23	24	25	26	27	28	29	30	31	
1,541	3,614	7,209	1,579	1,465	...	1,029	775	190	73	814	1,897	159	194	989	313	8,436	6,930	
1,424	3,538	7,150	1,517	1,444	...	955	723	167	53	295	1,733	151	188	944	310	7,979	6,647	
33	*60*	*380*	*62*	...	...	*56*	*38*	*25*	*7*	*1*	*11*	*26*	*9*	*80*	*35*	*405*	*359*	
26	29	342	41	...	...	46	32	23	5	1	7	25	8	76	31	338	240	1
...	...	...	...	...	...	...	...	...	...	..	...	...	...	...	..	...	...	2
7	28	33	20	...	...	10	5	2	2	...	4	1	1	4	4	55	69	3
...	3	5	1	...	...	...	1	...	...	...	...	...	...	...	...	12	50	4
538	*982*	*2,088*	*372*	*626*	...	*167*	*25*	*26*	...	*80*	*848*	*23*	*39*	*278*	*17*	*1,878*	*1,172*	
2	...	2	...	...	...	...	...	...	...	...	...	...	...	...	...	...	...	5
179	234	815	67	127	...	113	...	10	...	13	41	5	2	114	2	597	117	6
181	584	344	142	85	...	1	6	4	...	13	107	10	28	81	14	387	287	7
88	72	891	101	241	...	51	2	8	...	4	66	8	2	78	1	696	614	8
88	92	36	62	173	...	2	17	4	...	...	129	...	7	...	...	198	154	9
259	*962*	*2,347*	*597*	*195*	...	*96*	*48*	*11*	*4*	*114*	*868*	*22*	*28*	*197*	*26*	*1,134*	*1,544*	
51	197	116	142	...	...	26	15	...	3	12	93	1	1	14	24	243	262	10
98	259	559	284	195	...	1	20	1	...	31	263	10	12	57	2	270	706	11
13	75	267	54	...	...	1	1	1	...	21	7	11	...	31	...	169	147	12
17	225	418	78	...	...	...	...	...	...	12	1	...	15	31	...	201	286	13
80	206	987	39	...	...	68	12	9	1	38	4	...	...	64	...	251	143	14
209	*585*	*1,331*	*105*	*198*	...	*244*	*66*	*23*	*2*	*87*	*508*	*24*	*82*	*246*	*2*	*1,789*	*886*	
95	200	93	35	113	...	5	37	...	...	24	41	7	10	41	...	207	230	15
...	...	...	...	...	...	...	...	...	...	...	...	...	...	...	...	9	...	16
49	226	457	25	85	...	15	6	1	...	10	351	2	11	70	...	850	362	17
65	109	641	37	...	...	202	23	22	2	37	80	15	3	135	...	666	288	18
...	...	130	8	...	..	22	...	...	...	16	31	...	8	...	2	44	3	19
...	...	10	...	...	...	...	...	...	...	...	...	...	...	...	...	13	3	20
41	*111*	*62*	*28*	...	...	*6*	*16*	...	...	*11*	*120*	*4*	*8*	*32*	*4*	*800*	*434*	
...	5	19	2	...	...	...	...	...	...	2	1	...	...	...	...	31	44	21
11	19	10	1	...	...	...	...	...	...	2	49	...	...	3	...	58	18	22
14	58	29	15	...	...	6	16	...	...	5	59	1	5	23	4	136	277	23
16	29	4	10	...	...	...	...	...	...	2	11	3	3	6	...	75	95	24
60	*82*	*411*	*29*	...	...	*72*	*16*	*3*	*25*	*2*	*61*	...	*12*	*30*	...	*609*	*511*	
1	32	72	13	...	...	2	12	...	11	2	6	...	7	11	...	105	113	25
...	...	...	...	...	...	...	...	...	...	...	...	...	...	...	...	...	...	
1	...	22	4	...	...	...	1	...	...	...	18	...	...	3	...	103	239	26
3	...	37	4	...	...	14	3	...	4	...	..	...	...	4	...	74	27	27
52	26	262	7	...	...	51	...	...	...	...	7	...	2	11	...	55	52	28
3	24	18	1	...	...	5	...	3	10	...	30	...	3	1	...	272	80	29
117	*363*	*413*	*205*	*170*	...	*120*	*98*	*3*	*5*	*24*	*150*	*45*	*54*	*43*	*85*	*1,020*	*881*	
54	91	26	52	113	...	39	33	1	...	...	51	18	20	8	10	342	277	30
51	64	70	20	...	...	13	21	1	5	7	24	7	20	20	...	294	213	31
11	188	138	117	...	...	64	44	...	..	2	1	...	14	11	65	151	213	32
1	20	179	16	57	...	4	...	1	...	15	74	20	...	4	10	233	128	33
167	*448*	*118*	*119*	*255*	...	*194*	*416*	*76*	*10*	*26*	*177*	*7*	*6*	*43*	*141*	*844*	*910*	
114	371	64	11	45	...	143	346	1	...	...	41	...	...	17	124	261	312	34
39	49	20	43	136	...	29	66	65	10	18	...	5	4	5	7	278	186	35
7	9	11	47	29	...	2	2	9	...	7	36	...	...	1	8	214	236	36
7	14	23	18	45	...	20	2	1	...	1	100	2	2	20	2	91	176	37
117	76	59	62	21	...	74	52	23	20	19	164	8	6	45	3	457	283	
4	10	14	10	21	...	37	...	2	3	9	39	...	5	31	...	65	38	38
113	66	45	52	...	...	37	52	21	17	10	125	8	1	14	3	392	245	39
...	...	...	...	...	...	...	...	...	...	...	...	...	...	...	...	...	...	40
...	...	...	...	...	...	...	...	...	...	...	...	...	...	...	...	...	...	41

IMPERIAL TABLE XV.

Occupation or Means of Livelihood.

PART D.—DISTRIBUTION BY RELIGION.

NOTE 1.—The discrepancies between this table and Imperial Table VI are due to the exclusion of the populations of the Pakôkku Hill Tracts and of the estimated areas of Kokang, West Maunglûn, and the Brè Tracts of Karenni from the occupational census.

Class.	Sub-class.	Order and Group. Serial No.	Order and Group. Description.	Total number of workers and dependents.	Distribution by Religion. Buddhist.	Animist.	Hindu.	Mahomedan.	Christian.	Others.
1	2	3	4	5	6	7	8	9	10	11
			All Industries	12,039,083	10,384,544	625,539	389,528	420,769	210,077	8,626
A	...	...	Production of raw materials	8,639,688	7,658,157	535,186	98,224	200,022	147,796	303
	I	...	**Exploitation of the surface of the earth** ...	8,624,395	7,647,588	535,186	94,475	199,065	147,778	303
	II	...	**Extraction of Minerals**	15,293	10,569	...	3,749	957	18	...
B	...	...	Preparation and supply of material substances ...	2,403,804	1,998,892	70,343	156,031	155,541	20,251	2,746
	III	...	**Industry**	806,431	682,304	21,089	58,934	39,284	4,429	391
	IV	...	**Transport**	393,652	285,310	7,507	53,922	38,088	7,785	1,040
	V	...	**Trade**	1,203,721	1,031,278	41,747	43,175	78,169	8,037	1,315
C	...	...	Public Administration and Liberal Arts	445,846	360,502	6,818	25,412	21,400	26,919	4,795
	VI	...	**Public Force**	79,495	45,730	1,261	12,249	9,976	5,918	4,361
	VII	...	**Public Administration**	103,108	81,989	3,263	7,661	3,690	6,365	140
	VIII	...	**Professions and Liberal Arts**	256,276	228,559	2,207	4,753	6,845	13,643	269
	IX	...	**Persons living on their income**	6,967	4,224	87	749	889	993	25
D	...	...	Miscellaneous	549,745	366,993	13,192	109,861	43,803	15,111	782
	X	...	**Domestic Service**	85,771	36,613	2,208	27,438	12,862	6,387	263
	XI	...	**Insufficiently described occupations**	429,399	301,323	9,776	81,061	28,520	8,262	457
	XII	...	**Unproductive**	34,575	29,057	1,208	1,362	2,424	462	62
A.—Production of Raw Materials.	I.—Exploitation of the Surface of the Earth.	i	**Pasture and Agriculture**	8,472,391	7,506,898	532,867	91,486	193,507	147,362	271
		i(a)	**Ordinary Cultivation**	8,083,712	7,158,313	517,926	79,720	185,697	141,820	236
		1	Income from Rent of Agricultural Land ...	220,485	185,133	22,596	2,073	7,101	3,527	55
		2	Ordinary Cultivators	6,215,154	5,434,526	476,410	42,845	143,136	118,066	171
			(a) Cultivating their own land	3,810,610	3,396,978	238,024	20,169	91,452	63,831	156
			(b) Tenants	1,599,331	1,471,428	33,837	21,669	49,340	23,042	15
			(c) *Taungya* Cultivators	805,213	566,120	204,549	1,007	2,344	31,193	...
		3	Agents, Managers of landed estates, clerks, rent collectors, etc.	123	80	2	10	6	25	...
		4	Farm servants and field labourers	1,647,950	1,538,574	18,918	34,792	35,454	20,202	10
		i(b)	**Growers of special products and market gardening.**	238,511	216,857	9,282	5,787	2,828	3,741	16
		5	Tea, coffee, cinchona, indigo, and rubber plantations.	6,217	2,267	20	3,653	137	127	13
		6	Fruit, flower, vegetable, betel, vine, areca nut, etc., growers.	232,294	214,590	9,262	2,134	2,691	3,614	3
		i(c)	**Forestry**	42,765	40,699	1,241	158	192	474	1
		7	Forest officers, rangers, guards, etc.	5,116	4,554	70	54	112	325	1
		8	Wood cutters, firewood, lac, cutch and rubber collectors, and charcoal burners.	37,649	36,145	1,171	104	80	149	...
		i(d)	**Raising of farm stock**	105,944	89,715	4,399	5,819	4,667	1,326	18
		9	Cattle and buffalo breeders and keepers ...	2,645	1,073	464	991	93	23	1
		10	Sheep, goat, and pig breeders	12,232	10,067	1,679	59	13	412	2
		11	Breeders of other animals (horses, mules, etc.)	35	35	...	...	...	...	...
		12	Herdsmen, shepherds, goatherds, etc. ...	91,032	78,540	2,256	4,769	4,561	891	15
		i(c) 13	**Raising of small animals** (Birds, bees, silk-worms, etc.)	1,459	1,314	19	2	123	1	...
		ii	**Fishing and hunting**	152,004	140,690	2,319	2,989	5,558	416	32
		14	Fishing	151,601	140,342	2,311	2,989	5,555	373	31
		15	Hunting	403	348	8	...	3	43	1
	II.—Extraction of Minerals.	iii	**Mines**	8,173	3,750	...	3,567	846	10	...
		16	Coal mines and petroleum wells ...	3,319	1,104	...	1,589	623	3	...
		17	Mines and metallic minerals (gold, iron, etc.)	4,854	2,646	...	1,978	223	7	...
		iv (18)	**Quarries and hard rocks**—Other minerals (jade, rubies, limestone, etc.)	3,896	3,605	...	182	102	7	...
		v	**Salt, etc.**	3,224	3,214	...	...	9	1	...
		19	Rock, sea and marsh, salt	3,224	3,214	...	...	9	1	...
		20	Extraction of saltpetre, alum, and other substances soluble in water.	...	...	...	...	...	...	...

of Occupations by Religion.

Class.	Sub-class.	Order and Group. Serial No.	Order and Group. Description.	Total number of workers and dependents.	Distribution by Religion. Buddhist.	Animist.	Hindu.	Mahomedan.	Christian.	Others.
1	2	3	4	5	6	7	8	9	10	11
B.—Preparation and Supply of Material Substances.	III.—Industry.	vi	**Textiles**	155,050	150,811	581	2,377	1,221	60	...
		21	Cotton ginning, cleaning and pressing ...	2,282	584	9	1,376	313	...	...
		22	Cotton spinning, sizing and weaving ...	132,737	131,385	556	209	540	47	...
		23	Jute spinning, pressing and weaving ...	...	...	...	...	...	...	...
		24	Rope, twine and string	1,241	298	9	701	229	4	...
		25	Other fibres (cocoanut, aloes, flax, hemp, straw, etc.)	15	5	...	...	10	...	...
		26	Wool carders and spinners, weavers of woollen blankets, carpets, etc.	46	13	...	29	...	4	...
		27	Silk spinners and weavers	18,621	18,486	7	48	77	3	...
		28	Hair, camel and horse hair, bristles work, brush makers, etc.	...	...	...	...	...	...	...
		29	Persons occupied with feathers	...	...	...	...	...	...	...
		30	Dyeing, bleaching, printing, preparation and sponging of textiles.	62	...	...	13	49	...	...
		31	Other (lace, crape, embroideries, fringes, etc.) and insufficiently described textile industries.	46	40	...	1	3	2	...
		vii	**Hides, skins and hard materials from the animal kingdom.**	624	566	29	20	5	4	...
		32	Tanners, curriers, leather dressers, leather dyers, etc.	161	140	8	4	5	4	...
		33	Makers of leather articles, such as trunks, water bags, etc.	207	191	16	...	...	...	...
		34	Furriers	5	...	...	5	...	...	...
		35	Bone, ivory, horn, shell, etc., workers ...	251	235	5	11	...	...	...
		viii	**Wood**	191,686	178,553	6,856	2,732	2,957	534	54
		36	Sawyers, carpenters, turners and joiners, etc.	143,719	131,538	6,299	2,636	2,731	466	49
		37	Basket makers and other industries of woody material, including leaves.	47,967	47,015	557	96	226	68	5
		ix	**Metals**	34,912	30,420	772	2,402	1,207	96	15
		38	Forging and rolling of iron and other metals	483	199	...	194	90	...	...
		39	Plough and agricultural implement makers...	3	3	...	...	...	...	...
		40	Makers of arms, guns, etc.	67	15	...	35	...	17	...
		41	Other workers in iron and makers of implements and tools, principally or exclusively of iron.	29,040	25,560	743	1,995	680	47	15
		42	Workers in brass, copper and bell metal ...	554	528	...	22	4	...	...
		43	Workers in other metals (tin, zinc, lead, quick-silver, etc.).	4,759	4,115	29	156	427	32	...
		44	Workers in mints, die-sinkers, etc.	6	...	...	...	6	...	...
		x	**Ceramics**	18,821	16,193	...	2,107	490	30	1
		45	Makers of glass and crystal ware	192	189	...	...	...	3	...
		46	Makers of porcelain	12	8	...	...	3	1	...
		47	Potters and earthen pipe and bowl makers	15,323	14,990	...	233	88	11	1
		48	Brick and tile makers	3,242	954	...	1,874	399	15	...
		49	Others (mosaic, talc, mica, alabaster, etc., workers).	52	52	...	...	...	...	...
		xi	**Chemical products properly so called and analogous.**	10,560	2,480	2	5,595	2,406	75	2
		50	Manufacture of matches and explosive materials.	1	1	...	...	...	...	...
		51	Manufacture of aerated and mineral waters	132	...	...	16	115	1	...
		52	Manufacture of dyes, paint and ink ...	4	...	...	...	1	3	...
		53	Manufacture and refining of vegetable and mineral oils.	9,110	1,440	...	5,420	2,198	50	2
		54	Manufacture of paper, card board and *papier maché*.	168	127	...	41	...	...	...
		55	Others (soap, candles, lac, cutch, perfumes and miscellaneous drugs).	1,145	912	2	118	92	21	...
		xii	**Food industries**	178,255	147,973	1,980	14,923	12,597	749	33
		56	Rice pounders and huskers and flour grinders	110,623	85,278	1,500	14,075	9,204	564	2
		57	Bakers and biscuit makers	1,234	167	56	163	826	20	2
		58	Grain parchers, etc.	94	68	...	26	...	...	...
		59	Butchers	6,897	4,471	96	155	2,068	103	4
		60	Fish curers	20	7	13	...	...	...	...
		61	Butter, cheese and ghee makers	...	...	...	...	...	...	...
		62	Makers of sugar, molasses and *gur*	8,298	8,287	...	11	...	...	...
		63	Sweetmeat makers, preparers of jams and condiments, etc.	2,113	1,720	40	194	132	2	25
		64	Brewers and distillers	653	640	...	...	13	...	...
		65	Toddy drawers	35,152	34,966	20	98	59	9	...
		66	Manufacturers of tobacco, opium and *ganja*	13,171	12,369	255	201	295	51	...

Class.	Sub-class.	ORDER AND GROUP.		Total number of workers and dependents.	DISTRIBUTION BY RELIGION.					
		Serial No.	Description.		Buddhist.	Animist.	Hindu.	Mahomedan.	Christian.	Others.
1	2	3	4	5	6	7	8	9	10	11
B.—PREPARATION AND SUPPLY OF MATERIAL SUBSTANCES.	III.—INDUSTRY—concluded.	**xiii**	**Industries of dress and the toilet ... ...**	**116,056**	**77,660**	**9,907**	**16,042**	**11,377**	**946**	**124**
		67	Hat, cap and turban makers	364	191	110	38	18	7	...
		68	Tailors, milliners, dressmakers and darners, embroiderers on linen.	60,870	41,810	8,339	2,387	7,537	712	85
		69	Shoe, boot and sandal makers	11,972	9,313	972	1,422	217	34	14
		70	Other industries pertaining to dress, gloves, socks, gaiters, belts, buttons, umbrellas, canes, etc.	1,607	1,487	4	22	93	1	...
		71	Washing, cleaning and dyeing	23,742	12,356	266	9,326	1,629	159	6
		72	Barbers, hairdressers and wigmakers	4,877	187	191	2,658	1,799	23	19
		73	Other industries connected with the toilet (tattooers, shampooers, bath houses, etc.).	12,624	12,316	25	189	84	10	...
		xiv	**Furniture industries ... ...**	**1,862**	**462**	**81**	**57**	**1,245**	**16**	**1**
		74	Cabinet makers, carriage painters, etc. ...	1,820	420	81	57	1,245	16	1
		75	Upholsterers, tent makers, etc.	42	42	...	...	...	...	...
		xv	**Building industries .. ..**	**24,257**	**19,267**	**148**	**1,766**	**2,866**	**189**	**21**
		76	Lime burners, cement workers	1,167	1,158	...	9	...	...	...
		77	Excavators, plinth builders and well-sinkers ...	269	75	1	127	...	66	...
		78	Stone and marble workers, masons and brick-layers, *pucca* house-builders.	13,003	9,765	97	1,230	1,876	15	20
		79	Others (thatchers, building contractors, house painters, tilers, plumbers, lock-smiths etc.).	9,818	8,269	50	400	990	108	1
		xvi	**Construction of means of transport ... ...**	**2,187**	**1,601**	**51**	**312**	**148**	**75**	...
		80	Cart, carriage, *palki*, etc., makers and wheel-wrights.	1,198	954	46	29	111	58	...
		81	Saddlers, harness makers, whip and lash makers	144	126	...	10	7	1	...
		82	Ship and boat builders	845	521	5	273	30	16	...
		xvii (83)	**Production and transmission of physical forces** (Gas works, electric light and ice factories).	**180**	**57**	...	**2**	**9**	**108**	**4**
		xviii	**Industries of luxury and those pertaining to literature and the arts and sciences.**	**58,878**	**51,117**	**608**	**3,993**	**1,791**	**1,318**	**51**
		84	Printers, lithographers, engravers, etc. ...	2,981	929	17	1,114	230	684	7
		85	Newspaper and magazine managers and editors, journalists, etc.	114	21	1	23	...	67	2
		86	Bookbinders and stitchers, envelope makers, etc.	861	69	2	314	409	67	...
		87	Makers of musical instruments	307	2	275	7	...	23	...
		88	Makers of watches and clocks and optical, photographic and surgical instruments.	1,045	627	13	52	298	55	...
		89	Workers in precious stones and metals, enamellers, imitation jewellery makers, gilders, etc.	50,232	46,832	256	2,358	568	188	30
		90	Makers of bangles, rosaries, bead and other necklaces, spangles, lingams and sacred threads.	1,297	1,276	13	...	1	7	...
		91	Toy, kite, cage, fishing tackle, etc., makers, taxidermists, etc.	1,566	1,189	1	25	225	123	3
		92	Others, including managers, persons other than performers employed in theatres and other places of public entertainment, employés of public societies, race-course service, huntsmen, etc.	475	172	30	100	60	104	9
		xix (93)	**Industries concerned with refuse matter** (sweepers, scavengers, dust and sweeping contractors).	**13,103**	**5,144**	**74**	**6,606**	**965**	**229**	**85**
	IV.—TRANSPORT.	**xx**	**Transport by water ... ...**	**131,071**	**99,767**	**1,690**	**7,233**	**19,918**	**2,395**	**68**
		94	Harbour works, dockyards and pilots ...	695	129	...	83	358	124	1
		95	Shipowners and their employés, ship brokers, ships' officers, engineers, mariners and firemen.	11,539	1,412	585	1,877	5,644	2,015	6
		96	Persons employed on the maintenance of streams, rivers and canals (including construction).	66	...	...	...	63	3	...
		97	Boat-owners, boatmen and towmen	118,771	98,226	1,105	5,273	13,853	253	61
		xxi	**Transport by road ... ...**	**230,168**	**180,014**	**5,586**	**29,131**	**13,720**	**1,369**	**348**
		98	Persons employed on the construction and maintenance of roads and bridges.	91,541	62,893	3,347	20,105	4,348	799	49
		99	Cart-owners and drivers, coachmen, stable boys, tramway, mail, carriage, etc., managers and employés (excluding private servants).	132,099	112,355	2,142	8,908	8,194	346	154
		100	*Palki*, etc., bearers and owners	149	9	...	...	...	...	140
		101	Pack elephant, camel, mule, ass and bullock owners and drivers.	6,304	4,689	97	118	1,174	221	5
		102	Porters and messengers	75	68	...	...	4	3	...
		xxii	**Transport by rail ... ...**	**27,686**	**3,777**	**209**	**16,009**	**3,944**	**3,139**	**608**
		103	Railway employés of all kinds other than construction coolies	22,633	3,093	194	12,837	3,349	2,696	464
		104	Labourers employed on railway construction...	5,053	684	15	3,172	595	443	144
		xxiii (105)	**Post office, Telegraph and Telephone services**	**4,727**	**1,752**	**22**	**1,549**	**506**	**882**	**16**

of Occupations by Religion.

Class.	Sub-class.	Order and Group.		Total number of workers and dependents.	Distribution by Religion.					
		Serial No.	Description.		Buddhist.	Animist.	Hindu.	Mahomedan.	Christian.	Others.
1	2	3	4	5	6	7	8	9	10	11
B.—Preparation and supply of material substances.	V.—Trade.	**xxiv** (106)	**Banks, establishments of credit, exchange and insurance** (Bank managers, money lenders, exchange and insurance agents, money changers and brokers, and their employés).	17,345	11,054	204	3,152	1,678	1,135	122
		xxv (107)	**Brokerage, commission and export** (Brokers, commission agents, commercial travellers, warehouse owners and employés).	21,415	15,941	1,137	2,542	1,202	479	114
		xxvi (108)	**Trade in textiles** (Trade in piece-goods, wool, cotton, silk, hair and other textiles).	74,875	59,508	2,728	2,455	9,939	207	38
		xxvii (109)	**Trade in skins, leather and furs** (Trade in skins, leather, furs, feathers, horns, etc.).	1,481	1,043	80	92	250	16	...
		xxviii (110)	**Trade in wood** [Trade in wood (not firewood), cork, bark, etc.].	21,988	18,450	556	1,757	994	220	11
		xxix (111)	**Trade in metals** (machinery, knife, tool, etc., sellers).	1,644	1,365	2	39	232	6	...
		xxx (112)	**Trade in pottery**	10,386	10,122	115	62	63	24	...
		xxxi (113)	**Trade in chemical products** (drugs, dyes, paints, petroleum, explosives, etc.)	2,903	2,212	51	285	290	64	1
		xxxii	**Hotels, cafes, restaurants, etc.**	21,651	14,186	3,121	1,694	2,337	181	132
		114	Venders of wine, liquors, ærated waters, etc.	14,474	9,688	2,196	1,322	1,139	60	69
		115	Owners and managers of hotels, cookshops, *sarais*, etc., and their employés.	7,177	4,498	925	372	1,198	121	63
		xxxiii	**Other trade in food stuffs**	513,911	460,704	10,992	17,421	22,729	1,725	340
		116	Fish dealers	107,111	100,935	1,444	1,030	3,493	182	27
		117	Grocers and sellers of vegetable oil, salt and other condiments.	35,978	32,310	200	981	2,326	76	85
		118	Sellers of milk, butter, ghee, poultry, eggs, etc.	10,378	2,905	540	4,511	2,299	81	42
		119	Sellers of sweetmeats, sugar, *gur* and molasses.	108,839	95,867	1,271	5,471	5,943	254	33
		120	Cardamom, betel-leaf, vegetables, fruit and areca nut sellers.	117,309	106,788	4,267	1,919	3,917	417	1
		121	Grain and pulse dealers	105,332	96,187	2,618	2,303	3,638	448	138
		122	Tobacco, opium, *ganja*, etc., sellers ...	22,362	19,998	644	425	1,027	254	14
		123	Dealers in sheep, goats and pigs	1,058	1,008	6	22	21	1	...
		124	Dealers in hay, grass and fodder	5,544	4,706	2	759	65	12	...
		xxxiv (125)	**Trade in clothing and toilet articles** (clothing, hats, umbrellas, socks, ready-made shoes, perfumes, etc.).	6,531	5,674	486	84	235	41	11
		xxxv	**Trade in furniture**	13,496	12,320	190	110	843	23	10
		126	Trade in furniture, carpets, curtains and bedding.	7,137	6,835	63	12	209	18	...
		127	Hardware, cooking utensils, porcelain, crockery, glassware, bottles, articles for gardening, the cellar, etc.	6,359	5,485	127	98	634	5	10
		xxxvi (128)	**Trade in building materials** (stones, bricks, plaster, cement, sand, tiles, thatch, etc.).	3,057	2,914	20	37	83	3	...
		xxxvii (129)	**Trade in means of transport** (Dealers and hirers of elephants, camels, horses, cattle, asses, mules, etc., sellers (not makers) of carriages, saddlery, etc.).	15,661	11,971	997	425	2,220	45	3
		xxxviii (130)	**Trade in fuel** (Dealers in firewood, charcoal, coal, cowdung, etc.).	10,753	9,118	401	754	416	64	...
		xxxix	**Trade in articles of luxury and those pertaining to letters and the arts and sciences.**	10,961	8,166	574	560	1,539	64	58
		131	Dealers in precious stones, jewellery (real and imitation), clocks, optical instruments, etc.	8,591	6,269	437	476	1,334	17	58
		132	Dealers in common bangles, bead necklaces, fans, small articles, toys, hunting and fishing tackle, flowers, etc.	1,150	1,064	27	31	28	...	...
		133	Publishers, booksellers, stationers, dealers in music, pictures, musical instruments and curiosities.	1,220	833	110	53	177	47	...
		xl (134)	**Trade in refuse matter** (Dealers in rags, stable refuse, etc.).	94	46	...	30	7	6	5
		xli	**Trade of other sorts**	455,569	386,484	20,093	11,676	33,112	3,734	470
		135	Shopkeepers otherwise unspecified	450,939	383,758	19,969	10,767	32,741	3,304	400
		136	Itinerant traders, pedlars, hawkers, etc. ...	456	159	81	23	127	...	66
		137	Conjurors, acrobats, fortune tellers, reciters, exhibitors of curiosities and wild animals.	3,816	2,289	43	882	186	416	...
		138	Other trades (including farmers of pounds, tolls and markets).	358	278	...	4	58	14	4

IMPERIAL TABLE XV-D.—*Distribution of Occupations by Religion.*

Class.	Sub-class.	Order and Group: Serial No.	Order and Group: Description.	Total number of workers and dependents.	Distribution by Religion: Buddhist.	Animist.	Hindu.	Mahomedan.	Christian.	Others.
1	2	3	4	5	6	7	8	9	10	11
C.—Public Administration and Liberal Arts.	VI.—Public Force.	xlii (139)	**Army**	**24,984**	**2,844**	**264**	**7,736**	**6,157**	**4,402**	**3,581**
		140	Army (Native States)	...	...	...	...	...	...	..
		xliii (141)	**Navy**	**28**	**10**	..	**11**	...	**7**	...
		xliv	**Police**	**54,483**	**42,876**	**997**	**4,502**	**3,819**	**1,509**	**780**
		142	Police	54,266	42,669	991	4,502	3,819	1,505	780
		143	Village Watchmen	217	207	6	...	...	4	...
	VII.—Public Administration.	xlv	**Public Administration**	**103,108**	**81,989**	**3,263**	**7,661**	**3,690**	**6,365**	**140**
		144	Service of the State	34,294	22,151	215	5,428	2,123	4,259	118
		145	Service of Native and Foreign States ...	2,976	2,566	375	21	...	14	...
		146	Municipal and other local (not village) service	4,174	999	25	1,861	608	662	19
		147	Village officials and servants other than watchmen.	61,664	56,273	2,648	351	959	1,430	3
	VIII.—Professions and Liberal Arts.	xlvi	**Religion**	**140,834**	**132,378**	**1,407**	**705**	**2,240**	**4,059**	**45**
		148	Priests, ministers, etc.	128,642	121,588	1,286	569	2,024	3,130	45
		149	Religious mendicants, inmates of monasteries, etc.	11,638	10,722	44	118	156	598	...
		150	Catechists, readers, church and mission service	434	20	61	6	24	323	...
		151	Temple, burial or burning ground service, pilgrim conductors, circumcisers.	120	48	16	12	36	8	...
		xlvii	**Law**	**8,306**	**6,392**	**1**	**423**	**763**	**679**	**48**
		152	Lawyers of all kinds, including *kasis*, law agents and *mukhtiars*.	6,079	4,678	1	297	494	570	39
		153	Lawyers' clerks, petition writers, etc.	2,227	1,714	..	126	269	109	9
		xlviii	**Medicine**	**52,172**	**46,338**	**366**	**1,760**	**1,815**	**1,810**	**83**
		154	Medical practitioners of all kinds, including dentists, oculists and veterinary surgeons.	49,582	44,662	327	1,518	1,688	1,307	80
		155	Midwives, vaccinators, compounders, nurses, masseurs, etc.	2,590	1,676	39	242	127	503	3
		xlix (156)	**Instruction** (Professors and teachers of all kinds and clerks and servants connected with education).	**26,939**	**18,848**	**70**	**561**	**1,537**	**5,889**	**34**
		l	**Letters and arts and sciences**	**28,025**	**24,603**	**363**	**1,304**	**490**	**1,206**	**59**
		157	Public scribes, stenographers, etc.	1,866	1,383	...	272	112	93	6
		158	Architects, surveyors, engineers, and their employés.	3,998	2,664	70	371	184	688	21
		159	Others (authors, photographers, artists, sculptors, astronomers, meteorologists, botanists, astrologers, etc.).	5,666	5,025	203	223	57	139	19
		160	Music composers and masters, players on all kinds of musical instruments (not military), singers, actors and dancers.	16,495	15,531	90	438	137	286	13
	IX.—Persons living on their income.	li (161)	**Persons living principally on their income.** Proprietors (other than of agricultural land), fund and scholarship holders and pensioners.	**6,967**	**4,224**	**87**	**749**	**889**	**993**	**25**
D.—Miscellaneous.	X.—Domestic Service.	lii	**Domestic service**	**85,771**	**36,613**	**2,208**	**27,438**	**12,862**	**6,387**	**263**
		162	Cooks, water-carriers, doorkeepers, watchmen and other indoor servants.	82,197	36,163	2,202	25,136	12,084	6,351	261
		163	Private grooms, coachmen, dog boys, etc. ...	3,574	450	6	2,302	778	36	2
	XI.—Insufficiently described occupations.	liii	**General terms which do not indicate a definite occupation.**	**429,399**	**301,323**	**9,776**	**81,061**	**28,520**	**8,262**	**457**
		164	Manufacturers, business men and contractors otherwise unspecified.	10,852	5,151	382	1,733	3,159	382	45
		165	Cashiers, accountants, book-keepers, clerks and other employés in unspecified offices, warehouses and shops.	58,873	26,088	3,039	16,390	7,872	5,361	123
		166	Mechanics otherwise unspecified	8,240	2,448	31	1,193	3,178	1,305	85
		167	Labourers and workmen otherwise unspecified	351,434	267,636	6,324	61,745	14,311	1,214	204
	XII.—Unproduction.	liv (168)	**Inmates of Jails, asylums and hospitals** ...	**8,500**	**7,275**	**46**	**617**	**427**	**96**	**39**
		lv (169)	**Beggars, vagrants, prostitutes** (procurers, receivers of stolen goods, cattle poisoners, etc.).	**26,075**	**21,782**	**1,162**	**745**	**1,997**	**366**	**23**

IMPERIAL TABLE XV-E.

Statistics of Industries.

PART I.—PROVINCIAL SUMMARY.

IMPERIAL TABLE XV-E.—

PART I.—PROVINCIAL

Description of Factory, Mine or other Industrial Unit.			Classification of Factory, etc., according to number of persons employed (including management).	Number of Factories or Industrial unit.	Total number of persons employed.	
Class.	Group.	Whether mechanical power is used.			M	F
1(a)	1(b)	1(c)	2	3	4	5
GROWING OF SPECIAL PRODUCTS.	Rubber plantation ...	Not used ...	Total	10	3,896	151
			From 20 to 49 persons ...	2	68	1
			From 50 to 99 persons ...	1	79	4
			From 200 to 399 persons ...	3	767	63
			400 persons and over ...	4	2,982	83
MINES ...	Petroleum wells ... (Management units).	Used ...	Total	19	5,120	204
			From 20 to 49 persons ...	4	131	4
			From 50 to 99 persons ...	7	514	8
			From 100 to 199 persons ...	1	164	6
			From 200 to 399 persons ...	4	1,072	64
			400 persons and over ...	3	3,239	122
	Tin and Wolfram Mines.		Total	17	1,688	47
		Used ...	Total, 50 to 99 persons ...	1	58	...
		Not used ...	Total	16	1,630	47
			From 20 to 49 persons ...	8	258	2
			From 50 to 99 persons ...	2	110	34
			From 100 to 199 persons ...	4	495	10
			From 200 to 399 persons ..	1	330	...
			400 persons and over ...	1	437	1
	Silver and Lead Mine	Used ...	Total, 400 persons and over	1	1,845	...
	Galena Mine ...	Used ...	Total, 100 to 199 persons...	1	102	...
QUARRIES OF HARD ROCKS.	Ruby Mines ...	Used ...	Total, 400 persons and over	1	1,393	...
	Jade Mines ...	Not used ...	Total	12	1,128	8
			From 20 to 49 persons ...	5	196	8
			From 50 to 99 persons ...	5	362	...
			From 200 to 399 persons...	2	570	...
	Stone Quarry ...	Used ...	Total, 400 persons and over	1	1,442	154
TEXTILE INDUSTRIES.	Cotton Ginning Factories.	Used ...	Total	5	577	159
			From 50 to 99 persons ...	2	87	51
			From 100 to 199 persons...	2	213	73
			From 200 to 399 persons...	1	277	35
	Rope Factory ...	Used ...	Total, 100 to 199 persons...	1	136	17
WOODS AND ALLIED INDUSTRIES.	Saw Mills ...	Used ...	Total	82	9,523	310
			From 20 to 49 persons ...	26	903	48
			From 50 to 99 persons ...	31	2,015	139
			From 100 to 199 persons...	12	1,487	123
			From 200 to 399 persons...	8	1,995	...
			400 persons and over ...	5	3,123	...
METAL INDUSTRIES.	Iron Foundries ...	Used ...	Total	5	736	...
			From 20 to 49 persons ...	1	24	...
			From 50 to 99 persons ...	2	154	...
			From 100 to 199 persons...	1	118	...
			400 persons and over ...	1	440	...
	Arsenal	Used ...	Total, 200 to 399 persons...	1	292	...
	Engineering Workshops	Used ...	Total, 200 to 399 persons...	3	852	...
	Municipal Workshop ...	Used ...	Total, 50 to 99 persons ...	1	70	...
	Lead Smelting Workshop	Used ...	Total, 400 persons and over	1	477	59

Statistics of Industries.

SUMMARY.

CLASSIFICATION OF PERSONS EMPLOYED.												Remarks.	
Direction, supervision and Clerical work.				Skilled workmen.				Unskilled labourers.					
Europeans and Anglo-Indians.		Indians and other Asiatics.		Europeans and Anglo-Indians.		Indians and other Asiatics.		Age 14 and over.		Under 14.			
M	F	M	F	M	F	M	F	M	F	M	F	Nature of power used.	State of business on date of record (10-3-1911).
6	7	8	9	10	11	12	13	14	15	16	17	18(a)	18(b)
33	...	36	...	...	...	540	...	3,239	133	48	18	......	Normal.
...	...	2	..	...	...	...	...	66	1	...	...		
1	...	2	...	...	...	2	...	72	4	2	...		
10	...	9	...	..	...	58	...	684	55	6	8		
22	...	23	...	...	...	480	...	2,417	73	40	10		
81	...	161	...	300	...	1,074	6	3,498	198	6	...	Steam, 13 ... Steam and Oil, 3 Steam and Gas, 3	7 brisker than usual. 8 normal. 2 somewhat slacker than usual. 2 much slacker than usual.
3	...	9	...	8	...	26	...	85	4	...	...		
3	...	21	...	50	...	82	6	355	2	3	..		
2	...	5	...	11	...	16	...	130	6	...	...		
16	...	11	...	16	...	434	...	592	64	3	...		
57	...	115	...	215	...	516	...	2,336	122	...	...		
24	..	59	1	2	...	401	13	1,187	24	15	9		
1	...	2	...	...	...	14	...	41	...	..	...	Water.	
23	...	57	1	2	...	387	13	1,146	24	15	9	......	2 somewhat brisker than usual. 13 normal. 1 somewhat slacker than usual. 1 slacker than usual.
13	.	11	...	2	...	73	...	153	2	6	...		
2	...	4	...	...	...	90	9	9	19	5	6		
5	...	12	...	.	...	185	4	289	3	4	3		
...	...	12	...	...	...	9	...	309		...	...		
3	...	18	1	...	...	30	...	386	...	...	...		
12	...	10	...	6	...	91	...	1,726	...	...	...	Steam and Water	Brisker than usual.
2	...	...	...	...	...	30	...	70	...	...	...	Water and Steam	Much slacker than usual.
40	..	6	...	...	...	160	...	1,187	..	...	...	Electricity ...	Slacker than usual.
...	...	10	....	...	...	283	...	835	8	...	...	......	1 much brisker than usual. 1 brisker than usual. 1 somewhat brisker than usual. 3 normal. 1 somewhat slacker than usual. 5 slacker than usual.
...	...	6	...	...	...	63	...	127	8	...	...		
...	...	1	...	...	...	105	...	256	...	...	...		
...	...	3	...	...	...	115	...	452	...	...	...		
8	...	6	...	...	...	40	...	901	41	487	113	Steam ...	Normal.
...	...	85	...	...	...	96	13	375	116	21	30	Steam, 4 ... Steam and Oil, 1	1 much brisker than usual. 1 normal. 1 somewhat slacker than usual. 2 slacker than usual.
...	...	8	...	...	...	14	13	58	33	7	5		
...	...	34	...	...	...	46	...	124	63	9	10		
...	...	43	...	...	...	36	...	193	20	5	15		
...	...	4	..	...	...	60	10	70	4	2	3	Steam ...	Normal.
85	6	1,305	46	7	...	2,165	53	5,813	173	148	32	All Steam power	3 much brisker than usual. 1 brisker than usual. 2 somewhat brisker than usual. 33 normal. 12 somewhat slacker than usual. 20 slacker than usual. 11 much slacker than usual.
9	...	157	4	...	...	343	14	341	25	53	5		
41	6	322	6	1	...	282	20	1,296	102	73	5		
3	...	202	36	..	...	362	19	898	46	22	22		
15	...	363	...	6	...	342	...	1,269	...	...	...		
17	...	261	...	...	...	836	...	2,009	...	...	...		
19	...	19	...	22	...	345	...	331	...	...	...	Steam, 4 .. Oil, 1 ...	2 brisker than usual. 1 normal. 1 somewhat slacker than usual. 1 slacker than usual.
5	...	1	...	...	...	16	...	2	...	...	...		
3	...	9	...	3	...	69	...	70	...	...	...		
3	...	...	...	7	...	58	...	50	...	...	...		
8	...	9	...	12	...	202	...	209	...	...	...		
32	...	19	...	2	...	83	...	139	...	17	...	Steam ...	Normal.
28	...	27	...	4	...	550	...	243	...	...	...	Steam 2, Oil 1 ...	1 somewhat brisker than usual. 1 normal. 1 somewhat slacker than usual.
2	...	3	...	...	...	31	...	33	...	1	...	Steam ...	Normal.
9	...	21	...	11	...	98	...	338	59	...	...	Steam ...	Brisker than usual.

IMPERIAL TABLE XV-E.—
PART I.—PROVINCIAL

Description of Factory, Mine or other Industrial Unit.			Classification of Factory, etc., according to number of persons employed (including management).	Number of Factories or Industrial unit.	Total number of persons employed.	
Class.	Group.	Whether mechanical power is used.			M	F
1(a)	1(b)	1(c)	2	3	4	5
Glass and Earthenware Industries.	Brick and tile factories		Total	2	153	...
		Used ...	Total, 50 to 99 persons ...	1	87	...
		Not used ...	Total, 50 to 99 persons ...	1	66	...
Industries connected with Chemical Products.	Ice and ærated water factories.	Used ...	Total	4	277	...
			From 20 to 49 persons ...	1	32	...
			From 50 to 99 persons ...	3	245	...
	Petroleum Refineries ..	Used ...	Total	7	10,707	40
			From 20 to 49 persons ...	2	65	...
			From 50 to 99 persons ...	1	82	...
			400 persons and over ...	4	10,560	40
	Lac Refinery ...	Used ..	Total, 100 to 199 persons	1	117	9
Food Industries	Rice Mills ...	Used ...	Total	152	27,807	2,065
			From 20 to 49 persons ...	48	1,478	167
			From 50 to 99 persons ...	40	2,665	205
			From 100 to 199 persons...	24	3,296	196
			From 200 to 399 persons...	22	5,766	374
			400 persons and over ...	18	14,602	1,123
	Breweries	Used ...	Total, 100 to 199 persons	1	137	...
	Water works ...	Used ...	Total, 20 to 49 persons ...	2	50	...
Construction of means of transport.	Railway Workshops ...	Used ...	Total	2	2,944	...
			From 200 to 399 persons...	1	291	..
			400 persons and over ...	1	2,653	...
	Locomotive Running-Shed.	Not used ...	Total, 100 to 199 persons	1	184	...
	Railway Signal Workshop.	Used ...	Total, 50 to 99 persons ...	1	96	...
	Dockyards ..	Used ...	Total	2	1,070	108
			From 100 to 199 persons...	1	158	11
			400 persons and over ...	1	912	97
	Port Commissioners' Workshop.	Used ...	Total, 100 to 199 persons	1	191	...
	Marine Workshop ...	Used ...	Total, 100 to 199 persons	1	192	...
	Telegraph works ...	Used ...	Total, 50 to 99 persons ..	1	55	...
	Postal works ...	Not used ..	Total, 50 to 99 persons ...	1	67	. .
Production and Transmission of Physical Forces.	Electric power station ...	Used ...	Total, 50 to 99 persons ...	1	90	...
	Electrical Workshop ..	Used ...	Total, 100 to 199 persons	1	177	...
Industries of Luxury.	Printing Press ...		Total	8	1,746	9
		Used ...	Total	7	1,719	7
			From 20 to 49 persons ...	1	36	...
			From 50 to 99 persons ...	1	76	...
			From 100 to 199 persons...	2	362	6
			From 200 to 399 persons...	2	616	1
			400 persons and over ..	1	629	..
		Not used ...	Total, 20 to 49 persons ...	1	27	2

Statistics of Industries.

SUMMARY.

CLASSIFICATION OF PERSONS EMPLOYED.												Remarks.	
DIRECTION, SUPERVISION AND CLERICAL WORK.				SKILLED WORKMEN.				UNSKILLED LABOURERS.					
Europeans and Anglo-Indians.		Indians and other Asiatics.		Europeans and Anglo-Indians.		Indians and other Asiatics.		Age 14 and over.		Under 14.		Nature of power used.	State of business on date of record (10-3-1911).
M	F	M	F	M	F	M	F	M	F	M	F		
6	7	8	9	10	11	12	13	14	15	16	17	18(a)	18(b)
1	...	33	...	...	...	11	...	108	..	...	...	Steam ...	Brisker than usual.
1	...	...	...	...	...	6	...	80	...	...	...	......	Normal.
...	...	33	...	...	...	5	...	28	...	...	...		
5	...	33	...	3	...	63	...	173	...	...	...	Steam, 2 ... Gas and Electricity, 1. Steam, Oil and Gas, 1.	3 normal. 1 much slacker than usual.
1	...	2	...	1	...	4	...	24	...	...	...		
4	...	31	...	2	...	59	...	149	...	...	...		
211	...	233	...	8	...	2,878	...	7,223	40	154	...	Steam, 4 ... Steam, Oil and Electricity, 1. Steam and Oil, 2	1 brisker than usual. 1 somewhat brisker than usual. 4 normal. 1 slacker than usual.
2	...	3	..	...	...	4	...	56	...	...	...		
...		3	...	...	...	40	...	39	...	...	...		
209	...	227	...	8	...	2,834	...	7,128	40	154	...		
2	...	7	...	3	...	5	...	95	6	5	3	Steam ..	Normal.
147	...	1,268	35	208	13	3,452	71	22,245	1,701	487	245	Steam power generated by combustion of paddy husk.	6 much brisker than usual. 11 brisker than usual. 4 somewhat brisker than usual. 74 normal. 13 somewhat slacker than usual. 32 slacker than usual. 12 much slacker than usual.
19	...	303	4	17	11	270	...	816	135	53	17		
13	...	422	24	18	...	521	8	1,656	145	35	28		
11	...	240	7	70	...	396	...	2,507	155	72	34		
33	...	146	...	87	2	816	63	4,576	247	108	62		
71	...	157	...	16	...	1,449	...	12,690	1,019	219	104		
3	...	6	...	...	...	...	...	128	...	...	...	Steam ...	Slacker than usual.
4	...	...	...	...	...	12	...	34	...	...	...	Steam ...	2 normal.
40	...	187	...	68	...	1,941	...	708	...	...	...	Steam, 1 .. Steam and Electricity, 1.	2 normal.
2	...	14	...	1	...	207	...	67	...	...	...		
38	...	173	...	67	...	1,734	..	641	...	...	...		
4	...	4	...	11	...	80	...	85	. .	...	...	......	Brisker than usual.
2	...	6	...	3	...	48	...	37	...	...	...	Steam ...	Much brisker than usual.
30	14	7	...	3	...	331	...	699	94	...	...	Steam, 2 ...	1 brisker than usual. 1 slacker than usual.
...	...	7	...	3	...	79	...	69	11	...	...		
30	14	...	..	...	...	252	...	630	83	...	...		
4	...	10	...	5	...	90	..	82	...	...	...	Steam and Electricity.	Brisker than usual.
3	...	...	...	2	...	146	...	41	...	...	...	Steam ...	Normal.
36	...	12	..	...	...	7	...	...	...	...	...	Oil ...	Normal.
...	...	22	...	...	...	...	...	45	...	...	...	......	Normal.
7	...	1	...	1	...	27	...	54	...	...	...	Steam ...	Normal.
46	...	2	...	1	...	83	..	45	...	..	...	Electricity ...	Normal.
73	8	154	...	5	1	1,187	...	269	...	58	...	Steam, 2 ... Electricity, 1 ... Oil, 3 ... Steam and Electricity, 1.	8 normal.
71	7	152	...	4	...	1,169	...	267	...	56	...		
...	...	3	...	...	...	25	...	5	...	3	...		
...	...	2	...	...	...	73	...	...	...	1	...		
10	6	27	...	4	...	260	...	45	...	16	...		
40	1	11	...	...	..	432	...	115	...	18	...		
21	...	109	...	...	...	379	...	102	...	18	...		
2	1	2	...	1	1	18	...	2	...	2	...		

IMPERIAL TABLE XV-E.

Statistics of Industries.

Imperial Table XV-E.—*Statistics*

PART II.—DISTRIBUTION

Description of factory, mine or other industrial unit. Class.	Group.	District.	Number of Factories.	Total number of persons employed. M	F
1 (a)	1 (b)	2	3	4	5
Growing of special products.	Rubber Plantation	Total ...	10	3,896	151
		Hanthawaddy	2	908	23
		Amherst	3	429	42
		Mergui	4	2,335	80
		Toungoo	1	224	6
Mines ...	Petroleum Wells (Management units)	Total ...	19	5,120	204
		Pakôkku	6	996	64
		Minbu	1	98	...
		Magwe	9	2,750	50
		Mandalay	1	49	6
		Myingyan	2	1,227	84
	Tin and Wolfram Mines ...	Total ...	17	1,688	47
		Tavoy	11	1,394	45
		Mergui	5	167	2
		Southern Shan States ...	1	127	...
	Silver and Lead Mine	Northern Shan States Total	1	1,845	...
	Galena Mine	Northern Shan States Total	1	102	...
Quarries of hard rocks.	Ruby Mine	Ruby Mines ... Total	1	1,393	...
	Jade Mines	Myitkyina ... Total	12	1,128	8
	Stone Quarry	Amherst ... Total	1	1,442	154
Textile industries.	Cotton Ginning Factories ...	Myingyan .. Total	5	577	159
	Rope Factory	City of Rangoon ... Total	1	136	17
Wood and allied industries.	Saw Mills	Total ...	82	9,523	310
		City of Rangoon	17	4,680	...
		Hanthawaddy	1	47	...
		Tharrawaddy	2	145	28
		Pegu	3	157	...
		Prome	1	37	...
		Bassein	3	153	14
		Toungoo	13	671	32
		Thatôn	1	24	...
		Amherst	16	2,243	14
		Tavoy	1	40	...
		Mergui	1	37	...
		Mandalay	12	689	116
		Sagaing	1	40	4
		Lower Chindwin	1	23	9
		Yamèthin	9	537	93
Metal industries.	Iron Foundries	Total ...	5	736	...
		Akyab	1	70	...
		City of Rangoon	2	464	...
		Amherst	1	118	...
		Thatôn	1	84	...
	Arsenal	City of Rangoon ... Total	1	292	...
	Engineering Workshops ..	City of Rangoon ... Total	3	852	...
	Municipal Workshop ...	City of Rangoon ... Total	1	70	...
	Lead Smelting Workshop ...	Mandalay ... Total	1	477	59

of Industries.

BY DISTRICTS.

CLASSIFICATION OF PERSONS EMPLOYED.											
DIRECTION, SUPERVISION AND CLERICAL WORK.				SKILLED WORKMEN.				UNSKILLED LABOURERS.			
Europeans and Anglo-Indians.		Indians and other Asiatics.		Europeans and Anglo-Indians.		Indians and other Asiatics.		Age 14 and over.		Under 14.	
M	F	M	F	M	F	M	F	M	F	M	F
6	7	8	9	10	11	12	13	14	15	16	17
33	...	36	...	...	...	540	...	3,239	133	48	18
5	...	9	...	...	...	135	...	752	21	7	2
4	...	8	...	...	...	29	...	386	35	2	7
20	...	16	...	...	...	353	...	1,907	71	39	9
4	...	3	...	...	...	23	...	194	6	...	...
81	...	161	...	300	...	1,074	6	3,498	198	6	...
15	...	15	...	...	...	465	...	501	64	...	...
...	...	4	...	2	...	...	...	90	...	2	...
58	...	116	...	243	...	473	...	1,857	50	3	...
...	...	7	...	35	...	7	6	...	...	...	...
8	...	19	...	20	...	129	...	1,050	84	1	...
24	...	59	1	2	...	401	13	1,187	24	15	9
11	...	44	1	2	...	313	13	1,015	22	9	9
9	...	10	...	...	...	87	...	55	2	6	...
4	...	5	...	...	...	1	...	117	...	...	...
12	...	10	...	6	...	91	...	1,726	...	...	...
2	...	...	...	...	...	30	...	70	...	...	...
40	...	6	...	...	...	160	...	1,187	...	...	...
...	...	10	...	...	...	283	...	835	8	...	...
8	...	6	...	...	...	40	...	901	41	487	113
...	...	85	...	...	...	96	13	375	116	21	30
...	...	4	...	...	...	60	10	70	4	2	3
85	6	1,305	46	7	...	2,165	53	5,813	173	148	32
29	...	644	...	4	...	1,012	...	2,991	...	...	...
...	...	3	...	...	...	7	...	37	...	...	...
...	...	9	...	...	...	51	14	77	7	8	7
...	...	13	...	...	...	97	...	47	...	...	...
...	...	22	...	...	...	...	...	15	...	...	...
...	...	6	...	...	...	112	5	35	7	...	2
2	...	140	7	...	...	105	6	402	13	22	6
...	...	3	...	...	...	4	...	...	...	17	...
35	6	204	...	3	...	535	6	1,402	2	64	...
...	...	...	...	...	...	...	...	20	...	20	...
...	...	3	...	...	...	34	...	...	...	...	...
15	...	83	...	...	...	94	22	497	94	...	...
...	...	9	...	...	...	7	...	24	4	...	...
...	...	2	...	...	...	8	...	13	9	...	...
4	...	164	39	...	...	99	...	253	37	17	17
19	...	19	...	22	...	345	...	331	...	...	...
3	...	7	...	2	...	35	...	23	...	...	...
13	...	10	...	12	...	218	...	211	...	...	...
3	...	...	...	7	...	58	...	50	...	...	...
...	...	2	...	1	...	34	...	47	...	...	...
32	...	19	...	2	...	83	...	139	...	17	...
28	...	27	...	4	...	550	...	243	...	...	...
2	...	3	...	...	...	31	...	33	...	1	...
9	...	21	...	11	...	98	...	338	59	...	...

Imperial Table XV-E.—*Statistics*

PART II.—DISTRIBUTION

Description of factory, mine, or other industrial unit. — Class.	Group.	District.		Number of Factories.	Total number of persons employed. M	F
1 (a)	1 (b)	2		3	4	5
Glass and earthenware industries.	Brick and tile factories ...	Total	...	2	153	...
		Hanthawaddy ...	...	1	66	...
		Amherst ...	...	1	87	...
Industries connected with chemical products.	Ice and ærated water factories	City of Rangoon ...	Total	4	277	...
	Petroleum Refineries ...	Total	...	7	10,707	40
		City of Rangoon ...	...	4	1,707	...
		Hanthawaddy ...	...	3	9,000	40
	Lac Refinery	City of Rangoon ...	Total	1	117	9
Food industries	Rice Mills	Total	...	152	27,807	2,065
		Akyab ...	...	8	1,726	11
		City of Rangoon ...	...	53	16,755	1,469
		Hanthawaddy ...	...	5	129	8
		Tharrawaddy ...	...	3	194	20
		Pegu	...	9	366	19
		Prome ...	...	12	822	87
		Bassein ...	...	13	3,462	102
		Henzada ...	...	2	63	16
		Pyapôn ...	...	13	956	153
		Toungoo ...	...	3	144	6
		Thatôn ...	...	1	34	2
		Amherst ...	...	15	2,749	10
		Tavoy ...	...	5	157	53
		Mandalay ...	...	8	180	94
		Sagaing ...	...	1	44	15
		Yamèthin ...	...	1	26	...
	Breweries	Mandalay ...	Total	1	137	...
	Water-works	Total	...	2	50	...
		City of Rangoon ...	...	1	29	...
		Prome ...	...	1	21	...
Construction of means of transport.	Railway Workshops... ...	Total	...	2	2,944	...
		Hanthawaddy ...	...	1	2,653	...
		Sagaing ...	...	1	291	...
	Locomotive Running Shed ...	Mandalay ...	Total	1	184	...
	Railway Signal Workshop ...	City of Rangoon ...	Total	1	96	...
	Dock-yards	Total	...	2	1,070	108
		City of Rangoon ...	...	1	912	97
		Mandalay ...	...	1	158	11
	Port Commissioners' Workshop	City of Rangoon ...	Total	1	191	...
	Marine Workshop	Mandalay ...	Total	1	192	...
	Telegraph Workshop	Mandalay ...	Total	1	55	...
	Postal Workshop	Mandalay ...	Total	1	67	...
Production and transmission of physical forces.	Electric-power Station... ...	City of Rangoon ...	Total	1	90	...
	Electrical Workshop	City of Rangoon ...	Total	1	177	...
Industries of luxury.	Printing Presses	Total	...	8	1,746	9
		City of Rangoon ...	...	6	1,683	7
		Bassein ...	...	1	27	2
		Mandalay ...	...	1	36	...

of Industries.

BY DISTRICTS.

CLASSIFICATION OF PERSONS EMPLOYED.											
Direction, supervision, and clerical work.				Skilled workmen.				Unskilled labourers.			
Europeans and Anglo-Indians.		Indians and other Asiatics.		Europeans and Anglo-Indians.		Indians and other Asiatics.		Age 14 and over.		Under 14.	
M	F	M	F	M	F	M	F	M	F	M	F
6	7	8	9	10	11	12	13	14	15	16	17
1	...	33	...	...	...	11	...	108	...	...	...
...	...	33	...	...	...	5	...	28	...	...	...
1	...	...	...	...	...	6	...	80	...	...	...
5	...	33	...	3	...	63	...	173	...	...	...
211	...	233	...	8	...	2,878	...	7,223	40	154	...
26	...	6	...	...	...	631	...	1,044	...	...	...
185	...	227	...	8	...	2,247	...	6,179	40	154	...
2	...	7	...	3	...	5	...	95	6	5	3
147	...	1,268	35	208	13	3,452	71	22,245	1,701	487	245
14	...	41	...	1	...	138	...	1,524	8	8	3
72	...	331	11	15	...	2,129	63	13,849	1,221	359	174
...	...	21	3	...	...	19	...	88	4	1	2
...	...	25	3	...	...	70	7	96	4	3	6
1	...	146	...	16	...	45	...	141	19	17	...
...	...	152	2	70	...	87	...	509	73	4	12
23	...	89	...	2	...	517	...	2,816	98	15	4
...	...	7	...	...	...	6	...	50	15	...	1
1	...	146	13	...	...	68	...	686	100	55	40
2	...	43	4	...	...	30	1	69	1	...	...
...	...	3	...	...	...	15	...	16	2	...	...
20	...	184	...	87	2	277	...	2,162	8	19	...
4	...	8	...	15	11	16	...	108	39	6	3
10	...	55	...	2	...	20	...	93	94	...	...
...	...	12	...	...	...	8	...	24	15	...	...
...	...	5	...	...	...	7	...	14	...	...	...
3	...	6	...	...	...	...	...	128	...	...	...
4	...	...	...	...	...	12	...	34	...	...	...
2	...	...	...	...	...	2	...	25	...	...	...
2	...	...	...	...	...	10	...	9	...	...	...
40	...	187	...	68	...	1,941	...	708	...	...	...
38	...	173	...	67	...	1,734	...	641	...	...	...
2	...	14	...	1	...	207	...	67	...	...	...
4	...	4	...	11	...	80	...	85	...	...	...
2	...	6	...	3	...	48	...	37	...	...	...
30	14	7	...	3	...	331	...	699	94	...	...
30	14	...	...	...	...	252	...	630	83	...	...
...	...	7	...	3	...	79	...	69	11	...	...
4	...	10	...	5	...	90	...	82	...	...	...
3	...	...	...	2	...	146	...	41	...	...	...
36	...	12	...	...	...	7	...	...	...	...	...
...	...	22	...	...	...	...	...	45	...	...	...
7	...	1	...	1	...	27	...	54	...	...	...
46	...	2	...	1	...	83	...	45	...	...	...
73	8	154	...	5	1	1,187	...	269	...	58	...
71	7	149	...	4	...	1,144	...	262	...	53	...
2	1	2	...	1	1	18	...	2	...	2	...
...	...	3	...	...	...	25	...	5	...	3	...

Imperial Table XV-E.—*Statistics of Industries.*

Part III.—Particulars as to Ownership of Factories, etc.

Description of Factory.	Number of Factories.	Number owned by Companies of which the Directors are: Europeans or Anglo-Indians.	Indians.	Of both races.	Chinese.	Burmese.	Karen.	Number privately owned by: Europeans and Anglo-Indians.	Indians, Non-Indian Asiatics, Burmese, etc.: Hindus.	Mahomedans.	Bengalis.	Chinese.	Persian.	Burmese.	Talaing.	Karen.
1	2	3	4	5	6	7	8	9	10	11	12	13	14	15	16	17
Rice Mills	152	41	5	...	5	5	...	6	14	8	2	14	...	47	3	2
Saw Mills	82	14	3	...	7	1	1	...	11	14	4	8	1	18	...	...
Petroleum Wells ..	19	12	2	3	...	...	...	...	...	1	...	...	...	1	...	...
Petroleum Refineries ...	7	4	1	2	...	...	...	...	...	...	...	...	...	...	...	...
Tin and Wolfram Mines ...	17	9	...	...	...	...	...	1	...	...	...	6	...	1	..	...

Part IV.—Caste or Race of Managers of Factories, etc.

Description of Factory.	Number of Factories.	Number managed by: Europeans and Anglo-Indians.	Indians, Non-Indian Asiatics, Burmese, etc.: Hindus.	Mahomedans.	Bengalis.	Madrasis.	Chinese.	Persian.	Burmese.	Talaing.	Karen.
1	2	3	4	5	6	7	8	9	10	11	12
Rice Mills	152	45	8	17	1	1	19	...	57	2	2
Saw Mills	82	14	12	15	3	1	16	1	19	...	1
Petroleum Wells ..	19	16	1	1	...	...	...	...	1	...	..
Petroleum Refineries ..	7	4	1	1	...	...	..	...	1	...	...
Tin and Woltram Mines	17	10	..	...	...	...	5	...	2	...	...

IMPERIAL TABLE XVI.

Occupation by Selected Races.

NOTE 1.—The occupations pursued by the indigenous tribes and races in Burma are so uniform, and the Census records of the Immigrant Hindu Castes are so unreliable that a general preparation of this table has been deemed inexpedient. It has been prepared for Europeans, Anglo-Indians and Armenians only.

Imperial Table XVI.—*Occupation by Selected Races.*

	Occupation.	Europeans.		Anglo-Indians.		Armenians.	
		Males.	Females.	Males.	Females.	Males.	Females.
	1	2	3	4	5	6	7
	POPULATION DEALT WITH ...	9,878	3,292	6,039	5,067	146	127
	Actual workers	8,764	611	3,606	563	104	13
	Dependents	1,114	2,681	2,433	4,504	42	114
	PRINCIPAL OCCUPATION OF ACTUAL WORKERS.						
I	**Exploitation of the Surface of the Soil** ...	183	19	74	35	2	2
	Income from rent of land	36	15	8	26	...	2
	Cultivators of all kinds, including gardeners.	20	3	21	8	...	...
	Agents and managers of landed estates, planters, forest officers and their clerks, rent collectors, etc.	99	...	39	1	2	...
	Stock-breeders	1	1	1	...	...	...
	Fishing and hunting	27	...	5	...	...	...
II	**Extraction of Minerals**	425	...	31	...	...	...
	Owners, managers, clerks, etc.	403	...	26	...	...	...
	Artisans and other workmen	22	...	5	...	...	...
III	**Industries**	220	17	140	34	6	2
	Owners, managers, clerks, etc.	130	10	95	14	6	2
	Artisans and other workmen	90	7	45	20	...	...
IV	**Transport**	1,827	16	1,089	32	5	...
	Owners, managers, ship's officers, etc. ...	1,709	14	930	31	2	...
	Sailors, Railway Guards, Engine Drivers, etc.	118	2	159	1	3	...
V	**Trade**	743	45	381	94	35	2
VI	**Public Force**	3,467	19	132	...	...	...
	Commissioned and Gazetted Officers ...	270	1	38	...	...	...
	Others	3,197	18	94	...	...	...
VII	**Public Administration**	551	13	633	34	18	...
	Gazetted Officers	285	...	83	...	1	...
	Others	266	13	550	34	17	...
VIII	**Arts and Professions**	868	392	424	247	15	2
	Religious	133	79	18	5	1	...
	Lawyers, doctors and teachers	431	296	263	225	4	2
	Others	304	17	143	17	10	...
IX	**Persons living on their Income**	102	25	91	38	11	4
X	**Domestic Service**	50	44	133	8	...	...
XI	**Contractors, Clerks, Cashiers, etc., otherwise unspecified.**	266	5	237	28	10	1
XII	**Unspecified Warehousemen, Foremen and Storekeepers.**	52	...	226	13	1	...
XIII	**Beggars, Prostitutes, Criminals and Inmates of Jails and Asylums.**	10	16	15	...	1	...

IMPERIAL TABLE XVII.

Territorial Distribution of the Christian Population by Sect and Race.

NOTE 1.—The following persons of European and Anglo-Indian Race but not professing the Christian Religion are included in this Table under the heading "Indefinite beliefs" :—

Belief.	Persons.	Males.	Females.
Agnostic	50	45	5
Atheist	12	12	...
Secularist	4	4	...
Total ...	66	61	5

NOTE 2.—The sects included under Minor Protestant Denominations are :—

Denomination.	Number.
Plymouth Brethren ...	12
Reformed Church ...	4
Swedenborgian ...	9
Church of Christ ...	2
Christian Scientist ...	9
Church of Jerusalem ...	3
Seventh Day Adventist	6
Bible Christian ...	4
Total ...	49

Imperial Table XVII.—*Territorial Distribution*

Serial No.	District or State.	ALL DENOMINATIONS. Total. Persons.	Total. Males.	Total. Females.	Distribution by Race. Europeans and Allied Races. Males.	Europeans and Allied Races. Females.	Anglo-Indians. Males.	Anglo-Indians. Females.	Natives. Males.	Natives. Females.
	1	2	3	4	5	6	7	8	9	10
	Provincial Total	210,081	111,033	99,048	10,014	3,419	6,039	5,067	94,980	90,562
	Burma Proper	199,680	105,815	93,865	9,888	3,378	5,989	5,042	89,938	85,445
	Arakan Division	1,167	718	449	204	66	108	93	406	290
1	Akyab	605	433	172	185	52	88	80	160	40
2	Northern Arakan	7	4	3	4	1	...	1	...	1
3	Kyaukpyu	95	52	43	1	4	9	7	42	32
4	Sandoway	460	229	231	14	9	11	5	204	217
	Pegu Division	55,030	30,568	24,462	5,224	1,875	3,689	3,054	21,655	19,533
5	City of Rangoon	23,044	13,977	9,067	4,407	1,534	3,152	2,679	6,418	4,854
6	Hanthawaddy	12,647	6,733	5,914	634	230	354	257	5,745	5,427
7	Tharrawaddy	6,052	3,011	3,041	36	18	51	34	2,924	2,989
8	Pegu	12,316	6,341	5,975	89	62	110	65	6,142	5,848
9	Prome	971	506	465	58	31	22	19	426	415
	Irrawaddy Division ...	74,134	37,662	36,472	463	188	106	78	37,093	36,206
10	Bassein	27,927	14,111	13,816	323	137	28	25	13,760	13,654
11	Henzada	10,285	5,070	5,215	75	34	28	27	4,967	5,154
12	Myaungmya	18,157	9,218	8,939	20	7	27	16	9,171	8,916
13	Ma-ubin	10,474	5,217	5,257	23	6	14	5	5,180	5,246
14	Pyapôn	7,291	4,046	3,245	22	4	9	5	4,015	3,236
	Tenasserim Division ...	50,622	25,883	24,739	606	363	884	825	24,393	23,551
15	Toungoo	33,138	16,712	16,426	178	156	156	115	16,378	16,155
16	Salween	384	223	161	13	5	...	...	210	156
17	Thatôn	3,738	1,987	1,751	15	4	97	52	1,875	1,695
18	Amherst	6,884	3,531	3,293	212	138	590	627	2,729	2,528
19	Tavoy	1,999	1,070	929	86	1	14	7	970	921
20	Mergui	4,539	2,360	2,179	102	59	27	24	2,231	2,096
	Magwe Division	1,508	952	556	380	76	89	63	483	417
21	Thayetmyo	592	357	235	172	18	18	17	167	200
22	Pakôkku	284	166	118	57	25	17	7	92	86
23	Minbu	150	98	52	19	9	18	17	61	26
24	Magwe	482	331	151	132	24	36	22	165	105
	Mandalay Division .. .	9,503	5,658	3,845	1,973	600	781	664	2,904	2,581
25	Mandalay (including City) ...	6,571	3,870	2,701	1,466	511	687	596	1,717	1,594
26	Bhamo	1,785	1,030	755	271	39	12	12	747	704
27	Myitkyina	566	349	217	100	19	20	13	229	185
28	Katha	383	269	114	62	12	32	19	175	83
29	Ruby Mines	198	140	58	74	19	30	24	36	15
	Mandalay City	*4,032*	*2,234*	*1,798*	*605*	*334*	*379*	*260*	*1,250*	*1,204*
	Sagaing Division	4,229	2,436	1,793	652	106	140	94	1,644	1,593
30	Shwebo	2,746	1,617	1,129	566	63	37	40	1,014	1,026
31	Sagaing	1,013	492	521	46	26	57	42	389	453
32	Lower Chindwin ...	297	179	118	21	15	15	10	143	93
33	Upper Chindwin	173	148	25	19	2	31	2	98	21
	Meiktila Division	3,487	1,938	1,549	386	104	192	171	1,360	1,274
34	Kyauksè	679	345	334	22	15	23	17	300	302
35	Meiktila	678	451	227	224	42	45	38	182	147
36	Yamèthin	1,813	928	885	80	28	104	103	744	754
37	Myingyan	317	214	103	60	19	20	13	134	71
	Specially Administered Territories.	10,401	5,218	5,183	126	41	50	25	5,042	5,117
38	Northern Shan States ...	348	222	126	38	6	18	14	166	106
39	Southern Shan States ...	9,818	4,866	4,952	77	30	26	10	4,763	4,912
40	Pakôkku Hill Tracts ..	4	4	...	2	...	...	...	2	...
41	Chin Hills	231	126	105	9	5	6	1	111	99

of the Christian Population by Sect and Race.

ANGLICAN COMMUNION.									ARMENIAN.									
Total.			Distribution by Race.						Total.			Distribution by Race.						
			Europeans and Allied Races.		Anglo-Indians.		Natives.					Europeans and Allied Races.		Anglo-Indians.		Natives.		
Persons.	Males.	Females.	Males.	Females.	Males.	Females.	Males.	Females.	Persons.	Males.	Females.	Males.	Females.	Males.	Females.	Males.	Females.	Serial No.
11	12	13	14	15	16	17	18	19	20	21	22	23	24	25	26	27	28	
20,734	12,679	8,055	5,408	1,614	2,062	1,651	5,209	4,790	256	164	92	152	90	13	...	...	2	
20,512	12,533	7,979	5,323	1,588	2,044	645	5,166	4,746	256	164	92	152	90	13	...	...	2	
160	115	45	88	25	21	12	6	8	...	...	...	...	...	...	...	...	...	
130	94	36	79	24	13	11	2	1	...	...	...	...	...	...	...	...	...	1
6	4	2	4	1	...	...	...	1	...	...	...	...	...	...	...	...	...	2
4	4	...	1	...	2	...	1	...	...	...	...	...	...	...	...	...	...	3
20	13	7	4	...	6	1	3	6	...	...	...	...	...	...	...	...	...	4
8,518	5,420	3,098	2,794	947	1,278	1,014	1,348	1,137	206	140	66	127	64	13	...	...	2	
6,511	4,210	2301	2,415	846	1,107	901	688	554	204	138	66	125	64	13	...	...	2	5
1,631	983	648	301	69	108	79	574	500	2	2	...	2	...	...	...	...	...	6
103	55	48	15	5	27	18	13	25	...	...	...	...	...	...	...	...	...	7
131	94	37	35	13	33	13	26	11	...	...	...	...	...	...	...	...	...	8
142	78	64	28	14	3	3	47	47	...	...	...	...	...	...	...	...	...	9
2,191	1,281	910	282	56	43	23	956	831	6	3	3	3	3	...	...	...	...	
640	417	223	221	32	13	6	183	185	5	2	3	2	3	...	...	...	...	10
130	62	68	31	13	10	6	21	49	...	...	...	...	...	...	...	...	...	11
359	202	157	11	6	15	6	176	145	...	...	...	...	...	...	...	...	...	12
444	223	221	10	3	4	3	209	215	...	...	...	...	...	...	...	...	...	13
618	377	241	9	2	1	2	367	237	1	1	...	1	...	...	...	...	...	14
5,352	2,768	2,584	191	117	228	199	2,349	2,268	2	2	...	2	...	...	...	...	...	
4,272	2,159	2,113	63	69	66	31	2,030	2,013	...	...	...	...	...	...	...	...	...	15
4	4	...	4	...	...	...	...	...	...	...	...	...	...	...	...	...	...	16
73	36	37	2	1	34	19	...	17	2	2	...	2	...	...	...	...	...	17
620	322	298	64	43	118	141	140	114	...	...	...	...	...	...	...	...	...	18
49	36	13	34	1	2	5	...	7	...	...	...	...	...	...	...	...	...	19
334	211	123	24	3	8	3	179	117	...	...	...	...	...	...	...	...	...	20
355	269	86	198	43	41	28	30	15	...	...	...	...	...	...	...	...	...	
167	145	22	137	11	7	7	1	4	...	...	...	...	...	...	...	...	...	21
56	32	24	22	17	7	5	3	2	...	...	...	...	...	...	...	...	...	22
63	41	22	12	5	9	9	20	8	...	...	...	...	...	...	...	...	...	23
69	51	18	27	10	18	7	6	1	...	...	...	...	...	...	...	...	...	24
2,384	1,532	852	924	275	306	270	302	307	26	11	15	11	15	...	...	...	...	
1,761	1,064	697	545	216	274	254	245	227	26	11	15	11	15	...	...	...	...	25
331	260	71	240	28	...	3	20	40	...	...	...	...	...	...	...	...	...	26
95	77	18	59	10	6	1	12	7	...	...	...	...	...	...	...	...	...	27
117	76	41	41	9	14	5	21	27	...	...	...	...	...	...	...	...	...	28
80	55	25	39	12	12	7	4	6	...	...	...	...	...	...	...	...	...	29
783	*475*	*308*	*234*	*107*	*99*	*72*	*142*	*129*	...	...	...	...	...	...	...	...	...	
1,023	757	266	576	80	54	39	127	147	10	7	3	7	3	...	...	...	...	
811	620	191	527	50	15	16	78	125	1	1	...	1	...	...	...	...	...	30
124	80	44	26	16	24	15	30	13	9	6	3	6	3	...	...	...	...	31
67	36	31	14	14	7	8	15	9	...	...	...	...	...	...	...	...	...	32
21	21	...	9	...	8	...	4	...	...	...	...	...	...	...	...	...	...	33
529	391	138	270	45	73	60	48	33	6	1	5	1	5	...	...	...	...	
46	30	16	8	5	11	7	11	4	...	...	...	...	...	...	...	...	...	34
281	229	52	197	21	20	15	12	16	...	...	...	...	...	...	...	...	...	35
139	89	50	40	9	34	32	15	9	6	1	5	1	5	...	...	...	...	36
63	43	20	25	10	8	6	10	4	...	...	...	...	...	...	...	...	...	37
222	146	76	85	26	18	6	43	44	...	...	...	...	...	...	...	...	...	
45	35	10	22	2	9	4	4	4	...	...	...	...	...	...	...	...	...	38
159	98	61	53	20	7	1	38	40	...	...	...	...	...	...	...	...	...	39
3	3	...	2	...	...	...	1	...	...	...	...	...	...	...	...	...	...	40
15	10	5	8	4	2	1	...	...	...	...	...	...	...	...	...	...	...	41

IMPERIAL TABLE XVII.—*Territorial Distribution*

Serial No.	District or State.	BAPTIST. Total. Persons.	BAPTIST. Total. Males.	BAPTIST. Total. Females.	Distribution by Race. Europeans and Allied Races. Males.	Europeans and Allied Races. Females.	Anglo-Indians. Males.	Anglo-Indians. Females.	Natives. Males.	Natives. Females.	CONGREGATIONALIST. Total. Persons.	Total. Males.	Total. Females.	Distribution by Race. Europeans and Allied Races. Males.	Europeans and Allied Races. Females.	Anglo-Indians. Males.	Anglo-Indians. Females.	Natives. Males.	Natives. Females.
	1	29	30	31	32	33	34	35	36	37	38	39	40	41	42	43	44	45	46
	Provincial Total	122,265	61,753	60,512	467	292	541	416	60,745	59,804	5	5	...	1	...	...	...	4	...
	Burma Proper	117,068	60,195	58,873	452	283	533	411	59,210	58,179	5	5	...	1	...	...	...	4	...
	Arakan Division ...	506	266	240	7	2	6	5	253	233	...	...	...	...	...	...	...	...	...
1	Akyab	57	46	11	7	...	4	5	35	6	...	...	...	...	...	...	...	...	...
2	Northern Arakan ...	...	...	...	...	...	...	...	...	...	...	...	...	...	...	...	...	...	...
3	Kyaukpyu	40	21	19	...	2	2	...	19	17	...	...	...	...	...	...	...	...	...
4	Sandoway	409	199	210	...	...	...	...	199	210	...	...	...	...	...	...	...	...	...
	Pegu Division	27,522	14,304	13,218	187	129	285	219	13,832	12,870	5	5	...	1	...	...	...	4	...
5	City of Rangoon ...	3,114	1,793	1,321	110	78	189	172	1,494	1,071	5	5	...	1	...	...	...	4	...
6	Hanthawaddy	7,981	4,149	3,832	58	32	77	36	4,014	3,764	...	...	...	...	...	...	...	...	...
7	Tharrawaddy	5,145	2,623	2,522	6	8	4	...	2,613	2,514	...	...	...	...	...	...	...	...	...
8	Pegu	10,730	5,456	5,274	11	8	9	10	5,436	5,250	...	...	...	...	...	...	...	...	...
9	Prome	552	283	269	2	3	6	1	275	265	...	...	...	...	...	...	...	...	...
	Irrawaddy Division ...	55,564	27,804	27,760	26	16	9	6	27,769	27,738		...	...	...	...	...	...	...	...
10	Bassein	22,042	11,481	11,461	10	7	...	1	11,471	11,453	...	...	...	...	...	...	...	...	...
11	Henzada	5,059	2,467	2,592	9	8	2	5	2,456	2,579	...	...	...	...	...	...	...	...	...
12	Myaungmya	13,848	6,870	6,978	1	...	2	...	6,867	6,978	...	...	...	...	...	...	...	...	...
13	Ma-ubin	8,769	4,394	4,375	6	1	2	...	4,386	4,374	...	...	...	...	...	...	...	...	...
14	Pyapôn	4,946	2,592	2,354	...	...	3	...	2,589	2,354	...	...	...	...	...	...	...	...	...
	Tenasserim Division ...	31,972	16,044	15,928	71	77	119	89	15,854	15,762	...	...	...	...	...	...	...	...	...
15	Toungoo	18,598	9,283	9,315	30	23	18	11	9,235	9,281	...	...	...	...	...	...	...	...	...
16	Salween	368	213	155	6	...	...	...	207	155	...	...	...	...	...	...	...	...	...
17	Thatôn	2,945	1,446	1,499	...	1	13	6	1,433	1,492	...	...	...	...	...	...	...	...	...
18	Amherst	4,557	2,317	2,240	15	47	86	69	2,216	2,124	...	...	...	...	...	...	...	...	...
19	Tavoy	1,828	944	884	12	...	1	...	931	884	...	...	...	...	...	...	...	...	...
20	Mergui	3,676	1,841	1,835	8	6	1	3	1,832	1,826	...	...	...	...	...	...	...	...	...
	Magwe Division	503	268	235	76	13	12	6	180	216	...	...	...	...	...	...	...	...	...
21	Thayetmyo	236	100	136	9	2	...	...	91	134	...	...	...	...	...	...	...	...	...
22	Pakôkku	69	39	30	6	1	2	1	31	28	...	...	...	...	...	...	...	...	...
23	Minbu	30	14	16	1	4	4	3	9	9	...	...	...	...	...	...	...	...	...
24	Magwe	168	115	53	60	6	6	2	49	45	...	...	...	...	...	...	...	...	...
	Mandalay Division ...	1,811	972	839	53	30	65	50	854	759	...	...	...	...	...	...	...	...	...
25	Mandalay (including City) ...	570	293	277	35	23	58	48	200	206	...	...	...	...	...	...	...	...	...
26	Bhamo	780	410	376	6	4	2	...	402	372	...	...	...	...	...	...	...	...	...
27	Myitkyina	349	185	164	5	3	3	2	177	159	...	...	...	...	...	...	...	...	...
28	Katha	82	64	18	...	...	2	...	62	18	...	...	...	...	...	...	...	...	...
29	Ruby Mines	24	20	4	7	...	...	...	13	4	...	...	...	...	...	...	...	...	...
	Mandalay City	*374*	*185*	*189*	*26*	*14*	*35*	*14*	*126*	*161*	...	...	...	...	...	...	...	...	...
	Sagaing Division	596	234	362	14	9	18	14	202	339	...	...	...	...	...	...	...	...	...
30	Shwebo	447	147	300	12	8	3	3	132	289	...	...	...	...	...	...	...	...	...
31	Sagaing	56	28	28	...	...	12	11	16	17	...	...	...	...	...	...	...	...	...
32	Lower Chindwin ...	54	30	24	...	...	1	...	29	24	...	...	...	...	...	...	...	...	...
33	Upper Chindwin ...	39	29	10	2	1	2	...	25	9	...	...	...	...	...	...	...	...	...
	Meiktila Division	594	303	291	18	7	19	22	266	262	...	...	...	...	...	...	...	...	...
34	Kyauksè	63	30	33	1	2	1	...	28	31	...	...	...	...	...	...	...	...	...
35	Meiktila	109	60	49	8	2	13	13	39	34	...	...	...	...	...	...	...	...	...
36	Yamèthin	355	168	187	6	1	5	8	157	178	...	...	...	...	...	...	...	...	...
37	Myingyan	67	45	22	3	2	...	1	42	19	...	...	...	...	...	...	...	...	...
	Specially Administered Territories.	3,197	1,558	1,639	15	9	8	5	1,535	1,625	...	...	...	...	...	...	...	...	...
38	Northern Shan States ...	201	150	51	3	2	3	5	144	44	...	...	...	...	...	...	...	...	...
39	Southern Shan States ...	2,784	1,295	1,489	12	6	1	...	1,282	1,483	...	...	...	...	...	...	...	...	...
40	Pakôkku Hill Tracts ...	...	...	...	...	...	...	...	...	...	...	...	...	...	...	...	...	...	...
41	Chin Hills	212	113	99	...	1	4	...	109	98	...	...	...	...	...	...	...	...	...

of the Christian Population by Sect and Race.

GREEK.									LUTHERAN.									
Total.			Distribution by Race.						Total.			Distribution by Race.						
			Europeans and Allied Races.		Anglo-Indians.		Natives.					Europeans and Allied Races.		Anglo-Indians.		Natives.		
Persons.	Males.	Females.	Males.	Females.	Males.	Females.	Males.	Females.	Persons.	Males.	Females.	Males.	Females.	Males.	Females.	Males.	Females.	Serial No.
47	48	49	50	51	52	53	54	55	56	57	58	59	60	61	62	63	64	
49	41	8	39	8	...	...	2	...	328	216	112	61	8	2	...	153	104	
49	41	8	39	8	...	...	2	...	328	216	112	61	8	2	...	153	104	
...	...	...	...	...	...	...	...	...	...	...	...	...	...	...	...	...	...	
...	...	...	...	...	...	...	...	...	...	...	...	...	...	...	...	...	...	1
...	...	...	...	...	...	...	...	...	...	...	...	...	...	...	...	...	...	2
...	...	...	...	...	...	...	...	...	...	...	...	...	...	...	...	...	...	3
...	...	...	...	...	...	...	...	...	...	...	...	...	...	...	...	...	...	4
48	41	7	39	7	...	...	2	...	297	185	112	31	8	1	...	153	104	
48	41	7	39	7	...	...	2	...	297	185	112	31	8	1	...	153	104	5
...	...	...	...	...	...	...	...	...	...	...	...	...	...	...	...	...	...	6
...	...	...	...	...	...	...	...	...	...	...	...	...	...	...	...	...	...	7
...	...	...	...	...	...	...	...	...	...	...	...	...	...	...	...	...	...	8
...	...	...	...	...	...	...	...	...	...	...	...	...	...	...	...	...	...	9
...	...	...	...	...	...	...	...	...	...	...	...	...	...	...	...	...	...	
...	...	...	...	...	...	...	...	...	...	...	...	...	...	...	...	...	...	10
...	...	...	...	...	...	...	...	...	...	...	...	...	...	...	...	...	...	11
...	...	...	...	...	...	...	...	...	...	...	...	...	...	...	...	...	...	12
...	...	...	...	...	...	...	...	...	...	...	...	...	...	...	...	...	...	13
...	...	...	...	...	...	...	...	...	...	...	...	...	...	...	...	...	...	14
1	...	1	...	1	...	...	...	...	31	31	...	30	...	1	...	...	...	
...	...	...	...	...	...	...	...	...	...	...	...	...	...	...	...	...	...	15
...	...	...	...	...	...	...	...	...	...	...	...	...	...	...	...	...	...	16
1	...	1	...	1	...	...	...	...	1	1	...	...	...	1	...	...	...	17
...	...	...	...	...	...	...	...	...	29	29	...	29	...	...	...	...	...	18
...	...	...	...	...	...	...	...	...	1	1	...	1	...	...	...	...	...	19
...	...	...	...	...	...	...	...	...	...	...	...	...	...	...	...	...	...	20
...	...	...	...	...	...	...	...	...	...	...	...	...	...	...	...	...	...	
...	...	...	...	...	...	...	...	...	...	...	...	...	...	...	...	...	...	21
...	...	...	...	...	...	...	...	...	...	...	...	...	...	...	...	...	...	22
...	...	...	...	...	...	...	...	...	...	...	...	...	...	...	...	...	...	23
...	...	...	...	...	...	...	...	...	...	...	...	...	...	...	...	...	...	24
...	...	...	...	...	...	...	...	...	...	...	...	...	...	...	...	...	...	
...	...	...	...	...	...	...	...	...	...	...	...	...	...	...	...	...	...	25
...	...	...	...	...	...	...	...	...	...	...	...	...	...	...	...	...	...	26
...	...	...	...	...	...	...	...	...	...	...	...	...	...	...	...	...	...	27
...	...	...	...	...	...	...	...	...	...	...	...	...	...	...	...	...	...	28
...	...	...	...	...	...	...	...	...	...	...	...	...	...	...	...	...	...	29
...	...	...	...	...	...	...	...	...	...	...	...	...	...	...	...	...	...	
...	...	...	...	...	...	...	...	...	...	...	...	...	...	...	...	...	...	30
...	...	...	...	...	...	...	...	...	...	...	...	...	...	...	...	...	...	31
...	...	...	...	...	...	...	...	...	...	...	...	...	...	...	...	...	...	32
...	...	...	...	...	...	...	...	...	...	...	...	...	...	...	...	...	...	33
...	...	...	...	...	...	...	...	...	...	...	...	...	...	...	...	...	...	
...	...	...	...	...	...	...	...	...	...	...	...	...	...	...	...	...	...	34
...	...	...	...	...	...	...	...	...	...	...	...	...	...	...	...	...	...	35
...	...	...	...	...	...	...	...	...	...	...	...	...	...	...	...	...	...	36
...	...	...	...	...	...	...	...	...	...	...	...	...	...	...	...	...	...	37
...	...	...	...	...	...	...	...	...	...	...	...	...	...	...	...	...	...	
...	...	...	...	...	...	...	...	...	...	...	...	...	...	...	...	...	...	38
...	...	...	...	...	...	...	...	...	...	...	...	...	...	...	...	...	...	39
...	...	...	...	...	...	...	...	...	...	...	...	...	...	...	...	...	...	40
...	...	...	...	...	...	...	...	...	...	...	...	...	...	...	...	...	...	41

Serial No.	District or State.	METHODIST. Total. Persons.	Males.	Females.	Distribution by Race. Europeans and Allied Races. Males.	Females.	Anglo-Indians. Males.	Females.	Natives. Males.	Females.	MINOR PROTESTANT DENOMINATIONS. Total. Persons.	Males.	Females.	Distribution by Race. Europeans and Allied Races. Males.	Females.	Anglo-Indians. Males.	Females.	Natives. Males.	Females.
	1	65	66	67	68	69	70	71	72	73	74	75	76	77	78	79	80	81	82
	Provincial Total	1,675	974	701	202	79	102	113	670	509	49	21	28	7	11	10	14	4	2
	Burma Proper	1,165	689	476	201	77	101	112	387	287	43	21	22	7	8	10	11	4	2
	Arakan Division	2	...	2	...	2	...	...	...	...	...	...	...	...	...	...	...	...	...
1	Akyab	2	...	2	...	2	...	...	...	...	...	...	...	...	...	...	...	...	...
2	Northern Arakan	...	...	...	...	...	...	...	...	...	...	...	...	...	...	...	...	...	...
3	Kyaukpyu	...	...	...	...	...	...	...	...	...	...	...	...	...	...	...	...	...	...
4	Sandoway	...	...	...	...	...	...	...	...	...	...	...	...	...	...	...	...	...	...
	Pegu Division	570	337	233	121	36	65	86	151	111	43	21	22	7	8	10	11	4	2
5	City of Rangoon	407	238	163	89	24	62	73	87	72	43	21	22	7	8	10	11	4	2
6	Hanthawaddy	94	61	33	29	10	...	11	32	12	...	...	...	...	...	...	...	...	...
7	Tharrawaddy	21	9	12	1	1	...	...	8	11	...	...	...	...	...	...	...	...	...
8	Pegu	46	27	19	...	1	3	2	24	16	...	...	...	...	...	...	...	...	...
9	Prome	2	2	...	2	...	...	...	...	...	...	...	...	...	...	...	...	...	...
	Irrawaddy Division	12	7	5	1	...	...	...	6	5	...	...	...	...	...	...	...	...	...
10	Bassein	1	1	...	...	...	...	...	1	...	...	...	...	...	...	...	...	...	...
11	Henzada	5	3	2	...	...	...	...	3	2	...	...	...	...	...	...	...	...	...
12	Myaungmya	1	1	...	1	...	...	...	...	...	...	...	...	...	...	...	...	...	...
13	Ma-ubin	5	2	3	...	...	...	...	2	3	...	...	...	...	...	...	...	...	...
14	Pyapôn	...	...	...	...	...	...	...	...	...	...	...	...	...	...	...	...	...	...
	Tenasserim Division	179	103	76	9	23	13	8	81	45	...	...	...	...	...	...	...	...	...
15	Toungoo	76	40	36	7	23	7	5	26	8	...	...	...	...	...	...	...	...	...
16	Salween	...	...	...	...	...	...	...	...	...	...	...	...	...	...	...	...	...	...
17	Thatôn	96	56	40	...	...	6	3	50	37	...	...	...	...	...	...	...	...	...
18	Amherst	...	...	...	...	...	...	...	...	...	...	...	...	...	...	...	...	...	...
19	Tavoy	2	2	...	2	...	...	...	...	...	...	...	...	...	...	...	...	...	...
20	Mergui	5	5	...	...	...	...	...	5	...	...	...	...	...	...	...	...	...	...
	Magwe Division	7	4	3	3	2	1	...	...	1	...	...	...	...	...	...	...	...	...
21	Thayetmyo	...	...	...	...	...	...	...	...	...	...	...	...	...	...	...	...	...	...
22	Pakôkku	7	4	3	3	2	1	...	...	1	...	...	...	...	...	...	...	...	...
23	Minbu	...	...	...	...	...	...	...	...	...	...	...	...	...	...	...	...	...	...
24	Magwe	...	...	...	...	...	...	...	...	...	...	...	...	...	...	...	...	...	...
	Mandalay Division	168	118	50	48	9	17	16	53	25	...	...	...	...	...	...	...	...	...
25	Mandalay (including City) ...	135	90	45	37	9	14	14	39	22	...	...	...	...	...	...	...	...	...
26	Bhamo	12	9	3	3	...	...	1	6	2	...	...	...	...	...	...	...	...	...
27	Myitkyina	1	1	...	1	...	...	...	...	...	...	...	...	...	...	...	...	...	...
28	Katha	19	17	2	6	...	3	1	8	1	...	...	...	...	...	...	...	...	...
29	Ruby Mines	1	1	...	1	...	...	...	...	...	...	...	...	...	...	...	...	...	...
	Mandalay City	*107*	*62*	*45*	*17*	*9*	*13*	*14*	*32*	*22*	...	...	...	...	...	...	...	...	...
	Sagaing Division	55	32	23	8	...	2	1	22	22	...	...	...	...	...	...	...	...	...
30	Shwebo	5	5	...	4	...	...	...	1	...	...	...	...	...	...	...	...	...	...
31	Sagaing	1	...	1	...	...	...	1	...	...	...	...	...	...	...	...	...	...	...
32	Lower Chindwin	45	23	22	3	...	...	...	20	22	...	...	...	...	...	...	...	...	...
33	Upper Chindwin	4	4	...	1	...	2	...	1	...	...	...	...	...	...	...	...	...	...
	Meiktila Division	172	88	84	11	5	3	1	74	78	...	...	...	...	...	...	...	...	...
34	Kyauksè	21	9	12	1	...	2	...	6	12	...	...	...	...	...	...	...	...	...
35	Meiktila	23	10	13	5	5	...	1	5	7	...	...	...	...	...	...	...	...	...
36	Yamèthin	125	66	59	4	...	1	...	61	59	...	...	...	...	...	...	...	...	...
37	Myingyan	3	3	...	1	...	...	...	2	...	...	...	...	...	...	...	...	...	...
	Specially Administered Territories.	510	285	225	1	2	1	1	283	222	6	...	6	...	3	...	3	...	...
38	Northern Shan States ...	7	1	6	...	2	1	1	...	3	...	...	...	...	...	...	...	...	...
39	Southern Shan States ...	503	284	219	1	...	...	...	283	219	6	...	6	...	3	...	3	...	...
40	Pakôkku Hill Tracts ...	...	...	...	...	...	...	...	...	...	...	...	...	...	...	...	...	...	...
41	Chin Hills	...	...	...	...	...	...	...	...	...	...	...	...	...	...	...	...	...	...

of the Christian Population by Sect and Race.

PRESBYTERIAN.									PROTESTANT (UNSECTARIAN OR SECT NOT SPECIFIED).									
Total.			Distribution by Race.						Total.			Distribution by Race.						
			Europeans and Allied Races.		Anglo-Indians.		Natives.					Europeans and Allied Races.		Anglo-Indians.		Natives.		
Persons.	Males.	Females.	Males.	Females.	Males.	Females.	Males.	Females.	Persons.	Males.	Females.	Males.	Females.	Males.	Females.	Males.	Females.	Serial No.
83	84	85	86	87	88	89	90	91	92	93	94	95	96	97	98	99	100	
1,009	824	195	739	136	39	28	36	31	2,782	1,520	1,262	267	44	63	50	1,190	1,168	
1,000	806	194	734	136	36	27	36	31	2,782	1,520	1,262	267	44	63	50	1,190	1,168	
33	31	2	30	2	1	...	...	...	32	16	16	...	...	2	4	14	12	
33	31	2	30	2	1	...	...	...	2	...	2	...	...	...	2	...	...	1
...	...	...	...	...	...	...	...	...	...	...	...	...	...	...	...	...	...	2
...	...	...	...	...	...	...	...	...	30	16	14	...	...	2	2	14	12	3
...	...	...	...	...	...	...	...	...	...	...	...	...	...	...	...	...	...	4
644	496	148	452	101	19	21	24	26	775	491	284	244	34	36	22	211	228	
573	434	139	391	100	19	13	24	26	277	240	37	203	4	18	8	19	25	5
64	56	8	56	...	...	8	...	...	60	30	30	30	19	...	11	...	...	6
...	...	...	...	...	...	...	...	...	...	...	...	...	...	...	...	...	...	7
...	...	...	...	...	...	...	...	...	408	204	204	9	11	14	3	181	190	8
7	6	1	6	1	...	...	...	...	30	17	13	2	...	4	...	11	13	9
41	34	7	32	5	...	1	2	1	1,846	928	918	4	4	...	...	924	914	
16	14	2	14	2	...	...	...	...	1,681	852	829	4	4	...	...	848	825	10
4	4	...	3	...	...	...	1	...	165	76	89	...	...	...	...	76	89	11
...	...	...	...	...	...	...	...	...	...	...	...	...	...	...	...	...	...	12
8	5	3	5	2	...	1	...	...	...	...	...	...	...	...	...	...	...	13
13	11	2	10	1	...	...	1	1	...	...	...	...	...	...	...	...	...	14
31	25	6	20	4	5	2	...	...	71	46	25	9	4	24	17	13	4	
4	4	...	4	...	...	...	...	...	...	...	...	...	...	...	...	...	...	15
...	...	...	...	...	...	...	...	...	...	...	...	...	...	...	...	...	...	16
4	1	3	1	2	...	1	...	...	...	...	...	...	...	...	...	...	...	17
16	14	2	9	2	5	...	...	...	64	39	25	7	4	21	17	11	4	18
3	3	...	3	...	...	...	...	...	2	2	...	...	...	...	...	2	...	19
4	3	1	3	...	...	...	...	...	5	5	...	2	...	3	...	...	...	20
13	13	...	13	...	...	...	...	...	20	15	5	10	2	1	...	4	3	
...	...	...	...	...	...	...	...	...	...	...	...	...	...	...	...	...	...	21
13	13	...	13	...	...	...	...	...	20	15	5	10	2	1	...	4	3	22
...	...	...	...	...	...	...	...	...	...	...	...	...	...	...	...	...	...	23
...	...	...	...	...	...	...	...	...	...	...	...	...	...	...	...	...	...	24
201	177	24	164	19	7	3	6	2	38	24	14	...	...	...	7	24	7	
155	137	18	128	14	3	2	6	2	38	24	14	...	...	...	7	24	7	25
10	10	...	10	...	...	...	...	...	...	...	...	...	...	...	...	...	...	26
18	17	1	14	...	3	1	...	...	...	...	...	...	...	...	...	...	...	27
5	3	2	3	2	...	...	...	...	...	...	...	...	...	...	...	...	...	28
13	10	3	10	3	...	...	...	...	...	...	...	...	...	...	...	...	...	29
55	*43*	*12*	*41*	*10*	...	...	*2*	*2*	*38*	*24*	*14*	...	...	...	*7*	*24*	*7*	
8	7	1	5	1	1	...	1	...	...	...	...	...	...	...	...	...	...	
1	...	1	...	1	...	...	...	...	...	...	...	...	...	...	...	...	...	30
...	...	...	...	...	...	...	...	...	...	...	...	...	...	...	...	...	...	31
...	...	...	...	...	...	...	...	...	...	...	...	...	...	...	...	...	...	32
7	7	...	5	...	1	...	1	...	...	...	...	...	...	...	...	...	...	33
29	23	6	17	4	3	...	3	2	...	...	...	...	...	...	...	...	...	
4	3	1	...	...	1	...	2	1	...	...	...	...	...	...	...	...	...	34
6	5	1	3	1	2	...	...	...	...	...	...	...	...	...	...	...	...	35
10	8	2	8	2	...	...	...	...	...	...	...	...	...	...	...	...	...	36
9	7	2	6	1	...	...	1	1	...	...	...	...	...	...	...	...	...	37
9	8	1	5	...	3	1	...	...	...	...	...	...	...	...	...	...	...	
9	8	1	5	...	3	1	...	...	...	...	...	...	...	...	...	...	...	38
...	...	...	...	...	...	...	...	...	...	...	...	...	...	...	...	...	...	39
...	...	...	...	...	...	...	...	...	...	...	...	...	...	...	...	...	...	40
...	...	...	...	...	...	...	...	...	...	...	...	...	...	...	...	...	...	41

Serial No.	District or State.	ROMAN CATHOLIC.											
		Total.			Distribution by Race.						Total.		
					Europeans and Allied Races.		Anglo-Indians.		Natives.				
		Persons.	Males.	Females.	Males.	Females.	Males.	Females.	Males.	Females.	Persons.	Males.	Females.
	1	101	102	103	104	105	106	107	108	109	110	111	112
	Provincial Total	60,282	32,403	27,879	2,501	1,093	3,156	2,762	26,746	24,024	581	382	199
	Burma Proper	53,825	29,182	24,643	2,481	1,092	3,136	2,753	23,565	20,798	581	382	199
	Arakan Division	434	290	144	79	35	78	72	133	37	...	...	...
1	Akyab	381	262	119	69	24	70	62	123	33	...	...	...
2	Northern Arakan ...	1	...	1	...	...	...	1	...	...	...	...	...
3	Kyaukpyu	21	11	10	...	2	3	5	8	3	...	...	...
4	Sandoway	31	17	14	10	9	5	4	2	1	...	...	...
	Pegu Division	15,795	8,708	7,087	1,057	497	1,935	1,648	5,726	4,942	547	365	182
5	City of Rangoon ...	10,958	6,252	4,706	833	351	1,686	1,468	3,733	2,887	547	365	182
6	Hanthawaddy	2,815	1,452	1,363	158	100	169	112	1,125	1,151	...	...	...
7	Tharrawaddy	783	324	459	14	4	20	16	290	439	...	...	...
8	Pegu	1,001	560	441	34	29	51	37	475	375	...	...	...
9	Prome	238	120	118	18	13	9	15	93	90	...	...	...
	Irrawaddy Division ...	14,474	7,605	6,869	115	104	54	48	7,436	6,717	...	...	...
10	Bassein	2,642	1,344	1,298	72	89	15	18	1,257	1,191	...	...	...
11	Henzada	4,922	2,458	2,464	32	13	16	16	2,410	2,435	...	...	...
12	Myaungmya	3,949	2,145	1,804	7	1	10	10	2,128	1,793	...	...	...
13	Ma-ubin	1,248	593	655	2	...	8	1	583	654	...	...	...
14	Pyapôn	1,713	1,065	648	2	1	5	3	1,058	644	...	...	...
	Tenasserim Division ...	12,980	6,861	6,119	271	137	494	510	6,096	5,472	...	...	...
15	Toungoo	10,188	5,226	4,962	74	41	65	68	5,087	4,853	...	...	...
16	Salween	12	6	6	3	5	...	...	3	1	...	...	...
17	Thatôn	617	445	172	10	..	43	23	392	149	...	...	...
18	Amherst	1,534	807	727	85	41	360	400	362	286	...	...	...
19	Tavoy	114	82	32	34	...	11	2	37	30	...	...	...
20	Mergui	515	295	220	65	50	15	17	215	153	...	...	...
	Magwe Division	609	382	227	79	16	34	29	269	182	...	...	...
21	Thayetmyo	189	112	77	26	5	11	10	75	62	...	...	...
22	Pakôkku	119	63	56	5	3	6	1	54	52	...	...	...
23	Minbu	57	43	14	6	...	5	5	32	9	...	...	...
24	Magwe	244	164	80	44	8	12	13	108	59	...	...	...
	Mandalay Division ...	4,839	2,805	2,034	769	252	382	318	1,654	1,464	34	17	17
25	Mandalay (including City) ...	3,858	2,240	1,618	710	234	334	271	1,196	1,113	28	11	17
26	Bhamo	646	341	305	12	7	10	8	319	290	...	...	...
27	Myitkyina	95	61	34	17	6	8	9	36	19	6	6	...
28	Katha	160	109	51	13	1	12	13	84	37	...	...	...
29	Ruby Mines	80	54	26	17	4	18	17	19	5	...	...	...
	Mandalay City	*2,675*	*1,445*	*1,230*	*287*	*194*	*234*	*153*	*924*	*883*	...	...	...
	Sagaing Division	2,537	1,399	1,138	42	13	65	40	1,292	1,085	...	...	...
30	Shwebo	1,481	844	637	22	4	19	21	803	612	...	...	...
31	Sagaing	823	378	445	14	7	21	15	343	428	...	...	...
32	Lower Chindwin	131	90	41	4	1	7	2	79	38	...	...	...
33	Upper Chindwin	102	87	15	2	1	18	2	67	12	..	...	...
	Meiktila Division	2,157	1,132	1,025	69	38	94	88	969	899	...	...	...
34	Kyauksè	545	273	272	12	8	8	10	253	254	...	...	...
35	Meiktila	259	147	112	11	13	10	9	126	90	...	...	...
36	Yamèthin	1,178	596	582	21	11	64	63	511	508	...	...	...
37	Myingyan	175	116	59	25	6	12	6	79	47	...	...	...
	Specially Administered Territories.	6,457	3,221	3,236	20	1	20	9	3,181	3,226	...	...	...
38	Northern Shan States ...	86	28	58	8	...	2	3	18	55	...	...	...
39	Southern Shan States ...	6,366	3,189	3,177	11	1	18	6	3,160	3,170	...	...	...
40	Pakôkku Hill Tracts ...	1	1	...	...	...	...	...	1	...	...	...	...
41	Chin Hills	4	3	1	1	...	...	...	2	1	...	...	...

of the Christian Population by Sect and Race.

SECT NOT RETURNED.						INDEFINITE BELIEFS.									
Distribution by Race.						Total.			Distribution by Race.						
Europeans and Allied Races.		Anglo-Indians.		Natives.					Europeans and Allied Races.		Anglo-Indians.		Natives.		
Males.	Females.	Males.	Females.	Males.	Females.	Persons.	Males.	Females.	Males.	Females.	Males.	Females.	Males.	Females.	Serial No.
113	114	115	116	117	118	119	120	121	122	123	124	125	126	127	
122	41	29	31	221	127	66	61	5	49	3	12	2	...	...	
122	41	39	31	221	127	66	61	5	49	3	12	2	...	...	
...	...	...	...	...	...	...	...	...	...	...	...	...	...	...	
...	...	...	...	...	...	...	...	...	...	...	...	...	...	...	1
...	...	...	...	...	...	...	...	...	...	...	...	...	...	...	2
...	...	...	...	...	...	...	...	...	...	...	...	...	...	...	3
...	...	...	...	...	...	...	...	...	...	...	...	...	...	...	4
120	41	35	31	220	110	60	55	5	43	3	12	2	...	...	
120	41	35	31	210	110	60	55	5	43	3	12	2	...	...	5
...	...	...	...	...	...	...	...	...	...	...	...	...	...	...	6
...	...	...	...	...	...	...	...	...	...	...	...	...	...	...	7
...	...	...	...	...	...	...	...	...	...	...	...	...	...	...	8
...	...	...	...	...	...	...	...	...	...	...	...	...	...	...	9
...	...	...	...	...	...	...	...	...	...	...	...	...	...	...	
...	...	...	...	...	...	...	...	...	...	...	...	...	...	...	10
...	...	...	...	...	...	...	...	...	...	...	...	...	...	...	11
...	...	...	...	...	...	...	...	...	...	...	...	...	...	...	12
...	...	...	...	...	...	...	...	...	...	...	...	...	...	...	13
...	...	...	...	...	...	...	...	...	...	...	...	...	...	...	14
...	...	...	...	...	...	3	3	...	3	...	...	...	...	...	
...	...	...	...	...	...	...	...	...	...	...	...	...	...	...	15
...	...	...	...	...	...	...	...	...	...	...	...	...	...	...	16
...	...	...	...	...	...	...	...	...	...	...	...	...	...	...	17
...	...	...	...	...	...	3	3	...	3	...	...	...	...	...	18
...	...	...	...	...	...	...	...	...	...	...	...	...	...	...	19
...	...	...	...	...	...	...	...	...	...	...	...	...	...	...	20
...	...	...	...	...	...	1	1	...	1	...	...	...	...	...	
...	...	...	...	...	...	...	...	...	...	...	...	...	...	...	21
...	...	...	...	...	...	...	...	...	...	...	...	...	...	...	22
...	...	...	...	...	...	...	...	...	...	...	...	...	...	...	23
...	...	...	...	...	...	1	1	...	1	...	...	...	...	...	24
2	...	4	...	11	27	2	2	...	2	...	...	...	...	...	
...	...	4	...	7	17	...	...	...	...	...	...	...	...	...	25
...	...	...	...	...	...	...	...	...	...	...	...	...	...	...	26
2	...	...	...	4	...	2	2	...	2	...	...	...	...	...	27
...	...	...	...	...	...	...	...	...	...	...	...	...	...	...	28
...	...	...	...	...	...	...	...	...	...	...	...	...	...	...	29
...	...	...	...	...	...	...	...	...	...	...	...	...	...	...	
...	...	...	...	...	...	...	...	...	...	...	...	...	...	...	30
...	...	...	...	...	...	...	...	...	...	...	...	...	...	...	31
...	...	...	...	...	...	...	...	...	...	...	...	...	...	...	32
...	...	...	...	...	...	...	...	...	...	...	...	...	...	...	33
...	...	...	...	...	...	...	...	...	...	...	...	...	...	...	
...	...	...	...	...	...	...	...	...	...	...	...	...	...	...	34
...	...	...	...	...	...	...	...	...	...	...	...	...	...	...	35
...	...	...	...	...	...	...	...	...	...	...	...	...	...	...	36
...	...	...	...	...	...	...	...	...	...	...	...	...	...	...	37
...	...	...	...	...	...	...	...	...	...	...	...	...	...	...	
...	...	...	...	...	...	...	...	...	...	...	...	...	...	...	38
...	...	...	...	...	...	...	...	...	...	...	...	...	...	...	39
...	...	...	...	...	...	...	...	...	...	...	...	...	...	...	40
...	...	...	...	...	...	...	...	...	...	...	...	...	...	...	41

IMPERIAL TABLE XVIII.

Europeans, Armenians and Anglo-Indians by Race and Age.

NOTE.—The discrepancies between the totals of Columns 6, 19 and 32 of this table and Column 5 of Table XVII are due to the inclusion of ten European Buddhists in this Table and their exclusion from Table XVII.

IMPERIAL TABLE XVIII.—*Europeans, Armenians*

Serial No.	District or State.	TOTAL.			EUROPEANS AND									
					British Subjects.									
					All Ages.			0—12		12—15		15—30		
		Total.	Males.	Females.	Total.	Males.	Females.	Males.	Females.	Males.	Females.	Males.	Females.
	1	2	3	4	5	6	7	8	9	10	11	12	13
	Provincial Total ...	**24,549**	**16,068**	**8,486**	**11,828**	**8,904**	**2,924**	**726**	**756**	**102**	**122**	**4,706**	**941**
	Burma Proper ...	**24,307**	**15,887**	**8,420**	**11,683**	**8,795**	**2,888**	**716**	**746**	**102**	**120**	**4,668**	**936**
	Arakan Division ...	*471*	*312*	*159*	*256*	*195*	*61*	*18*	*15*	...	...	*68*	*18*
1	Akyab	405	273	132	225	177	48	15	11	...	...	64	14
2	Northern Arakan ...	6	4	2	5	4	1	...	...	...	...	1	...
3	Kyaukpyu ...	21	10	11	4	1	3	...	...	...	...	...	...
4	Sandoway ...	39	25	14	22	13	9	3	4	...	...	3	4
	Pegu Division ...	*13,852*	*8,923*	*4,929*	*6,212*	*4,623*	*1,589*	*378*	*382*	*55*	*49*	*2,229*	*511*
5	City of Rangoon ...	11,782	7,569	4,213	5,162	3,866	1,296	286	296	37	34	1,852	429
6	Hanthawaddy ...	1,475	988	487	791	595	196	67	64	18	10	328	50
7	Tharrawaddy ...	139	87	52	45	31	14	7	1	...	1	5	4
8	Pegu	326	199	127	132	77	55	11	15	...	...	27	21
9	Prome	130	80	50	82	54	28	7	6	...	4	17	7
	Irrawaddy Division ...	*835*	*569*	*266*	*494*	*357*	*137*	*32*	*34*	*3*	*3*	*138*	*68*
10	Bassein	513	351	162	332	242	90	14	20	3	1	95	49
11	Henzada	164	103	61	87	57	30	15	12	...	1	15	8
12	Myaungmya ...	70	47	23	24	17	7	1	1	...	...	6	2
13	Ma-ubin	48	37	11	26	20	6	...	...	...	1	9	2
14	Pyapôn	40	31	9	25	21	4	2	1	...	...	8	2
	Tenasserim Division ...	*2,678*	*1,490*	*1,188*	*725*	*435*	*290*	*84*	*96*	*22*	*28*	*115*	*87*
15	Toungoo	605	334	271	298	163	135	53	41	18	16	35	40
16	Salween	18	13	5	12	11	1	...	...	...	...	6	1
17	Thatôn	168	112	56	8	4	4	...	1	...	...	2	2
18	Amherst	1,567	802	765	237	112	125	11	46	2	12	39	38
19	Tavoy	108	100	8	84	83	1	12	1	1	...	15	...
20	Mergui	212	129	83	86	62	24	8	7	1	...	18	6
	Magwe Division ...	*608*	*469*	*139*	*340*	*272*	*68*	*13*	*26*	*1*	...	*160*	*16*
21	Thayetmyo	225	190	35	181	166	15	7	5	...	...	113	2
22	Pakôkku	106	74	32	62	38	24	3	10	...	...	17	5
23	Minbu	63	37	26	27	18	9	...	5	1	..	7	2
24	Magwe	214	168	46	70	50	20	3	6	...	...	23	7
	Mandalay Division ...	*4,018*	*2,754*	*1,264*	*2,469*	*1,916*	*553*	*123*	*135*	*12*	*34*	*1,276*	*185*
25	Mandalay (including City).	3,260	2,153	1,107	1,891	1,418	473	101	113	8	31	991	153
26	Bhamo	334	283	51	302	266	36	7	10	2	...	201	15
27	Myitkyina	152	120	32	116	99	17	3	5	...	1	42	8
28	Katha	125	94	31	67	59	8	4	...	2	1	20	4
29	Ruby Mines	147	104	43	93	74	19	8	7	...	1	22	5
	Mandalay City ...	*1,591*	*988*	*603*	*892*	*577*	*315*	*72*	*85*	*7*	*29*	*320*	*100*
	Sagaing Division ...	*992*	*792*	*200*	*731*	*635*	*96*	*38*	*28*	*3*	*2*	*472*	*29*
30	Shwebo	706	603	103	623	560	63	34	19	3	2	447	18
31	Sagaing	171	103	68	52	35	17	2	4	...	...	8	7
32	Lower Chindwin ...	61	36	25	36	21	15	2	4	...	...	4	4
33	Upper Chindwin ...	54	50	4	20	19	1	...	1	...	...	13	...
	Meiktila Division ...	*853*	*578*	*275*	*456*	*362*	*94*	*30*	*30*	*6*	*4*	*215*	*27*
34	Kyauksè	77	45	32	30	16	14	5	4	...	1	2	3
35	Meiktila	349	269	80	265	224	41	13	15	5	2	170	16
36	Yamèthin	315	184	131	99	77	22	10	5	...	...	30	7
37	Myingyan	112	80	32	62	45	17	2	6	1	1	13	1
	Specially Administered Territories.	**242**	**176**	**66**	**145**	**109**	**36**	**10**	**10**	...	**2**	**38**	**5**
38	Northern Shan States	76	56	20	35	29	6	1	2	...	...	10	...
39	Southern Shan States	143	103	40	95	69	26	9	8	...	2	24	3
40	Pakôkku Hill Tracts	2	2	...	2	2	...	...	...	...	...	1	...
41	Chin Hills	21	15	6	13	9	4	...	...	...	...	3	2

and Anglo-Indians by Race and Age.

ALLIED RACES.

30—50		50 and over.		OTHERS. All Ages.			OTHERS. 0—12		OTHERS. 12—15		OTHERS. 15—30		OTHERS. 30—50		OTHERS. 50 and over.		
Males.	Females.	Males.	Females.	Total.	Males.	Females.	Males.	Females.	Males.	Females.	Males.	Females.	Males.	Females.	Males.	Females.	Serial No.
14	15	16	17	18	19	20	21	22	23	24	25	26	27	28	29	30	
2,929	940	441	165	1,342	974	368	65	60	18	22	382	118	419	127	90	41	
2,875	921	434	165	1,320	957	363	62	60	18	22	378	118	411	125	88	38	
95	*20*	*14*	*8*	*14*	*9*	*5*	...	...	...	...	*8*	...	*4*	*4*	*2*	*1*	
84	18	14	5	12	8	4	...	...	...	...	2	...	4	3	2	1	1
3	1	...	...	...	...	...	...	...	...	...	...	...	...	...	...	...	2
1	1	...	2	1	...	1	...	...	...	...	...	...	...	1	...	...	3
7	...	...	1	1	1	...	...	...	...	...	1	...	...	...	...	...	4
1,700	*552*	*261*	*95*	*676*	*489*	*187*	*30*	*31*	*12*	*9*	*209*	*57*	*195*	*74*	*43*	*16*	
1,468	467	223	70	570	431	139	24	24	9	7	194	44	169	54	35	10	5
157	52	25	20	71	37	34	4	6	...	2	10	10	15	12	8	4	6
18	6	1	2	9	5	4	...	...	...	...	1	1	4	2	...	1	7
30	17	9	2	19	12	7	2	...	3	...	3	2	4	4	...	1	8
27	10	3	1	7	4	3	...	1	...	...	1	...	3	2	...	...	9
153	*33*	*36*	*4*	*151*	*103*	*48*	*2*	*1*	...	*7*	*48*	*30*	*42*	*9*	*11*	*1*	
103	18	27	2	123	79	44	...	1	...	7	41	30	31	5	7	1	10
25	9	2	...	22	18	4	2	...	...	...	4	...	9	4	3	...	11
8	3	2	1	3	3	...	...	...	...	...	1	...	1	...	1	...	12
7	2	4	1	3	3	...	...	...	...	...	2	...	1	...	...	...	13
10	1	1	...	...	...	...	...	...	...	...	...	...	...	...	...	...	14
180	*61*	*34*	*18*	*242*	*169*	*73*	*26*	*23*	*6*	*6*	*65*	*14*	*54*	*15*	*18*	*15*	
46	31	11	7	36	15	21	2	4	1	...	4	4	4	5	4	8	15
5	...	...	...	6	2	4	...	4	1	...	...	...	1	...	...	...	16
2	...	...	1	9	9	...	1	...	...	...	2	...	6	...	...	...	17
48	22	12	7	113	100	13	4	1	2	...	47	5	37	5	10	2	18
49	...	6	...	3	3	...	...	...	...	...	...	...	1	...	2	...	19
30	8	5	3	75	40	35	19	14	2	6	12	5	5	5	2	5	20
92	*26*	*6*	...	*116*	*108*	*8*	...	...	...	...	*32*	*4*	*72*	*4*	*4*	...	
42	8	4	...	9	6	3	...	...	...	...	2	2	3	1	1	...	21
16	9	2	...	20	19	1	...	...	...	...	1	...	15	1	3	...	22
10	2	...	...	1	1	...	...	...	...	...	...	...	1	...	...	...	23
24	7	...	...	86	82	4	...	...	...	...	29	2	53	2	...	...	24
444	*170*	*61*	*29*	*76*	*46*	*30*	*2*	*1*	...	...	*13*	*10*	*24*	*15*	*7*	*4*	
272	150	46	26	58	37	21	2	...	...	...	11	8	20	10	4	3	25
51	9	5	2	8	5	3	...	1	...	...	1	...	1	2	3	...	26
50	2	4	1	3	1	2	...	...	...	...	...	1	1	1	...	...	27
30	3	3	...	7	3	4	...	...	...	...	1	1	2	2	...	...	28
41	6	3	...	...	...	...	...	...	...	...	...	...	...	...	...	...	29
152	*85*	*86*	*16*	*47*	*28*	*19*	*1*	...	...	...	*9*	*7*	*14*	*9*	*4*	*3*	
110	*32*	*12*	*5*	*17*	*10*	*7*	*2*	*3*	...	...	*1*	*1*	*6*	*3*	*1*	..	
72	21	4	3	5	5	...	...	...	...	...	...	...	4	...	1	...	30
21	5	4	1	11	5	6	2	2	...	...	1	1	2	3	...	...	31
12	6	3	1	...	...	...	...	...	...	...	...	...	...	...	...	...	32
5	...	1	...	1	...	1	...	1	...	...	...	...	...	...	...	...	33
101	*27*	*10*	*6*	*28*	*28*	*5*	...	*1*	...	...	*7*	*2*	*14*	*1*	*2*	*1*	
7	6	2	...	7	6	1	...	...	...	...	...	1	4	...	2	...	34
35	5	1	3	1	...	1	...	...	...	...	...	1	...	...	...	...	35
35	8	2	2	3	2	1	...	...	...	...	1	...	1	...	...	1	36
24	8	5	1	17	15	2	...	1	...	...	6	...	9	1	...	...	37
54	19	7	...	22	17	5	3	...	...	...	4	...	8	2	2	3	
15	4	3	...	9	9	...	...	...	...	...	3	...	5	...	1	...	38
34	13	2	...	12	8	4	3	...	...	...	1	...	3	2	1	2	39
1	...	...	...	...	...	...	...	...	...	...	...	...	...	...	...	...	40
4	2	2	...	1	...	1	...	...	...	...	...	...	...	...	...	1	41

	District or State.	ARMENIANS.												
		All Ages.			0—12		12—15		15—30		30—50		50 and over.	
Serial No.		Total.	Males.	Females.	Males.	Females.	Males.	Females.	Males.	Females.	Males.	Females.	Males.	Females.
	1	31	32	33	34	35	36	37	38	39	40	41	42	43
	Provincial Total	273	146	127	23	39	5	7	56	36	45	26	17	19
	Burma Proper	273	146	127	23	39	5	7	56	36	45	26	17	19
	Arakan Division	...	...	...	...	...	...	...	...	...	...	...	...	...
1	Akyab	...	...	...	...	...	...	...	...	...	...	...	...	...
2	Northern Arakan ...	...	...	...	...	...	...	...	...	...	...	...	...	...
3	Kyaukpyu	...	...	...	...	...	...	...	...	...	...	...	...	...
4	Sandoway	...	...	...	...	...	...	...	...	...	...	...	...	...
	Pegu Division	*221*	*122*	*99*	*19*	*29*	*3*	*4*	*46*	*27*	*37*	*22*	*17*	*17*
5	City of Rangoon ...	219	120	99	19	29	3	4	46	27	37	22	15	17
6	Hanthawaddy ...	2	2	...	...	...	...	...	...	...	...	...	2	...
7	Tharrawaddy... ...	...	...	...	...	...	...	...	...	...	...	...	...	...
8	Pegu	...	...	...	...	...	...	...	...	...	...	...	...	...
9	Prome	...	...	...	...	...	...	...	...	...	...	...	...	...
	Irrawaddy Division ...	*6*	*3*	*3*	*1*	...	...	*1*	*1*	*2*	*1*	...	...	...
10	Bassein	5	2	3	1	...	...	1	...	2	1	...	...	...
11	Henzada	...	...	...	...	...	...	...	...	...	...	...	...	...
12	Myaungmya	...	...	...	...	...	...	...	...	...	...	...	...	...
13	Ma-ubin	...	...	...	...	...	...	...	...	...	...	...	...	...
14	Pyapôn	1	1	...	...	...	...	...	1	...	...	...	...	...
	Tenasserim Division ...	*2*	*2*	...	...	...	...	...	*1*	...	*1*	...	...	...
15	Toungoo	...	...	...	...	...	...	...	...	...	...	...	...	...
16	Salween	...	...	...	...	...	...	...	...	...	...	...	...	...
17	Thatôn	2	2	...	...	...	...	...	1	...	1	...	...	...
18	Amherst	...	...	...	...	...	...	...	...	...	...	...	...	...
19	Tavoy	...	...	...	...	...	...	...	...	...	...	...	...	...
20	Mergui	...	...	...	...	...	...	...	...	...	...	...	...	...
	Magwe Division ...	...	...	...	...	...	...	...	...	...	...	...	...	...
21	Thayetmyo	...	...	...	...	...	...	...	...	...	...	...	...	...
22	Pakôkku	...	...	...	...	...	...	...	...	...	...	...	...	...
23	Minbu	...	...	...	...	...	...	...	...	...	...	...	...	...
24	Magwe	...	...	...	...	...	...	...	...	...	...	...	...	...
	Mandalay Division ...	*28*	*11*	*17*	*1*	*6*	*2*	*1*	*8*	*5*	...	*3*	...	*2*
25	Mandalay (including City).	28	11	17	1	6	2	1	8	5	...	3	...	2
26	Bhamo	...	...	...	...	...	...	...	...	...	...	...	...	...
27	Myitkyina	...	...	...	...	...	...	...	...	...	...	...	...	...
28	Katha	...	...	...	...	...	...	...	...	...	...	...	...	...
29	Ruby Mines	...	...	...	...	...	...	...	...	...	...	...	...	...
	Mandalay City	*13*	*4*	*9*	...	*2*	...	*1*	*4*	*2*	...	*2*	...	*2*
	Sagaing Division ...	*10*	*7*	*3*	*2*	...	...	*1*	...	*2*	*5*	...	...	...
30	Shwebo	1	1	...	...	...	...	...	...	...	1	...	...	...
31	Sagaing	9	6	3	2	...	...	1	...	2	4	...	...	...
32	Lower Chindwin ...	...	...	...	...	...	...	...	...	...	...	...	...	...
33	Upper Chindwin ...	...	...	...	...	...	...	...	...	...	...	...	...	...
	Meiktila Division ...	*6*	*1*	*5*	...	*4*	...	...	...	...	*1*	*1*	...	...
34	Kyauksè	...	...	...	...	...	...	...	...	...	...	...	...	...
35	Meiktila	...	...	...	...	...	...	...	...	...	...	...	...	...
36	Yamèthin	6	1	5	...	4	...	...	...	...	1	1	...	...
37	Myingyan	...	...	...	...	...	...	...	...	...	...	...	...	...
	Specially Administered Territories.	...	...	...	...	...	...	...	...	...	...	...	...	...
38	Northern Shan States	...	...	...	...	...	...	...	...	...	...	...	...	...
39	Southern Shan States	...	...	...	...	...	...	...	...	...	...	...	...	...
40	Pakôkku Hill Tracts	...	...	...	...	...	...	...	...	...	...	...	...	...
41	Chin Hills	...	...	...	...	...	...	...	...	...	...	...	...	...

and Anglo-Indians by Race and Age.

ANGLO-INDIANS.													
All Ages.			0—12.		12—15.		15—30.		30—50.		50 and over.		
Total.	Males.	Females.	Males.	Females.	Males.	Females.	Males.	Females.	Males.	Females.	Males.	Females.	Serial No.
44	45	46	47	48	49	50	51	52	53	54	55	56	
11,106	6,039	5,067	1,765	1,688	444	407	1,860	1,688	1,600	980	870	804	
11,031	5,989	5,042	1,755	1,678	443	407	1,844	1,677	1,579	976	868	804	
201	*108*	*93*	*40*	*37*	*7*	*9*	*34*	*28*	*21*	*14*	*6*	*6*	
168	88	80	28	33	7	8	31	23	17	12	5	4	1
1	...	1	...	...	...	...	...	1	...	...	...	...	2
16	9	7	7	1	...	1	...	2	2	2	...	1	3
16	11	5	5	3	...	...	3	2	2	...	1	...	4
6,748	*3,689*	*3,054*	*1,007*	*997*	*283*	*227*	*1,246*	*1,071*	*942*	*591*	*211*	*168*	
5,831	3,152	2,679	866	856	263	205	1,085	945	765	520	173	153	5
611	354	257	88	102	18	18	111	76	113	50	24	11	6
85	51	34	15	15	...	1	9	11	23	5	4	2	7
175	110	65	33	22	2	3	35	31	33	8	7	1	8
41	22	19	5	2	...	...	6	8	8	8	3	1	9
184	*106*	*78*	*22*	*18*	*3*	*1*	*28*	*38*	*44*	*20*	*14*	*6*	
53	28	25	5	4	1	1	8	15	10	5	4	...	10
55	28	27	8	11	...	...	6	8	10	7	4	1	11
43	27	16	8	2	1	...	5	7	11	5	2	2	12
19	14	5	1	...	...	...	3	2	8	2	2	1	13
14	9	5	...	1	1	...	1	1	5	1	2	2	14
1,709	*884*	*825*	*280*	*247*	*46*	*84*	*246*	*248*	*241*	*178*	*71*	*78*	
271	156	115	52	38	6	12	43	36	45	20	10	9	15
...	...	...	...	...	...	...	...	...	...	...	...	...	16
149	97	52	15	15	2	3	34	18	38	12	8	4	17
1,217	590	627	205	181	37	69	158	178	142	135	48	64	18
21	14	7	3	3	1	...	2	3	6	1	2	...	19
51	27	24	5	10	...	...	9	8	10	5	3	1	20
152	*89*	*63*	*29*	*25*	*6*	*4*	*18*	*20*	*32*	*11*	*4*	*3*	
35	18	17	9	7	2	1	2	4	5	4	...	1	21
24	17	7	4	2	2	1	1	2	9	1	1	1	22
35	18	17	7	7	2	2	2	4	7	4	...	...	23
58	36	22	9	9	...	...	13	10	11	2	3	1	24
1,445	*781*	*664*	*265*	*238*	*90*	*68*	*194*	*208*	*189*	*126*	*48*	*30*	
1,283	687	596	241	207	89	61	169	182	146	116	42	30	25
24	12	12	2	6	...	...	4	5	5	1	1	...	26
33	20	13	6	4	1	1	6	7	7	1	...	...	27
51	32	19	9	9	...	...	7	7	16	3	...	...	28
54	30	24	7	12	...	1	8	7	15	4	...	...	29
639	*379*	*260*	*190*	*82*	*52*	*25*	*98*	*80*	*89*	*58*	*26*	*15*	
284	*140*	*94*	*88*	*42*	*1*	*7*	*30*	*27*	*60*	*18*	*11*	*5*	
77	37	40	10	16	...	6	10	11	13	5	4	2	30
99	57	42	14	17	1	1	12	15	28	7	2	2	31
25	15	10	5	7	...	...	3	1	4	1	3	1	32
33	31	2	9	2	...	...	5	...	15	...	2	...	33
363	*192*	*171*	*74*	*74*	*7*	*12*	*53*	*47*	*50*	*29*	*8*	*9*	
40	23	17	8	6	1	3	7	3	6	3	1	2	34
83	45	38	20	20	...	1	9	9	13	6	3	2	35
207	104	103	42	42	5	8	30	31	23	17	4	5	36
33	20	13	4	6	1	...	7	4	8	3	...	...	37
75	50	25	10	10	1	...	16	11	21	4	2	...	
32	18	14	4	6	...	...	8	6	6	2	...	...	38
36	26	10	5	3	...	...	6	5	13	2	2	...	39
...	...	...	...	...	...	...	...	...	...	...	...	...	40
7	6	1	1	1	1	...	2	...	2	...	...	...	41

PROVINCIAL TABLE I.

Area and population of Townships, States and Special Tracts.

NOTE 1.—The names of 47 Townships have been changed since 1901. A second part has been added to Column 1 of the Statement to indicate the original designations of such Townships.

NOTE 2.—Nine extra Townships have been formed since 1901 by the subdivision of one or more previously existing Townships. On the other hand, there have been amalgamations resulting in the abolition of the Townships of—

Kangyidaung	...	(Bassein District).
Wetwun	...	(Mandalay District).
Pyintha	...	(Mandalay District).
Malè	...	(Shwebo District).
Padu or Sadaung	...	(Sagaing District).
Dayegaung	...	(Kyauksè District).

NOTE 3.—In addition to the nine extra, and the six amalgamated, Townships, there have been changes in the boundaries of the following 69 Townships :—

Townships.	Serial No.	Townships.	Serial No.	Townships.	Serial No.	Townships.	Serial No.
Rathedaung	2	Einmè ...	58	Thanbula ...	105	Kanbalu ...	149
Insein ...	18	Wakèma ...	59	Pakôkku ...	106	Kyunhla ...	150
Taikkyi ...	19	Ma-ubin ...	61	Yesagyo ...	107	Sagaing ...	155
Twante ...	21	Pantanaw ...	62	Seikpyu ...	111	Myinmu ...	157
Kyauktan ...	23	Bogalè ...	66	Sagu ...	114	Myaung ...	159
Kayan ...	25	Kyaiklat ...	67	Pwinbyu ...	115	Ngazun ...	160
Letpadan ...	27	Toungoo ...	70	Salin ...	117	Masein ...	168
Minhla ...	28	Leiktho ...	71	Sidôktaya ...	118	Kale ...	170
Gyobingauk	29	Oktwin ...	73	Magwe ...	119	Maingkaing	175
Nattalin ...	30	Shwegyin ...	76	Yenangyaung	120	Kyauksè ...	176
Monyo ...	31	Pa-an ...	82	Taungdwingyi	121	Myittha ...	178
Pegu ...	33	Moulmein ...	84	Satthwa ...	122	Myingyan ...	188
Kawa ...	34	Mudôn ...	88	Myothit ...	123	Natogyi ...	190
Hlègu ...	35	Thayetmyo ...	100	Natmauk ...	124	Pagan ...	191
Nyaunglèbin	37	Mindôn ...	101	Mogaung ...	133	Salè ...	192
Hmawza ...	40	Kama ...	102	Kamaing ...	134		
Thabaung ...	46	Minhla ..	103	Mawlu ...	137		
Myaungmya	57	Allanmyo ...	104	Kin-u ...	147		

The population for 1901 has been adjusted, as far as the available information would permit, to the Township areas as constituted on the 10th March 1911.

NOTE 4.—It has been impossible to carry the adjustments of population for changes in township areas beyond 1901. Consequently Column 11 has been left blank for 'recently formed townships'. In cases where township areas have changed, the percentage in Column 11 is the percentage of variation of the corresponding townships as constituted in 1901.

NOTE 5.—Separate figures for the populations of the specially administered Kachin Tracts attached to various townships in the Mandalay Division are not available for the years 1891 and 1901. They have, therefore, been amalgamated with the populations of the normal township jurisdictions for the purpose of calculating the percentages of variation.

NOTE 6.—The separate areas of the Kachin Tracts and the normal township jurisdictions in such townships are not available. The density of population shown in Column 12 is the resultant density of the amalgamated specially and normally administered jurisdictions.

NOTE 7.—The areas of the Sinbo, Sadôn and Sima Kachin Hill Tracts are not available, and their density of population cannot be calculated.

NOTE 8.—All areas of Kachin Hill Tracts in Bhamo, Myitkyina and the Katha Districts, and the areas of most of the Northern and Southern Shan States are estimated.

NOTE 9.—The double figures in Column 10 for the Northern Shan States indicate the percentages of increase excluding and including the areas brought within the census operations for the first time.

PROVINCIAL TABLE I.

Serial No.	Township. 1911.	Township. 1901.	Area in Square Miles.	Number of Towns.	Number of Village Tracts.	Number of Occupied Houses.	Population 1911 Persons.	Population 1911 Males.	Population 1911 Females.	Population 1901 Persons.	Percentage of Variation 1901 to 1911.	Percentage of Variation 1891 to 1901.	Number of Persons per Square Mile in 1911.
	1		2	3	4	5	6	7	8	9	10	11	12
	Arakan Division.		14,807	2	1,959	175,791	839,896	441,925	397,971	762,102	+ 10	+ 12	57
	AKYAB DISTRICT.		5,136	1	1,106	108,835	529,943	289,474	240,469	481,666	+ 10	+ 16	103
1	Akyab ...	......	72	1	25	9,546	49,539	35,904	13,635	47,427	+ 4	− 2	688
2	Rathedaung ...	......	361	...	90	12,197	56,789	29,196	27,593	53,021	+ 7	− 43	157
3	Ponnagyun ...	Urittaung ...	783	...	177	11,999	51,805	26,666	25,139	49,555	+ 4	+ 11	66
4	Pauktaw ...	......	656	...	105	10,470	45,350	23,904	21,446	43,395	+ 4	+ 6	69
5	Minbya ...	......	899	...	168	10,452	47,795	26,205	21,590	41,663	+ 14	+ 19	53
6	Kyauktaw ...	Kaladan ...	562	...	118	12,389	55,820	30,668	25,152	53,303	+ 4	+ 18	99
7	Myohaung ...	......	567	...	154	12,680	58,032	31,895	26,137	49,978	+ 16	+ 15	102
8	Buthidaung ...	(Recently formed)	796	...	110	11,210	63,679	33,479	30,200	60,078	+ 6	...	80
9	Maungdaw ...	Na-af ...	440	...	159	17,292	101,134	51,557	49,577	83,247	+ 21	+ 27	230
	NORTHERN ARAKAN. (Not divided into Townships.)		1,500	...	38	5,456	22,234	11,405	10,829	20,682	+ 7	+ 41	15
	KYAUKPYU DISTRICT.		4,387	1	594	41,699	184,916	89,571	95,345	168,827	+ 10	+ 3	42
10	Kyaukpyu ...	......	594	1	131	10,945	46,195	22,330	23,865	42,424	+ 8	+ 1	78
11	Myebon ...	......	1,008	...	84	5,961	28,880	14,960	13,920	24,109	+ 19	+ 13	29
12	An	......	1,877	...	201	7,483	32,855	16,800	16,055	29,337	+ 12	+ 5	17
13	Ramree ...	......	600	...	103	10,632	46,789	21,363	25,426	46,058	+ 1	− 3	78
14	Cheduba ...	......	308	...	75	6,678	30,197	14,118	16,079	26,899	+ 12	+ 6	98
	SANDOWAY DISTRICT.		3,784	1	221	19,801	102,803	51,475	51,328	90,927	+ 13	+ 16	27
15	Taungup ...	Northern ...	1,663	...	81	7,402	37,625	18,620	19,005	32,948	+ 14	+ 13	23
16	Sandoway ...	Central ...	1,318	1	86	8,188	43,215	21,640	21,575	30,542	+ 9	+ 16	33
17	Gwa	Southern ...	803	...	54	4,211	21,963	11,215	10,748	18,437	+ 19	+ 20	27
	Pegu Division.		13,258	10	2,576	407,945	2,073,737	1,136,192	937,545	1,880,638	+ 14	+ 20	156
	RANGOON TOWN DISTRICT. (Not divided into Townships.)		28	1	...	49,476	293,316	208,111	85,205	245,430	+ 20	+ 35	10,476
	HANTHAWADDY DISTRICT.		3,048	2	820	106,456	539,109	295,886	243,223	474,262	+ 14	+ 20	177
18	Insein ...	......	359	1	125	18,045	88,092	50,179	37,913	76,342	+ 15	− 11	245
19	Taikkyi ...	......	539	...	79	13,486	58,221	29,795	28,426	49,127	+ 18	+ 2	108
20	Tantabin ...	(Recently formed)	449	...	110	12,165	60,227	30,581	29,646	51,778	+ 16	...	134
21	Twante ...	......	404	...	144	14,168	83,702	47,468	36,234	74,892	+ 11	+ 7	207
22	Kungyangôn ...	......	438	...	129	16,210	81,149	43,142	38,007	71,017	+ 14	+ 11	185
23	Kyauktan ...	......	304	1	90	13,076	68,887	41,489	27,398	61,875	+ 11	+ 1	227
24	Thôngwa ...	(Recently formed)	219	...	71	8,920	46,228	25,027	21,201	42,031	+ 10	...	211
25	Kayan ...	Thabyegan ...	336	...	72	10,386	52,603	28,205	24,398	47,200	+ 11	− 46	157
	THARRAWADDY DISTRICT.		2,863	3	642	88,057	433,320	216,442	216,878	396,870	+ 10	+ 17	151
26	Tharrawaddy ...	(Recently formed)	377	1	67	12,148	59,592	29,807	29,785	53,110	+ 12	..	158
27	Letpadan ...	......	528	1	112	15,656	81,443	41,256	40,187	69,599	+ 17	− 15	154
28	Minhla ...	......	629	...	145	17,395	82,454	41,224	41,230	74,268	+ 11	− 1	131
29	Gyobingauk ...	......	433	1	146	19,160	94,552	46,906	47,646	87,085	+ 8	+ 3	218
30	Nattalin ...	Tapûn ...	696	...	121	15,046	73,453	36,547	36,906	70,059	+ 4	+ 16	106
31	Monyo ...	......	200	...	51	8,652	41,826	20,702	21,124	41,449	+ 1	+ 19	209
	PEGU DISTRICT.		4,404	1	515	83,221	429,121	229,540	199,581	339,572	+ 26	+ 43	97
32	Thanatpin ...	(Recently formed)	415	...	59	8,938	48,367	26,084	22,283	37,135	+ 30	...	117
33	Pegu ...	Payagalè ...	1,394	1	98	17,134	88,747	48,124	40,623	73,439	+ 20	+ 5	64
34	Kawa ...	......	423	...	87	11,068	66,730	36,015	30,715	56,134	+ 18	− 7	158
35	Hlègu ...	......	479	...	110	13,231	65,353	34,218	31,135	55,731	+ 17	+ 24	136
36	Daik-u ...	Pyuntaza ...	870	...	88	15,252	76,557	41,139	35,418	52,952	+ 44	+ 120	88
37	Nyaunglèbin ...	......	823	...	79	17,598	83,367	43,960	39,407	64,201	+ 29	+ 63	101
	PROME DISTRICT.		2,915	3	599	80,536	378,871	186,213	192,658	365,804	+ 4	+ 1	130
38	Prome ...	(Recently formed)	9	1	...	4,857	27,011	14,485	12,526	27,375	− 1	− 9	2,990
39	Paukkaung ...	......	694	...	77	6,321	28,603	14,357	14,246	29,797	− 4	− 7	41
40	Hmawza ...	......	273	...	134	16,178	73,256	35,567	37,689	68,581	+ 7	− 13	270
41	Thègôn ...	......	241	...	77	13,691	66,718	32,438	34,280	60,982	+ 9	+ 25	277
42	Paungdè ...	......	379	1	96	13,669	66,189	32,817	33,372	60,604	+ 9	+ 7	175
43	Shwedaung ...	......	300	1	112	14,218	63,503	30,333	33,170	65,743	− 4	+ 1	212
44	Padaung ...	......	1,019	...	103	11,601	53,191	26,326	26,865	51,712	+ 3	− 1	52

PROVINCIAL TABLE I.

Serial No.	Township. 1911.	Township. 1901.	Area in Square Miles.	Number of Towns.	Number of Village Tracts.	Number of Occupied Houses.	Population 1911. Persons.	Population 1911. Males.	Population 1911. Females.	Population 1901. Persons.	Percentage of Variation. 1901 to 1911.	Percentage of Variation. 1891 to 1901.	Number of Persons per Square Mile in 1911.
	1		2	3	4	5	6	7	8	9	10	11	12
	Irrawaddy Division.		13,408	17	2,757	262,406	1,869,485	962,913	906,572	1,663,669	+ 12	+ 28	139
	Bassein District.		*4,127*	*3*	*711*	*82,592*	*440,988*	*226,773*	*214,215*	*391,427*	+ *13*	+ *22*	*107*
45	Bassein ...	......	499	1	160	22,117	122,487	67,221	55,266	110,836	+ 10	+ 18	245
46	Thabaung ...	......	1,252	...	102	9,269	48,295	24,263	24,032	41,613	+ 16	+ 7	38
47	Ngaputaw ...	......	1,457	...	110	9,268	46,379	23,802	22,577	37,126	+ 25	+ 25	32
48	Ngathainggyaung	Yegyi ...	336	1	142	14,108	77,324	37,916	39,408	64,891	+ 19	+ 15	230
49	Kyônpyaw ...	......	320	1	118	16,053	90,704	45,404	45,300	82,144	+ 10	+ 64	283
50	Kyaunggôn ...	......	263	...	79	11,177	55,799	28,167	27,632	54,817	+ 2	+ 6	212
	Henzada District.		*2,843*	*5*	*689*	*104,600*	*532,357*	*264,319*	*268,038*	*484,558*	+ *10*	+ *11*	*187*
51	Henzada ...	......	370	1	161	25,990	140,205	70,047	70,158	131,698	+ 6	+ 11	379
52	Zalun ...	......	288	1	111	14,543	77,378	38,285	39,093	69,502	+ 11	+ 11	269
53	Lemyethna ...	......	226	1	91	12,493	64,242	31,980	32,262	60,314	+ 6	+ 6	284
54	Kanaung ...	......	871	1	99	22,323	106,943	52,797	54,146	92,365	+ 16	+ 16	123
55	Kyangin ...	......	208	1	62	10,954	50,329	25,289	25,040	46,633	+ 8	+ 2	242
56	Ingabu ...	Ôkpo	880	...	105	18,297	93,260	45,921	47,339	84,046	+ 11	+ 14	106
	Myaungmya District.		*2,642*	*2*	*635*	*65,113*	*334,852*	*176,465*	*158,387*	*282,932*	+ *18*	+ *56*	*127*
57	Myaungmya ...	......	1,025	1	205	16,928	83,915	44,772	39,143	75,343	+ 11	— 1	82
58	Einmè ...	Thigwin ...	287	...	113	13,784	71,790	36,606	35,184	59,307	+ 21	+ 42	250
59	Wakèma ...	......	721	1	184	18,204	95,103	49,978	45,125	77,456	+ 23	+ 20	132
60	Mawlamyaingyun	(Recently formed)	609	...	133	16,197	84,044	45,109	38,935	70,766	+ 19	...	138
	Ma-ubin District.		*1,648*	*3*	*398*	*59,611*	*305,073*	*155,715*	*149,358*	*278,309*	+ *10*	+ *30*	*185*
61	Ma-ubin ...	......	511	1	117	16,111	79,608	41,572	38,036	72,979	+ 9	+ 58	156
62	Pantanaw ...	......	507	...	89	13,334	71,700	36,341	35,359	62,374	+ 15	+ 29	141
63	Yandoon ...	......	326	1	70	12,840	61,872	31,460	30,412	57,923	+ 7	— 2	190
64	Danubyu ...	......	304	1	122	17,326	91,893	46,342	45,551	85,033	+ 8	+ 40	302
	Pyapôn District.		*2,148*	*4*	*384*	*50,490*	*256,215*	*139,641*	*116,574*	*226,443*	+ *13*	+ *95*	*119*
65	Pyapôn ...	Pyindayè ...	334	1	76	9,739	50,178	28,198	21,980	43,922	+ 14	+ 79	150
66	Bogale ...	......	1,165	1	68	11,348	58,919	32,600	26,319	43,756	+ 35	+ 52	51
67	Kyaiklat ...	......	284	1	117	14,754	75,676	40,331	35,345	71,770	+ 5	+ 65	266
68	Dedayè ...	......	365	1	123	14,649	71,442	38,512	32,930	66,995	+ 7	+ 36	196
	Tenasserim Division.		35,886	7	1,864	276,532	1,429,294	750,626	678,668	1,159,558	+ 23	+ 27	40
	Toungoo District.		*6,172*	*2*	*632*	*76,531*	*351,076*	*181,488*	*169,588*	*279,315*	+ *26*	+ *32*	*57*
69	Yedashe ...	......	853	...	74	11,291	49,550	25,229	24,321	42,456	+ 17	+ 34	58
70	Toungoo ...	Myoma ...	270	1	68	11,773	53,032	28,220	24,812	42,227	+ 25	— 15	196
71	Leiktho ...	...	794	...	138	3,951	18,050	8,878	9,172	16,382	+ 10	+ 54	23
72	Pyu	(Recently formed)	773	...	68	15,049	70,300	36,227	34,073	58,215	+ 21	...	91
73	Oktwin ...	......	924	...	75	10,736	49,753	25,217	24,536	44,169	+ 13	— 8	54
74	Tantabin ...	......	889	...	76	9,201	41,568	21,246	20,322	24,686	+ 68	+ 38	47
75	Kyaukkyi ...	......	1,048	...	72	8,591	40,447	20,966	19,481	32,226	+ 25	+ 25	39
76	Shwegyin ...	......	621	1	61	5,929	28,376	15,505	12,871	18,954	+ 50	— 38	46
	Salween District.		*2,666*	...	*85*	*10,755*	*46,608*	*24,741*	*21,867*	*37,837*	+ *23*	+ *29*	*17*
77	Papun ...	......	2,666	...	85	10,755	46,608	24,741	21,867	37,837	+ 23	+ 29	17
	Thatôn District.		*4,892*	*2*	*415*	*76,508*	*416,975*	*217,770*	*199,205*	*343,510*	+ *21*	+ *29*	*85*
78	Kyaikto ...	......	508	1	58	10,502	52,522	27,454	25,068	45,082	+ 16	+ 35	103
79	Bilin ...	......	738	...	55	12,690	60,269	31,325	28,944	55,112	+ 9	+ 24	82
80	Thatôn ...	......	453	1	53	12,822	75,817	40,079	35,738	67,928	+ 12	+ 20	167
81	Paung ...	......	422	...	59	10,675	65,125	34,949	30,176	55,071	+ 18	+ 19	154
82	Pa-an ...	......	1,007	...	115	18,965	102,490	52,772	49,718	76,591	+ 34	+ 0	102
83	Hlaingbwè ...	......	1,764	...	75	10,848	60,752	31,191	29,561	43,726	+ 39	+ 54	34
	Amherst District.		*7,059*	*1*	*366*	*64,423*	*367,918*	*198,430*	*169,488*	*300,173*	+ *23*	+ *29*	*52*
84	Moulmein ...	......	30	1	7	12,712	65,383	39,293	26,090	55,004	+ 19	— 12	2,179
85	Chaungzôn ..	Bilugyun ...	193	...	52	8,910	49,271	25,556	23,715	41,880	+ 18	+ 23	255
86	Kyaikkami ...	Wagaru ...	928	...	20	3,780	23,105	12,395	10,710	15,676	+ 47	+ 21	24
87	Yelamaing ...	......	1,258	...	30	5,740	35,580	19,243	16,337	25,973	+ 38	+ 43	28
88	Mudôn ...	Zaya ...	230	...	66	9,886	59,808	30,781	29,027	51,882	+ 15	+ 27	260
89	Kawkareik ...	Haungtharaw ...	1,963	...	78	8,712	46,902	24,858	22,044	31,192	+ 50	+ 39	24
90	Kyaikmaraw ...	Ataran ...	2,457	...	113	14,683	87,867	46,304	41,563	78,616	+ 12	+ 84	36
	Tavoy District.		*5,308*	*1*	*199*	*27,811*	*135,293*	*68,667*	*66,626*	*109,979*	+ *23*	+ *16*	*25*
91	Yebyu ...	Northern ...	1,602	...	41	2,971	17,132	9,226	7,906	12,550	+ 36	+ 11	11
92	Tavoy ...	Central ...	2,412	1	38	7,884	39,222	20,083	19,139	33,818	+ 16	+ 31	16
93	Launglôn ...	Western ...	313	...	57	8,075	41,081	20,417	20,664	33,187	+ 24	+ 22	131
94	Thayetchaung ...	South-Eastern ...	981	...	63	8,881	37,858	18,941	18,917	30,424	+ 24	— 1	38
	Mergui District.		*9,789*		*167*	*20,509*	*111,424*	*59,530*	*51,894*	*88,744*	+ *26*	+ *20*	*11*
95	Mergui ...	......	1,377	1	58	9,530	53,466	29,139	24,327	43,070	+ 24	+ 33	39
96	Palaw ...	......	785	...	42	5,243	28,588	14,407	14,181	22,442	+ 27	+ 15	36
97	Tenasserim ...	......	4,033	...	24	2,478	12,583	6,744	5,839	10,712	+ 18	+ 28	3
98	Bôkpyin ...	Lenya ...	2,605	...	25	1,681	8,575	4,609	3,966	7,255	+ 18	+ 26	3
99	Maliwun ...	......	989	...	18	1,577	8,212	4,631	3,581	5,265	+ 56	— 38	8

Provincial Table I.

Serial No.	Township 1911	Township 1901	Area in Square Miles	Number of Towns	Number of Village Tracts	Number of Occupied Houses	Population 1911 Persons	Population 1911 Males	Population 1911 Females	Population 1901 Persons	Percentage of Variation 1901 to 1911	Percentage of Variation 1891 to 1901	Number of Persons per Square Mile in 1911
	1		2	3	4	5	6	7	8	9	10	11	12
	Magwe Division.		17,575	9	2,472	257,258	1,239,032	603,614	635,418	1,078,317	+ 15	+ 8	70
	Thayetmyo District.		*4,750*	*2*	*703*	*55,959*	*248,275*	*122,231*	*126,044*	*239,706*	+ *4*	− *4*	*52*
100	Thayetmyo ...	......	455	1	97	9,909	44,775	22,620	22,155	41,128	+ 9	− 1	98
101	Mindon ...	......	1,033	...	120	8,791	36,598	18,022	18,576	35,774	+ 2	+ 2	35
102	Kama ...	......	503	...	101	8,068	34,103	16,605	17,498	33,981	+ 0	− 18	68
103	Minhla ...	......	1,007	...	125	7,672	37,030	18,379	18,651	35,420	+ 5	+ 6	37
104	Allanmyo ...	......	912	1	126	13,737	62,216	29,873	32,343	60,646	+ 3	− 22	68
105	Thanbula ...	Sinbaungwè ...	840	...	136	7,782	33,553	16,732	16,821	32,757	+ 2	+ 48	40
	Pakôkku District.		*6,210*	*1*	*862*	*84,696*	*409,909*	*196,159*	*213,750*	*357,632*	+ *15*	+ *14*	*66*
106	Pakôkku ..	......	403	1	92	17,438	86,501	41,180	45,321	72,829	+ 11	+ 1	215
107	Yesagyo ...	......	377	...	165	22,165	95,756	44,424	51,332	88,834	+ 8	+ 65	254
108	Myaing ...	......	780	...	163	16,661	78,969	36,460	42,509	71,976	+ 10	+ 53	101
109	Pauk ...	......	977	...	111	9,094	50,137	24,917	25,220	41,021	+ 22	+ 12	51
110	Saw ...	Pasók ...	1,011	...	95	4,645	22,462	11,588	10,874	19,868	+ 13	− 11	22
111	Seikpyu ...	......	774	...	80	6,223	30,693	14,708	15,985	26,721	+ 15	− 44	40
112	Gangaw ...	Hkunhnaywa ...	1,400	...	98	5,817	30,739	15,418	15,321	24,200	+ 27	+ 7	22
113	Tilin ...	......	488	...	58	2,653	14,652	7,464	7,188	12,183	+ 20	+ 11	30
	Minbu District.		*3,302*	*3*	*430*	*55,589*	*263,939*	*128,837*	*135,102*	*234,271*	+ *13*	+ *8*	*80*
114	Sagu ...	......	787	1	78	11,732	62,791	30,971	31,820	54,635	+ 15	+ 23	80
115	Pwinbyu ...	Legaing ...	456	...	70	13,069	61,233	30,216	31,017	56,116	+ 9	+ 56	134
116	Ngape ...	......	355	...	54	4,010	16,735	8,441	8,294	16,033	+ 4	+ 22	47
117	Salin ...	......	777	2	154	21,392	100,231	47,732	52,499	87,472	+ 15	− 12	129
118	Sidôktaya ...	......	927	...	74	5,386	22,949	11,477	11,472	20,015	+ 15	− 18	25
	Magwe District.		*3,313*	*3*	*478*	*61,014*	*316,909*	*156,387*	*160,522*	*246,708*	+ *28*	+ *13*	*96*
119	Magwe ...	......	637	1	85	14,119	71,594	35,240	36,354	56,993	+ 26	+ 36	112
120	Yenangyaung .	......	384	1	51	9,395	50,302	26,511	23,791	35,721	+ 40	+ 55	131
121	Taungdwingyi ...	......	223	1	52	7,201	35,531	17,305	18,226	29,434	+ 20	− 45	159
122	Satthwa ...	Myingun ...	563	...	77	6,467	32,811	16,037	16,774	25,016	+ 31	+ 3	58
123	Myothit ..	......	626	...	87	10,844	53,454	25,852	27,602	40,730	+ 31	+ 20	85
124	Natmauk ...	......	880	...	126	12,988	73,217	35,442	37,775	58,814	+ 24	+ 38	83
	Mandalay Division.		30,476	6	2,760	177,295	832,969	426,776	406,193	778,466	+ 7	+ 21	26
	Mandalay District (including City).		*2,117*	*3*	*385*	*77,181*	*340,770*	*170,750*	*170,020*	*366,507*	− *7*	− *2*	*161*
	Mandalay City ...	......	25	1	...	31,518	138,299	69,718	68,581	183,816	− 25	− 3	5,532
125	Amarapura ...	......	85	1	54	10,285	44,021	21,064	22,957	43,884	+ 0	− 14	518
126	Patheingyi ...	......	213	..	73	7,769	34,837	16,647	18,190	28,546	+ 22	− 10	163
127	Madaya ...	......	321	...	111	12,635	54,550	26,832	27,718	53,212	+ 3	+ 4	170
128	Singu ...	Ngasingu ...	712	...	82	8,904	40,898	20,001	20,897	35,670	+ 14	− 4	57
129	Maymyo ..	{ Maymyo ... Wetwun ... Pyintha ...	761	1	65	6,018	28,165	16,488	11,677	21,379	+ 32	+ 36	37
	Bhamo District.		*6,903*	*1*	*721*	*22,118*	*107,811*	*55,528*	*52,283*	*79,515*	+ *36*	+ *90*	*16*
130	Bhamo	...	3,643	1	123	7,182	36,558	20,697	15,861	57,572	+ 40	+ 119	10
	Sinlun, Kachin Hill Tracts ...	...	1,600	...	401	9,745	44,035	20,868	23,167				28
131	Shwegu—												
	(a) Township ...	...	448	...	116	4,030	21,149	11,055	10,094	21,943	+ 24	+ 34	47
	(b) Kachin Hill Tracts ...	...	1,212	...	81	1,161	6,069	2,908	3,161				5
	Myitkyina District.		*10,977*	*1*	*666*	*17,242*	*85,577*	*47,863*	*37,714*	*68,527*	+ *25*	+ *32*	*8*
132	Myitkyina—												
	(a) Township ...	...	4,500	1	82	3,724	18,067	10,547	7,520	19,581	+ 23	...	5
	(b) Myitkyina, Kachin Hill Tracts ...			...	88	818	3,896	1,964	1,932				
	(c) Sinbo, Kachin Hill Tracts	...		...	51	434	2,168	1,059	1,109				
133	Mogaung—												
	(a) Township ...	...	3,490	...	52	2,870	14,150	7,908	6,242	19,039	+ 13	...	6
	(b) Kachin Hill Tracts ...	...		...	16	1,519	7,391	3,672	3,719				
134	Kamaing—												
	(a) Township ...	...	2,987	...	27	2,036	9,666	6,626	3,040	10,643	+ 40	...	5
	(b) Kachin Hill Tracts ..	...		...	14	1,004	5,272	2,864	2,408				
	Sadon, Kachin Hill Tracts ...	...	Not obtainable.	...	199	2,741	13,066	6,683	6,383	11,991	+ 9	...	...
	Sima, Kachin Hill Tracts ...	...		...	137	2,096	10,253	4,892	5,361	7,273	+ 41	...	...
	Military Camps and Expedition	...		...	..	...	1,648	1,648	...	...	...	...	...
	Katha District.		*7,001*	...	*580*	*41,157*	*198,193*	*98,148*	*100,045*	*176,223*	+ *12*	+ *95*	*28*
135	Katha—												
	(a) Township ...	...	1,152	...	52	4,085	20,464	10,689	9,775	20,062	+ 26	+ 7	22
	(b) Kachin Hill Tracts ...	...		...	30	876	4,964	2,359	2,605				
136	Tigyaing	...	352	...	46	3,609	17,582	8,850	8,732	16,046	+ 9	+ 1	50
137	Mawlu—												
	(a) Township ...	...	1,353	...	45	3,915	19,593	9,952	9,641	17,178	+ 20	+ 177	15
	(b) Kachin Hill Tracts ...	...		...	11	167	1,015	522	493				
138	Indaw	...	416	..	45	3,160	15,572	7,863	7,709	14,208	+ 9	+ 26	37
139	Wuntho	...	592	...	78	5,976	23,664	11,797	11,867	22,934	+ 3	...	40
140	Kawlin	...	536	...	85	7,596	33,135	16,650	16,485	28,114	+ 18	...	62
141	Pinlebu	...	1,368	...	102	6,088	32,615	15,599	17,016	29,321	+ 11	...	24
142	Banmauk	...	1,232	...	86	5,683	29,589	13,867	15,722	28,360	+ 4	...	24
	Ruby Mines (including Möng Mit State).		*5,478*	*1*	*408*	*19,597*	*100,618*	*54,487*	*46,131*	*87,604*	+ *15*	...	*18*
	I.—*Ruby Mines (District Proper).*		*1,916*	*1*	*149*	*9,720*	*47,404*	*27,247*	*20,157*	*42,896*	+ *10*	+ *157*	*25*
143	Mogôk	..	610	1	81	5,368	26,381	15,806	10,575	24,590	+ 7	+ 31	43
144	Thabeikkyin	...	688	...	33	2,153	10,238	5,807	4,431	9,787	+ 5	+ 21	15
145	Tagaung	...	618	...	35	2,199	10,785	5,634	5,151	8,609	+ 25	+ 21	17
	II.—*Möng Mit State.*		*3,562*	...	*259*	*9,877*	*53,214*	*27,240*	*25,974*	*44,708*	+ *19*	...	*15*
	(a) State Proper ...	...	2,802	...	116	4,729	24,085	13,092	10,993	22,581	+ 27	...	10
	(b) Ngadaung Hill Tracts	...				968	4,672	2,323	2,349				
	(c) Kodaung Hill Tracts	...	760	...	143	4,180	24,457	11,825	12,632	22,127	+ 10	...	32

Provincial Table I.

Serial No.	Township 1911.	Township 1901.	Area in Square Miles.	Number of Towns.	Number of Village Tracts.	Number of Occupied Houses.	Population 1911. Persons.	Population 1911. Males.	Population 1911. Females.	Population 1901. Persons.	Percentage of Variation 1901 to 1911.	Percentage of Variation 1891 to 1901.	Number of Persons per Square Mile in 1911.
	1		2	3	4	5	6	7	8	9	10	11	12
	Sagaing Division.		26,182	4	2,020	257,828	1,155,271	543,289	611,982	994,466	+ 16	+ 22	44
	Shwebo District.		*5,714*	*1*	*669*	*80,921*	*356,363*	*168,070*	*188,293*	*286,891*	*+ 24*	*+ 24*	*62*
146	Shwebo ..	......	428	1	86	13,299	60,292	29,947	30,345	51,248	+ 18	+ 12	141
147	Kin-u ...	Chaukya ...	309	...	85	9,486	42,404	20,153	22,251	31,499	+ 35	+ 12	137
148	Wetlet ...	Sheinmaga ..	512	...	88	12,301	54,675	26,172	28,503	39,255	+ 38	+ 21	107
149	Kanbalu ...	Myedu ...	1,536	...	132	11,76)	51,895	25,462	26,433	44,783	+ 16	+ 85	34
150	Kyunhla ...	Indaing ...	988	...	39	2,743	13,742	6,873	6,869	8,560	+ 61	+ 37	14
151	Ye-u ...	......	140	...	62	7,086	29,472	13,251	16,221	24,190	+ 22	+ 21	210
152	Tabayin ...	Mayagan ...	613	...	95	10,43[illegible]	45,859	20,658	25,201	39,340	+ 17	+ 20	75
153	Tamadaw ...	Shwegyin ...	600	...	37	5,8[illegible]8	23,820	9,956	13,864	19,634	+ 21	+ 42	40
154	Tazè ...	......	588	...	45	7,907	34,204	15,598	18,606	28,382	+ 21	+ 46	58
	Sagaing District.		*1,825*	*1*	*340*	*70,751*	*312,111*	*147,816*	*164,295*	*277,769*	*+ 12*	*+ 15*	*17*
155	Sagaing ...	......	474	1	88	21,010	87,842	42,152	45,690	76,531	+ 15	+ 95	185
156	Tada-u ...	Ava ...	360	...	61	11,656	54,326	26,052	28,274	46,661	+ 16	+ 19	151
157	Myinmu ...	......	295	...	46	8,966	41,314	19,397	21,917	38,572	+ 7	+ 21	140
158	Chaung-u ...	......	188	...	29	7,113	33,512	15,288	18,224	33,134	+ 1	+ 10	178
159	Myaung ...	Kyaukyit ...	177	...	50	9,889	40,498	19,100	21,398	34,181	+ 18	+ 34	229
160	Ngazun ...	Myotha ...	331	...	65	12,108	54,619	25,827	28,792	48,690	+ 12	+ 8	165
	Lower Chindwin District.		*3,480*	*1*	*523*	*70,623*	*316,175*	*141,262*	*174,913*	*276,383*	*+ 14*	*+ 18*	*91*
161	Budalin ...	......	451	...	94	13,487	64,050	27,368	36,682	55,447	+ 16	+ 9	140
162	Mônywa ...	......	487	1	112	22,114	99,388	44,170	55,218	90,164	+ 10	+ 25	204
163	Kani ...	......	1,788	...	125	13,403	57,131	26,283	30,848	48,717	+ 17	+ 18	32
164	Salingyi ..	......	296	...	118	13,629	60,361	27,183	33,178	50,814	+ 19	+ 16	204
165	Palè ...	......	458	..	74	7,990	35,245	16,258	18,987	31,241	+ 13	+ 21	77
	Upper Chindwin District.		*15,163*	*1*	*488*	*35,533*	*170,622*	*86,141*	*84,481*	*153,423*	*+ 11*	*+ 39*	*11*
166	Kindat ...	......	1,088	1	38	3,886	15,225	7,968	7,257	13,946	+ 9	+ 22	14
167	Tamu ..	Kalaw... ...	540	...	22	1,652	5,918	3,162	2,756	5,264	+ 12	+ 19	11
168	Massein ...	Balet	768	...	45	3,073	13,909	6,911	6,098	12,012	+ 15	— 5	18
169	Kalewa ...	(Recently formed)	176	...	8	793	4,013	2,186	1,827	3,675	+ 9	...	23
170	Kale ...	Kale	812	...	50	3,134	15,054	8,072	6,982	12,804	+ 18	— 5	19
171	Mingin ...	......	872	...	51	4,819	22,336	11,101	11,235	19,941	+ 12	— 5	26
172	Kyabin ...	Taungdwingyaung	640	...	47	2,732	11,234	5,672	5,562	9,954	+ 13	+ 36	18
173	Paungbyin ...	......	1,516	...	59	5,512	30,440	15,289	15,151	26,409	+ 15	+ 38	20
174	Homalin ...	......	2,524	...	51	4,419	23,608	11,673	11,935	17,624	+ 34	+ 60	9
175	Maingkaing ...	Uyu	4,665	...	50	3,618	18,618	9,115	9,503	22,275	— 16	+ 102	4
	Kampti State ...	......	983	...	22	430	2,560	1,287	1,273	2,048	+ 25	...	3
	Thaungdut State	Hsawnghsup State	579	...	45	1,465	7,697	3,705	3,992	7,471	+ 3	...	13
	Meiktila Division.		10,829	7	2,231	256,711	1,170,572	567,380	603,292	995,659	+ 18	+ 10	108
	Kyauksè District.		*1,274*	*1*	*336*	*27,777*	*141,426*	*68,868*	*72,558*	*141,253*	*+ 0*	*+ 12*	*111*
176	Kyauksè ...	......	180	1	117	3,475	52,348	25,586	26,762	52,147	+ 0	+ 46	291
177	Singaing ...	......	851	...	81	9,647	39,791	19,093	20,698	38,475	+ 3	— 16	47
178	Myittha ...	......	243	...	138	14,655	49,287	24,189	25,098	50,631	— 3	+ 79	203
	Meiktila District.		*2,183*	*1*	*473*	*56,930*	*279,822*	*134,170*	*145,652*	*252,305*	*+ 11*	*+ 16*	*128*
179	Meiktila ...	......	470	1	130	16,720	83,257	39,711	43,546	76,656	+ 8	+ 17	177
180	Mahlaing ...	......	426	...	92	14,271	67,805	31,455	36,350	62,890	+ 8	+ 13	159
181	Thazi... ...	......	817	...	115	11,414	59,487	30,096	29,391	49,824	+ 19	+ 27	73
182	Wundwin ...	......	470	...	136	14,525	69,273	32,908	36,365	62,935	+ 10	+ 11	147
	Yamèthin District.		*4,255*	*3*	*642*	*77,616*	*307,419*	*153,223*	*154,196*	*243,197*	*+ 26*	*+ 18*	*72*
183	Yamèthin ...	......	1,114	1	161	16,838	80,588	40,014	40,574	67,872	+ 18	— 4	72
184	Pyawbwè ...	......	336	1	101	9,380	47,525	23,021	24,504	42,495	+ 12	+ 2	141
185	Yanaung ...	Yindaw ...	551	...	122	9,435	49,265	23,904	25,361	40,694	+ 21	+ 7	89
186	Pyinmana ...	......	1,474	1	157	16,893	80,380	41,137	39,243	61,578	+ 31	+ 34	54
187	Lewè ...	......	780	...	101	25,070	49,661	25,147	24,514	30,558	+ 62	+ 20	64
	Myingyan District.		*3,107*	*2*	*780*	*94,388*	*441,905*	*211,119*	*230,786*	*358,904*	*+ 23*	...	*142*
188	Myingyan ...	......	414	1	116	19,202	93,317	45,292	48,025	81,978	+ 14	+ 4	225
189	Taungtha ..	......	516	...	125	16,383	73,046	34,840	38,206	57,729	+ 27	— 0	142
190	Natogyi ...	......	471	...	120	16,289	72,439	34,195	38,244	60,854	+ 19	+ 15	154
191	Pagan ...	......	579	1	119	14,846	70,805	34,021	36,784	57,035	+ 24	+ 15	122
192	Sale ...	......	356	...	105	9,894	42,617	20,177	22,440	33,265	+ 28	— 27	120
193	Kyaukpadaung ...	......	771	...	195	17,774	89,681	42,594	47,087	68,043	+ 32	+ 2	116

PROVINCIAL TABLE I.

Serial No.	State.	Area in Square Miles.	Number of Towns.	Number of Village Tracts.	Number of Occupied Houses.	Population 1911 Persons.	Population 1911 Males.	Population 1911 Females.	Population 1901 Persons.	Percentage of Variation 1901 to 1911.	Percentage of Variation 1891 to 1901.	Number of Persons per Square Mile in 1911.
	1	2	3	4	5	6	7	8	9	10	11	12
	Specially Administered Territories.	66,428	...	19,038	300,432	1,504,961	750,779	754,182	1,237,749	22	...	23
	Northern Shan States. Census Area ... Total Area ...	*14,294* *16,594*	...	*6,109*	*84,140*	*458,952*	*230,545*	*228,407*	*321,090*	+29 +43	...	*32*
i	*North Hsenwi State.* Census Area ... Total Area ...	*6,830* *9,130*	...	*3,051*	*39,862*	*215,682*	*107,222*	*108,460*	*118,325*	+45 +82	...	*24*
	(a) Shan Tracts ...	Separate figures not available.	..	1,093	16,959	96,095	48,180	47,915	73,198	+31	...	...
	(b) Kachin Tracts ...		...	1,231	14,773	75,421	36,592	38,829	45,127	+67	...	...
	(c) Kokang ...		Estimated.	409	4,968	25,604	13,389	12,215	...	...	...	...
	(d) West Manglün ...	500		318	3,162	18,562	9,061	9,501	...	...	...	37
	(e) East Manglün ...	2,300	...	...	Omitted from Census Operations				...	...	...	...
ii	South Hsenwi State ...	2,281	...	1,080	14,155	85,110	42,402	42,708	67,836	+25	...	37
iii	Hsipaw State ...	4,400	...	1,734	24,433	122,129	62,250	59,879	112,248	+ 9	...	28
iv	Tawngpeng State ...	778	...	243	4,887	31,976	15,980	15,996	22,681	+41	...	41
	Lashio (Notified Area) ...	5	...	1	803	4,055	2,691	1,364	...	...	...	811
	Southern Shan States.	*40,434*	..	*12,118*	*185,291*	*900,202*	*448,705*	*451,497*	*816,354*	+10	...	*22*
	South-Eastern Subdivision.	*8,288*	...	*1,785*	*20,199*	*104,230*	*51,587*	*52,643*	*95,467*	+ 9	...	*13*
i	Möngnai	2,904	...	761	6,783	35,623	17,639	17,984	34,429	+ 3	...	16
ii	Kengtawng		...	206	2,252	12,225	6,103	6,122	9,497	+29	...	
iii	Mawkmai	2,200	...	483	6,571	31,892	15,786	16,106	29,454	+ 8	...	14
iv	Möng-Pan	2,988	...	203	3,439	18,554	9,196	9,358	16,629	+12	...	6
v	Kenghkam	196	...	42	1,154	5,936	2,863	3,073	5,458	+ 9	...	30
	North-Eastern Subdivision.	*6,543*	...	*3,294*	*34,207*	*176,287*	*87,066*	*89,221*	*161,352*	+ 9	...	*27*
vi	Loi-Hkä	1,552	...	652	5,478	30,196	14,902	15,294	25,811	+17	...	19
vii	Möng-Küng	1,593	...	625	6,834	35,222	17,529	17,693	30,482	+16	...	22
viii	Ke-Hsi-Mansäm	497	...	369	3,864	18,393	9,096	9,297	22,062	−17	...	37
ix	Keng-Lön	54	..	101	1,208	5,291	2,596	2,695	4,259	+24	...	98
x	Möng-Hsü	470	...	336	4,095	20,913	10,286	10,627	17,480	+20	...	44
xi	Möng-Nawng	1,646	..	801	7,794	42,538	20,890	21,648	39,102	+ 9	...	26
xii	Möng-Sit	357	...	162	1,734	7,838	3,879	3,959	9,013	−13	...	22
xiii	Möng-Pawn	366	...	247	3,014	15,145	7,489	7,656	13,143	+15	...	41
	Loi-Lem (Notified Area) ...	8	...	1	186	751	399	352	...	...	...	94
	Central Subdivision.	*4,526*	...	*1,413*	*24,036*	*114,084*	*56,741*	*57,343*	*107,740*	+ 6	...	*25*
xiv	Samkä	314	...	205	3,731	15,742	7,766	7,976	17,643	−11	...	50
xv	Hsä-Htüng	471	...	156	1,988	11,453	5,692	5,761	10,584	+ 8	...	24
xvi	Namhkok	108	...	72	1,360	6,920	3,428	3,492	6,689	+ 3	...	64
xvii	Nawng-Mawn	28	...	71	1,024	4,143	2,000	2,143	4,805	−14	...	148
xviii	Möng-Pai	730	...	165	4,653	20,287	10,093	10,194	19,358	+ 5	...	28
xix	Wan-Yin	219	...	168	2,347	11,254	5,567	5,687	11,297	+ 0	...	51
xx	Sa-koi	82	...	34	501	2,162	1,101	1,061	1,387	+56	...	26
xxi	Ho-Pöng	212	...	162	2,593	13,153	6,475	6,678	11,140	+18	...	62
xxii	Lawksawk	2,362	..	380	5,839	28,970	14,619	14,351	24,839	+17	...	12
	Karenni Subdivision.	*4,280*	...	*721*	*16,177*	*63,628*	*31,468*	*32,160*	*45,795*	+39	...	*15*
xxiii	Kantarawadi	3,000	...	448	9,693	39,198	19,834	19,364	26,333	+49	...	13
xxiv	Bawlake	500	...	77	2,267	8,649	4,448	4,201	5,701	+52	...	17
xxv	Kyebogyi	700	Enumerated. Estimated	70 69	1,808 1,590	7,068 5,717	3,116 2,606	3,952 3,111	9,867	+30	...	18
xxvi	Naungpale	30	...	21	322	1,153	559	594	1,265	− 9	...	38
xxvii	Nammekon	50	...	36	497	1,843	905	938	2,629	−30	...	37
	Kengtüng Subdivision.	*12,400*	...	*2,575*	*41,561*	*200,344*	*101,342*	*99,002*	*190,698*	+ 5	...	*16*
xxviii	Kengtüng State	12,400	...	2,575	41,561	200,344	101,342	99,002	190,698	+ 5	..	16
	Western Subdivision.	*4,397*	...	*2,329*	*48,088*	*236,449*	*117,645*	*118,804*	*214,667*	+10	...	*54*
xxix	Hsamonghkam	293	...	203	3,432	15,509	8,227	7,282	12,561	+23	...	83
xxx	Kyöng	24	...	21	541	2,577	1,274	1,303	2,340	+10	...	107
xxxi	Pwela	102	...	55	1,884	8,835	4,356	4,479	7,866	+12	...	87
xxxii	Mawson	43	...	39	943	3,792	1,796	1,996	3,557	+ 7	...	88
xxxiii	Pangtara	86	...	95	3,082	16,789	8,092	8,697	15,014	+12	...	195
xxxiv	Kyawkku	76	...	32	792	4,636	2,238	2,348	4,771	− 3	...	61
xxxv	Yengan	359	...	60	1,946	10,107	5,101	5,006	9,958	+ 1	...	28
xxxvi	Maw	741	...	61	1,646	8,262	4,190	4,072	7,743	+ 7	...	11
xxxvii	Yawnghwe	1,302	...	1,027	22,304	106,377	52,843	53,534	95,339	+12	...	82
xxxviii	Mawnang	39	...	45	971	4,644	2,236	2,408	3,755	+24	...	119
xxxix	Pangmi	30	...	34	705	3,529	1,778	1,751	3,456	+ 2	...	118
xl	Loi-Maw	48	...	56	1,007	5,045	2,443	2,602	4,576	+10	...	105
xli	Loi-Ai	156	...	72	1,198	5,939	3,014	2,925	5,442	+ 9	...	38
xlii	Namkai	86		71	1,442	7,841	3,811	4,030	6,780	+16	...	91
xliii	Loi-Löng	998	...	445	5,903	31,657	15,736	15,921	30,731	+ 3	...	32
xliv	Namtop	14	...	13	232	910	460	450	778	+17	...	65
	Taunggyi (Notified Area) ...	...	...	1	1,083	5,180	2,856	2,324	...	...	...	...
	Bampon Civil Station ...	...	...	...	...	...	...	...	326	...	...	...
	Survey Party Camps ...	...	...	...	...	...	...	...	309	...	...	...
	Pakôkku Hill Tracts.	*3,700*	...	*333*	*5,459*	*26,251*	*12,967*	*13,284*	*13,116*	+100	...	7
	Administered Area ...	2,200	...	295	3,559	17,128	8,489	8,639	13,116	+31	...	8
	Unadministered Area ...	1,500	...	38	1,900	9,123	4,478	4,645	...	...	...	6
	Chin Hills.	*8,000*	...	*478*	*25,542*	*119,556*	*58,562*	*60,994*	*87,189*	+37	-	*15*
	Falam Subdivision ...	890	...	180	10,551	43,213	20,554	22,659	36,858	+17	...	49
	Haka Subdivision ...	5,100	...	154	9,852	44,425	22,177	22,248	33,896	+31	...	9
	Tiddim Subdivision ...	2,010	...	144	5,139	31,918	15,831	16,087	16,435	+94	...	16

PROVINCIAL TABLE II.

Population of Townships and States by Religions.

PROVINCIAL TABLE II.

Serial No.	Township. 1911.	1901.	DISTRIBUTION OF POPULATION BY RELIGION. Buddhist. Males.	Buddhist. Females.	Animist. Males.	Animist. Females.	Hindu. Males.	Hindu. Females.	Mahomedan. Males.	Mahomedan. Females.	Christian. Males.	Christian. Females.	Others. Males.	Others. Females.
	1		2	3	4	5	6	7	8	9	10	11	12	13
	Arakan Division.		280,251	280,997	38,626	36,449	14,755	1,242	107,506	78,817	728	449	69	17
	AKYAB DISTRICT.		*154,935*	*147,592*	*17,501*	*16,395*	*13,418*	*1,036*	*103,124*	*75,257*	*433*	*178*	*63*	*17*
1	Akyab ...	......	9,922	9,186	345	47	8,710	291	16,516	3,937	350	158	61	16
2	Rathedaung ...	......	22,650	22,421	506	493	347	6	5,692	4,673	1	...	...	...
3	Ponnagyun ...	Urittaung ...	21,364	22,190	2,6[illegible]2	2,623	540	5	1,039	321	31	...	...	...
4	Pauktaw ..	......	20,750	19,621	327	303	213	...	2,606	1,522	8	...	...	...
5	Minbya ...	......	17,687	16,102	4,323	4,058	638	15	3,553	1,413	3	2	1	...
6	Kyauktaw ...	Kaladan ...	14,890	13,956	3,471	3,353	646	137	11,657	7,703	4	3	...	...
7	Myohaung ...	......	23,47[illegible]	21,550	2,23[illegible]	2,137	730	14	5,455	2,435	1	1	...	...
8	Buthidaung ...	(Recently formed)	13,126	12,349	2,236	2,113	56[illegible]	114	17,545	15,622	2	1	1	1
9	Maungdaw ...	Na-af ...	10,067	10,217	1,371	1,268	1,035	454	39,061	37,631	33	7	...	...
	NORTHERN ARAKAN. (Not divided into Townships.)		*997*	*798*	*9,977*	*9,844*	*391*	*176*	*36*	*8*	*4*	*3*	...	...
	KYAUKPYU DISTRICT.		*79,099*	*86,765*	*7,718*	*7,008*	*572*	*18*	*2,130*	*1,511*	*52*	*43*	...	...
10	Kyaukpyu ...	......	21,427	23,355	110	65	192	16	584	415	17	14	...	...
11	Myebôn ...	......	12,485	12,334	1,457	1,386	277	...	729	189	12	11	...	...
12	An	......	10,824	10,665	5,884	5,367	53	1	17	4	22	18	...	...
13	Ramree ...	......	20,365	24,3[illegible]6	221	153	19	1	758	876	...	...	...	...
14	Cheduba ...	......	13,9[illegible]8	16,015	46	37	51	...	42	27	1	...	...	...
	SANDOWAY DISTRICT.		*45,220*	*45,842*	*3,430*	*3,202*	*374*	*12*	*2,216*	*2,041*	*229*	*231*	*6*	...
15	Taungup ...	Northern ...	16,183	16,803	2,144	2,084	95	1	144	53	54	64	...	...
16	Sandoway ...	Central ...	18,633	18,8[illegible]6	755	634	216	10	1,931	1,941	105	94	...	...
17	Gwa ...	Southern ...	10,404	10,143	531	484	63	1	141	47	70	73	6	...
	Pegu Division.		844,606	843,575	21,131	7,832	169,747	42,648	67,554	18,164	30,568	24,462	2,586	864
	RANGOON TOWN DISTRICT. (Not divided into Townships.)		*52,137*	*45,330*	*5,936*	*1,281*	*89,028*	*19,322*	*45,106*	*9,528*	*13,977*	*9,067*	*1,927*	*677*
	HANTHAWADDY DISTRICT.		*227,611*	*220,027*	*4,024*	*651*	*44,951*	*12,186*	*12,023*	*4,284*	*6,733*	*5,914*	*544*	*161*
18	Insein ...	......	34,399	31,363	952	141	9,830	3,135	2,435	1,071	2,207	2,065	356	138
19	Taikkyi ...	......	25,747	26,430	332	35	1,445	273	1,186	563	1,080	1,123	5	2
20	Tantabin ...	(Recently formed)	27,405	27,767	400	87	1,2[illegible]7	456	261	66	1,215	1,270	3	...
21	Twante ...	......	35,500	33,8[illegible]	511	68	8,[illegible]97	1,238	1,875	573	584	466	1	...
22	Kungyangón ...	......	36,[illegible]67	35,15[illegible]	426	77	3,7[illegible]8	1,197	1,730	969	821	605	...	...
23	Kyauktan ...	......	24,744	23,63[illegible]	494	66	12,022	2,740	3,583	713	476	225	170	21
24	Thôngwa ...	(Recently formed)	20,368	19,452	450	68	3,460	1,378	411	161	329	142	9	...
25	Kayan ...	Thabyegan ...	23,081	22,324	459	109	4,102	1,779	542	168	21	18	...	...
	THARRAWADDY DISTRICT.		*202,639*	*210,945*	*1,965*	*411*	*6,125*	*1,281*	*2,667*	*1,190*	*3,011*	*3,041*	*35*	*10*
26	Tharrawaddy ...	(Recently formed)	26,195	27,614	261	37	1,179	260	759	520	1,405	1,350	8	4
27	Letpadan ...	......	37,269	38,523	498	47	2,000	514	761	310	714	789	14	4
28	Minhla ...	......	39,069	40,491	424	70	930	171	417	113	382	384	2	1
29	Gyobingauk ...	......	44,169	46,674	524	232	1,356	267	544	156	306	316	7	1
30	Nattalin ...	Tapûn ...	35,519	36,633	228	25	556	67	162	88	82	93	...	...
31	Monyo ...	......	20,418	21,010	30	...	104	2	24	3	122	109	4	...
	PEGU DISTRICT.		*188,279*	*181,333*	*4,110*	*1,281*	*25,357*	*8,993*	*5,399*	*1,985*	*6,341*	*5,975*	*54*	*14*
32	Thanatpin ...	(Recently formed)	21,781	20,650	428	65	3,438	1,387	405	152	32	29	...	...
33	Pegu ...	Payagale ...	37,580	36,803	1,147	437	7,210	2,281	1,679	596	477	407	31	9
34	Kawa ...	......	30,261	28,254	522	81	3,984	1,598	643	220	604	562	1	...
35	Hlègu ...	......	28,419	27,429	359	78	2,031	631	815	387	2,585	2,610	9	...
36	Daik-u ...	Pyuntaza ...	34,367	32,952	1,027	442	3,688	654	936	352	1,117	1,017	4	1
37	Nyaunglebin ...	......	35,871	35,155	627	178	5,006	2,442	921	278	1,526	1,350	9	4
	PROME DISTRICT.		*173,940*	*185,940*	*5,096*	*4,208*	*4,286*	*866*	*2,359*	*1,177*	*506*	*465*	*26*	*2*
8	Prome ...	(Recently formed)	10,628	11,063	484	74	1,919	600	1,149	589	196	199	9	1
39	Paukkaung ...	......	12,894	12,8[illegible]2	1,400	1,328	34	9	21	14	8	3	...	...
40	Hmawza ...	......	34,775	37,872	274	175	332	47	137	66	39	39	...	...
41	Thègôn ...	......	31,255	34,067	59	5	731	48	300	85	93	75	...	...
42	Paungdè ...	......	31,189	33,060	262	25	8[illegible]4	96	397	144	64	46	11	1
43	Shwedaung ...	......	29,772	32,[illegible]08	53	9	266	59	219	182	20	12	3	...
44	Padaung ...	......	23,427	24,078	2,564	2,592	110	7	136	97	86	91	3	...

PROVINCIAL TABLE II.

Serial No.	Township 1911.	1901.	Buddhist. Males.	Buddhist. Females.	Animist. Males.	Animist. Females.	Hindu. Males.	Hindu. Females.	Mahomedan. Males.	Mahomedan. Females.	Christian. Males.	Christian. Females.	Others. Males.	Others. Females.
	1		2	3	4	5	6	7	8	9	10	11	12	13
	Irrawaddy Division.		856,877	856,062	10,449	1,219	36,513	5,593	21,115	7,156	37,662	36,472	297	70
	Bassein District.		*194,614*	*196,413*	*1,864*	*185*	*10,471*	*1,351*	*5,680*	*2,427*	*14,111*	*13,816*	*33*	*23*
45	Bassein ...	......	48,592	47,148	782	82	8,461	1,181	4,107	1,714	5,250	5,118	29	23
46	Thabaung ...	......	20,579	20,020	70	8	206	16	91	19	3,316	3,069	1	...
47	Ngaputaw ...	......	21,480	20,861	167	8	202	12	95	29	1,768	1,667	...	...
48	Ngathainggyaung	......	35,088	38,171	274	30	623	70	448	197	880	940	3	...
49	Kyônpyaw ...	......	42,550	43,500	337	31	685	52	457	221	1,375	1,496	...	...
50	Kyaunggôn ...	......	25,725	25,813	234	26	204	20	482	247	1,522	1,526	...	...
	Henzada District.		*248,922*	*260,388*	*1,309*	*157*	*5,912*	*688*	*3,074*	*1,583*	*5,070*	*5,215*	*32*	*7*
51	Henzada ...	......	63,555	67,367	446	38	2,975	489	1,375	620	1,682	1,631	14	4
52	Zalun ...	......	35,298	37,279	263	36	798	44	543	298	1,381	1,436	2	...
53	Lemyethna ...	......	31,011	31,824	170	15	342	44	186	103	266	274	5	2
54	Kanaung ...	......	50,248	52,800	181	23	981	56	570	334	815	932	2	1
55	Kyangin ...	......	24,404	24,735	70	3	442	16	205	136	159	150	9	...
56	Ingabu ...	Ôkpo ...	44,406	46,383	179	42	374	39	195	83	767	792	...	...
	Myaungmya District.		*153,362*	*147,153*	*2,683*	*239*	*5,486*	*642*	*5,694*	*1,409*	*9,218*	*8,939*	*22*	*5*
57	Myaungmya ..	......	39,635	36,393	687	53	1,254	186	860	228	2,330	2,282	6	1
58	Einmè ...	Thigwin ...	31,505	31,877	550	31	694	170	1,281	583	2,571	2,520	5	3
59	Wakèma ...	......	43,014	42,086	771	72	1,804	112	1,764	431	2,617	2,425	8	...
60	Mawlamyaingyûn	(Recently formed)	3[illegible],208	36,797	675	83	1,734	175	1,789	167	1,700	1,712	8	1
	Ma-ubin District.		*140,611*	*142,058*	*1,475*	*176*	*4,775*	*617*	*3,615*	*1,249*	*5,217*	*5,257*	*22*	*1*
61	Ma-ubin ..	......	36,470	36,344	614	87	2,203	284	1,254	380	1,011	941	...	...
62	Pantanaw ...	......	33,314	33,320	263	33	329	44	683	248	1,750	1,713	2	1
63	Yandoon ...	......	28,740	29,365	411	28	1,056	204	714	269	539	546	...	...
64	Danubyu ...	......	42,067	43,029	187	28	1,187	85	964	352	1,917	2,057	20	...
	Pyapôn District.		*119,368*	*110,050*	*3,118*	*462*	*9,869*	*2,295*	*3,052*	*488*	*4,046*	*3,245*	*188*	*34*
65	Pyapôn ...	Pyindayè ...	22,714	20,521	1,089	197	2,718	764	1,069	154	504	331	104	13
66	Bogale ...	......	28,178	24,559	585	51	1,801	402	473	27	1,524	1,273	39	7
67	Kyaiklat ...	......	35,132	33,472	818	111	2,223	334	812	163	1,333	1,261	13	4
68	Dedayè ...	......	33,344	31,498	626	103	3,127	795	698	144	685	980	32	10
	Tenasserim Division.		611,494	593,105	35,970	27,217	44,807	14,565	32,293	18,984	26,883	24,729	279	58
	Toungoo District.		*138,220*	*136,650*	*12,815*	*10,140*	*10,070*	*4,150*	*4,170*	*2,199*	*16,712*	*16,426*	*101*	*23*
69	Yedashe ...	Myoma ...	23,649	23,624	371	167	597	91	262	104	345	331	5	4
70	Toungoo ...	......	21,019	21,338	941	405	2,821	761	1,926	1,140	1,387	1,147	96	19
71	Leiktho ...	(Recently formed)	862	848	3	1	2	...	4	...	8,007	8,323	...	...
72	Pyu ...	......	29,818	29,959	647	281	4,307	2,958	973	432	482	443	...	...
73	Ôktwin ...	......	22,497	22,715	1,455	1,193	641	152	333	177	291	299	...	...
74	Tantabin ...	......	14,072	13,609	2,189	2,001	85	14	61	21	4,839	4,677	...	...
75	Kyaukkyi ...	......	12,974	12,360	6,509	6,070	386	59	40	10	1,057	982	...	...
76	Shwegyin ...	......	13,299	12,197	100	22	1,231	115	571	315	304	222	...	...
	Salween District.		*11,213*	*9,261*	*12,725*	*12,343*	*231*	*43*	*349*	*59*	*223*	*161*	...	...
77	Papun ...	......	11,213	9,261	12,725	12,343	231	43	349	59	223	161	...	...
	Thatôn District.		*192,749*	*187,495*	*3,840*	*2,118*	*12,131*	*4,674*	*7,054*	*3,167*	*1,987*	*1,751*	*9*	...
78	Kyaikto ...	......	24,233	23,778	708	246	1,689	703	780	305	42	36	8	...
79	Bilin ...	......	29,203	28,403	472	140	990	173	634	213	26	9	...	...
80	Thatôn ...	......	34,641	33,485	725	299	2,659	835	1,703	878	348	241	3	...
81	Paung ...	......	27,945	26,938	257	79	5,122	2,206	1,473	877	148	76	4	...
82	Pa-an ..	......	48,602	47,776	357	128	1,539	715	1,583	523	601	576	...	...
83	Hlaingbwè ...	......	28,035	27,115	1,321	1,226	132	36	881	371	822	813	...	...
	Amherst District.		*158,436*	*151,468*	*3,441*	*897*	*18,402*	*5,462*	*14,560*	*8,333*	*3,531*	*3,293*	*60*	*35*
84	Moulmein ...	......	16,559	17,060	1,803	432	12,116	3,180	7,180	3,584	1,575	1,499	60	35
85	Chaungzôn ...	Bilugyun ...	23,168	22,443	175	43	1,032	449	1,087	740	34	35	...	...
86	Kyaikkami ...	Wagaru ...	11,079	10,284	136	9	669	54	400	269	111	94	...	...
87	Yelamaing ...	......	17,504	16,075	181	18	948	69	521	102	89	53	...	...
88	Mudôn ...	Zaya ...	27,200	27,170	594	97	1,704	737	1,058	815	225	208	...	...
89	Kawkareik ...	Haungtharaw ...	22,502	20,891	143	32	723	213	1,342	798	149	110	...	...
90	Kyaikmaraw ...	Ataran ...	40,424	37,525	410	261	1,150	460	2,972	2,025	1,348	1,294	...	...
	Tavoy District.		*64,908*	*64,597*	*991*	*383*	*781*	*61*	*908*	*656*	*1,070*	*929*	*3*	...
91	Yebyu ...	Northern ...	8,446	7,473	312	33	44	1	10	11	414	388	...	...
92	Tavoy ...	Central ...	17,898	18,202	298	16	665	53	715	490	504	378	3	...
93	Launglòn ...	Western ...	20,101	20,876	23	2	28	6	60	77	5	4	...	...
94	Thayetchaung ...	South-Eastern	18,263	18,346	364	333	41	1	123	78	147	159	...	...
	Mergui District.		*45,968*	*43,634*	*2,752*	*1,336*	*3,192*	*175*	*5,252*	*4,570*	*2,360*	*2,179*	*6*	...
95	Mergui ..	......	21,641	20,518	1,522	756	2,692	153	2,588	2,243	690	577	6	...
96	Palaw ...	......	12,667	12,665	294	159	16	3	33	13	1,397	1,341	...	...
97	Tenasserim ...	......	6,060	5,393	139	22	155	3	301	319	87	102	...	...
98	Bôkpyin ...	Lenya ...	3,230	2,806	357	265	27	3	857	755	138	137	...	...
99	Maliwun ...	......	2,370	2,172	440	134	302	13	1,171	1,240	48	22	..	...

PROVINCIAL TABLE II.

DISTRIBUTION OF POPULATION BY RELIGION.

Serial No.	Township. 1911.	1901	Buddhist. Males.	Buddhist. Females.	Animist. Males.	Animist. Females.	Hindu. Males.	Hindu. Females.	Mahomedan. Males.	Mahomedan. Females.	Christian. Males.	Christian. Females.	Others. Males.	Others. Females.
	1		2	3	4	5	6	7	8	9	10	11	12	13
	Magwe Division.		577,817	619,779	12,819	12,004	7,420	1,219	4,050	1,686	952	556	556	174
	THAYETMYO DISTRICT.		*111,290*	*116,768*	*7,594*	*7,638*	*1,605*	*581*	*1,361*	*803*	*357*	*235*	*24*	*19*
100	Thayetmyo ...	......	20,651	21,004	179	103	893	430	637	469	254	147	6	2
101	Mindon ...	......	15,176	15,672	2,813	2,895	6	4	19	...	8	5	...	...
102	Kama ...	......	15,440	15,366	1,058	1,075	16	..	44	19	37	38	...	...
103	Minhla ...	......	16,727	17,240	1,376	1,355	105	15	159	35	12	6	...	...
104	Allanmyo ...	......	28,616	31,788	127	93	574	130	495	280	43	35	18	17
105	Thanbula ...	Sinbaungwè ...	14,080	14,698	2,031	2,117	11	2	7	...	3	4	...	...
	PAKÔKKU DISTRICT.		*192,432*	*211,605*	*1,831*	*1,641*	*1,016*	*154*	*681*	*213*	*166*	*118*	*33*	*19*
105	Pakôkku ...	......	39,530	44,841	181	38	743	128	568	201	138	100	20	13
107	Yesagyo ...	......	44,379	51,323	15	4	16	1	6	...	6	4	2	...
108	Myaing ...	......	36,416	42,503	...	...	13	1	20	...	9	5	2	...
109	Pauk ...	......	24,768	25,209	24	...	107	6	9	2	5	2	4	1
110	Saw ...	Pasök ...	11,120	10,479	436	393	30	...	1	...	1	...	...	...
111	Seikpyu ...	......	14,690	15,982	3	...	10	...	3	...	...	...	2	3
112	Gangaw ...	Hkunhnaywa ...	14,119	14,109	1,146	1,175	74	18	69	10	7	7	3	2
113	Tilin ...	......	7,410	7,159	26	29	23	...	5	...	...	...	...	...
	MINBU DISTRICT.		*122,133*	*131,794*	*3,056*	*2,702*	*2,449*	*202*	*775*	*286*	*98*	*52*	*326*	*66*
114	Sagu ...	......	29,805	31,441	150	15	438	85	373	182	78	51	127	45
115	Pwinbyu ...	Lègaing ...	27,788	30,735	224	184	1,786	57	255	30	20	1	143	10
116	Ngape ...	......	6,178	6,105	2,216	2,186	45	1	2	2	...	...	...	..
117	Salin ...	......	47,042	52,192	317	166	175	59	142	72	..	...	56	10
118	Sidôktaya ...	......	11,320	11,321	149	151	5	...	3	...	...	...	...	...
	MAGWE DISTRICT.		*151,962*	*159,612*	*338*	*23*	*2,350*	*282*	*1,233*	*384*	*331*	*151*	*173*	*70*
119	Magwe ...	......	34,084	36,038	133	4	451	87	352	128	57	36	163	61
120	Yenangyaung .	......	23,696	23,354	150	13	1,752	173	681	170	229	74	3	7
121	Taungdwingyi ...	......	17,002	18,111	39	..	99	17	137	75	21	21	7	2
122	Satthwa ...	Myingun ...	15,998	16,751	8	5	2	...	11	...	18	18	...	...
123	Myothit ...	......	25,814	27,593	5	1	1	...	31	8	1	...	...	...
124	Natmauk ...	......	35,368	37,765	3	...	45	5	21	3	5	2	...	...
	Mandalay Division.		320,444	327,099	60,471	57,661	20,539	7,310	17,435	9,919	5,658	3,845	2,229	359
	MANDALAY DISTRICT (INCLUDING CITY).		*141,480*	*153,424*	*1,278*	*219*	*11,192*	*4,879*	*12,236*	*8,609*	*3,870*	*2,701*	*694*	*188*
	Mandalay City ...	......	51,687	57,548	1,197	187	5,269	2,615	8,696	6,267	2,238	1,807	631	157
125	Amarapura ...	......	18,496	20,992	10	5	1,072	450	1,454	1,498	26	11	6	1
126	Patheingyi ...	......	15,955	17,537	...	...	563	532	126	120	3	1	...	...
127	Madaya ...	......	26,398	27,596	...	...	286	28	133	85	15	9	...	...
128	Singu ...	Ngasingu ...	19,912	20,830	1	...	15	2	70	65	3	...	...	...
129	Maymyo ...	{ Maymyo ... Wetwun ... Pyintha ... }	9,032	8,921	70	27	3,987	1,252	1,757	574	1,585	873	57	30
	BHAMO DISTRICT.		*27,182*	*26,308*	*23,244*	*24,478*	*1,404*	*248*	*1,852*	*390*	*1,030*	*755*	*816*	*104*
130	Bhamo ...	... ...	14,235	13,767	2,169	953	1,150	190	1,516	331	811	516	816	104
131	Shwegu—													
	(a) Township ...	...	10,394	9,728	474	318	46	8	133	37	8	3	...	...
	(b) Kachin Hill Tracts ...	...	...	...	2,508	3,161	...	...	...	...	...	...	...	...
	Sinlum Kachin Hill Tracts ...	...	2,553	2,813	17,693	20,046	208	50	203	22	211	236	...	...
	MYITKYINA DISTRICT.		*16,518*	*13,653*	*24,098*	*21,952*	*4,617*	*1,575*	*1,618*	*288*	*369*	*217*	*663*	*29*
132	Myitkyina—													
	(a) Township ...	...	5,296	4,805	1,734	1 200	2,282	1,083	739	200	263	209	233	23
	(b) Kachin Hill Tracts ...	...	18	3	1,792	1,921	50	5	18	...	3	...	83	3
133	Mogaung—													
	(a) Township ...	...	6,409	5,852	454	110	790	200	193	73	21	7	41	...
	(b) Kachin Hill Tracts ...	...	...	...	3,672	3,719	...	...	...	...	...	...	...	...
134	Kamaing—													
	(a) Township ...	...	4,440	2,855	1,797	135	196	41	123	10	1	1	69	...
	(b) Kachin Hill Tracts ...	...	8	3	2,856	2,405	...	...	...	...	...	...	...	...
	Sinbo Kachin Hill Tracts ...	...	...	...	1,059	1,109	...	...	...	...	...	...	...	...
	Sadon Kachin Hill Tracts ...	...	293	97	5,988	6,165	305	113	49	5	13	...	35	3
	Sima Kachin Hill Tracts ...	...	37	40	4,508	5,188	326	133	4	...	12	...	5	...
	Military Camps and Expedition	...	17	...	238	...	668	...	492	...	36	...	197	...
	KATHA DISTRICT.		*92,871*	*96,263*	*2,984*	*3,105*	*1,268*	*161*	*754*	*402*	*269*	*114*	*2*	...
135	Katha—													
	(a) Township ...	...	9,812	9,472	31	1	418	79	220	167	136	56	2	...
	(b) Kachin Hill Tracts ...	...	...	...	2,359	2,605	...	...	...	...	...	...	...	...
136	Tigyaing	..	8,732	8,653	22	4	16	1	72	65	8	9	...	...
137	Mawlu—													
	(a) Township	...	9,648	9,582	1	...	202	14	83	41	18	4	...	...
	(b) Kachin Hill Tracts ...	...	...	...	522	493	...	...	...	...	...	...	...	...
138	Indaw	...	7,484	7,621	9	...	268	25	84	47	18	16	...	...
139	Wuntho	...	11,459	11,803	11	...	197	24	96	31	34	9	...	...
140	Kawlin	...	16,491	16,429	2	1	78	6	56	32	23	17	...	...
141	Pinlebu	...	15,509	16,994	13	...	31	7	37	15	9	...	...	...
142	Banmauk	...	13,736	15,709	14	1	58	5	36	4	23	3	...	...
	RUBY MINES (INCLUDING MÖNG MIT STATE).		*42,393*	*37,451*	*8,867*	*7,907*	*2,058*	*447*	*975*	*230*	*140*	*58*	*54*	*38*
	I.—Ruby Mines (District Proper).		*21,890*	*18,602*	*2,361*	*834*	*1,913*	*422*	*906*	*204*	*123*	*57*	*54*	*38*
143	Mogôk	...	11,538	9,073	1,987	833	1,649	385	469	183	109	57	54	38
144	Thabeikkyin	...	4,807	4,397	372	1	223	25	395	8	10	...	...	...
145	Tagaung	...	5,545	5,132	2	...	41	12	42	7	4	...	...	...
	II.—Möng Mit State.		*20,503*	*18,849*	*6,506*	*7,073*	*145*	*25*	*69*	*26*	*17*	*1*	...	...
	(a) State Proper ...	...	12,418	10,679	457	262	133	25	68	26	16	1	...	...
	(b) Kodaung Hill Tracts ...	...	6,167	6,300	5,644	6,332	12	...	1	...	1	...	...	...
	(c) Ngadaung Hill Tracts	...	1,918	1,870	405	479	...	...	...	...	...	...	...	...

Provincial Table II.

Serial No.	Township: 1911.	Township: 1901.	DISTRIBUTION OF POPULATION BY RELIGION. Buddhist. Males.	Buddhist. Females.	Animist. Males.	Animist. Females.	Hindu. Males.	Hindu. Females.	Mahomedan. Males.	Mahomedan. Females.	Christian. Males.	Christian. Females.	Others. Males.	Others. Females.
	1		2	3	4	5	6	7	8	9	10	11	12	13
	Sagaing Division.		526,593	602,348	2,240	1,767	5,207	1,524	6,640	4,463	2,436	1,793	273	87
	Shwebo District.		*161,070*	*183,782*	*101*	*10*	*1,841*	*464*	*3,424*	*2,902*	*1,617*	*1,129*	*17*	*6*
146	Shwebo ...	......	26,797	29,137	90	10	1,062	354	979	357	1,002	481	17	6
147	Kia-u ...	Chaukywa ...	19,875	22,049	2	...	57	4	96	75	123	123	...	...
148	Wetlet ...	Sheinmaga ...	25,869	28,379	...	...	147	27	135	88	21	9	...	...
149	Kanbalu ...	Myedu ...	21,941	24,021	5	...	367	48	2,064	2,260	85	104	...	...
150	Kyunhla ...	Indaing ...	6,791	6,799	4	...	7	1	67	68	4	1	...	...
151	Ye-u ...	......	12,701	15,842	...	...	174	28	78	54	298	297	...	...
152	Tabayin ...	Mayagan ...	20,647	25,201	...	...	10	...	...	...	1	...	...	...
153	Tamadaw ...	Shwegyin ...	9,952	13,863	...	...	...	...	...	...	4	1	...	...
154	Tazè ...	......	15,497	18,401	...	...	17	2	5	...	79	113	...	...
	Sagaing District.		*144,311*	*162,105*	*75*	*20*	*1,228*	*544*	*1,710*	*1,105*	*492*	*521*	...	...
155	Sagaing ...	......	39,867	44,343	43	19	996	507	1,094	691	152	130	...	...
156	Tada-u ...	Ava ...	25,911	23,176	...	...	39	1	101	97	1	...	...	...
157	Myinmu ...	......	18,944	21,770	31	1	106	14	300	126	16	6	...	...
158	Chaung-u ...	......	15,059	18,027	...	...	67	21	5	2	155	174	...	...
159	Myaung ...	Kyaukyit ...	18,900	21,169	...	...	8	...	24	18	168	211	...	...
160	Ngazun ...	Myotha ...	25,630	28,610	1	...	10	1	186	171	...	...	...	...
	Lower Chindwin District.		*139,518*	*174,321*	*74*	*8*	*629*	*155*	*635*	*241*	*179*	*118*	*227*	*70*
161	Budalin ...	......	27,281	36,672	1	...	67	7	18	3	1	...	...	...
162	Mônywa ...	......	42,747	54,665	65	8	450	131	525	228	156	116	227	70
163	Kani ...	......	26,201	30,841	2	...	35	4	38	5	6	...	...	...
164	Salingyi ...	......	27,066	35,159	4	...	71	13	31	4	11	2	...	...
165	Palè ...	......	16,221	18,584	2	...	6	...	23	2	5	..	...	...
	Upper Chindwin District.		*81,694*	*82,140*	*1,990*	*1,729*	*1,409*	*361*	*871*	*215*	*148*	*25*	*29*	*11*
166	Kindat ...	......	7,095	7,048	65	9	470	100	274	84	35	5	29	11
167	Tamu ...	Kabaw ...	2,776	2,454	204	229	130	66	20	5	32	2	...	...
168	Masein ...	Balet ...	6,876	6,992	5	...	19	3	8	3	3	...	...	...
169	Kalewa ...	(Recently formed)	2,003	1,780	15	...	75	20	84	23	9	4	...	...
170	Kale ...	Kale ...	7,370	6,664	302	231	293	66	93	30	14	1	...	...
171	Mingin ...	......	10,918	11,183	1	1	60	23	96	23	26	5	...	...
172	Kyabin ...	Taungdwingyaung	5,659	5,558	...	...	12	4	1	...	...	...	...	...
173	Paungbyin ...	......	15,105	15,108	5	1	119	38	52	4	7	...	...	...
174	Homalin ...	......	10,831	11,486	426	379	196	36	209	32	11	2	...	...
175	Maingkaing ...	Uyu ..	9,062	9,488	...	...	12	1	30	8	11	6	...	...
—	Kampti State ...	......	810	852	477	421	...	...	...	...	...	...	...	...
...	Thaungdut State ..	Hsawnghup State	3,188	3,527	490	458	23	4	4	3	...	...	...	...
	Meiktila Division.		543,267	589,651	2,697	1,062	7,822	1,487	12,492	9,301	1,938	1,549	274	143
	Kyaukse District.		*65,293*	*69,635*	*24*	*1*	*682*	*133*	*2,509*	*2,445*	*345*	*334*	*15*	*10*
176	Kyauksè ...	......	23,747	25,265	24	1	333	78	1,328	1,269	141	140	13	9
177	Singaing ...	......	17,076	19,553	...	...	69	9	863	955	184	181	1	...
178	Myittha ...	......	23,570	24,817	...	...	280	46	318	221	20	13	1	1
	Meiktila District.		*128,307*	*143,467*	*80*	*15*	*2,474*	*457*	*2,800*	*1,453*	*451*	*227*	*58*	*23*
179	Meiktila ...	......	37,544	42,451	32	8	789	224	910	636	388	184	49	33
180	Mahlaing ...	......	31,250	36,298	34	2	86	10	79	30	6	10	...	...
181	Thazi ...	......	26,802	28,408	3	...	1,471	203	1,762	753	55	27	5	...
182	Wundwin ...	......	32,711	36,370	12	5	125	20	49	34	4	6	4	...
	Yamèthin District.		*141,650*	*146,397*	*1,433*	*1,019*	*3,068*	*698*	*5,956*	*5,101*	*928*	*885*	*188*	*96*
183	Yamèthin ...	......	37,162	38,730	164	108	803	171	1,652	1,359	228	204	5	2
184	Pyawbwè ...	......	21,502	23,638	102	9	403	119	819	635	15	9	180	94
185	Yanaung ...	Yindaw ...	22,506	23,875	1	...	5	...	1,389	1,486	3	...	...	..
186	Pyinmana ...	......	36,268	36,233	998	730	1,490	339	1,741	1,908	637	639	3	...
187	Lewè ...	......	24,212	23,921	168	172	367	69	355	319	45	33	...	...
	Myingyan District.		*207,917*	*230,152*	*160*	*26*	*1,588*	*199*	*1,227*	*302*	*214*	*103*	*13*	*4*
188	Myingyan ...	......	43,697	47,651	136	18	746	139	589	147	111	66	13	4
189	Taungtha ...	......	34,703	38,165	2	2	64	5	68	31	9	3	...	...
190	Natogyi ...	......	34,157	38,232	...	...	5	...	31	12	2	...	...	...
191	Pagan ...	......	33,012	36,640	21	6	652	38	273	67	63	33	...	...
192	Sale ...	......	19,815	22,394	...	...	99	10	235	35	28	1	...	...
193	Kyaukpadaung ...	......	42,533	47,070	1	...	28	7	37	10	1	...	...	...

PROVINCIAL TABLE II.

Serial No.	State.	DISTRIBUTION OF POPULATION BY RELIGION. Buddhist. Males.	Buddhist. Females.	Animist. Males.	Animist. Females.	Hindu. Males.	Hindu. Females.	Mahomedan. Males.	Mahomedan. Females.	Christian. Males.	Christian. Females.	Others. Males.	Others. Females.
	1	2	3	4	5	6	7	8	9	10	11	12	13
	Specially Administered Territories.	**552,210**	**558,504**	**184,740**	**188,120**	**5,950**	**1,441**	**2,343**	**859**	**5,218**	**5,183**	**318**	**76**
	NORTHERN SHAN STATES.	*167,904*	*167,532*	*59,217*	*60,103*	*2,250*	*357*	*952*	*289*	*222*	*126*	...	...
i	North Hsenwi State	52,041	52,377	54,412	55,932	620	57	57	15	92	79	...	...
	(a) Shan Tracts	42,124	42,327	5,433	5,478	475	16	57	15	91	79	...	...
	(b) Kachin Tracts	9,917	10,050	26,529	28,738	145	41	...	..	1	...	...	...
	(c) Kokang	...	...	23,389	12,215	...	...	...	...	...	...	...	...
	(d) West Manglün	...	...	9,061	9,501	...	...	..	...	...	..	...	...
	(e) East Manglün				Omitted from Census Operations.							...	...
ii	South Hsenwi State	39,984	40,441	2,289	2,249	55	7	68	11	6	...	...	...
iii	Hsipaw State	65,489	59,157	721	500	563	38	410	156	67	28	...	...
iv	Tawngpeng State	13,877	14,546	1,761	1,407	265	29	47	3	30	11	...	...
	Lashio (Notified Area)	1,513	1,011	34	15	747	226	370	104	27	8	...	...
	SOUTHERN SHAN STATES.	*384,220*	*390,936*	*55,696*	*54,435*	*2,638*	*644*	*1,274*	*526*	*4,866*	*4,952*	*11*	*4*
	South-Eastern Subdivision.	*50,092*	*51,195*	*1,303*	*1,331*	*80*	*16*	*53*	*20*	*59*	*81*	...	...
i	Möngnai	17,483	17,850	32	32	44	14	23	7	57	81	...	
ii	Kengtawng	5,944	5,963	155	159	3	..	1	...	...	...	...	...
iii	Mawkmai	15,183	15,523	556	569	21	1	26	13	...	...	...	...
iv	Möng-Pan	8,629	8,786	559	571	4	1	2	...	2	...	...	...
v	Kënghkam	2,853	3,073	1	...	8	..	1	...	...	...	...	...
	North-Eastern Subdivision.	*86,312*	*88,762*	*515*	*353*	*142*	*55*	*72*	*40*	*18*	*21*	*7*	...
vi	Loi-Hkä	14,850	15,257	12	4	4	17	27	9	9	7	...	...
vii	Möng-Küng	17,518	17,687	1	...	2	...	8	6	...	...	...	...
viii	Kè-Hsi-Mänsäm	9,039	9,259	21	35	6	2	..	...	...	...	...	...
ix	Këng-Lön	2,595	2,695	...	...	...	...	...	...	1	...	...	...
x	Möng-Hsu	10,284	10,627	1	...	...	...	1	...	...	...	...	...
xi	Möng-Nawng	20,764	21,644	91	4	31	...	4	...	...	...	...	...
xii	Möng-Sit	3,844	3,939	34	20	1	...	...	...	...	...	...	...
xiii	Möng-Pawn	7,171	7,368	314	288	1	...	3	...	...	...	...	...
	Loi-Lem (Notified Area)... ...	247	286	11	1	97	36	29	25	8	4	7	...
	Central Subdivision.	*48,220*	*48,818*	*6,496*	*6,410*	*49*	*8*	*27*	*8*	*1,949*	*2,099*	...	...
xiv	Samkä	7,643	7,844	117	131	1	...	5	1	...	...	...	...
xv	Hsä-Htüng	5,658	5,728	33	31	...	...	1	2	...	...	...	...
xvi	Namhkok	3,426	3,492	2	...	...	...	...	...	...	...	...	...
xvii	Nawng-Mawn	1,986	2,142	...	...	9	1	5	...	...	...	..	...
xviii	Möng-Pai	2,002	2,094	6,142	6,001	...	...	...	...	1,949	2,099	...	...
xix	Wan-Yin	5,501	5,616	58	70	5	...	3	1	...	...	...	...
xx	Sa-Kol	961	884	140	177	...	...	...	...	...	...	...	...
xxi	Ho-Pong	6,437	6,670	...	...	29	6	9	2	...	...	...	...
xxii	Lawksawk	14,606	14,348	4	...	5	1	4	2	...	...	...	...
	Karenni Subdivision.	*11,394*	*10,612*	*17,846*	*19,602*	*159*	*19*	*203*	*49*	*1,865*	*1,875*	*1*	*3*
xxiii	Kantarawadi	9,852	9,025	9,632	10,265	151	19	167	43	31	9	1	3
xxiv	Bawlakè	880	656	1,773	1,759	8	...	35	5	1,752	1,781	...	...
xxv	Kyebogyi ... { Enumerated ...	121	386	2,982	3,561	...	...	1	1	12	4	...	...
	{ Estimated ...	...	...	2,606	3,111	..	..	...	...	...	...	...	...
xxvi	Naungpale	203	2[illegible]0	286	313	...	...	...	...	70	81	...	...
xxvii	Nammekon	338	345	567	593	...	...	...	...	...	...	...	...
	Kengtung Subdivision.	*72,866*	*73,058*	*26,964*	*25,035*	*603*	*112*	*85*	*19*	*822*	*777*	*2*	*1*
xxviii	Kengtung State	72,866	73,058	26,964	25,035	603	112	85	19	822	777	2	1
	Western Subdivision.	*113,799*	*116,786*	*2,493*	*1,696*	*764*	*101*	*535*	*181*	*53*	*40*	*1*	...
xxix	Hsamonghkam	7,118	7,205	565	1	391	48	130	24	20	4	1	...
xxx	Kyong	1,274	1,303	...	...	...	...	...	...	...	...	...	...
xxxi	Pwela	4,351	4,479	...	...	3	...	2	...	...	...	...	...
xxxii	Mawson	1,796	1,996	...	...	..	...	...	...	...	...	...	...
xxxiii	Pangtara	8,078	8,687	...	...	6	...	8	10	...	...	...	...
xxxiv	Kyawkku	2,886	2,348	...	...	...	...	1	...	1	...	...	...
xxxv	Yengan	5,101	5,005	...	...	...	1	...	...	...	...	...	...
xxxvi	Maw	4,190	4,072	...	...	...	...	...	...	...	...	...	...
xxxvii	Yawnghwe	51,991	53,293	70	10	358	49	392	146	32	36	...	...
xxxviii	Mawnang	2,236	2,408	...	...	...	...	...	...	...	...	...	...
xxxix	Pangmi	1,778	1,751	...	...	...	...	...	...	...	..	...	...
xl	Loi-Maw	2,443	2,602	...	...	...	..	...	..	...	...	...	...
xli	Loi-Ai	3,013	2,974	...	...	...	...	1	1	...	...	...	...
xlii	Namkhai	3,811	4,032	...	...	...	...	...	..	...	...	..	...
xliii	Loi-Long	13,901	14,267	1,830	1,651	4	3	1	...	...	..	...	...
xliv	Namtop	432	416	28	34	...	...	...	...	...	...	...	...
	Taunggyi (Notified Area) ...	1,537	1,705	79	8	841	333	269	209	100	69	...	...
	PAKÔKKU HILL TRACTS.	*22*	*13*	*12,817*	*13,234*	*115*	*36*	*7*	*1*	*4*	...	*2*	...
	Administered Area	22	13	8,339	8,589	115	36	7	1	4	...	2	...
	Unadministered Area	...	...	4,478	4,645	...	...	...	...	...	...	...	...
	CHIN HILLS.	*64*	*23*	*57,010*	*60,348*	*947*	*404*	*110*	*43*	*126*	*105*	*305*	*71*
	Falam Subdivision	46	14	19,787	22,409	453	177	33	15	9	3	226	48
	Haka Subdivision	9	1	21,892	22,139	177	80	66	19	33	19	...	...
	Tiddim Subdivision	9	8	15,331	15,827	317	147	11	9	84	83	79	23

G. B. C. P. O.—No. 33, S. C. O., 24-4-1912,—1,204—J.T.N.